Intranet Web Development

John Desborough

Contribution by Brian Croft

New Riders

New Riders Publishing, Indianapolis, Indiana

Intranet Web Development

By John Desborough

Published by:
New Riders Publishing
201 West 103rd Street
Indianapolis, IN 46290 USA

Printed in the United States of America 1 2 3 4 5 6 7 8 9 0

Library of Congress Cataloging-in-Publication Data

Desborough, John, 1960-
    Intranet Web Development John Desborough
        p. cm.
    Includes index.
    ISBN 1-56205-618-2
    1. Intranets (Computer networks) 2. World Wide Web
(Information retrieval system) I. Title
TK5105.875.I6D47 1996
005.2--dc20   96-35507
                                                   CIP

Warning and Disclaimer

Publisher	*Don Fowley*
Publishing Manager	*Julie Fairweather*
Marketing Manager	*Mary Foote*
Managing Editor	*Carla Hall*

Acquisitions Editor
Julie Fairweather

Senior Editor
Sarah Kearns

Development Editors
Ami Frank
Suzanne Snyder

Project Editor
Ami Frank

Copy Editors
Charles Gose
Sarah Kearns
Greg Pearson

Technical Editor
Richard Harris

Associate Marketing Manager
Tamara Apple

Acquisitions Coordinator
Tracy Turgeson

Administrative Coordinator
Karen Opal

Cover Designer
Karen Ruggles

Cover Production
Aren Howell

Book Designer
Sandra Schroeder

Production Manager
Kelly D. Dobbs

Production Team Supervisor
Laurie Casey

Graphics Image Specialists
Casey Price, Clint Lahnen

Production Analysts
Jason Hand
Bobbi Satterfield

Production Team
Dan Caparo
David Garratt
Aleata Howard
Beth Rago
Erich J. Richter
Megan Wade
Christy Wagner

Indexer
Andrew McDaniel

About the Author

John Desborough has had extensive involvement in the development of the overall business strategies of several organizations including the development of intranets in support of mission-critical business processes. John currently brings his understanding of business process innovation and intranet technologies together in this book, as well as in his consulting practice—designing and implementing intranets in support of mission-critical business processes.

If John had his druthers, he and his troll-like sense of humor would be found wandering the fairways of the local golf courses with his wife or walking through the forest with his children. In the early morning hours you can find John practicing his troll-dancing along the river. Some people mistakenly think he is running.

You can find John most easily by visiting his e-home at http://www.intranomics.com.

Trademark Acknowledgments

All terms mentioned in this book that are known to be trademarks or service marks have been appropriately capitalized. New Riders Publishing cannot attest to the accuracy of this information. Use of a term in this book should not be regarded as affecting the validity of any trademark or service mark.

Dedication

To Andrea: Thank you for being there and not being there when I needed it most. You *are* the light at the end of the tunnel.

Mon Bisou: je t'aime ma belle.

Mon P'tit Bucko: Thank you for smiling. When you grow up you'll understand.

Acknowledgments

When I started this book I had "*no worries*," as they say in Australia, about its eventual completion. At this point in time, I am thankful to have had support from many people to handle all the "*no worries*" that raised their ugly heads along the way. I would like to take this opportunity to thank them.

My wife and children: The house is yours again. Enfin, Papa est sorti du cave. I promise not to work 22-hour days again or stay awake all through the weekend. I thank you for helping me take the chance.

The staff at Papou's Paladi: Thank you for boarding your daughter and grandchildren while I wandered through these pages. Thanks for everything Nona, including the prayers. Really!

Richard Harris: Thanks for the use of the server space and for agreeing to be the technical editor of the tome.

Guy Vales: See what happens when you jump? Thanks for being a good sounding board.

The Crew at NRP: Julie Fairweather for offering me the chance to work twice as hard and four times as long as I ever thought I could. Ami Frank for putting up with soapbox diatribes and troll-isms and for not letting me throw in the towel. Suzanne Snyder for starting me on the straight and narrow and keeping me on the straight but somewhat-wider. Thanks for finding some humor in my words. Greg Pearson for his copy editing and his semantic jousting; Webster's is not the only dictionary—if it sounds like it fits, like "firstpersonating," let's use it! It is always a challenge when developing a new language, but we did it: troll-speak. All the rest of you folks at NRP who are too shy and/or quiet to be overheard from the background but contributed to this book: THANKS!

Brian Croft: For saving some bacon by providing the chapter "Human Resources Issues for Intranets." I hope we get the chance to collaborate more fully in the future. I look forward to it!

James Gale: You will never see these words, but you helped to shape them.

Ann Gale: You told me to take the opportunity and do it right. I did the best I could. I think you would have liked it. Be at peace with your brother.

Contents at a Glance

PART 5: Additional Information Servers

Appendices

Table of Contents

Part 1: Intranet Concepts and Architecture— Server

Part 2: Intranet Concepts and Architecture— Client

Part 3: Application Building Blocks

Part 4: Constructing Information Resources

Part 5: Additional Information Servers

Appendices

Client/Server, Groupware, and the Collaborative Network Communications Revolution

The intranet is in the news nearly everywhere you look. *Business Week* has done a cover story on its rise. *Information Week* has discussed it as a means of making client/server computing finally work. Recent reviews of large companies in America have indicated that over two-thirds of all large companies are thinking of implementing some form of intranet over the next year.

Because more and more organizations are acquiring Web-server software for internal use rather than for external use, the intranet phenomenon is best described by the "iceberg" metaphor: just as you see only a small portion of an iceberg above water, the Web servers you see that are external to organizational walls are really only a small portion of the total number of Web servers out there. The majority of the Web servers are below the surface, like the bulk of the iceberg, behind the firewalls and available only for internal information distribution.

The Concept Behind the Intranet

Web servers for corporate purposes began initially as an internal Web site, in other words, an IntraWeb for distribution of organizational information. Incorporating access to data in a variety of corporate applications from the IntraWeb creates the functional rationale for the intranet.

The intranet's big brother—the now famous Internet—was developed with technologies that enable diverse machines and operating platforms to interoperate on a global basis. Adoption and implementation of these same technologies by an organization for its internal information holdings creates the framework for the intranet.

The ever-changing economic landscape forces companies to constantly seek new business models to meet the demands of day-to-day operations. Because of downsizing, many companies have had to do more with less—small workforces that need to work in close cooperation in order to meet a project's requirements are often spread across large geographical areas. Working as a team in a single physical location is often demanding enough without adding the geographic disbursement of integral staff members! Workgroup computing, therefore, is one of the critical success factors in distributed organizations. Through the intranet, it is now possible to implement "real" workflow applications across an organization's communications/information systems.

What this Book Will Cover

This book shows you that four basic intranet models exist that provide solutions for individual organizations. In order for the intranet to offer itself as an enterprise alternative to client/server computing, a progression must be made from the "Simple IntraWeb" model toward the "Enterprise Intranet" model. The four intranet models are as follows:

- **Simple IntraWeb**—an internal Web server that publishes static pages of HTML text. The browser opens up a connection to the server, and the server returns the page and closes the connection. A measure of interaction can be added by creating lists of links to sites that the user may be interested in reviewing.

- **Interactive IntraWeb**—contains forms, fields, and buttons (all outlined in Chapter 9) that take input from the user before opening a connection to the server to allow the data and choices to be transmitted. The HTTP server passes the information to a custom server program or script for processing, and then, in turn, a new page is passed back to the browser for viewing. The connection between browser and server is then broken.

- **Distributed IntraWeb**—takes into account and utilizes the current infrastructure of the organization with its distributed data sources throughout the organization. The simple action of opening an HTML file invokes a procedure on behalf of the user. Through the introduction of the Java programming language, small programs called *applets* can be incorporated into the pages sent to the browser.

- **Enterprise Intranet**—will be replete with true open client/server applications as the Java programming language matures and companies begin to develop truly useful applications. Picture this: instead of loading an HTML page, the client is coded in downloadable Java and runs in any Java-capable browser. When a page containing a Java applet is downloaded to the browser by an HTTP server, the applet runs in the browser, opening its own communications session with the server.

Note

If a company makes the decision that it will implement client/server technology through the intranet, then by default the full-scale Enterprise Intranet will be developed.

This book will take you through the evolution of the intranet, from a corporate IntraWeb to an alternative business model that connects people to people and people to information.

Part 1: Intranet Concepts and Architecture—Server

The first two parts of this book show you how to implement a Simple IntraWeb and expand it into an Interactive IntraWeb. This is done by means of presenting the following information:

- Concepts behind the IntraWeb and how it can eventually become a full-fledged intranet (Chapter 1)

- How to develop the business case for an intranet and the planning process for its implementation (Chapter 2)

- A short examination of the important Web components: the HTTP protocol, fundamentals of TCP/IP, and intranet security (Chapters 3, 4, and 5)

Part 2: Intranet Concepts and Architecture—Client

Part 2 continues your exploration and familiarization with important Web considerations, such as the following:

- How to set up the client browser for cross-platform requirements (Chapter 6)

- The advantages of browser/server communications (Chapter 7)

Part 3: Application Building Blocks

In order to expand your IntraWeb to an intranet, the understanding of several key building blocks is necessary. In this part you will be exposed to the following components:

- An introduction to the HyperText Markup Language (HTML) (Chapter 8)

- Forms and information handling, including a quick look at a Java-Script application (Chapter 9)

- An introduction to Common Gateway Interface (CGI) programming for both database and text search and retrieval (Chapter 10)

- The integration of the Open Database Connectivity (ODBC) interface and gateway programming (Chapter 11)

- Alternative corporate information models that incorporate CGI (Chapter 12)

Part 4: Constructing Information Resources

In order to provide required information at the right time and in the right location, you need to know where the information is located within your organization and how to get it into the hands of others. This part of the book addresses the following aspects of this need:

- How to structure your organization's information resources (Chapter 13)

- Document and content management demands and requirements (Chapter 14)

- The role of the "IntraMaster," in contrast to the role of the traditional "WebMaster" (Chapter 15)

- How to convert data for use within an intranet (Chapter 16)

- Workflow implementation through an examination of groupware versus intranet (Chapter 17)

- How Lotus Notes and the intranet can simultaneously be put to good use: a case study (Chapter 18)

- How the intranet can support a company's Human Resources department, with a brief look at Silicon Graphics' Intranet implementation as an example (Chapter 19)

Part 5: Additional Information Servers

The final part of this book reflects on several components that play an important part in the operation of the intranet:

- The possible role of newsgroups within the intranet framework (Chapter 20)

- Using a Chat Server to provide real-time online intra-company conferencing (Chapter 21)

- File storage and archives through the use of File Transfer Protocol (ftp) servers (Chapter 22)

- The future of the intranet: who and what to watch (Chapter 23)

This Book's Mission

The goal of this book is to assist you in discovering the possibilities of the intranet as an alternative to the traditional client/server models of the past. In doing so, this book provides the tools and framework for you to create a simple, yet productive intranet—one that works when launched. Keep in mind, however, that the basic tenet of intranet planning has been "Remember, even the Titanic had a successful launch." The adoption of the intranet as *the* new business model will keep the ship afloat.

Author's Note

Although every care has been taken to portray the functionality of software products as accurately as possible, the software applications will have most likely undergone improvements and alterations between the time this is written and the time you read this book. Given the explosive growth rate of the Internet and intranet worlds, it is virtually impossible to represent the "absolute latest information," but I have given it my best shot.

Intranet Concepts and Architecture—Server

1

Intranet: Building the Corporate-Wide Web

The Internet is enjoying rapid growth. More and more businesses are beginning to create a presence on the Internet because "our competitors are out there—if we don't get on the Net, we'll lose." Many of these businesses are also in the process of establishing their own internal Web sites to share information across their own infrastructures.

In the November 13, 1995 edition of *Inter@ctive Week Magazine*, Netscape reported that most of its server sales to corporations are for internal use. It is widely believed that the relationship of external to internal Web sites is much like an iceberg—the part we can see (external sites) is only a small part of the whole market.

Increasingly, corporations are implementing intranets to assist their people in finding information, in collaborating with each other, and in distributing the results of this collaboration throughout the organization. The term "intranet" is defined as follows:

     ❝ the use of Internet technologies to link together the information resources of an organization, from text to legacy databases to workflow and document management. ❞

Through the use of a single universal interface, corporate users can now access information from across a company's systems or from around the world on the Internet. Figure 1.1 below, shows, as a sample, an intranet home page of a project in which the author was involved.

Figure 1.1

Main page of an intranet.

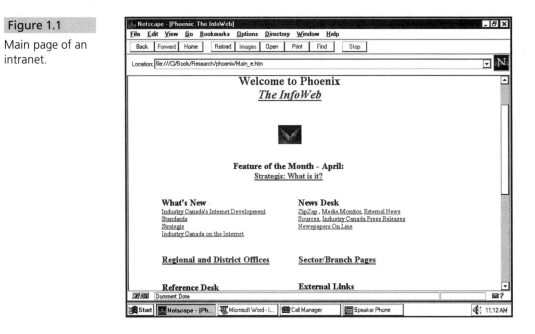

The results of the implementation of an intranet within an organization can be dramatic. Advantages of an intranet include:

- A reduced learning curve in accessing information held in a variety of systems. That is, the interface is always the same for the user—an Internet Web browser.

Note

> A browser is a graphical user interface (GUI) designed for use within the World Wide Web. There are browsers for almost every possible combination of platform and operating systems. While most are mouse-driven, there are also line-oriented browsers for non-graphical usage. Documents will be displayed differently between browsers, depending on the underlying formatting of the document. Even within the same browser, documents might be displayed differently between platforms (Macintosh or Windows).

- The abolishment of geographic and departmental compartmentalization. Users are only a phone call away—all they need is a computer with a modem, a password, and a phone line to access the organization's information.

- A dynamic space that enables local and global groups to collaborate and do business efficiently and effectively.

- Low deployment and maintenance costs. The intranet uses the existing architecture of the Web and can be established using public domain software.

- The use of a single interface software package—an Internet Web browser—to access complicated applications and complex information across many computer platforms.

If the implementation of an intranet allows an organization to increase productivity and lower costs while distributing decision making and flattening its hierarchies, it isn't surprising that stories about the growth of intranets abound in the media. What is astounding is that only just now are companies realizing that they can do more with available Internet technologies than set up an internal Web site; they can create an *IntraWeb*. The technologies available are capable of providing an enterprise alternative to the client/server computing applications that have been all the rage over the past years.

Note

Two components define client/server architecture:

- A client: interacts with the user by accepting input and displaying data/responses to the user

- A server: performs the tasks as instructed by the client by gaining access to data on behalf of the client, manipulating the data as required, and then returning the data or response to the client.

Both the client and the server will be discussed later in the book.

Join in moving along with the corporate revolution through the development of an IntraWeb and to a simple, yet full-blown, intranet.

Note

An *IntraWeb* is an internal Web site, with access to text-based documents and any other multimedia components contained within these documents. An *intranet* is all those features of the IntraWeb, plus access to an organization's other information servers (databases held on a variety of hardware and software platforms, for example).

IntraWebs tend to be housed on one server, with all the documents held within the physical boundaries of the server. An intranet, on the other hand, includes data from disparate servers throughout the organization.

This chapter considers the following issues:

- The IntraWeb as a corporate Web site

- The differences between an IntraWeb and the intranet

- The rise of the intranet and its appeal

The IntraWeb: A Corporate Web Site

Go ahead. Try to register a domain name for your business on the Internet. In all likelihood there will be a problem or a delay—someone may already have registered the same domain name.

A domain name, for those not familiar with the term, is the character-based representation of an Internet address. An Internet address is similar to a mailing address in that it tells the computers on the network where to deliver a company's mail. When establishing a presence on the Internet, a company applies for and receives a numeric Internet Protocol (IP) address that defines the company's location within the Internet (see Chapter 4, "Fundamentals of TCP/IP: Understanding the Transport Layer," for more details). Instead of having clients remember the numeric version, it is possible to register a name for your location that can be somewhat descriptive. For example, the author's *domain name* is www.intranomics.com, and Microsoft's is www.microsoft.com (among others they have registered).

There has been explosive growth in the number of companies who have registered domain names for themselves. It is not uncommon to hear "What's your address on the Net?" in any gathering. Many businesses are establishing a Web presence because their competitors are there. From a marketing perspective, this is a relatively inexpensive form of advertising—an Internet service provider can put up a "virtual home page" for its clients at a cost to the client of about $500/year. Being able to reach a potential market the size of the Internet user-base for such a small amount is usually seen to be a cost effective approach to incremental marketing.

Note

If you have not registered a domain name for an external Internet site, try out the following address for the InterNic Registration Services: http://rs.internic.net.

Many of these same companies have also created Web sites internally to inform their staffs about what is happening throughout the organization. The first phase of development in this area was to quickly put corporate information (human resource documents, policy and procedure manuals, and the like) onto a Web site for the internal staff to access. For many of these companies, the money saved by electronic distribution of these materials paid for the initial development expenditures of the Web site. The driving forces behind these early sites tended to be the Human Resources, Finance, and Corporate Communications (in really big organizations) divisions, which typically spent large dollars in printing documents and manuals for distribution.

Thus the basis for the Corporate Web was formed.

The next phase was expansion, typically looking outward for information. To be competitive in a global market, people need to be apprised of general market conditions, industry news, and competitor information. In addition to putting up their own sales and marketing information for all employees to see, companies usually established links to competitors' and customers' sites. Clipping services and news groups filled out the rest of the information typically made available during the expansion phase.

At the same time as companies were providing access to the publicly available marketing information, they came to realize that all staff need to know what is in development within the organization. In order to keep everyone abreast of products in the pipeline, divisions and project teams were provided with space on the corporate Web to post status reports, minutes from meetings, and member lists, for example. This allowed the rest of the organization to stay up-to-date about where the company is going so that the latest facts were available when dealing with clients and potential clients.

At this point, the standard corporate Web is a reasonably robust information distribution system expanded from one being driven by the center of the organization to one that is driven by those within the organization with information to share. By developing this IntraWeb, employees of the company can now access the latest documents from

Human Resources and Finance, review competitive marketing literature, keep abreast of the latest internal product developments, and keep
tabs on what the competition is saying to the client community, all on
their Web site.

However, this flow of information is one way—from the provider/
creator to the reader. Typically, at this phase in the development of an
IntraWeb, no interaction takes place other than "mail to:" responses for
questions and feedback to the content provider or the WebMaster.

The "IntraWeb" Versus the "Intranet"

According to the musical group The Talking Heads, "facts don't have a
point of view." This is a fundamental principle to keep in mind. When
interpreted within a specific context, a fact either has value or is neutral.
Given a context that combines them, facts can be pulled together into
an information set—a document or a database of facts, for example.

When creating a collection of information to meet the needs of an entire organization, no person or machine could ever collect, organize,
and present the facts in every conceivable context (or combination). In
addition, the storage requirements of a complete information set would
be prohibitive.

This inability to present the "perfect information resource collection" is
the basic reason why many companies are expanding from an IntraWeb
to an intranet.

Instead of trying to publish the facts in every conceivable context, the
shift is now toward making the raw facts accessible for the user to review, search, and query in his own context at that given instant in time.
By making the databases (both textual and relational) of facts available
through one user interface, a company can enable its employees to create customized, dynamic, context-sensitive reports that are as accurate
and up-to-date as the raw facts within the databases.

Taking that one step further, if an organization used the same interface to: (a) distribute internal documents and provide links to competitive information (the IntraWeb concept) and, (b) create context-sensitive reports from a variety of raw fact databases, that organization would have created a true intranet.

This is the intranet—accessing information resources that are held throughout the organization by using Internet technologies. This does not mean that all collections must be maintained on a local or wide-area network. Usage of the existing Internet infrastructure, combined with passwords and other appropriate security measures (discussed in Chapter 5), extends the network of the enterprise far beyond any four walls.

The Rise of the Intranet

Read the popular press any morning and you will find articles on the Internet. Read the business press and you will see articles on the "intranet Phenomenon." A year ago, the press contained many articles about companies creating their own Web sites (read the label of your favorite beverage; chances are that its producer's Web address is printed somewhere). Over the last year, a large number of those companies were covered in the news as ground breakers and pioneers in establishing internal Web sites. Now these same early entries have grasped the need for and are leading the charge in the development of intranets. This section will explain what an intranet is in detail and what makes it appealing for organizations.

What Is an Intranet?

The "classic" definition of an intranet is the application of Internet technologies to internal business applications. In the media, most refer to the intranet in terms of applying Web technologies to information systems. In reality, an intranet consists of computers, communications equipment and cables, software to make the machines work, a business framework or model to drive the applications on the intranet, and people.

People are the most important part of the whole equation. People create the context in which the facts are presented. People talk with other people (clients, suppliers, and colleagues) and develop new contextual references by which to organize the facts. Without people there would be no need for communication. And since knowledge is the biggest asset a company can have, it is imperative that relevant knowledge be shared throughout the organization.

An intranet is really part of an expanding knowledge spiral—putting people in touch with people and putting company-related information into the hands, and heads, of people in or connected to your organization.

Why are Intranets So Appealing to Organizations?

The early Internet was accused of being for "techies and geeks" who understood Unix and drank Jolt cola—it was full of functional capacity but only a small amount of badly organized, business-related content. Then came the graphical user interfaces, created by those same techies and geeks, that made it very easy to use the Internet and the growing Web presence of information sources.

Then average people were offered the opportunity to create their own home pages with quick and easy utilities! Personal pages spread throughout the Internet like wildfire. Not only were companies catching on, but their employees were creating their own pages at home and, in some cases, moonlighting by helping other companies and individuals to "get on the Internet." Somehow we ended up with whole groups of people experimenting with Web page design and HyperText Markup Language (HTML) and lobbying their management to permit them to create a home page for the division. The "vanity publishing" aspect of the internal Web site had begun.

The front-runners in establishing the framework for intranets realized the demands being made by the employees. The smart organizations capitulated, but in a controlled fashion. They agreed to implement internal Web sites, but only under some form of corporate standards and control. Most of these organizations worked with the proponents of the internal system to establish an overall framework, screen, menu, and document template and successfully launched prototypes with participation from across the organization.

Many organizations were faced with employees demanding to use a Web-based interface for searching. Their clients and suppliers began building their own Web sites and attempting to create links among the various pages. With all of the preceding, combined with a burgeoning group of HTML programmers within the organization, a universal front-end (or interface) to internal and external searching was not far away.

To satisfy the needs and demands of the "information age" and the "information literate," the application of Internet technologies to create intranets has enormous appeal. The basic reasons for this appeal include:

- Universal communications—People can connect to others throughout the organization and to people in client, supplier, or partner organizations.

- High-bandwidth—Usually allows the inclusion of video and audio clips to increase the effectiveness of the communications. Multimedia can be used to get the message across in the most appropriate ways. (See Chapter 6, "Cross-Platform Client Browser Setup," to see how multimedia is set up within the user interface, the browser.)

- Proven technologies—HTTP, TCP/IP, Telnet, FTP, and SMTP are some of the proven, highly robust, and reliable Internet technologies. (These acronyms will be discussed in more detail throughout the book.)

- Low cost—Internet technologies are inexpensive when compared to proprietary networking environments—most large organizations already have established TCP/IP networks.

- Communication and adaptation—The use of standard protocols and programming interfaces such as TCP/IP, FTP, HTML, and

MIME can deliver tools that enable internal infrastructures to adapt to changing business needs as well as permit communication with the systems of external partners, clients, and suppliers.

Note

A *protocol*, in our universe, is a set of rules that defines the format of the information packets and the semantics for their use.

On TCP/IP networks, as on most others, the information sent across the network is divided into pieces, or *packets*, to allow a variety of resources to share the same network cables and to assist in the performance of error detection and correction.

The underlying appeal of the intranet rests in these key items: (a)the standards-based approach to produce interoperability and, (b)the creativity of people, unleashed to use these approaches to create feature- and content-rich solutions within the available hyperspace.

Standards-Based Delivery

Driven, for the most part, by the technology features of the Web, information containing a variety of data formats—from text to graphics to audio to video—can be transferred across any TCP/IP-based network. Navigation from one fact to another or from page to page is done by selecting, or clicking, a hypertext link embedded within the document.

The three key Web-related standards that oversee movement of facts, data, or information between the user's Browser and the Web Server are as follows:

- HTML—HyperText Markup Language defines the formatting of the pages of information and how the Web browser should "display" the information to the user.

- HTTP—HyperText Transport Protocol defines how the Web browser and Web server exchange pages of information and other data objects.

- CGI—Common Gateway Interface is a method of defining or describing how dynamic information is exchanged between external applications (outside the Web site) and the Web server.

These standards allow for immense flexibility in introducing new types of data to be shared, such as Java scripting for interactive objects and the Virtual Reality Markup Language (VRML) that defines virtual reality objects. HTML, HTTP, and CGI are discussed in more detail in later chapters.

Interoperability

Interoperability is a problem in organizations when information from diverse systems needs to be brought together in a single interface. This sounds a lot like what has already been discussed relative to intranets.

With a given number of information systems to make "interoperable," you can calculate the number of translation algorithms that you need as follows: $.5(n(n-1))$, where n is the number of systems that need to become interoperable.

Note

A translation algorithm is, in essence, an application that is written between any two computer systems so they can "converse" with each other transparently. For example, an individual sells her house and moves into another: she has access to an application at work in which she can change her coordinates in her employee record. Because the company has many locations, each with its own local Human Resources software, the changes are posted locally in one database application; but when they are rolled up into the corporate system at headquarters, the data in the local system is retrieved by an application locally that extracts the new information and passes it over to the corporate database, that is running on a completely different platform and database software program.

This means that, as in figure 1.2, for five systems to become interoperable, 10 translation algorithms are required—each line connecting a system represents one algorithm.

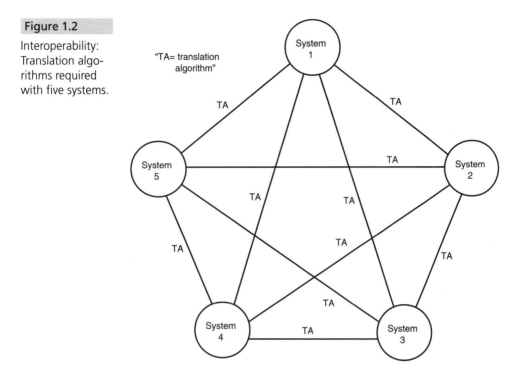

Figure 1.2

Interoperability: Translation algorithms required with five systems.

The math is simple—with 10 systems, 45 translation algorithms are required. This is expensive to create and maintain.

By selecting a standard, or a set of standards, through which all information sources must be made available, a company can reduce the number of translation algorithms that have to be developed and maintained to make all its information systems interoperable. Figure 1.3 shows the number of translation algorithms required to make the five previously mentioned systems accessible through the Web-based intranet that you are proposing.

Creating and maintaining five algorithms in this model is a more effective and efficient model. More on how to create these translation algorithms can be found in Chapter 10, "Introduction to CGI."

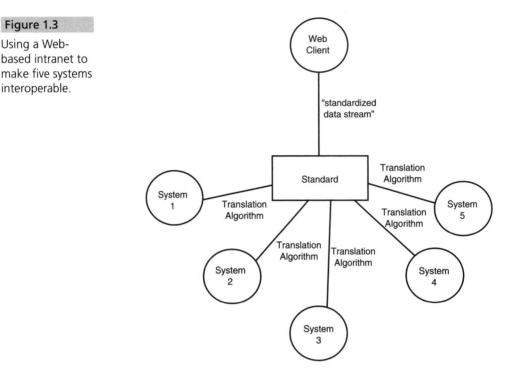

Features

From the perspective of the Information Systems management, the important features of the intranet are as follows:

- It uses TCP/IP for local-area and wide-area transport of information.

- It uses HTML, Simple Mail Transfer Protocol (SMTP), File Transfer Protocol (FTP), and other Internet-based standards to move information between clients and servers.

- It is inside the firewall of the corporation and, therefore, not accessible to the general public via the Internet.

- It is owned by the company and managed by IS with similar sets of tools and procedures as its legacy systems.

These features will be discussed in further detail in other chapters, but for the moment, a brief discussion of each will help set the stage.

1. The intranet uses TCP/IP for local- and wide-area transport.

   TCP/IP stands for Transmission Control Protocol/Internet Protocol, which are the names of the two most popular protocols in the suite of protocols that enable the networks of the Internet to communicate. Although they are not the only protocols in the suite, TCP/IP is the generic name given to the suite.

   The TCP/IP protocol suite includes, in addition to those mentioned above, the following protocols, the majority of which will be covered in this book: Domain Name System (DNS), Simple Mail Transfer Protocol (SMTP), File Transfer Protocol (FTP), User Datagram Protocol (UDP), and numerous others.

   The Internet protocol (IP) is where TCP and UDP are encapsulated, like a letter in an envelope. The IP packet provides the address required to ensure that the data gets to the right Internet (or in your case, intranet) computer.

   TCP provides guaranteed delivery and serialization of the data (making sure that the data arrives in the same order in which it was sent). Using sequence numbers assigned to the UP packets by the sender, the recipient's computer reorders the IP packets according to their TCP sequence numbers, if they were shuffled in transit. If any data is missing, TCP arranges for the missing packets to be resent.

2. The intranet uses HTML and other Internet-based standards to move information between clients and servers.

   Aside from SMTP and ftp, which are part of the TCP/IP protocol suite, the movement of information between servers and clients needs to done in a consistent fashion. Documents for Web browsers are written in HyperText Markup Language (HTML).

Looking at an HTML text file, you would think that something had gone wrong with the word processor used to create the file—the text is interspersed with formatting commands that look like the following: *<format_command>*.

HTML includes ways to specify links to ftp archives, Gopher servers, and other Web servers. HTML documents are transferred between Web servers via the HyperText Transport Protocol (HTTP).

Graphical Web browsers take the HTML-tagged document from the Web server and present it to the user based on the formatting specified by the HTML commands. Hypertext links to other documents, other Web servers, or other Internet services are usually displayed with a visual cue, such as an underlined phrase.

Graphics, audio, and video clips can also be displayed by the Web browser to the user by separate programs when the browser receives data of the appropriate type. All browsers will handle GIF and JPEG file formats. Some browsers require helper applications in order to process images for viewing within the browser.

3. The intranet is inside the firewall of the corporation and not accessible to the general public via the Internet.

   A firewall is a combination of hardware and software which acts to prevent unauthorized access between networks. A firewall is used to protect intranets from unauthorized use. Chapter 5 discusses firewalls in greater detail.

   Even though the same technologies are used on the Internet, the intranet is designed to be used only within the organization. If you have a network in place within your organization and have more than one local area network, you will probably have at least two routers involved in moving information between end nodes of your network. By having routers in your networks, you allow more devices to be interconnected through the introduction of multiple network numbers (this will be covered in greater detail in Chapters 4 and 5).

Routers enable the separation of one group of computers from another. Many routers have the ability to filter the IP addresses that can access or pass information through a network. Thus, the network administrator can put very strict controls on who uses what on the network.

4. The intranet is owned by the company and managed by IS with similar sets of tools and procedures as its legacy systems.

   Within an intranet, the company decides which information it wants to make available to its employees and how it wants to make the information available. By controlling the development and implementation of the access tools, the company can use its traditional computer systems management or life cycle development procedures. This keeps the company working with the development methodology it is accustomed to using for the creation and maintenance of its legacy systems. There is no learning curve relative to the implementation of a new methodology dictated by external factors.

   The implementation of an intranet is just another programming application or project that IS would undertake. The underlying concept of the intranet is a non-traditional alternative to client/server systems implementation. The analysis, design, development, testing, and evaluation processes that are traditionally used for the company's systems can be used here. It is the use of "traditional" Internet server and client software that makes the implementation of the solution different from the "usual" client/server implementation.

The company does not have to buy a tremendously expensive software program, nor does it have to purchase tremendously expensive consultants/integrators to make the system work. Many of the CGI tools that can be used are in the public domain. You will learn, later in this book, that you can implement modest CGI scripts effectively and efficiently.

Making Your Case

We live, work, and breathe in a competitive global market. "Innovate or die," we have been told in the press. The terms "downsizing," "rightsizing," and "re-engineering" have been used so often that the meaning behind the words has been blurred. (Recently a colleague was overheard saying that his group was going through "re-engineering," their computers were being upgraded to 486s. His interpretation was not that the business processes of his work group were being re-engineered but rather the technology they used was being re-engineered.)

In this chapter, you will review the business needs that intranets address and how the intranet can be judged as to whether it can meet these needs or not. Before implementing an intranet, the company should analyze the *value* that the intranet could bring to the organization in support of its business processes. That value may be measurable through a formal Return on Investment process, or it may be less tangible, qualitative benefits that arise.

Following this look at the *value proposition* for an intranet, the *business case* for the intranet will be discussed, including some suggestions as to what other companies have found to be successful intranet applications. Once the business case has been established, the process of planning the intranet must take place. The chapter outlines a number of the items to be taken into account when planning for the implementation of the intranet.

Preparing a Value Proposition

A value proposition is a document that outlines the rationale for pursuing a project, from both a quantitative and a qualitative point of view. In considering the implementation of an intranet to support the business processes of an organization, the financial impact, or the quantitative point of view, is generally supported by a Return on Investment analysis. One of the primary reasons for implementing an intranet is the qualitative benefits that accrue from the intranet.

This section of the chapter will explore both the financial impact as well as some of the compelling qualitative benefits that many organizations have already realized through their intranet implementations. Many organizations stop short of doing the qualitative analysis and rely on Return on Investment when considering intranet implementations. The most significant point to be made here is that in order to have significant impact on the bottom line, companies must change the way in which they work. This statement is more properly addressed by the qualitative analysis than the financial returns alone.

Business Needs Addressed by Intranets

Businesses have to face the realities of the '90s. They have to be efficient and effective. Intranets have an inherent ability to increase productivity, lower costs, and reduce delivery times to market.

- **Reducing time-to-market**:

  - Allows staff to access the information they need when they need it; they should not have to spend their time searching for information but rather analyzing the information—this reduces the *opportunity cost* associated with the time spent researching

  - Enables working with suppliers, vendors, and clients to develop new products and strategies as *partners*

- Permits staff to search and access previous work to reduce redundant efforts

- Allows geographically dispersed staff to participate in "virtual teams" and to access the project information instantaneously

- **Customer service:**

  - Encourages (and requires) sharing of information, from problem reports to new product development, so that any staff member can converse intelligently with any client

  - Provides direct access to the client, through a hyperlink to the client's external Web site

  - Permits staff to review what the client is saying to its customers

  - Ensures that feedback mechanisms are globally available and shared by all

  - Makes results and comments available on more than just one desk so that all can review and provide their own comments and feedback

- **Sales efforts:**

  - Permits information about competitor products to be accessed via links or to be distributed from one individual or group to all staff

  - Makes current product literature as well as "in-the-pipeline" information available at everyone's fingertips, turning every staff member into a potential salesperson

  - Allows "just-in-time" training about new and existing products or about the potential client (through examination of the client's Web site)

  - Permits access to the knowledge of a distributed sales team

Evaluating the Financial Impact of an Intranet

Staying ahead of the pack, in order to survive or succeed, means that you need the ability to run on intuition and your best judgments, as well as the ability to analyze the financial impact of your actions. Some call this ability "running on intuition" and Return on Investment (ROI).

If you are under strict budgetary control, ROI is an important tool for ensuring that the actions you take are the most profitable ones available. This has obvious implications for both the company's future as well as your own. You will read more about ROI later in this chapter.

Return on Investment is a good starting point, but you must also weigh the financial return against risk, timing, competition, and feasibility considerations.

Many companies are realizing that their needs for corporate and market information are not being met by their current environment. These major communications hurdles must be overcome in the competitive environment. With significant investment in the current systems, and a constrained financial policy, many companies are running on instinct and have turned to the intranet to solve their communications problems.

Given the amounts of money typically invested in their legacy systems, senior management is generally cautious about adopting new business models. In order to get real management support—the funding required for implementation—a business case will have to support the value proposition presented to management. The business case and the process to get the green light from management will be discussed more later in the chapter. Focus for the moment on the value proposition on which you will base your efforts.

Intranet projects are bought into by senior management based on two aspects:

- Harvestable savings

- Qualitative benefits

How the harvestable savings are demonstrated by setting up an intranet in an organization will be discussed in the following sections.

Cost Savings of Implementing an Intranet

Savings can be identified easily when looking at candidate applications for an intranet. They can very quickly add up to attractive numbers and easily convince management to adopt the strategy. Remember, however, that unless you already have the basic infrastructure in place, there will be incremental costs in setting up the facilities required.

Here are a few classic examples of savings realized through the implementation of an intranet.

Example 1: Employee Manuals

Traditionally, all employees are issued manuals covering financial and human resource policies, including benefit entitlements. These cost approximately $20 each (in this real organization) to print and distribute. As changes are made to the policies, copies are printed and mailed to all individuals.

By publishing the manuals and the changes on the intranet, the users can access the documents whenever they need them. Notices about changes can be posted in the "What's New" section, instructing the staff to review the changes as necessary.

The savings realized are the printing and distribution costs for new manuals and the ensuing changes. Say that approximately 400 of an organization's 4,500 staff turn over annually. The estimated annual savings of using an intranet therefore equals $8,000 in new manuals. An estimated six changes per year are made to the policy manual. At $2 per employee per change for printing and distribution, the estimated annual savings equals $54,000.

Example 2: Telephone Directories

In this scenario, the 2,000 person organization publishes a printed phone book quarterly for internal use. The information on each individual consists of a phone number, office coordinates, and after-hours contact information. Staff surveys indicate that, on average, nine out of ten clients who were referred to a particular phone or desk by switchboard personnel or other staff should have been referred to someone else. The "I think so-and-so is responsible for doing such-and-such..." syndrome drove staff crazy and frustrated clients. A six month project to incorporate the "Duties as assigned" section from every individual's job description into the printed version failed—in only a handful of cases were the descriptions representative of what the people actually did in their job. The intranet solution takes the published phone book database and, using forms (discussed in Chapters 9, 10, and 11), enables the individuals to maintain their own phone numbers and addresses and to input, in their own words, a description of their roles and responsibilities. This information base is searchable (via a form), and the incentive to the individuals to keep their job profile accurate and current is the ability to reduce the amount of noise or incorrect referrals. The Client Satisfaction Survey of the marketing department shows a marked increase in the "happiness rating" of the clients.

Savings are estimated to be about $45 per employee per year for updates of the phone book—or $90,000 per year. This does not take into account the time saved dealing with erroneous referrals, nor does it reflect the happier clients.

Example 3: Catalog/Price Publishing

A parts clearance company printed and distributed its catalog and price book on a monthly basis to its 75 headquarters-based tele-sales staff and 50 road sales representatives (in addition to the marketing, accounting and purchasing staff). The staff at headquarters had access to the inventory levels of each part through their workstations, but the road reps did not. Road reps were required to call the tele-sales staff, on priority lines, to find out inventory positions on potential orders. Servicing the road reps took an estimated 20 percent of the tele-sales staff time, and the headquarters staff did not receive any compensation for sales made by road reps.

The solution for this company was to put the catalog and price list onto the intranet, which could be accessed by the tele-sales staff and also the road reps, who dialed a toll-free number from their notebook computers (appropriate security measures were established). A CGI (Common Gateway Interface) script was written to allow staff to check the inventory position of a given part and to commit a quantity to an order. This made it possible for the road reps to see if a given part was in the current catalog and, if it was in stock, to place an order from the intranet.

The savings realized in this example were an estimated $40 per month per employee for the 125 tele-sales and road rep staff—that is $60,000 of savings per year for the printing and distribution of the catalog and price book alone. This solution also allowed the company to change the way in which it worked, giving all its sales staff more time to do what they did best—sell to clients.

The examples just outline savings realized. There were costs involved in setting up the intranets in the first two examples (both under $20,000 for initial phase and example discussed) and in developing the CGI-based application in the last example (an intranet pilot was already up and running). However, all three examples were still profitable. As seen in the third example, other qualitative benefits can arise from the implementation of an intranet. These benefits are usually discussed under the title of a value proposition.

Qualitative Benefits of Implementing Intranets

The value propositions most often submitted by those implementing intranets tend to focus on the following qualitative benefits:

- Creating a technology-enabled workforce

- Changing the corporate culture

- Abolishing geographical/divisional barriers

- Establishing a corporate memory

- Creating organizational flexibility

All of these qualitative benefits can be arrived at through the implementation of an intranet. Before moving to the business case to discuss how to start your organization along this path, examine each of these benefits, and consider why each is worth the effort.

Creating a Technology-enabled Workforce

Most companies would rather have their staff doing their job rather than searching for the information needed to do the job. Having their staff comfortable in accepting, receiving, sharing, and distributing information electronically is believed to be of significant value. Once people have become comfortable with receiving information electronically, they often tend to provide the results of their work electronically (sometimes even refusing to accept requests for their input unless the notice comes in electronically). This tends to increase the productivity of the individuals who look for other ways to apply the same skills to all projects.

Changing the Corporate Culture

Unlike electronic mail where people tend to create noise and traffic by copying everyone on their recipient list, an intranet encourages people to post their efforts in a central space for others to come to—in other words, it provides "information on demand." The benefits include the following:

- The productivity of individuals is demonstrated in this sharing space because the artifacts of their efforts are now in the corporate domain. Non-productive people have nowhere to hide in this new environment and, as a result, the overall productivity level of every employee increases.

- People will realize that they can no longer hoard information— they have to share what they know (knowledge is *not* power, but rather *shared* knowledge is power).

Abolishment of Geographic and Divisional Barriers

Information wants to be free. If it is not free to travel from one area to another, misunderstandings and friction can occur between groups. Many companies are moving their compensation/reward systems away from individual and group profitability toward contribution to overall corporate objectives and goals. Intranets allow the contributions to be documented and recognized publicly, encouraging behavior that benefits the corporate goals.

Solving Corporate Amnesia

If every individual in the organization can access the problem solving records, past and present, they each can realize a reduction in the resources expended to solve recurring or similar situations. This scenario enables the entire organization to develop creative solutions to any situation. Instead of assigning ownership and restricting the communications flow, unlimited creativity and information flow and multiple ownership are now possible.

Organizational Flexibility

Most companies want to assemble their best people into teams to address projects that can last from one day to several years. They want to bring their best resources to bear on each issue. This physical problem can be solved with an intranet. Here are some of the advantages demonstrated by this flexibility:

- Intranet tools provide easy communication between groups, allow mobile workers to participate, and accommodate the concept of a disconnected work model from a technological perspective.

- Key staff can move in and out of projects when their skills are required or no longer needed.

- Having the project history documented and available on demand reduces the time spent on the learning curve for newly arrived project members.

- Intranets permit organic configuration and reconfiguration of "virtual" workgroups from the human-ware perspective.

The benefits discussed in the previous sections are desired by almost every organization in order to compete in the global marketplace. Companies need to implement the changes necessary to bring about these qualitative benefits—it is the premise of this book that an intranet can permit an organization to travel this path. How these changes are implemented are the subject of the next section on the Business Case.

Building the Business Case

In order to address the critical pressures that a business faces today, you must realize that significant changes in the business will not be brought about by the applications running on the intranet, but rather from changes in how you work. The intranet allows you to alter how you work.

Your business case will be built around an initial project demonstrating the realizable benefits of an intranet. Remembering that you want to enable changes in the way staff work, your goal is to increase performance of the worker by incorporating concepts of performance technology, information management, and intelligent, intuitive interface design.

The press has presented arguments against the implementation of intranets, focusing on what the authors call "hidden costs" (refer to

"Intranets: A Thicket of Hidden Costs," *Computerworld,* May 6, 1996). This book proposes that the intranet presents an alternative to client/server that mitigates the costs of implementing an intranet.

The premise of this book is that the intranet is *a* solution but may not be *the* solution for any given organization. The book outlines tools, methods, and procedures through which an effective and efficient means of supporting the mission-critical business processes of an organization can be created where none have been perceived before. It is through the creation of the value proposition and the business case that the organization will be able to decide if the intranet is its best solution. If the intranet is selected as the appropriate solution, this book should be a valuable guide in putting in place the required pieces.

The remainder of this section discusses the categories of strategic applications that have been successfully implemented in existing intranets, how to pick the *right* applications for an initial pilot, and a brief discussion of Return on Investment.

Strategic Applications

The intranet has no value without the applications that take advantage of it. These applications must address the needs of the business relative to its strategic direction. There is a virtually limitless number of applications that can be created for specific industries or for a demonstrated need.

Note

In order to avoid confusion, programs are defined as a series of instructions that are followed to achieve a given result—the printing of a statistical report, for example. Applications are defined as a *context* within which a program or series of programs is exercised to achieve an objective or goal. A sales management application, for example, might contain a program to print a statistical report.

The two terms are often used interchangeably. In this book the author refers to applications from the contextual perspective.

The majority of intranet applications fall into the following categories:

- *One-to-many publishing applications,* such as easily outdated manuals, newsletters, and so on, where the payback is immediate in the reduction of printing and distribution costs.

- *Two-way interactions,* such as obtaining office supplies or the organizational phone book where the individual updates his or her own position profile (for search purposes), thereby reducing improper referrals or paper pushing by knowledge staff.

- *Many-to-many applications,* such as a work group's newsgroup to facilitate the exchange of information among the members, organized by topic or "thread." People can subscribe to internal or external newsgroups based on their interests at the time.

The secret to the initial success of an intranet is to pick the right initial pilot applications. Pick a business process and design the intranet to be the enabler of that process. The right blend of immediate payback and "agent of change" applications have to be selected in order to convince senior management of the economic benefits in the short term and the longer term strategic benefits.

Picking the Right Initial Pilot(s)

When you are deciding upon the initial applications to implement, keep in mind the following recurring themes that were seen in numerous successful intranet implementations:

- **Passion**—Success demands passion; you have to be able to stand in front of senior management and sell them on the concept. If you have emotional ownership of the project, then you are on the right track.

- **Lasting difference**—An immediate impact on the daily routines of users, especially in automating mundane administrative tasks, will encourage them to seek new applications for development for the intranet.

- **User empowerment**—Reduce the barriers to automating processes through experimentation. Development costs are not high; therefore if an idea doesn't work, it can be noted, archived, and stopped easily. Visual presence of results of individual efforts allows the shy and retiring among us to put forward ideas in a forum where no one can see us blush.

- **Change of ownership**—By providing staff with the means by which to increase their productivity, where they are an active part of the change process, change becomes a positive way of doing business. If staff can see that their work is published and that their peers can provide feedback, comments, and accolades, they will continue to seek new and improved ways to incorporate the intranet into the fabric of their jobs.

Depending upon which area is the driving force behind the implementation of the intranet, you can develop applications for the major areas of any company. Here is a quick run-down of some specific types of applications that could drive your intranet.

- **Sales and Marketing (a one-to-many type application)**—The biggest hurdle in this area is to have accurate and timely information in the hands of a sales force that is often spread across the country or around the world. Publishing applications for this group indicate that having critical information at the exact moment you need it can make, or break, a sale.

- **Product development (a many-to-many type application)**—Up-to-date information is essential for the successful management of a project. With team members updating project schedules and progress reports, the success of the project often depends upon how effectively the participants communicate among themselves. Password protection keeps sensitive information restricted to the team members, but in the principle of "shared knowledge is power," any member of the company, including those outside the project team, may be an integral component in the process.

- **Customer Service (a many-to-many type application)**—To provide the highest quality service and support in the industry, in an efficient cost-effective manner, an intranet enables the sharing of customer and problem information in order to create a corporate-wide support system.

- **Human Resources (a two-way interaction type application)**—Keeping employees attuned to their corporate and personnel well-being, publishing corporate information, and using transactional applications to provide personal data, human resource departments can free up their staff from answering routine questions and basic processing tasks.

- **Finance (a two-way interaction and one-to-many type application)**—Secure access to important financial information in an easy-to-use format can be provided through the use of forms-based queries; travel authorizations and claims can be completed and processed quickly and efficiently; and financial indicators and clear financial objectives can be set and posted for restricted or general internal review.

When selecting the initial pilot, you must incorporate applications that convince senior management of the economic benefits in the short term and the strategic benefits in the long term. You will, therefore, move along the lines of the intranets that have been adopted by pioneers, but ensure that you enable change to happen, moving from a simple IntraWeb to enterprise intranet.

1. Publishing—Select the group in the company that prints and distributes the most paper-based information for distribution to all employees. Propose the following: we won't reduce their preparation costs, initially, but we can significantly reduce their print and distribution expenditures. Target the human resources and sales and marketing departments. Once you have the "big ticket" items on your side, you can focus on any other area that produces any document of value within the corporate entity.

2. Searchable directories—Develop the means to provide rapid access to the corporate phone book, including the corporate "yellow pages" (employee-generated and -maintained profiles of areas of

individual responsibilities and expertise). You will also work to develop the skills necessary to implement an application to provide access to client/customer profiles. These skills provide the ability to allow employees to attach a note to the profile, outlining meetings, contacts, status of sale/project, and so on, in addition to creating discussion forums that can be used to track thoughts and ideas.

3. Information links—Hyperlinks to Internet sites of competitors, clients, and suppliers keep staff abreast of what *they* are saying to *their* client community. They also will provide pointers and links to industry news feeds, research sites, and external newsgroups based on employee demand and availability.

4. Simple groupware application—Select a project in the company that is just getting started or, if there are no others, use the intranet project to put in place a project-based intranet application. The project's schedules, status reports, and information base will be made available for all to see, participate in, and comment on.

By starting with these initial areas of applications, you will demonstrate fiscal benefits of implementing an intranet as well as the power of the intranet and its ability to foster change. First you need to understand the concept of Return on Investment.

Return on Investment

In the world of limited resources and too many projects, Return on Investment, or ROI (mentioned earlier in this chapter), has become a requirement for significant investments in new technologies. Many will argue that the ROI process will slow down, and possibly kill, the adoption process of an intranet. Evidence suggests that the completion of a formal ROI does not slow down the full-scale implementation of the intranet, but rather it provides a structured methodology for the implementation to all aspects of the organization.

The key to a successful implementation of an intranet is to identify a base application that justifies the necessary technology and infrastructure required to support the intranet. This application will be used in the initial pilot. Most companies are comfortable with allowing the initial pilot to take place before a formal ROI relative to widespread implementation has to be completed. That is one of the primary reasons to select the Publishing application(s) in the initial pilots above.

Just a brief example, from "Example 1: Employee Manuals" in the section "Value Proposition" earlier on in the chapter, the costs to put in place the intranet technologies were $20,000. The resulting ROI for this project was 310 percent ($62,000 savings divided by $20,000 of incremental costs). This was well above the company's threshold for investment in the project.

Intranet Planning Process

The planning process for the intranet is similar to that for other computer systems/applications—the traditional life cycle methodology. The differences that will be focused on here relate to the technologies used within the initial pilot and what you hope to achieve at the end of the pilot. The basic components of the intranet planning process include the following:

- Strategy planning

- Analysis and design

- Implementation

- Marketing

- Evaluation

These steps are not one-time-only steps. Because the intranet deals with changing business requirements, changing information needs, and changing technology, among other things, the planning process is indeed a cyclical process.

Before discussing the components of the planning process, consider for a few minutes the principles involved with planning the intranet.

Principles of Intranet Planning

You are proposing that what is put into place is a methodology that focuses on building the processes and skills that enable and encourage adaptive innovation.

1. The methodology should be focused on the functional business and management requirements of the business rather than on the technology available.

2. The technology will likely change from month to month, so it is recommended you not base solutions on the available technology.

Traditionally when we hear the word "methodology," visions of slow-moving bureaucratic volumes of dos and don'ts dance through our heads. With the intranet, you are proposing the following:

3. That the focus is on the strategic business or mission of the company, not on the techies' desire to create a marvel implementation of the latest technology.

4. Movement is imperative—continuous new information and new innovative services are absolute requirements if the intranet is to keep the company's employees using the intranet as their primary source of information.

In your proposal for the initial pilots, focus on four items that are easy to implement within a short time frame (from a technological point of view): publishing, searchable directories, information links, and simple groupware. From a humanware side of things, the applications that you are proposing are not onerous, nor do they require painstaking effort on the part of the individuals. They are designed to free up individuals to perform those roles for which they are employed.

Strategy Planning

The basic premise here is that every application you implement through the intranet will be in line with the company's overall business strategy and will further the ability of the employees of the firm to achieve corporate objectives.

Selecting the initial applications for the intranet has been discussed earlier in the development of the business case for the intranet. It is prudent to discuss the following project management strategies that should be kept in mind throughout the intranet planning process:

1. Charismatic leaders are a must. They can clear the way of politics and demonstrate that the intranet has senior management support. Emotional commitment by management is often more important that financial commitment.

2. IS support, not IS control. To get the ownership of the intended changes, IS has to remember that users tend to perceive IS as wanting to control the systems and how they can be used. The intranet is about helping everyone do their jobs in the most effective fashion. IS has to walk a narrow path between requiring standards and suggesting policies. The suggested approach is to develop "standard" templates and routines for users to incorporate in designing their own proposals for applications on the intranet. By providing the framework and assisting others in exploiting all the features of that framework, IS can work with the rest of the organization in the development of applications that not only meet corporate business needs, but also still work on the platforms.

3. Affect the daily lives of users. The first intranet applications have to be compelling enough to convince the users that the intranet is the preferred application development environment. If this can be achieved, then the creative genius in each employee will kick in and staff will repeatedly come up with new applications that improve productivity. For the users to develop ownership of the intranet, they must have, ultimately, multiple applications and a long-term strategic view. This means that the rate of new application development in the early stages will have to be rapid in order to keep the momentum going.

4. Define, then harvest the benefits. Companies with the highest ROI from intranet implementation tend to be those that most precisely articulated the business benefits they expected from their intranet prior to the implementation of the intranet. The more

numerical goals you can attach to the specific benefits, the more likely you are to obtain the desired benefit. In times of scarce budgets, the intranet project management can always propose to develop the application on behalf of the proponent and split the harvested benefits. This gives both sides the added incentive to do the job as effectively and efficiently as possible.

5. Involve the users throughout the process. Get them involved early and at every stage throughout the process. Providing them the mechanisms for good two-way communications and getting them to use the intranet project management capabilities will have them hooked in without much effort.

6. Success can kill. The success of the intranet implementation can generate an unexpected demand for new applications and product enhancements. Resources can be overwhelmed and original project deadlines can slip if pressure from outside is not resisted. IS must be a key player in ensuring that the original phase-in approach is followed.

7. Central coordination, not control. All applications should have a similar look and feel, minimizing productivity downtime in learning new applications. This also ensures that there is no wasted time and effort in terms of application duplication.

These are all elements that have to be considered in the strategy planning phase of the intranet. These are systematic, but they must be incorporated into each application proposed for the intranet in order for overall success to be achieved.

Analysis and Design

The decision to pursue an intranet is assumed to have settled a couple of important issues:

- There is a business process or need for the intranet.

- Sufficient resources are available to obtain the required equipment for the pilot.

This book will focus on the four application areas that were identified for your initial pilot (publishing, searchable directories, information links, and simple groupware) and accept the fact that these four applications represent the business needs to be addressed by your intranet implementation.

In terms of analysis and design, this book is not designed to be a treatise on the subject. Instead, the areas that need to be addressed will be identified so that you can make your own analysis relative to your specific situation. In later chapters, this book will delve further into several of these areas and explore in more detail the areas that you will want to pull back into the overall planning process.

The areas to be explored, which you can apply depending upon your unique situation, cover the following:

- Basic infrastructure requirements

- Maintaining the server

- Operations

- Special publishing

Basic Infrastructure Requirements

At the technical end of the project, several areas need to be addressed under the title of basic infrastructure requirements. In many cases, the firms putting in place intranets already provide access to the Internet for their staff and will already have implemented an external Internet site. If this is the case, the information below may be redundant. For those who are starting an intranet from scratch, the following presents the basic components of the infrastructure that are required for the intranet.

- Server software—Unless you already have it, you will need to evaluate and choose server software based on needed features: concurrent users, seamless integration, and modularity. Chapter 3 discusses in more detail the HyperText Transport Protocol server required for the intranet, and Appendix C provides a list of the currently available server products. If changes are required to the server software implemented in the Internet server to integrate with the intranet, changing the server software vendors should be transparent to the end users. The server software must run on server hardware.

- Server hardware—If you do not already have a server, select one based on processor, memory, disk space, and clock speed. Remember that a successful intranet will need room to grow, so selecting hardware based on scaleability (the capability to add components to existing hardware systems in order to improve performance) and speed is recommended.

- Communications/network—You need to know how your staff will be connected to the server. If you currently have a network in place that supports TCP/IP, go with this. TCP/IP *is* the protocol of the intranet technologies and is discussed further in Chapter 4, "Fundamentals of TCP/IP: Understanding the Transport Layer." It is possible to have all users employ dial-up to get to the server, but if applications in mind are bandwidth intensive (such as video), network access becomes an issue and dial-up is dead in the water.

- Server Services—What server services are to be enabled? Do the applications or users require ftp, Telnet Gopher, or something else? If ftp service is to be provided, you will need to decide on the types of files that will be available and if the service is something other than anonymous ftp.

- Browsers—If one is not already selected within your organization, select a browser that works across all your platforms (Mac, Windows, Unix). Browsers are becoming a commodity, but certain features are important depending upon the features that you wish to implement in your intranet (Netscape helper applications and plug-ins and proxy authorization, for example). Chapter 6 discusses the issues involved in cross-platform browser setup in further detail.

- Installing client—Determine how you will get the client software (browser) installed on the machines of your staff (diskette, electronic, mail in of hard drive, and so on). You will need to have procedures and support structures in place and be prepared to update these as the client software is upgraded.

- Organize the server—You will need to establish the directories, backups, archiving, permissions/security, searching and purging procedures, and documentation.

- Organize the development environment—As the proponent of the intranet, staff will be looking to you for the tools, methods, standards, and procedures to use and follow. These need to be selected and established based in part on the quantity and type of publishing work that will be undertaken.

- Organize the support environment—There are four levels of support that you will have to provide: the end user, the developer, the server, and the network. It is recommended that you publish your service standards for all to see in order to ensure that everyone understands the process of support. Use the intranet for publishing these standards.

- Organize the intranet server master hierarchy of pages and access—You will need to decide on what types of information will be displayed first and how the navigation through the site will take place.

This list is not all-inclusive. Please review your own technical platform for items that already exist in your other applications and see if they need to be addressed in the above or another area.

Maintaining the Server

Several areas surrounding the server have to be incorporated into the planning process. They include, but are not limited to, the following:

- Indexing—Information holdings must be indexed so that searching across a knowledge base is possible. Select and implement the software, ensuring that it runs automatically each time new information is loaded onto the server. Support for indexing alternatives should be available—users should be able to specify a search of total holdings or a limited search. Searching should support multiple file types and should incorporate sub-directory searching as well. Wide Area Information Server (WAIS), described in Chapter 10, "Introduction to CGI," is a good example of this search technology.

- Purging—Information should not reside on the server indefinitely. Pages of information should expire and be archived and then deleted off the server. This prevents stale information from slipping through maintenance cracks. It also forces the providers of the content to keep an eye on their information space on the off chance that nothing is there!

- Security/Access—Universal access to information may not be possible—some information may be limited to certain groups or individuals. User accounts and passwords may need to be assigned and maintained, and security levels may need to be implemented. Security levels normally allow individuals to access information at their own divisions or domains or subordinate levels within, but they do not permit access to the same or higher levels in another division/domain.

- Directory maintenance—Directories need to be created, deleted, or renamed. The directories should be organized by application, by department/division, and by function (jointly or separately depending upon the scope of the directory).

- Monitoring disk space usage—If disk space usage approaches capacity, either the server will require additional space (scaleability) or a server reorganization will be required.

- Monitoring system throughput—Minimum acceptable levels should be set for response times. If response times are slow, better server software or hardware should be considered as well as the option of setting up additional servers to handle the flow. Also, a review of the content on the server is warranted. Large images and huge documents may be the reason the system is slow.

- Upgrading of software—New releases of software, as well as the development tools, search engines, and the operating system, will occur. Processes for the implementation of the upgrades and distribution of the new releases of the tools need to be established within the framework of the plan.

- Backing up/restoring server—The server software and the data files should be backed up regularly, with verified methods of restoration that impose minimal disruption and downtime. Having a backup machine ready for cross-over will be a must as the intranet grows—plan for it now.

Tip

The intranet is an efficient way of distributing new releases of software to users.

Operations

Under this heading the planning for creating the content for the intranet is covered. The following topics must be considered:

- Authoring—It is prudent to recommend a single methodology for authoring documents from each type of input program. This topic is discussed in Chapters 13, 14, and 16 of this book. For example, outline how your corporate standard word processing program, your spreadsheet application, your presentation software, and your standard database application will be designed for provision across the intranet.

- Publishing/republishing—There are several items to cover in this section including the means of transporting an authored page from the author to the output directory on the server. An authorization process for the release of information should be put in place that gives ownership of "information space" to the content providers. The tools and techniques for this process are discussed within a later discussion in Chapter 17, "Workflow Software, Groupware, and the Intranet." It is essential that the publishing process is not onerous on the authors—you want them to publish, and it is your job to provide a service to them.

- Linking of new documents—As new documents are added to a collection, a method and process for adding the document links to the collection's page are required. If the intranet has information collections that are managed by different groups within the company and presented on sub-sites within the intranet, it is recommended that you incorporate a recommendation in which the owners of each information space have a person designated as the local "IntraMaster." This person would need to be trained in the use of a basic HTML authoring tool, allowing them to update the required pages and add the new document links. This process is not difficult to learn or an added burden.

- Removal of obsolete links—The corollary of adding new links and a process to remove old links and documents automatically should be developed.

- Succession planning—A procedure (or a set of procedures) should be established to provide for organizational changes, IntraMaster resignations or additions, and so on. This should include a procedure to transfer the permissions for access to server directories.

Author's Note

In the development of an intranet publishing system, consider Michael Porter's *value chain* approach in developing the intranet. The intranet is an agglomeration of technology, information, and people. Each plays a different role in adding value to the document as it moves through the publication process from authoring to distribution. In putting together the intranet, strive to be only a distribution service provider even though you have to plan, implement, and assist the rest of the organization in the development of the skills and procedures they require. Getting the right information to the right people at the right time and in the right place is a big enough challenge. The ultimate goal of the intranet is to provide a structure that supports the business processes of the organization, not one that *is* one of the business processes. Try to get out of the normal document publishing loop of research, author review, edit, approve, and publish. The provision of products and services that facilitate this process is the what the intranet should be about.

Special Publishing

When the application calls for access to information stored in another computer application external to the intranet server, IS personnel are often called upon to implement the required solution. In the overall strategy of the intranet, the information systems of the organization that are external to the intranet, but required within the final intranet solution, should be identified so that the analysis and design stage can explore the best means to achieve the desired solution. Some possible solutions are ODBC access or Lotus Notes access.

- Open Database Connectivity (ODBC) access—In order to implement access to an ODBC database, an established standard for accessing data within databases, you need to ensure that you have IS personnel who understand HTML, CGI tools, drivers, and the external database that you wish to access. This topic is covered in greater detail in Chapter 11, "Integrating ODBC and CGI." For each separate database to which you wish to provide access, the following must be accomplished:

  - The user interface must be designed

  - The gateway scripting must be written

  - The appropriate drivers must be installed

  - The procedures must be tested and the results integrated and linked into other intranet pages

The contents of the ODBC database are current, so the results may differ for a query today and the same query tomorrow.

- Lotus Notes access—For data stored in Lotus Notes applications, a process is currently required to convert the data from the native Notes format to HTML documents that are then placed on the intranet server. This conversion process requires good analysis skill and experience in Notes application development, HTML programming, and the application used to convert from Notes to HTML (Lotus InterNotes Web Publisher or TILE are two possible applications).

Note

> At the time of writing, Lotus is in a beta test of the Lotus Domino Web Server, a version of Lotus Notes that incorporates dynamic access to Notes data from a browser. The user connects to the appropriate IP address, and the Notes page at that address is dynamically converted to HTML and presented to the user. The user cannot only read the records within the Notes database with appropriate security permissions, but can also use the browser to modify existing records or input new records. The significance of this development is that no longer will conversion to HTML be necessary to get data held by Lotus Notes onto an intranet. The data will be directly accessible from the browser at the user's computer.

Access to other databases of information, be they ODBC, Lotus Notes, or some other format, is possible. However, significant effort in maintaining the accessibility of this information is required. The other applications will be upgrading their software as time passes and, with each change that they make to their systems, you must have a change control process in place to handle the required changes at the intranet end.

The preceding four sections pose a great deal of the questions you have to consider in the preparation of the analysis and design portion of the intranet planning process. By the time you have finished answering all these questions, you will have a good understanding of the current capabilities within the company and what you need to implement in order to support the intranet. You should know the following as you move into the planning stage for implementation:

- How many users you will connect, where they are, the method by which they will connect to the intranet (dial-up or network), and the operating system and browser that they will be using

- The hardware and software for the server, how it will be configured, the services that will be offered (FTP, Telnet, and so forth), the access/security framework that will be implemented, and how the usage of the server will be monitored

- How the content providers will be creating and delivering information to the output area(s) for placement on the server and how the information will be maintained for currency

- The IS resources required to implement and maintain special publishing applications where information is obtained from databases external to the intranet server

Implementation

The implementation plan will be very simple in this initial pilot portion of the intranet—just get it done. You don't want the user community to get too excited too early in the development cycle because managing user expectations will be difficult enough without adding the hype on top of the work.

With the answers to each of the questions raised in the previous section, the implementation plan for the technology will normally consist of one-line items with a completion date, such as the following: Obtain and install Netscape server by Fri. 13th.

The secret to successful implementation will be to put the technology components into place before you start to get involved with the content providers. Once you start assisting the content providers, your time and effort will be pulled away from the technical aspect of setting up and testing the infrastructure.

Here are some of the other areas that you will have to address in the implementation plan for the intranet.

- **Support.** Initial requirements will address how to set up the browser and how to connect the users to the server so that they can navigate through the site. Content providers will be looking for support in getting their information to the server and will be trying to push the envelope of functionality for their content—how to put in image maps, Java applets, video, and so on.

- **Training.** This will be a big issue if the intranet is the first exposure to Internet technologies for the organization. If the company has already provided for Internet access for staff, the training plan will already be complete. Otherwise, you need to consider training procedures such as showing users how to use the browser, search, print, and use passwords; showing local IntraMasters how to publish; showing the help desk staff how to use a browser and instruct them on HTML creation and publishing and interaction with intranet support staff; and, showing all staff the policies and procedures of working on the intranet.

Note

> An IntraMaster is a person designated with the responsibility of operating the intranet or a portion of the intranet. Chapter 15 is a discussion on the roles and responsibilities of the IntraMaster.

- **Policies.** The policies relating to the publishing of information electronically should be defined and published for all to access. These should include the code of ethics, an acceptable use policy, what types of information should be published, guidelines about look and feel (have you developed a template for them to use?), and policies on the introduction of new software into the intranet—both at the client end as well as at the server. It is recommended that there be a small policies committee that has representation from the users, the content providers, IS, and senior management. The committee should be responsible for the establishment and maintenance of the policies of the intranet. Samples of several policies are included within Appendix A.

Your implementation plan for these last three issues is important, not so much as an impact on the development of the intranet, but rather as a parallel with the implementation of the technology components. When you go live with the intranet, these items need to be available to all staff as a framework in which the intranet will work.

Marketing

Marketing of the intranet is not a trivial task. While some employees will grab hold of the intranet and use it (pushing you to enhance both the content and the technology), others will be reluctant to use it at all.

The marketing plan for the intranet needs to incorporate announcements, demonstrations, and hands-on tutorial/training sessions, and it has to spell out in plain language that the intranet is the way the organization will be communicating. This last aspect needs to be stressed, but from the perspective that this is not top-down. The intranet is a means for everyone to communicate with everyone else. Information may be organized from a top-down perspective, but it is what the staff does with that information that is the key.

The intranet is about enabling employees to work more effectively and efficiently, providing just-in-time information instead of just-in-case information. The marketing efforts of the intranet need to ensure that each employee is aware that the intranet is not there to replace them, but to help them do their work.

Evaluation

Evaluation of the intranet will help to continually refine and improve both the services and the content. Automated mechanisms can be put in place to track the usage of the intranet, counting the number of times a document was accessed and by whom, for example. User surveys to determine the use of collections of information along with feedback mechanisms embedded into the pages of the intranet can assist the content providers and the IntraMaster in determining new content demands.

Earlier on the concept of ROI and its importance in the investment strategies of the organization were discussed. With these targets firmly in mind, your evaluation plan must incorporate a process for measuring the parameters that were identified and determining where the intranet is positioned relative to financial requirements.

The secret of evaluation is that it is a multiple occurrence. Evaluation is an ongoing process that can only help to increase the value of the intranet, both in achieving its financial objectives and in realizing the qualitative benefits that were outlined at the beginning of the chapter.

3

The HTTP Protocol: Understanding the Application Layer

This chapter is geared toward getting you started on building your own intranet. It will start immediately by covering how HyperText Markup Language (HTML) documents are normally moved between a server and a client (browser). The more complex processes involving scripts and forms will be covered in detail in later chapters.

In the course of normal interaction, a Web browser requests a document from a Web server, processes the HTML codes, applies the appropriate formatting, and displays the document to the user. If the returned document contains a hyperlink to another document and is activated by the user, the Web browser will retrieve and display the linked document. Figure 3.1 depicts the scenario.

Figure 3.1

Web browser
connected to
two Web (HTTP)
servers.

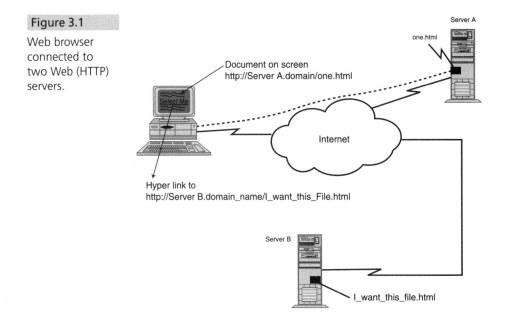

The browser running on Desktop 1 obtains a document from Server A that contains a link to a document on Server B.

By activating the link, the client requests the file from the HTTP server running on Server B and presents it to the user at the desktop.

The communications between the browser and the HTTP server are defined by the HyperText Transfer Protocol. Before you move into setting up the intranet servers, you need to review HTTP in detail so that you have an understanding of how the HTTP server will work before you set up your service. To this end, this chapter will discuss the following topics:

- Purpose of HTTP

- Requirements of HTTP

- HTTP terminology

- HTTP's overall operation

- Access authentication with HTTP

- Security considerations with HTTP

- HTTP's relationship to MIME

After you have become acquainted with HTTP and the operation of an HTTP server, the remainder of the chapter will guide you through the process of setting up the Netscape Communications Server on the Windows NT and Unix servers.

What is HTTP?

The HyperText Transfer Protocol (HTTP) has been in use on the World Wide Web since 1990. The first version, HTTP 0.9, allowed for the transfer of raw data across the Internet. Since then, HTTP 1.0 has evolved to provide messages in Multipurpose Internet Mail Extensions (MIME)-like formats that contain metadata about the data that is being transferred. MIME is discussed in more detail later in the chapter.

Note

Metadata is information about a piece of information. For example, the file format of the information, the requester's location, the server's address, the size of the file, and the version of the browser software being used to view the information are all metadata for the piece of information stored within a file.

Given the demand for new functionality and features, a revised specification, HTTP 1.1, is under development. This new specification seeks to address functions and services and is necessary in order to enable two communicating applications to determine each other's real capabilities (such as determining whether a browser supports extended HTML tags or Java). The new version (HTTP 1.1) will be backward compatible with HTTP 1.0, but has tightened up the requirements to ensure more reliable implementation of HTTP's features.

Author's Note

The HTTP protocol can be looked at simply as the browser sending out a message that roughly says the following:

```
"This is who I am: my name and address
```

```
This is the version of software that I am operating under:
➡product  X version y.z
```

```
These are the file formats that I can display dynamically within
➡my display: formats a, b, c, d, ...
```

```
This is the file that I would like to receive from you, the
➡server, if it is one of the file formats that I can use: name
➡of file"
```

The server's response is along the lines of:

```
"OK, this is what you told me: name, address, file requested
```

```
Here is the file that you wanted, in the following file format
➡that you, the browser, can use"
```

A great deal more is involved within the HTTP protocol, but the whole of it revolves around the negotiation process of the request/ response format until the information requested by the browser is delivered to the browser, or until the browser determines that the server that the information requested is just not accessible by the user.

The Purpose of HTTP

In obtaining information by the Web browser, to indicate the purpose of the browser's request—today's information systems require more than just retrieval, they need to be able to search, update, and annotate —HTTP permits an open-ended set of methods to be used. Open-ended refers to the ability to add new functionality to the methods of passing information, such as GET and POST (discussed in detail in Chapter 10, "Introduction to CGI"). To indicate the resource on which to apply a given method, HTTP builds on the reference discipline provided by the Uniform Resource Identifier (URI) as a location (URL) and a name (URN).

Note

Independent of any protocol, the URI discipline is a philosophy or methodology of indicating the resource (file, server, and so on) that should be addressed to implement the instructions indicated by the method chosen. The URI is simply a formatted string of characters that identify a network resource. The Uniform Resource Locator (URL), the physical location of the resource in question, and the Uniform Resource Name (URN), the name of the resource (the file name), are combined to form the URI. Within the HTTP protocol, the semantics for the HTTP URL (http://host [:port#]/absolute path) assumes a location of port 80 for the Web server. When the name of a file (an URN) is added to the preceding URL location, a fully developed URI has been created. The de facto nomenclature in use within the Internet and intranet worlds is to use the term *URL* as a blanket for URIs, URNs, and URLs.

The messages transmitted are passed along in a MIME-like format.

The Uniform Resource Locator (URL) of the document on Server B might appear something like:

```
http://ServerB.domain_name.orginization_type/i_want_this_file.html
```

In other words, something has to enable you to retrieve different types of documents on a variety of different machines running a variety of different operating systems and server programs. To this end, HTTP allows the browser to select a resource by selecting a hypertext link, and the responding server responds with not only the file but with information about what the browser should do with the file or how it should be displayed. Because there are many file formats that people want to provide and this number is increasing rapidly as we explore new ways to prepare and deliver information, the current version of HTTP is being rewritten to accommodate new file formats and to provide greater functionality within the Internet and the intranet.

HTTP also permits other Internet protocols (SMTP, FTP, Gopher, and so on) to communicate with browsers. This provides hypermedia access to a wide range of resources in a variety of application types.

HTTP Requirements

As you go through the implementation of the intranet, the first thing you have to do is ensure that you have the intranet Web server up and running. Since this is an HTTP server, you need to make certain that you understand the basics of how the HTTP protocol works and have the equipment necessary to put the server into place.

There are several "flavors" of HTTP servers that can be implemented as the heart of the intranet in your organization; a list of currently available servers is provided in Appendix C, "Intranet-Compatible HTTP Server Products." Several of the servers have, traditionally, been free of charge in terms of acquiring and implementing them, as well as being "unsupported" by the authoring groups. More and more, however, commercial versions of HTTP servers are appearing on the market and are fully supported. The demands of companies putting in place mission-critical applications on these servers have caused businesses to move toward the selection and implementation of a "commercial" server.

In this book, the Netscape Communications Server will be used as the HTTP server for example and demonstration purposes.

Note

> Appendix C provides a list of other available HTTP servers that are intranet-compatible. While this list may not be exhaustive, or even completely accurate at the time it is read, every effort was made at the time of writing to create the list for your review.

Terminology of HTTP

Based on the HTTP 1.0 specification, the following terms are presented so that you have a understanding from which to proceed and can understand the roles played by the participants in and the objects of the HTTP communication:

- **connection**—a transport layer "virtual circuit" created between two programs for the purpose of communication

- **message**—the basic unit of HTTP communication, consisting of a structured sequence of octets (see Chapter 4 for a description of octets) matching the syntax defined in HTTP 1.0 specification and transmitted via the connection

- **request**—an HTTP request message

- **response**—an HTTP response message

- **resource**—a network data object or service that can be identified by a URI

- **entity**—a specific instance of a data resource, or a reply from a service resource, which may be enclosed within a request or response message. An entity consists of metadata in the form of entity headers and content in the form of an entity body

- **client**—a program that establishes connections for the purpose of sending requests

- **user agent**—the client that initiates a request. These are often browsers, editors, spiders (Web-traversing robots), or other end-user tools

- **server**—a program that accepts connections in order to service requests by responding to clients

- **origin server**—the server on which a given resource resides or is to be created

- **proxy**—an intermediary program that acts as both a server and a client for the purpose of making requests on behalf of other clients. Requests are serviced internally or by passing them on, with possible translation, to other servers. A proxy must interpret and, if necessary, rewrite a request message before forwarding it. Proxies are often used as client-side portals through network firewalls and as helper applications for handling requests via protocols not implemented by the user agent

- **gateway**—a server that acts as an intermediary for some other server. Unlike a proxy, a gateway receives requests as if it were the origin server for the requested resource. The requesting client may not be aware that it is communicating with a gateway. Gateways are often used as server-side portals through network firewalls and as protocol translators for access to resources stored on non-HTTP systems

- **tunnel**—an intermediary program that acts as a blind relay between two connections. Once active, a tunnel is not considered a party to the HTTP communication, although the tunnel may have been initiated by an HTTP request. The tunnel ceases to exist when both ends of the relayed connections are closed. Tunnels are used when a portal is necessary and the intermediary cannot, or should not, interpret the relayed communication

- **cache**—a program's local store of response messages and the subsystem that controls its message storage, retrieval, and deletion. A cache stores cacheable responses in order to reduce the response time and network bandwidth consumption on future equivalent requests. Any client or server may include a cache, although a cache cannot be used by a server while it is acting as a tunnel

At any given time, a program may be capable of being both a client and a server. The terminology listed is used to define the role being performed by the program for a specific connection. Servers can switch behavior based on the specific nature of a request. A server may be a proxy, gateway, tunnel, or an origin server as required.

Overall Operation of HTTP

The HTTP metaphor is based on this request/response sequence of events:

1. The client connects to the server and passes a request to it. The request contains the form of the request method, URI, and version of the protocol.

2. The request modifiers, client information, and any possible content follow in a MIME-like message.

3. The server responds with a status line indicating its protocol version and a success or error code.

4. Again, a MIME-like message follows containing server information, entity metadata, and possible body content.

The most basic form of HTTP communication is where a user agent initiates a request applied to a resource on some origin server (such as selecting a file for retrieval and display). Figure 3.2 demonstrates the simple chains of request and response from the client to the origin server (in order to select a document, for example).

Figure 3.2

The basic form of HTTP communication.

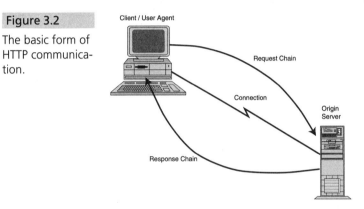

However, it is often more complicated than this. There can be one or more intermediaries present in the chain—common ones being proxy, gateway, and tunnel. Here is a possible sequence of events:

1. Acting as a forwarding agent, the proxy takes the request for a URI, rewrites all or part of the message as necessary, and passes the message along to the server identified in the URI.

2. A gateway acts as an agent working on behalf of another server and may be required to translate the request into the other server's protocol in order to facilitate the communication.

3. A tunnel is used to pass a message between two connections without changing the message—through a firewall, for example.

Figure 3.3 outlines a more complex request that is sent from the desk of the Marketing manager, through the Marketing Department's server on the intranet, to the corporate server, then on to the server in Finance, which connects to the server containing the latest financial figures the Marketing manager has requested.

Figure 3.3

A more complex communication chain.

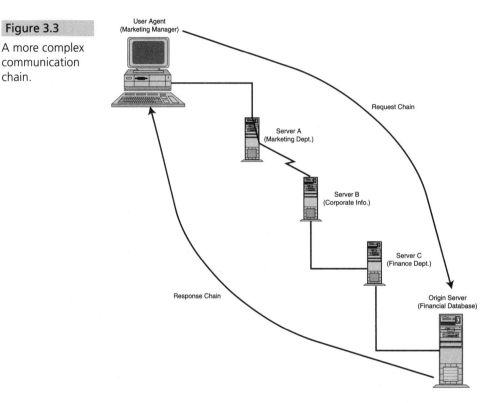

Keep in mind that at any point in time, the servers in figure 3.3 may be servicing other requests. A request that travels the whole length of the chain must pass through four separate connections. This is significant because some of the HTTP communications options may apply differently depending upon the nature of the request.

For example, any party that is not acting as a tunnel may use an internal cache for storing and handling requests. If one of the participants in the chain has the response to the request cached, it returns the response and shortens the chain. Not all responses are cacheable, and some requests may contain modifiers placing restrictions on cache behavior.

HTTP communication occurs over TCP/IP connections, generally, and the default port used is TCP 80. Other ports can be used, but the port would have to be specified in the request in this event. HTTP presumes a reliable transport and, thus, could be implemented on top of any other protocol on the intranet or other networks that guarantee reliable transport.

Note

> The mapping of the HTTP request and response structures onto the transport data units of other protocols is beyond the scope of this book. For more information on the topic, review the Web site of HTTP Working Group, http://www.w3.org.

Access Authentication

HTTP uses a relatively simple challenge/response mechanism for authentication. The server challenges a client request, and a client provides authentication information. In other words, in response to a request, the server asks for the user-ID and password, provided by the user.

The basic principle here is that there is a protected space (realm) to which one desires access. The user must provide a user-ID and a password for each protected realm. The ID and password sent by the user agent are passed back to the server in this non-secure method of filtering unauthorized access to the resources on the HTTP server. The basic authentication scheme is based on the assumption that the connection between the client and the server can be trusted, something uncertain in an open network. In this light, if the intranet put in place uses connections outside of the organization's firewall, some form of security, another firewall for example, should be put in place to protect the organization's resources even further. Firewalls and other security measures are discussed in Chapter 5, "Intranet Security."

In spite of all this, clients should implement this form of basic authentication in order to communicate with the servers that use it. The results of the analysis and design phase of the intranet planning process should determine if this basic level of authentication is sufficient and, if applicable, where it is not. For the moment, suffice it to say that HTTP permits the authentication function to exist, and the implementation of the function may need to be explored further as the breadth and reach of your intranet expand.

HTTP Security Considerations

As previously mentioned, the basic authentication scheme is not a secure method of user authentication. It does not prevent the entity-body, the resource requested from the server, from being transmitted in clear text across the physical network used as the carrier, but it is possible to implement additional authentication schemes and encryption mechanisms to increase security. Chapter 5 discusses these mechanisms briefly, but for a fuller understanding of security measures that can be put into place, please refer to *Actually Useful Internet Security Techniques* by Larry Hughes, Jr. (New Riders, 1995).

Within the software development community, the convention has been established that the GET and HEAD methods of the HTTP protocol only perform retrieval. These methods are considered "safe." This allows user agents to represent other methods, such as POST, in order to make the user aware of the fact that a possibly unsafe action is being requested. The user can then decide whether or not to pursue it.

Used typically within *forms*, the GET method of passing information to the server appends the input from the browser to the end of the URL in the following format:

```
http://host/resource_name?query_string
```

An example of this would be:

```
http://host/search.cgi?sasquatch
```

The resource that matches the criteria is passed directly back.

During a POST submission from a form, the input data is encapsulated within a character string which must be interpreted before the appropriate actions, as dictated by the resource, are undertaken. It is because of this interpretation of the character string that POST is considered less safe.

Chapter 10 discusses the use of both GET and POST methods of passing data from forms to various resources and outlines how the POST method can be made safe.

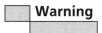
Warning

> HTTP cannot regulate the content of the data that is transferred, nor is there a method of determining the sensitivity of any particular piece of information within the context of any given request. Applications that use the POST method should supply as much control over this information as possible to the provider of that information.

This chapter only briefly touched some of the security limitations of the HTTP protocol. For more information regarding security issues, please see Chapter 5. For more information on GET and POST and how they are implemented, see Chapter 10.

Relationship to Multipurpose Internet Mail Extensions (MIME)

While HTTP 1.0 uses many of the MIME constructs to allow entities to be transmitted in an open variety of representations, HTTP has several features that differ from the Internet Mail and MIME standards.

MIME will be discussed in more detail from the client perspective in Chapter 6, "Cross-Platform Browser Setup."

Note

> Please refer to "MIME (Multipurpose Internet Mail Extensions) Part One: Mechanisms for Specifying and Describing the Format of Internet Message Bodies" RFC 1521, (by N. Borenstein and N. Freed, Bellcore, Innosoft, September 1993) for a detailed discussion of the Internet Mail standards. This can be found at http//:www.cis.ohio-state.edu/htbin/rfc/rfc1521.html.

Here are some of the basic differences to keep in mind:

- HTTP allows for line breaks to be represented as CRLF (carriage return, line feed), bare CR (carriage return), and bare LF (line feed) within the input.

- HTTP 1.0 date formats are from a restricted set to simplify the process of date comparison. Proxies and gateways from servers running on other protocols need to ascertain that the Date header conforms to HTTP 1.0 formats.

More details concerning the client perspective of MIME can be found in Chapter 6.

Getting Up and Running

Finally you can get the show on the road! This section will guide you through setting up the Netscape Communications Server on both a Windows NT and a Unix server. The processes described in this section pertain to Netscape products, but they are similar across the realm of the available commercial intranet server products listed in Appendix C.

Requirements for Installing an HTTP Server

The following basic requirements must be met in order to successfully implement a sever:

- The minimum computer system requirements for installing the Netscape Communications Server (see table 3.1) are in place.

- The TCP/IP protocol is configured on the server and all of its clients.

Note

This chapter assumes that the TCP/IP protocol has been installed as required. Chapter 4 will cover the basics of TCP/IP, including the installation of the protocol stack on the server(s).

- The server and the clients have had no previous versions of HTTP installed.

- The Netscape Communications Server software has been acquired —based on the computer and operating system platforms.

Table 3.1

Unix Platforms

Any CPU with access to a CD-ROM running a supported Unix operating system.

> DEC (OSF/1 2.0 and 3.x)
>
> HP-UX 9.03, 9.04, 10.x, and series 700, 800, and 9000 hardware
>
> IBM RS/6000 (AIX 3.2.5 and 4.x)
>
> SGI (IRIX 5.2 and 6.2)
>
> Sun (SunOS 4.1.3)
>
> Sun (Solaris 2.3, 2.4, and 2.5)
>
> 386/486/Pentium (BSDI 2.0)

Minimum 32 MB RAM, 64 MB or more is recommended for machines that will handle a lot of traffic.

5 MB hard disk space for the server, plus 2–3 MB for log files.

A forms-capable browser (such as Netscape Navigator, which is included with the server).

WINDOWS NT Platforms

Windows NT workstation with a 486 or a Pentium chip.

> Windows NT version 3.5
>
> Minimum 16 MB RAM (more RAM is recommended for serving large numbers of clients or high levels of transactions)

continues

Table 3.1	
	Windows NT Platforms, continued
	A swap size at least as large as the RAM size (for high-load servers, this should be between 100-150MB)
	30MB free disk space for the installation
	30MB free disk space for log files (for approximately 300,000 accesses per day)
	A forms-capable browser (such as Netscape Navigator, which is included with the server).

Now that the basic requirements to put the server in place have been defined, and in some cases you have just placed the orders for the necessary equipment, return to the HTTP protocol itself to further understand what you are about to undertake.

Information Necessary for Successful Installation

You need to do a few things to make the setup and configuration of the Netscape product much easier:

- Implement or choose a Domain Name Service.

- Create a home page.

- Create an alias for the server.

- Create a user account.

Implement or Choose a Domain Name Service (DNS)

When you install the Netscape Communication Server, you will be asked for either a hostname or an IP address as an input string.

Note

> A *hostname* is a name for a specific computer in the form *machine.subdomain.domain*, and is translated into a dotted IP address by a Domain Name Service (DNS). Chapter 4 covers TCP/IP and the assigning of IP addresses to networks and machines and explains the significance and composition of the dotted IP address.

A Domain Name Service is required if you want to be able to access external servers or if multiple servers are put in place within the intranet. The DNS converts the name of the URI you seek into the numeric IP address. DNS provides your server an identity to the intranet/ Internet, allowing clients to navigate their way to your site.

Because your organization should already have access to the Internet, you may want to have your Internet service provider maintain your domain information. Most will do this for a fee, but you will probably want to access and manage your own DNS from your own LAN as your intranet grows in size. Commercial DNS server products can be obtained and implemented should you require them.

Note

> It is possible to set up a DNS relatively easily on a Windows NT server by installing the software provided in the Windows NT 3.5 Resource Kit.

Create a Home Page for the Intranet

The home page is the first document users will see when they access the intranet. If you have someone who can pull a quick prototype together, use the prototype page as a temporary home page. Creating pages in HTML will be covered in Chapter 8, "Introduction to HyperText Markup Language (HTML)." Otherwise, you can use the page the installation process creates and edit it after installing the server.

Create an Alias for the Server

If your server will run on one machine among many in your network, you should set up an alias (such as www) that points to the actual server machine. This way, if you have to move the intranet "home" off the original server, you can change the actual hostname or IP address of the server machine without having to change all your URLs.

Author's Note

> You may start the intranet server running on a computer that runs several other servers (FTP or other HTTP servers). As the usage grows, you may be required to move the intranet server software to another computer altogether. The actual name of the physical server does not have to be used within the URL to the intranet server. It is recommended that you establish an alias so that when and if you move the intranet server to another computer, you will not have to change each and every URL to point to the new address. It is common to see *www* used as the alias for Web-based sites, such as
>
> www.intranomics.com
>
> This is my corporate site and it actually resides on a server named alice.intranomics.com. This is the third physical computer that has housed the Web site, and I have learned from experience about the effort required to change all the URLs to point to the new computer.

For example, you might call the server intranet.anycompany.com and then use an alias like www.anycompany.com: the URLs of documents on your server would use the *www* alias instead of *intranet*.

Create a User Account

In order to attach the server to the network, a user account for the server must be created. This account identifies the server as a network resource and will enable the server to be found by users. For security reasons, the server should have restricted access; for example, it should not be able to write to the configuration files. The user account of the server should have *read-write access* only to the directories that are dictated from within the applications running on the server. Consult your system manual if you are not familiar with setting up such an account.

After installation, you can change the user account your server uses, and you should do so on a regular basis in order to reduce the potential of the system being "hacked" by unauthorized users.

For Windows NT

The installation process uses the LocalSystem user account, which has a limited set of privileges by default. After the installation process is complete, it is recommended that you change the user account for the server for security reasons and configure this new user account to have permissions to get files on another machine. This enables your server to serve files that are mounted from another machine. It is recommended that you use a dedicated user account for the server in order to isolate the permissions and privileges of the server.

For Unix

A Unix server also requires a user account that has restricted access to your system resources and runs under a non-privileged system user account. The account needs read permissions for the configuration files and write permissions for the log file directory. When the server starts for the first time, it runs with this Unix user account that was input and identified during installation.

Warning

For security reasons, do not allow the user account assigned to the server to have write permissions to the configuration files. This preserves the configuration in the unlikely event someone compromises the security of the server.

You can use the account with the name *nobody*, but this might not work on some systems as they will not accept this username. Some machines ship with a *uid* parameter of –2 for the user *nobody*. A uid parameter less than zero generates an error during installation. Check the /etc/passwd file to see if the uid parameter for nobody exists, and make sure it is greater than zero. Regardless of the name selected, the account should be dedicated for use by the server and not by any other computer in the network.

Choose Unique Port Numbers

TCP provides a feature called port numbers. *Port numbers* are almost another layer of address below the IP address. Whereas IP addresses uniquely identify computers, port numbers are used to identify the services within a computer. Port numbers below 1024 are called *privileged ports* in Unix because only the root user account can start servers that listen to them. This is done for increased security.

For the implementation of the Netscape Communications Server you need two port numbers: one for the administration server and one for the Communications Server of your intranet. The administration server is a separate daemon that lets you manage the potentially multiple servers of the intranet from a single forms-based interface.

Note

> A server can be run standalone as a daemon. A server running as a daemon continuously listens to its assigned port and spawns a copy of itself to handle each request that arrives.

For Windows NT

The standard HTTP port number is 80. This is the default port, but you can install the server to any port. You should choose a random number (for example, 14532) for the administration server to make it harder for anyone to breach your server's security. When you access the administration forms, use the administration server's port number.

For Unix

Port numbers for all network-accessible services are maintained in the file /etc/services. The standard HTTP port number is 80, but you can install the server to any port. You should choose a random number (for example, 14532) for the administration server to make it harder for anyone to breach your server. When you gain access to the administration forms, use the administration server's port number. Make sure the port you choose isn't in use. Look at the file /etc/services on the server machine to make sure you don't assign a port number that is used by another service. The server will not function properly should two services contend for data coming in on the same port number.

Installing Netscape Communications Server for Windows NT

The installation process consists of two processes: copying files from the Netscape Communications Server CD-ROM to your hard disk, and then configuring and starting the server. This section discusses the installation and configuration of the server.

Note

Errors that occur during installation or when the server is starting are logged in the Event Viewer. The server logs errors to the normal error log file once it has started.

Installation Instructions

To install the server, you need to do the following:

1. Put the Netscape Communications Server CD-ROM in the drive, and then choose File, Run from the main menu.

2. In the dialog box that appears, enter D:\SETUP, where *D:* is the drive letter for your CD-ROM drive.

3. A message box appears with information about technical support. Read this information, then click on Continue.

4. A dialog box appears asking you for the directory where you want to install the server. The default is C:\NETSCAPE. You can enter another drive and directory if you like. This is the server root directory where you install all servers (if you plan to have more than one server installed on your machine). Click on Continue.

Warning

You can't use long directory names. The directory name must be eight characters or fewer. Also, do not rename the directory after the installation because the server uses the directory name for log and error files and for the document root.

5. A dialog box appears asking if your machine has a DNS entry in a DNS server. If you choose DNS Configured, the installation process assumes you want to use host names (you can still use IP addresses if you like). If you choose No DNS Entry, the installation process uses only IP addresses.

Warning

> If your machine doesn't have access to a DNS server that can do DNS lookups, or if your machine does not have an entry in the DNS map of a DNS server, you must click No DNS Entry and use IP addresses throughout installation.
>
> Also, if your machine has an entry in the DNS server, but your machine is not configured to do DNS lookups on the DNS server, you should click No DNS Entry. This means clients can gain access to your server using your hostname, but the server will use IP addresses instead of DNS host names (for example, it uses IP addresses for user authorizations).

6. The installation program goes to your computer's Registry and determines your host name or IP address. Confirm the entry or change it in the dialog box, then click on Continue.

7. The installation program copies all the files to your hard disk and starts a service called Netscape Install. This service runs on a random port and is automatically destroyed after the installation process. A message appears about configuring the server using the Server Manager forms. Click on OK.

Tip

> The rest of the configuration process is done through forms you use with Netscape Navigator.

8. Netscape Navigator appears, displaying a form. Click Install New Server. You will see three buttons.

   • The Server Config button takes you through a series of forms that configure the server.

- The Document Config button displays a form for configuring the document root directory and the types of documents your server can send to clients.

- The Admin Config button displays a form for configuring the administration server.

You can specify which users have permission to use the administration forms to configure all your installed servers.

9. Once you have completed all the installation forms, click on the link called Go For It. The actual installation now takes place, creating a Windows group with three icons: Administration, Navigator, and Netscape Server Help. The software is installed as requested through the steps above.

Results of the Installation Process

Note

During the installation, a number of things happen that you should know about. Some temporary files are written to C:\TEMP. These are removed after installation. No other files or directories are modified in any way.

The installation process places all the files under the server root directory specified in the installation. The following directories and files are created under the server root directory:

- **admserv**—contains the server administration files, the user name and password for the administration account, and the binary files for running the server manager

- **bin**—contains the binary files for the server, such as the actual server, the administration forms, and so on

- **[type]-[port#]**—are the directories for each server you have installed on the machine. The directory name uses the server type and the server's port number, for example httpd-80. Each server directory has the following subdirectories and files:

- **config**—contains the file mime.types. It also contains the server key and other encryption certificates

- **logs**—contains any error and access log files

- **userdb**—contains all user databases. This central directory enables any number of servers to use the same user databases

- **mc-icons**—contains icons for FTP listings and Gopher menus

- **extras**—contains utilities such as a log file analyzer

- **nsapi**—contains header files and example codes for creating your own functions using the Netscape API

Changing the User Account of the Server

After the server installation is complete, change the user account assigned to the server. By default, the user account is LocalSystem. For extra security, change the user account to something more challenging for hackers to work through.

To change the user account after installation, perform the following steps:

1. Go to the Administration Manager and click on System Specifics.

2. Enter the server user account you want to use.

3. Scroll down the form and click on Make These Changes.

4. Go to the Control Panel and double-click on the Services icon.

5. Select the server name Netscape Httpd.

6. Click on the StartUp button.

7. In the "Logon as" section, enter the account name you want to use.

8. Enter the password for that account, then enter it again to confirm the password.

9. Click on OK.

10. Restart the server either by using the Services program or by using the Administration Manager. The next section explains how to do just that.

Starting and Stopping the Server

Once installed, the server should run properly, listening for and accepting requests. If the computer ever crashes or is taken off-line, the server stops, and any requests it was servicing are lost. There are three ways to restart the server:

• Use the Administration Manager to restart any server.

• Use the NT Control Panel Services to restart any server.

• Use the Control Panel Services to configure the operating system to restart the server each time the machine is rebooted.

Choosing between the Administration Manager or the Control Panel Services to restart the computer depends upon the systems administrator's preferences. Both are equally effective and efficient in getting the server back up and running. While the first two methods are more manual in nature, you can configure the operating system to restart the server each time the machine is started or rebooted. Doing so takes only a few steps once and will save time and effort in the future.

1. In the Main group, double-click on the Control Panel icon.

2. Double-click on the Services icon.

3. Scroll through the list of services and select the service called Netscape Httpd.

4. Click on the Start Up button. A dialog box appears.

5. Check Automatic to have your computer start the server each time the computer starts or reboots.

6. Click on OK.

If your intranet is in an area where there are frequent power outages, for example, you may want to use this method to ensure that the server is fired up once the power returns to the computer.

The Server Manager

The Netscape Communications Server should run smoothly after installation. If you need to change any of the configuration information, such as adding a new file server to which the intranet server should have access, or perform general maintenance on the server, you will want to use the Server Manager application of the Netscape Communications Server.

Any remote machine will allow systems administration-level access. However, before you can do any server configuration, you must start the administration server and then use a browser to view the Administration Manager forms. The administration server must be running before you can do any configuration, including remote configurations. For security reasons, do not leave the administration server running if you're not using it. Unauthorized users could cause havoc within the intranet if they were to stumble across the administration server running unattended.

Double-click on the Administration icon to start the administration server and then start Netscape Navigator (it was also installed) with the correct URL for the Administration Manager. The Administration Manager contains links to the Server Manager for each server installed on the computer.

Because the administration server runs as a service, you can use the Windows NT Control Panel to start and view it directly.

In order to access the Server Manager, do the following steps:

1. Double-click on the Administrator icon in the Netscape Server group. If you're doing remote configuration, then you need to do this manually. Use a forms-capable browser to point to the appropriate URL:

   ```
   http://[servername].[yourdomain].[domain]:[port]/
   ```

Use the port number for the administration server that you specified during installation. For example, enter **:14532**, which was used as the example.

2. You'll be prompted for a username and password. This is the administration username and password you specified during the installation process. The Administration Manager appears listing all of the servers you have installed on the computer.

3. Click on the link for the server you want to configure.

That completes the basic installation procedures for the Netscape Communications Server on a Windows NT computer. It is beyond the scope of this book to go further into the details of maintaining and operating the server because each installation will have different configuration requirements based on your organization. For more information and assistance, please refer to the Netscape Web site at: http://www.netscape.com.

Installing Netscape Communications Server for Unix

The installation consists of two processes: copying files from the Netscape Communications Server CD-ROM to your hard disk, and then configuring and starting the server. This section discusses the installation and configuration of the server.

Note

Errors that occur during installation or when the server is starting are logged in the Event Viewer. The server logs errors to the normal error log file once it has started.

Installation Instructions

In order to install the Unix version of the Netscape Communications Server, you must be logged in as the *root* user or plan to install the server on a port number greater than 1024 *and* have a user account has the necessary permissions to write to the directory in which the server software will reside. Otherwise, your user account does not have sufficient permissions to install the Communications Server software.

To install the Netscape Communications Server, perform the following steps:

1. Put the Netscape Communications Servers CD-ROM in the drive and change to the drive and directory for the Unix operating system your computer uses. For example, enter **cd solaris**. The directories available are:

    aix

    bsdi

    irix

    hp_ux

    osf_1

    sun4_nis (see note)

    sun4_dns (see note)

    solaris

Note

There may be a contention problem with NIS (Network Information Service) for the SunOS and DNS services running on the same machine. Netscape does not provide any details within the manual regarding the cause, but because of it, there are two separate tar (compressed) files for SunOS—one with the resolver library linked in, and one without.

The tar file in the sun4_dns directory contains the resolver library (libresolv). Start with this tar file, especially if running DNS. If the server experiences problems locating hosts or if access control doesn't work correctly, re-install with the tar file in the sun4_nis, which doesn't use the resolver library and should solve the problems concerning the NIS.

2. Run the installation program directly from the CD-ROM or copy the installation program to your hard disk and run it there.

- From the CD enter **cd httpd**, then enter **cd install** to change to the installation directory.

- To install from the hard drive, copy the httpd.tar file from the CD-ROM directory to the directory on the hard drive where you want the installation program to run.

The install needs about 10 MB of disk space and should be a temporary directory instead of the destination directory where you will install the server.

Warning

> If you use the Solaris operating system, don't use the /tmp directory because you might encounter problems later in the install process. The installation process copies files to the /tmp directory and could overwrite an existing file required by the operating system. Use another directory name to avoid this problem.

3. Unpack the tar file by typing **tar xvof httpd**. This unpacks the server files and creates a temporary directory structure under the current directory. "o" is an optional argument you may wish to use.

4. Enter **cd httpd** to change to the new directory. Review the contents of the README file before continuing. This will provide you with the latest information about the server.

5. Enter **cd install** to change to the httpd/install directory from which the software will be installed.

6. Enter **./ns-setup** to start the server installation.

Warning

> As stressed earlier in this section, you must be logged in as root or have sufficient write permission to perform the installation. Otherwise, your user account will be unable to install the software to the computer.

7. Accept the default (Netscape Navigator) or enter the name of your browser. The browser starts and loads the installation forms. If you don't understand a setting, accept the default value. Make any necessary changes later via the administration forms, after you have determined the proper settings.

   The installation HTML forms collect data that the install process later uses to generate the configuration files magnus.conf and obj.conf, which are used to control the performance of the server.

8. Once you have completed all the installation forms, click on the link called Go For It to start the actual installation procedures.

Temporary files are written to /tmp and removed after the installation is finished. No other files or directories are modified in any way.

What Happens During the Installation Process?

The installation process places all the files under the server root directory specified in the installation forms. The following directories and files are created under the server root directory:

- **start-admin and stop-admin**—start the server manager, which permits configuration of all servers installed in the server root directory

- **admserv/**—contains the server administration files, the username and password for the administration account, and the binary files for running the server manager

- **bin/**—contains the binary files for the server, the administration forms, and so on

- **[type]-[port#]/**—are the directories for each server you have installed on the machine. The directory name uses the server type and the server's port number (httpd-80, for example). Each server directory has the following subdirectories and files:

- **config/**—contains the server's configuration files: magnus.conf, obj.conf, and mime.types. It also contains the server key and other encryption certificates

- **logs/**—contains any error and access log files. Shell scripts to start, stop, and restart the server and a script to rotate log files are also created and located here

- **userdb/**—contains all user databases, acts as a central directory, and lets any number of servers use the same user data bases

- **mc-icons/**—contains icons for ftp listings and Gopher menus

- **extras/**—contains utilities such as a log file analyzer

- **nsapi/**—contains header files and example codes for creating your own functions using the Netscape API (Application Programming Interface). See the *Netscape Programmer's Guide* for more information

Starting the Server

Once up and running, the server and its child processes run constantly, listening for and accepting requests. If the computer ever crashes or is taken off-line, the server processes are lost. There are four ways the server can be restarted:

- Automatically restart it from inittab.

- Automatically restart it with other rc scripts; in other words, with daemons in /etc/rc.local when the machine reboots.

- Restart it manually.

- Soft restart.

Because the installation forms of the Netscape Communications Server cannot edit the /etc/rc.local or /etc/inittab files, edit those files with a text editor to make the required changes. If you don't know how to edit these files, consult your system administrator or system manual.

The method chosen to restart the computer depends upon the preferences of the systems administrator. In order to automatically restart the server, use the inittab procedure; however, you will need the appropriate access permissions to edit the inittab file. The rc scripts function is much the same matter if it is identified to run during startup of the computer. You can use the command line approach to manually start a server or to restart a *hung* server.

Restarting with Inittab

Inittab will automatically restart the server whenever the computer reboots. In order to set up this feature you need to:

1. Put the following text on one line in the /etc/inittab file in order to restart the server from inittab:

```
http:2:respawn:[ServerRoot]/[type-port#]/start -i
```

   The "–i" option prevents the server from putting itself in a background process.

2. Replace [ServerRoot] with the directory in which the server was installed.

3. Replace [type-port#] with the server's directory

Remove this line before stopping the server by editing the inittab file. Otherwise, the server will boot up again automatically.

Warning

If you are using a version of Unix not derived from the System V version (such as SunOS 4.1.3), you won't be able to use the inittab option. Check the Unix documentation for information regarding this feature.

Restarting the System with rc Scripts

In order to restart the server with rc scripts, the following steps are necessary:

1. Place the following line in /etc/rc.local:

```
[ServerRoot]/[type-port#]/start
```

2. Replace [ServerRoot] with the directory in which the server was installed and the [type-port#] with the appropriate directory information.

Restarting Manually

To restart manually, do the following:

1. Log in as root or with the server's user account.

2. At the command-line prompt, enter the following command:

```
[ServerRoot]/[type-port#]/start
```

3. Replace [ServerRoot] and [type-port#] with the appropriate directory names. Optional parameters that can be used include:

   - **–p XX**—starts the server on a specific port number. This overrides the setting in magnus.conf.

   - **–i**—runs the server in inittab mode. If the server process crashes, the inittab will restart the server. It also prevents the server from putting itself in a background process.

Warning

> Manually starting the server using the preceding syntax will fail if the server is already running on the port. Stop the server first, then use the *start* command. If server startup fails, kill the process before trying to restart in order to reset all the computer's parameters.

Soft Restart

To restart the server while it is running, such as in the case of a "hung" process, enter:

```
[ServerRoot]/[type-port#]/restart
```

[ServerRoot] and [type-port#] are replaced with the appropriate directory names.

This script finds the parent process ID, located in the logs/pid file, and sends the hang-up (–HUP) signal with this process ID.

Stopping the Server Manually

In the event that you wish to stop the server manually, such as to implement changes to the configuration of the server, follow these steps:

1. Log in as root and enter the following at the command-line prompt:

   ```
   [ServerRoot]/[type-port#]/stop
   ```

   [ServerRoot] and [type-port#] are replaced with the appropriate directory names.

2. If you used inittab to restart the server, remove the line added to /etc/inittab by editing the inittab file before stopping the server. Otherwise, the server will restart automatically.

The Server Manager

The Server Manager is a set of forms used to change options and control the server. The Server Manager is available immediately after installation and can be used from any remote machine to make configuration changes.

The administration server must be started before the Server Manager can be accessed. Go to the /admserv directory in the server root directory and enter start-admin. The administration server is started using the port number you specified during installation. For security reasons, the administration server should not be allowed to run unattended. Unauthorized users could cause havoc within the intranet if they were to stumble across the administration server running unattended.

To view the Server Manager, perform the following steps:

1. Use a forms-capable browser to point to the appropriate URL:

   ```
   http://[servername].[yourdomain].[domain]:[port]/
   ```

   Use the port number for the administration process specified during installation (the example used was 14532) and not the port number for an individual server.

2. Enter the administration username and password you specified during the installation process. The administration manager appears listing all of the servers you have installed on the computer.

3. Click on the link for the server you want to configure.

That completes the basic installation procedures for the Netscape Communications Server on a Unix computer. It is beyond the scope of this book to go further into the details of maintaining and operating the server because each installation will have different configuration requirements based on your organization. For more information and assistance, please refer to the Netscape Web site at: http://www.netscape.com.

Status Check

At this point in the process of building the framework for an intranet, you have learned the underlying concepts of the intranet, looked at the value proposition for your implementation, and built the business case and implementation plan for an initial intranet pilot project. This chapter has begun to put the nuts and bolts of the intranet in place.

By going through the process of building the Netscape Communications Server, you have given yourself a computer with the means (HTTP) to communicate with other computers and pass information among your organizations. The next step along the path is to understand the transportation layer of the Internet technology model, TCP/IP. This will be a review of the basic concepts and will aid in the development of the understanding of how data moves between the computers.

Fundamentals of TCP/IP: Understanding the Transport Layer

The TCP/IP, or Transmission Control Protocol/Internet Protocol, is the data communications protocol of the Internet and is used to coordinate the exchange of information between two network devices. Thus, by default, TCP/IP is also the protocol of the intranet. TCP/IP is so important to the intranet (and Internet) that Microsoft has included TCP/IP support in the base Windows NT system. Before setting up the intranet within an organization, it is a good idea to understand the basic fundamentals of TCP/IP and how it is used within the intranet. In the previous chapter, the HTTP server was installed and set up for work. Before you could install the HTTP server software, you first had to actually set up the physical computer as a server. One of the elements involved in that process is the installation and configuration of the TCP/IP "stack" on the server. This chapter briefly describes this process of establishing a Windows NT computer for use as a server.

Most Unix implementations already include TCP/IP support as part of the operating system. When you boot a new Unix machine, you are asked if the workstation will be used as part of a network. A positive response invokes a request for the information needed to configure all the networking features properly. Should you be required to make changes to the configuration of the Unix workstation or server relative to the implementation of the TCP/IP stack, please see your system's manual or system administrator.

This chapter will provide steps for the configuration of the TCP/IP protocol stack on a Windows 95 desktop as well. Users of the intranet will need to have TCP/IP in order to access the system, and Windows 95 is the example used. This chapter also uses Windows 95 to demonstrate the basic requirements of configuring a desktop for dial-up networking to the intranet.

Introduction

With its roots in the Advanced Research Projects Agency Network (ARPAnet) of the United States Department of Defense, the Internet grew from its 1971 base requirements—a means for ARPAnet to transfer files and support remote logins. The first requirement led to the File Transfer Protocol (ftp) and the second to the development of Telnet.

In 1983, the University of California at Berkeley released a version of Unix that incorporated TCP/IP as a transport protocol. Because of the extensive use of Unix at ARPAnet, the adoption of TCP/IP was widely accepted within ARPAnet—the Internet boom was on.

As previously stated, TCP/IP stands for the Transmission Control Protocol/Internet Protocol. It is actually a suite, or stack, of protocols, and aides in the movement of data between computers.

As the de facto standard of Internet communication, it is supported by almost all computer systems manufactured today.

The design of the TCP/IP protocol is based on a layered model. With each layer independent of the others, changes in the services affecting one layer should not affect the others. The layered model also enables the development of a number of small services for a specific task. Initially more difficult to design, a layered model is easier to maintain and enhance. As such, it is more efficient.

According to the original model, as information moves from one computer to another through the protocol, control over the data passes from one layer to the next, starting at the application layer in one of the systems. The data proceeds down through the stack on the first computer, travels across the wires to the second computer, and then travels up the stack in the second system. Figure 4.1 outlines this process and lays out the hierarchy of the TCP/IP stack.

Figure 4.1

Transport of data across the TCP/IP stack.

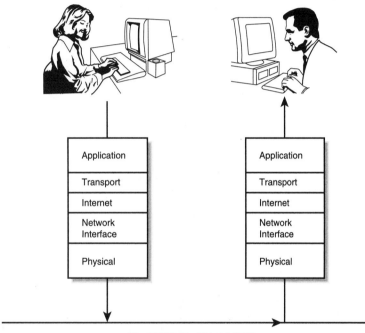

Physical Media - Network Cable

There are five layers to the TCP/IP protocol. Each adds its own header and trailer data, encapsulating the message from the layer above. At the receiving end, the data is stripped one layer at a time and the information is passed up the stack to the application layer. The layers are as follows:

- **Application Layer (Layer 5)**—applications such as ftp, Telnet, and SMTP relate to this layer.

- **Transport Layer (Layer 4)**—TCP and User Datagram Protocol (UDP) add transport data to the information packet and pass it to the Internet layer.

- **Internet Layer (Layer 3)**—this layer takes the packet from the transport layer and adds IP information before sending it off to the Network Interface layer.

- **Network Interface Layer (Layer 2)**—this is the network device as the local computer (or host) sees it and through which the data is passed to layer 1, the Physical layer.

- **Physical Layer (Layer 1)**—this is the layer where the ethernet, Point-to-Point Protocol (PPP), or Serial Line Interface Protocol (SLIP) protocols exist and permit the use of TCP/IP over the wires connecting the computer to the intranet—the LAN cables or the phones lines.

Basic Concepts of TCP/IP

The Internet Protocol is the base upon which the other major protocols of the TCP/IP stack are built. TCP and UDP are encapsulated within IP like an invitation in an envelope. In order to get to the recipient, the envelope needs to be addressed to arrive at the correct destination. IP provides the address required to get the data packet to the correct intranet computer.

Addressing in TCP/IP

An analogy to the addressing scheme of TCP/IP is the corporate phone system that includes an automated voice response system. Companies with many employees often publish one main number in the phone book. Each employee has his or her own extension. Thus when someone calls the main number, he is instructed to dial the extension of the person he is trying to reach.

If you look at a phone number, it is made up of an area code, the local phone number, and the extension of the individual in question. TCP/IP is similar in nature in that the addresses are divided into components that help to specify the location of an individual resource on the network.

An *IP address* is a 32-bit number, but is broken down into four segments of eight bits each. These 8-bit segments are called an *octet*, and are converted into decimal numbers separated by dots ("."). The result is a "dotted octet," such as 205.211.4.4.

The IP address is made up of two parts: the network portion and the host portion. To make efficient use of the addresses available, the designers divided the IP addresses into classes based on the demand for the number of hosts on a network. The most important classes of addresses are A, B, and C. Figure 4.2 provides a quick review of these classes, and the number of nodes per network. The figure also provides a tip as to how to determine the corresponding class of an IP network address.

The information in figure 4.2 indicates that a class B network, with an IP address of 135.113.210.2, has an upper limit of two bytes worth of hosts. Each of these would share the same two beginning octets or bytes, and must have unique host portions.

Figure 4.2

IP address classes.

Class	Sample Address	Number of Devices	Class Indicator (First Byte Range)
A	15. 17.232.8	16,777,216	0 – 127
B	135.113.210.2	65,534	128 – 191
C	205.211.4.4	254	192 – 223

In building an intranet that will provide access to external sites, such as customer or competitor sites, your organization should, if it has not done so already, contact the InterNIC registration services at Network Solutions, Inc. The InterNIC will assign an official, unique network number to the company. You can now assign the host IDs for that network as you see fit.

Note

Registration with InterNIC requires that you first try to have IP addresses assigned to you by your local provider in order to stem the number of addresses being used and to prevent a situation where there is a shortage of IP addresses. New addressing schemes are being developed, but until they are in use, InterNIC will only grant IP addresses in special cases. See their site for more information.

Currently, InterNIC also requires that you provide them with two IP addresses for each domain name. This system provides redundancy so in case one name server goes down, clients will still be able to negotiate their way to your site.

If you do not already have an IP address, it may be simpler to obtain an IP address by connecting through an Internet Service Provider. Having the service provider set you up with the network number that is part of their network address space is called *sub-netting*.

If you already have Internet connectivity, an internal network administrator may be responsible for assigning IP addresses to individuals. Check with your system administrators to determine the appropriate solution.

Once you have been assigned an IP network number, you can start to assign specific addresses (from that network) to individual devices on your network. An electronic log book is the most efficient way to keep a record of assigned IP addresses and their corresponding devices. If it is on the intranet, appropriately protected, your system administrator will be able to check the list from any machine in the organization.

Networks grow in size. New users with new computers, printers, and servers to support their work efforts are added. As you build the intranet, keep in mind two things when configuring new devices into the network:

- All devices on the network must have the IP address configured with the same network number.

- Each device must have a unique host portion of the IP address; otherwise, the two or more devices with the same IP address will not work properly.

Once the IP addresses are properly installed and configured for all the devices on the network, a "node" uses the IP address to determine which packets to receive and which to ignore. Only the nodes with the same network ID portion accept each other's broadcasts. In determining which part of the IP address represents the network ID and which represents the host ID, *netmasks* are used.

Netmasks are used primarily to split the network into subnets when there are a number of Local Area Networks (LANs) within your network. For example, instead of applying for class C network addresses for each LAN—and dealing with the cost and maintenance of each of these distinct networks—you could apply for a class B network address, which allows for multiple LANs to have class C-like functionality. Netmask numbers resemble an IP address, using the dotted octet form, but use only two numbers, 255 and 0.

An octet of 255 indicates that this is reserved for the network ID. A 0 indicates that the octet is reserved for the host ID. For example, the default netmask for a class C network is 255.255.255.0—the first three positions signify the network ID and the last is the host ID. This netmask enables you to effectively break a class B address into class C subnets. You can accomplish this by using the third position to assign a network ID to the individual LANs to use across their nodes. Nodes are assigned unique host IDs by using the last position only and the netmask of 255.255.255.0. They will discard any packets that do not match its network ID.

In the final analysis, communications by computers take place by moving data from node to node on a network using some form of link. Some of the more common links are ethernet, Token Ring, FDDI, and Point-to-Point Protocol (PPP). The addressing schemes of these links are different from that of IP addresses—most of the addresses used here are built right into the hardware of the device (usually a Network Interface Card) by the manufacturer.

On an ethernet network, for example, every device on the network has a built-in ethernet address that is assigned to the device: the first three bytes identify the vendor of the device and the last three are unique to each device manufactured by that vendor.

Because not all computers, or other network devices, have ethernet support, IP addresses enable devices connected to other types of links to communicate. IP addresses are based on network topology and not on the vendor—this makes for a much more effective routing scheme to move data from point to point. Ethernet connects network hardware—users and services on a network communicate with other users and services, not network devices.

In order for an IP node on an ethernet network to communicate with another IP node with the same network number, the assumption is made by IP that the two nodes are on the same segment of wire. Ethernet sends out a broadcast message that all ethernet devices hear—this is a specific ethernet address that all devices accept as if it were addressed to them. Each device receiving the packet and supporting IP checks its own IP address to see if it matches the "recipient" IP address in the message. If this is the case, that device sends a response back to the ethernet address of the originator with the correct ethernet address of the intended recipient. The originator then encapsulates the IP packet in an ethernet packet and sends it on its way to the correct ethernet address.

Routing

Sending packets along the wire of a network is not really a difficult concept to grasp. But what about sending information between two networks (LANs, or even corporate networks)? If the destination is on another network, how do you send the packet from "your wire" to "their wire" when you are not directly connected?

Routers are used to connect networks. To interconnect networks, the router is a network device whose duty it is to get the IP packet from one end node to another in a series of *hops* between routers.

In the ethernet example, the originating node would encapsulate the IP packet in an ethernet packet addressed specifically to the router.

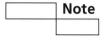

Note

TCP/IP end nodes need to be configured with the address of at least one router—the *default gateway*. This is usually a manual task when installing the stack on the node.

Upon receipt, the router would examine the internally stored *routing table* to determine where it should forward the packet. If the network is not directly connected to the router, the routing table indicates which router is the next one to send to. The router sends a request to the next "hop router" and encapsulates the packet in the link layer packet, addressed to the next router. The receiving router checks its routing table to determine if it needs to route the packet to yet another router or can deliver the packet to a node on a network that is directly connected to this router.

Routing tables can be set in two ways: manually or through dynamic acquisition. Manual configuration and maintenance is difficult in a changing network environment and downright impossible in a large network. Dynamic acquisition of routing tables is usually done through the Routing Information Protocol. This protocol enables the router to communicate with other routers about its routing table and to receive reciprocal information from them. In addition, many routers are clumped together in default route, the IP network 0.0.0.0, and advertise their connectivity to this default route. If a router does not see a specific network address anywhere, it can send the packet to this default route and the packet should be delivered from there.

TCP/IP Addresses and Names

In terms of finding and using services on the intranet, the people behind the keyboards are not good at remembering numbers. What is your Social Security number? What is your partner's? See? It is much easier to remember names. TCP/IP services are usually found by names—at least, that is how the users ask for these services. For example, it is easier to remember *www.magmacom.com* than *204.191.36.1.*

Because IP packets cannot be addressed to a name, a service name can be mapped to an IP address and maintained in a *hosts file*. This works for small networks, but an up-to-date file on each single IP device in a large network would not be practical to maintain. As mentioned earlier in Chapter 3, "The HTTP Protocol: Understanding the Application Layer," the Domain Name Service (DNS) is one way to maintain a network-accessible database of name-to-IP mappings.

In order to maintain such a database, you should designate a machine to be the DNS site and have all other machines send requests to these servers to have names converted to an IP address or vice versa. In configuring each device on the network during the installation of the TCP/IP stack, enter the address of the machine to which the device should go to use the DNS service. This chapter will discuss shortly how to configure a Windows 95 desktop to access a DNS service.

So concludes this discussion of the basics of TCP/IP, addressing, and routing. For a more in-depth discussion of these topics, please refer to George Eckel's *intranet Working* (New Riders, 1996).

Installing TCP/IP on the Windows NT Server

In order to connect to the services that utilize the TCP/IP protocol, you must have the TCP/IP stack installed on every machine that you want to connect to the intranet—this includes the server. This topic will be covered only briefly in this chapter. Several excellent books, including *Building a Windows NT Internet Server*, by Eric Harper, Matt Arnett, and R. Paul Singh (New Riders, 1995), go into greater detail on the topic.

Microsoft recognized the importance of TCP/IP as the most accepted transport mechanism in the world, and provided native support for TCP/IP in Windows NT. This means that the tools to connect NT systems to the intranet are already in the NT software.

Note

The discussion here assumes that you have already installed the NT software and are adding the TCP/IP functionality.

1. Log in as the Administrator.

2. Open the Control Panel and select the Networks icon.

3. Click on Add Software.

4. Select TCP/IP Internetworking, Connectivity Utilities, and Simple TCP/IP Services.

5. Click on Continue.

Windows NT will copy over the file necessary for the installation of the TCP/IP protocol stack. After the software has been copied to the NT computer, you must provide some basic configuration information in order for the computer to function within the intranet. The information that is requested follows:

- Windows NT asks for a valid IP address. Enter the IP address of this machine.

- Enter the subnet mask (see the discussion earlier in this chapter).

- Enter default gateway, or router, address (see discussion earlier in this chapter).

At this time, you should set up the access to the Domain Name Service that will resolve the system names with IP addresses. Follow these steps to set up the system:

1. Click on DNS.

2. If you have a HOSTS file on the computer, enter the name of the file.

3. Enter the DNS server's IP address, then click on Add.

Note

Up to three IP addresses can be entered, but ensure that they are listed in the order you want the server to search. Use the arrow buttons on the side to change order.

4. Enter up to six domain suffixes to be used in resolving host names. Six suffixes are helpful if, for example, there are several domains within the intranet that you want to have searched. More suffixes help to identify to the DNS which domains it should search first.

Note

> The domain suffixes are added to the host names during resolution to create a Fully Qualified Domain Name (FQDN) of host_name.domain_name. Thus, if the host name is *subscription* and the domain name is *busint.com*, the FQDN is *subscription.busint.com*.

5. Click on OK to close DNS Configuration.

6. Click on OK to close the TCP/IP Configuration dialog box.

Following these steps should enable the TCP/IP stack on the computer so that the computer will operate as the heart of the intranet.

Configuring TCP/IP on Windows 95 Desktops

The Windows 95 software is widely used across the United States and around the world on the desktop. It is relatively simple to add TCP/IP support to the desktop by following these steps:

1. From the default Windows 95 desktop, select My Computer, followed by Control Panel.

2. Select the Network icon.

3. Click on Add.

4. Choose Adapter (see figure. 4.3).

5. From the list of adapters, choose Microsoft from Manufacturer's box and Dial-Up Adapter from the Network Adapter box. Click on OK.

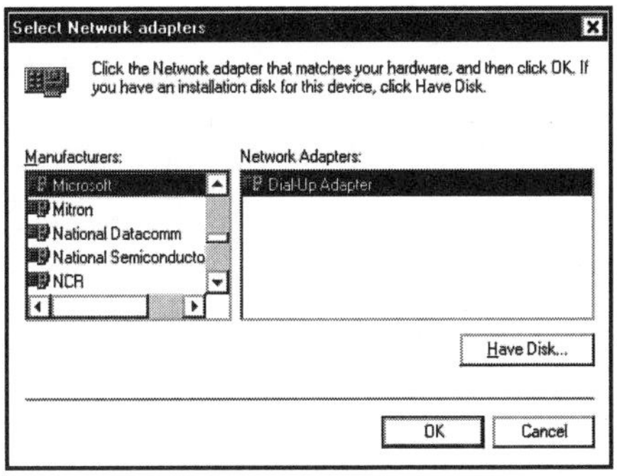

Figure 4.3

Selecting the Microsoft Dial-Up Adapter.

6. Choose Add—this takes you back to the Select Network Component Type window.

7. Choose Protocol.

8. Select Microsoft from the Manufacturer's box and TCP/IP from the Network Protocol box. Click on OK (see figure 4.4).

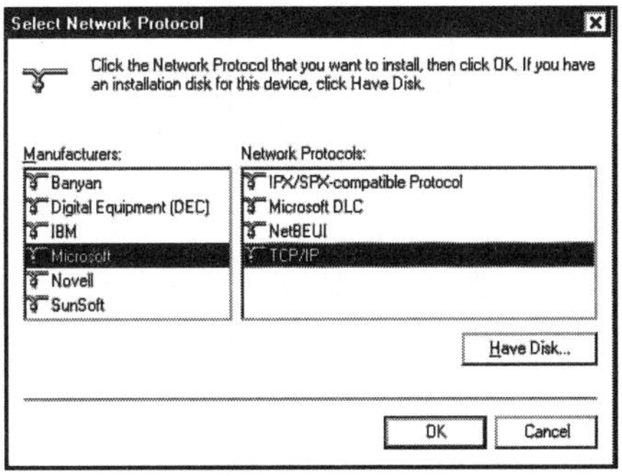

Figure 4.4

Selecting the Microsoft TCP/IP protocol.

9. From the Network window, select TCP/IP from the list and click on Properties. The TCP/IP Properties window appears with six tabbed pages: Bindings, Advanced, DNS, Gateway, WINS, and IP Address.

10. Select IP Address and choose Obtain IP Address Automatically (see figure 4.5).

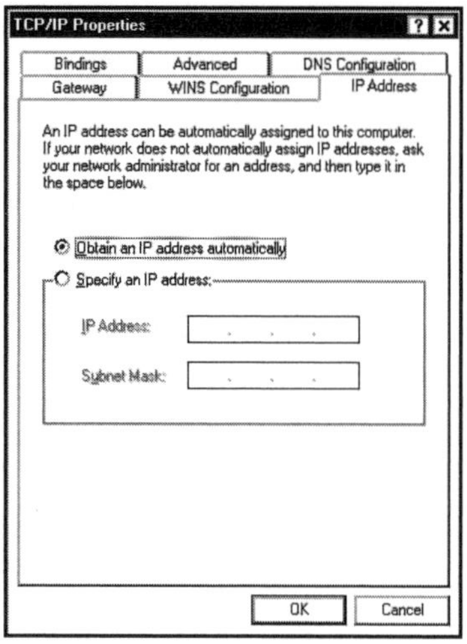

Figure 4.5

Selecting an
IP address
automatically.

11. Under Gateway, enter the address of the gateway (for example, 204.191.36.1) as shown in figure 4.6. Click on Add.

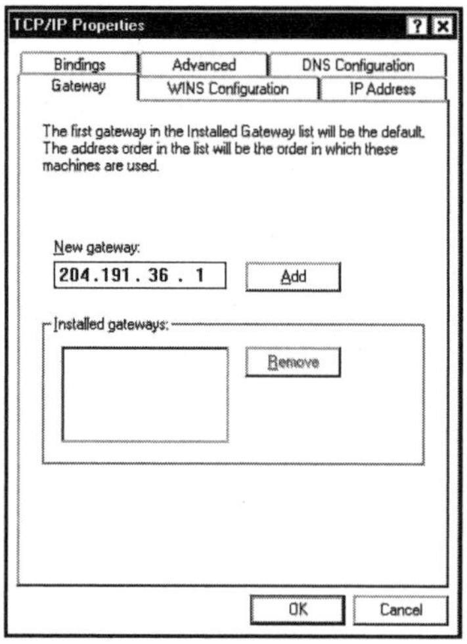

Figure 4.6

Entering the
Gateway Address.

12. Under Bindings, leave Client for Microsoft Networks selected.

13. Under DNS Configuration, select Enable DNS. For the HOST field, enter the user name you have been assigned (for example, a person). Under domain, enter the domain to which you will be connecting (for example, magmacom.com).

14. In the DNS Server Search Order, enter the addresses of the DNS servers that you want to use, in order of preference (for example, 204.191.36.5 and 198.63.64.14), as shown in figure 4.7.

Figure 4.7

Depicting DNS Configuration.

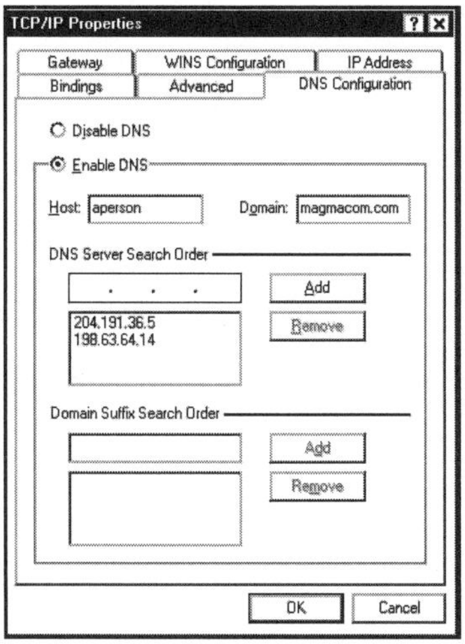

15. Click on OK.

16. Click on OK to leave the Network window.

17. Restart Windows when prompted for changes to take effect.

This has now enabled your desktop to access the world of the intranet. If you are connected to the network where the intranet server is located, you are off and running. If you are dialing in to the intranet, the next section discusses the configuration of the Window 95 desktop for dial-up access.

Configuring Dial-up Networking for Windows 95 Desktops

What happens if you are out of the office at a meeting and you want to connect to the intranet? How can you connect to the intranet across the phone lines?

All you need to do is set up a Windows NT Remote Access Server connected to the intranet. This server needs to be equipped with a pool of IP addresses that the remote users can access. Remote users will need to have their machines configured to permit dial-up networking.

Note

Please refer to the Windows NT documentation for establishing a Remote Access Server, or refer to *Building a Windows NT Internet Server* (New Riders, 1995) by Eric Harper, Matt Arnett, and R. Paul Singh.

To configure the desktop for remote access, perform the following:

1. From the default Windows 95 desktop, select My Computer, followed by Dial-Up Networking.

2. Select the Make New Connection icon.

3. Enter the name of the target system in the first field (for example, Business Interactive). The modem field should already indicate the modem installed in the machine.

4. Click on Next.

5. Fill in the area code and telephone number as appropriate and select the appropriate country listing from the Country Code list.

6. Click on Next, Finish. You now have an icon in the Dial-Up Networking window entitled Business Interactive.

7. Point to the new icon and press the RIGHT MOUSE BUTTON.

8. Select Properties.

Note

You may want to de-select the Use Country Code and Area Code option, but check with the system administrator first to determine the configuration requirements. Typically, these two options are not used except for users who are traveling internationally and need to dial in.

9. Choose Configure, and then review General and Connection pages for compatibility with your hardware. Make any changes that are required to ensure that your computer's settings are compatible with the options selected previously. If you have any doubts or questions, please contact the system administrator.

10. Under Options, de-select Bring Up Terminal Window Before Dialing and Bring Up Terminal Window After Dialing unless specified by your systems administrator.

    Figure 4.8 that shows the Properties windows the configuration of the Server Type for this particular connection is started from.

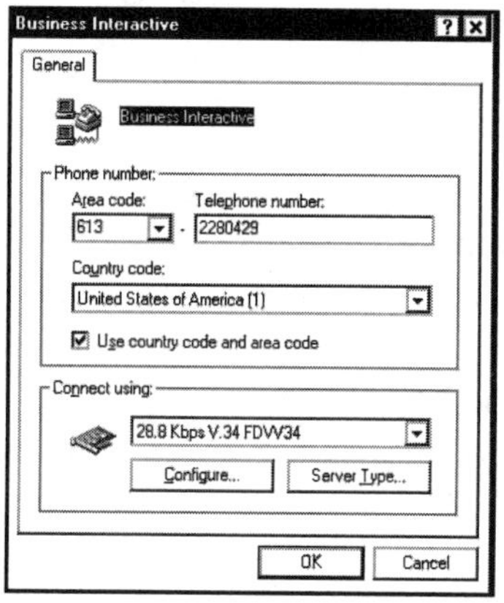

Figure 4.8

Configuring the Dial-Up Networking Properties.

11. Click on OK.

12. Select Server Type. Ensure that TCP/IP is selected under Allowed network protocols and de-select NetBEUI and IPX/SPX.

13. De-select Log on to the Network and select Enable Software Compression. Leave Require Encrypted Password disabled unless you have a requirement for this feature.

14. Click on OK twice.

Congratulations! You should now be ready to dial in to the intranet. The parameters that you have selected are the usual configuration features that are installed. Please check with your system administrator to obtain the required parameters. The actual performing of the configuration is not difficult at all.

Status Check

By now you should have an understanding of the basics of the addressing and routing aspects of TCP/IP. It is not expected that you immerse yourself in all the various components of the protocol, but you really do need to understand the basics of how the computers connect and send information to one another.

In addition, the value of the Domain Name Service is apparent. In the initial stages of an intranet, you may want to have your Internet Service Provider manage your DNS. As your intranet grows in size and the services it offers, it is highly probable that you will find it more efficient to run your own DNS. Plan for that eventuality now, but start with your service provider if at all possible.

At this point, you still have your Netscape Commercial Server up and running on the Windows NT server. You should now understand how this machine was configured to enable TCP/IP to work, and should also understand the addressing and routing basics. You are just about ready, from the server point of view, to take on the actual creation of a home page from which to access your databases of information and other applications.

The last thing you need to ensure before getting started is to review the security aspects of the service. You need to understand how to allow people to access the information that they need, how to restrict access in some cases (like personnel records), and how to secure dial-up access. Security is the last concept that will be covered in this book with respect to getting the server up and going.

Intranet Security

n terms of looking at security and computers, George Eckel said it best in his *Intranet Working* (New Riders, 1996):

> " A secure network does not exist; nor does a secure computer. The only secure computer is one that is unplugged, locked in a secure vault that only one person knows the combination to, and that person died last year. When you move beyond that scenario, you must expect lapses in security. "

Anytime you connect a computer to the outside world, you create the potential for someone to damage your internal systems.

A truly internal intranet, with no access outside of corporate connections, is secure from direct attacks from people outside the organization. Because neither the computers on your network nor your intranet servers would be connected to a computer or network outside your organization, in theory you should be safe. The biggest security concerns at this point should be from an inexperienced user trying to make a computer system within the intranet do something it is just not capable of doing, thereby causing a crash. Other than inexperienced drivers, viruses that are unwittingly brought into the organization on portable media or through dial-up to an infected computer are a major concern.

However, the discussion in Chapter 2, "Making Your Case," of the intranet as a source of knowledge about your organization views the intranet from a vertical perspective—including access to the sites of your suppliers, vendors, and customers, as well as those of your competitors. This means that you have to allow access to your internal systems to the Internet at-large.

Assuming that you have an external Web site to make your corporate information available to your customers, the assumption is also made that the external Web site is a stand-alone computer outside of your corporate firewall. This setup would indicate that you have people already focusing on the security of the company's information.

The remainder of this chapter will focus on the basics of security as they surround the establishment and operation of an intranet that does connect to the external world. The following topics will be discussed:

- HTTP's Basic Authorization Scheme

- Implementing access control

- Setting up user authorization

- Implementing subnets

- Employing encryption

- Introducing firewalls

- Implementing dial-up access

It is important to have an understanding of the security features that can be built into your intranet in order to maintain the security of your networks and the integrity of your data.

An Introduction to Intranet Security

Figure 5.1 shows the basic configuration of the assumed intranet with access to the outside world. The question mark represents the concerns about how to protect the intranet and its critical systems (financial records, human resource records, and so on). It is entirely possible to buy new hardware to replace old or damaged pieces. It is sometimes impossible to replace the data.

Basic intranet configuration.

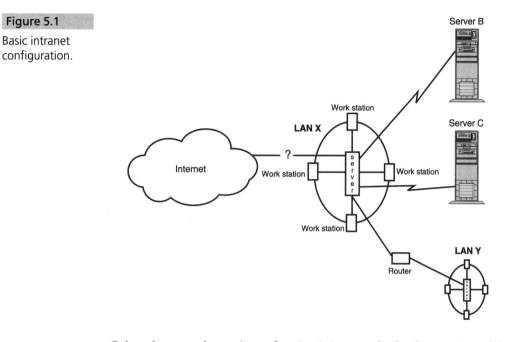

Other than good practices of maintaining regular backup copies of data in secure (and off-site) storage, the book will cover how to address several of the concerns about security to the systems and to the data on the systems.

In looking at security, it is recommended you start with the HTTP server and the Basic Authorization Scheme in place there.

Basic Authorization Scheme

The chapter on the HTTP protocol briefly touched on the Basic Authorization Scheme of the HTTP 1.0 specification. This scheme is simply an encoding scheme, not an encryption scheme. It is designed to ensure the integrity of authorization data in transit between computers; it is not designed to be secure—all the information the potential intruder needs is available in response to the server's challenge. This challenge-response metaphor is depicted in figure 5.2.

Note

As an encoding scheme, the authorization data being transferred between computers is broken down into "chunks," complete with headers and footers, that are then transmitted across the network. The chunks are then re-assembled into the complete entity-body of the authorization data. The only encrypted part is the password field. The data can be re-assembled by ordering the chunks that arrive.

An encryption scheme would take the content being transferred and, using an encryption algorithm, convert the data to an "unreadable mess" to those without the ability to decrypt the message. This encrypted message, if sent as authorization data, would still be encoded for transport to another computer.

Figure 5.2

Challenge-
response of Basic
Authentication
Scheme.

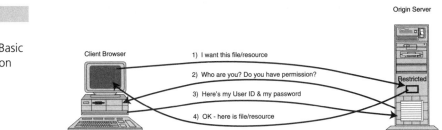

The most basic option for security is the Basic Authentication Scheme of the HTTP protocol. It assigns differing levels of access privileges to users, relative to realms of its data structure and the access permissions of the users. When a file is requested from a restricted area of the server, an authorization transaction is initiated by the server. The challenge issued by the server consists of the authorization scheme—in this mode the authorization scheme would be "basic"—and an identifier that represents the realm of the restricted file(s).

The browser will prompt the user for an ID and password and send the response back to the server. The response contains the credentials of the user for access within that area of the server. The server compares the credentials supplied by the user with those stored in its database to determine if they are valid. The user will be provided the requested data—if the server is satisfied with the credentials—or will receive a notification that access is forbidden.

Implementing Access Control

The majority of servers use an Access Control File to configure how the server operates when it receives requests. In the Netscape Communications Server, Access Control lets you restrict access to a resource according to the client hostname or IP address. An advantage of this is that you can pick and choose the resources that you want to protect or you can protect the entire server.

To implement this type of control in the Windows NT version of the Netscape Communications Server, you must first create a database of users on the system. To do so, follow these instructions:

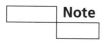

Note

The server stores its databases in the \userdb directory in the server root and stores its user files in a .pfw file. The format of each line in the file is username:encryptedpassword.

1. Start the Administration Manager and select the appropriate Server Manager to configure from the list of servers.

2. Select the link to create a user database.

3. Enter a name for the database—up to 255 characters in length—but do not include a path.

4. Select the appropriate type of database to create—the NCSA-style database encrypts the passwords—and create the line format of user:password.

5. Enter a password of up to eight characters and re-enter for accuracy.

6. Click on Make These Changes.

You can now add the new users to the database. The names the user employs for authenticating with the server can be up to 255 characters in length. The password for the user can be up to eight characters, and you will have to enter it twice for confirmation purposes. When finished, click on the Make These Changes button and the user will be added.

Setting Up User Authorization

Once the users have been established in the server database, you can set up the access control required for your server. There are some areas of the server, or other servers, that you may wish to prevent people from seeing unless they have the proper credentials to view the data. For example, the personnel files in Human Resources containing confidential information should not be accessible to staff in general.

To set up user authorization with the Netscape Communications Server (both NT and Unix versions) choose the Access Control option from the Server Manager and perform the following steps:

1. Choose the database used to look up user names and passwords.

2. Enter the users who will have access to this resource. All the users from this database will have access if the field is left blank.

3. Create a realm describing the part of the server where access control is being used. This string will help the user to understand what they are trying to access. An example of a realm would be the part of the directory structure that would pertain to and would be called "Confidential Employee Records"—this could be one directory or an entire tree of a directory and its subdirectories.

These steps enable you to restrict access by user authorization. You can limit access to the intranet based on the hostname or IP address of the requester. Address restriction is one way to control who will see what documents. With a request, the server knows the IP address of the requester. It uses a Domain Name Server (DNS) to look up the hostname that corresponds with that IP address and then checks its address restrictions. For more information on DNS, refer to Chapter 4, "Fundamentals of TCP/IP: Understanding the Transport Layer."

The server first tries to match the incoming hostname with the restriction hostname. If the client fails the test, the server checks the IP address against IP address restrictions. If the hostname matches a restriction, the server takes appropriate action. Even if the name fails, if the IP address is not on the restricted list, the file will be served. Figure 5.3 depicts the process.

Figure 5.3

Access restrictions
by IP address.

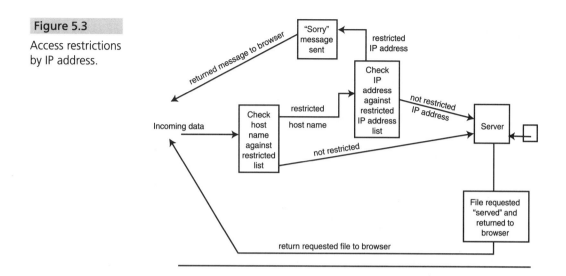

Normally, the server will send "Not Found," which also happens when the requested document does not exist. You can specify another file to be sent back by the server, but make certain that the file name to be sent back to the user is the absolute path to the file, such as /usr/local/messages/notfound.html.

Note

If the server does not have DNS or is not configured to do DNS lookups, you are limited to restricting by IP address only.

All servers will have some form of access control and authentication scheme, from the Basic Authentication Scheme of HTTP 1.0 to the Secure Sockets Layer (SSL) protocol and others that are intended to send private information over the Net.

Please review your server documentation to determine the authentication capabilities of the server. Use this information in conjunction with the security needs of your intranet to implement the method or combination of methods from above and to implement the appropriate authentication scheme.

Subnets

Subnets were mentioned briefly in Chapter 4, during a discussion about the breaking of a Class B IP network into smaller Class C networks that all start with the same addresses in the first three positions of the IP address. Subnets can also be implemented to improve security in response to the issues of *time savers* and over-burdened system administration personnel.

Users of the intranet will always be looking for ways to speed up access to the data they require. One way is to use the TCP/IP feature, which enables you to establish a file of hosts that permit users who have successfully logged into one of these hosts to log into your server remotely. Even though the users of your intranet will appreciate the time-saving aspect of not having to log into other internal systems once they have connected to the intranet, it is a potential security hazard, and it usually indicates that you have all the servers, from different work groups, on the same network. Using a subnet strategy, breaking these different work groups into separate subnets of the intranet, and the IP address authorization scheme described earlier in the chapter provide a more secure environment without reducing the functionality available to the users. This strategy means that you do not have to use the /etc/hosts.equiv files that would have been used otherwise.

On a human level, it is almost impossible for a single system administrator to be responsible for all the various components and activities that relate to security for a large network with many servers. Trying to maintain or even cope with a large network causes system administrators more headaches than smiles. A feasible solution is a subnet strategy, where each subnet is managed by a system administrator.

Subnets can be established and a system administrator assigned to each subnet. This apportions the workload across the series of system administrators and, with a smaller number of machines, people, and applications to worry about, security will stand a better chance of being implemented as it should be, not as time allows.

In addition, on the automated front, subnets can be utilized to partition groups of users into logical or strategic units for the purposes of
access control. For example, in restricting access to the personnel files
of the organization, only the HR staff can be permitted to access the
HR databases based on their IP addresses—"only permit access to
unique hosts on the 205.238.206" is the requirement that would be
converted into the syntax for the computer to implement. In addition
to this level of security, remember that routers are used to connect networks to each other. Because most routers now have the ability to apply
filters to the IP addresses passing through, the routers in place in a
subnet strategy add an additional layer of security of the IP address
authorization variety.

Figure 5.4 shows, conceptually, what a subnet would look like as compared to one large network.

Figure 5.4

Subnet strategy
versus one large
network.

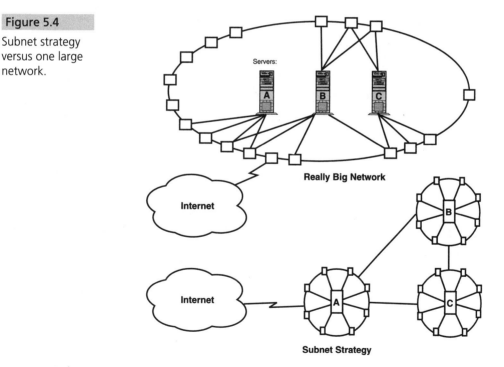

Encryption

Protecting the contents of information transmitted over the intranet may be a concern, especially if you are planning to link remote offices across the Internet. Because many companies use the Internet as a proxy for their wide area network, the transmission of confidential information is important.

As mentioned during the discussion on the Basic Authentication Scheme, encoding is not secure for the transmission of contents of the message. Basic authentication uses the encoding scheme on the authentication portion only, leaving the body in clear text. Should anyone be "sniffing" the message and its response, attempting to obtain passwords or data, he will be able to obtain the user ID and the password included in the response.

Note

Sniffing is a term used for eavesdropping on the flow of data across the network. There are legitimate reasons for sniffing software, such as virus checking. However, many managers of networks where sensitive data, such as credit card numbers, are transmitted are very worried about hackers sniffing out card numbers or passwords to their systems.

As mentioned previously, the authorization data is already encoded but not encrypted, and the body data is neither encoded nor encrypted. Encryption can be employed to make it more difficult to break both the user ID and password transmission as well as the body text. A great deal of work is under way in this field to make the Internet secure for commercial transactions. For more information on this subject, visit the CommerceNet site at http://www.commerce.net.

Note

CommerceNet is a not-for-profit organization that brings together companies from all industry sectors to promote and advance the use of electronic commerce. CommerceNet has a series of task forces and interest groups that are working to solve problems facing companies

continues

participating in the electronic commerce arena. The Web site has a series of White Papers and other documents that discuss data encryption and security in general.

If you believe that your intranet will require the use of encryption to protect your data during transmission, you should go to the CommerceNet site at http://www.commerce.net (or others like it) to review literature on encryption. Officials at CommerceNet can be contacted through the site to answer questions that you may have or provide you with the appropriate contacts in the industry. It is beyond the scope of this book to go into further detail on this topic.

Forms of Encryption

There are two basic forms of encryption (or cryptography): secret- and public-key. Both will be covered briefly here.

Secret-key encryption works on the principle that the sender and the recipient of the message know and use the same secret key to encrypt and then decrypt the message. The U.S. government's Data Encryption Standard (DES) is one example of a secret-key algorithm. Many secret-key algorithms are available free-of-charge on the Internet, but be aware of export restrictions that are in place. For example, no product containing encryption technology greater than 40-bit encryption (using 40 bits to encrypt each character of the data) can be exported from the United States to countries that have not signed an agreement with the U.S. government. The state-of-the-market encryption at the time of writing is based on 256-bit encryption algorithms.

The management and administration of keys is critical to the success of all cryptographic systems. If someone has been able to obtain a secret key, he will be able to read all messages encrypted with that key.

Warning

Getting the key into the hands of the sender and the receiver, especially if they are in physically separate locations, means trusting someone not to disclose the key.

Public-key encryption entails each individual generating a pair of keys—a public and a private key. The public key is published while the private key is just that, private. The private keys are not shared—all communications involve only the public key. In order to decrypt a message sent to a published public key, the associated private key is required. It is possible for people sniffing around to intercept the message, but they cannot read the information unless they possess the private key.

As mentioned earlier, the generation and storage of these keys is paramount to the security. An infrastructure is required to maintain and manage the whole public-key process. This is where the work of organizations such as CommerceNet is proving invaluable.

Secret-key encryption lends itself to use for transactions within an organization because the organization can choose the secret-key algorithm it wishes to use and implement it across the organization. Secret-key becomes difficult to implement in international organizations or among international partners (including clients and suppliers) due to the export restrictions on the technology.

The direction private industry seems to be leaning toward is the public-key infrastructure. Issues still need to be solved, especially pertaining to the cross-border certification of certificates; but organizations like the CommerceNet are working with government and industry groups around the world to work out a solution.

For more information on the topic, please refer to the CommerceNet site at http://www.commerce.net.

Verifying Public Key Certificates

Public key certificates are issued and registered with a Certificate Authority. During a transaction, the public key input by the participants in a transaction needs to be verified to satisfy both ends of the transaction so that they know they are in fact dealing with the intended parties.

Note

This verification process is analogous to a retail store "swiping" your credit card through a machine when you wish to purchase goods—the swipe machine reads the information from the magnetic strip on the card and transmits it over the phone lines in order to check the validity of the card and its usage, in other words, a verification.

Implementing Security in Netscape Servers with SSL

As an example of how security has been used on a commercial product, Netscape Communications Corp. has implemented the Secure Sockets Layer (SSL) protocol to provide secure data communication in its Netscape Commerce Server.

SSL is an encryption system that works at the protocol level and provides authentication, encryption, and data integrity. SSL should not be confused with the access-control type of user authentication.

A digital certificate from a Certification Authority is required. It contains two sets of information: 1) the certificate information including the name of the server, the public key assigned, the validity dates of the certificate, and the name of the Certification Authority; and 2) the digital signature. To obtain the certificate you must do the following:

1. Start the Netscape Commerce Server's Server Manager and select Generate a Key from the Security Configuration options.

2. Enter the path where you will store the key file. It is recommended that this be stored in a directory that the *root* user or the server's user account can access.

3. Enter an eight-character password, containing at least one non-alpha character, for the key file, for example r2D2c3Po. The security of the server is only as good as the security of the key file, so make sure that you remember it and do not write it down. Save the changes.

4. Contact one of the Certificate Authorities on the list you received with the Netscape Commerce Server and obtain the details regarding the specific format of the information they need.

5. Select Request or Renew a Certificate from the Server Manager.

6. Enter the e-mail address of the Certificate Authority with whom you are dealing and specify if this is a new certificate or a renewal.

7. Enter the location and password of your key file.

8. Enter the information specified by the Certificate Authority relative to the distinguished name, the name to be used on the face of the Certificate.

9. Enter your phone number, including area code and any international code required.

10. Click on Make These Changes.

The server will send an e-mail to the Certificate Authority, complete with the digital signature created by the private key. This is used to determine that the e-mail was not tampered with en route. After you have received the response from the Certificate Authority you can continue to install the security features. You do so with the following procedure:

1. Save the e-mail message containing the certificate from the Certificate Authority in a protected area on the server.

2. From Server Manager select Install a Certificate.

3. Enter the full pathname to the saved e-mail.

4. Specify a destination directory for the certificate—you can accept the default suggested by application, but do not put the file in the document root directory or any generally available directory.

5. Click on Make These Changes.

Now you are ready to activate the security features to enable the encryption capabilities. Here's how:

1. From Server Manager select Activate Security and Specify Ciphers.

2. Check the appropriate radio button to enable security.

3. Specify port 443 with secure server.

4. Enter the path to the key file.

5. Enter the path to the certificate for server authentication.

6. Activate the ciphers. These are used during client and server negotiations regarding which encryption method to use.

7. Click on Make These Changes and re-start the server.

These steps will put the security features of the Netscape Commerce Server in place. The secure server marketplace is getting new members regularly. Appendix C, "Intranet-Compatible HTTP Server Products," lists products that are intranet-compatible.

Cross-Certification Issues

One of the big problems at the moment is cross-certification of the Certificate Authorities. If the two parties in this form of transaction use certificates that are issued and managed by the same Certificate Authority, the validity can be verified relatively easily. But what happens when the two parties have had their public keys issued by different Certificate Authorities? How do you resolve the validity of these certificates in this case? What about cross-border certification? In this world of global economies, transactions requiring this form of security are becoming commonplace—especially if you have regional or international offices that wish to access confidential records through the intranet.

Organizations such as CommerceNet are working on these issues through their issue task forces and through international affiliations with groups around the globe also working to solve these and other related problems.

Firewalls

Firewalls are a gateway to your company's information resources. This gateway protects the intranet by monitoring traffic on the connection between networks. The IP address and port number of each IP packet moving between the two networks is monitored and the firewall implements the security policies of the organization as required.

There are several kinds of firewalls, but the two most popular are the Inline Host and Monitoring Host varieties. Other configurations include a simple screening router, the screened subnet (two screening routers and a host firewall), as well as many commercial vendor solutions. For more information on firewalls and security, refer to *Internet Firewalls and Computer Security* (New Riders, 1996). This section will focus on the Inline Host and Monitoring Host.

An Inline Host puts a computer on the link between the two networks and uses proxies to pass data between them. These proxy programs are transparent to the user and usually run on the inline host. They can be set up to allow or prevent access based on the source address, the destination address, and the source/destination ports. A password and ID are usually required to pass into the internal system.

A Monitoring Host is set up as in figure 5.5, with a router sitting on the direct connection and the monitoring host listening to all the traffic. Because most routers can be configured to filter the traffic based on the IP address, they provide the security. The monitoring host records the traffic and needs to be managed.

Figure 5.5

A monitoring host hateway.

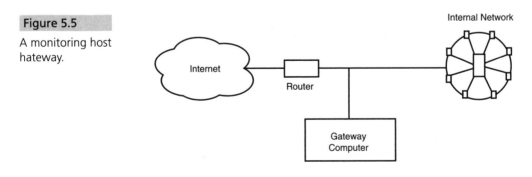

In the world of your intranet, you have to consider a couple of issues regarding the use of gateways and where you want to put them. Your primary needs are as follows:

- Make the intranet available to staff throughout the organization.

- Do not allow people outside of the organization access to the intranet.

- Allow internal staff access to the Internet to review other sites and seek information and intelligence for your competitive advantage.

- Allow staff in regional and international offices access to the resources of the intranet through the usage of the Internet infrastructure.

- Permit traveling staff access to the intranet through remote/dial-up access.

In order to accomplish all the issues securely, take the approach that links between internal LANs that are directly connected by routers and use router filtering. This is done to allow access to the resources only to those people whose IP addresses match the company's IP network address. In cases where the information is of a confidential nature and a subnetting strategy has been implemented to separate people into authorized groups, the subnet's IP address will be utilized in the router filtering as well.

As part of the router-based internal strategy, configure your intranet gateway as in figure 5.6, with a router on both sides of the gateway. This will provide you the ability to permit people from the regional offices to gain access to the intranet resources at headquarters through two filtering routers. The inconvenience of this second router inside the gateway, which may slow the transfer of data while checking the addresses, provides an added level of security should there be a breach in the gateway computer. There will always be a trade-off between ease of use and security, but by placing the intranet server shown in figure 5.6, it is relatively safe from outside attacks and is isolated enough in case either the outside router or the gateway computer is compromised.

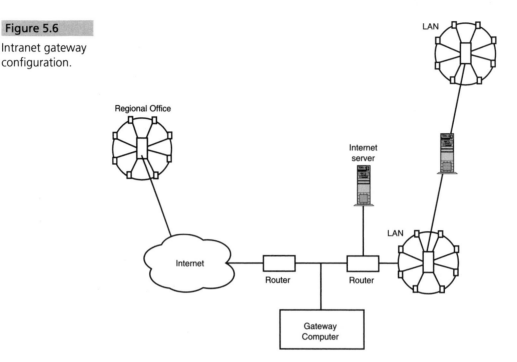

Figure 5.6

Intranet gateway configuration.

If your organization already has an external Web site in place, it is highly probable that the implementers of the Web site will have already looked at the issue of a firewall. For more information on security and firewalls, refer to *Internet Firewalls and Computer Security.*

Dial-up Access

This section is not designed to show you how to implement dial-up access security systems, but rather to indicate that, in the event that you have users who want or require dial-up access, methods exist that make this type of access possible and are brought forward in this section.

Making the intranet accessible to people outside the office presents some security risks. It is possible to create a communications server to handle the inbound dial-up and the logging and connection requirements to have access to the intranet. Some people may want to attach a modem to their desktop computer so that they can access their desktop from home using applications like PCAnywhere by Symantec. If these individuals have access to the intranet from their desktop via this dial-up, appropriate security measures need to be put in place in order to prevent the service from being compromised.

For users who are on the road or others who must connect via modem, consider adding another password in the connection scheme or setting up a Remote Access Server.

In the Unix world, dial-up passwords can be created and are encrypted like other passwords, but they reside in a separate file. The user is asked to provide his user-ID, then his password, and a final dial-up password. Implemented by the dpasswd utility, an error in any three of the items causes the user to be asked to log in again without knowing which item was incorrect. In a Windows NT environment, a Remote Access Server can be set up to handle the dial-up traffic. Please refer to *Building a Windows NT Internet Server* (New Riders) for a step-by-step guide to installing the server.

The decision to establish remote access to the intranet via dial-up can be done through methods as inexpensive as a modem on a desktop computer that is running on the network, or methods costing hundreds of thousands of dollars for computers to handle hundreds of simultaneous callers. The ease of implementation and management of these extremes also varies greatly. If a company has traveling people requiring a connection to the intranet, it is a good idea to put in place a communications server/remote access server. The configuration of the computer required and the telephony requirements must address the current needs as well as the growth expected by the company.

Not only does this remote access service provide connectivity to those who are out of the office, thereby increasing their productivity; but the implementation of a remote access service increases the security protection of your intranet. Someone accidentally dialing the number of a modem attached to a computer connected to the network could, to paraphrase Clint Eastwood, "Make your day!"

Status Check

At this point, this book has covered all the basic requirements of getting the intranet's primary server up, running, and protected. The security features offered by the hardware and software have been discussed, and you have decided on what you want to offer the users in the initial pilot project.

You may want to incorporate several different types of file formats that are not plain text. There are images, audio clips, video clips, and database access that potentially need to be incorporated into the documents that will sit within the intranet. In order for the users to be able to see and use the various formats that you may want to incorporate and those your outside contacts may be using, you need to ensure the desktop applications and browsers that they will be using are compatible with the formats (and security measures) this book has discussed.

The next chapter will discuss how to set up the browser.

Intranet Concepts and Architecture—Client

6

Cross-Platform Client Browser Setup

The Hypertext Transfer Protocol does something that is really neat before the transfer of information takes place. Negotiations between the server and the browser take place to determine what the browser can display and the server can deliver.

The HTTP server generally awaits requests at port 80, which is reserved for its services. The client allocates an arbitrary, unused, and non-reserved port for its communications when it makes a request. Because the time connected to the server is minimal, just long enough to have a file returned in response to the user's request, HTTP is often described as a "stateless" protocol—one that does not remain connected to the server with an established circuit. In order to be efficient and handle multiple requests, HTTP allows transfer representations to be negotiated between the client and the server with the results being returned in a MIME body part.

This chapter will discuss in greater detail the Multipurpose Internet Mail Extensions (MIME) that has been mentioned in previous chapters, and why you need to be aware of what it does in the intranet. It will also discuss the usage of multimedia over the intranet and follow up with how to get the users' browsers up and running properly. It will also review the browsers that are currently available on the market (current to the publication date).

Multipurpose Internet Mail Extensions (MIME)

In the embryonic stages of the Internet, there were several attempts to define the specifications of the structure of the Internet mail message in order to facilitate transfer of information. The first "official" standard was the Request For Comments (RFC) 822 by Dan Crocker of the University of Delaware. RFC 822 dealt with the specifications for Internet Mail. In 1988, the Request For Comments 1049 document outlined work to extend the capabilities of Internet Mail through the use of Multipurpose Internet Mail Extensions (MIME). These extensions to Internet Mail revolved around the development of the content-type field within the header of the message. More details about this content-type field are available in the following section.

Throughout the development of the Internet, as research on the development of technological standards was published, RFC documents were placed in the public domain, on the Internet, for comments and contributions to further develop the concepts of the RFC into a standard. This convention still exists today with two groups being the central figures in the advancement of Internet technologies.

The World Wide Web Consortium (W3C) is now the home of Tim Berners-Lee, the "creator" of the World Wide Web. If you review the history of the World Wide Web, you will note numerous references to CERN. This is where Berners-Lee was located when he started the development of what is known today as "the Web."

The Internet Engineering Task Force (IETF) is a loosely self-organized group of people who make technical and other contributions to the engineering and evolution of the Internet and its technologies. It is the principal body engaged in the development of new Internet standard specifications. Its mission includes

- Identifying and proposing solutions to pressing operational and technical problems of the Internet

- Specifying the development or usage of protocols and the near-term architecture to solve such technical problems for the Internet

- Making recommendations to the Internet Engineering Steering Group (IESG) regarding the standardization of protocols and protocol usage on the Internet

- Facilitating technology transfer from the Internet Research Task Force (IRTF) to the wider Internet community

- Providing a forum for the exchange of information within the Internet community between vendors, users, researchers, agency contractors, and network managers

The IETF meeting is not a conference, although it holds technical presentations. The IETF is not a traditional standards organization, although it produces many specifications that become standards. The IETF is made up of volunteers who meet three times a year to fulfill the IETF mission.

As previously stated, these two groups make significant contributions to the development and enhancement of the standards utilized within Internet technologies.

One of the standards used is Internet Mail. RFC822, the official document outlining Internet Mail, specifies that a mail message has two sections—a header and a body. The specification details that the header contains information about the message (such as the message sender, the recipient, the subject), but nothing about the contents of the body.

In order to facilitate the exchange of electronic mail containing different character sets and multimedia objects, MIME extends the description of the body of the mail message. Using the MIME specification, Web authors on different computer systems and using Internet e-mail standards can mark non-text elements of HTML documents. Using the file extensions to recognize the specific file formats, MIME ensures that the appropriate application program can be executed when the data is transferred.

MIME Content Types

MIME content types are specific file formats, recognized by their file extensions, that are known by Web clients and servers.

A standardized content-type field allows mail-reading systems to automatically identify the type of a structured message body and to process it for display accordingly. The structured message body must still conform to the RFC 822 requirements concerning allowable characters. A mail-reading system, as well as the browsers of the intranet, need not take any specific action upon receiving a message with a valid Content-type header field. The ability to recognize this field and invoke the appropriate display process accordingly improves the readability of messages and allows the exchange of messages containing mathematical symbols or foreign language characters.

Note

Seven valid MIME content-types exist at this time. To propose a new content-type, new subtypes must be registered with the Internet Assigned Numbers Authority (IANA) (to avoid name conflicts) and specified in a formal document available from that organization. Currently, the method of extending the content-types is to define new subtypes of established content-types.

An example would be the content-type images and the creation of a new subtype called *johnspec*. This would mean that images created with the johnspec format would be usable, if the subtype is accepted, along with the *jpg*, *gif*, *pcx*, and *tiff*, and other image subtypes.

Registering a new subtype is typically done through the Request For Comments process, and the time frame for obtaining official status is nebulous.

The media type of the message or the body part is described by the content-type identifier. This is a major change in the definition of new content-types that was outlined in RFC1049, introduced above. In the event that a browser does not recognize the subtype specified in conjunction with the content-type field, the browser attempts to perform the action that is associated with the base content-type in an attempt to act rather than return an error message. Typically, this means the browser displays a message indicating that it "does not have a specific action associated with this content-type/subtype combination," and asks "would the user like to save the file to disk?" Content-types and subtypes are explained in more detail later within this chapter.

Note

See http://home.netscape.com/assist/helper_apps/rfc3.html for the RFC that outlines the steps necessary for submitting a new subtype.

The seven defined content-type values are text, image, audio, video, message, multipart, and application. They all have different specifications, which are detailed in the following list:

- Text (the default content-type)—The default subtype is plain text, with subtypes associated with particular rich text formats. A browser vendor might use content-type: text/product-name for rich text-based mail, with the understanding that recipients using other mail software might read the raw rich text representation. MIME defines a subtype of text, *richtext*, which provides a very simple base for those who wish to experiment in multifont formatted e-mail. HTML is another subtype that you need for the intranet.

- Image—Subtypes are image format names. "image/gif" and "image/jpeg" are defined by MIME. Browsers that do not recognize an image format will at least know that it is an image and that showing the raw data to the recipient results in "garbage" being shown on the screen.

- Audio—Subtypes are audio format names. Subtype "audio/basic" denotes single channel 8000 HZ u-law audio data, an intended standard for telephone-quality e-mail audio.

- Video—Subtypes correspond to video format names, such as the one defined by MIME, "video/mpeg."

- Message—Used to encapsulate an entire RFC 822 format message. It can be used in forwarding or rejecting mail. The standard defines two subtypes of message "message/partial" can be used to break a large message into several pieces for transport. The pieces are put back together automatically on the other end. "message/external-body" can be used to pass a very large message body by reference, rather than including its entire contents. It should be noted that a message with "content-type: message" may contain a message that has its own different content-type field—the message structure may be recursive.

- Multipart—Used to assemble several parts, potentially of differing types and subtypes, into a single RFC 822 message body. The content-type field specifying type multipart also includes a delimiter, that is used to separate each consecutive body part. Each body part is itself an RFC 822 message in miniature. It usually contains its own content-type field to describe the type of the part. Subtypes of multipart are specifically required to have the same syntax as the basic multipart type, thus guaranteeing that all implementations can successfully break a multipart message into its component parts. Subtypes of multipart are used to further add structure to the parts in order to permit a more integrated structure of multipart messages among cooperating user agents.

- Application—Used for most other kinds of data that do not fit into any of the other content-type variables. List servers, mail-based information servers, and mail-based application languages are some examples.

The MIME types are inferred from a mapping table based on the file extension. Table 6.1 shows which file extensions are mapped onto which MIME types and provides an example of a Helper Application that can be used to view the file if it cannot be viewed directly within the browser. *Mapping* is the term used for the process by which one matches the file extensions with the appropriate MIME type.

Table 6.1

A MIME Type Mapping Table

File	MIME Type/Subtype Helper	Description	Extension Application
HTM	text/html	ascii text with HTML markup	none
TXT	text/plain	ordinary ascii text	none
PS	application/postscript	Adobe PostScript data	Ghostscript
RTF	application/rtf	Microsoft Rich Text Format	Ghostscript
PDF	application/pdf	Adobe Portable Document Format	Acrobat
ZIP	application/zip	Pkware compression	Pkunzip
DOC	application/msword	MS Word Format	MS Word
WAV	applications/wav	Waveform sound format	Windows media player
JPG	image/jpeg	jpeg graphics format	none
JPEG	image/jpeg	jpeg graphics format	none
GIF	image/gif	Compuserve graphics inter-change format	none
TIF	image/tiff	Tagged Image File Format	Vueprint
TIFF	image/tiff	Tagged Image File Format	Vueprint
AU	audio/basic	Sun/Next sounds	none
MPG	video/mpeg	mpeg video	VMPEG

continues

Table 6.1

A MIME Type Mapping Table, continued

File	MIME Type/Subtype Helper	Description	Extension Application
MPEG	video/mpeg	mpeg video	VMPEG
MOV	video/quicktime	Apple Quicktime video	Eviewer
Default	application/octet-string	any binary string of data	user customizable

Note

In Table 6.1 above, in the Helper application column, "none" means the browser can display the datatype without an external application being used. The list is neither complete nor exhaustive. The Helper Applications listed within the table are examples of software that have been created for the viewing of particular file formats. A more complete list of helper applications is provided later in the chapter.

A file is maintained on the server which indicates the types of documents that correspond to various file extensions. When the server gets a request for a URL leading to a file which has one of these extensions, a single line is sent to the browser indicating the MIME type and subtype of the file. This is the extent of the server's work with MIME.

Browsers maintain a list of MIME types and subtypes but also include the name of the application which will be used to display that type. Figure 6.1 is a screenshot of Netscape Navigator 2.01's Helper Application screen. You can see the type/subtype pairs as well as the helper application that has been established for this particular browser implementation.

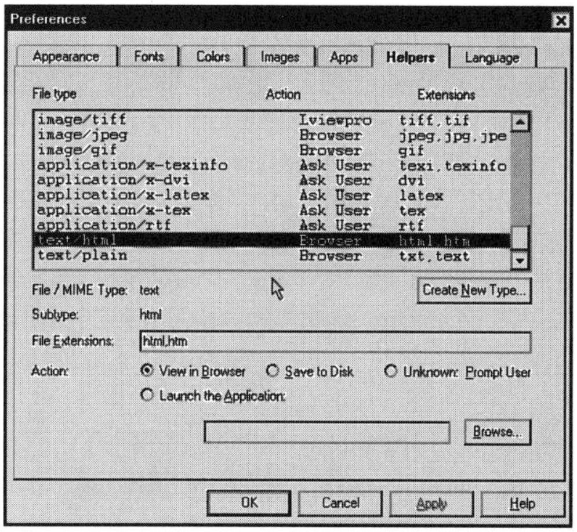

Figure 6.1

Netscape Navigator 2.01—MIME Types and Helper Applications.

Why is MIME Required?

The HTTP protocol contains simple commands the browser uses to tell the server what types of data it is capable of receiving. The server starts sending the requested data to the browser once the handshake is complete. The client "caches" the file temporarily on disk and then calls the associated application using the temporary file as the argument.

The browsers we use have internal helpers that will handle a basic and increasingly wider variety of MIME subtypes. These helper applications handle anything from remote log-ins to hearing or viewing audio, video, text, image, and graphics files. If you want to incorporate additional formats into your intranet for which you do not have the helper application, you can obtain the appropriate application and configure and test it for your browser. See the list provided later in the chapter for helper applications available at the time of writing.

Because of the rapid development of file subtypes, MIME plays an important role in allowing the browser and server to negotiate a successful transfer. In the event that it is not capable of handling a certain file type, the browser can usually be configured to save the file with an advisory message so that you will be able to find the appropriate helper application and install and configure it in order to use the file just received.

Multimedia and the Intranet

There are tremendous advantages to being able to incorporate a wide variety of media types into the intranet. A video of a technician installing a modem could be used to assist a user in performing the task without the help of a technician. Interactive videos and training software can be used to prepare staff for certification exams. These examples outline a couple of useful applications that use multimedia on the intranet.

However, companies should avoid the temptation to use multimedia just for the sake of the media type. Multimedia formats can meet certain business requirements, such as virtual meetings where none of the participants are in the same room, and the development of new products by a dispersed work group. As one moves from the traditional document delivery metaphor through to operational requirements, workflow within the framework of the intranet the implementation of multimedia can have a dramatic effect on the way work is done within an organization. One caveat is that too much multimedia can slow down the network and distract users from the completion of their tasks. One example of the latter would be to make cable TV available over the intranet—the temptation might be too great for some users (particularly the author during football season).

With respect to the business processes that can be affected through the intranet, you can, for example, play video and audio for interactive training on the usage of a software product, or you can make the department's annual budget spreadsheet available. The users of the budget would have the spreadsheet application in their possession for their input and manipulation and for their own records.

Small-scale video conferencing, telephone conversations, real-time audio—these "high-bandwidth" applications may have a place within your intranet, but focus here on the two main ways to get your browser to work with the variety of formats that exist. These two ways are through helper applications and plug-ins.

Helper Applications

Helper Applications are used in conjunction with the browser to enable you to utilize data files that your browser cannot interpret directly.

If you are building this function into the intranet from the HTML pages where you want to invoke the helper application, you should do the following:

1. Create the hyperlink with the href set to the data file within the HTML page.

2. Ensure the browser can locate the application required to interpret the file. Make certain that the helper application has been obtained and is located on the user's computer or on the network where it can be invoked by the user.

When the link is activated, the file is copied by the browser to a temporary file, and then the browser starts the application needed.

Helper applications are not interactive. In other words, no activity can be taken by the browser based on the user's input. Helper applications just display the file for viewing. HTML forms (discussed in Chapter 9) are used to implement interactivity and security. By passing the user's input to another routine on the server, processes can act upon the user's response away from the control of the user. The response to the user is usually an HTML document that is dynamically created and returned to the browser submitting the form.

Warning

You should be aware of a few security issues when setting up helper applications on users' desktops. If files with a bat extension are associated with MIME type *application/msdos-script* and the user has already configured the browser to launch such scripts with COMMAND.COM as the helper application, the file requested will be retrieved and executed. Any DOS command can be put into a batch file, which may include the deletion of all files and the installation of viruses in exe files and MIME types application/msdos-app.

Following is a non-exhaustive list of helper applications that you can obtain for use by the users of your intranet (Windows users only). These are the products and addresses available at the time of writing and will most likely have changed by the time the reader sees these words. They are provided as examples only and you should act accordingly.

Table 6.2

Helper Applications for Windows

Product Type	URL
Graphics Viewers	
Paint Shop Pro	.http://www.jasc.com/psp.html
LView Pro	http://world.std.com/~mmedia/lviewp.html
Movie Viewers	
Apple's Quicktime	http://quicktime.apple.com/form-qt2win.html
Video for Windows	ftp://gatekeeper.dec.com/pub/micro/msdos/win3/desktop/avipro2.exe
MPEG	ftp://gatekeeper.dec.com/pub/micro/msdos/win3/desktop/mpegwin.zip
MPEG	http://random.chem.psu.edu/mpeg.html
Sound Players	
Goldwave	ftp://oak.oakland.edu/SimTel/win3/sound/gldwav21.zip
Live Internet Video	
CU See Me	http://cu-seeme.cornell.edu/
VDO Live	http://www.vdolive.com/index.html
Live Internet Audio	
Xing Streamworks	http://www.xingtech.com/streams/index.html
Real Audio	http://www.realaudio.com/

Type Product	URL
Internet Telephone	
Speak Freely	http://www.fourmilab.ch/netfone/ windows/speak_freely.html
News & Mail	
FreeAgent 1.0 Newsreader	ftp://ftp.forteinc.com/pub/forte/ free_agent/fagent10.zip
Eudora E-mail	ftp://ftp.qualcomm.com/quest/windows/ eudora/1.5/eudor154.exe
TCP/IP Applications	
WS_FTP32 (32 bit FTP utility)	ftp://mirrors.aol.com/mir01/CICA/ pub/pc/win3/winsock/ws_ftp32.zip
EWAN105 (TELNET utility)	ftp://mirrors.aol.com/mir01/CICA/ pub/pc/win3/winsock/ewan105.zip
WS_PING (PING utility)	ftp://mirrors.aol.com/mir01/CICA/ pub/pc/win3/winsock/ws_ping.zip
WS_CHAT (CHAT utility)	ftp://mirrors.aol.com/mir01/CICA/ pub/pc/win3/winsock/ws_cha30.zip
WSIRCV20 (IRC utility)	ftp://mirrors.aol.com/mir01/CICA/ pub/pc/win3/winsock/wsircv20.zip
WSFNGR15 (FINGER utility)	ftp://mirrors.aol.com/mir01/CICA/ pub/pc/win3/winsock/wsfngr15.zip
TcpSpeed (measures network bandwidth)	http://maximized.com/
Compression Tools	
WinZip 6.0 (16 bit)	ftp://ftp.winzip.com/winzip/ wz16v6116.exe
WinZip 6.0 (32 bit)	ftp://ftp.winzip.com/winzip/ wz326116.exe

Many of these helper applications are available free-of-charge. However, these freebies are also *free-of-support*. Other than finding others who have implemented these applications and are willing to share their experiences, you may be on your own in using them. The commercial products are well supported and most provide online as well as voice support. It is only through obtaining the various helper applications and testing them with your users, for ease of use, for example, that you will determine the best of the helper applications upon which to standardize.

The other alternative that will be discussed in the next section is the in-line plug-in which operates in a different manner than the helper applications.

In-line Plug-ins

Plug-ins are a newer feature that have seen rapid growth over the past few months. Popularized for use with Netscape Navigator, the plug-ins are dynamic code modules that are associated with MIME types and subtypes for which Netscape Navigator has no native support. When Navigator encounters a data type that is unknown, it first looks for a plug-in associated with that MIME type and then loads it. Once an HTML page is closed, the plug-in is closed. When the Navigator loads, it checks the directory/folder netscape\plugins (because the existence of a plug-in is recognized by the browser, each plug-in is displayed briefly on the browser's splash, or introductory, screen). If the browser encounters a MIME type/subtype that requires a plug-in, the plug-in loads automatically.

The basic difference between in-line plug-ins and the helper applications is that the plug-ins operate within the browser, not a separately running application as is the case under a helper application.

Note

Plug-ins are software programs that extend the abilities of the browser by allowing you to, for example, play audio samples or view a video movie from within the browser.

Table 6.3 outlines a non-exhaustive list of plug-ins available for the Windows platform.

Table 6.3

Plug-ins Available for Netscape Navigator

Category	Product	URL
Animation		
	FutureSplash	http://www.futurewave.com
	Live3D	http://home.netscape.com/ comprod/products/navigator/ live3d/download_live3d.html
	mBED	http://www.mbed.com/
	Play3D	ftp://magna.com.au/pub/users/ mark_carolan/HeadsOff.html
	Shockwave	http://www.macromedia.com/tools/ shockwave/index.html
	Sizzler	http://totallyhip.com/
	Topper	http://www.ktx.com/products/ hyperwire/index.html
	Viscape	http://www.superscape.com
	VR Scout	http://www.chaco.com
	Vrealm	http://www.ids-net.com
	WebXpresso	http://www.dvcorp.com/webexpres so/index.html
	WIRL	http://www.vream.com
Basic Productivity		
	Amber	http://www.adobe.com/
	ActiveX	http://www.microsoft.com/ intdev/sdk
	Carbon Copy/ Net	http://www.microcom.com/
	Chemscape Chime	http://www.mdli.com/
	Concerto	http://www.alphasoftware.com

continues

Table 6.3

Plug-ins Available for Netscape Navigator, continued

Category	Product	URL
	EarthTime	http://www.starfishsoftware.com
	Envoy	http://www.twcorp.com
	Formula One/ NET	http://www.visualcomp.com
	ISYS HindSite	http://www.isysdev.com
	Look@Me	http://www.farallon.com/
	NET-Install	http://www.twenty.com
	OpenScape	http://www.busweb.com/
	PointCast Network	http://www.pointcast.com
	PointPlus	http://www.net-scene.com/
	QuickServer	http://www.wayfarer.com/
	Techexplorer	http://www.internet.ibm.com/
	Word Viewer	http://www.inso.com
Presentation		
	ASAP WebShow	http://www.spco.com/default.htm
	Astound Web Player	http://www.golddisk.com
	PowerMedia	http://www.radmedia.com
Audio/Video		
	ACTION	http://www.open2u.com/action
	CoolFusion	http://www.iterated.com
	Crescendo	http://www.liveupdate.com/
	Echospeech	http://www.echospeech.com
	Koan	http://www.sseyo.com/
	Moviestar	http://www.beingthere.com/
	PreVu	http://www.intervu.com/

Quicktime	http:// quicktime.apple.com/pt/ sw/license.html
RapidTransit	http://monsterbit.com/rapidtransit/
RealAudio	http://www.realaudio.com/
ToolVox	http://www.voxware.com/
VDOLive	http://www.vdolive.com/
VivoActive	http://www.vivo.com

Image Viewers

ABC Quicksilver	http://www.micrografx.com
CMX	http://www.corel.com
DWG/DXF	http://www.softsource.com
FIGleaf Inline	http://www.ct.ebt.com/
Fractal Viewer	http://www.iterated.com/
InterCAP	http://www.intercap.com
KEYview	http://www.ftp.com
Lightening Strike	http://www.infinop.com
Shockwave/ Freehand	http://www.macromedia.com
SVF	http://www.softsource.com
ViewDirector	http://www.tmsinc.com
Wavelet Image	http://www.summus.com/
WHIP!	http://www.autodesk.com/

Tip

For the latest in information on plug-ins, check out:

- "Plug-In Plaza" at http://www.browserwatch.com

- "Tucows' Plug-ins for Windows" at http://home.texoma.com/ mirror/tucows/plug95.html

continues

- "SlaughterHouse's Browser Plug-ins" at http://www.magpage.com/~cwagner/plugins.html

- "Windows95.com's Plug-ins and Utilities" at http://www.windows95.com/apps/plugins.html

- "MacWeek's List of Mac Plug-ins" at http://www.zdnet.com/macweek/mw_1007/plugins.html

Both the helper application and the inline plug-ins make it easier to get more out of your browser and easier to use a greater variety of file formats to present your information across the intranet. There is a tradeoff, however. Each of the applications, either helpers or plug-ins, utilize system resources when operating. This slows down the response time somewhat with the current versions, but the next releases of many of these applications are being re-designed to work more efficiently within the browser paradigm.

Keep in mind that there are costs to implementing each of these internally, such as for training, acquiring the software, and production which may be external if you buy these services. Be sure that the usage of these tools solves a business process problem and is not there for "vanity" purposes.

The next section covers how to get a browser system up and running so you can solve your business problems.

Browser Configuration

Now that you have an idea of what you can incorporate to extend the native capabilities of your browser to handle all the potential formats of information, the chapter turns to walking you through the configuration of the browser. Netscape Navigator 2.01 will be the primary example in setting up the browser to work across the variety of file formats that you will employ within the framework of your initial intranet pilot project.

Tip

It is recommended that, for ease of support and maintenance, you standardize on one browser for the company. People will have used a variety of browsers within your company, but it is much easier to enable support for one browser than it is to support a variety of browsers. This is especially true when you are planning to work with helper applications and plug-ins.

All browsers have configuration options that can be set to the user's preferences. They will vary from those that will be demonstrated here, but the basic type of configuration options and the method of going through the configuration process are all similar.

From the Chapter 2 discussion relative to the strategic applications of the initial pilot, this book suggests that the initial intranet that is built should address the following four primary areas:

1. Publishing internal information

2. Links to information sites

3. Simple groupware application

4. Access to the phone directories and client/company profiles

If you already have an external Web site, the people creating information for that site have probably already adopted some software tools and product formats for the preparation and distribution of information. You can build on the tools that they have used, especially if the information they have already created is meant to be distributed across the company.

A variety of tools and processes can be used to create information products for distribution. Many of these products will create output in a format that can be used within the intranet. Several of them can save to multiple formats. Because the Intranet is internal to the company, you can "standardize" on a file format type, or a small number of formats, for a given application or business process solution.

Note

Although there are people who will cry "foul" at the mention of a standard, this will provide people a technological framework to unleash their innate creativity. Just tell them that if there is another standard they feel is warranted in order to solve the business process problem, you will test the application with them to try to make it work.

This chapter does not deal with the creation tools but rather how the users will access the files they want to retrieve. Although you may be able to control the formats of files created internally, you will have no control over those created externally. What will be discussed here is the basic configuration of the browser and obtaining and configuring the helper applications and in-line plug-ins that you feel may be helpful, using Netscape Navigator 2.01 for a case study.

Configuring Internal Applications

The following example is based on Netscape Navigator 2.01 and assumes that you have obtained and installed the software using the defaults. Figure 6.2 shows the Netscape Navigator Options Menu. The areas that will be dealt with are as follows:

- General Preferences

- Mail and New Preferences

- Network Preferences

- Security Preferences

General Preferences

The General Preferences menu option allows the user to configure the Netscape Navigator for their own personal preferences. There are seven pages within the General Preferences area that enable the user to configure the browser in the following areas:

- Appearance

- Fonts

- Colors

- Images

- Apps (supporting applications)

- Helpers (helper applications)

- Language

Each preference is considered in terms of setting up the Navigator browser in the fashion the user requires and works within the parameters of the intranet technology.

Figure 6.2

Netscape Navigator Options Menu.

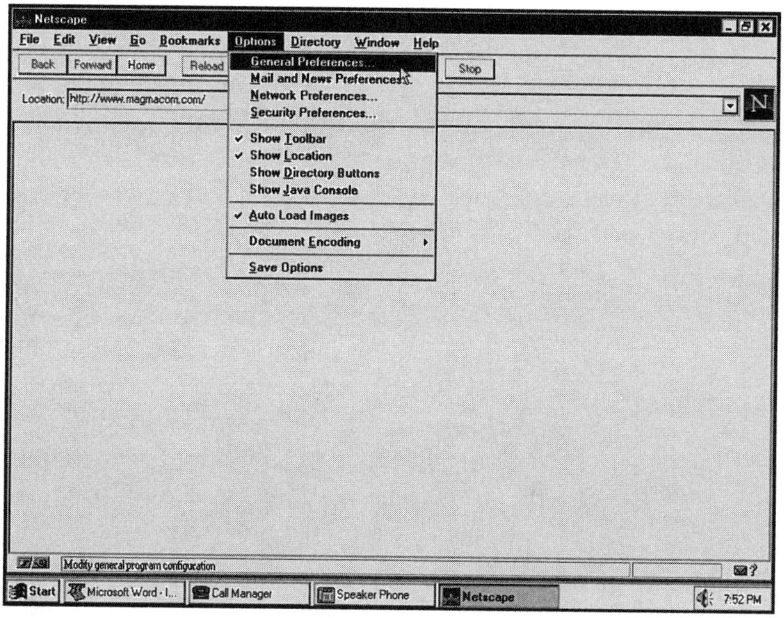

Appearance

The settings in the appearance menu establish how Netscape will look when you start it up relative to the way the Navigator's Toolbar appears on the screen, the home page the browser should connect to, and how the hyperlinks available should be portrayed and managed. The following procedure deals with the items that appear on the screen, as shown in figure 6.3.

1. The toolbar can be set up to display pictures, text, or both. To maximize the space available for document display, select Text—only the text description of the buttons appears. Using Pictures displays the graphic description or icon for the function on the button. The Pictures and Text option displays both the text and icon. Regardless of the method specified, the toolbar will function in a consistent manner.

2. Select Netscape Browser as the launch window for the browser in the Startup area. Choosing either the Netscape News or Netscape Mail options starts the browser in the mode selected, pointing to the respective servers as defined under the Mail and News Preferences menu option. Regardless of the option selected, the Navigator allows the user to open all three windows.

3. Check the Home Page Location button and enter the URL of the intranet's main server. Upon launching the browser, this is the file that will be automatically retrieved and displayed on the user's browser.

4. Make sure the Underlined box is selected under Link Styles. This allows the user to see the hypertext links more clearly.

5. Followed Links can be set to either Never Expire or Expire After XX Days. When a link is selected or followed, the color in which the link is displayed to the user changes as per the parameters selected under the Colors window of the General Preferences options. If you set the Followed Links to some form of expiration, the followed links will revert back to the color of the unfollowed links after the specified time period.

Note

Once you have selected or followed a link, the color of the followed link, as specified under the Colors Window of the General Preferences options, changes. If you set the Followed Links option to Never Expire, this link will always remain the color of a followed link. If you allow the link to expire, the color will revert to that of an unfollowed link. Depending upon the users that you will set up on the intranet, set the links to expire after 30 days. This may trigger the user to follow the link in your intranet because it appears they have not been there; if the link appears to be "unfollowed," based on the color, many people will automatically assume that there is "new" material there and follow the link in order to stay abreast of what is going on. Many users will not retrace their steps to see if anything new has been added to the intranet if a link has not been "reset." This is a tricky way of getting them to keep using the intranet to see what new developments there are within the system. One caveat with this approach: you better make sure that there is new information within the system in order to keep the users' interest level up.

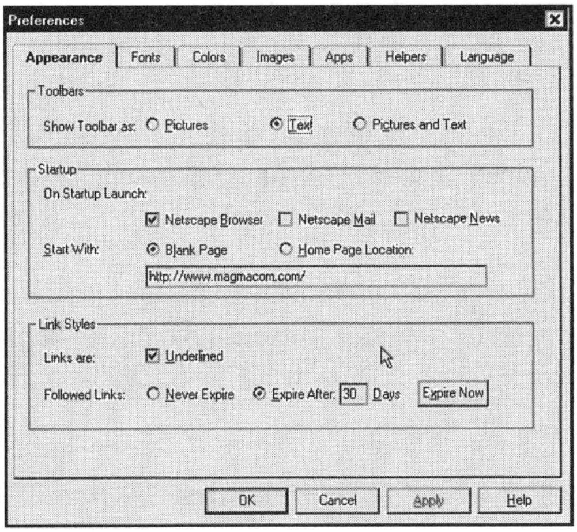

Figure 6.3

Netscape Navigator General Preferences| Appearances.

Fonts

Netscape enables you to choose a character set that governs the display of text on the desktop. The default, Latin1, is recommended with the proportional font of Times 12 and fixed font Courier 10, as shown in Figure 6.4. Latin1 allows the inclusion of accents and other characters that are associated with the use of many foreign languages. If this choice does not fit the specific needs of your users, choose one of the alternate solutions which best matches your circumstances.

Figure 6.4

Netscape Navigator General Preferences|Fonts.

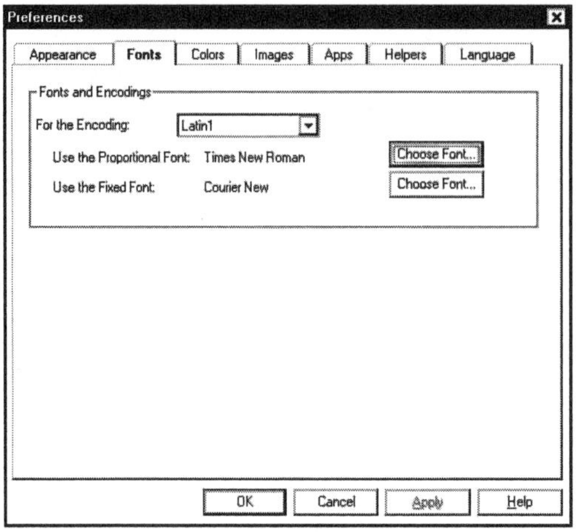

Colors

The use of color is contingent upon a couple of things: that the users can see the screen and discern the colors, and that the users want to customize the colors on their browser.

Figure 6.5 shows this Preferences panel. The settings can be customized, and the Choose Color buttons enable you to pick the colors that you wish to use for the available options: links, followed links, text, and background.

You can also enter the name of an image file (jpg or gif file format) to which the user has access to be used as the background for the browser. If you always want to have this image appear in the background, check off the Always Use My Colors, Overriding Document box.

Note

Two things to remember if you use an image for the background of the browser: the text of every document retrieved will be placed on top of this image, and the text may be awkward to read with the image in the background. If you are establishing the environment for all users, please remember that roughly five percent of humans are color blind (red/green mostly). Don't mix these colors together on the screen, or else the users may see nothing but a blob.

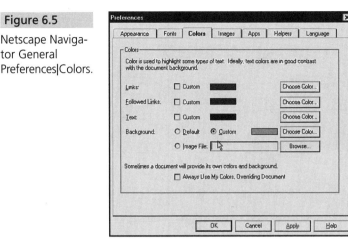

Figure 6.5

Netscape Navigator General Preferences|Colors.

Images

Because the creators of images use a variety of software programs, it is difficult to perfectly match the colors used to create an image. Several options are available for the user to facilitate the display of color images. There is a trade-off between speed of display and the quality of the color displayed within the browser. The user should specify the method of color selection to be used while the images are loaded. Automatic (the default) determines the most appropriate type of image display, and it is usually the fastest of the three options to load. Use dithering to the color cube to most closely match your computer's available colors. Dithered images may offer a closer match to an image's intended colors, but they take longer to display. To substitute colors with the closest match in the color cube, select the Substitute Colors option. Figure 6.6 shows the default (and recommended) settings for the intranet.

Apps

Use this panel to input any applications that support Netscape in getting connected to your data sources. This is where the supporting applications for establishing Telnet or terminal emulation sessions, with a mainframe, for example, are identified. Figure 6.7 shows an example of completed fields.

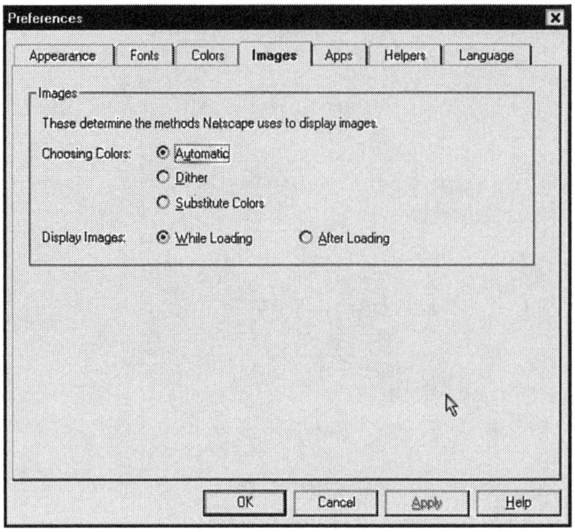

Figure 6.6

Netscape Navigator General Preferences|Images.

To input applications, you must take the following steps:

1. Enter the location of the Telnet software you use. Telnet provides a means to connect to and run a terminal session (data entry into a financial system, for example) on another computer as if you were just a remote terminal on that system.

2. Enter the location of your TN3270 application if the intranet is connected to an IBM mainframe via a Telnet session.

3. Enter the location of the viewer application you wish to use to view the source code behind the HTML files displayed in the browser. If it is something other than the default viewer of the browser, enter the name, including directory path, of the executable file to start the chosen software.

4. Enter the name of a directory to be used for temporary storage of application files on your computer. These files will be deleted by Netscape once the application has finished.

Helpers

This is the area where you can see the Helper Applications, as described earlier in the chapter, that Netscape has built-in and the actions associated with applications the program does not handle by default. When Netscape needs to read a file with a format that it cannot read by itself, an external helper application is sought.

Figure 6.7

Netscape Navigator General Preferences|Apps.

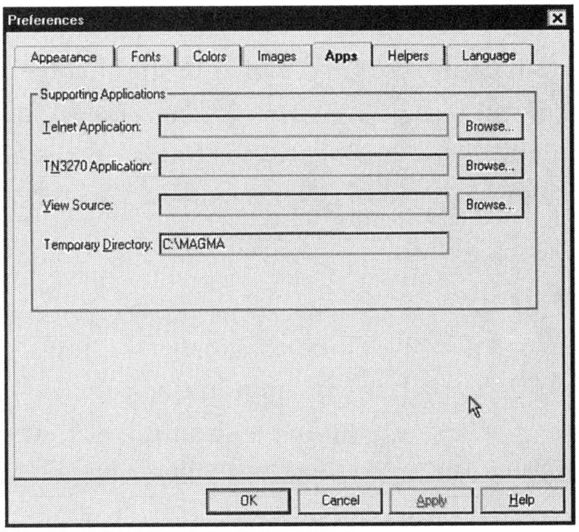

To install Lview Pro, MMedia Research Corp., for example, the following steps are required and are shown in figure 6.8:

1. In the General Preferences|Helpers panel, scroll down and select "image/tiff."

2. Select Launch the Application in the Action area.

3. In the associated box, enter the program name or use Browse to select the program name. In the example you would enter **C:\lview pro\lviewpro**.

Figure 6.8

Netscape Navigator General Preferences|Helpers.

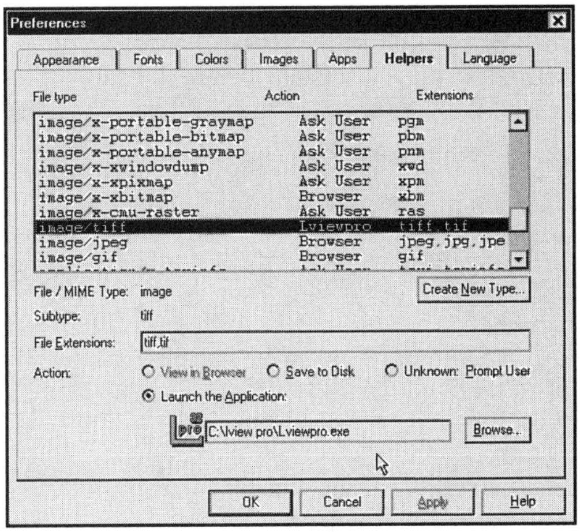

These steps take you through the process of selecting the MIME content-type/subtype, as discussed earlier in the chapter, and specifying what the browser should do when it encounters a file of the specified type. In the example, the browser is instructed to take the action of Launch Application by invoking the Lview_Pro software to view the file.

Language

Your language priorities can be sent as part of the HTTP request header if you have established them in this panel. If you establish the capability to receive pages in multiple languages, servers capable of providing files in multiple languages will do so. The following steps enable you to build the Accept List that is shown in figure 6.9:

1. Highlight the language required in the Language/Region field.

2. Click the Right arrow button to insert the selected language into the Accept List.

Tip

Should you wish to define your own Language/Region code, you may do so with the User Define area. Enter the code you wish to create in the user define box and press the down arrow to include the code in the Accept List.

Figure 6.9

Netscape Navigator General Preferences| Language.

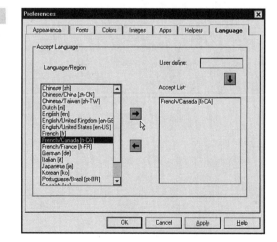

Mail and News Preferences

The Mail and News Preferences enable you to establish the parameters for accessing and reading information from news servers and mail servers. The user can configure the parameters within the following sections to their specific needs, within the framework of the intranet. The following panels represent the configuration options for this section:

- Appearance

- Composition

- Servers

- Identity

- Organization

Appearance

This panel permits customization of the font and text/quoted text styles, as well as a selection of mail client, with Netscape being the default. Changes should be made as per the user's preference and the availability of alternate mail client software.

Composition

The Composition panel permits the user to automatically store a copy of every sent message to a user-specified directory and forward copies of mail or news messages to another e-mail address, among other actions. This reduces the need for the user to save copies to disk themselves, and it ensures an audit trail of all sent messages. In order to complete the configuration of the Composition panel, complete the following steps:

1. Select Allow 8-bit for the widest range of e-mail servers in the U.S. and Europe.

2. Enter an e-mail address in Mail Messages or News Messages to automatically forward a copy of a message to the address. Copies of sent messages are, by default, copied to the Sent Mail file.

3. Select Automatically Quote Original Message when replying in order to include the original message in any response.

Servers

In order to utilize Netscape Navigator to read news and mail servers, you must complete the information on the Servers panel. This panel contains all the parameters required by the browser to properly read and post information to the servers indicated, provided that the user has the permission to participate. You have the following options:

1. Enter the names of the Outgoing Mail (SMTP) Server and Incoming Mail (POP) Server in order to send and receive mail via Netscape (check with the Internet Service Provider or your internal e-mail gurus). The remaining mail parameters are to be individually setup for each person.

2. Enable news services through the inclusion of the News (NNTP) Server name and a directory in which the news files should be stored.

Figure 6.10 shows the Mail and News Preferences|Servers panel with the author's information displayed.

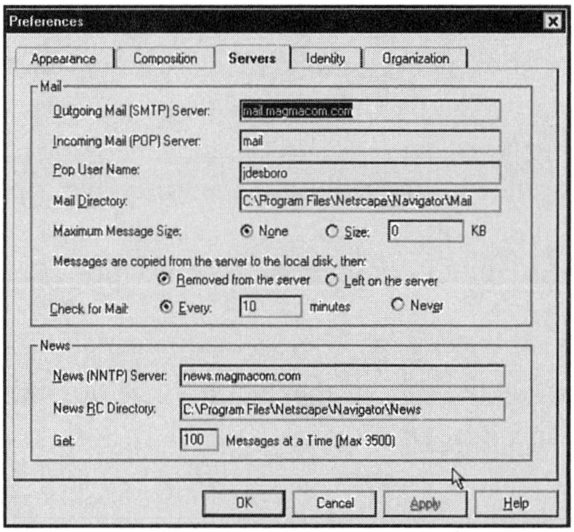

Figure 6.10

Netscape Navigator Mail and News Preferences| Servers.

Identity

If you choose to participate in news groups and send e-mail from the browser, netiquette dictates that you identify yourself to the readers and recipients of your postings and e-mail. The following points outline the basic steps required to complete the panel, which is shown in figure 6.11:

1. Enter the requested information in the Your Name and Your Email fields.

2. Use the Your Organization and Signature File fields to advertise yourself at the bottom of the e-mail message automatically. Remember, this signature file goes to all recipients.

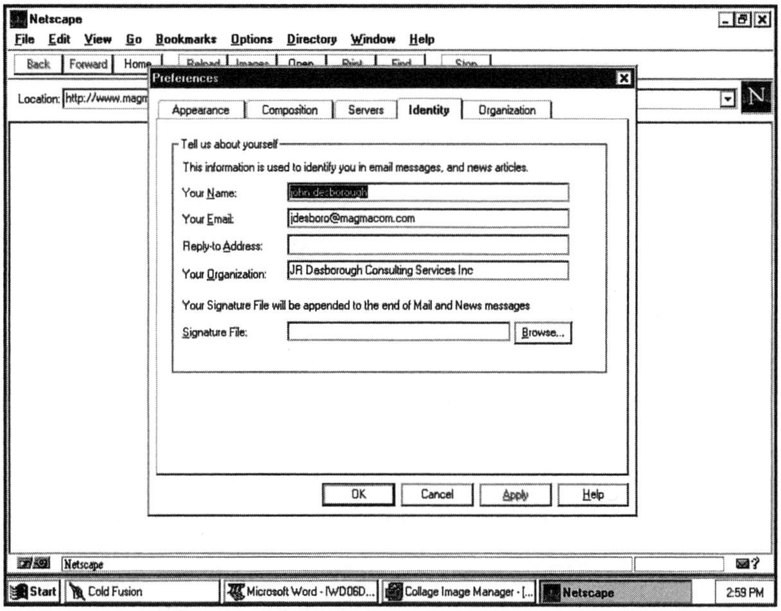

Figure 6.11.

Netscape Navigator Mail and News Preferences|Identity.

Organization

Do the following to permit the organization of mail and news messages by subject/topic threading:

1. Select the appropriate parameters based on individual preference.

2. Select Remember Mail Password to stop Netscape from requesting a password each time the Mail window is opened.

Network Preferences

The Network Preferences panel needs to be completed to enable both the memory and disk cache of Netscape. The cache function is used to store frequently accessed documents. When Reload is pressed from the toolbar, Netscape compares the cached document to the network document and shows the most recent one. The number of simultaneous connections and proxy information are also handled in this area.

Within the intranet, you are running Netscape on an internal network from behind a firewall, so you need to ascertain from the system administrator the names and associated port numbers for the server running proxy software for each network service and put them into the Proxies panel.

Following are the panels within the Network Preferences menu option within which the network parameters can be configured.

- Cache—Accept the defaults for Memory Cache and Disk Cache size, as well as the Disk Cache Directory (unless you wish to set up another directory) and set the Verify Documents to Once per Session.

- Connections—Accept the default maximum Number of Connections (4) and the Network Buffer Size (32K).

- Proxies—Enter the Proxy information as required for your intranet. An example is shown in figure 6.12.

Because the intranet is behind a firewall, a proxy server may be needed to allow Netscape running on the intranet to access information beyond the firewall. In order to complete the Proxies panel, you will need to have names or IP addresses of the various services available as well as the port number to which each has been assigned. To bypass the firewall's restriction, you must set the No Proxy For field to include any internal server in the intranet.

When discussing access, it is important to take a look at security. The next section will outline the main options in security preferences.

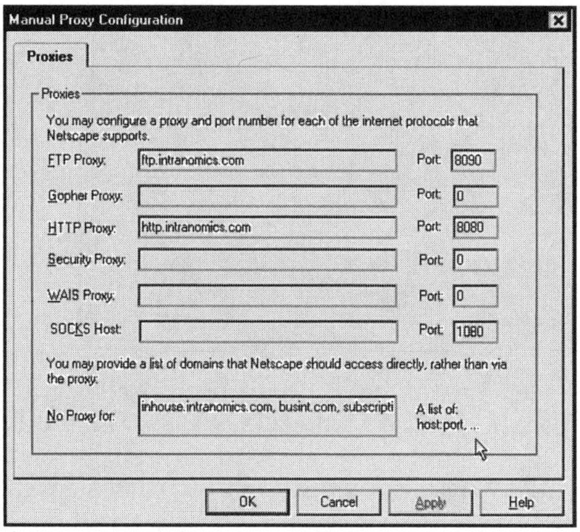

Figure 6.12

Netscape Navigator Network Preferences|Proxies.

Security Preferences

The Security Preferences General panel allows you to disable the automatic running of Java applets and to specify when you want to receive security alerts. The Site Certificates panel identifies the Certificates you have obtained. To review the discussion regarding certificates and Certificate Authorities, please return to Chapter 5, "intranet Security."

- **General**—Unless you are using Java applets within your intranet, check Disable Java. Ensure that all the Security Alert choices are selected, with the exception of Submitting a Form Insecurely. The Security Alert choices provide an extra level of security notification to users when they are interacting with documents that are secure.

- **Site Certificates**—To change the parameters of an individual Site Certificate, select the entry and Edit Certificate. Make any changes that are required.

Figure 6.13 shows the Site Certificate for a user's machine with CommerceNet. Note that the certificate allows for the connection to sites certified by the authority.

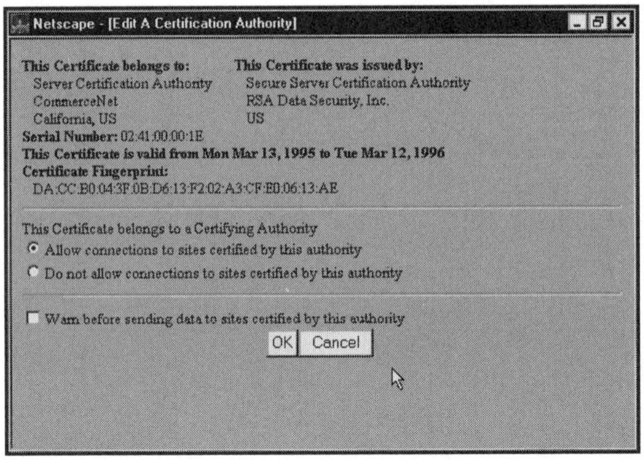

Figure 6.13

Netscape Naviga-
tor Security
Preferences|Site
Certificate.

Configuring External Applications

The following two sections outline how to ensure that Plug-ins for
Netscape Navigator 2.01 have been installed and how to configure
external applications for NCSA Mosaic 2.1.1.

Plug-ins for Navigator

An earlier discussion covered Inline Plug-ins for Netscape and how they
are loaded into Netscape when the browser is loaded. In the earlier
section dealing with the General Preferences|Helpers, the set up for a
Helper Application was covered. Following are the standard steps required to get the plug-ins up and running:

1. Decide on the plug-in that is required (for example, NET-
   Install, by 20/20 Software).

2. Obtain the appropriate copy of the software (see the non-exhaustive list of products and locations provided earlier).

3. Follow the instructions of the software company regarding the
   installation (generally, decompress in a separate directory and then
   copy required files to the plug-in directory, for example,
   \netscape\navigator\plugins). Refer to the manual or documentation provided with the plug-in, if necessary.

4. Restart Netscape.

5. From the Netscape menu, select Help|About Plug-ins to see a list of the plug-ins which you have installed for your browser to use.

The preceding steps will display a file that lists the plug-ins you have available on Netscape in the MIME-like format of type/subtype.

Note

NET-Install, by 20/20 Software, is a plug-in designed specifically for distributing software from Web pages. By clicking one link, Netscape Navigator users can download, decompress, and install software. The software is available for Windows 95, Windows NT, and Windows 3.1 at the time of this writing. The application can be implemented to facilitate the distribution of software versions already configured to be used on company-standard machines. For more information, please contact the vendors directly at http://www.twenty.com.

External Applications for NCSA Mosaic 2.1.1

NCSA Mosaic uses external viewers to display files which it does not have the native ability to display. They are set up in a process that is similar to that of Netscape Navigator Helper Applications. To install these external applications for use by Mosaic, follow these steps:

1. Obtain and install the required software. (For example, Lview Pro, by MMedia Research Corp.)

2. Start NCSA Mosaic.

3. Select Preferences from the Options menu.

4. Select the Viewers Preference sheet.

5. Select Add.

6. Enter MIME type (such as image) in the Associated MIME Type Of field.

7. Enter Description of MIME Type, if desired.

8. Enter appropriate file extensions in the With This/These Extensions field (for example, .tiff, .tif).

9. Enter, or use the Browse button to enter, the name of the application in the To this Application field (for example, C:\lview pro\lviewpro.exe).

10. Click on Add and OK to save information and close the Preferences window.

Figure 6.14 shows the NCSA Mosaic for Windows Preferences panel and, specifically, the Viewers panel where the previous example has been shown.

Figure 6.14

NCSA Mosaic for Windows Preferences.

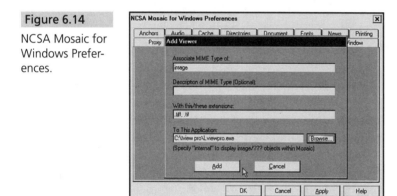

Available Browsers

A large number of browsers are available for use in the intranet. Rather than printing a long list, figure 6.15 is a look at the BrowserWatch site (http://www.browserwatch.com/browsers.html), which is the first place to look when trying to find out more about browsers.

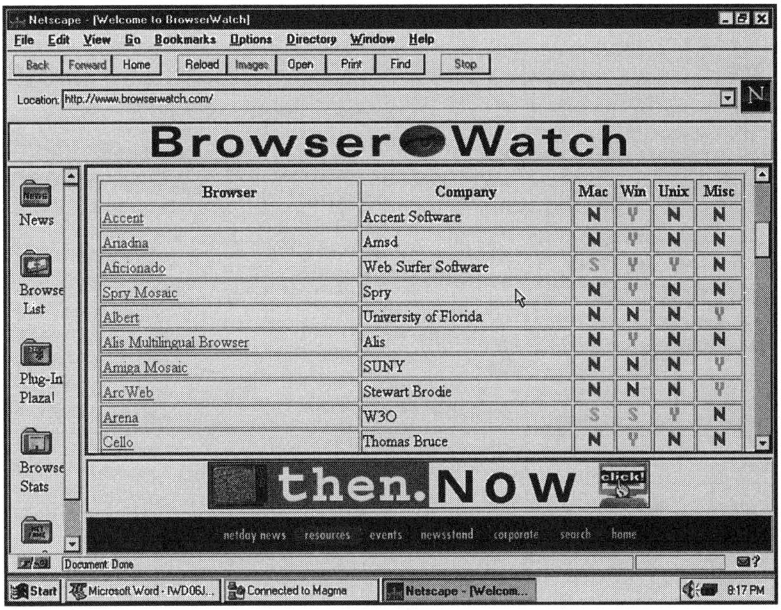

Figure 6.15

BrowserWatch
Browser List,
Courtesy of
iWorld.

Status Check

At this point, you should be able to evaluate the various file formats you will be incorporating into the intranet and set up the browser to handle the various non-native file formats it encounters. A fair number of browsers are on the market at the time of this writing— Browser-Watch listed 42 separate browsers available. Make sure the browser you select for your organization is robust and has the capability to enable external helper applications for file formats that are non-native.

The next chapter looks at the advantages of browser/server communications to understand the hype and the reality of the intranet. Specifically, the following questions will be answered:

- What is client/server computing?

- What is browser/server computing?

- What does the future hold for the intranet?

7

Understanding the Advantages of Browser/Server Communications

A movement is being made to utilize the technologies of the intranet/Internet to provide a means of connecting all of an organization's information sources. The goal is to use the intranet browser as the user's interface to the information held within the organization's servers, regardless of platform. This means that the browser and server must be capable of communicating with each other across the network. This is where the value of TCP/IP comes into play: the ability to communicate between browser and servers on different operating platforms and within different storage software is the forte of the TCP/IP protocol at the communications level.

A server is a program that offers a service and can be reached across the network. Servers accept requests via the network, perform a function in response to the requests, and then return the responses to the requesters. Servers can operate on any network using TCP/IP by implementing a server as an application level program.

A client is a program that can send a request to a server, wait for a response, and then reply to that response. In the world of the intranet, the browser is the client.

During the early 1990s, "client/server computing" was the buzzword the computer industry press touted as the answer to many business problems. "To increase productivity, go client/server." "Cost reductions required, go client/server." Et cetera.

Recently, the same press has published stories of how client/server computing has not worked or solved the problems as predicted. Why is it, then, that there is now a feeling that the intranet model of client/server, or rather browser/server, will work? This chapter answers that question by considering the following:

- The hype vs. the reality of the client/server system

- How the browser/server system works and its advantages over the client/server system

- What to expect from browser/server related systems in the future

Client/Server

There are probably as many definitions of client/server communications as there are vendors. The original basic concept, though, was that there should be movement away from the "corporate computing center" toward putting information and processing capacity on the users' desks. No matter where the users are located, they are the center of the information universe in the client/server system.

The Hype

During the 1980s, desktop computer prices sank and users became impatient with delays in getting access to information held within the "big iron" of the Information Technology (IT) shops. Part and parcel of the IT shops, the user service group within the IT shop was often called Electronic Data Processing and usually consisted of keypunch operators and mainframe programmers. The technology changed regularly within the IT shops, thus improving the capabilities of the technology. As the 1980s drew to a close, the rate of change of the technology was rapidly increasing. One of the problems was that the type of user services changed much more slowly. Even though the name of the user services group changed from Electronic Data Processing (EDP) to Information Systems (IS) to reflect the increasing integration of data and technology, the impatience levels of the users looking for strategic information grew with the perspective that the maintenance of the data by IS was not for the benefit of the users. By the time the information was generated and provided to the end user, it was often out of date and the next request had already been submitted.

Author's Note

In one organization in which I worked in the mid-1980s, any time part of the organization wanted a new report or a modification to an existing report, they prefaced their requests like this:

"Even though it will take 3 years and $3 million dollars to do this, could you....."

The whole information technology and services group was looked upon as a roadblock to "real success" when in reality it was trying to implement a client/server solution, installing approximately 800 desktop computers over 8 months and developing the programs to support access to the data the users required, all while maintaining the current operating environment.

By the time the users had received the new reports or modifications, they *were* out of date.

End users started developing their own solutions to their problems of information access and timeliness. As companies grappled with running the central information systems and installing desktop computers, empowered users pulled computers and software together to begin inputting their data, expanding and enhancing it to their own customized needs. As the requirements of these users grew and the capabilities of IS expanded, often they did not grow in the same general direction, and the systems would not work together.

Consider the following hypothetical example: an organization has a database of client profiles and activities running on a mainframe at headquarters. The regional staff submits to the central system update information on clients within the regional offices. The central system verifies and enters the changes. Turnaround time is approximately four weeks. Because several regional office staff may deal with a company in their region, the turnaround time on updates to the profiles is unacceptable to the regional office because it cannot keep track of its dealings with the client. The regional office creates a database of clients and the supporting application and makes the data available on its LAN. This allows the regional office staff to update the client records immediately so that everyone in the office can see the latest information on dealings with the client. The only problem is that the regional application can neither accept data from the corporate application, nor can it feed the data from the regional system to the headquarters database.

The solution was to try to bring the wide variety of tools and data together at the desktop—in the users' hands—and centralize the generally expensive (but reliable) corporate systems and data. The combined Information Technology and Information Systems departments, now calling themselves strictly Information Systems (IS), and their skills were needed to bring together the end users' tools and data into reliable networks in order to simultaneously share knowledge and provide access to corporate systems that worked with the end users' system.

Given the range of tools and data on the desktop and the demands from management to provide information systems that kept up with the changing business environment, the new IS groups were swamped trying to keep the old systems up and running while moving them to new platforms so they would work with the end users' systems. The rapid expansion of integrator consulting firms that promised to bring your old and new systems in touch with each other created lots of stories for the industry trade magazines. The late 1980s and early 1990s were boom years for the integrators as they grew rapidly to meet the demands of their clients.

Companies with expertise in linking "Brand A" applications with "Brand B" applications began to pop up. University graduates with diplomas still damp with ink were hired by these firms if they could write code. It did not matter if they had little or no business experience, as long as they knew code. Many integrator firms hired project managers and business analysts who could look at the business processes that needed to be fixed and then organize the team around getting the code written to make it all possible.

Business was good. Whatever the media called the phenomenon—re-engineering, downsizing, or right-sizing—all of a company's information access problems could be solved by a switch to client/server computing. The client/server system put the tools in the hands of the users and provided access to the data and logic stores so the end users would be able to structure the results package they needed. The media offered more and more stories of companies "going client/server"—with integrator assistance.

What went wrong with client/server computing? Why have recent media reports come back saying that many organizations are not happy with their client/server implementation? What is the reality of client/server?

The Reality

The client/server system was most commonly used in order to create a globally integrated data model for an organization's data. The environment tended to occur as follows:

1. A client application is started on a remote desktop that opens a connection across the network to be able to access the required information.

2. The user requests that the client application perform a function.

3. The application evaluates the request and figures out what demands it has to make of the data that resides on the server.

4. The client program formulates the demand and sends the request to the server.

5. The server, upon receipt of the request, determines which data meets the request and then sends the data back to the client desktop across the network.

Figure 7.1 is a pictorial representation of the points just covered. The numbers in the figure correspond to the numbered points in the list.

Figure 7.1

Simple depiction of client/server model.

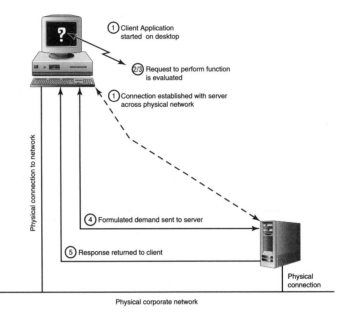

This environment is most appropriately suited for a transactional system, an order-entry application, for example, where the amount of data transferred is small and is completed quickly. A non-client/server environment would require sending the entire file across the network so that the client could sort through the information until it found the information required, if any.

As espoused by the vendors of client/server software and the integrators, the benefits that can be achieved by a successful client/server implementation are as follows:

- Geographic dispersion—Individuals can access the resources they need from wherever they are located.

- Multi-platform—Data stores and logical processes can be run on big, fast, powerful computers away from the desktop.

- Data integrity—Having the data on stable platforms where back-up routines are well-established means that the users don't have to worry about hardware or power failures.

- Security—Database administrators can structure the rights of access and manipulation of data much better with the client/server database systems than they can with end user applications like FoxPro or dBase. With the data residing centrally, rather than on the users' desktops, the security and access-control features of both the network and the server-based database engine can be established and implemented to protect the integrity of the data.

- Compliance—Having all the data stores in a database compliant with the client/server solution selected makes integration with other applications possible. It is through the database compliance that the interoperability among the various data stores is achieved.

In the framework for determining to "go client/server," several factors have to be considered:

- The learning curve—If a company does not already have the client/server database, a full implementation plan is required to establish the practices and procedures to ascertain the integrity of the data, to train staff for appropriate and required usage efforts, and even to learn the database itself.

- Cost—The cost of purchasing and implementing client/server databases can be very high, not only for the engine but for the means to access the engine.

- Complexity—Client/server adds another layer of application and complexity which is translated into higher support and maintenance requirements.

- Expertise—Although plenty of code writers may be out there, there is a shortage of experts who have overseen the successful implementation of client/server architecture. Then once someone has done it successfully for one firm, he or she tends to leave that firm to become a "high-priced integrator."

The facts of client/server implementation are that it is expensive, it requires a lot of training for both developers and users, and it can take a relatively long time if you are starting from scratch.

Many companies have applications that put data into databases quickly, safely, and efficiently. Retrieving information in the format the user wants at a specific moment in the time-space continuum proves more difficult. Then, with the complexity of pulling data from multiple platforms and formatting it for distribution to multiple platforms within an organization, it is no wonder that people are starting to look at Internet technologies, bundled as an intranet, to provide a simpler, less expensive solution.

The intranet offers an enterprise alternative to the traditional implementation of client/server computing. In this chapter and throughout the remainder of the book, the use of a browser/server-based intranet will be demonstrated. It is believed that for many organizations a browser/server model based on intranet technologies will provide a cost-efficient and cost-effective means to provide access to the organization's information resources.

Browser/Server

The browser sitting on the user's desktop computer is the intranet "client." When the user fires up the browser, it is pointed at, connects to, and retrieves the "home page" from the intranet server.

Defining Browser/Server Computing

In all reality, the intranet is just another instance of client/server computing. The difference is that the browser and its functionality deal with and can request information from both internal and external servers, as opposed to the client/server system that required the creation of servers. The servers may be in a variety of locations, running a variety of operating systems, with a variety of information types available for delivery to the user through the browser.

The browser/server architecture of the intranet information services is what enables any computer connected to the intranet to provide services to any other. To the user this concept appears to be the same as that of CompuServe, the commercial information service (http://www.compuserve.com), that provides all information services (except e-mail) from its own network. However, the intranet and CompuServe information services are vastly different.

The TCP/IP protocol enables the machines of the intranet to get information to each other even though one may be completely different from the other. HTTP enables the server and browser to negotiate the file format(s) they can send each other. Helper applications and in-line plug-ins for Netscape extend the browser's ability to utilize file formats that are not native.

How Browser/Server Computing Works

Within the framework of the intranet, the most basic functions are request and response. At the risk of being pedantic, here is a walk through a hypothetical situation:

1. Sit down in front of the computer and fire up the browser.

2. If you have entered the URL of a home page to start up with automatically, the browser creates an HTTP request and sends it off to the intranet server.

3. The server responds by sending you back the home page, which appears on your screen.

4. Select What's New in the Paper to review the articles about the company in today's press.

5. The browser sends a request to the server that is referenced in the URL, asking for the document/file in the URL to be returned to the screen. (If you need to familiarize yourself with this process, refer to Chapter 3, "The HTTP Protocol: Understanding the Application Layer," for a discussion of the HTTP protocol.)

6. The server accepts the request, checks to see if the document is available within its storage space, and, if so, bundles the document into the response and returns it to the requesting browser.

7. The browser receives the response and reviews the header information to see if it is in a format that can be displayed directly. If so, the document is displayed within the browser. If not, but if there is a helper application available, the browser copies the file to a temporary directory, launches the helper application, and displays the file within the helper application.

8. The browser waits for your next instructions. The server is ready to receive the next request from any browser.

The above transaction was pretty basic. The link that was activated returned a static document, one that had been created by some process, converted to a format acceptable to the intranet, and stored within the server's storage space. Other types of transactions take place when you select a link. The link you select may be more process-oriented: what the browser sends to the intranet server may start a process on another server altogether.

Consider the following hypothetical scenario: You need to speak to one of your colleagues in the Western Regional Office, but you do not know the phone number. You turn to the intranet to find the answer, perhaps using the following steps:

1. Select the Inter-Office Phone Book link.

2. Click on the arrow adjacent to the Employee Last Name field on the form the browser displays. Scroll down and choose the name of your colleague.

3. Click on the Get Info button.

4. Read the form the browser displays containing the name, address, phone number, and a brief description of the roles and responsibilities of the individual. There is also a link on this form to send an e-mail to the individual.

5. Pick up the phone and call.

In the previous scenario, you requested and received a form from the intranet server, selected a name, and when you clicked on the Get Info button, you sent a request to another server in the Intranet where the phone book application resides. The application then read your parameters, passed them to a database application, got the results from the database engine, and passed them back to the browser, formatted for display.

That was a simple transaction with a relatively static database. On the other hand, if you wanted to obtain a list of all the customers who had purchased a specific product between two dates sorted by geographic region and by volume of purchase, you could use the same basic principles to obtain the information. The information that is retrieved from the database is, hopefully, dynamic—if you ran the same request again tomorrow, you'd hope to see greater quantities for the customers listed on today's report and see new customers and their purchases.

Note

Chapter 9 will discuss the creation of forms for handling information and Chapters 10 and 11 will explore getting information into and out of databases.

But what you should see from these examples is that you are not stuck with retrieving a basic, plain old document. In fact, you are able to fill out a travel authorization request form, have it routed to the appropriate person for approval, then have it routed to the individual who makes the travel arrangements on your behalf. At the same time, a copy is routed to the finance group who, in turn, sends someone up with a cash advance that has been recorded in the financial ledgers. A whole business process has been initiated and actions have occurred as a result of the request and submission of the forms.

The possibilities are endless. Just find a business process that needs support of information resources, and develop the application required to get the right information required into the hands of the people who need it then and there. Please refer to Chapter 2, "Making Your Case," and Chapter 13, "Structuring Company Information Resources," for discussions on supporting the business processes of the organization.

Why Browser/Server is Better Than Client/Server

The need for a browser/server solution can be caused, for example, by an information or knowledge resource system for your business growing from a simple contact manager to multiple information sets in each division of your company. The growth in magnitude and complexity of the applications can cause several changes in the platform upon which the applications run. It would be prudent to start with a standard language that would be the base for work on any machine, no matter where the data is stored. That way, there would be no worries when trying to connect from anywhere in the world.

Is browser/server any better? There are a number of reasons why large companies across the United States and around the world are implementing intranets as a step toward solving their client/server problems. Some of the reasons include the following aspects of intranets:

- A single point of access to all the company's databases from anywhere the staff is traveling

- A single interface to all information sources, whether text or data

- All information available to users through one interface, regardless of varieties of platforms

Numerous articles have cited the advantages of adopting an intranet strategy and referenced several companies that are doing so:

- *Business Week*, Feb. 26, 1996, featured the intranet phenomenon as its cover story. The article talked about intranet developments at FedEx, Compaq Computer Corp., Ford Motor Co., Levi Strauss, 3M, and others.

- *Information Week*, Jan 29, 1996, outlined intranet plans of Visa International, Inc., drug maker Eli Lilly and Co., and MCI, where re-usable software kernels are stored. Booz-Allen has one administrator, according to the article, to run its intranet.

- *Web Week*, April 29, 1996, featured an article about J.P. Morgan, one of the top commercial banks in the process of completing a testing phase for the use of an internal Web site that they hope will expand to a full-fledged intranet.

These are only a few of the literally hundreds of articles appearing daily about firms who are adopting intranet technology. In fact, according to Zona Research Inc., Redwood City, California, the predicted sales of software to run intranet servers will be $4 billion in 1997, up from $476 million in 1995. This does not cover the applications packages being created and announced daily. For example, Information Advantage, Inc. of Minneapolis and Red Brick Systems of Los Gatos, CA, have recently released their partnership effort WebOLAP Content Server, "the first packaged ready-to-use offering for putting the data warehouse on the Net." This type of application seems to answer some of the concerns that were raised earlier about transaction-oriented systems being the basic type of client/server applications available on the intranet.

Author's Note

The information about the Information Advantage, Inc./Red Brick Systems product is from their marketing literature. I am using this as an example only. I have not, at the time I write this, had the luxury of working with the product to see if it works as advertised other than to try their Web site at http://www.infoadvan.com. However, this type of software will open the door for many companies to implement support tools for the decision-maker in mission-critical business processes.

Companies have adopted intranets for four simple reasons:

1. Browser-based intranets rely on HTML to present information to users on their computers. HTML enables programmers to extract available information from almost any kind of computer. This is also an advantage because the programmer only has one language to learn and then can put up pages of information that will be upwardly accessible by newer versions of browsers and HTML. By using the Common Gateway Interface (covered in Chapter 10,

"Introduction to CGI"), HTML can be extended to call external programs from within the HTML program.

2. Cross-platform support for browsers, available for almost every type of machine, enables you to create an information application on one type of computer and then obtain the browsers you need for each of the various computer types on your network. As new versions of the browsers come out with added functionality, all you have to do is replace the old ones with the new versions.

3. Because HTML browsers and HTTP servers are designed for working on the Internet and the intranet, no proprietary solutions are required to implement the networking of computers. No learning curve in the network support area!

4. For most Web browsers, the use of a Graphical User Interface (GUI) makes it much easier to access information, especially database resources. By picking a commercial product like Netscape Navigator to run on your flavor of machine, you have the ability to run HTML programs written for other platforms. You also do not have to develop a custom GUI for your client/server application. All you have to do is create the forms that are required to collect the information to be passed to the database application, and the form to be used to present the results back to the user via the browser.

In other words, the combination of HTML, CGI, HTTP, and TCP/IP-based networks provides a base of simple standards upon which to build the intranet. If you follow the KISS (Keep It Simple, Sam) principle, it seems that this *is* the better way.

What Does the Future Hold?

If the numbers from the Zona Research study are correct, the predicted sales volumes for intranet servers will be $4 billion in 1997 and $8 billion in 1998. This does not include the application packages, programming tools, and other "stuff" that goes into intranets. The amounts are staggering. Everyone wants a piece of the pie.

But what does this mean to the KISS principle in action? With all this money to be spent, how many different mousetraps will be created to do the same thing? Will you be able to focus on the core elements, with a set of clearly defined standards? Or will you be in a constant state of flux as hardware and software change and open up new avenues for companies to propose changes to the "standards?" Before you finally get to creating your intranet, a few comments are in order on the "state of the nation" relative to the technologies of the intranet. This section covers the following topics:

• Standards compliance

• Published Application Programming Interfaces (APIs)

• Things to watch for

Standards Compliance

The basis of the growth of the Internet, and subsequently the intranet, was based upon the TCP/IP standard and the Unix operating system. Once the HTML-based graphical user interfaces showed up and the HTTP protocol arrived, the intranet changed forever.

The TCP/IP Standard

It is unlikely that the TCP/IP standards will change much in the foreseeable future. Given the length of time they have been in place and the need for a ubiquitous standard, computer users will probably use something in the future very similar to the TCP/IP stack that they have today. The machines used and the application systems implemented will be changing, and this may lead to changes in the protocol, but the crystal ball is cloudy on this.

The HTTP Standard

If you read the latest versions of the HTTP 1.1 specification, you will see that the "authors" recognize that they were not able to think of everything when they first concocted the HTTP protocol. At the time, it solved problems for them. But like for any good thing, a satisfied customer will tell two people, and they will tell two people, and so on. The more people see the potential in something, the more they will push the edge of the envelope.

It is likely that within the 1996/97 time frame you will see an adoption of an HTTP 1.1 standard that will then be implemented over the following six to eight months. In fact, many of the changes between HTTP 1.0 and HTTP 1.1 are already in the labs of the software houses in anticipation of the final results.

The HTML Standard

Within the world of hard copy information, a philosophy or methodology was developed over time that allowed the creation of documents around a standard set of criteria for the structure and format of the information contained within the document. This methodology was implemented through what is now called the Standard Generalized Markup Language (SGML) and has been adopted as an ISO standard.

SGML is used to define the structural elements of a document and the format of the content of those elements. In defining the various elements of the document structure, one of the parameters that is stated for each structural element is the *tag*, or delimiter, that is used to define the structural element. These tags can be defined in any manner the person creating the document chooses, but the syntax of the tags, usually paired, is as follows:

```
<start_tag>structural element contents</end_tag>
```

The structural definition, including the tag names, is maintained in a file called a Document Type Definition (DTD). The basic theory behind the use of SGML to create the hard copy document was that the Document Type Definition file and the document to be printed, structured using the appropriately defined tags, could be given to any printer using SGML printing software. The printer's software would format the *tagged document* based on the information contained within the DTD file.

The development of SGML meant, in theory, that documents could be created and formatted independent of any proprietary software, based on the DTD of that particular document.

When trying to develop a means to organize and display documents electronically, the philosophy of SGML was borrowed for use with the development of HTML. Using the philosophy of tagging the elements of the document in a consistent manner, Tim Berners-Lee and others working at the CERN laboratories in Europe developed the HTML language for displaying documents transported across the wires via the HTTP protocol.

In reality, what these people had done was create a Document Type Definition that was transparent to the user. The tags that were permitted for use and display within the HTML browsers were defined and published in the public domain. It has been described that HTML is one instance of an implementation of SGML. The biggest difference is that HTML was not created to be independent of the printer—it was designed for use on the HTTP protocol.

HTML has its own concerns about compliance to standard. Those people who hail from the Standard Generalized Markup Language (SGML) world and the "enlightened" HTML world have realized that the philosophies behind SGML and HTML have the same end-goals and objectives. They realize that the two sides must come together and find the middle ground to bring both the print and electronic world into harmony. Already, in the early HTML 3.0 version, the Document Type Definition of the SGML world has been incorporated.

The next standard for HTML is a tricky issue in some corners. A group has been working toward, and has almost arrived at, an official HTML 3.0 specification that could be adopted. The issue at stake here is one that you can see throughout the Web right now—many sites advertise that they are optimized for Netscape extensions. With approximately 70 percent of the browser market, Netscape has the potential leverage to dictate to some degree the shape of future versions of what the HTML standards look like.

Netscape Communications has stated that it will continue to work with the appropriate standards bodies (including the World Wide Web Consortium (W3C)—this is where Berners-Lee and the other "fathers" of HTML now reside) and the authors of other WWW browsers in an attempt to have these extensions available in all browsers in the near future. All of the Netscape Navigator extensions to HTML take the form of additional tags and attributes added to the HTML specification and, according to Netscape, are specifically designed not to break existing WWW browsers.

In the latest versions of the browsers on the street, you will find HTML 2.0-compliance as a minimum level of standard. Many of the browsers incorporate the elements of HTML 3.0 that are stable and unlikely to be dismissed. With its large market share behind it, Netscape has been working with the Internet Engineering Task Force and the W3C to finalize the HTML 3.0 specification. Netscape's own literature indicates that it is committed to the HTML standard and that it has added new areas of HTML functionality to its Netscape Navigator software that are not currently in the HTML 3.0 specification. Client-side Image Maps and HTTP File Upload are two examples of what Netscape has been proposing.

As these and other future functional enhancements are incorporated into the HTML standards, new products and services will become available on the market. Adding to the capabilities of the browser can move some of the processing burden from the servers to the workstation. Realistically, this can only be done across the multiplicity of platforms that exist if the functionality is incorporated into the standard. Otherwise, the meltdown that happened in the client/server world will also occur in the browser/server world.

Timeline of Standards Revisions

Like at any other large gathering, consensus is sometimes hard to achieve, especially surrounding the issue of standards. It is believed that the new and improved HTTP and HTML standards will be in place before long, probably by the end of 1996. It is also believed that there will be another set of revisions of these standards underway the day the announcement of acceptance is made.

Relative to their usage within the intranet as you are building it, the software and hardware that should be used must, at a minimum, work with HTTP 1.0 and HTML 2.0 and should be able to accept and address ODBC databases.

Published Application Programming Interfaces

Application Programming Interfaces (APIs) are libraries of functions that programmers use to create applications that gain access to the data or resources of an application. This section looks at several things relative to published APIs and how they can be used within the intranet:

• Third-party APIs and plug-ins

• Common Gateway Interfaces

• JavaScript

Third-party APIs and Plug-ins

By publishing these libraries of computer code, third party applications can be developed that utilize the resources of the publisher's application. In other words, the company that publishes the APIs makes it possible for someone else to create a separate program that acts as the interface to the publisher's software. For example, Netscape Client APIs enable developers to write applications on native operating systems that can communicate and remotely control a client application such as the Netscape Navigator. Following is a list of some of the applications types that have been created using the Netscape APIs to integrate the browser and the "back end" application:

• Database access

• Development tools

• Full-text search engines

• Information and document management

- Legacy systems connectivity tools

- Site monitoring tools

- User tracking and log analysis tools

By publishing these APIs, both Netscape and the providers of the software at the server end have tacitly encouraged the use and adoption of their respective tools. Not only does the strategy enhance the functionality of the intranet, it is good marketing strategy on the part of the software companies.

The Common Gateway Interface

It is possible to use the functionality provided by the published APIs in conjunction with Common Gateway Interface (CGI) programming to extend even further the reach of the intranet. On the server side of things, the Common Gateway Interface is the Internet standard for invoking server-based scripts or programs at the request of clients. This is the most common way today to provide clients with dynamic content from databases.

WebOLAP, the product from Information Advantage, Inc. and Red Brick Systems that was mentioned previously, is an example of the user communicating with a data warehouse through an HTML page and through the CGI to one application, which in turn obtains data from another through the use of the API published by the warehouse vendor.

The ability to layer a Web interface over the top of a CGI interface combined with APIs beyond the CGI program creates the potential for a wonderfully robust and information-rich environment. Products that use this approach are just starting to reach the market now and should become even more robust as more and more companies publish their APIs.

JavaScript

JavaScript, developed in conjunction with Java programming language by Sun Microsystems, is a simple scripting language that permits the creation of simple applications embedded entirely within HTML documents and can be used to define objects that allow developers access to databases. Many of the major SQL database companies, including Oracle, are committed to open Web systems and have published their APIs for incorporation into third-party products.

JavaScript can be used in combination with APIs and CGI techniques to extend the reach and functionality of the browser in terms of data access. JavaScript is relatively new to the marketplace; the full extension of its capabilities has not yet been explored by programmers implementing intranets. It is foreseeable that JavaScript, in conjunction with APIs and CGI, will enable the user to develop applications that will run in the background, transparent to the user. For example, it could be used to automatically pull up stock prices from a news feed every fifteen minutes instead waiting until the user selects that link.

Note

For more information regarding JavaScript and its programming uses, see *Programming with JavaScript* by Tim Ritchey (New Riders, 1996).

APIs are not limited to the Web/intranet environment. They are applicable with almost any software product where the developers have realized that third-party application development will extend the reach and functionality of their particular product. These enlightened companies are now in a position to participate in the growth of the intranet and are rapidly working to develop products.

Things to Watch For

The future of the browser/server communications strategy of the intranet will see some interesting developments.

Much more work in dynamic documents, incorporating both client-pull and server-push strategies, is forthcoming. One simple example of how to create a dynamic document is to use the META HTTP-EQUIV="Refresh" tagging statement within the header of the document. This forces the browser to update the screen, simulating selecting the View|Refresh menu option from the Netscape Navigator menu.

For example, updating a document on the screen every ten seconds could be done by using the client-pull technique. To do this, the header of an HTML document should contain the HTML 3.0 tag META. The following code sample tells the browser to pretend that the HTTP response, when the document was loaded, included the directive "Refresh: 10" in the header:

```
<META HTTP-EQUIV="Refresh" CONTENT="10;
   URL=http://www.subscription.com/new-info.html">
```

The use of "refresh" in the header tells the browser to reload the document after ten seconds have elapsed. The second line of code shows the valid HTML tag that would utilize this concept and actually tells the browser to get another file after ten seconds, rather than reload the original.

More extensions to the HTML 3.0 standard will be developed in response to user demands in order to assist in providing solutions as intranets are implemented to support business processes. Client-side imagemaps and HTTP file uploads will be pushed by Netscape.

Alternative methods of describing information will be enhanced. For example, DBML (Database Markup Language) is used extensively in applications like Cold Fusion, by Allaire Corp., for getting information out of a database and into the browser. (Chapter 11, "Integrating ODBC and CGI," will demonstrate how Cold Fusion can be used to access database information.) VRML, Virtual Reality Markup Language, is in its second version and may be enhanced and expanded as more research is done in the behavioral responses area. One use of VRML today is in the new house construction business: using technological aids like a virtual reality "helmet," the potential home buyer walks through the layout of a model home selecting colors, cabinets, and placing furniture through computer-assisted methods. At the end of the walk-through, the potential buyer has been able to "see" what the new home would look like once built and furnished. Another real-world example of the benefits of VRML is the development of more sophisticated flight simulators for pilot training.

From the base technology front that concerns the browser/server aspect, the technologies to keep an eye on to expand the functionality of the intranet will be as follows:

- Discussion and conferencing software—Chapters 18, 21, and 23 of this book discuss some of the current products and the future of these areas.

- Intranet Web server creation and management tools—Appendix C provides a list of HTTP servers that are intranet-compatible, but the field of management tools for intranet servers is just beginning to draw the attention of the software developers.

- Content search tools—Chapter 10 discusses WAIS text searching, but search engine products like Excite for Web Servers, by Excite, Inc., which is available free of charge, are now starting to add complex searching abilities to intranets.

- Turnkey intranet server products where the purchaser plugs the server into the network and all the applications necessary for an intranet implementation—This is an "intranet-in-a-box," so to speak.

- Interactive applets and browser extensions—As the ability to create Java applets and JavaScript scripts and as the whole realm of third party plug-ins for browsers become more widespread, the ways the resulting products are used will be more and more oriented to supporting mission-critical business processes.

One of the interesting by-products of the intranet is the process of knowledge manufacturing. By using the intranet's information services that are accessed and analyzed in the specific context of the user, combined with the user's experience and knowledge, a new value-added piece of information can be created for sharing with the rest of the organization. This, in turn, may spark another person's creative or analytical genius.

This knowledge manufacturing process can have a huge impact on an organization, both at the business and the social/people end of the organization. There will be a great deal more attention paid to the people end of the spectrum over the next few years. People drive the browsers and seek the information that is required in order to get their jobs done. It has to be easy. It has to be quick. And it has to be able to support analytical processes, not just static documents or traditional transactional systems.

Status Check

It's time to roll up your sleeves and get your hands dirty.

Now that your server is primed and your browser tuned, you can start to really build the intranet. Even though you have discussed accesses to databases and mentioned workflow, you still have to start by building the foundation for your intranet.

You know where you are going with your initial intranet pilot project, and now it's a question of building the pieces to get there. The first stop is the nuts and bolts of the HyperText Markup Language (HTML) and the creation of pages.

p a r t

3

Application Building Blocks

8

Introduction to HTML

The World Wide Web (or "the Web") is the graphical Internet/ intranet service and has powerful linking abilities. Because of its ease of use and graphical capabilities, the implementation of Web-based information services has spurred the growth of the Internet and intranet worlds. As has been previously stated within the book, the HyperText Markup Language (HTML) is *the* language of the intranet and the Internet.

Tim Berners-Lee led the development work on the Web from CERN, a particle physics lab in Geneva, Switzerland. Starting in 1989, Berners-Lee's initial development focus was on the definition of the HTTP protocol, the development of a sample server, and a programming library called wwwlib. The library was placed in the public domain in 1992, at which point many university computing departments and a number of organizations grabbed hold of the concepts. Several of these organizations, including the National Center for Supercomputer Applications (NCSA) at the University of Illinois in Urbana-Champaign, began developing browsers for different operating platforms with additional features such as the ability to display inline graphics or call an executable file. The most notable of these products was Mosaic, developed at NCSA.

Marc Andreessen, now at Netscape Communications, led the work on Mosaic from the NCSA. The NCSA Web server and related utilities remain in the public domain to this date. They can be used with no licensing problems, even if you do manage to make a profit through the venture.

The common thread to all the development that took place as a result of the work initiated by Berners-Lee and his colleagues was the use of the HTML language to create the pages of information shown on the user's display and the use of the HyperText Transfer Protocol (HTTP) to get the pages from the server to the browser.

In order to implement an intranet, an understanding of HTTP is necessary. Chapter 3, "HTTP: Building the Application Layer," provided you with the required level of understanding of how information is moved between the browser and the server. The use of HTML to create the interface screens that the users of the intranet see within the browser is the thrust of this chapter. In order to ensure that you obtain a thorough understanding of the HTML language, this chapter will cover:

- An introduction to the concepts of HTML tagging

- Basic document design for your intranet pages

- The necessary steps in programming the various elements of your intranet pages

- The philosophy of template design

In order to set the stage for accessing data stored in the organization's databases, you need a basic understanding of how pages and hyperlinks are created and how information is formatted for display on the screen. Throughout the following four chapters, you will learn to create basic HTML pages, HTML forms for accepting data input, Common Gateway Interface programs to take information from and return results to HTML pages, and the HTML pages that will format and display data returned by a search of a database. All of the development through these four chapters (Chapters 8 through 11) builds upon the work of the previous chapters. The base building block is the HTML language. Now to start building the foundation.

Introduction to the HTML Language

It is possible to display a file incorporating different sizes of typeface on the intranet, show an image, incorporate an active hyperlink, or play back an audio track, among other possibilities discussed in Chapter 6, "Cross-Platform Client Browser Setup." In order to prepare the document for use within the intranet, the original document must be modified by inserting the HTML codes necessary to invoke all those features. These HTML codes are called *tags*. This section will introduce the reader to the basic syntax of HTML and how these tags are applied.

Within the intranet, what you see displayed on the browser's screen in front of you is in reality an ASCII file that has had a series of HTML codes, or *tags*, embedded in it. These files are referred to as HTML files and the file extension is usually *.HTML*.

HTML files can be created in an ASCII text editor, converted to this format by a conversion program, or generated dynamically by the server or by a script. The structure of the HTML document is provided by the tags, which are in turn interpreted by the browser for display. Figure 8.1 shows the ASCII-text source file for the document that you see using Netscape Navigator (figure 8.2).

There are two main elements to understand when discussing tagging that will be discussed in this chapter. These elements are the relationship between HTML and SGML as discussed in Chapter 7, "Understanding the Advantages of Browser/Server Communications," and the syntax of tagging.

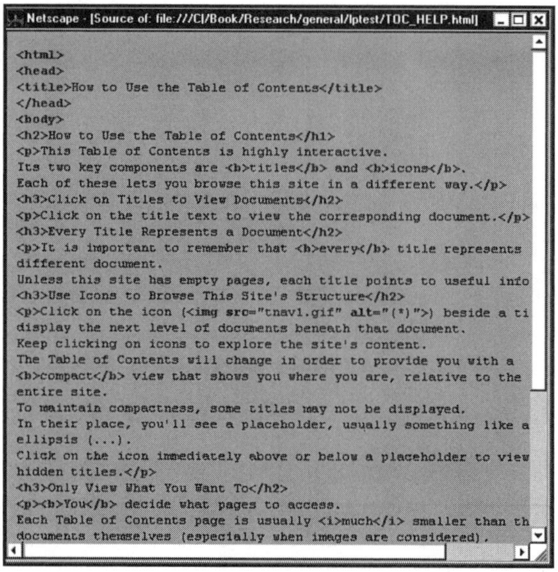

Figure 8.1

ASCII-text
HTML file,
TOC_HELP.html.

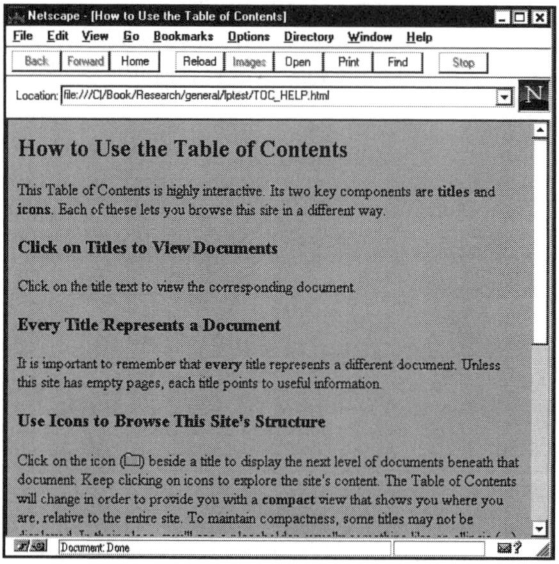

Figure 8.2

Netscape Naviga-
tor displaying
TOC_HELP.html.

Note	
	All the HTML files that are created within the context of this chapter are available on the CD included with this book.

SGML vs HTML

As discussed in Chapter 7, Standard Generalized Markup Language (SGML) is an ISO standard for specifying both the structure of the document and the content. SGML was designed to enable document interchange among organizations, computing platforms, and application software packages independent of any proprietary software solution.

SGML is used to define the structural elements of a document and the format of the content of those elements. In defining the various elements of the document structure, one of the parameters that is stated for each structural element is the *tag*, or delimiter, that will be used to define the structural element. These tags can be defined in any manner the person creating the document chooses; but the syntax of the tags, usually paired, is as follows:

```
<start_tag>structural element contents</end_tag>
```

The structural definition, including the tag names, is maintained in a file called a Document Type Definition (DTD). The basic theory behind the use of SGML in creating the hard copy document is that the Document Type Definition file and the document that was structured using the appropriately defined tags can be printed on any printer using SGML software. The printer's software formats the *tagged document* based on the information contained within the DTD file.

When an attempt was made to develop a means to organize and display documents electronically, the philosophy of SGML was borrowed for use with the development of HTML. By using the philosophy of tagging the elements of the document in a consistent manner, Tim Berners-Lee and others working at the CERN laboratories in Europe developed the HTML language for displaying documents transported across the wires via the HTTP protocol.

In reality, what these people had done was create a Document Type Definition that was transparent to the user. The tags that were permitted for use and display within the HTML browser(s) were defined and published in the public domain. HTML has been described as one instance of an implementation of SGML. The biggest difference here is that HTML was not created to be independent of the printer; it was designed for use on the HTTP protocol.

As you can see now, HTML is based on some of the concepts of SGML relative to structuring the document's content. However, HTML was designed specifically for the HTTP protocol. The current version of HTML is 2.0. The HTML 3.0 specification that has been proposed includes features and structures that would make HTML fully compatible with SGML (other than the reliance on the HTTP protocol). These similarities include a definable Document Type Definition that will facilitate features like the displaying of tables of data returned from database queries. In fact, there is movement toward a merger of the HTML specifications into the SGML specifications as an ISO-recognized instance of SGML.

Note

Many people look at SGML as a philosophy of how to compose and define the structure of the document; they see HTML as an instance or implementation of SGML and a subset of the "fully compliant features" of SGML. These features include all the elements of print documents from footnotes to sidebars to the incorporation of tables into the HTML specification. Although it is not in the HTML 2.0 specification, many browser developers added the functional ability to recognize table constructs within HTML pages—making the presentation of tabular data much easier to do on the fly.

Within HTML or SGML documents, you can use tags to easily identify the following:

- The title

- The structure of the document, through header levels

- Many types of lists

- The insertion point for graphic images

- What has been selected as a hyperlink and where it is designed to take you

Note

Although the tag names may differ for each SGML document depending upon their definition within the Document Type Definition, HTML tags are always the same for each HTML document. For example, the <TITLE> tag in HTML is always used for the title of the document. In a sample of SGML documents, the following variety of tags were among those used to represent the titles of the documents: <TI>, <DOCTITLE>, <TITLE>, and <TITLE_OF_DOCUMENT>.

The browser governs the font used to display text, the size of that font, the width and height of the screen, and the colors used for the background, foreground, and highlights. These attributes are handled in the SGML world when the DTD is used to interpret the associated document for printing. Within the browser-based HTML world, even though you may specify a specific background image or color within your HTML document, most browsers give users the opportunity to override the document choices and use their own personal preferences.

Syntax of HTML Tagging

Tags are used within HTML documents as instructions to the browser regarding how to display the items on the screen. Two basic tag types within HTML invoke the associated formatting within the browser: standalone and paired.

A paired tag type is composed of a start-tag component and an end-tag component. Both components of the tag pair are required. The same name is given to both components, but the end tag is prefaced by the slash (/) character. The following example shows the HTML paired tag used for the document's title:

```
<TITLE>This is a sample title</TITLE>
```

You will notice that the components of the tag pair surround the text to be used as the title. In all instances of paired tags, the information is enclosed between the start- and end-tag components.

A standalone tag is only one tag functioning as a start-tag component. The tag invokes the associated formatting within the browser until another standalone or paired start-tag is encountered. An example of a standalone tag is the line-break tag (<BR>), which is used to force a new line of text on the screen.

Each tag is encapsulated by angle brackets, that is, the less-than (<) sign and the greater-than (>) sign. The following are examples of how the two types are written:

standalone tag   <TAGNAME>

paired tags   <TAGNAME></TAGNAME>

To reiterate, you will notice the second of the paired tags contains a forward slash (/) character. This indicates to the browser to end the tag's function. In a verbal description of the above paired tags, you would refer to the tags as "tagname" and "end tagname"—the forward slash (/) is pronounced "end." For example:

<B> .... </B> is read "bold" .... "end bold."

The use of a tag implies a function that is being applied to an object within the document. For example, to make the first part of the phrase bold-faced and leave the remaining text in the normal font, use the following:

<B>This is bold text</B> while this is not

Many of the tag constructs in HTML have options that can be included. These options are used only within the standalone tags and the start tag of paired tags. The complete syntax for these tags would be:

<TAGNAME option1 option2 option3 ... optionX>

Warning

The most common mistake in manually authoring HTML documents is to forget to put in the end tag altogether or to leave out the forward slash (/) in the end tag. If this happens you will usually see the result on the browser screen fairly easily. These mistakes are simple to correct once you see the results on the screen. Simply edit the HTML file and insert the "/" where it is needed.

Figures 8.3 and 8.4 show a very simple example. In figure 8.3, the HTML page in the browser has omitted the "/" character to end the <B> formatting of the word "bold" in the middle of the sentence. Figure 8.4 shows the corrected file. Following is the line of text that will be displayed; first with the error that is displayed in figure 8.3, then the corrected version of figure 8.4:

```
the only word in this sentence that is in <B>bold<B> text should
be in the middle
```

The corrected version reads:

```
the only word in this sentence that is in <B>bold</B> text should
be in the middle
```

Figure 8.3

An HTML file with tagging error.

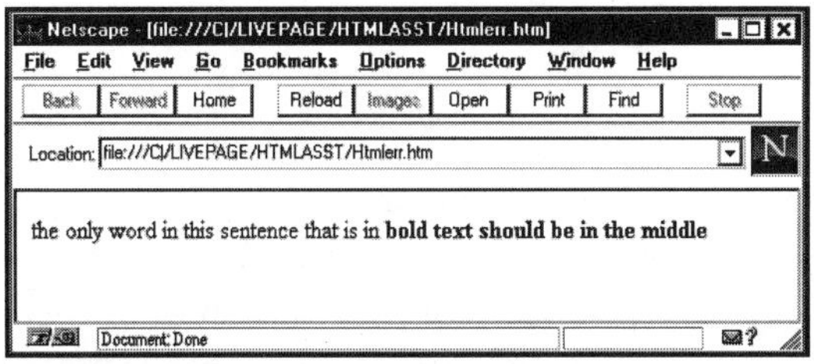

Figure 8.4

An HTML file with no error.

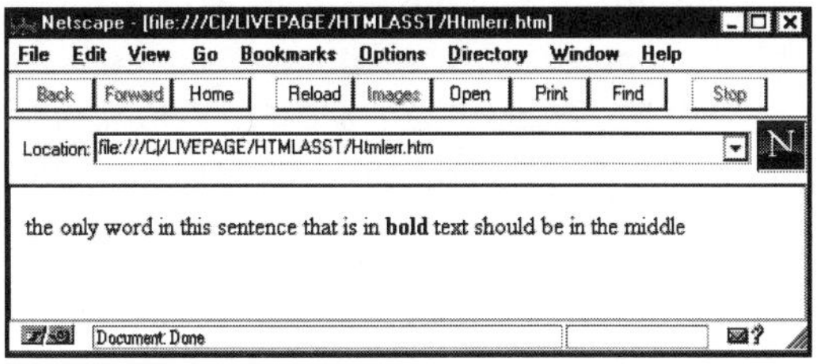

With these thoughts in the back of your mind, move on to creating your basic intranet home page.

Basic Document Design

Three tag pairs are used to create the basic structure of an HTML document. They are:

```
<HTML> entire HTML document is inside </HTML>
<HEAD> document header information is here </HEAD>
<BODY> body of the HTML document </BODY>
```

When you actually write the ASCII-text HTML file, the basic document described above will look something like the following:

```
<HTML>
<HEAD>
     Information that belongs in the header
</HEAD>
     <BODY>
          Body elements and textual content go here
     </BODY>
</HTML>
```

Remember that regardless of how you lay out the physical HTML file for your creation and editing ease, the browser will display the document in the physical fashion it has been directed to use. In the example above, nesting or indentation of elements is good programming practice to facilitate the reading of the code but will not do anything within the browser. Figure 8.5 shows what the preceding lines of HTML actually generate when you look at the file in Netscape Navigator 2.01. This will be covered in more detail later on in the chapter when a sample home page is created through the exploration of the HTML language.

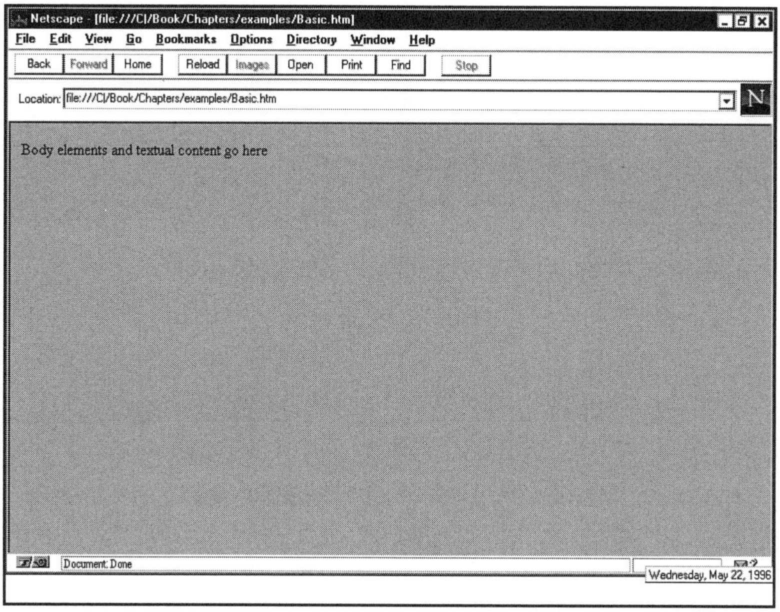

Figure 8.5

The very basic HTML file.

A Sample HTML Page

In the day-to-day creation of pages for the Intranet, you will most likely have to create a whole set of home pages. You will have to create one for the very top level of your site and, usually, one for each main subsection of that level.

The author has created the following HTML file that he uses as a template for the creation of home pages within the intranets he works on. Though it is designed for a subsection home page, with a few quick modifications it becomes the top-level home page. Figure 8.6 shows the HTML page in the browser.

Figure 8.6

The sample HTML page displayed by Netscape Navigator.

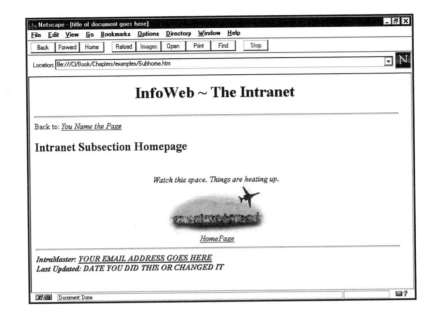

The HTML file behind the image looks like this:

```
<HTML>
<HEAD>
<TITLE>title of document goes here</TITLE>
</HEAD>


<BODY  bgcolor=#FFFFFF text="#000000"> .
<CENTER><H1>InfoWeb ~ The Intranet</H1></CENTER>
<HR>
Back to: <A HREF="Somemenu.html"><I>You Name the Page</I></A>
<!--...........your heading (if graphical) should be called
➥subhead.gif...........-->
<!--...........body content goes here..........-->
<H2>Intranet Subsection Homepage</H2><BR>
<!--...........body content ends here..........-->
<!-- Anchor takes the user back to InfoWeb -->
<I><CENTER>
Watch this space. Things are heating up.<BR>
<A HREF="mainmenu.htm"><img src="bomb.jpg" BORDER=0 alt="fire bomb
➥dropped by plane"></A><BR>
<A HREF="mainmenu.htm">HomePage</A></I>
</CENTER>
```

```
<HR>
<ADDRESS>
<EM>IntraMaster: <A HREF="mailto:your email address">YOUR EMAIL
➥ADDRESS GOES HERE</A>
<BR>
<B>Last Updated: DATE YOU DID THIS OR CHANGED IT</B></EM><P>
C:\intranet\subhome.html
</ADDRESS>
</BODY>
</HTML>
```

Warning

> On some computer systems, when you are creating HTML files, you can only use a three-letter file extension to save your files. The end result is that although your code lines may refer to files with ".HTML" extensions, your system is only capable of working with and creating ".HTM" files. You may experience errors within the HTML files created here when retrieving ".HTML" files. Simply edit the files and change the file extension reference to ".HTM." For example, the following hyperlink may give you an error message:
>
> <A HREF="Somemenu.html">.
>
> By rewording the text to read: <A HREF="Somemenu.htm">, you should be able to avoid this problem.
>
> The author uses the ".htm" file extension in his code examples from this point on so that they can be retrieved more easily. It is a simple matter of using the file extension that works for the user.

Here is an examination of the new tags used in the file.

- The <TITLE> tag pair is used once per document and is located within the <HEAD> section. If you look at the very top of figure 8.6, you will see the title listed after the word Netscape, in this example "title of document goes here." The title is encapsulated in square brackets ([ ]). This is the document name that shows up in the users' bookmark list, after they add the page to their list.

  ```
  <TITLE>title of document goes here</TITLE>
  ```

- The <CENTER> tag pair is used to center the text or images within the pair when seen on the browser.

```
<CENTER><H1>InfoWeb ~ The Intranet</H1></CENTER>
```

- The <HR> tag causes the browser to create a horizontal rule (line) across the screen. Use this tag to create logical divisions on the screen.

```
<HR>
```

- This tag is used to indicate the start of a paragraph and is, in reality, the lead tag in a paired tag set. The </P> tag is often omitted. The <P> tag also generates a blank line on the display of most browsers.

```
<P>
```

- The <H1> tag pair is used as an indication of the structure of the document. There are six levels of headers, H1 through H6, with H1 being the highest level (with the largest font size). You can compare the results of the <H1> tag with those of the <H2> tag, which is surrounding the "Intranet Subsection Homepage" text in figure 8.6.

```
<H1>InfoWeb ~ The Intranet</H1>.
```

- The comment tag is used to include comments within the text. There can be spaces between the "--" and ">," but not between the "<!" and "--." If spaces are there, the line will not be interpreted as a comment, but rather it will be treated as text to display in the browser. Any instance of "-->" will stop the comment. The following example is a comment to the user of the file and indicates that the body content of the HTML file is to follow this comment:

```
<!--.......body content goes here.....-->
```

- The <I> tag pair puts the text into italics. This can be nested within other tags, but some browsers may only read the innermost tags.

```
<I> Watch this space...</I>
```

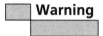
Warning

Because of the proliferation of browsers and their varied abilities, it is recommended that any HTML pages that will be displayed within the intranet be tested with the browsers that may be in use within the organization. This testing will ensure that the tagging used will be displayed consistently across the browsers in use.

- The line break tag breaks the current line of text. There is no </BR> tag.

```
<BR>
```

- The <EM> tag pair marks the phrase to be displayed with generic emphasis. The browser controls how the text is to be displayed within its environment.

```
<EM>IntraMaster:...<?EM>
```

- The <ADDRESS> tag pair is used to give an address or contact information and is usually displayed in italics at the bottom of the page.

```
<ADDRESS> text </ADDRESS>
```

A couple of other tags are found in this document—the <IMG> inline image tag and the <A> anchor tag. These will be covered in more detail shortly.

Building a Sample Home Page

Because it is a lot easier to start with a sample document that is relatively close to what you want, steal the code written for the file above, SUBHOME.HTM. Modify it slightly so that you create your top-level page and set up the page to provide access to the basic sub-areas for your initial pilot project.

Start with the changes to the code. Below is the "finished" file, HOMEPAGE.HTM, in which the changes from the SUBHOME.HTM file have been outlined using the comment tag construct of "<!-- comment -->."

```
<HTML>
<HEAD>
<TITLE>InfoWeb Home Page</TITLE>   <!-- replaced "title of document
➥goes here" -->
</HEAD>

<BODY  bgcolor=#FFFFFF text="#000000">
<CENTER><H1>InfoWeb ~ The Intranet</H1></CENTER>
<HR>

<!-- removed "Back to: <A HREF="Somemenu.html"><I>You Name the Page</
➥I></A>" -->

<!--..........your heading (if graphical) should be called
➥subhead.gif..........-->
<!--..........body content goes here..........-->
<H2>Your Knowledge Resource Center</H2>

<UL>
<LI>Documents and Manuals<BR>
<LI>Company Phone List<BR>
<LI>Information Links<BR>
<LI>Projects and Workgroups<BR>
</UL>

<!--..........body content ends here..........-->
<!-- Anchor takes the user back to InfoWeb -->
<I><CENTER>
Watch this space. Things are heating up.<BR>

<!-- remove the anchor <A HREF="mainmenu.htm"></A> -->

<IMG SRC="bomb.jpg" BORDER=0 ALT="fire bomb dropped by plane">

<!-- removed <A HREF="mainmenu.htm">HomePage</A> -->
</I>
  </CENTER>
```

```
<HR>
<ADDRESS>

<!-- below the email address is changed to the address of the contact
-->

<B>IntraMaster: <A
HREF="mailto:jdesboro@magmacom.com">jdesboro@magmacom.com</A>
<BR>
Last Updated: May 21, 1996</B>
<P>
c:\intranet\homepage.htm    <!-- file name is changed to the
➥homepage.html file name -->

Graphic by: Fish      <!-- give attribution where attribution is
➥due -->
</ADDRESS>
</BODY>
</HTML>
```

The file above makes a few changes to the contents and adds an Unordered List with the <UL></UL> tag pair. The results of this file are shown in figure 8.7. Now you have a place to call a home page.

Figure 8.7

"InfoWeb" Home Page.

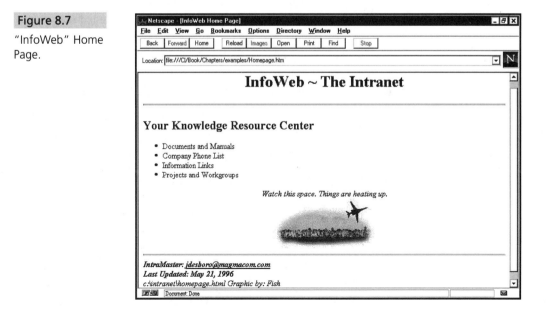

Now that the first home page has been created, you can move on to enhance the look and feel of your intranet. The next section covers the addition of hyperlinks between documents, including images and documents, and implementing lists and tables to enhance the HTML pages created for the intranet. For more information on designing your HTML pages, please refer to *Web Concept and Design* by Crystal Waters (New Riders, 1996).

Enhancing the Basic HTML Home Page

Now that you can create a home page, review the things that you have to do to get it into shape for general release to the rest of the organization as a working model. In order to get the intranet ready for release, you need to understand and include the following within the HTML pages of the Intranet:

- Hyperlinking documents

- Incorporating graphics

- Including lists and tables

The <IMG> and <A> tags were mentioned earlier. You need to be certain that you understand the hyperlinking capabilities of the tags you plan to use in order to make navigation through the site as simple, yet elegant, as possible. This section also will have a brief introduction to lists and tables in order to help make things look a little prettier, and more functional, down the road.

Hyperlinking Documents: Creating Links and Anchors

The hyperlink is one of the most important features of the Intranet—it is the basic means of navigation between documents. When the user clicks on a hyperlink displayed on the screen, the browser retrieves the resource identified within the HTML file. The remainder of this section will explore the differences between links and anchors as they are used in the creation of hyperlinks; it will discuss the syntax of the hyperlink, examples of how to create hyperlinks, and how to reference other documents within the hyperlink.

But first, quick basic definitions of links and anchors are in order. An *anchor* is used to identify a specific place within a document. This anchor is identified with a *name*. A *link* is, basically, an instruction to the browser that when it is selected, the browser is to move the reader from the current location to the location identified within the link. The location identified within the link is an *anchor name*.

The usage of links and anchors is discussed in greater detail in the following sections.

The Syntax of the Hyperlink

In order to appreciate the syntax of the hyperlink, it is necessary to start with an understanding of the anchor tag. The anchor tag can be used as follows:

```
<A NAME="name_of_anchor">link text</A>

<A HREF="#name_of_anchor">link text</A>

<A HREF="URL">link text</A>

<A HREF="url#name_of_anchor">link text</A>
```

Note

The anchor tag defines either a link or an anchor in a document. The anchor tag must contain a NAME attribute or an HREF attribute, or both. In order to create a link, the HREF attribute must be used.

Creating Anchors and Links Within a Single HTML File

The most simple usage of the anchor tag is to define a location within a document using the following syntax:

```
<A NAME="name_of_anchor">link text</A>
```

This syntax provides a location to which a link could move the user, and it is occasionally referred to as a *link-to point*. An example would be to put an anchor at the top of a very long document to which users would be returned if they selected a link elsewhere in the document that said "Return to Top." The syntax required to implement the anchor could be as follows:

```
<A NAME="top">text at top of page</A>
```

In order to create the link to move the user to the location identified by the anchor-name from within the same document, the following syntax is used:

```
<A HREF="name_of_anchor">text to describe the link</A>
```

Continuing with the long document example from the preceding paragraph, to create a link to return the user to the *anchor* named "top," the following syntax would be used:

```
<A HREF="#top">Return to Top</A>
```

The pound (#) symbol is used to denote an anchor name as opposed to a variable in memory. If the document being displayed by the browser is seven or eight screens of information, including the Return to Top link in several locations throughout the document enables the user to quickly jump to the top of the document simply by selecting one of the links.

Consider an online book of six chapters contained in one HTML file. Each chapter heading has the appropriate version of the following anchor name/link-to point:

```
<A NAME="Chapterx">Chapter x</A>
```

To hyperlink to the start of Chapter 6 from anywhere within the document itself, create the following hyperlink:

```
For more details, please refer to <A HREF="#Chapter6">Chapter 6</A>
```

This brief example shows that the anchor or link-to point does not have to be at the top of a file but can be in any location within the file.

Creating Hyperlinks to Other Documents

When the user sees and activates a hyperlink within an HTML document, the HTML code to implement the hyperlink uses the following syntax to create the link:

```
<A HREF="URL">description-of-link text</A>
```

The description-of-link text is displayed in the browser and is generally underlined. When you look at the SUBHOME.HTM file, the following line of text is shown near the top of the file:

```
Back to: <A HREF="Somemenu.htm"><I>You Name the Page</I></A>
```

The phrase "You Name the Page" becomes the description-of-link text for a hyperlink to a file named Somemenu.html.

In the SUBHOME.HTML file, an example of an image used as the hyperlink anchor is also demonstrated. Now look at it a little more closely.

```
<A HREF="mainmenu.htm"><IMG SRC="bomb.jpg" BORDER=0 ALT="fire bomb
➥dropped by plane"></A>
```

Here you can see that the image file BOMB.JPG has been used as the hyperlink anchor back to the MAINMENU.HTM file. If you load the SUBHOME.HTML file and move your mouse pointer over the image, you will see that the pointer changes shape, indicating an active link is connected with the image.

The options that are included in the <IMG> tag will be discussed in a later section.

A hyperlink, by default, points to the top of the document referred to in the URL. You can create hyperlinks that transport you to other locations within an HTML document, but first you must identify and name the anchor or link-to point in the target document. The NAME option described in the preceding section is used to do this within the anchor tag. To review, the following syntax is used to create the anchor within the target file:

```
<A NAME="anchor-name">Location text</A>
```

With the anchor location now defined, the hyperlink to this point in the target document can now be defined. From an external document, a hyperlink could be established directly to the Chapter 6 location in the book example by using a hyperlink referencing the anchor location as follows:

```
<A HREF="URL#Chapter6">Chapter 6 of the Dissertation</A>
```

The URL can be a fully qualified URL, for example http:// www.intranomics.com/whitepaper.html, or a relative URL, as in whitepaper.html. In a fully qualified URL, the syntax is as follows:

```
access method://server-name/directory/file
```

The use of fully qualified URLs is usually reserved for calling resources on another server. For example:

```
http://www.inforium.com/inforium.html
```

This uses the HTTP protocol to contact the server called "www.inforium.com" and retrieve a file stored in the root directory of the server called "inforium.html."

Note

Regardless of the type of file or server upon which it is located, each and every file in the intranet can be addressed by its URL.

Referencing Documents Within Hyperlinks

When you create your intranet files, you are probably like most people—working on your own computer. Unless you also control the directory assignments of the server on which the intranet files you are creating will be located, you may not know the final path name of the directory. By using relative URLs, which assume the same access method, server name, and directory path, you can refer to another document in the same directory simply as:

```
<A HREF="book2.html">Sequel to Book One</A>
```

The server assumes that you will be looking in the current directory, using the HTTP protocol for a file called book2.html. Thus, if you moved that whole collection of books to another directory, you would only have to change the location pointers to the home page of the collection. All references, provided they used the same syntax as the example above, would be consistent and lead to the documents required.

One can also use a special URL to send e-mail back to a contact, as designated on the screen. In your HOMEPAGE.HTML file, you used the following construct to create the feedback possibility at the bottom of the page:

```
IntraMaster: <A HREF="mailto:jdesboro@magmacom.com">
➥jdesboro@magmacom.com</A>
```

Figure 8.8 shows a slightly different version of the HOMEPAGE.HTML file, called HOMEPG2.HTM, which incorporates anchors and hyperlinks to the subsection home pages. The hyperlinks can be identified as the underlined text.

Figure 8.8

HOMEPG2.HTM
with hyperlinks.

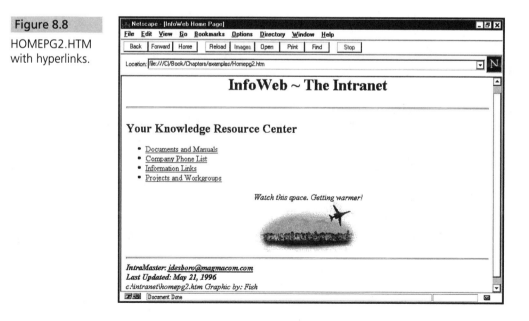

Just to be consistent with the other examples, the ASCII-text HTML file HOMEPG2.HTM follows:

```
<HTML>
<HEAD>
<TITLE>InfoWeb Home Page </TITLE>
</HEAD>

<BODY  bgcolor=#FFFFFF text="#000000">
<CENTER><H1>InfoWeb ~ The Intranet</H1></CENTER>
<HR>

<!--...........body content goes here..........-->

<H2>Your Knowledge Resource Center</H2>

<UL>
<LI><A HREF="docshome.htm">Documents and Manuals</A><BR>
<LI><A HREF="fonehome.htm">Company Phone List</A><BR>
<LI><A HREF="infohome.htm">Information Links</A><BR>
<LI><A HREF="workhome.htm">Projects and Workgroups</A><BR>
</UL>

<!--...........body content ends here..........-->
<!-- Anchor takes the user back to InfoWeb -->
<I><CENTER>
Watch this space. Getting warmer!<BR>

<IMG SRC="bomb.jpg" BORDER=0 ALT="fire bomb dropped by plane">

</I>
</CENTER>

<HR>
<ADDRESS>
<!-- below the email address is changed to the address of the contact
➥-->
<B>IntraMaster: <A
HREF="mailto:jdesboro@magmacom.com">jdesboro@magmacom.com</A>
<BR>
Last Updated: May 21, 1996</B>
<BR>
c:\intranet\homepg2.htm    <!-- file name is changed from the
➥homepage.html file name -->
```

```
Graphic by: Fish   <!-- give attribution where attribution is due -->
</ADDRESS>
</BODY>

</HTML>
```

By loading the HOMEPG2.HTM file from the CD-ROM and selecting the Documents and Manuals link, the file DOCSHOME.HTM is retrieved via a relative URL and is displayed. Figure 8.9 shows the DOCSHOME.HTM file, as seen by Netscape Navigator. The HTML coding behind the displayed file is what will be used to discuss the <IMG> tag.

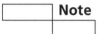

Note

> You will find the HTML files for this chapter located on the CD for this book. For a complete listing of what the CD-ROM includes, please see Appendix D, "What's on the CD."

Netscape - [Document Source Home Page]
File Edit View Go Bookmarks Options Directory Window Help
Back Forward Home Reload Images Open Print Find Stop
Location: file:///C|/Book/Chapters/examples/docshome.htm
InfoWeb ~ The Intranet
Back to: InfoWeb Home Page
Documents and Manuals
Marketing and Sales Literature
Research and Technical Reports
Human Resource Manuals
Financial Policies and Procedures
Watch this space. Starting to sizzle now!
InfoWeb Home Page
Document: Done

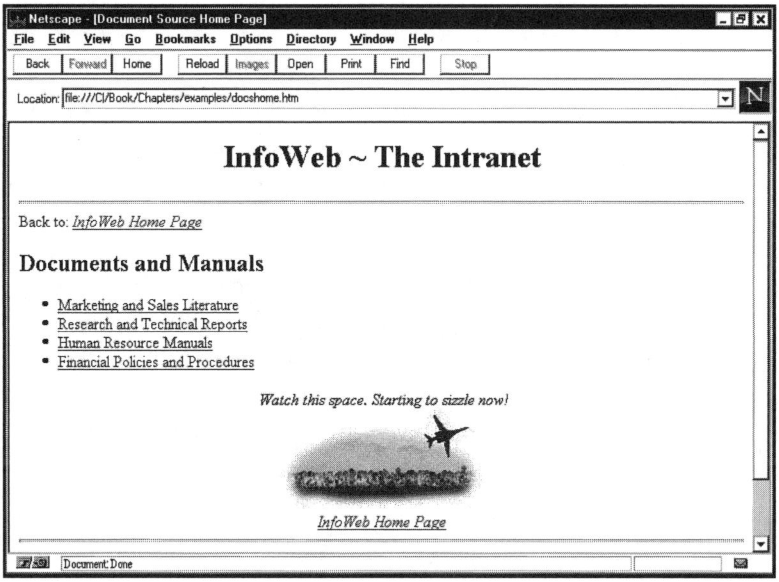

Figure 8.9

Selecting "Documents and Manuals" shows the DOCSHOME.HTM file.

Incorporating Graphics: Inline and External Images

There are two basic forms in which to display graphics in Web browsers:

- Inline images

- External images

To keep the nomenclature fairly straightforward, the words graphic or graphics will be used to refer to external images and the words image or images will be used to refer to inline images. External images or graphics are displayed by launching a separate viewer program—a helper application or a plug-in—that is specifically requested by activating a hyperlink.

Inline images are included in the autoflow and autowrap of the HTML on the browser screen. Treated just like a word, the image can be smack dab in the middle of a paragraph. If you want it to stand alone, put paragraph or break tags around the image. All browsers support image file formats of GIF and XBM, and most browsers now support the JPG image format as well for inline images. For more information on the image formats, helper-applications, and plug-ins, please refer to Chapter 6, "Cross-Platform Client Browser Setup."

Because they are treated just like words, images are loaded into the document and displayed as they are received. However, because they are a separate file, a separate connection to the server is implemented to bring down the image file at the same time as the text of the document. This is why you may notice the status bar of your browser flipping back and forth between files showing how much of a file, percentage-wise, has been loaded. The DOCSHOME.HTM file contains one inline image. Therefore, when you request the file to be shown on your browser, you actually have to download two files, the DOCSHOME.HTM file and the BOMB.GIF file.

Note

> The larger the file size, the longer it will take to download to the browser. As a rule of thumb, keep the image size under 40k if you can. Larger files take too long because most users will have their browsers configured to Autoload images, which means the users have to wait until the files are all loaded. Also, not everyone has Macs or even 256-color capabilities. See how well the images look in 16-color and, if you are really keen, create parallel sites designed for both levels.

Even though the "really cool sites" on the Internet tend to be heavily graphics-oriented, it takes a long time to deal with all those graphics (see note). If people have the graphics turned off on their browsers, they won't see all the effort that has been put into the graphics work. For an Intranet, the best combination for a page is a mix between the simple and the elegant: one clean, crisp image balanced with text that is not
to heavily played with relative to font size and color (if the browser is capable).

Now that you understand more about the image itself, the next step is to actually put in place the tags to call the images to the screen.

Retrieving and Displaying Images

The <IMG> tag displays an image referred to by an URL. This is done through the SRC attribute as in the following line of text from DOCSHOME.HTM:

```
<IMG SRC="bomb.jpg" BORDER=0 ALT="fire bomb dropped by plane">
```

Attributes that are part of the HTML 2.0 specification include:

- ALIGN—TOP, MIDDLE, or BOTTOM are the choices, causing the top, middle, or bottom of the image to be aligned with the text containing the IMG tag.

- ALT—for text to be displayed by browsers that do not display images or to be used when image display is suppressed.

- ISMAP—indicates that an image is an imagemap.

- SRC—here the "URL" identifies the image source, usually a GIF or JPEG file.

The line of code from the DOCSHOME.HTM file contains a BORDER=0 attribute that is a Netscape extension to the IMG tag. The number in the BORDER attribute refers to the border thickness in pixels.

Tip

> It is not recommended that you set the BORDER=0 for images that are to be used as hyperlinks because the users have no idea that the image is a link unless they move the mouse pointer over the image and see the pointer change shape, indicating the fact that the image is an active link. Many sites use this type of "hidden door" to permit special users to get access to information sets not generally available for everyone else.

As stated earlier in the chapter, images can be used as links to other documents, such as in the DOCSHOME.HTM file. The author has even used the "hidden door" type of image (see preceding tip), in that the BORDER=0 attribute is used within the file.

```
<A HREF="homepage.htm"><IMG SRC="bomb.jpg" BORDER=0 ALT="fire bomb
➥dropped by plane"></A>
```

However, by putting a text link directly underneath the image, with the same hyperlink assigned to the text as to the image, it is slightly more palatable.

Here is the actual code behind figure 8.9, the DOCSHOME.HTM file.

```
<HTML>
<HEAD>
<TITLE>Document Source Home Page</TITLE>
</HEAD>

<BODY  bgcolor=#FFFFFF text="#000000">
<CENTER><H1>InfoWeb ~ The Intranet</H1></CENTER>
<HR>
Back to: <A HREF="homepage.htm"><I>InfoWeb Home Page</I></A>


<!--..........body content goes here..........-->

<H2>Documents and Manuals</H2>

<UL>
<LI><A HREF="mktpage.htm">Marketing and Sales Literature</A><BR>
<LI><A HREF="techpg.htm">Research and Technical Reports</A><BR>
<LI><A HREF="hrpage.htm">Human Resource Manuals</A><BR>
<LI><A HREF="finpage.htm">Financial Policies and Procedures</A>
</UL>


<!--..........body content ends here..........-->
<!-- Anchor takes the user back to InfoWeb -->
<I><CENTER>
Watch this space. Starting to sizzle now!<BR>

<A HREF="homepage.htm">
<IMG SRC="bomb.jpg" BORDER=0 ALT="fire bomb dropped by plane"></A>
<BR>

<A HREF="homepage.htm">InfoWeb Home Page</A>
</I>
</CENTER>

<HR>
<ADDRESS>
<!-- below the email address is changed to the address of the contact
-->
<B>IntraMaster: <A
HREF="mailto:jdesboro@magmacom.com">jdesboro@magmacom.com</A>
<BR>
Last Updated: May 21, 1996</B>
<BR>
```

```
c:\intranet\docshome.htm    <!-- file name is changed to the
docshome.html file name -->

Graphic by: Fish   <!-- give attribution where attribution is due -->
</ADDRESS>
</BODY>
</HTML>
```

Including Lists and Tables in HTML Pages

This section takes a look at including different styles of lists and the use of tables to display information on HTML pages. The lists enable the user to create bulleted, numerically-ordered, and definition lists, which can be used to create "tables of contents" for gaining access to other documents and other functions. Each type of list will be explored briefly.

Using Lists in HTML Documents

You can create the following three types of lists by using HTML language:

- Unordered, or *bulleted*

- Numeric, or *ordered*

- Definition

In two files that have been developed so far, HOMEPAGE.HTM (including the HOMEPG2.HTM version) and DOCSHOME.HTM, you have seen unordered (bulleted) lists. This used the following construct to surround the list of bulleted items:

```
<UL> list </UL>
```

Within the <UL></UL> tag construct, the <LI> list item tag is used to precede each list entry so that the browser knows where to put the bullets. Here is an example of what was used in a previous example:

```
<UL>
<LI><A HREF="mktpage.htm">Marketing and Sales Literature</A><BR>
<LI><A HREF="techpg.htm">Research and Technical Reports</A><BR>
```

```
<LI><A HREF="hrpage.htm">Human Resource Manuals</A><BR>
<LI><A HREF="finpage.htm">Financial Policies and Procedures</A>
</UL>
```

The constructs of the other two list types are:

Ordered lists—<OL> list </OL>

Definition lists—<DL> list </DL>

The ordered list also uses the <LI> tag to identify the items within the list. However, when the browser interprets the tags used, the <LI> tag is replaced with numbers instead of the bullets. The following is an example of how the ordered list might be presented:

```
<OL>
   <LI>heading 1
   <LI>heading 2
   <LI>heading 3
</OL>
```

The definition list does not use the <LI> tag but uses <DT> and <DD> tagging pairs to identify the term (<DT>) and definition (<DD>). The definitions are generally indented under each item, with no blank lines between them. For example:

```
<DL>
<DT>A good day's work
<DD>a day when your children sleep in and then allow you put in a
➥twenty hour day before having to go outside and cut the grass; or a
➥day in which you get more than 4 consecutive hours of sleep
<P>
<DT>a marathon
<DD>for some it's a nice drive
</DL>
```

Figure 8.10 below shows the definition list from above, as well as a combination of nested ordered and unordered lists. The portion of the HTML file used to create these samples follows figure 8.10.

Figure 8.10

List examples.

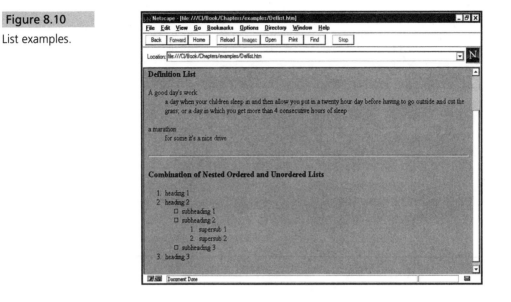

The code from the HTML file DEFLIST.HTM:

```
<H2>List samples</H2>
<HR>
<H3>Definition List</H3>
<DL>
<DT>A good day's work
<DD>a day when your children sleep in and then allow you put in a
➡twenty hour day before having to go outside and cut the grass; or a
➡day in which you get more than 4 consecutive hours of sleep<P>
<DT>a marathon
<DD>for some it's a nice drive
</DL>
<HR>
<H3>Combination of Nested Ordered and Unordered Lists</H3>
<OL>
<LI>heading 1
<LI>heading 2
<UL>
    <LI>subheading 1
    <LI>subheading 2
      <OL>
        <LI>supersub 1
        <LI>supersub 2
      </OL>
    <LI>subheading 3
```

```
</UL>
<LI>heading 3
</OL>
```

Incorporating Tables Into HTML Documents

The last item to cover is the <TABLE></TABLE> tag pair. At the time of writing, many of the browsers on the market support the use of tables within HTML documents even though the table tag pair is not part of the official HTML 2.0 specification. Because of user demand for this feature, this tag pair will be part of the HTML 3.0 specification. In the meantime, this section of the book will go through a brief introduction to creating a table in order to provide you with the ability to implement the table feature as required by users. You can work with a version of the DOCSHOME.HTM file called DOCTABLE.HTM that is found on the CD included with the book.

Figure 8.11 shows how the use of a table with the border turned on, as viewed by Netscape Navigator, can perform the same type of logical separation of information on the screen as tables with <HR> tags do. Figure 8.12 shows the same file as seen by NCSA Mosaic. Notice the differences in the way the same codes are interpreted by the browsers. Keep in mind that not all browsers will show a file in an identical fashion. Test your HTML documents with all the browsers that you plan to use within the intranet.

Figure 8.11

DOCTABLE.HTM—example of table usage, Netscape Navigator.

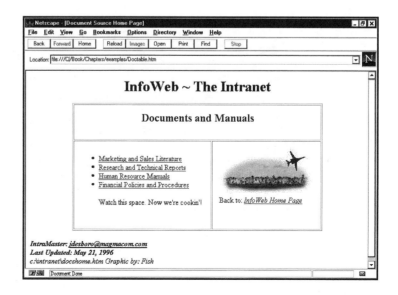

Figure 8.12

DOCTABLE.HTM—
example of table
usage, NCSA
Mosaic

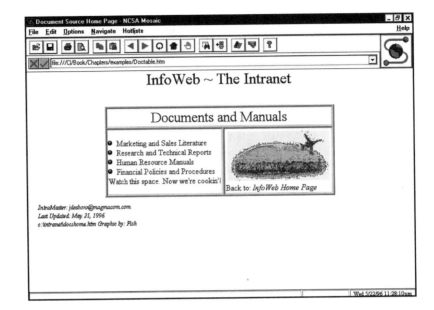

When you look through the ASCII-text version of the
DOCTABLE.HTM file, you should look at how the constructs are
used. The <TABLE attributes> tag uses only the BORDER attribute to
frame the table and each cell entry. The <TR></TR> (table row) tag
pair is used to indicate the elements of a row and the <TD></TD>
(table data) tag pairs define the cells in a given row.

```
<HTML>
<HEAD>
<TITLE>Document Source Home Page</TITLE>
</HEAD>

<BODY  bgcolor=#FFFFFF text="#000000">
<CENTER><H1>InfoWeb ~ The Intranet</H1></CENTER>

<!--..........body content goes here..........-->
<CENTER>
<TABLE CELLPADDING=15 BORDER><TR CELLPADDING=5>
<TD COLSPAN=2 ALIGN=center>

<H2>Documents and Manuals</H2>

</TD>
</TR>
```

```
<TR>
<TD>
<UL>
<LI><A HREF="mktpage.htm">Marketing and Sales Literature</A><BR>
<LI><A HREF="techpg.htm">Research and Technical Reports</A><BR>
<LI><A HREF="hrpage.htm">Human Resource Manuals</A><BR>
<LI><A HREF="finpage.htm">Financial Policies and Procedures</A>
➥<BR><BR>
Watch this space. Now we're cookin'!
</UL>
</TD>
<TD>
<A HREF="homepage.htm">
<IMG SRC="bomb.jpg" BORDER=0 ALT="fire bomb dropped by plane"></A>
<BR>
Back to: <A HREF="homepage.htm"><I>InfoWeb Home Page</I></A>
➥<BR><BR><BR>
</TD>
</TR>
</TABLE><P>
</CENTER>

<ADDRESS>
<!-- below the email address is changed to the address of the contact
➥-->
<B>IntraMaster: <A
HREF="mailto:jdesboro@magmacom.com">jdesboro@magmacom.com</A>
<BR>
Last Updated: May 21, 1996</B>
<BR>
c:\intranet\docshome.htm    <!-- file name is changed to the
docshome.html file name -->
Graphic by: Fish    <!-- give attribution where attribution is due -->
</ADDRESS>
</BODY>
</HTML>
```

The first row of the table in DOCTABLE.HTM uses the COLSPAN attribute to join the two cells so that the contents of the <TD> tag pair appear as a two-column header or title row. Because the table only contains two rows, you will notice the flexibility of the browser to handle the bulleted list in the first cell and both the image and text in the second cell.

Many things can be done with the TABLE tag set, including turning off the BORDER so that your table data cells appear to be nicely positioned relative to your graphic images. Figure 8.13 shows the same file without the BORDER attribute turned on.

Figure 8.13

DOCTABLE.HTM— no border around table, Netscape Navigator.

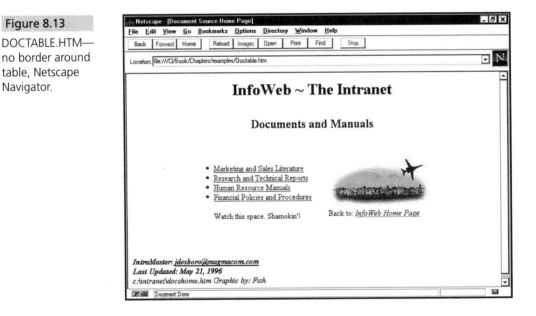

Philosophy of Template Design

When you start to develop your intranet pages, you and your team will work close together to assemble the prototype of the various pages that you will need and the features of each page. Once you get the Intranet up and going in beta for the rest of the company to see, you will very quickly find that everyone wants to help out. Well, maybe not everyone!

Those who do want to help usually want to put together the pages for their own area, with their own design and tools. Put your foot down hard and fast and make a lot of noise with that one stomp. Get their attention. You really do want them to work with you, but you have to let them know that they have to play in your ballpark. Here are some suggestions to prevent an intranet without consistency:

- As done with the examples in this chapter, start with a template of the basic layout that you would like all the participating groups to use. This includes elements such as navigation buttons, logos, and watermarks to allow for a consistent user interface across the site, as well as HEADER and FOOTER information for all files.

- Define the standard color schemes for background and text.

- Let them know what helper applications and plug-ins (if you can use them) are in place and how those applications and plug-ins help them to define the file formats they can use.

- Because your employees will need help creating tables for their pages, it is a good idea to create a series of templates for tables with two to eight columns and make them available.

The best way to make the templates available is to create a subsection home page file for each group to use, a sub-subsection page for them to copy, and the collection of table files mentioned previously. Make them available on the intranet in a heading off the main menu (Templates to Design Your Space on the intranet, or something similar).

Most of all, help the employees in any way you can to get their stuff up in a hurry. As the excitement builds, more and more people will want to set up and need your help.

Status Check

Hopefully you are now able to get through the development of the basic home page for the Intranet. The examples that were worked through in the chapter, from HOMEPAGE.HTM to

HOMEPG2.HTM, with its links to the next level of pages, to
DOCSHOME.HTM and DOCTABLE.HTM as examples of a second
level page, should provide you with the flavor for what is needed to
create the various pages required within the basic intranet.

If you stick to the four basic areas of your initial intranet pilot project—
document publishing, searchable directories, information links, and
simple groupware—you should be able to create all the pages for accessing the publications and manuals of the company and for links to
internal and external information sites. The searchable directories and
simple groupware applications will be discussed in Chapters 10 and 17.
Next will be a look at how to get the interaction into the system by
starting the development of forms for collecting and receiving
information.

9

Beyond Basic HTML: Using Forms to Handle Information

Forms provide a means for the browser to prompt the user for information and enable the user to enter the information into the intranet page. A Common Gateway Interface (CGI) program is usually required to process the information after the user enters it, and then to receive results displayed back on the screen. This chapter will cover the basics of form creation, and then it will move on up to making it work. The next chapter in the book covers the use of CGI programs and how these programs work with forms.

Several HTML tags can be used in the creation of forms. (For a review of HTML tags, please refer to Chapter 8, "Introduction to HTML.") Forms can be used to obtain names and addresses or to order multiple items in a "shopping cart." Figure 9.1 is an example of a form to complete for an employee phone list.

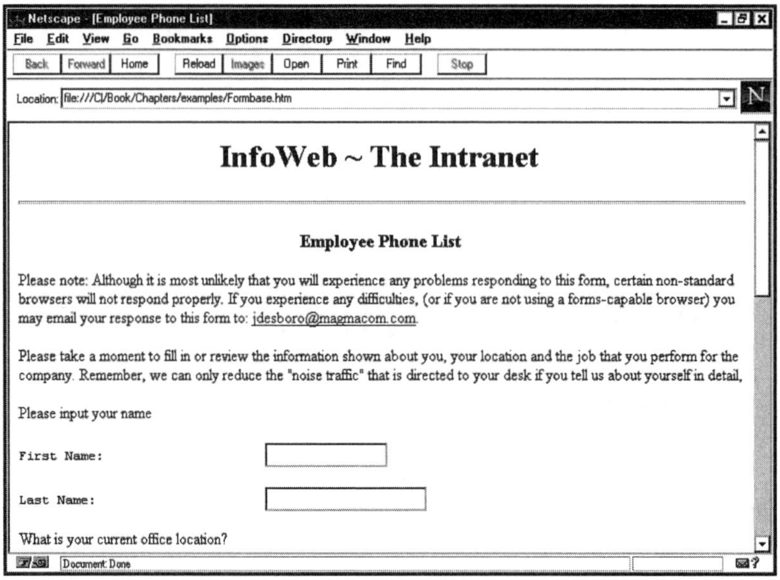

Figure 9.1

Sample form,
Netscape
Navigator.

```
Netscape - [Employee Phone List]                                    _ 8 X
File  Edit  View  Go  Bookmarks  Options  Directory  Window  Help
Back  Forward  Home    Reload  Images  Open    Print  Find      Stop
Location: file:///C/Book/Chapters/examples/Formbase.htm
```

InfoWeb ~ The Intranet

Employee Phone List

Please note: Although it is most unlikely that you will experience any problems responding to this form, certain non-standard browsers will not respond properly. If you experience any difficulties, (or if you are not using a forms-capable browser) you may email your response to this form to: jdesboro@magmacom.com.

Please take a moment to fill in or review the information shown about you, your location and the job that you perform for the company. Remember, we can only reduce the "noise traffic" that is directed to your desk if you tell us about yourself in detail.

Please input your name

First Name:

Last Name:

What is your current office location?

```
Document Done
```

In this chapter, the following topics are covered:

- Planning and designing the form

- The elements of a form

- Creating a basic form

- Obtaining and handling input from the user

- Adding finishing touches to the form

Creating Forms: Getting Started

Forms are HTML documents that are designed not only to display information to the user but to obtain information, or input, from the user. In essence, the author of the form creates a document prompting users to provide input into blanks called *fields*. Several different types of blanks can be used within forms, and they will be discussed later in this chapter.

In order to obtain input from the user, an HTML document that contains the form must be created. Forms are created using HTML tags. Each form must have a <FORM> start and </FORM> end tag. The basic syntax of the tag pair is as follows:

```
<FORM ACTION=action base> form tags </FORM>

<FORM METHOD=method> form tags </FORM>

<FORM ENCTYPE=media type> form tags </FORM>
```

These tag types will be discussed in greater detail in the section "Elements of a Form." But before getting into the details of how to implement all the detailed elements of a form, a discussion of form planning and design is in order.

Planning and Design

When sitting down to look at collecting information via a form, there are two things to keep in mind: you use a form in conjunction with a CGI program to pass information to and receive information back from another application, or you can create a form that will have the responses mailed back to you via e-mail. You must then *do* something with those responses.

The look and feel of your form can be enhanced by having it professionally designed and laid out, incorporating artwork and custom logos from a graphic artist. However, the purpose of this book is to get you started on your own. It will cover the basics of what is needed—a checklist of things to prepare in order to get your form right.

The following are items that you need to have in hand when planning and designing your form. The specifics of how these items are tagged and put into the form are covered in the next section.

Establishing General Information About the Form

In establishing the HTML document that contains the form, a few pieces of information fall into the "general" category. Although not exactly specific to the form, the HTML document requires a title, as do all other HTML forms that have been covered thus far. Also, depending upon the "look-and-feel" guidelines you have established for your intranet, you may wish to alter the background color or add a background image to the HTML documents that contain forms. This provides a visual cue to the user that this document is not just an information item but rather an interactive form.

Following are the items that should be collected under the precept of general information:

- **Title**—What is the title of the form? It will appear in the browser's header (in most browsers).

- **Heading**—What is the form heading? It will appear at the top of the form.

- **Background color**—What background color do you want to have for your form? Some samples are listed here with their respective codes:

    - red   FF0000

    - green   00FF00

    - blue   0000FF

    - black   000000

    - white   FFFFFF

    - gray   888888

    - yellow   FFFF00

- **Text color**—What is the color of the text to be on the form (choose color from the preceding list or another color)?

- **Text placement**—Do you want the text centered on the form?

- **Response address**—To which address should any e-mail responses be directed?

- **Button titles**—What do you want the *submit* and *reset* buttons to read?

- **Background image**—Do you want an image to appear in the background of the form? If so, what is the name of the image file?

Preparing Leading Text

Leading text is a string of text which appears beneath your form's heading. It should appear above any text inserts or fields you place in your form. The following is the text used in the sample form (see fig. 9.1):

```
Please note: Although it is most unlikely that you will experience
any problems responding to this form, certain non-standard browsers
will not respond properly. If you experience any difficulties (or
if you are not using a forms-capable browser), you may e-mail your
response to this form to:
<a href="mailto:jdesboro@magmacom.com">jdesboro@magmacom.com</a>.
Please take a moment to fill in or review the information shown about
you, your location, and the job that you perform for the company.
Remember, we can only reduce the noise traffic that is directed to
your desk if you tell us about yourself in detail.
```

Developing Text Inserts

Text inserts are the "kind and gentle" instructions that you put in front of the fields you want completed. For example, in figure 9.1 you can see two text inserts: "Please input your name" and "What is your current office location?" These serve to guide the user in completing the form.

Determining Text Fields

Text fields are the fields where the users enter text from their keyboards. Typically, any information that will require typing on behalf of the user falls into this category.

Make a list of the fields of information that you need to collect. Also, assign a length to these fields so you can create the input fields appropriately. Keep in mind that some database applications have a field length limit of 255 characters.

Note

> If you are dealing with a CGI program, there may be a list of prescribed field names for you to use. Check with the database administrator for more information. Chapter 10, "Introduction to CGI," and Chapter 11, "Integrating ODBC and CGI," discuss CGI programming in greater detail.

Defining Comment Fields

A comment field enables users to respond beyond the length of a text field, as described previously. Comment fields are usually incorporated to provide a feedback section on the same form as the real input.

Comment fields are used, for example, in forms that collect user feedback or in "suggestion box" forms where the creator of the form wants the user to input as much information into the form as the user feels necessary. In an example created later in this chapter, a comment field is implemented to obtain feedback.

Implementing Check Boxes

Are you planning to have a list from which a user can select one or more items? Check Boxes are logically grouped items, shown in a list on the form, from which the user can click and select one or more entries. An example of logically grouped items would be, "Which of the following golf courses have you played in the last three years (check all that apply): course A, course B, course C," and so on.

Because these groups/lists of items appear on the form, you may want to limit the number of items or the number of groups of check boxes that you want to have appear. (See the list box discussion for other possibilities.)

Defining Radio Buttons

Radio buttons are similar to check boxes in that they are items organized in groups. The difference comes from the fact that you can only select one of the options. Organize your information requirements where you would like to use these features into logical groups. For example, "What would you prefer to drink with your meal: coffee, tea, juice, water, soda (select one)."

Note

> The difference between check boxes and radio buttons is in the number of options you can check within each category. Check boxes enable you to select more than one item in the list while radio buttons enable you to select only one item in the list.

List Boxes

List boxes are used to create a list that appears in a scrollable window-box. This reduces the space required for the display of the possible options from which the user can choose. For example, "Select the country you would most like to visit from the following list:" The list of all countries in the world would not be shown for size and space reasons.

Organize the information that you want to have in these types of boxes into the logical lists that are required. You can select multiple entries from the list and can specify the number of lines within the window box that can be seen on the form. If you are going to enable only one entry to be selected, then plan on leaving the window box at a size of 1 (more on this later). This is an alternative to placing a long list of check boxes on the screen.

Including Graphics

Within the body of the form, it is possible to use graphics to create a visual image (a company logo perhaps). Many organizations utilize graphic symbols to indicate important or required information types on the form itself. If you plan to use graphics for your form, make a list of all the graphics you want to have displayed on the form. A couple of things to keep in mind: the file formats should be either *gif* or *jpg* so that they can be read by all browsers, and the size of the graphics should be kept under or close to 40k in size. The size is important because of the time required to load the files into the browser.

Listing Hyperlinks

As discussed in Chapter 8, hyperlinks can be inserted into HTML documents to enable the user to jump from one location in a document to another or jump between the current document and the document that is identified in the hyperlink. Make a list of all hyperlinks to appear on the form that you want the user to be able to access. You should have the URL and the text that you want as the anchor text available.

Outlining Tables

Tables are often used to display columns and rows of information within a document. They are used to organize information visually for the user. For example, consider three columns representing the three days of a conference and four rows representing four time slots for presentations. This particular table provides a very quick means for the user to cross-reference information.

If you have information that could benefit from tabular format and display, sketch out the column and row headings and define how they relate.

Note

If you think that you are going to have a table on the form, remember that not all browsers can display them. Because of this factor, it is a good idea not to incorporate input fields into a table on a form. If the browser cannot display the table, the input cannot be entered by the user.

To determine if your browser can display tables, use the example that is created at the end of this chapter, available on the CD included with the book, and retrieve the document with your browser. If the browser displays the table, things are fine. If the table is not displayed, your browser does not display tables.

For your table you should come up with a caption, the basic structure (numbers of rows and columns) including column headers, the content of each cell (can include URLs for hyperlinking), the location of the table relative to the margins (left, right, or center), and whether you want to have the table borders shown (refer to Chapter 8 for an introduction to tables and borders). With these ideas in mind, you should be prepared to put in the tables required.

Defining Trailing Text

In order to have the input data accepted and acted upon according to the FORM ACTION, which will be discussed in detail shortly, a *submit* button must be placed on the form. The *reset* button is often displayed next to the submit button to enable the user to clear the information from the form and re-input before submitting the information.

At the end of your form, just above where the submit and reset buttons are located, you should place a message regarding what to do with the buttons or, better yet, a note thanking the user for having filled in the form: "Thanks for helping us keep the intranet up-to-date!"

Really Neat Things

Note

This section is included here to give you a hint of what can be done with the products that are now reaching the market. A simple example will be demonstrated later in the chapter of how JavaScript can be used. For more information on Java and JavaScript, please refer to Tim Ritchey's *Programming JavaScript for Netscape 2.0* (New Riders, 1996).

If you want to incorporate some of the features that JavaScript allows, such as a scrolling status bar message which will be demonstrated in this chapter, you will need two things—someone who can write the JavaScript for you, and the understanding that not all browsers can currently handle this type of feature. If this doesn't stop you from proceeding, decide on what you want to incorporate into the status bar message that will be created in this chapter.

At this point you have all the pieces that you want to include on the form. The next step is to organize it into a file that provides the look and feel that you want. There are several ways to do this in the beginning.

If you have never designed a form or newsletter before, you need to know the secret of the trade—do a quick mock-up on a white board or with a paper and pencil. Try to get a good gut feeling at some point about one particular design relative to the layout of the form, the order in which the information you have collected previously should be displayed, and where graphics should be placed. Once you have completed this "storyboard," you are ready to proceed to a first pass at creating the required HTML file to incorporate the pieces.

Author's Note

IMHO (In my humble opinion) the white board is the best place to quickly sketch out the pieces in a column on one side and then sketch them into place on the other side on the board, crossing them off the column as you go. This process should take all of five minutes. My rationale for this length of time is that I would rather get something together quickly on the machine that I can let others play with than spend my time trying to create something artistic that I can't very well get to people located around the building or across an ocean. Use the HTML file as the white board, keeping the filename to six characters (the last two can be reserved for VX, where V equals "version" and X equals the version number you are up to. If it isn't final after ten versions, delegate the task to someone else).

Understanding the <FORM> tag

Now that you have collected the elements that you want to put into the form, how does this relate to the HTML tags that can be used within the form? Before you do the actual work, a discussion of some tags is in order.

In this section the following tags will be discussed to ensure that the reader understands the way in which forms are created:

- The <FORM> </FORM> tag pair and its attributes: METHOD, ACTION, and ENCTYPE

- The <INPUT> tag and its attributes: CHECKBOX, FILE, HIDDEN, IMAGE, PASSWORD, RADIO, RANGE, RESET, SUBMIT, and TEXT

- The <SELECT> tag and its counterpart, the <OPTION> tag

- The <TEXTAREA> tag and its attributes: COLS and ROWS

The Basic Form Tag

The basic form tag was discussed at the beginning of the chapter, but to review, here is an example:

```
<FORM METHOD=POST ACTION="http://www.intranomics.com/cgi-bin/
comments" >
</FORM>
```

A form is designed to pass the input to another function, a mail message, a database for storage, or a CGI program for the purpose of extracting records that match the input criteria. The attributes define the *method* by which the data passes and to what *action* the information should be passed. You will see a much more detailed discussion of how this is used in Chapter 10, "Introduction to CGI," and Chapter 11, "Integrating ODBC and CGI."

Following is a detailed description of the attributes of the form tag:

- The METHOD attribute determines how the data will be sent to the CGI program. The possible methods are GET or POST. GET specifies a query form used to get data from a server. POST specifies a form that gives information to the server and perhaps instigates the updating of a database or sending of a message.

Note

For complete information on the differences between the GET and POST methods, please refer to *The CGI Book* by William E. Weinman (New Riders, 1996).

- The ACTION attribute is used to give the URL of the CGI program that will process the form.

- The ENCTYPE default media type is "application/x-www-form-urlencoded," which specifies how the browser assembles the user responses and the form to create a response URL that is then submitted to the server.

The INPUT Tag and its Attributes

Now that you understand the basic form tag, this section will cover the input tag. The <INPUT> tag is used to define the type of input field that is placed on the form. The basic syntax of the <INPUT> tag is as follows:

```
<INPUT TYPE=input_type [parameters specific to input_type]>
```

The <INPUT> tag has a variety of types that will be covered:

- CHECKBOX

- FILE

- HIDDEN

- IMAGE

- PASSWORD

- RADIO

- RANGE

- RESET

- SUBMIT

- TEXT

The TYPE=CHECKBOX attribute

The CHECKBOX type attribute allows the user to select zero, one, or several of the choices offered. The NAME attribute is required to identify the data for the field. The VALUE attribute specifies the value that is returned if the box is checked. The CHECKED attribute, if specified, shows that the box is initially selected. The syntax for the CHECKBOX attribute is:

```
<INPUT TYPE=CHECKBOX NAME=name VALUE=value>

<INPUT TYPE=CHECKBOX NAME=name VALUE=value CHECKED>
```

The TYPE=FILE attribute

The FILE attribute allows the user to attach one or more files to the form for submission. The NAME attribute is the required field used to identify the data for the field. The ACCEPT attribute is a list of MIME-types that will be accepted, for example "image/gif, image/jpeg." The syntax for this attribute is:

```
<INPUT TYPE=FILE NAME=name ACCEPT=MIME type list>
```

The TYPE=HIDDEN attribute

The HIDDEN type attribute specifies a hard-coded name-value pair within the form. This field is not displayed to the user. Both the NAME and VALUE are required attributes. The syntax for this INPUT type is:

```
<INPUT TYPE=HIDDEN NAME=name VALUE=value>
```

The TYPE=IMAGE attribute

The IMAGE type attribute specifies an image to be presented to the user. As soon as the user clicks on the image, the form is submitted with the selected x-y coordinates of the spot on the image and the data for the other form fields. The NAME attribute is a required field used to identify the data for the field. The SRC and ALIGN attributes are the same as the <IMG> tag (in Chapter 8). The syntax is as follows:

```
<INPUT TYPE=IMAGE NAME=name SRC="URL">
```

```
<INPUT TYPE=IMAGE NAME=name SRC="URL" ALIGN="alignment">
```

The TYPE=PASSWORD attribute

The PASSWORD type attribute specifies a single-line text entry field within the form that contains it. The value entered by the user will be obscured—it is entered in the form of asterisks (*******). The NAME attribute is a required field used to identify the data for the PASSWORD attribute. The MAXLENGTH attribute indicates the maximum length of the field—if a length is not specified, then there is no limit on the number of characters that can be entered. The SIZE attribute defines the size of the text field that is open to input. Text entered into the field will scroll appropriately if more information is entered than can be displayed in the window. The browser will limit the default SIZE. The VALUE attribute specifies the initial value of the field. The syntax is as follows:

```
<INPUT TYPE=PASSWORD NAME=name>

<INPUT TYPE=PASSWORD NAME=name MAXLENGTH=length>

<INPUT TYPE=PASSWORD NAME=name SIZE=size>

<INPUT TYPE=PASSWORD NAME=name VALUE=value>
```

 Warning

Remember that this is not a secure method of using passwords for network security purposes. It is just an added feature of the HTML tag set.

The TYPE=RADIO Attribute

The RADIO type attribute allows for a single choice among multiple options. Within the logical grouping, each radio button will appear with the same name. The user can select only one of the choices. The NAME attribute is a required field and the VALUE attribute specifies the value that is returned if the box is checked. If one of the options has been CHECKED, it will be initially selected. The syntax is as follows:

```
<INPUT TYPE=RADIO NAME=name VALUE=value>

<INPUT TYPE=RADIO NAME=name VALUE=value CHECKED>
```

The TYPE=RANGE attribute

The RANGE type attribute allows the user to enter a number restricted to a set range. The NAME attribute is a required field used to identify the data for the field. The MIN and MAX attributes specify the minimum and maximum values that can be entered. The VALUE attribute specifies an initial value and must be in the range specified. The syntax is as follows:

```
<INPUT TYPE=RANGE NAME=name MIN=min MAX=max>
```

```
<INPUT TYPE=RANGE NAME=name MIN=min MAX=max VALUE=value>
```

The TYPE=RESET attribute

The RESET type attribute specifies a button which resets all the fields in the form to their initial values. You can specify what the face of the button says by using the VALUE attribute. The syntax is as follows:

```
<INPUT TYPE=RESET>
```

```
<INPUT TYPE=RESET VALUE=value>
```

The TYPE=SUBMIT attribute

The SUBMIT type attribute also specifies a button that submits the form when clicked. The NAME attribute is used to identify the data for the field. If no NAME attribute is given, the element does not form part of the submitted response. The VALUE attribute allows you to specify what the button says on its face. The syntax is as follows:

```
<INPUT TYPE=SUBMIT>
```

```
<INPUT TYPE=SUBMIT NAME=name>
```

```
<INPUT TYPE=SUBMIT VALUE=value>
```

The TYPE=TEXT attribute

The TEXT type attribute specifies a single-line text entry field within the form. The NAME attribute is a required field used to identify the data for the field. The MAXLENGTH attribute specifies the number of characters to be entered and, if absent, allows an unlimited length of the field. The SIZE attribute specifies the length of the input field window, will scroll if the text entered goes beyond the number of characters that can be displayed in the field. The VALUE attribute specifies the initial value of the field. The syntax is as follows:

```
<INPUT TYPE=TEXT NAME=name>
```

```
<INPUT TYPE=TEXT NAME=name MAXLENGTH=length>
```

```
<INPUT TYPE=TEXT NAME=name SIZE=size>

<INPUT TYPE=TEXT NAME=name VALUE=value>
```

The SELECT tag

Once you have considered all the options for the INPUT tag attributes, there is also a method of selecting information from a multiple-line selection box field, or list box. If the MULTIPLE attribute is specified, the user is able to select multiple entries from the available list. For example, "Select the Olympic sporting events for which you would like tickets (you may select as many as you wish): archery, badminton, cow chip toss," and so on. The SIZE attribute here applies to the number of lines of the selection box that are visible.

Tip

Depending upon the design of your form, you may wish to display only one line or several in the selection box. If you display only one line, users tend to think that only one choice is allowed. If you have a box of several lines, people tend to think there may be more than one choice allowed.

The SELECTED attribute of the option tag specifies that the option is to be initially selected. The VALUE attribute specifies the value to be returned upon selection. If the VALUE attribute is not specified, the content of the option is used. The syntax possibilities are as follows:

```
<SELECT NAME=name> option entries </SELECT>

<SELECT NAME=name MULTIPLE> option entries </SELECT>

<SELECT NAME=name SIZE=size> option entries </SELECT>

<OPTION> content

<OPTION SELECTED> content

<OPTION VALUE=value> content
```

The TEXTAREA tag

This tag specifies a multiple-line text area field within the form. The NAME attribute is a required field used to identify the data for the field. The COLS and ROWS attributes specify the width and height in characters. The content part of the syntax example below is used for the initial value of the field. The field can be scrolled beyond the specified rows and columns.

```
<TEXTAREA NAME=name COLS=#columns ROWS=#rows> content </TEXTAREA>
```

These tags and their attributes and options give you the grammar you need to implement in order to get on the road to designing your own form and making it work.

Putting the Form to Work

Now that you have collected the information you want to put onto the form and have an understanding of its elements, it should be easy to bring it all together.

There are three basic areas of the form—the header, the body, and the footer. These are not to be confused as replacing the same three elements of an HTML page. The form itself is the "body" element of the HTML page.

The header area of the form is where you put the heading for the form, and a notice to the users that includes general instructions about the usage of the form and any other pertinent information. It is also a good idea to provide a "mailto:" address in the event that someone is not using a forms-capable browser.

The footer area of the form is where you have your final instructions and comments and usually includes the submit and reset buttons.

The body area of the form is where the input, selection, and text areas are located.

Within the remaining sections of the chapter, the following topics will be covered en route to completing your understanding of the basic form:

- Creating the basic layout

- Getting the user to input information

- Handling the user's input

- Incorporating the finishing touches

Creating the Basic Layout

Sleeves rolled up? Coffee hot and just beyond the keyboard? Good! Now you are going to take everything this chapter has covered and create the physical layout of your form. This involves several components:

- The outline

- General information

- Text fields

- Insertion codes

The Outline

The first step is to lay out the basic outline of the form. The HTML file to start with, FORM1.HTM, contains the following lines of HTML code:

```
<HTML>
<HEAD>
<TITLE>Employee Phone List</TITLE>
</HEAD>
<BODY>
<CENTER><H1>InfoWeb ~ The intranet</H1></CENTER>
<HR>
```

```
<FORM ACTION="mailto:jdesboro@magmacom.com" METHOD=POST >
This where we will build the form

</FORM>
<P>
<HR>

<ADDRESS>
<!-- below the email address is changed to the address of the contact
-->
IntraMaster: <A HREF="mailto:jdesboro@magmacom.com">jdesboro@
magmacom.com</A>
<BR>
Last Updated: May 25, 1996
<BR>
c:\intranet\form1.htm
</ADDRESS>
</BODY>
</HTML>
```

As you can see from the code, the form is set up with a mailto: AC-TION. The concept behind this type of form is to mail the information entered to another point where it will be read into another application which will then process the information. For example, say you wish to take your summer vacation and retrieve the HTML document that the Human Resources branch has prepared for the intranet. Within this document is a form that you complete indicating the number of days you plan to be away, the starting and ending dates, and your current office phone number. When you click on the submit button at the bottom of the screen, the information that you entered is e-mailed to the appropriate personnel in Human Resources to book your vacation.

Figure 9.2 shows the form the lines of code create, as seen by Netscape Navigator. You will notice the same basic template layout from the previous chapter—the page heading separated from the body by a rule which is, in turn, separated from the footer area of the form by a rule. By using the same basic template for all page designs, you achieve consistency in look and feel.

Figure 9.2

FORM1.HTM, as
seen by Netscape
Navigator.

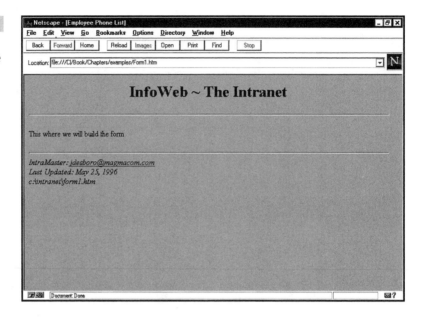

General Information

Start with the general information for the form. Where you put each of
the items will be reflected by its location in the HTML file:

- The TITLE of the form will be "Employee Information Sheet"
  because you are asking for input from the employee as well as
  providing some information to the staff.

- The form heading will be set to the <H3> tag pair and will read
  "Employee Information Sheet."

- The background color will be white and the text black.

- All the general information text will be centered.

- The submit button will read "Information is OK" and the reset
  button will read "Reset Information."

- The same graphic image from the intranet Home Page will be
  used and centered on the page just before the form—the file name
  is BOMB.JPG.

The HTML code to use is outlined below, and the resulting file is shown in Figure 9.3. Please note that the <BODY> color attributes for text and background must be stated before the first line of text outside of the <HEAD> tag pair.

In addition to the general information items that have been collected, the form also incorporates the leading text before the actual user input areas, the incorporation of a graphic image, and the trailer text—just above the buttons.

```
<HTML>
<HEAD>
<TITLE>Employee Information Sheet</TITLE>
</HEAD>
<BODY BGCOLOR="FFFFFF" TEXT="000000">

<CENTER><H1>InfoWeb ~ The intranet</H1></CENTER>
<HR>

<CENTER><H3>Employee Information Sheet</H3>
</CENTER>

<P>Please note: Although it is most unlikely that you will experience
any problems responding to this form, certain non-standard browsers
will not respond properly. If you experience any difficulties (or if
you are not using a forms-capable browser), you may email your
response to this form to:
<A HREF="mailto:jdesboro@magmacom.com">jdesboro@magmacom.com</A>.
<P>
Please take a moment to fill in or review the information shown about
you, your location and the job that you perform for the company.
Remeber, we can only reduce the "noise traffic" that is directed to
your desk if you tell us about yourself in detail.<BR>
<CENTER><IMG SRC="bomb.jpg" ALIGN=""></CENTER>
<HR>

<FORM ACTION="mailto:jdesboro@magmacom.com" METHOD=POST >

<P>
Thank you for making our company a fine place to work!
```

```
<P><INPUT TYPE="submit" VALUE="Information is OK"> <INPUT
TYPE="reset" VALUE="Reset Information ">

</FORM>

<P>
<HR>

<ADDRESS>
<!-- below the email address is changed to the address of the contact
-->
IntraMaster: <A
HREF="mailto:jdesboro@magmacom.com">jdesboro@magmacom.com</A>
<BR>
Last Updated: May 25, 1996
<BR>
c:\intranet\form1.htm
</ADDRESS>
</BODY>
</HTML>
```

Figure 9.3

FORM2.HTM—
Incorporating the
general informa-
tion into form.

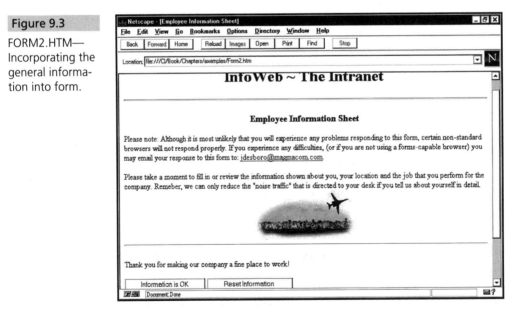

Text Fields

Keeping one eye on the white board where the storyboard design of the form is located, you can now start to lay out the text inserts and place the fields you expect the user to complete. Figure 9.4 shows the form after this step has been completed.

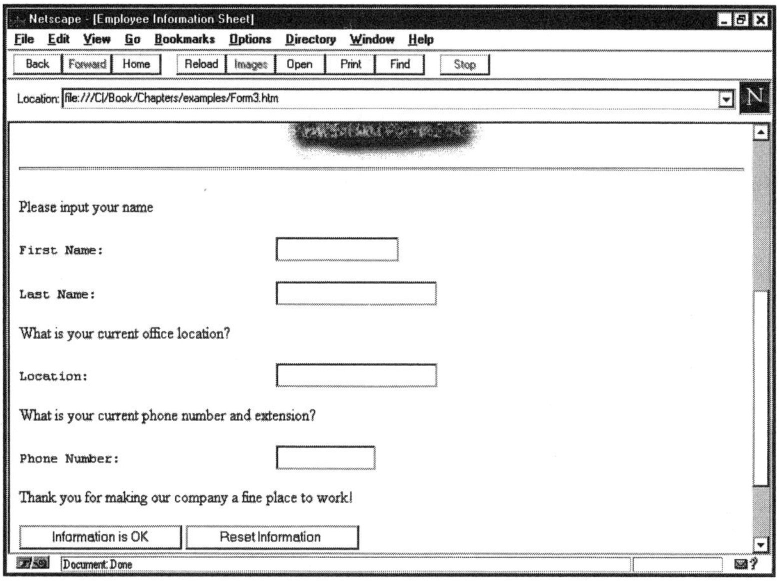

Figure 9.4

FORM3.HTM— Adding in text fields.

The HTML file includes the <PRE> pre-formatted tag which defines text that should be shown in a fixed font width, with line breaks and white space as specified by the file author. Multiple spaces are displayed as multiple spaces. In many HTML files, this tag is used to show lines of program code. The HTML file, in its progression, now looks like the following:

```
<HTML>
<HEAD>
<TITLE>Employee Information Sheet</TITLE>
</HEAD>
<BODY BGCOLOR="FFFFFF" TEXT="000000">

<CENTER><H1>InfoWeb ~ The intranet</H1></CENTER>
<HR>
```

```
<CENTER><H3>Employee Information Sheet</H3>
</CENTER>

<P>Please note: Although it is most unlikely that you will experience
any problems responding to this form, certain non-standard browsers
will not respond properly. If you experience any difficulties (or if
you are not using a forms-capable browser), you may email your re-
sponse to this form to: <A
HREF="mailto:jdesboro@magmacom.com">jdesboro@magmacom.com</A>.
<P>
Please take a moment to fill in or review the information shown about
you, your location and the job that you perform for the company.
Remeber, we can only reduce the "noise traffic" that is directed to
your desk if you tell us about yourself in detail.<BR>
 <CENTER><IMG SRC="bomb.jpg" ALIGN=""></CENTER>
<HR>

<FORM ACTION="mailto:jdesboro@magmacom.com" METHOD=POST >

<P>Please input your name<BR>
<P><PRE>First Name: <INPUT TYPE="TEXT" NAME="firstname"
SIZE=15></PRE>
<P><PRE>Last Name: <INPUT TYPE="TEXT" NAME="lastname" SIZE=20></PRE>
<P>What is your current office location?<BR>
<P><PRE>Location: <INPUT TYPE="TEXT" NAME="location" SIZE=20></PRE>
<P>What is your current phone number and extension?<BR>
<P><PRE>Phone Number: <INPUT TYPE="TEXT" NAME="phonenumer" SIZE=12></
PRE>

<P>
Thank you for making our company a fine place to work!

<P><INPUT TYPE="submit" VALUE="Information is OK"> <INPUT
TYPE="reset" VALUE="Reset Information ">

</FORM>

<P>
<HR>

<ADDRESS>
```

```
<!-- below the email address is changed to the address of the contact
-->
IntraMaster: <A
HREF="mailto:jdesboro@magmacom.com">jdesboro@magmacom.com</A>
<BR>
Last Updated: May 25, 1996
<BR>
c:\intranet\form1.htm
</ADDRESS>
</BODY>
</HTML>
```

Now you have the areas for the user to input text field information. Note that the length of the fields has been included as the SIZE attribute.

On your "Employee Information Sheet" you want to have the employees describe, in their own words, what it is exactly that they do within the confines of the organization. In order to do that, you need to add a TEXTAREA tag to the form.

To fit this into the HTML form, the following line is added to the code:

```
<P>Please outline, in as much detail as possible, what it is that you
do within the framework of the company.<BR>
<P><TEXTAREA NAME="duties" ROWS=10 COLS=60></TEXTAREA><P>
```

This now creates the input area for your personnel to input their information. The section of the file FORM4.HTM that has the input text fields and the text has the following coding syntax:

```
<P>Please input your name<BR>
<P><PRE>First Name: <INPUT TYPE="TEXT" NAME="firstname" SIZE=15>
</PRE>
<P><PRE>Last Name: <INPUT TYPE="TEXT" NAME="lastname" SIZE=20></PRE>
<P>What is your current office location?<BR>
<P><PRE>Location: <INPUT TYPE="TEXT" NAME="location" SIZE=20></PRE>
<P>What is your current phone number and extension?<BR>
<P><PRE>Phone Number: <INPUT TYPE="TEXT" NAME="phonenumer" SIZE=12>
</PRE>
```

```
<P>Please outline in as much detail as possible, what it is that you
do within the framework of the company.<BR>
<P><TEXTAREA NAME="duties" ROWS=10 COLS=60></TEXTAREA><P>
```

The addition of this <TEXTAREA> coding creates the text box as shown in figure 9.5. By adding the two lines of code that deal with the text area, the "text insert" text and the actual TEXTAREA tag, to the HTML file FORM3.HTM, you will have created the FORM4.HTM file that was used for figure 9.5.

Figure 9.5

FORM4.HTM—adding the text box.

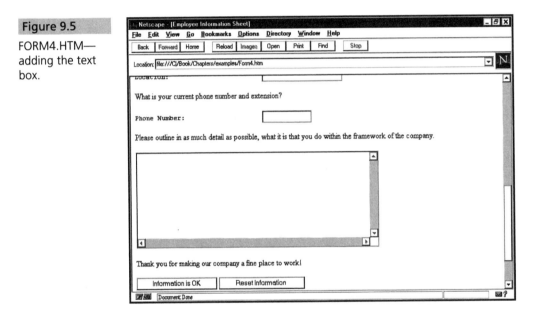

Sit back for a minute now, freshen up that cup of coffee, and look at what you have done.

You have created the basic form that allows for text field input and a text area for longer entry. If you look back at the <FORM> tag area in the HTML file, you will see that the ACTION attribute was set to "MAILTO:jdesboro@magmacom.com." After the user fills in the fields on the form and hits the submit button that you have labeled "Information is OK," the browser takes the information that was entered and mails it to the address in the MAILTO attribute.

Figure 9.6 shows the fields of information filled in and ready to be sent by clicking on the Information is OK button. The act of submitting the information creates an e-mail that the browser then sends off to the address as described previously. The message that was sent containing the data you see in figure 9.6 is as follows:

```
firstnamejohn+&lastnamedesborough&location=camp+misfortune%2C+
canada&phonenumer=819-595-1783&duties=I+get+to+sit+in+the+
basement+and+write+many+words+on+paper%0D%0Ahoping+that+
someday+I+will+get+some+people+calling+to+have%0D%0Ame+come+
and+help+them+put+in+place+intranets.+However%2C+I+%0D%0Aworry
+that+the+words+I+write+may+make+it+so+easy+for+them+to
+%0D%0Aset+up+their+own+intranets%2C+that+I+will+be+like+the
+Maytag%0D%0Arepair+man.+Sigh%21
```

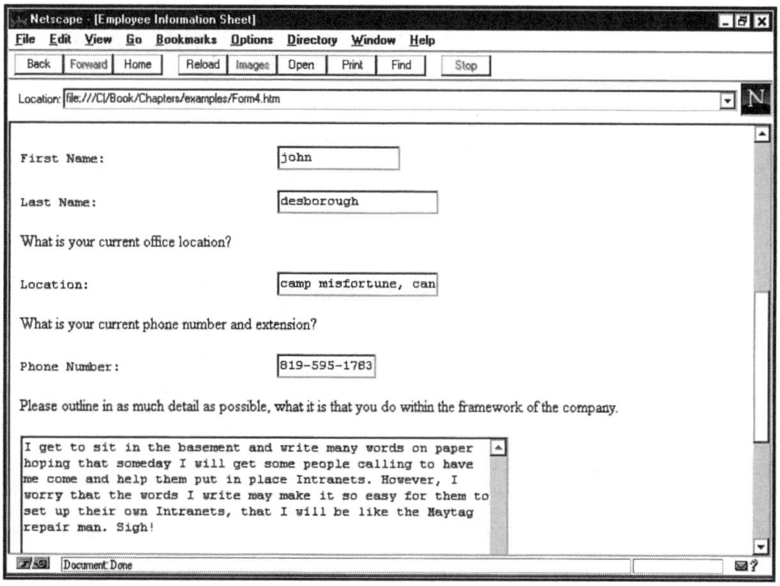

Figure 9.6

The completed text area.

Insertion Codes

You can see that the contents of all the fields completed were concatenated into one long string using the following syntax:

```
fieldname=content
```

The following are a series of insertion codes which have been used in the preceding text.

- &—delimits the content of one field from the start of the field-name of the next

- +—represents spaces between words in the text

- %2C—represents the comma

- %0D%0A—represents carriage return and linefeed (I used a hard return to end the lines)

- %21—represents the exclamation mark

Your browser's help manuals will have a complete list of the insertion codes that are used by the browser when it sends the message.

Tip

> You don't have to input insertion codes into your computer; it is done automatically. Don't worry about them if you don't have to.

Handling of the Input

In response to the burning question "What happens to the message that is sent by the browser?" the answer is straightforward: nothing at this time. The form you have been building demonstrates a form that actually sends the message somewhere.

The next chapter will discuss how the message can be sent to the CGI program which, in conceptual terms, takes the message and passes the field names and their contents to a query engine within the data application. The query engine processes the request and sends the information back to your browser through the CGI.

At this time, you can take the response string and create a macro within your word-processing software to search, cut, and paste the response information into a more traditional and recognizable "fieldname=content" structure for importing into a software package for storage or analysis.

If you have created the form used earlier, completed the fields, and mailed it to yourself (try replacing the e-mail address with your own), you will notice that there is no visible sign that you have done anything at all, success or failure. However, a couple of ways exist to provide feedback to the user.

One of the ways to provide some feedback outside of the form itself is to configure the e-mail address to which the file is being sent with an autoreply message thanking them for their input. This requires two things: 1) an e-mail application that allows autoreply, and 2) an e-mail address that is used for this purpose only.

Warning

> If you use your own address and have autoreply set up for this application, any other e-mail message coming to your desktop for other purposes will get the autoreply that you had designed for the form reply. To avoid people receiving thank you notes for participating in one area when it is not appropriate, establish a dedicated e-mail account for the application.

Finishing Touches

So far the form is looking pretty good, but someone just brought you a double-long Espresso and you are going to be up for a while. What can you do to add a few more features to the form and explore some of the other options that are available?

Check Boxes, Radio Buttons, and List Boxes

By adding in a CHECKBOX feature you can provide users the opportunity to select one or more options from a list. One of the more appreciated things within an intranet is to have access to newsgroups that pertain to topics of interest. Given the nature of some of the newsgroups external to the organization, you may wish to establish a series of newsgroups that the intranet gains access to on behalf of the organization, and then offer the users the chance to subscribe to these newsgroups internally via the form.

Figure 9.7 shows a sample of how you could implement this type of request into the MAILTO form that has been worked on. The code lines that were added to FORM4.HTM to create the FORM5.HTM containing the check boxes are as follows:

```
<HR>
<P>Select the news groups that you want to have automatically
configured for access.<BR>
<P>
<INPUT TYPE="CHECKBOX" NAME="News_Groups" VALUE="intranet"
CHECKED>intranet <BR>
<INPUT TYPE="CHECKBOX" NAME="News_Groups" VALUE="HTML">HTML <BR>
<INPUT TYPE="CHECKBOX" NAME="News_Groups"
VALUE="Autoconverting">Autoconverting <BR>
<I>Multiple items may be chosen.</I>
<HR>
```

Note the first CHECKBOX item has the attribute CHECKED. This indicates, as you can see in figure 9.7, that the Intranet box is checked initially when you load the form.

Figure 9.7

FORM5.HTM—
Check boxes in
the form.

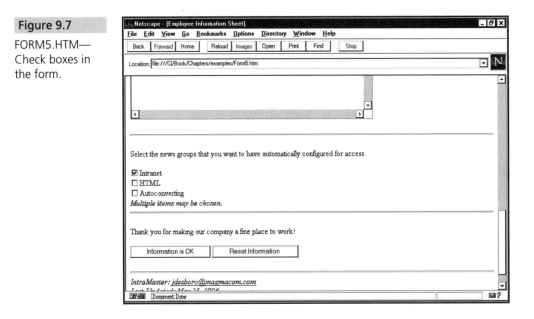

Radio buttons work in somewhat the same fashion as check boxes except that only one can be selected. In your list of items to select, you typically put the "Choose one only" or similar text insert to accompany a radio button grouping. Each option has the same NAME attribute within the logical group. FORM6.HTM is the progression from FORM5.HTM that contains the lines of code that demonstrate how to use this feature. The appropriate lines of code added to create FORM6.HTM are presented next, and the results are shown in figure 9.8.

```
<CENTER>
<P>Would you like to receive all the documents from all the
projects?<BR>
<P><MENU>
<INPUT TYPE="RADIO" NAME="All_Mailings" VALUE="Yes" CHECKED>Yes<BR>
<INPUT TYPE="RADIO" NAME="All_Mailings" VALUE="No" >No<BR>
</MENU>
</CENTER>
```

Figure 9.8

FORM6.HTM—
Radio buttons on
the form.

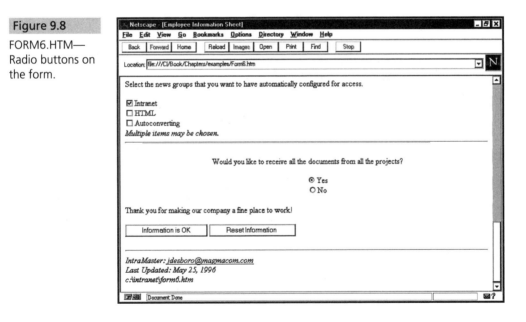

You will also note here that the radio button with the VALUE attribute of Yes is also checked. This indicates that there is a default setting of "Yes" as the value. Note that the NAME attribute is the same in both cases, thus rendering the logic here to "either/or." In addition, the <MENU> tag is used creating a list of items but putting neither bullets nor numbers in front of them. Most likely HTML 3.0 will replace this tag with <UL PLAIN>, but at the moment <MENU> is valid.

Creating a long list of items using checkbox or radio button features may take up more space on the screen than you want to devote to the feature. A list box may be a better alternative. List boxes can be set up to enable the selection of a single item or to enable multiple items to be selected. The lines of code to facilitate the single selection option are shown here:

```
<HR>
<P>Select the Project Team that interests you<BR>
<P><SELECT NAME="Project_Teams">
<OPTION SELECTED> Wide Area Network
<OPTION> Interface Look and Feel
<OPTION> Server Construction
<OPTION> Browser Setup and Testing
<OPTION> Forms and CGI
</SELECT>
```

Note the NAME attribute in the <SELECT> tag—all the options available to this logical grouping are listed here. This example is a single-choice only list—the user scrolls down the list and selects only one option. Note that one OPTION is already SELECTED—this indicates the default setting. The following adaptation, containing the attribute MULTIPLE in the SELECT tag, represents the multichoice list coding:

```
<HR>
<P>Select the Project Team that interests you<BR>
<P><SELECT NAME="Project_Teams" MULTIPLE>
<OPTION SELECTED> Wide Area Network
<OPTION> Interface Look and Feel
<OPTION> Server Construction
```

```
<OPTION> Browser Setup and Testing
<OPTION> Forms and CGI
</SELECT>
<BR>
```

Figure 9.9 shows the FORM7.HTM file with the MULTIPLE selection list box on the screen.

Really Neat Stuff—A Really Quick Introduction

Here is a short script that can be incorporated into the intranet home page that will play a scrolling message to wow your friends and impress the boss. (This book is not about the writing and implementing of JavaScript, so this is probably the only place you will see this done in the book. And now for something completely different!)

```
<SCRIPT LANGUAGE="JavaScript">
<!-- Beginning of JavaScript Applet -----------
/* Copyright 1996 JR Desborough Consulting Services Inc.
```

```
All Rights Reserved.
*/
function roll_bar (start)
{
    var msg = "This message should be rolling across your screen—
change it as you wish";
    var out = " ";
    var c = 1;
    if (150 < start) {
            start--;
            var cmd="roll_bar(" + start + ")";
            timerTwo = window.setTimeout(cmd, 25);
    }
    else if (start <= 150 && 0 < start) {
            for (c=0 ; c < start ; c++) {
                    out+=" ";
            }
            out+=msg;
            start--;
            var cmd="roll_bar(" + start + ")";
                window.status=out;
            timerTwo=window.setTimeout(cmd,25);
    }
    else if (start <= 0) {
            if (-start < msg.length) {
                    out+=msg.substring(-start,msg.length);
                    start--;
            var cmd="roll_bar(" + start + ")";
                    window.status=out;
                    timerTwo=window.setTimeout(cmd,25);
            }
            else {
                    window.status=" ";
                    timerTwo=window.setTimeout("roll_bar(150)",25);
            }
    }
}
// -- End of JavaScript code -------------- -->

</SCRIPT>
<BODY BGCOLOR="FFFFFF"
onLoad="timerONE=window.setTimeout('roll_bar(100)',50);">
```

If you are using a browser that supports JavaScript and Java, you should see the message *"This message should be rolling across your screen— change it as you wish"* rolling across the browser's status bar. Figure 9.10 shows the message scrolling across the bottom of the screen, as seen by Netscape Navigator 2.01. The screen is supposed to be blank, but the pointer is visible in the image, just above the message that rolls across the screen.

Figure 9.10

ROLLBAR.HTML— JavaScript "Rolling status bar" Message.

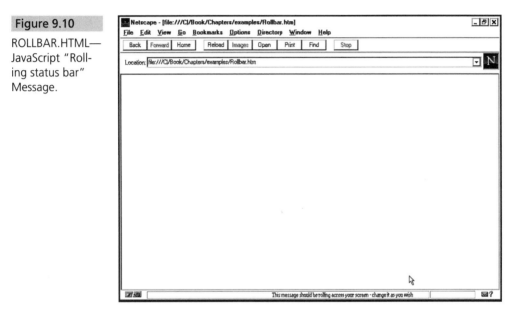

This is but one example of what you can do with JavaScript. However, in setting up the intranet, focus first on getting the information out to the users when they want it. When you have the demand for more and greater functionality in areas such as the use of JavaScript, you should start by bringing in someone to help out and create the initial nuggets of any reusable code.

Status Check

You now have the basic means to collect information from users. Some of the information you want for your own records and research, but most of the forms that will be implemented will be to request data from non-HTML sources. The next two chapters cover the Common

Gateway Interface and Open Database Connectivity—the means to get the information from your form to the query engine of the data collection you are targeting, and the means to get the results displayed back in front of you.

10

Introduction to CGI

The Common Gateway Interface is the meat in the sandwich. Between the HTTP server of the intranet and the other services and resources available, CGI is a set of agreed-upon named variables and conventions for moving information between the browser and the server and back again.

The development work around the CGI took place primarily at the National Center for Supercomputer Applications (NCSA) at the University of Illinois, Urbana-Champaign. In order to provide access to dynamic data through the NCSA HTTPd server in conjunction with the Mosaic browser, a program of some sort was needed. The Common Gateway Interface, currently in version 1.1, was developed to provide access to Unix databases held on the NCSA HTTPd server.

Over the ensuing years, many extensions and variations have been developed by numerous people and organizations, extensions that may or may not work with the browser/server combination within an intranet. The only official definition of CGI is the NCSA version 1.1.

The previous chapter explored the creation of forms and developed a "mailto:" type form that transmitted the input data to the addressee "as-is" and that did not require the use of a CGI program in order to be processed. What was seen from that exercise was a response string that was mailed to a user. The body of the message was a combination of the field name and the user's input.

For the recipient of the e-mail to make use of the information in the response string, the content of the e-mail would have to be read and broken down into the component parts, and then the recipient would perform some action based on receiving the input. In the example used, the requirement to the form was a completed Employee Information Sheet and, therefore, it is probable that the data would have then been added to a database or used to update an existing employee record.

It is possible to automate this process by developing CGI programs that work between the HTML forms and the database. CGI programs can be created to search for, modify, and add new data to databases. In order to work with this data and to manipulate the input string into a format that can be used with a database, CGI programs are created. This chapter will attempt to demystify the CGI experience for you by walking you through the following:

- A brief overview of the CGI including how data is passed using CGI programming.

- The significance of *environment variables* that are passed with each message in CGI programming.

- The two principle methods of passing data from forms to CGI programs (GET and POST), and how the input data is extracted from the environment variables.

- The programming languages that can be used to write CGI programs.

- A discussion of gateway programming for text search and retrieval.

By the end of the chapter you will have created an HTML form to pass data to a CGI program and several CGI programs that display data on the user's screen. You will understand how to extract the input data from the environment variables that are passed between the browser and server. All these skills and understandings are necessary in order to move to the next step of extracting data from a database using CGI programs, which will be covered in Chapter 11, "Integrating ODBC and CGI."

The Common Gateway Interface—What Is it?

The Common Gateway Interface is a standard for interfacing your intranet HTTP server with external applications. Instead of retrieving a static HTML document, the URL might identify a file that contains a program or script that is executed when the user selects the link identified by the URL.

One example of this external nature that is frequently implemented is a page counter program that increases by one each time the file is retrieved. On the Internet, one often sees "You are visitor number XXX,XXX to this site." When you select the link to download this particular page to your browser, the CGI program runs, looks at the number currently stored in a variable in the CGI program file, adds one to the number, and then displays the number within the HTML file that you see.

Another use of external applications can be demonstrated in two phases, the selection and completion of a form in an HTML document. The input data is passed to a CGI program when the user clicks on Submit. Then the CGI program performs whatever activity it has been written to undertake.

Note

Trying to be consistent throughout, both scripts and programs will be referred to as programs for the simple fact that not all programs are scripts but all scripts are programs. A *script* is a type of program that is interpreted at runtime, whereas a *program* is a set of instructions to follow in an prescribed manner.

The basic method of invoking a CGI program is as follows:

1. The user clicks on a link from an HTML page.

2. The browser contacts the server for permission to run the CGI program.

3. If the user has the appropriate permission, the server runs the CGI program (if it actually exists).

4. The output of the CGI program is returned to the browser.

5. The browser displays the output.

Figure 10.1 demonstrates the process. This process assumes that the CGI program is located on the server; however, the CGI program could be located elsewhere.

Figure 10.1

The CGI process.

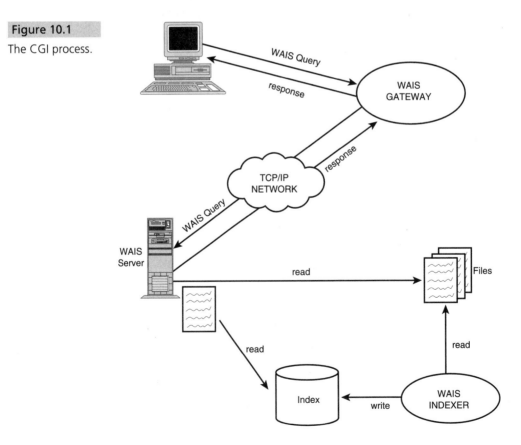

A CGI Example Form

To get your thoughts in order, this chapter is going to work with the form shown in figure 10.2 to develop a simple CGI program that will process the information that your form collects.

Note

Several good publications are devoted to CGI programming, including William Weinman's *The CGI Book* (New Riders, 1996) and Jeff Rowe's *Building Internet Database Servers with CGI* (New Riders, 1996). Because those publications cover CGI programming comprehensively, this book will not go into depth about it. It will take you instead through the process and show you how relatively easy it is to unleash your intranet by enabling your users to communicate with the organization's database applications. This capability extends the utility and functionality of the intranet to better support mission-critical business processes.

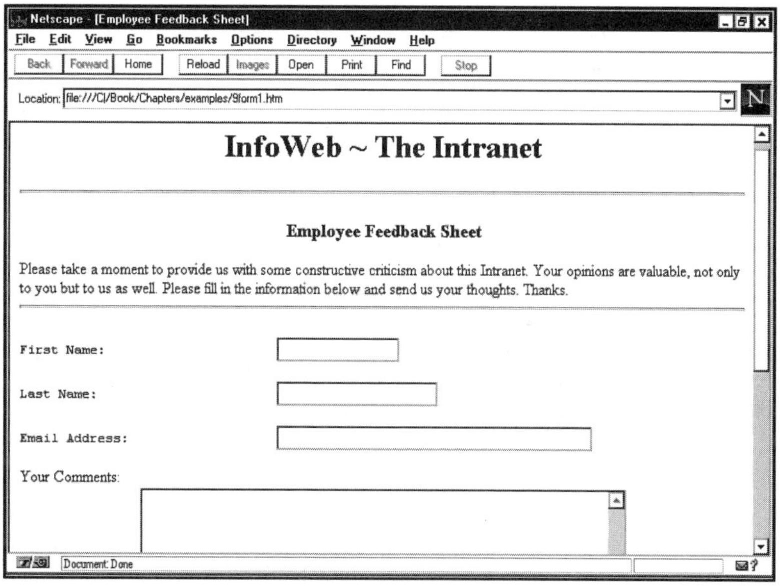

Figure 10.2

Example form for CGI demonstrations.

The form shown in figure 10.2 is similar to the forms developed in Chapter 9. As you see it now, the FORM ACTION is set to be a "mail-to:" type; before the end of this chapter, you will develop and test the capability of the form to send the data input to a CGI program that you will create, which, in turn, sends you back an output message. This sets the stage for the automation of adding data into and extracting data from the databases of your organization, instead of mailing the information to someone else who then has to add the data into the database in question. This automated interaction with databases is explored in Chapter 11.

As a reference point, the HTML code for the form is shown below:

```
<HTML>
<HEAD>
<TITLE>Employee Feedback Sheet</TITLE>
</HEAD>
<BODY BGCOLOR="FFFFFF" TEXT="000000">
<CENTER><H1>InfoWeb ~ The intranet</H1></CENTER>
<HR>
<CENTER><H3>Employee Feedback Sheet</H3>
</CENTER>
<P>
Please take a moment to provide us with some constructive criticism
about this intranet. Your opinions are valuable, not only to you but
to us as well. Please fill in the information below and send us your
thoughts.  Thanks.
<HR>
<FORM ACTION="mailto:jdesboro@magmacom.com" METHOD=POST >
<P><PRE>First Name:<INPUT TYPE="text" NAME="firstname" SIZE=15></PRE>
<P><PRE>Last Name:<INPUT TYPE="text" NAME="lastname" SIZE=20></PRE>
<P><PRE>Email Address:<INPUT TYPE="text" NAME="email" SIZE=40></PRE>
<P>Your Comments:
<CENTER>
<P><TEXTAREA NAME="feedback" ROWS=10 COLS=60></TEXTAREA><P>
</CENTER>
Thank you for making our company a fine place to work!
<P><INPUT TYPE="submit" VALUE="Information is OK"> <INPUT
TYPE="reset" VALUE="Reset Information ">
```

```
</FORM>
<P>
<HR>
<ADDRESS>
<!-- below the email address is changed to the address of the contact
-->
IntraMaster: <A
HREF="mailto:jdesboro@magmacom.com">jdesboro@magmacom.com</A>
<BR>
Last Updated: June 5, 1996
<BR>
c:\intranet\9form1.htm
</ADDRESS>
</BODY>
</HTML>
```

Once completed and submitted, the form returns the following sample e-mail message to the recipient as indicated within the ACTION parameter of the form:

```
firstname=Ennie&lastname=Parson&email=ennie.parson@busint.com&feedback=
I+would+like+to+take+this+opportunity+to+thank+all+those%0D%0Awho+
made+this+possible.++My+wife+Andrea%2C+my+children+Zo%EB+%0D%0Aand
+Evan%2C+Guy+and+his+%22mafia%22+at+Business+Interactive+and+%0D%0Athe
+academy.
```

What you will do is create a CGI program that takes that input stream and sends you back a message in the form of an HTML page, and then breaks the input string into the component parts of fieldname and associated content. The next step is to build the base necessary to be able to do this.

Introduction to CGI Programming Languages

In order to create a CGI program, some form of programming language needs to be used. In this section, and for the remainder of the examples you will see, Perl (Practical Extension and Reporting Language) is the programming language used. Perl was developed as a systems management tool for Unix and is one of the most popular choices for CGI development.

According to available literature, over 60 percent of servers on the Internet are operating on some flavor of Unix. Within the intranet market, Windows NT is starting to challenge Unix for dominance. Depending on the type of operating system you choose to run, your choices for programming languages range from Perl to C to Visual Basic to *shell scripts* (a type of programming language) of which the Bourne Shell (sh) is the common denominator. Perl and C tend to be widely used because of their inherent robust functions—Perl for built-in operators and functions and C for its system-level operations to create powerful applications using minimal resources.

As this book is being written, Java is gaining a lot of popularity as the "language of the future" that will probably make CGI programming as it is known today obsolete. Until that happens, this book will focus on Perl for its examples.

There are some basic things to remember when choosing a CGI programming language:

- The language should be supported by the operating system behind your HTTP server.

- The language has to be robust enough to allow you to write CGI programs that perform the tasks you desire.

- You have to be comfortable enough with the language to program proficiently—you can always hire out this part of the job, but it helps to understand exactly what is going on in the background.

Later on in this chapter, a brief discussion will show you examples of Perl, sh, and C programs and examine the similarities of the programming among the languages.

Basics of Passing Data

In order to start down the road of passing data, here is a very simple program written in Perl, fitting for a first attempt:

```
#!/usr/local/bin/perl

# File: firstscript.perl.cgi
# (c) 1996 John Desborough

print "Content-type: text/html\n\n";

# Because this comes back as HTML we put into a format
# that is understandable, including a title
print "<HTML><HEAD><TITLE>First Script Response</TITLE></HEAD>\n";

# And now the body of the HTML page we will see returned
print "<BODY><H1>My First Script</H1><HR>Congratulations! You pro-
grammed your first CGI script!</BODY></HTML>\n";
```

The purpose of the program is to have the CGI program send a message back to the browser when the program is invoked. In order to explain the anatomy of the code, here are a few words about the program written in Perl:

- The first line of the Perl script must specify where on the server the Perl interpreter can be found.

- Lines that start with # are comments and are not acted upon by the Perl interpreter.

- The Print command sends the text to the standard output.

- The text strings are enclosed in quotes.

- Required *newlines* are indicated by "\n."

- All statements in Perl must end with a semicolon (;).

This is an example of how the CGI program causes the server to pass information back to the user's browser. In order to invoke this CGI program, the hyperlink that calls the CGI program has to be placed within an HTML file, and a user would have to click on the hyperlink. The CGI program file needs to be placed on the server so the users can activate the hyperlink pointing to the program.

There are several ways to get the CGI program file onto the server. Using the File Transfer Protocol (FTP) to transfer the CGI program is the most popular method unless your server is connected to the LAN and you have access to copy the CGI program file into the appropriate directory. The /usr/cgi-bin directory is the most common place for the CGI files to be stored.

Invoking the CGI Program

As was mentioned in the previous section, the simplest method to invoke this CGI program and others is to put a hyperlink into your HTML document that calls the CGI program. If a form is being used to pass data to the CGI program, as will be developed during this chapter, the FORM ACTION attribute calls the CGI program when the Submit button is clicked.

Using a variation of the template file you developed for the creation of your home page, create a page from which you can test CGI programs. The hyperlink that is created for the first CGI program is embedded in the HTML document as follows:

```
Invoke the simple Perl script: <A HREF="usr/cgi-bin/
firstscript.perl.cgi">firstscript.perl.cgi</A><BR>
```

Figure 10.3 shows the HTML page that has been adapted for this purpose. The HTML code behind the page, containing that code line, follows.

Figure 10.3

CGI test page.

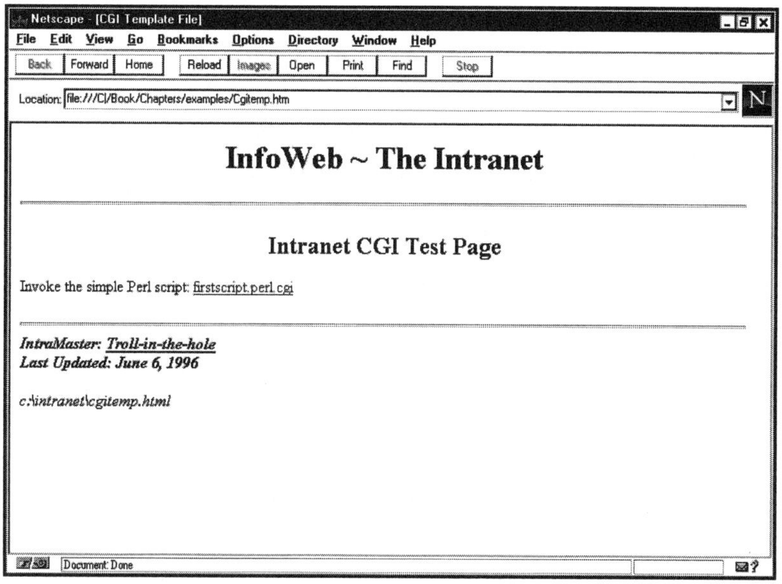

And here is the code:

```
<HTML>
<HEAD>
<TITLE>CGI Template File</TITLE>
</HEAD>
<BODY  BGCOLOR=#FFFFFF TEXT="#000000">
<CENTER><H1>InfoWeb ~ The intranet</H1></CENTER>
<HR>
<CENTER>
<H2>intranet CGI Test Page</H2>
</CENTER>
Invoke the simple Perl script: <A HREF="usr/
cgi-bin/firstscript.perl.cgi">firstscript.perl.cgi</A><BR>
<P>
<HR>
<ADDRESS>
<B>IntraMaster: <A HREF="mailto:jdesboro@magmacom.com">Troll-in-the-
hole</A>
<BR>
Last Updated: June 6, 1996</B>
c:\intranet\cgitemp.html
</ADDRESS>
</BODY>
</HTML>
```

As you can see in figure 10.4, the results are returned in an HTML page that is displayed by your browser.

Note

For your convenience, the HTML files and the CGI Programs are included on the CD included in the book. You may have to make minor edits to the CGI files and the HTML files in order to incorporate your intranet structure and naming conventions.

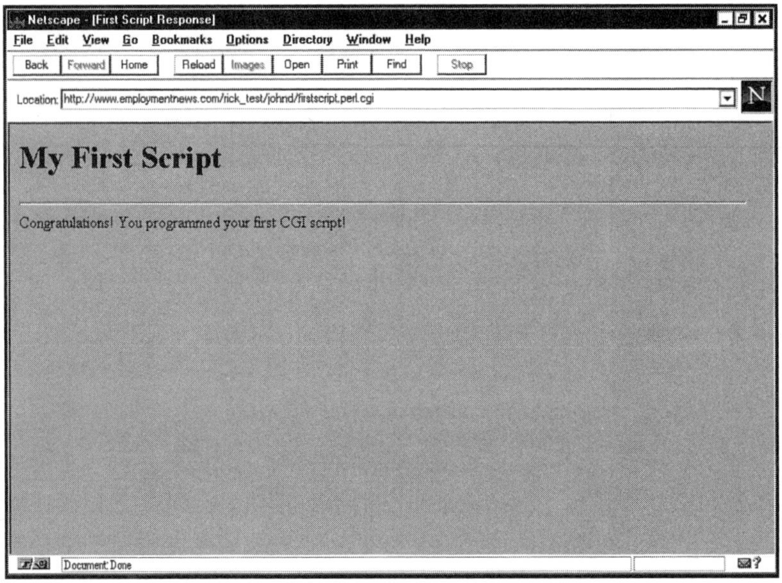

Figure 10.4

First CGI Script results in Netscape Navigator.

This should now give you the basic idea of how to create a program in Perl and create the link on the intranet's HTML page in order to call the CGI program from the server. This has been a simple but valuable start. Move on to find out how the input is actually bundled up and moved between the browser and CGI program.

Environment Variables—Understanding the Basics

The HTTP server (the intranet server) sets up a bunch of environment variables whenever a CGI program is called. Data can be passed to a

CGI program through the use of these environment variables. Not all environment variables pertain to all browsers, servers, sites, and so on. Some programs, including CGI programs, look at these environment variables to ascertain the values therein, including the data input into a form by the user. In some cases a default value will be used if the variable does not exist in the environment; at other times the program may fail until you set the variable.

Once you are familiar with the environment variables that exist and what information these variables pass to the server, Perl programs will be created to utilize the information contained therein. Table 10.1 outlines some of the variables that are passed by the HTTP server.

Table 10.1

Environment Variables from HTTP Server

Variable	Brief Description
AUTH_TYPE	contains the authentication method used to validate the user
CONTENT_LENGTH	number of bytes of data
CONTENT_TYPE	used for POST queries and contains the MIME type of the data as *type/subtype*
GATEWAY_INTERFACE	contains the CGI revision specification, for example CGI 1.1
HTTP_ACCEPT	contains the MIME formats that the browser can accept in *type/subtype, type/subtype,...* format
HTTP_REFERER	contains the last page the user accessed before arriving at the page
HTTP_USER_AGENT	contains the name and version number of the user's browser as *name/version library/version*; may contain information about any proxy gateways through which the user may be passing

continues

Table 10.1

Environment Variables from HTTP Server, continued

Variable	Brief Description
PATH_INFO	contains additional path information to the CGI application that is not necessarily recognized by the HTTP server
PATH_TRANSLATED	contains the PATH_INFO appended to document root path of the server
QUERY_STRING	most common method of passing information to CGI program, usually indicated by adding "?" followed by additional information in the URL: http://www.busint.com/cgi/showme.cgi?subscription.com—creating the variable value of subscription.com. The QUERY_STRING variable is never encoded or decoded before it is received by the CGI program
REMOTE_ADDR	contains the IP address of the user
REMOTE_HOST	may contain the text-equivalent host name of the address; many servers turn off the feature because it reduces performance in having to send requests to the DNS server for the host name; most often it is blank or filled in with value of REMOTE_ADDR
REQUEST_METHOD	contains the method used for the request, usually POST or GET
SCRIPT_NAME	contains the file name of the CGI program
SERVER_NAME	contains the server's host name, DNS alias, or IP address
SERVER_PORT	contains the number of the port through which the request came

Environment Variables from HTTP Server, continued

Variable	Brief Description
SERVER_PROTOCOL	contains the name and revision number of the protocol the request comes in from, in the format *protocol/revision*
SERVER_SOFTWARE	contains the name and version of the server software

Programming with Perl to Display Environmental Variables

To provide you with a little practice in writing another Perl program, and to show how the environment variables pass data, you will create your second Perl program to have the server display the values stored within the environment variables. The code for this program is shown below.

```
#!/usr/local/bin/perl

# Filename: printvars.perl.cgi
# (c) 1996 John Desborough

print "Content-type: text/plain\n\n";

#display the CGI environment variables
print qq(AUTH_TYPE = $ENV{"AUTH_TYPE"}\n);
print qq(CONTENT_LENGTH = $ENV{"CONTENT_LENGTH"}\n);
print qq(CONTENT_TYPE = $ENV{"CONTENT_TYPE"}\n);
print qq(GATEWAY_INTERFACE = $ENV{"GATEWAY_INTERFACE"}\n);
print qq(HTTP_ACCEPT = $ENV{"HTTP_ACCEPT"}\n);
print qq(HTTP_REFERER = $ENV{"HTTP_REFERER"}\n);
print qq(HTTP_USER_AGENT = $ENV{"HTTP_USER_AGENT"}\n);
print qq(PATH_INFO = $ENV{"PATH_INFO"}\n);
print qq(PATH_TRANSLATED = $ENV{"PATH_TRANSLATED"}\n);
print qq(QUERY_STRING = $ENV{"QUERY_STRING"}\n);
print qq(REMOTE_ADDR = $ENV{"REMOTE_ADDR"}\n);
print qq(REMOTE_HOST = $ENV{"REMOTE_HOST"}\n);
print qq(REQUEST_METHOD = $ENV{"REQUEST_METHOD"}\n);
print qq(SCRIPT_NAME = $ENV{"SCRIPT_NAME"}\n);
print qq(SERVER_NAME = $ENV{"SERVER_NAME"}\n);
```

```
print qq(SERVER_PORT = $ENV{"SERVER_PORT"}\n);
print qq(SERVER_PROTOCOL = $ENV{"SERVER_PROTOCOL"}\n);
print qq(SERVER_SOFTWARE = $ENV{"SERVER_SOFTWARE"}\n);
```

In order to activate this CGI program, a hyperlink was created and placed on the HTML page "CGI Test Page," created as cgitemp.html (the files are available on the CD that comes with the book). Selecting this link causes the following to be returned to the browser, as shown in figure 10.5.

Figure 10.5

CGI environment variables returned (Perl).

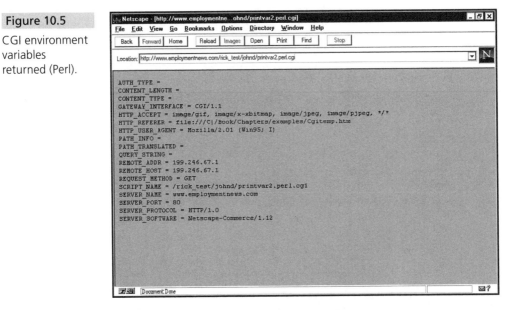

<table>
<tr><td>Note</td></tr>
</table>

You may have noticed a slight difference between the program listing and the program previously created. If you look closely at the Print commands, you will see that in the latter case qq(......) is used instead of putting the entire string in double quotes (" "). This is a Perl directive that means to treat the following character as a double quote and, in many cases, is used to reduce the confusion between single and double quotes. You *could not*, for example, write the character sequence as follows:

```
"SERVER_SOFTWARE = $ENV{"SERVER_SOFTWARE"}\n";
```

> Variables will be expanded from within a string if the string is enclosed in double quotes—but you cannot use double quotes within double quotes.

Defining Standard Input

Using HTML forms to pass data from text fields, check boxes, radio buttons, and text areas implies the use of *standard input* (stdin) to send the information to the HTTP server. By default, standard input is the method that the user employs to input data into any program, or, in the case of the intranet browser, the terminal used. Once you enter the information requested by the program, it is passed to the server via standard input. Standard input is simply a data channel for connecting an input device to a running program.

The HTTP server of the intranet is one example of a running program—it takes the data entered by the user and sends it off to the CGI program. The results of the CGI program are returned via standard output. *Standard output* (stdout) is how the output stream comes to the user's computer. The HTTP server does not process the arguments you pass to the CGI program—the arguments arrive at the server encoded the way the browser sent them.

Although the significance of this is not yet apparent, when the section on the GET and POST methods of FORM ACTION are discussed, the use of standard input becomes clearer.

Fundamentals of CGI Programming

Now that you have created a program that returns the environment variables to the screen, how can you tell if there are any data there for you to work with? And how do you deal with the data?

If you take a quick look back at figure 10.5, you will notice that the CONTENT_LENGTH, CONTENT_TYPE, and QUERY_STRING variables are empty—nothing in the way of data has been passed into these variables. This book has already talked briefly, in Chapter 9,

"Beyond Basic HTML: Forms and Information Handling," about the GET and POST methods of passing input to the CGI program, so start there. This section will contain these topics:

- A more in-depth discussion about GET and POST

- Breaking the input out of the environment variables

At the end of this section, you will be able to create a Perl-based CGI program to separate the input data from the environment variables from forms that use the GET and the POST method of passing the data to the CGI program.

Understanding GET and POST

Take a look at the GET and POST methods for a few moments and see what the difference is between them. This example will work with the code listing that was presented back at the beginning of the chapter, the mailto: form that had been developed for figure 10.2. Within the HTML code, the following line was found:

```
<FORM ACTION="mailto:jdesboro@magmacom.com" METHOD=POST >
```

This example will use the same HTML page to test the GET and POST method by changing the <FORM ACTION= > combined with the use of the two methods to show you the differences between each. But first, you must create the actual CGI program that will be used to show the variables passed to the server. The following Perl program is created to work with the forms:

```
#!/usr/local/bin/perl

# Filename: form.feedback.perl.cgi
# (c) John Desborough 1996
```

```
print "Content-type: text/plain\n\n";
print "This is the form.feedback.perl.cgi program output\n";

#display the CGI environment variables
print qq(HTTP_USER_AGENT = $ENV{"HTTP_USER_AGENT"}\n);
print qq(REQUEST_METHOD = $ENV{"REQUEST_METHOD"}\n);
print qq(SCRIPT_NAME = $ENV{"SCRIPT_NAME"}\n);
print qq(QUERY_STRING = $ENV{"QUERY_STRING"}\n);
print qq(REMOTE_HOST = $ENV{"REMOTE_HOST"}\n);
print qq(REMOTE_ADDR = $ENV{"REMOTE_ADDR"}\n);
print qq(CONTENT_TYPE = $ENV{"CONTENT_TYPE"}\n);
print qq(CONTENT_LENGTH = $ENV{"CONTENT_LENGTH"}\n);
print qq(GATEWAY_INTERFACE = $ENV{"GATEWAY_INTERFACE"}\n);
```

This program is invoked when the Submit button is clicked on either of the forms shown in the following two figures. Figure 10.6 shows the form that contains the <FORM METHOD=GET ....> tag, as is shown on the face of the form; figure 10.7 shows the form that uses the POST method.

Figure 10.6

HTML form for GET CGI program.

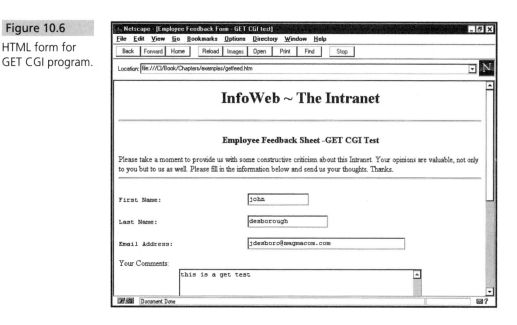

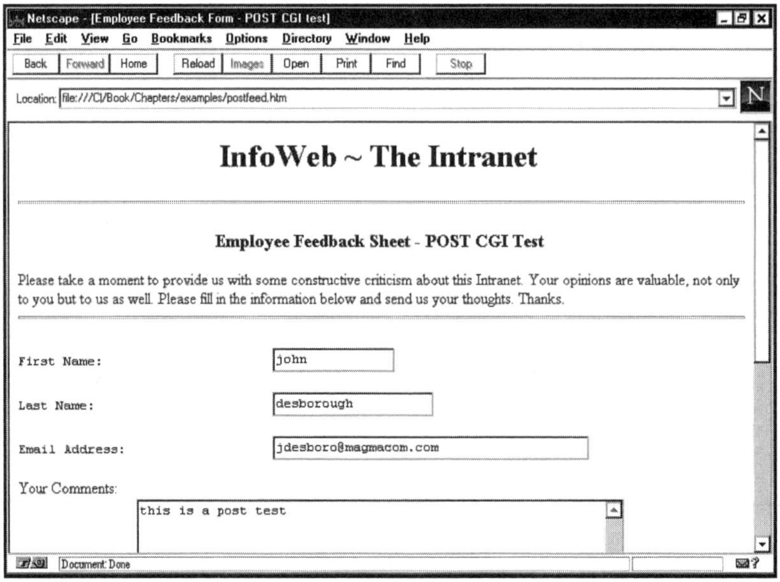

Figure 10.7

HTML form
for POST CGI
program.

As you can see from the two forms, you can't tell the difference from the outside other than the headings that tell you which method you are using.

The results returned by the programs, however, are different. Figure 10.8 shows the results of the CGI program replying to the GET method submission. You will notice in the Location window of the browser that the address for the CGI program is followed by a "?" and the input from the form is in the format of a *name=value* pair. This is known as the QUERY_STRING and is displayed in the list of environment variables returned to the browser.

Figure 10.9, the results of the POST method, does not have a QUERY_STRING variable, but it does have CONTENT_TYPE and CONTENT_LENGTH variables. The GET method, however, did not have CONTENT_TYPE and CONTENT_LENGTH variables. The CONTENT_LENGTH variable, as previously stated, contains the number of bytes of information in the input stream. The CONTENT_TYPE indicates the MIME type as *application/x-www-form-urlencoded*.

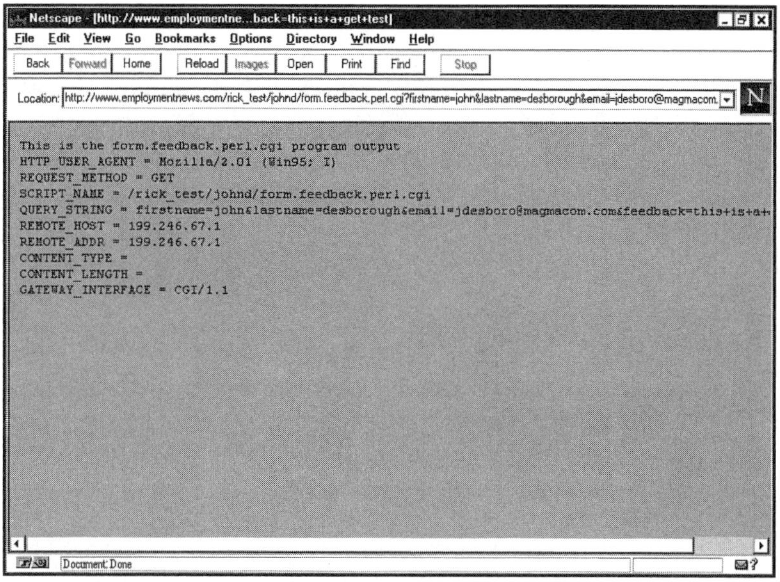
Netscape - [http://www.employmentne...back=this+is+a+get+test]
File Edit View Go Bookmarks Options Directory Window Help
Back Forward Home Reload Images Open Print Find Stop
Location: http://www.employmentnews.com/rick_test/johnd/form.feedback.perl.cgi?firstname=john&lastname=desborough&email=jdesboro@magmacom.
This is the form.feedback.perl.cgi program output
HTTP_USER_AGENT = Mozilla/2.01 (Win95; I)
REQUEST_METHOD = GET
SCRIPT_NAME = /rick_test/johnd/form.feedback.perl.cgi
QUERY_STRING = firstname=john&lastname=desborough&email=jdesboro@magmacom.com&feedback=this+is+a+
REMOTE_HOST = 199.246.67.1
REMOTE_ADDR = 199.246.67.1
CONTENT_TYPE =
CONTENT_LENGTH =
GATEWAY_INTERFACE = CGI/1.1
Document: Done

Figure 10.8

Environment variables returned by GET Method.

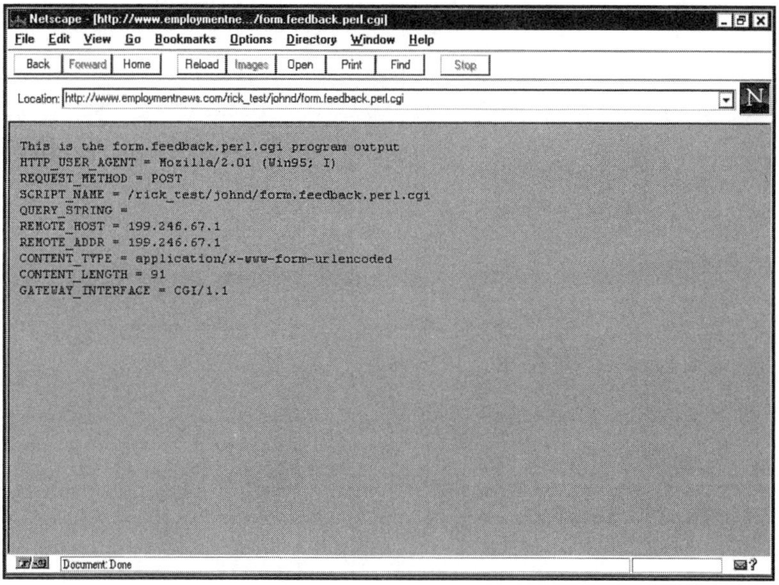
Netscape - [http://www.employmentne.../form.feedback.perl.cgi]
File Edit View Go Bookmarks Options Directory Window Help
Back Forward Home Reload Images Open Print Find Stop
Location: http://www.employmentnews.com/rick_test/johnd/form.feedback.perl.cgi
This is the form.feedback.perl.cgi program output
HTTP_USER_AGENT = Mozilla/2.01 (Win95; I)
REQUEST_METHOD = POST
SCRIPT_NAME = /rick_test/johnd/form.feedback.perl.cgi
QUERY_STRING =
REMOTE_HOST = 199.246.67.1
REMOTE_ADDR = 199.246.67.1
CONTENT_TYPE = application/x-www-form-urlencoded
CONTENT_LENGTH = 91
GATEWAY_INTERFACE = CGI/1.1
Document: Done

Figure 10.9

Environment variables returned by POST Method.

Again, the significance of the manner in which the input data is delivered to the CGI program is not readily apparent. However, there may be instances when the input data that the form is passing to the CGI program needs to be secure, as in a user identification name. If the GET method is used to pass this information, anyone seeing the input data string in the Location window of the browser would see the user identification name displayed in the input string following the "?." Using the POST method is slightly more secure in that the input is not readily visible. Someone would have to intercept the data and then break out the input from the environment variables.

Breaking Out the Input from Environment Variables

This now brings you to the point where you are able to create forms and CGI programs that provide you with form content as an e-mail message, a QUERY_STRING environment variable, and an input stream of a specified CONTENT_LENGTH and CONTENT_TYPE. In all cases, the input from the form is in an input string or stream of name/value pairs. To be able to make any use of this input data, you must now separate these name/value pairs—break them out of the environment variables—in order to be able to do something "intelligent" with the input.

As has been discussed earlier in the chapter, GET and POST methods deliver the input data to the CGI program in different fashions. The remainder of this section covers two actions:

- Retrieving the input data from the GET method

- Retrieving the input data from the POST method

Retrieving the Input Data from the GET Method

Review the returned variables in figure 10.8, focusing especially on the QUERY_STRING variable. You need to take the content of the variable and break it out into meaningful name/value pairs.

To do that, create a simple Perl program that employs the *split* function to separate the individual components, and then follow with the creation of the associative array of the input elements. This array will be used for further processing of the data.

```perl
#!/usr/local/bin/perl

# Filename: breakout.get.perl.cgi
# (c) John Desborough 1996

print "Content-type: text/plain\n\n";
print "CGI program filename: breakout.get.perl.cgi\n";
print "To demonstrate the breakout of input\n\n";

#display the CGI environment variables
print qq(HTTP_USER_AGENT = $ENV{"HTTP_USER_AGENT"}\n);
print qq(REQUEST_METHOD = $ENV{"REQUEST_METHOD"}\n);
print qq(SCRIPT_NAME = $ENV{"SCRIPT_NAME"}\n);
print qq(QUERY_STRING = $ENV{"QUERY_STRING"}\n);
print qq(REMOTE_HOST = $ENV{"REMOTE_HOST"}\n);
print qq(REMOTE_ADDR = $ENV{"REMOTE_ADDR"}\n);
print qq(CONTENT_TYPE = $ENV{"CONTENT_TYPE"}\n);
print qq(CONTENT_LENGTH = $ENV{"CONTENT_LENGTH"}\n);
print qq(GATEWAY_INTERFACE = $ENV{"GATEWAY_INTERFACE"}\n);

# copy the contents of the QUERY_STRING into a variable
$breakqs = $ENV{"QUERY_STRING"};

# break up the input stream into an array using "&" character
@breakqs = split(/&/,$breakqs);

foreach $i (0 .. $#breakqs)
  {
  # now we convert the plus characters to spaces
  $breakqs[$i] =~ s/\+/ /g;

  # convert the hex characters to alphanumeric
  $breakqs =~ s/%(..)/pack("c",hex($1))/ge;

  # separate into the name/value pairs
  ($name, $value) = split(/=/,$breakqs[$i],2);
```

```
# establish the associative elements
$breakqs{$name} = $value;
}

print "\nVariables listing:\n\n";

for each $name (sort keys(%breakqs))
  { print "$name=", $breakqs{$name}, "\n" }
```

Figure 10.10 shows the output resulting from the CGI program, as seen in the browser, with the form completed as in the previous example.

Figure 10.10

QUERY_STRING variable breakout from GET input.

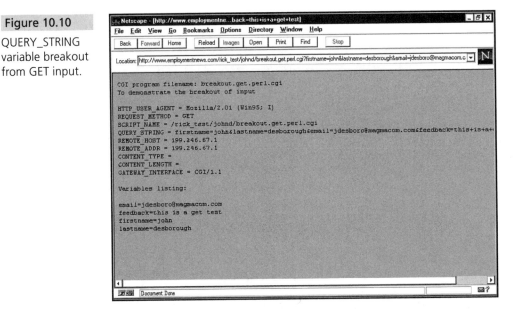

Having been able to obtain the name/value pairings from the input data, you are set for the work in Chapter 11 where the name portion of the name/value pair corresponds to a fieldname in the database. After the CGI program has been able to break the input data out from the environment variables, the input data, in the name/value pairing, as shown in figure 10.10, can be used to enter into or extract data from a database.

Retrieving the Input Data from the POST Method

Now for the other half of the dynamic duo, POST. Please refer to figure 10.9, the listing of environment variables returned by the POST program. There is no QUERY_STRING variable, but you do have the CONTENT_TYPE and CONTENT_LENGTH to work with.

The CGI program developed here will be very similar to that for the GET method with the exception that you will get the data input from the standard input device instead of the QUERY_STRING variable. Keep in mind that you will have to read exactly the number of bytes of the stdin as indicated in the CONTENT_LENGTH variable because it is not guaranteed that there will be an end-of-file marker in the data stream. Once you have the data input from stdin, break it out in the same fashion as for the GET program above. The CGI program you will use is as follows:

```perl
#!/usr/local/bin/perl

# Filename: breakout.post.perl.cgi
# (c) John Desborough 1996

print "Content-type: text/plain\n\n";
print "CGI program filename: breakout.post.perl.cgi\n";
print "To demonstrate the breakout of input\n\n";

#display the CGI environment variables
print qq(HTTP_USER_AGENT = $ENV{"HTTP_USER_AGENT"}\n);
print qq(REQUEST_METHOD = $ENV{"REQUEST_METHOD"}\n);
print qq(SCRIPT_NAME = $ENV{"SCRIPT_NAME"}\n);
print qq(QUERY_STRING = $ENV{"QUERY_STRING"}\n);
print qq(REMOTE_HOST = $ENV{"REMOTE_HOST"}\n);
print qq(REMOTE_ADDR = $ENV{"REMOTE_ADDR"}\n);
print qq(CONTENT_TYPE = $ENV{"CONTENT_TYPE"}\n);
print qq(CONTENT_LENGTH = $ENV{"CONTENT_LENGTH"}\n);
print qq(GATEWAY_INTERFACE = $ENV{"GATEWAY_INTERFACE"}\n);

# create working variables for type and length
$type = $ENV{"CONTENT_TYPE"};
$long = $ENV{"CONTENT_LENGTH"};
```

```perl
# make sure the content type is acceptable for processing
if($type ne "application/x-www-form-urlencoded")
  {
  print "Invalid content-type: %s\n", $type;
  exit 1;
  }

# read the contents of stdin into a variable
read(STDIN, $breakqs, $long);

# break up the input stream into an array using "&" character
@breakqs = split(/&/,$breakqs);

foreach $i (0 .. $#breakqs)
  {
  # now we convert the plus characters to spaces
  $breakqs[$i] =~ s/\+/ /g;

  # convert the hex characters to alphanumeric
  $breakqs =~ s/%(..)/pack("c",hex($1))/ge;

  # separate into the name/value pairs
  ($name, $value) = split(/=/,$breakqs[$i],2);

  # establish the associative elements
  $breakqs{$name} = $value;
  }

print "\nVariables listing:\n\n";

foreach $name (sort keys(%breakqs))
  { print "$name=", $breakqs{$name}, "\n" }
```

Figure 10.11 shows the environment variables and the name/value pairs that are associated with the data input stream. The input values are the same as for figure 10.9 (as seen in figure 10.7).

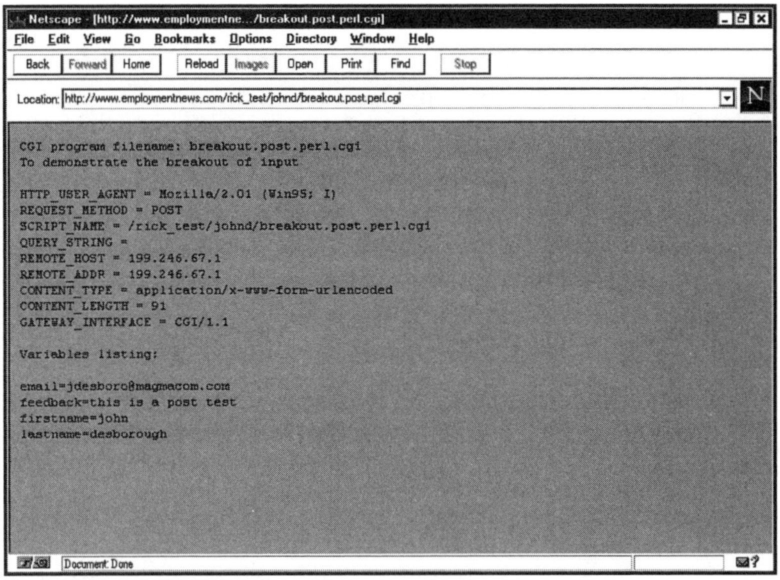

Figure 10.11

Variable breakout from POST input.

```
Netscape - [http://www.employmentne.../breakout.post.perl.cgi]
File   Edit   View   Go   Bookmarks   Options   Directory   Window   Help

Back   Forward   Home      Reload   Images   Open   Print   Find      Stop

Location: http://www.employmentnews.com/rick_test/johnd/breakout.post.perl.cgi


CGI program filename: breakout.post.perl.cgi
To demonstrate the breakout of input

HTTP_USER_AGENT = Mozilla/2.01 (Win95; I)
REQUEST_METHOD = POST
SCRIPT_NAME = /rick_test/johnd/breakout.post.perl.cgi
QUERY_STRING =
REMOTE_HOST = 199.246.67.1
REMOTE_ADDR = 199.246.67.1
CONTENT_TYPE = application/x-www-form-urlencoded
CONTENT_LENGTH = 91
GATEWAY_INTERFACE = CGI/1.1

Variables listing:

email=jdeaboro@magmacom.com
feedback=this is a post test
firstname=john
lastname=desborough


Document: Done
```

Using Perl Libraries

This now gives you two CGI programs to break out the name/value pairs from the input stream. In the next chapter, you will see how to integrate this ability with queries to a database. But is there a better, more efficient way to implement these two CGI programs you have just created? By bringing in the concept of a library of Perl programs or subprograms, routine operations, such as obtaining the input data in the appropriate name/value pairs, can be reused by many CGI programs. This section of the chapter describes how a library of Perl routines is used to facilitate the creation of the CGI program.

Tying it Together with cgi-lib.pl

Having separate CGI programs to break out the name/value pairs works, but there is a more efficient way to do this. Instead of creating a new CGI program every time you need to extract the input data, consider creating a library of stored reusable programs, or subprograms, that perform a generic function, such as extracting input data from the environment variables.

As you can do in many other programming languages, there are ways to create libraries of routines for Perl. The simplest is to review and test someone else's library first to get a feel for what is required.

Here you will utilize a library of Perl routines that has already been created. Within the CGI program that is created for the example in this part of the chapter, the library is referenced by inserting the following line into the CGI program you will see shortly:

```
require "cgi-lib.pl";
```

Many programmers use Steven Brenner's library, cgi-lib.pl, to process information sent to CGI programs. Brenner also has co-authored a book, *Introduction to CGI/Perl* (MIS:PRESS), that is an excellent source of knowledge and tips on how to use the cgi-lib.pl library. Brenner's book also covers the details of creating your own library. Following this discussion of the use of the cgi-lib.pl library, a brief discussion is held showing you how to create a library of Perl routines.

Note

You will find a copy of Steven Brenner's library on the CD. For a complete list of what is on the CD, see Appendix D, "What's on the CD."

Like many other texts on this subject, this section will share the Read-Parse() function of this library with you. This function first determines the method by which the browser is communicating, and then breaks out the input into the name/value pair associative array called "%in." Here is a quick example of how these features are used to process the form data to close this section.

The ReadParse() function by Steven Brenner is seen in the following:

```
#!/usr/local/bin/perl -- -*- C -*-

# Perl Routines to Manipulate CGI input
# S.E.Brenner@bioc.cam.ac.uk
# $Header: /cys/people/seb1005/http/cgi-bin/RCS/cgi-lib.pl,v 1.7
1994/11/04 00:17:17 seb1005 Exp $
```

```
#
# Copyright 1994 Steven E. Brenner
# Unpublished work.
# Permission granted to use and modify this library so long as the
# copyright above is maintained, modifications are documented, and
# credit is given for any use of the library.
#
# Thanks are due to many people for reporting bugs and suggestions
# especially Meng Weng Wong, Maki Watanabe, Bo Frese Rasmussen,
# Andrew Dalke, Mark-Jason Dominus and Dave Dittrich.


# see http://www.seas.upenn.edu/~mengwong/forms/    or
#      http://www.bio.cam.ac.uk/web/ for more information


# ReadParse
# Reads in GET or POST data, converts it to unescaped text, and puts
# one key=value in each member of the list "@in"
# Also creates key/value pairs in %in, using '\0' to separate mul-
tiple
# selections

# If a variable-glob parameter (e.g., *cgi_input) is passed to
ReadParse,
# information is stored there, rather than in $in, @in, and %in.

sub ReadParse {
    local (*in) = @_ if @_;


    local ($i, $loc, $key, $val);

    # Read in text
    if ($ENV{'REQUEST_METHOD'} eq "GET") {
    $in = $ENV{'QUERY_STRING'};
    } elsif ($ENV{'REQUEST_METHOD'} eq "POST") {
    read(STDIN,$in,$ENV{'CONTENT_LENGTH'});
    }

    @in = split(/&/,$in);
```

```
foreach $i (0 .. $#in) {
    # Convert plus's to spaces
    $in[$i] =~ s/\+/ /g;

    # Split into key and value.
    ($key, $val) = split(/=/,$in[$i],2); # splits on the first =.

    # Convert %XX from hex numbers to alphanumeric
    $key =~ s/%(..)/pack("c",hex($1))/ge;
    $val =~ s/%(..)/pack("c",hex($1))/ge;

    # Associate key and value
    $in{$key} .= "\0" if (defined($in{$key})); # \0 is the multiple
    separator
    $in{$key} .= $val;

}

return 1; # just for fun
}
```

If you examine the code closely you will see that it is very similar to the code you created for your GET and POST examples earlier. What the use of this component of the library does for you is eliminate the need to create CGI programs for each GET and POST operation that you create. The ReadParse() subroutine evaluates the environment variables to determine the method (GET or POST) used and then performs the appropriate process relative to the method used. This library subroutine can be used over and over to break the input data out of the environment variables for use within further processing. This will save you countless hours in writing and testing Perl programs to perform this task within different applications.

Now in order to bring all of the fundamentals you have developed into a meaningful package, bring back an "Employee Feedback Form," shown in figure 10.12.

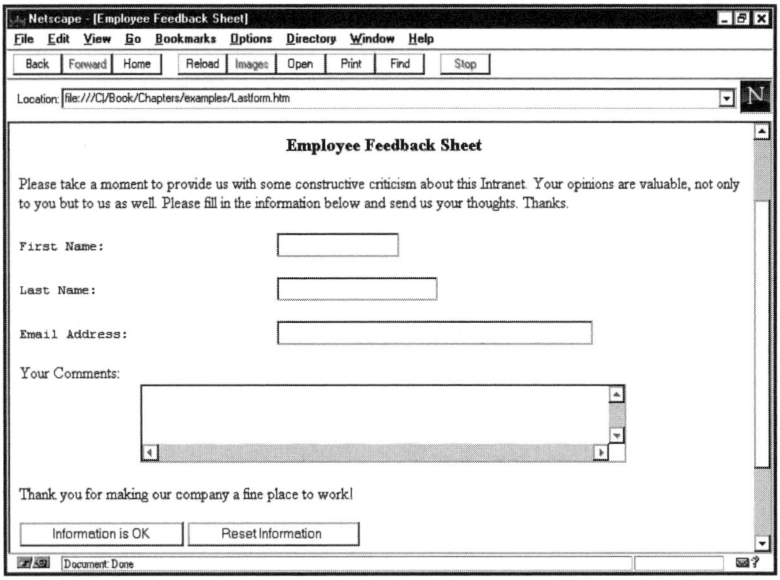

Figure 10.12

Employee feedback form—tying it together.

When the user clicks the Information is OK button, the Perl program *intranet.feedback.perl.cgi* is called up. The source code for this program is as follows:

```
#!/usr/local/bin/perl

# Filename: intranet.feedback.perl.cgi
# (c) John Desborough 1996

# Use Steven Brenner's library
require "cgi-lib.pl";

# Print the standard html header - from Brenner's library
print &PrintHeader();

#Read data from standard input and put it in associative array
&ReadParse();

# Use the name/value pairs generated to verify minimum user
# input has been provided
if ( !$in{"lastname"} || !$in{"firstname"} || !$in{"email"} )
   {
```

```
        print "<HEAD><TITLE>intranet Feedback Form</TITLE></HEAD>";
        print "<BODY><H1>Not Enough Information</H1><HR><BR>";
        print "You must fill in your name and email address. Thanks.<BR>";
        exit 1;
        }

# So what are we going to do with the feedback? we can send it to the
# IntraMaster using the following technique to create quasi unique
# mail messages for the user
$message = "IntraMaster:\n\n";
$message .= "Our employee, ";
$message .= "$in{\"firstname\"} " if $in{"firstname"};
$message .= "$in{\"lastname\"}, " if $in{"lastname"};
$message .= "whose email address is: \n$in{\"email\"}," if
$in{"email"};
$message .= "\nprovides the following feedback about our
intranet:\n\n";
$message .= $in{"feedback"} if $in{"feedback"};

$unique = time + rand;
$mail_file = "/tmp/tempfile.".$unique;

open(DUMMY, ">mail_file");
print DUMMY $message;
close(DUMMY);

system("/bin/mail -s \"intranet Feedback\" http < $mail_file");

unlink($mail_file);

# Being kind and gentle people we will compose a response to our
# employee, thanking them for their input
$reply = "Thanks, ";
$reply .= "$in{\"firstname\"} " if $in{"firstname"};
$reply .= "$in{\"lastname\"}." if $in{"lastname"};
$reply .= "<BR>The following message was emailed to the IntraMaster.
";
$reply .= "Our employees make this company a great place to work ";
$reply .= "and we promise to respond to your comments within 48
hours.";
```

```
# Now we create the HTML page to respond to our user and show the
email # that was sent to the IntraMaster

print "<HEAD><TITLE>intranet Feedback</TITLE></HEAD>";
print "<BODY><H1>Thanks for your feedback!</H1><P>";
print "$reply";
print "<P>*** The following message was sent to the IntraMaster
***<BR>";
print "<PRE>";
print "$message";
print "</PRE>";
print "*** End of the message ***";
```

The program thanks the user for the input and allows the user to see the content of the e-mail message before sending it to the IntraMaster. Figure 10.13 shows the response to the user, as viewed through the browser.

Figure 10.13

Response form—
tying it together.

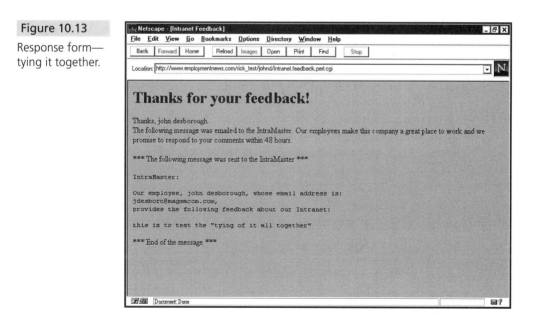

As you can see, the CGI program returns the response to the user after sending the e-mail to the IntraMaster. You are able to take the input stream, break out the input data from the environment variables, and by using the resulting name/value pairs in the associative array, create a response to the user that displays the values stored in those elements.

The next chapter will show you how to utilize these abilities to extract data from a database and return the results to the user through the CGI program.

Creating a Library of Perl Programs

As you can see from the previous example, the capability to include a library of reusable programs into the development environment is extremely useful. Once a Perl program has been tested and completed, it can be added to a library and reused over and over. To create your own library, one that meets the programming needs of your intranet environment, review the CGI programs that you will build or have built and see if there are any components or functions that are used repeatedly.

If you discover that there are, pull a copy of the components out of the CGI program and create a generic version that could be used across all your applications. It is beyond the scope of this book to determine what those needs and components are, given the unique circumstances of your situation. To incorporate these collected program components into a library, the following steps are offered as an example of how one could create a library of routines:

1. Using a text editor, create a file to hold the library and name it accordingly, for example, *myperl-lib.pl.*

2. Because this library is a Perl program unto itself, the first line of the library must be the location of the Perl interpreter:

```
#!/usr/local/bin/perl -- -*- C -*-
```

3. Incorporate the Perl programs or sub-programs into the library in the following manner, providing each with a name for the subroutine, as shown below:

```
sub YOUR-SUBROUTINE-NAME {
the program or subroutine goes between the brace/curly
brackets
}
```

4. When all the components have been added to the library file, complete the file with the following line, as required by the Perl interpreter:

```
1; #return true
```

5. Save the library file.

6. In the your CGI programs, you need to include the library by inserting the following line into the CGI program:

```
require "library-name";
```

   Library-name is the name of the library file that you just created in steps one through five.

7. To call the subroutine located within the library file, use the following syntax, inserted at the correct location within the CGI program, to invoke the library file's subroutine:

```
SUBROUTINE-NAME()
```

   where SUBROUTINE-NAME is the name of the library file component you wish to execute.

These steps show you how to create a library file of Perl subroutines that can be used repeatedly. It is suggested that you begin by exploring libraries by reviewing the cgi-lib.pl from Steven Brenner that can be found on the CD included with this book. This is a good place to start, and as the content of the file indicates, it may be modified as long as the user maintains the original copyright notice.

Comparing CGI Programming Languages

As mentioned earlier in the chapter, several languages can be used to write CGI programs. The choice of the language used is a combination of two elements: programming languages the creator of the programs already knows, and the functionality offered by the language as compared to the requirements of the program. The author recommends you review William Weinman's *The CGI Book* (New Riders, 1996) or *HTML and CGI Unleashed* (sams.net, 1995). Both books offer several examples and contain in-depth discussions about the merits of various programming languages and CGI.

Just to compare the Perl, C, and sh programming languages, samples have been included of the C and sh versions of the code listing needed to print the environment variables. To provide a point of reference for comparison, the Perl program developed earlier in the chapter is presented again.

Printing the Environment Variables with the Perl code:

```perl
#!/usr/local/bin/perl/cgi-bin

# Filename: printvars.perl.cgi
# (c) 1996 John Desborough

print "Content-type: text/plain\n\n";

#display the CGI environment variables
print qq(AUTH_TYPE = $ENV{"AUTH_TYPE"}\n);
print qq(CONTENT_LENGTH = $ENV{"CONTENT_LENGTH"}\n);
print qq(CONTENT_TYPE = $ENV{"CONTENT_TYPE"}\n);
print qq(GATEWAY_INTERFACE = $ENV{"GATEWAY_INTERFACE"}\n);
print qq(HTTP_ACCEPT = $ENV{"HTTP_ACCEPT"}\n);
print qq(HTTP_REFERER = $ENV{"HTTP_REFERER"}\n);
print qq(HTTP_USER_AGENT = $ENV{"HTTP_USER_AGENT"}\n);
print qq(PATH_INFO = $ENV{"PATH_INFO"}\n);
print qq(PATH_TRANSLATED = $ENV{"PATH_TRANSLATED"}\n);
print qq(QUERY_STRING = $ENV{"QUERY_STRING"}\n);
print qq(REMOTE_ADDR = $ENV{"REMOTE_ADDR"}\n);
print qq(REMOTE_HOST = $ENV{"REMOTE_HOST"}\n);
print qq(REQUEST_METHOD = $ENV{"REQUEST_METHOD"}\n);
```

```
print qq(SCRIPT_NAME = $ENV{"SCRIPT_NAME"}\n);
print qq(SERVER_NAME = $ENV{"SERVER_NAME"}\n);
print qq(SERVER_PORT = $ENV{"SERVER_PORT"}\n);
print qq(SERVER_PROTOCOL = $ENV{"SERVER_PROTOCOL"}\n);
print qq(SERVER_SOFTWARE = $ENV{"SERVER_SOFTWARE"}\n);
```

Printing the environmental variables with the sh code:

```
#!/bin/sh

# Filename: printvars.sh.cgi
# (c) 1996 John Desborough

echo Content-type: text/plain
echo

#display the CGI environment variables
echo AUTH_TYPE = $AUTH_TYPE
echo CONTENT_LENGTH = $CONTENT_LENGTH
echo CONTENT_TYPE = $CONTENT_TYPE
echo GATEWAY_INTERFACE = $GATEWAY_INTERFACE
echo HTTP_ACCEPT = $HTTP_ACCEPT
echo HTTP_REFERER = $HTTP_REFERER
echo HTTP_USER_AGENT = $HTTP_USER_AGENT
echo PATH_INFO = $PATH_INFO
echo PATH_TRANSLATED = $PATH_TRANSLATED
echo QUERY_STRING = $QUERY_STRING
echo REMOTE_ADDR = $REMOTE_ADDR
echo REMOTE_HOST = $REMOTE_HOST
echo REQUEST_METHOD = $REQUEST_METHOD
echo SCRIPT_NAME = $SCRIPT_NAME
echo SERVER_NAME = $SERVER_NAME
echo SERVER_PORT = $SERVER_PORT
echo SERVER_PROTOCOL = $SERVER_PROTOCOL
echo SERVER_SOFTWARE = $SERVER_SOFTWARE
```

Printing the environmental variables with the C code:

```
/*
Filename: printvars.c
(c) 1996 John Desborough
*/
```

```
#include <stdio.h>
#include <stdlib.h>

/* create temporary storage for environment variable */
char * qs;
char * nul = "<empty>";

main(int argc, char ** argv)
{
/* send the mime-type */
printf("Content-type: text/plain\n\n");

/* create a macro to display environment variables and check
to see if a null pointer was returned, if so, replace with "empty" */
#define okenv(a) ((qs = getenv(a)) ? qs : nul)

/* now we dispay the CGI environment variables */
printf("AUTH_TYPE = %s\n", okenv("AUTH_TYPE"));
printf("CONTENT_LENGTH = %s\n", okenv("CONTENT_LENGTH"));
printf("CONTENT_TYPE = %s\n", okenv("CONTENT_TYPE"));
printf("GATEWAY_INTERFACE = %s\n", okenv("GATEWAY_INTERFACE"));
printf("HTTP_ACCEPT = %s\n", okenv("HTTP_ACCEPT"));
printf("HTTP_REFERER = %s\n", okenv("HTTP_REFERER"));
printf("HTTP_USER_AGENT = %s\n", okenv("HTTP_USER_AGENT"));
printf("PATH_TRANSLATED = %s\n", okenv("PATH_TRANSLATED"));
printf("QUERY_STRING = %s\n", okenv("QUERY_STRING"));
printf("REMOTE_ADDR = %s\n", okenv("REMOTE_ADDR"));
printf("REMOTE_HOST = %s\n", okenv("REMOTE_HOST"));
printf("REQUEST_METHOD = %s\n", okenv("REQUEST_METHOD"));
printf("SCRIPT_NAME = %s\n", okenv("SCRIPT_NAME"));
printf("SERVER_NAME = %s\n", okenv("SERVER_NAME"));
printf("SERVER_PORT = %s\n", okenv("SERVER_PORT"));
printf("SERVER_PROTOCOL = %s\n", okenv("SERVER_PROTOCOL"));
printf("SERVER_SOFTWARE = %s\n", okenv("SERVER_SOFTWARE"));
}
```

Note

If you are really keen on programming in C, pick up *The C Programming Language,* by Kernighan and Ritchie. This is the standard text for C language programming.

You can see from the code samples that there are many similarities among the programming languages, at least in this simple program. If the user were to execute the C and sh programs, the results returned to the browser would be the same—the input data would be broken out of the environment variables and presented to the user in name/value pairs.

A number of excellent resources on the subject of CGI programming discuss the idiosyncrasies of each language. It is the author's opinion, however, that the Java language will be the next hot language to watch for moving programing data between browsers and data stores.

Gateway Programming for Text Search and Retrieval

The previous work has been done mainly to prepare you to access the more traditional, structured databases from your CGI programs. One of the things you need to remember is that a large part of your holdings is text-based. With these files at your disposal, what can you do with the files to ensure that they will be accessible to the intranet users?

There are several alternatives to the creation of searchable text-bases, from commercial search engines to the Wide Area Information Server (WAIS) storage and retrieval program. The WAIS engine is one of the most widely used on the Internet and is a trademark of WAIS, Inc. Although WAIS, Inc. now offers a commercial version of the WAIS program, several free-of-charge WAIS-like programs have been developed using the same ANSI Z39.50 protocol.

Instead of providing you with a list that is sure to be outdated by the time you read this, the following URL will invoke a search of the Yahoo site looking for a current listing of the available WAIS software:

```
http://search.yahoo.com/bin/search?p=wais+software
```

Some of the programs that will be listed are free-of-charge and some will be commercial. If you are in the process of considering a WAIS-like implementation, start with the Yahoo search above, and then review the information that is returned by the search. Once that is complete, you can experiment with the software you believe best meets your needs in order to determine the appropriate fit between the organization's needs and the software capabilities.

The core of the WAIS software is the indexer, which creates the full-text indexes of files fed into it, and a server that uses those indexes to perform keyword or full-text searches. The other components required to make the WAIS server work within an intranet are the database created by the indexer and the WAIS client. The WAIS client passes the information between the browser and the server.

The acquisition and setup of the WAIS will not be covered here. This topic is covered in great detail in several other books, including George Eckel's *Intranet Working* (New Riders, 1996) and Jeff Rowe's *Building Internet Database Servers with CGI* (New Riders, 1996). Setting up the WAIS service and creating searchable indexes for use with a WAIS gateway will be briefly discussed.

For the moment, however, look briefly at how things are set up to enable searching a WAIS collection.

Introductory Thoughts and Principles of Text Searching via WAIS

Once you have built your intranet home page and established links to a wide variety of documents, many of which are stored on the system, how do you allow the users to search these holdings? If you create a WAIS index of all the files within the intranet, you enable users to search for the file they want rather than require them to inspect each of the HTML pages to find the link to the correct document.

In order to enable users to search this way, you must do the following:

- Acquire the WAIS-like software and install and configure it.

- Gather the files you want to index on the intranet server into a hierarchical tree.

- Implement a gateway (WAIS client) that enables the browser to pass a query along to the WAIS search engine.

- Create the form that will accept the input to be passed along to the gateway.

Once these are done, you should be off to the races.

Introduction to WAIS

This is a brief run-through of how the WAIS service is built and works. To get WAIS to run on your site, assuming that you have acquired the WAIS server software, the following script will search the documents on the intranet server and create the searchable database:

```
set rootdir = /usr/local/www
#       This is the root directory of the Web tree you want to index.

set index = /usr/local/httpd/wais/sources/index
#       This is the name your WAIS indexes will be built under.
#       Index files will be called index.* in the /usr/local/httpd/
wais/sources
#       directory, in this example.

set doindex = /usr/local/httpd/wais/waisindex
#       The full pathname to your waisindex program.

set nonomatch
cd $rootdir
set num = 0
foreach pathname ('du $rootdir ¦ cut -f2 ¦ tail -r')
```

```
        echo "The current pathname is: $pathname"
        if ($num == 0) then
                set exportflag = "-export"
        else
                set exportflag = "-a"
        endif
        $doindex -l 0 -nopairs -nocat -d $index $exportflag
        $pathname/*.html
        $doindex -l 0 -nopairs -nocat -d $index -a $pathname/*.txt
        $doindex -l 0 -nopairs -nocat -d $index -a $pathname/*.c
        $doindex -nocontents -l 0 -nopairs -nocat -d $index -a
        $pathname/*.ps
        $doindex -nocontents -l 0 -nopairs -nocat -d $index -a
        $pathname/*.gif
        $doindex -nocontents -l 0 -nopairs -nocat -d $index -a
        $pathname/*.au
        $doindex -nocontents -l 0 -nopairs -nocat -d $index -a
        $pathname/*.hqx
        $doindex -nocontents -l 0 -nopairs -nocat -d $index -a
        $pathname/*.xbm
        $doindex -nocontents -l 0 -nopairs -nocat -d $index -a
        $pathname/*.mpg
        $doindex -nocontents -l 0 -nopairs -nocat -d $index -a
        $pathname/*.pict
        $doindex -nocontents -l 0 -nopairs -nocat -d $index -a
        $pathname/*.tiff
        @ num++
end
echo "$num directories were indexed."
```

This script uses the waisindex program to create the searchable database of the intranet files you will allow to be searched. The WAIS configuration file needs to be edited to establish the parameters that you want to operate under. The basic parts of the configuration file are as follows:

- **PageTitle**—specifies an HTML file that will be prefixed to the results of the search.

- **SelfURL**—the self-referencing URL that WAIS might use.

- **MaxHits 40**—the maximum number of results that can be returned from the WAIS search.

- **SortType**—how you want the information returned to the user. You can implement the sort type to return values of either lines, bytes, title, or score. Score is the most popular because it returns the most relevant information.

- **SwishBin**—the full path to your swish program. (If you are using WAIS software that incorporates swish program functionality, review the documentation that comes with the software.)

- **AddrMask**—allows everyone to use the database if the value is set to All, or if you only want a specific address accessing the information, sets the mask to the address that you want to let into the search engine.

- **WAISSource/SwishSource**—tells WAIS which files you will let the users search from. For WAIS servers, you must give the complete server name and a port number to access. For swish servers, you must give the complete path and the index.swish file to gain access to.

- **TypeDef**—tells the client and WAIS which types of files are going to be returned as results to a search. Because it is possible that WAIS can return pictures, sound, text, and even movie file formats, you must use the TypeDef configuration option to tell which mime.types are accessible for use in the database scheme. On a single TypeDef line, you need to specify the suffix for the particular type (with a period), a short description to include results (no more than two to three words), the URL to the icon representing the file type, and the MIME type corresponding to the particular type.

Once you have downloaded, compiled, configured, and indexed the data on your server (pretend you have waved the magic wand), access to the data can be permitted via an HTML form. Before you create the form that you need to use, you need to make certain that you have something in place that will act as a gateway between the programs that have created the indexed catalogs of files on the intranet site and the forms-capable browser.

Gateway Access to WAIS Indexes

WWWWais is a C program written by Kevin Hughes of Enterprise Integration Technology (EIT). It is loosely based on the Perl waisq interface program that comes with NCSA's HTTPd. You can obtain more information about the program at:

```
http://www.eit.com/software/wwwwais
```

It is an excellent program and permits you to create HTML forms and pass the input to the WAIS search engine. The simplest form would be one with the coding as follows:

```
<FORM METHOD="POST" ACTION="http://your.site.name.here/cgi-bin/
wwwwais/wwwwais">
<INPUT TYPE="TEXT" NAME="keywords" SIZE=40>
<INPUT TYPE="SUBMIT" VALUE="Submit">
</FORM>
```

This is a very simple form and, as always, there are options that can be used to expand the capabilities through the use of forms. WWWWais can be called with the following options, in the following format:

```
/cgi-bin/wwwwais?option=value
```

- **host**—specifies the host machine to search (works only when using waissearch)

- **iconurl**—specifies the master URL where WWWWais can find the icons to be used (if useicons is set to Yes)

- **isindex**—specifies the search keywords

- **keywords**—specifies the search keywords

- **maxhits**—determines the maximum number of URLs to return after a search

- **port**—specifies the port of the WAIS server that will be doing the searching (works only with waissearch)

- **searchprog**—specifies the program to do the searching (waisq, waissearch, or swish)

- **selection**—specifies the index source to use

- **sorttype**—determines the fashion in which WWWWais sorts the output (valid types are score, lines, bytes, title, and type)

- **source**—specifies the index database to search

- **sourcedir**—specifies the directory in which the index database resides

- **useicons**—indicates whether WWWWais should use icons to identify different file types

- **version**—gives the version information only for WWWWais and the waisq or waissearch program that it runs

- **<keywords only>**—keywords can be specified by themselves using isindex forms and will work only if no other options are used

- **<no arguments>**—called with no arguments, program brings up a blank field into which the users can enter search keywords

Figure 10.14 shows an HTML form that allows the user to enter keywords into the appropriate area and select from a series of indexes that they desire to be searched. Figure 10.15 shows the beginning of a list of the returned documents within the HTML page. By selecting one of the document URLs that were returned, you would retrieve that document and it would be displayed in the browser, as appropriate.

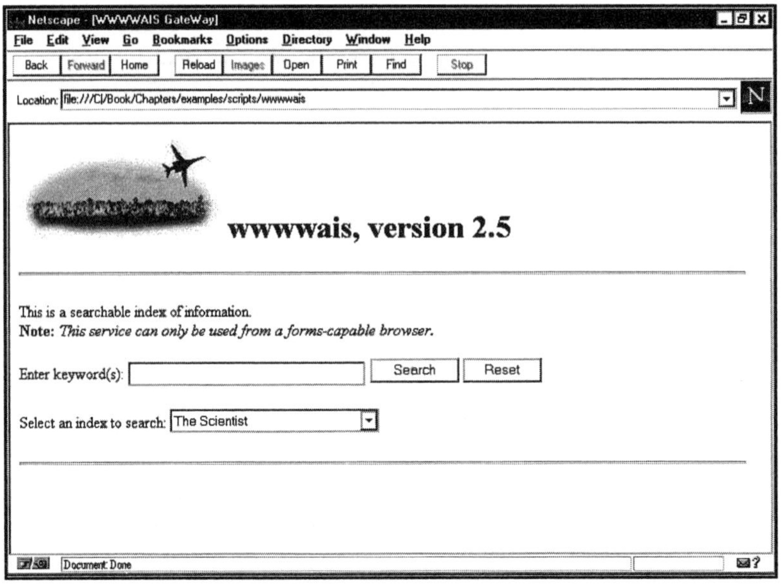

Figure 10.14

WWWWais HTML form for searching WAIS-indexed data.

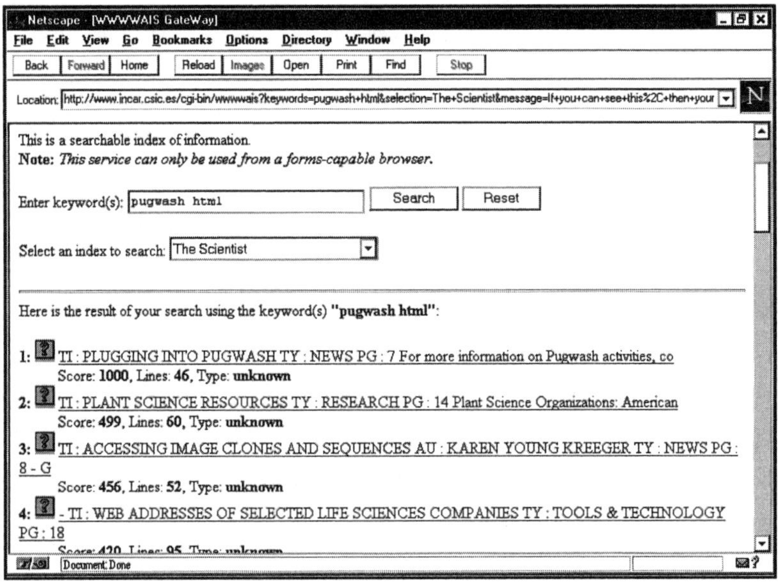

Figure 10.15

Results of WAIS query through WWWWais gateway.

Creating Your Own Form to Use the WAIS Search Engine

In order to provide you with a template for the creation of a form similar to the one used in figure 10.14, the basic code follows shortly. Please make certain to change the code to reflect your particulars. For example, make certain that you change *your.site.here* to your specific address and *YourIndex* to the appropriate index name, and specify any of the other options for which you have configured your system. In addition, you will need to change the <OPTION> tags to the appropriate labels for your information collections (Marketing Literature, for example) should you choose to use the code below.

```
<HTML>
<HEAD>
<TITLE>WWWWAIS GateWay</TITLE>
</HEAD>
<BODY>
<H1><IMG SRC="bomb.jpg" ALT="[*]">  wwwwais, version 2.5</H1>


<HR><FORM METHOD="GET" ACTION="http://your.site.here/cgi-bin/
wwwwais">
This is a searchable index of information.<BR>
<B>Note:</B> <I>This service can only be used from a forms-capable
browser.</I><P>
Enter keyword(s): <INPUT TYPE=text NAME="keywords" VALUE="" SIZE=30>
<INPUT TYPE=submit VALUE="  Search  "> <INPUT TYPE=reset VALUE="  Re-
set  ">
<P>
Select an index to search: <SELECT NAME="SELECTion">
<OPTION SELECTed>Collection one
<OPTION> Collection two
<OPTION>Collection three

</SELECT>
<P>
<INPUT TYPE=hidden NAME=message VALUE="If you can see this, then your
browser can't support hidden fields.">
<INPUT TYPE=hidden NAME=source VALUE="YourIndex">
<INPUT TYPE=hidden NAME=sourcedir VALUE="">
<INPUT TYPE=hidden NAME=maxhits VALUE="40">
```

```
<INPUT TYPE=hidden NAME=sorttype VALUE="score">
<INPUT TYPE=hidden NAME=host VALUE="your.site.here">
<INPUT TYPE=hidden NAME=port VALUE="210">
<INPUT TYPE=hidden NAME=searchprog VALUE="waissearch">
<INPUT TYPE=hidden NAME=iconurl VALUE="/icons">
<INPUT TYPE=hidden NAME=useicons VALUE="yes">
</FORM><HR>
```

The preceding code will create a form for you that enables you to pass the input to the WAIS search engine and receive the information back. One thing that you will notice in the code is that the HTML tag is used to start the page but is not closed within the framework of the code. The WWWWais program provides the returned document URLs and the finishing HTML code required to close out the page. Following are the final few lines of the document listing that was returned as figure 10.15 to demonstrate what the program does to display the found documents and close out the HTML document.

```
<A HREF="http://www.incar.csic.es/cgi-bin/
wwwwais?getdesc=yes&host=ds.internic.net&port=210&source=the-
scientist&searchprog=waissearch&SELECTion=none&docnum=39&keywords=pugwash+html">TI:
Researchers</A>
<DD> Score: <B>52</B>, Lines: <B>288</B></B>, Type: <B>unknown</B>
<DT> <B>40:   </B><IMG SRC="/icons/unknown.xbm" ALIGN="bottom" ALT="">
 <A HREF="http://www.incar.csic.es/cgi-bin/
wwwwais?getdesc=yes&host=ds.internic.net&port=210&source=the-
scientist&searchprog=waissearch&SELECTion=none&docnum=40&keywords=pugwash+html">TI
: Gene Patenting Is On The Rise, But Scientists Are Unimpressed
Buoyed by enabl</A>
<DD> Score: <B>44</B>, Lines: <B>291</B></B>, Type: <B>unknown</B>
</DL>
<HR>
<I>This search was performed by <A HREF="http://www.eit.com/software/
wwwwais/wwwwais.html">wwwwais 2.5</A>.</I>
</BODY>
</HTML>
```

This closes the brief introduction to the world of WAIS and getting access to the stores of documents that you can include into the intranet for searching. At this point you should have an understanding of how WAIS works and how to establish a form to access the WAIS indexes through the WWWWais gateway.

Status Check

You have come a long way in this chapter. It has covered the basics of creating CGI programs to pass data between the browser and the server, including separating the input stream from the environment variables. It has also established an understanding of how to access the data stored in a WAIS service.

The table is now set for the main course—getting the CGI program to pull information out of a database. The next chapter covers the integration of ODBC and CGI programming. It will cover the techniques to get the query input into the database system and how to return the results to the browser for the user to see. *Allons-y!* as the French would say. Let's go!

11

Integrating ODBC and CGI

This chapter focuses on expanding the integration of HTML forms with Common Gateway Interface CGI programs, which you learned in the last chapter. In order to get at the mountains of information that are stored within the databases of your organization, your intranet must be able to access the database engine to extract the correct information. This chapter explores the way data is extracted via CGI programs from databases that are compliant with Open Database Connectivity (ODBC).

To make a truly successful and complete intranet, you have to be able to get information out of the variety of sources that you operate inside the organization and put it into the hands of the staff who need to use it. When you consider the relational database world, you have several options that you can pursue to provide you with the ability to extract information and present it to the user. These will be discussed shortly; but first, look at the basics of getting to the data.

Figure 11.1 shows how a query is passed to and results are passed from the target database. The following list is a walk-through of the steps that normally take place when sending a query to a database from the intranet and that are captured in figure 11.1:

1. When the user clicks on the submit button on the form or selects the hyperlink on an HTML page, either the form or the URL is sent as a request to the HTTP server.

2. The HTTP server invokes the CGI program and, provided the user can access the CGI program, passes the request, including the information input in the user's browser, to the gateway program.

3. The gateway reads the data, formats it for the database being used, and forwards it to the database interface (provided by the database software) for an evaluation of accuracy.

4. If the data passed to the database interface is accurate, the database interface passes the query to the database for execution, and the results are passed back to the gateway program through the database interface.

5. The gateway program generates the HTML file required to display the results, and then passes the results to the HTTP server via the CGI.

6. The results are then passed to the user's browser for display.

Figure 11.1

A quick view of getting information from a database.

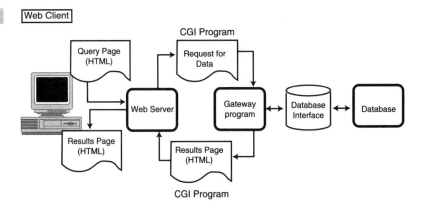

From this starting point, this chapter will develop your understanding of how to use CGI programs to extract data from ODBC databases by discussing the following topics:

- The building blocks of gateway programming

- Extracting information from the database

- Integrating CGI and ODBC databases

- Future directions in this marketplace

Building Blocks of Gateway Programming

This chapter works under the following assumption: you currently have existing relational database information sets or you will be creating some databases that you want to make accessible via the intranet.

Why would you choose the intranet method, making use of the Web technologies, to provide access to your data? You would choose the intranet method to make databases accessible because it can provide access to information sources regardless of where they are currently (or soon to be) located, the operating system of the host computer, or what type of computer from which you access the data. Following are the basic building blocks that you need to gain access to databases using the intranet method:

- Understanding of relational databases

- HTML

- CGI

- SQL (Structured Query Language)

- ODBC (Open Database Connectivity)

With these building blocks you can start to integrate data systems into the available collections of information that you offer your colleagues on the intranet. HTML was discussed in Chapters 8 through 10, and should have a good grasp of the fundamentals by this point. The basic fundamentals of CGI were discussed in Chapter 10, "Introduction to CGI." However, relational databases, SQL, and ODBC must be discussed before moving on. The following sections will cover these last three topics.

Toward Understanding Relational Databases

For those not familiar with the term "relational database," a few words are offered to explain the concept in brief.

Just as an accounting department can be broken down into, for example, accounts receivable, accounts payable, payroll, and inventory, the data lumped together within the "accounting database" can be organized into sets of information relating to the same organizational breakdown. These sets of information, called *tables* in the database world, all belong to the database called "accounting."

The term relational is applied to databases when the information in a database is broken down into tables of information that can be related to each other. For example, the following list shows an example of three tables in a database and how they are related:

- Customer information—Customer information is entered into the database once and is stored within the table called customer_info. The fields of information that make up each customer record can include, for example, the customer number, name, address, phone number, and fax number.

- Product information—Information about the products the company sells is entered into the database once and is stored within a table called product_info. The fields of information that make up each product record can include the product number, product description, and selling price.

- Invoice information—An invoice is created when a customer buys a product from the company, and the information for this purchase is stored within the invoice_info table of the database. The field of information that makes up the record of each transaction can include invoice number, invoice date, customer number, product number, quantity, and salesman ID number.

When you look at the information stored within the invoice information, you will notice that the only item stored about the customer is the customer number. It is through the use of this customer identification number that the invoice table record can be *related* to the appropriate customer record within the customer information database. Similarly, the product number from the invoice table is used as the key to relating the product information table to the invoice record.

That simple example should demonstrate to you the basics of what is called a relational database model. By taking all the pieces of data of a company and organizing the elements into logical groupings (customer information, product information, and so on), relationships can be sought and defined between these tables. This relational database model is the key building block behind the SQL query language for extracting data.

If you are just getting started in the database application area, review the literature on the available types and capabilities and pick a database engine that matches the needs of your organization and the intranet in which it will reside. The big names, such as Oracle, Sybase, and Informix also tend to come with big prices and big capabilities. The shareware and freeware database software are the opposite of the big name products. Often the software is unsupported by the developer, but there might be an active development community using the program from which you can seek support. These development communities can be found by looking through listings to see if there is an existing newsgroup or by using an Internet search facility such as Yahoo or AltaVista.

There are many things to look at when choosing a database, especially if you want to support database applications that will have users modifying existing records. Some of these things are crucial, given the nature of the technology, and they have to be given additional thought. It is advantageous, though, to understand that you will be making your data available through the intranet. This enables you to focus on the pieces of the puzzle that match your needs.

You need to make sure that you evaluate the options fairly so that you don't acquire too much or too little database solution. You need to evaluate the database engines based on the following features:

- ANSI compliance—As discussed earlier, compliance with the ANSI SQL standard is a critical element. Ascertain the extent to which the database engine complies with or deviates from the standard before making a choice.

- Data types—Make certain that the database can store the types of data that you will need to use in the intranet.

- Transaction support—If you are going to implement a full-scale intranet transaction system (order entry, for example) the database must be able to *roll back* all of the operations undertaken within the transaction. It is also prudent to ensure that the database engine supports user-defined transactions if there are sequential operations within the database during the transaction.

- Concurrence control—Record-locking is important if users have the ability to modify the contents of a record, enabling only one user to access and update the record at any given instant. Given the nature of intranet technologies, the record-locking feature is important.

- Views—The ability to use the relational capabilities of the database to pull together fields from a variety of tables in order to present data to the user in a "virtual table" is important. The ability to define views of the data for individual purposes allows only the parts of the database appropriate for the activity to be seen.

- ODBC compliance—Last, but not least, the database should be ODBC compliant in order to allow for the growth of the system into the intranet environment as the future unfolds.

An Introduction to SQL

Structured Query Language (SQL) is an industry standard language used to interact with relational databases. While the advanced features of SQL (pronounced officially as "sequel," or by some as "squeal," just for fun) are extremely powerful and relatively complex to master, the basics can be readily handled.

If you already have a relational database in-house (for example, Oracle, Sybase, or Ingres) you most likely have a database administrator (DBA) to take care of the database structure and its operation. If access to these information bases is a critical success factor of your intranet, then treat your DBA like your best friend. Although you will learn how to pass queries to and receive data from the database, the development of complex queries will most likely require the assistance of the DBA in getting it right.

Note

> If you are in the process of making the decision about which database to acquire for the intranet, read Jeff Rowe's *Building Internet Database Servers with CGI* (New Riders, 1996). Although the title says "Internet," the intranet uses the same technologies, and the book does an excellent and thorough job of walking you through the process of creating databases accessible by Internet and intranet technologies.

SQL is the standard relational database query language for the industry. In theory, the development of a single industry standard should mean that an application designed for one database can be ported to another with no change in the SQL statements. However, although all the databases incorporate many of the standard SQL features, most have defined their own extensions to the language that are not portable.

The American National Standards Institute (ANSI) leads, or rather referees, the continuing work to define the standard SQL database language. The ANSI SQL standard defines the command set, how each command should work, and the command parameters. If features offered by a database are not covered by the standard, this means that the database is not fully ANSI compliant. If you already have multiple databases to access within your intranet, make sure that you have a bottle of headache medicine handy as you work through the SQL access requirements of the various systems.

Gaining access to databases through SQL is not really *that* difficult, but a multiplicity of database systems with differing degrees of ANSI compliance means that you will have to be attentive to the details when modifying the programs that access the data held in those systems. A good DBA is invaluable in helping with the vagaries of the database world.

There have been vast improvements in the creation of SQL queries or statements for databases. A large number of SQL utilities are available to help you create your SQL statements visually (the Microsoft Access query builder, for one). You can create and test the queries beforehand and then cut and paste them into the request/results chain as depicted in figure 11.1.

The Basic SQL Commands

This section is provided as a very basic introduction to SQL. In order to understand fully how to implement a SQL database within the framework of the intranet, please refer to Jeff Rowe's *Building Internet Database Servers with CGI* (New Riders, 1996). It is beyond the scope and mandate of this book to provide a detailed review of SQL.

Following are the basic SQL commands that will give all the basic functionalities:

- **Create**—produces a new database, table, index, or view, depending upon the parameters you include

- **Drop**—eliminates a database or elements thereof, such as tables, indexes, and views, which cannot be recovered later

- **Insert**—puts data into the database

- **Update**—changes existing data record

- **Delete**—removes data from the database

- **Select**—retrieves data from the database based on parameters supplied

Later in this chapter you will see how the SQL commands are used in conjunction with a gateway programming tool to extract information from a database.

This chapter will focus on retrieving information because most of your legacy systems will already have a data entry/update module. This section will, however, discuss how to add information to the database system.

Retrieving Data from a SQL Database

In order to understand how to create the intranet facility that accesses databases and extracts the data demanded by the user, a SQL command, or *statement*, has to be sent to the database engine. This can be done from the intranet by incorporating the SQL statement into a CGI program that, when invoked, sends the SQL statement to the database engine. The statement includes the input string from the HTML form after the CGI program has extracted the name/value pairs of input data. Please see Chapter 10, "Introduction to CGI" for a review of this topic.

A SQL statement involves an operation followed by clauses and arguments that detail how to carry out the operation. The following is the basic syntactical structure of a SQL statement:

```
OPERATION clause argument
```

Take a look at the following discussion on the SELECT operation. SELECT is the most important operation for you at this time because it is used to select, or obtain, records from the database.

The basic syntax is as follows:

```
SELECT fields FROM table
```

The *fields* portion is a list of fieldnames separated by commas, and *table* is the name of the database table containing the fields in question. To select the firstname, lastname, email, and phone fields from the table emptable, the following syntax would be used:

```
SELECT firstname, lastname, email, phone FROM emptable
```

To retrieve all the fields in a table, use this:

```
SELECT * FROM emptable
```

In that statement, the asterisk (*) indicates that you want to select all the fields in the table.

All of this will present you with the complete listing of records within the table. In order to specify the record(s) you desire, the WHERE *clause* is used:

```
SELECT fields FROM table WHERE criteria
```

Criteria represents a combination of comparison and Boolean operators to determine the records that should be returned to the user. An example within the Human Resources area would be as follows:

```
SELECT position, salary FROM payscale WHERE salary > 35,000
```

This would return the position title and salary fields from the payscale table where the salary is greater than 35,000. To look at a Boolean example, from the inventory figures you would use this:

```
SELECT prodname, description, qty_on_hand FROM inventory WHERE
prodname='putter' or prodname='driver'
```

To organize the results in an orderly fashion, the ORDER BY clause may be used. If the WHERE clause is used to select specific records, the ORDER BY clause must appear after the WHERE clause in the

SQL statement. ORDER BY can also be used without the WHERE clause being present. The syntax for the use of ORDER BY is as follows:

```
SELECT fields FROM table WHERE criteria ORDER BY field order
```

The default order is ASCENDING. To specify a descending order, the qualifier DESC must be added. An example of the syntax would be as follows:

```
SELECT * FROM payscale
    WHERE salary > 20,000
    ORDER BY position, salary DESC
```

This would select all the fields from the payscale table where the value of the salary field was greater than 20,000 and would organize them by position (ascending) and by salary (descending) within each of the positions.

Entering New Data into a Database Using SQL

Now that you can see how to get information out of a database, at least in a simple, introductory fashion, how do you get new information into the database using a SQL statement? Because of the variety of SQL database systems and the minor variations among them, the following command line shows the most basic of the INSERT operation, independent of any specific SQL system:

```
INSERT INTO emptable VALUES( 1, 'John', 'Desborough',
'jdesboro@magmacom.com', '891-595-1783')
```

This command line would insert the comma-separated values into the *emptable* table which contains these fields: emp_id, firstname, lastname, email, and phone. This type of operation will be used later to demonstrate how to add the contents of the Employee Feedback Form (developed in the preceding chapter) on the intranet to the appropriate database table.

This chapter will cover a few more bits and pieces of the SQL environment as you progress through the chapter, but for the moment, you should have enough of a grasp on the subject to be able to proceed.

ODBC—What Exactly Is It?

Open Database Connectivity (ODBC) is a database standard that has been proposed and developed by Microsoft to provide a uniform interface to disparate database systems. This would allow one application to communicate with all ODBC database systems. Originally developed for the Windows 3.1 platform, it has been ported to Windows NT, Windows 95, Macintosh, and several Unix platforms. Most Windows-based development tools, report writers, and other applications dealing with databases now support ODBC.

ODBC's architecture is parallel to that of the printer drivers that have been created for use with Windows. When printing under Windows, applications issue printing commands without knowing the specifics of which printer is being used or where the printer is located. The Printer Control Panel is the location where the printer driver is set up, including the logical name for the printer. This allows all applications to be compatible with all printers.

ODBC works with drivers provided by the database vendors that implement the specifics of interacting with their database system. Users then use the ODBC Administrator Control Panel to provide logical names for the data sources. Gateways that interact with ODBC interfaces can do their work without knowing the specifics of the database system being used. This allows the applications to be compatible with all databases. In the cases where a SQL database has added proprietary extensions to the SQL language, their ODBC driver handles the necessary interactions. What this means for the intranet is that if all the database resources to which you must provide access are ODBC compliant, then you need to concentrate on the implementation of an ODBC compliant gateway program. The rationale here is that regardless of the database used for any access to information, the interaction between the database interface and the gateway program will be based on ODBC.

The selection of the gateway program then becomes important because it will be the key element between the CGI program and the input/ request data it is carrying and the database with which you need to interact. More on this aspect can be found later in the chapter.

ODBC on the Net—The Hype and The Reality

ODBC is offered by multiple vendors, such as Oracle, SQL Server, Sybase, Watcom, and Microsoft Access. It is supported by numerous applications and is used in a wide variety of production instances. ODBC drivers have been developed that perform identically to existing native database Application Programming Interfaces (APIs). ODBC offers the ability to incorporate multiple platforms (including Macintosh, Unix, OS/2, and Windows) into the information schema. ODBC drivers have been optimized to the point where independent studies have shown negligible performance differences between ODBC drivers and native APIs. All of this seems to indicate that the use of ODBC with Internet/intranet technologies is the next big trend within the intranet world.

The hype: ODBC vendors claim that their products will work over the intranet. Some pundits believe that any database networking "middle-ware" supporting ODBC and communicating over TCP/IP qualifies for the "it works on the intranet" category.

The reality: The tools enabling access to ODBC databases on the intranet have improved significantly over the last several months and will continue to improve. The second generation of secure server software and the deployment of industrial-strength encryption software enables forms to be used to pass information to servers on a secure basis. This will open the door to company-wide access to critical information for use within business processes.

Forms on the intranet were not designed for serious database access. The beauty of the intranet forms approach is that the deployment of the application is simple—just load the file with your Web browser.

One big drawback is the security of the forms. In many cases the login authentication passwords to the databases are out in the clear and easy for someone sniffing the wire to pull (in the event of a remote connection to the intranet via the Internet, this could be a disaster). No longer!

Well, there is an argument for some form of database middleware that would fit into the HTTP protocol and the Web browser. What is available is considered to be movement in the right direction. The middleware class, as discussed previously, is starting to flesh itself out. The concept of ODBC on the intranet will work for now. The security issues can be handled by the newer generation of secure servers, but at the moment there are issues that still need to be examined. For example, public key encryption will work, but the cross-certification of the keys of the various certificate houses, domestic and international, needs to be worked out. For more information on public-key encryption within this book, please refer to Chapter 5, "Intranet Security."

Note

Organizations, such as CommerceNet and their international affiliates, are working on issues such as these within the framework of electronic commerce. The main issues that CommerceNet is focusing on, in addition to public-key encryption, include EDI transaction automation and interoperability, payment method and protocol definition, smart catalogs architecture, and interoperability and access service level definition and agreements. Keeping tabs on these issues at CommerceNet is as easy as connecting to http://www.commerce.net.

The growing sophistication of commercial gateway products is providing the impetus and growth for the successful links between ODBC and CGI programs. To provide the information that the user requires to make business decisions, one simply needs to incorporate an HTML form defining the input requirement. The CGI program is called by the form, and the gateway program accepts the parsed data from the CGI program. The gateway program also does the final preparation of the data input/request before passing to the database interface. Programs such as Cold Fusion and dbWeb function at the gateway level and have the ability to deal with almost every database application scenario imaginable.

The secret to the success of applications such as Cold Fusion and dbWeb lies in the ability of the organization's database administrator to develop the SQL statement shells that will handle the user's possible database queries. The DBA and IntraMaster must keep the following in mind:

1. The DBA can create a series of SQL statement templates with which the user can eventually interact in order to access the required data.

2. The DBA, the IntraMaster, and the client/user need to sit down and define the output requirements, the comparison variables, the sorting order, and any other criteria that the user might need to shape their request and the results.

3. The DBA creates the required SQL statements which are then pasted into the gateway application.

4. From the other end, the IntraMaster creates the HTML form that allows the user to input the various criteria and allows the CGI program to parse the data and prepare it for delivery to the gateway program.

5. In addition, the display of the returned information is programmed within an HTML document.

As stated earlier, the ability of the DBA to extract information in accurate, timely, and efficient statements is one of the keys to the success of this part of the intranet. The other key element is the IntraMaster's ability to create the form and CGI script required to pass the information along.

Note

> Keep an eye on Java—the way to go in the future, rendering ODBC obsolete. Many providers of database products, report writers, and utilities are announcing intentions to move in this direction over the next period.

Extracting Information from the Database— A Primer

There are a variety of methods for extracting data out of the database for presentation within the intranet. The methods include, but are not limited to, the following:

- Employing the Application Programming Interface (API) provided by the vendor, (which will only work for the database in question). Also, any applications designed to extract information using the API will not be portable to any other database system.

- Placing the SQL statements directly in the HTML files. The HTML files are passed to and read by the CGI program. When the results are returned to the browser, the SQL commands are replaced by the actual results of the CGI program. This requires that the SQL statement be hard-coded into the HTML file and entails keeping a SQL expert on hand to assist the users as they create the requests to access data to place in the files that they maintain.

- Using CGI programs that call stored procedures within the database. These collections of SQL commands are stored internally to the database and can be invoked by external programs, passing the results to the browser for display. This option requires that someone write and maintain the stored procedures as well as the external programs that call them. This can be done, but is time consuming and relatively costly.

- Using ODBC abilities to connect. This enables connection to several databases using the same access application. Using the ODBC abilities, called by a CGI program, permits use of the HTML pages (mostly forms) to take the input that comes from one intranet screen, and uses the CGI program to pass a request for data to several databases within the organization. This option utilizes one interface to which the databases in question would make the information structure available in order to create the appropriate input mechanisms.

Because of its basic premise of "open connectivity," ODBC allows the implementation of a single user interface that connects to a variety of ODBC databases. By using this single standard for connectivity to databases, it is much easier to create the programs to interact with the variety of databases. In theory, only one access program would need to be written, instead of one for each database.

The following section focuses on the ODBC method and provides an example of a commercial gateway to obtain access to the required data sources. But first, a few paragraphs will discuss DBML (Database Markup Language), which is used by Cold Fusion, the gateway product in this chapter, and which Oracle has developed and presented to the IETF (Internet Engineering Task Force) and W3C (World Wide Web Consortium) for discussion. These two organizations are the official Internet standards-making bodies, and their approval of DBML would recognize it as the standard for marking up database data for presentation in HTML documents.

An Introduction to DBML (Database Markup Language)

In order to dynamically generate HTML pages on the fly based on user queries, DBML was developed to extend the HTML language when dealing with database-held data. The dynamic pages are usually created using a template file, which employ a mix of HTML and DBML tags. The HTML tags are used to format the page headers and footers as well as determine how the results should be formatted—putting a field in italics or a horizontal rule separating each returned record, for example. The DBML tags are used to specify the queries to send to the database and to define where and how you want to display the results of the query.

For example, earlier in the chapter you saw how to extract data from a database by sending the SQL query "SELECT lastname, phone FROM emptable" to the database. DBML wraps the SELECT statement inside one of the DBML commands in order to work with the HTML document that is created to send a pre-formatted table of the extracted data back to the user's browser. In the demonstration of how this concept works, Cold Fusion, the commercially available gateway that will be used for demonstration purposes, uses DBML in the creation of the template files used to process the queries. The four core DBML tags used within Cold Fusion follow, along with a brief description of each:

- DBQUERY—submits a SQL query to the database

- DBINSERT—inserts a record in a database

- DBUPDATE—updates a record in a database

- DBOUTPUT—displays the results of the query and can incorporate result set fields and HTML tags

The next section will cover the DBML tags and their syntax in more detail, demonstrating the products mentioned earlier. It will also explore the world of database access with some practical examples.

Integrating ODBC and CGI

The user does not care! As long as the intranet produces the results the users expect, they don't care *how* it happens. The users might not even know that the information they are receiving in their browsers can come from a variety of different database products on a variety of operating platforms in a variety of locations around the organization. Your goal within the intranet is to provide a single user interface to the information resources of the organization, and ODBC compliant databases are the elements key to allowing you to achieve your goal in this realm.

There are two methods you can employ to get the user's query to the ODBC data source:

- Write your own gateway.

- Use a third-party gateway (commercial or otherwise).

Given the need to get your information sources up quickly and efficiently, and the probable lack of a programmer who is fluent in CGI-to-ODBC API programming, it is recommended that you look at commercial gateway products. Commercial products are recommended because of the availability of support by the developer/vendor and the fiscal realities of business—they will maintain and improve their products if they want to stay in business.

In the exploration of how to extract data from an ODBC database, this chapter will use the Cold Fusion product of Allaire Corp. as the gateway product. The examples will use the following additional hard/software setup to demonstrate the products: O'Reilly's WebSite Server, running on a 100 Mhz Pentium with 16 MB RAM under Windows 95, and Netscape Navigator as the browser.

Making It Look Easy—A Practical Example

Your work to date has provided you with the skills to create HTML input forms and CGI programs to process that information. Understanding how these two elements work is key to putting the ODBC access to work. In this example, using Cold Fusion as the ODBC gateway, no detailed knowledge of CGI is required. Cold Fusion contains a CGI program internally that handles all client requests, interacts with the intranet server and database, and dynamically generates the HTML to be returned to the user's browser. Instead of writing CGI programs, the IntraMaster is asked to create a *template file* that is used to process the data, run the necessary database queries, and generate the HTML page to be sent back to the user.

Here are the basic steps by which the process works:

1. Upon clicking the submit button or selecting the hyperlink, the browser sends a request to intranet server.

2. The intranet server opens a Cold Fusion process, passes the process the submitted data, and points the process at the correct template file.

3. Cold Fusion reads the data and processes the DBML commands used in the template (including the format for the response on the results page and the type of request to be sent to the database).

4. Using ODBC, Cold Fusion interacts with the database and dynamically generates an HTML page, which contains the results, that is returned to the intranet server.

5. The intranet server returns the results page to the browser.

Now that you understand that Cold Fusion incorporates a CGI program, the traditional chain of data passing is still preserved. Following is a walk through the process of creating the process with the tools at your disposal.

HTML Front End

Once again, a standard HTML file will be used to provide input to the gateway program. Figure 11.2 is a slight variation of the feedback form you developed in Chapter 10. The "name" format has been modified to a single field and a "subject" field has been added. This allows the potential development of an application that lists, by subject, the comments received by the administrator, comments which could subsequently be selected for viewing.

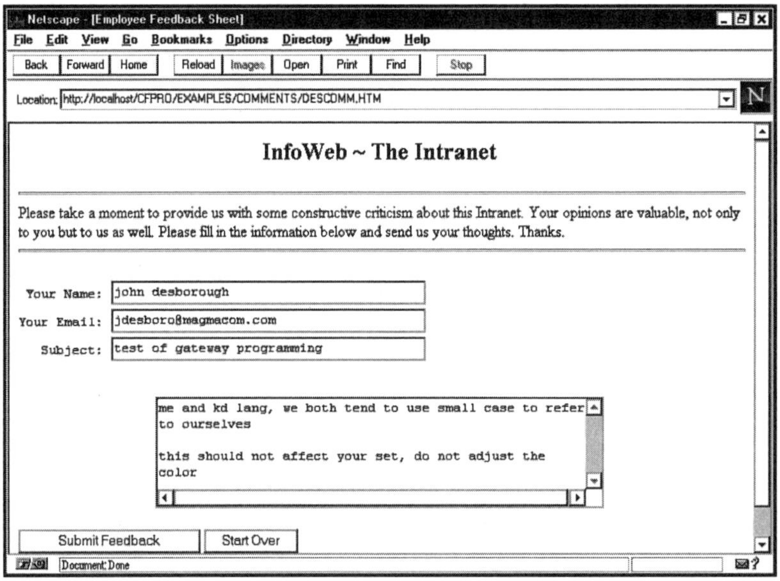

Figure 11.2

Feedback form, gateway programming example.

The HTML file that was used to create the form displayed in figure 11.2 is as follows:

```
<HTML>
<HEAD>
<TITLE>Employee Feedback Sheet</TITLE>
</HEAD>
<BODY>
<CENTER>
<H2>InfoWeb ~ The intranet</H2></CENTER>
<HR>
Please take a moment to provide us with some constructive criticism
about this intranet. Your opinions are valuable, not only to you, but
to us as well. Please fill in the information below and send us your
thoughts.  Thanks.
<HR>

<P>

<FORM ACTION="http://localhost/cgi-shl/dbml.exe?Template=/cfpro/ex-
amples/comments/dthanks.dbm" METHOD=POST>

<!-- Using SQL INSERT, collect comment information on person, e-mail,
subject, and actual text.
Also, using hidden fields, time-stamp the input for later use  -->

<INPUT TYPE="hidden" NAME="Posted" VALUE="CurrentDateTime()">
<PRE>
Your Name: <INPUT SIZE=40 NAME="FromUser">
Your Email: <INPUT SIZE=40 NAME="EMail">
Subject: <INPUT  SIZE=40 NAME="Subject">
</PRE>
</PRE>
<CENTER>
<TEXTAREA ROWS=5 COLS=55 NAME="MessageText"></TEXTAREA><P>
</CENTER>
<INPUT TYPE="submit" VALUE="  Submit Feedback  ">
<INPUT TYPE="reset" VALUE="Start Over"><BR>
```

```
<!--use hidden fields to require that certain fields have values be-
fore submission: E-mail address and user name are required
    before the entry can be submitted   -->

<INPUT TYPE="hidden" NAME="EMail_required"
    VALUE="You must enter an E-Mail Address.">

<INPUT TYPE="hidden" NAME="FromUser_required"
    VALUE="You must enter your name.">

</FORM>

<P>
<P>
<HR>
<ADDRESS>
<!-- below the email address is changed to the address of the contact
-->
IntraMaster: <A
HREF="mailto:jdesboro@magmacom.com">jdesboro@magmacom.com</A>
<BR>
Last Updated: June 17, 1996
<BR>
c:\intranet\descomm.htm
</ADDRESS>
</BODY>
</HTML>
```

There are a couple of things to take note of in this HTML file. The first
is the FORM ACTION tag:

```
<FORM ACTION="http://localhost/cgi-shl/dbml.exe?Template=/cfpro/ex-
amples/comments/dthanks.dbm"  METHOD=POST>
```

The "cgi-shl" is in bold text to highlight the fact that you may need to
change the location of the dbml.exe file if your server's CGI path is
different. Insert the appropriate location for the CGI programs, if it is
not the cgi-shl directory. You will also note the GET-like passing of the
input through the use of the "?" followed by the
template=templatename value pair.

Creating the Cold Fusion Template File

The template file is a text file that contains both HTML and DBML tags and is interpreted by Cold Fusion before the file is sent to the browser to be viewed. The differences between your traditional HTML files and the templates used by Cold Fusion are as follows:

- The templates are normally stored in the\CFUSION\TEMPLATE directory unless you change the default location at installation. The HTML files that refer to these templates can be located anywhere on any computer as long as they refer to the correct template location when the template file is called.

- The templates contain DBML tags as well as the HTML tags required for presentation.

- The templates are processed by the Cold Fusion Engine before they are returned to the client for viewing.

To create the template files, any text editor, such as Notepad, can be used. The template file referred to in the code above, dthanks.dbm, is shown below.

```
<!-- Insert the data passed from the form into the database -->
<DBINSERT DATASOURCE="CF Examples" TABLENAME="Comments">

<!-- Display a message to the user indicating that the comment was
received -->
<HTML>
<HEAD>
<TITLE>Thanks for the Feedback!</TITLE>
</HEAD>
<BODY>
<H1>Thanks for the Feedback!</H1>
<P>
<HR>
<P>
Thank you for sending us your thoughts. We will act upon them
immediately and get back to you within 48 hours. Your participation
is greatly appreciated.
<P>
```

```
<HR>
</BODY>
</HTML>
```

You will see in the template file the use of the DBML tag DBINSERT. The following command line instructed the gateway program to insert the contents of the form in figure 11.2 into the ODBC database "CF Examples," and, more specifically, into the "Comments" table within the database (those two attributes of the DBINSERT tag are required):

```
<DBINSERT DATASOURCE="CF Examples" TABLENAME="Comments">
```

Once the data has been inserted into the database, a message is returned to the user. Figure 11.3 shows the resulting file that is returned to the user's browser.

Figure 11.3

Results returned by the template file.

Querying the Database

Turning to getting information out of the database, now that you have been able to develop a means of adding records, look through the following template file used by Cold Fusion to obtain the user's input for passing to the database engine and returning the results to the browser:

```
<!-- first query template -->

<HTML>
<HEAD>
<TITLE>
User Feedback
</TITLE></HEAD>
<BODY>

<H2>User Feedback</H2>
<HR>

<!-- Run a query to get the names of all people who have made com-
ments -->

<DBQUERY NAME="FeedbackQuery" DATASOURCE="CF Examples"
    SQL="SELECT * FROM Comments">

<H3>Feedback Messages Have Been Received From</H3>

<!-- Note that in the DBTABLE use escape quotes and pound signs -->

<DBTABLE QUERY="FeedbackQuery" COLHEADERS HEADERLINES=2 COLSPACING=2>

<DBCOL HEADER="Subject" WIDTH=28 ALIGN=left
     TEXT="#Subject#>">
<DBCOL HEADER="User" WIDTH=16 ALIGN=left TEXT="#FromUser#">
<DBCOL HEADER="Date" WIDTH=10 ALIGN=left TEXT="#DateFormat(Posted)#">

</DBTABLE>

<P>
<HR>
<ADDRESS>
<!-- below the email address is changed to the address of the contact
-->
IntraMaster: <A
HREF="mailto:jdesboro@magmacom.com">jdesboro@magmacom.com</A>
<BR>
Last Updated: June 5, 1996
<BR>
c:\intranet\desrev.dbm
</ADDRESS>
```

```
</BODY>
</HTML>
```

The template file shown here is designed to look at the Comments table of the database and list the subject, the user name, and the date for each record in the database. The actual query definition is hard-coded into the template file as follows:

```
<DBQUERY NAME="FeedbackQuery" DATASOURCE="CF Examples" SQL="SELECT *
FROM Comments">
```

The syntax of the preceding DBQUERY tag indicates the following attributes:

- NAME—A name given to the query that will be used when displaying the results—in this case, later in the code in the <DBTABLE QUERY=queryname> tag.

- DATASOURCE—Indicates in which of the ODBC databases accessible to Cold Fusion it should look to invoke the SQL statement.

- SQL—The actual SQL command to invoke—in this example, SELECT all the records from the Comments table.

To display the results in the user's browser, the data needs to be formatted. In this particular example, the results are placed in a tabular format when returned to the browser. The code used is as follows:

```
<DBTABLE QUERY="FeedbackQuery" COLHEADERS HEADERLINES=2 COLSPACING=2>

<DBCOL HEADER="Subject" WIDTH=28 ALIGN=left TEXT="#Subject#>">
<DBCOL HEADER="User" WIDTH=16 ALIGN=left TEXT="#FromUser#">
<DBCOL HEADER="Date" WIDTH=10 ALIGN=left TEXT="#DateFormat(Posted)#">

</DBTABLE>
```

Here you see the DBTABLE tag with the instruction as to which named query should be displayed (QUERY="FeedbackQuery"), to display the column headers above each column (COLHEADERS), the number of lines to use for the column headers (HEADERLINES=2), and the number of spaces to insert between the columns (COLSPAC-ING=2).

Now that the basic table layout has been defined, the definition of each of the columns that you choose to display must be established. Using the last of the columns as an example, here is a breakdown of the DBML tags used and what they accomplish:

- Column definition tag, <DBCOL>—Defines the text to be displayed as the column header (HEADER="Date"), the width of the column for display purposes (WIDTH=10), the column alignment (ALIGN=left), and the text to be displayed within the column (TEXT="#DateFormat(Posted)#").

- Double quote (" ") delimited text—Determines what will be displayed within the column.

- Pound sign (#) delimiter—Indicates that the text enclosed is a place holder for the actual values of the field within the record when displayed (this is a little more evident in the two preceding column definitions).

- Last column definition—Indicates that the contents of the Posted field is to be displayed using the DateFormat formatting function.

This was brought out to show that within a column you can have combinations of literal text, HTML tags, and query result set field references.

Figure 11.4 shows the results of this template file after invocation using the following code line that was incorporated in a test file:

```
<a href="/cgi-shl/dbml.exe?Template=/cfpro/examples/comments/
first.dbm>
```

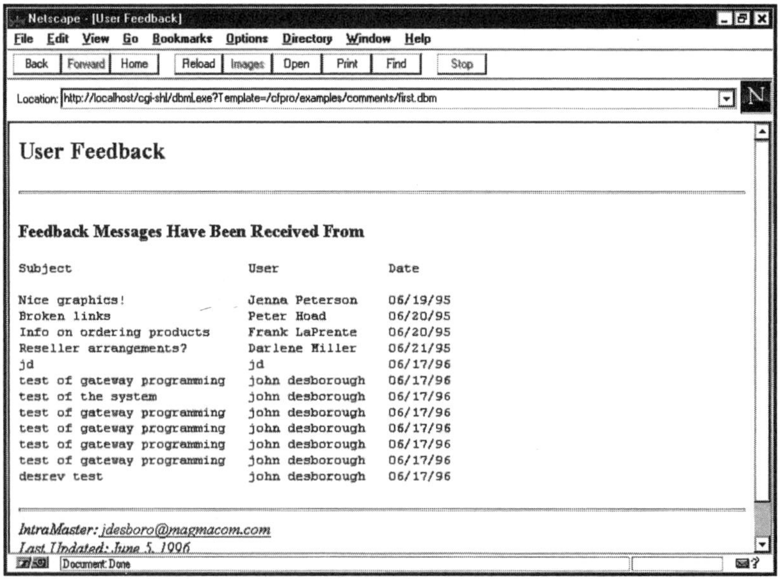

Figure 11.4

First Cold Fusion
query results.

Displaying the Output from the Query

In the previous template, your query results were returned as a table showing the columns of information from the records in the database. Now expand the functionality of the template file somewhat to include the actual feedback comments of the users. The following code file produces the results that you see in figure 11.5:

```
<!--second query template -->

<HTML>
<HEAD>
<TITLE>
User Feedback
</TITLE></HEAD>
<BODY>

<H2>User Feedback</H2>
<HR>

<!-- Run a query to get the names of all people who have made com-
ments -->
```

```
<DBQUERY NAME="FeedbackQuery" DATASOURCE="CF Examples"
    SQL="SELECT * FROM Comments">

<H3>Feedback Messages Have Been Received From</H3>

<!-- Note that in the DBTABLE use escape quotes and pound signs -->

<DBTABLE QUERY="FeedbackQuery" COLHEADERS HEADERLINES=2 COLSPACING=2>

<DBCOL HEADER="Subject" WIDTH=28 ALIGN=left
      TEXT="#Subject#">
<DBCOL HEADER="User" WIDTH=16 ALIGN=left TEXT="#FromUser#">
<DBCOL HEADER="Date" WIDTH=10 ALIGN=left TEXT="#DateFormat(Posted)#">

</DBTABLE>

<!-- detailed output for each comment in the feedback box.  -->

<DBOUTPUT QUERY="FeedbackQuery">

<HR>
<P>
<A NAME="#CommentID#"></A>
<PRE>
<B>Subject:</B>  #Subject#
<B>User:   </B>  <A HREF="mailto:#EMail#">#FromUser#</A>
<B>Date:   </B>  #DateFormat(Posted)#
</PRE>
<P>
#ParagraphFormat(MessageText)#

</DBOUTPUT>

<P>
<HR>
<ADDRESS>
<!-- below the email address is changed to the address of the contact
-->
IntraMaster: <A
HREF="mailto:jdesboro@magmacom.com">jdesboro@magmacom.com</A>
<BR>
Last Updated: June 5, 1996
```

```
<BR>
c:\intranet\second.dbm
</ADDRESS>

</BODY>
</HTML>
```

As you can see from the code and figure 11.5, the template that you
have developed includes the <DBOUTPUT> tag to display the actual
comments that people made. The QUERY attribute uses the same
name that was given during the DBQUERY command earlier in the
template file and discussed in the last section. What you have done here
is return to the user the list of comments that have been made using
the example form, as in the previous template file, as well as display the
fields of data from each of the records.

The inclusion of the "mailto:" action in a hyperlink provides the opportunity to respond directly to the user who provided the comments. The
content of the <TEXTAREA> tag from the form was stored in the
MessageText field and is displayed in the returned file through the use
of the syntax *#ParagraphFormat(MessageText)#*. This indicates that
the contents of the field *MessageText* should be displayed in paragraph
format.

Note

To create a query wherein the user can search the database of comments for comments submitted by a particular user, you would create a template containing code lines similar to the following:

```
<DBQUERY NAME="whodunnit" DATASOURCE="CF Examples"

    SQL="SELECT * FROM Comments

        WHERE FromUser LIKE '#Form.FromUser#%'">
```

The use of the LIKE operator permits "pattern-matched" searches. The percent sign (%) is a wildcard character in this search.

The DBOUTPUT section of the results might need to be formatted appropriately, but it should not require any significant modifications. Using a radio button to select an input option from a form would cause the syntax of the query to be similar to:

```
WHERE fieldname = '#fieldvalue#'
```

For more details on how to piece together query statements, please consult the user manuals from your database engine and the Cold Fusion (or your gateway) software.

Bringing It All Together

This section will discuss the enhancement of the Cold Fusion template to provide you with the following:

1. A list of "new" feedback messages to be addressed by the IntraMaster

2. Hyperlinks to take you from the list of messages to a specifically selected message

3. A DBUPDATE activity that marks the record as "processed" and calls the template file again to show an updated list of messages still outstanding.

This should provide you with the ability to modify the context of the feedback application shown here to create a similar application to handle a discussion group application, as discussed later in Chapter 17, "Workflow Software, Groupware and the Intranet." But first look at the HTML page you created to provide access to both the Employee Feedback Form and this IntraMaster Action application. Figure 11.6 shows what the HTML file looks like through the Netscape Navigator browser.

Figure 11.6

HTML page to invoke Cold Fusion templates.

Here is the code for the HTML page:

```
<HTML>
<HEAD>
<TITLE>InfoWeb Feedback Home Page</TITLE>
</HEAD>

<BODY>
<CENTER>
<H3>InfoWeb Feedback Home Page</H3>
<IMG SRC="bomb.jpg">

<HR>
<P>

<P>This intranet Page has two functions: 1) for users to submit
feedback and 2) for the IntraMaster to review submitted comments for
any required actions on their part.
```

```
<H4>To provide us with some feedback</H4>
<UL>
<LI><A HREF="descomm.htm">Give Us Some Feedback</A><P>
</UL>

<H4>Intramaster Action Required</H4>
<UL>
<LI><A HREF="/cgi-shl/dbml.exe?Template=/cfpro/examples/comments/
desrev.dbm">Bouquets and Bricks</A>
</UL>

</CENTER>
<P><P>
<HR>
<P>
<ADDRESS>
<!-- below the email address is changed to the address of the contact
-->
IntraMaster: <A
HREF="mailto:jdesboro@magmacom.com">jdesboro@magmacom.com</A>
<BR>
Last Updated: June 5, 1996
<BR>
c:\intranet\dmain.htm
</ADDRESS>

</BODY>
</HTML>
```

Extending the Functionality of the Application

You have already looked at how to input a comment into the database system using the template file, which corresponds to the first of the two choices available to the user as shown in figure 11.6. In order to develop the programming behind the second user option in figure 11.6, the template file that will be reviewed here is the one that is called "desrev.dbm" in the code line:

```
<A HREF="/cgi-shl/dbml.exe?Template=/cfpro/examples/comments/
desrev.dbm">Bouquets and Bricks</A>
```

To demonstrate the results of making this example a functional tool for the use of the hypothetical employee responsible for responding to the feedback provided by the first example template, activate the link and review what comes back to the browser. Figure 11.7 shows the results.

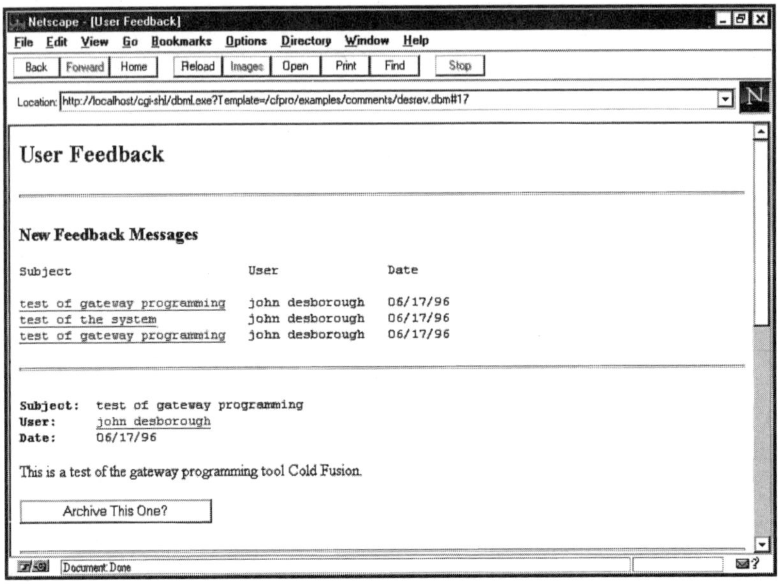

Figure 11.7

Bringing it all together with Cold Fusion.

Note the hyperlinks in the New Feedback Messages area. They are linked to the appropriate message based on a field that was hidden at the time of input, *CommentID*. Also, the button labeled "Archive This One?" is the trigger that marks the associated record as processed and calls the template file again. Figure 11.8 is the result of clicking the Archive This One? button in figure 11.7.

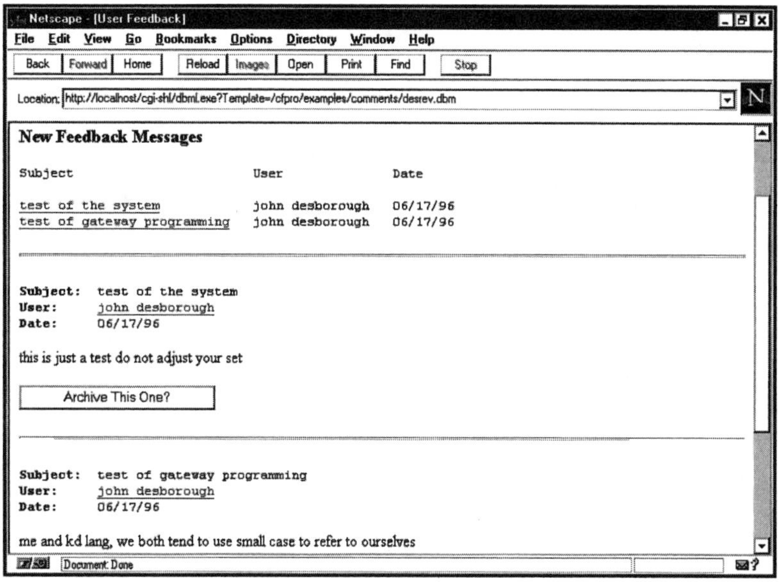

Figure 11.8

After clicking on
the Archive This
One? button on
message in figure
11.7.

Taking a Closer Look at the Details

In order to go over the details of what was added to the previous template to achieve these results, the template file is displayed here:

```
<!--- check to see that if we come to this page as a result of an
"Archive This One?" action then do the appropriate
database update to archive the comment. --->

<DBIF #ParameterExists(Form.CommentID)# is "Yes">
<DBUPDATE DATASOURCE="CF Examples" TABLENAME="Comments">
</DBIF>

<!-- Show the unarchived comments -->
```

```
<HTML>
<HEAD>
<TITLE>
User Feedback
</TITLE>
<BODY>

<H2>User Feedback</H2>
<HR>

<!-- Run a query to get unprocessed comments -->

<DBQUERY NAME="FeedbackQuery" DATASOURCE="CF Examples"
    SQL="SELECT * FROM Comments WHERE (Comments.Processed=No)">

<!-- Using a DBIF statement inform administrator if there are no new
messages-->

<DBIF #FeedbackQuery.RecordCount# is 0>

<P>There are no new comments to review.

<DBELSE>

<A NAME="Top"></A>

<H3>New Feedback Messages</H3>

<!-- Note that in the DBTABLE use escape quotes and pound signs -->

<DBTABLE QUERY="FeedbackQuery" COLHEADERS HEADERLINES=2 COLSPACING=2>

<DBCOL HEADER="Subject" WIDTH=28 ALIGN=left TEXT="<A
HREF=""###CommentID#"">#Subject#</A>">
<DBCOL HEADER="User" WIDTH=16 ALIGN=left TEXT="#FromUser#">
<DBCOL HEADER="Date" WIDTH=10 ALIGN=left TEXT="#DateFormat(Posted)#">

</DBTABLE>

<!-- detailed output for each comment in the feedback box. Using in-
ternal anchors, it is possible to create 'Threaded' views of
postings. Note also that in order to use
```

internal anchors, one must escape out pound signs with an
additional pound sign. That sends Cold fusion a cue to ignore
the other pound -->

```
<DBOUTPUT QUERY="FeedbackQuery">

<HR>
```

<!-- You can use an UPDATE statement to process comments. After
processing the comment, the database no longer sees messages
as new. All processed comments are stored in the COMMENTS
table as an archive. -->

```
<P>
<A NAME="#CommentID#"></A>
<PRE>
<B>Subject:</B>  #Subject#
<B>User:    </B>  <A HREF="mailto:#EMail#">#FromUser#</A>
<B>Date:    </B>  #DateFormat(Posted)#
</PRE>
<P>
#ParagraphFormat(MessageText)#
```

<!-- This template calls itself to implement an Update. This allows
the update to occur and the new list to be displayed at the same
time. -->

```
<FORM ACTION="/cgi-shl/dbml.exe?Template=/cfpro/examples/comments/
desrev.dbm" METHOD="POST">
<INPUT TYPE="hidden" NAME="CommentID" VALUE="#CommentID#">
<INPUT TYPE="hidden" NAME="Processed" VALUE="Yes">
<INPUT TYPE="submit" VALUE="  Archive This One?  ">

</FORM>

<P>

</DBOUTPUT>

</DBIF>

<P>
```

```
<HR>
<ADDRESS>
<!-- below the email address is changed to the address of the contact
-->
IntraMaster: <A
HREF="mailto:jdesboro@magmacom.com">jdesboro@magmacom.com</A>
<BR>
Last Updated: June 5, 1996
<BR>
c:\intranet\desrev.dbm
</ADDRESS>

</BODY>
</HTML>
```

Starting from the top of the file, the first section of the code looks to see if there are any messages that have just had their Archive This One? button pushed. The ParameterExists function returns the string "Yes" if the named parameter has been passed to the template. When the Archive This One? button is clicked, the CommentID field is indeed passed as a hidden input, and therefore the code line condition that follows would be met and the DBUPDATE would take place (otherwise the template file continues).

```
<DBIF #ParameterExists(Form.CommentID)# is "Yes">
```

Another <DBIF> operator is called to evaluate if there are any new records to be reviewed by the IntraMaster. If there are no new records to view the code, the following response appears:

```
<DBIF #FeedbackQuery.RecordCount# is 0>

<P>There are no new comments to review.

<DBELSE>
```

If new records exist, they are displayed as in the previous template example.

Making Internal Hyperlinks Work

Cold Fusion uses the pound sign (#) as a delimiter. Thus, any time that the use of the pound sign is required within a DBML tag, you must indicate to Cold Fusion that the pound sign is not to be used as a delimiter. For example, the HTML syntax to hyperlink to a named location within a document (an internal hyperlink) uses distinct tags as follows:

- The anchor or link-to point, defined as: <A NAME=top>

- The link reference to go to the anchor, defined as
  <A HREF=#top>Go to top of page</A>

In order to make the internal hyperlinks work, you need to "escape out" the pound sign with an additional pound sign—this cues Cold Fusion to ignore the other pound sign by telling it that the character is literal and not a delimiter. The way this is implemented in the code here is as follows:

```
<DBCOL HEADER="Subject" WIDTH=28 ALIGN=left TEXT="<A
HREF=""###CommentID#"">#Subject#</A>">
```

This points to the anchor with:

```
<A NAME="#CommentID#">link text</A>
```

Because the CommentID is a variable name in the code line, the template uses the pound sign on both sides to indicate this information to Cold Fusion. Because the HTML syntax requires a pound sign in the anchor name (such as in #top), in order to display a pound sign with the text of a Cold Fusion template, two pound signs (##) are required to tell Cold Fusion that this is a literal presentation of a pound sign, not a delimiter.

The requirements to show double quotes within the same Cold Fusion statement, in a *TEXT* attribute, are similar—double quotes ("").

This example set has shown how to create a template for use by Cold Fusion and HTML forms to populate the SQL activities outlined in those forms. Because this chapter is not about Cold Fusion and how to put it through the extreme paces, but rather about combining ODBC and CGI, the work will be completed with the examples here.

Just a few final notes about one of Cold Fusion's advanced features, DBTRANSACTION, and ODBC drivers. Not all the ODBC drivers support transactions. SQL Server and Access, for example, do support transactions while FoxPro, dBase, and Paradox do not at the time this is written. Similarly, not every driver that supports transactions supports all the ISOLATION levels of DBTRANSACTION (READ_COMMITTED, READ_UNCOMMITTED, REPEATABLE_READ, SERIALIZABLE, and VERSIONING). The Microsoft Access driver supports only the READ_COMMITTED level.

If you plan to implement a transaction system within the intranet, consult the ODBC driver's documentation form for more detailed information on the isolation levels supported and the behavior of the driver at each level.

Note

In the interest of not killing any more trees than really necessary here, Jeff Rowe, author of *Building Internet Database Servers with CGI* (New Riders, 1996), has outlined a list of available products and provided a brief description of them in Chapter 7 of his text. Jeff also keeps tabs on the rapidly changing list at the following address:

```
http://cscsun1.larc.nasa.gov/~beowulf/db/
existing_products.html
```

It is by far the best list that I have found on the Web covering the breadth of products available.

Future Directions

During the time it took to write this chapter, it is likely that at least two new gateway products hit the market. In the time between thrashing these words together and the time you read them, an entire generation of intranet products will have been displaced by a new generation.

However, select a commercial gateway program such as Cold Fusion today and use it to provide access to the variety of data systems that you have in your organization. The skills you develop and the time you invest will not be lost on the new generation of products. The investment will only increase your understanding of how your organization's data resources are stored and are made available and your understanding of how the users of your intranet want to play with and see your data holdings. All this will provide you with a better base from which to work.

Status Check

"In the beginning there was a concept, and that concept begot a plan which, in turn, begot...."

All of that aside, you have come a long way in a short time frame. Your intranet server is established. Your users' browsers have been configured, and all the helper applications and plug-ins have been acquired and installed. You have built your intranet home page and forms to take user input and do something with it. In this chapter, you have seen how to take that user input and add it to an ODBC-compliant database and how to get it back out again in a simple format.

The previous chapter demonstrated how to search text holdings of information. After completing the work in this chapter, you now have the ability to extract information from ODBC relational databases. The basics of getting the information out of databases have been identified. The intricacies of developing the SQL statements used to get exactly the data the user wants to see are beyond the scope of this book. However, combining the skills just acquired with those of the DBA who shepherds your databases, there should be no stopping you now.

Your next steps are to look at the intranet from the perspective of new, alternative information models to those currently existing. Once you have developed your model for the "new world," you need to set about structuring your information resources to fit into this new model.

12

Alternative Corporate Information Models

In the previous chapter you were shown the basics of mining data from the databases that exist within the company through the use of Common Gateway Interface (CGI) programming. Using CGI in this way means that the entire set of information resources of the company is available from one interface. Now that this capability exists, the way in which information is stored, accessed, and managed can and must be changed to permit efficient and effective utilization of those resources.

The establishment of companies whose real currency is their information requires a cultural change. Training, champions, and support are three key elements to the success of an information transformation that is nothing but a wheel—change is coming around again. Regardless of the technology implemented, you have to train the people not only in how to use it, but also *why* to use it. You need the champions running around behind the trainers continuously pushing the changes and the cultural benefits back onto the desks of the staff. And behind the champion comes the support flock. Their job is to make certain that the intranet helps change the way in which they do their work.

Significant changes will not come from the applications within the intranet—they will come from changing the way the work is done.

Through the establishment of an Enterprise intranet, the ability to support a corporate knowledge architecture can be established. As businesses search for and implement new business models to compete in the global marketplace, the information model must change as well. The new information model need not support only the new business model—information can be a driving force in *enabling* the new business model. This chapter will discuss the need for a new information model in which knowledge is created and unleashed in support of the business model. In particular, four models will be discussed: the simple IntraWeb, the interactive IntraWeb, the distributed IntraWeb, and the enterprise intranet.

Author's Note

As an example of needing to change the way work is done, I offer the following epithet: A "new computerized system" developed for a client allowed significant reductions in the time it took to complete two major tasks—the calculations of the standard costs of a given product line and the creation of a new price book reflecting any changes as a result of new standard costs. The new application enabled the accounting staff to complete in 15 minutes what was previously a three-week job for two clerks.

Now, the new pricing scheme was ready to be implemented during the second week of the month instead of the beginning of the next month. The manager responsible for the next step, the review and acceptance of the proposed price changes, initially refused to look at the resulting report when it was delivered at the start of the second week of the month because his input to the next stage had not been required until the end of the month under the previous process. Why should he alter the way things were done just because of a new computer system?

Based on the results of the work, the prices for the product lines in question were adjusted and the new price books had always been printed for distribution on the 1st of the month. By having the clerks select four separate links from a two-desktop, one-server intranet site, the clerks were now able to do the following:

1. Obtain a report on products where the average purchase price over the preceding month had increased beyond a 3 percent threshold;

2. Initiate a process to send the report from the previous point as the set of parameters from which to generate the new marked-up sales price for the products that maintained their required margins;

3. Generate a price book by product that was available on their desktops for them use to review pricing; and

4. Generate the report that went to the manager for his approval to change the prices for those products.

After three months of waiting for the manager to take action during the second week rather than at the end of the month, the clerks presented him with a report outlining the opportunity cost of his delay—net of commissions that would have been paid. The delay had cost the company over $235,000 in profit. That made the manager sit up and take notice.

By making the price changes at the start of the second week and e-mailing the electronic price book to the sales staff on that day, the company was able to realize an increase in profits of $850,000 in the first year. The two clerks became the custodians of the company's internal Web site developed to avoid e-mailing the price book.

Moral of the story: change the way in which things have always been done in order to make changes in the bottom lines.

Corporate models are changing. In order to support the business processes, and indeed to drive them yourself, you need to bring about the convergence of the Internet technologies and those of the internal networks to provide the users access to the knowledge bases they require to do their jobs.

This chapter discusses the need for the development and adoption of alternative information models in the face of changing business demands and processes. The topics this chapter covers on the subject are:

- "Shared knowledge is power"

- Information models in support of a knowledge architecture

- Other issues to consider in establishing a new information model

Shared Knowledge is Power

Silos belong on a farm!

It used to be said that knowledge was power. Hoarded information represented the silos of internal groups. This hoarding caused unnecessary expenditure in the development of parallel and redundant systems. Individuals and groups held their knowledge assets close to the chest so that they could succeed; this was certainly true when companies rewarded people on their individual performance and not on how their efforts helped to advance the company toward its overall objectives and goals.

As companies got smaller, smarter, and tougher in order to survive in the global marketplace, they discovered the hoarders and started to ferret them out of their holes, forcing them to share in the development of the knowledge base of the company. Compensation based on how the company does as a whole is more of the norm these days than is rewarding individual performance, except when people are rewarded with promotions. The advances in technology that have enabled people in remote locations to participate in "virtual teams" has also meant that hoarding knowledge and not participating in the team is visible to all the others much more rapidly.

Shared knowledge is power. The synergy of bringing together the knowledge and experiences of a group of people focusing on the same problem is real. With all the team members participating, the increase in the knowledge base of the individuals as well as that of the company is significant. But how do you manage and support this tautology?

Paradigms for a New Information Model

With the changes that you are seeing in the way your business must compete in the global economy, there is a driving rationale to support or lead the charge for change. You live in a knowledge economy and, as such, you need to facilitate the flow of knowledge to all people in the company.

The new information model must do the following:

- Accelerate the spread of knowledge throughout the organization

- Make the best practices and methods available to all in order to increase their abilities to create knowledge assets

- Support process improvement and accelerate process innovation, to borrow from Tom Davenport, author of *Process Innovation* and a business re-engineering guru

- Make the experiences and the understandings of staff accessible to others

- Foster the "knowledge manufacturing process" or "knowledge spiral" (as opposed to the death spiral)

Fiscal restraint and rapidly changing demands of time and resources present some challenges to achieving those goals. The new information models put in place must enable the user to work smarter and faster in order to survive in the global marketplace. There is never enough time or money allocated to take a slow waltz through the business day. To succeed, companies must be lean, efficient, and effective in going about their business.

The Challenge: The Need for a Knowledge Architecture

Sally Helgesen offers the following insight in her book *Web of Inclusion: a New Architecture for Building Great Organizations*:

“ The science and art of architecture lie in skillfully relating parts to a greater whole, creating a form uniquely appropriate for the exercise of a specific set of functions. ”

The role of knowledge architecture is to optimize the integration of knowledge into the fabric of the way business is done.

Charles Savage, in his book *Fifth Generation Management*, has the following definition for knowledge:

“ Knowledge is more than just knowing something. It comes in a variety of forms:

Know-how = procedures that get things done

Know-who = key resources to call upon

Know-what = the ability to discern key patterns based on knowledge

Know-why = understanding the larger context, the visions

Know-when = a sense of rhythm, timing, and realism. ”

These five points form the foundation for the knowledge architecture and for the intranet.

To optimize and maximize the use of the intranet, you must make certain that the technology and the facts pertaining to each point are available.

Know-how

In order to develop and implement new business processes and support them with intranet technologies, the identification of the processes for redesign can be assisted by information technology. Systems modeling and simulating process flows are two functions that are critical in the design of information systems and can be transported to the knowledge architecture. Aiding in the design and enabling new processes, technological solutions to support those processes are easily put in place.

The ability to extract data from a variety of sources, analyze the data, and deliver the data to the user in the format of their choice is a stock-in-trade of intranet technologies and the people who implement them.

Know-who

With rapid changes in technology and new products and services coming at the reader every day, it difficult to be able to "do it all." Specialization is a necessity, especially to add value to a process. In order to be effective and efficient, companies are forced to call in specialists or subcontractors for short periods of time to provide a solution to a particular problem.

Knowing who to bring in to write a Perl program to link together the intranet browser and the PeopleSoft human resource database application is a valuable skill. Combine that with a willingness to bring the expert in and you will be able to accomplish even more. It is imperative that the experts in all aspects of the applications of the intranet that support the mission-critical business process of the company are identified and are willing to support the company's efforts.

Know-what

Knowledge is created through the combination of facts and experience. Facts are neutral. People looking at facts are generally looking at them with a specific frame of reference or context based on past experiences. The synergy created by bringing together a fact and an individual's context can create a new fact, which has value added to it due to the application of the user's previous experiences.

This ability to recognize that a fact matches the context of the one seeking it is based on patterns that have been developed. By capturing these patterns into applications running on the intranet, the automation of the collection of facts that are in support of the business processes can be put in place. These applications are the so-called artificial intelligence applications (or knowledge engines) that are now starting to surface in decision support systems for the intranet. An example of such a program is WebOLAP from Information Advantage and Red Brick Systems.

Know-why

Understanding the flow of the current business processes and assisting in the design of the new business process enables those implementing the technologies of the intranet to see the overall context within which the intranet will operate.

It is also important to understand how competitors will be building their systems to achieve competitive advantage. In order to retain competitive advantage, a solid grasp of the overall vision of the company must be developed and maintained. In short, know why your company is implementing an intranet, from details to vision.

Know-when

It is not "speed kills" any more. The ability to get a new product to market more quickly, effectively, and efficiently are the keys to success. The abilities to analyze corporate and competitive data, recognize patterns that present opportunities for the organization, and act upon them quickly and effectively are required. Intranet technology permits such reactions.

The Need for a Knowledge Architecture

All the relevant information of, about, and for the business must be accessible through a single tool. That single tool has to enable the employee to do his or her job and add to the base of knowledge assets.

Significant changes will not come from the applications that are within the intranet—they will come from changing the way in which the work is done. A knowledge architecture that becomes an intranet can provide the base from which to start.

The Internet will be used by employees of the company each and every day to find information. Along the way they will stumble across a fact or two that they had not anticipated finding, and that will expand their knowledge base. Browsing is a good way to broaden your understanding of a subject. If this activity were focused on the corporate environment, your staff would be examining the company's own data stores to find information to do their job better. This sounds profitable and kicks off a little knowledge manufacturing in the individuals themselves.

If your organization can develop a rich enough source of information to keep the employee's interest in digging for and harvesting nuggets of gold from the company's own information systems, why doesn't it?

The users want Internet technologies, the browser in particular. Once the user learns how to use the browser, the user can get at almost everything that is on the Internet. Why not do that at your own company internally? The more the staff knows about the operations of their own organization, the greater the pool of knowledge assets at the company's disposal. To do this right, knowledge assets must be built properly. These assets are not just facts, but they are also people. In order to build these assets, a knowledge architecture—the intranet—must be put in place.

This architecture must support the goals and objectives of the business. The business processes that are defined and implemented within the knowledge architecture must be rewarded for their contribution to the knowledge assets of the company, and evaluation methods and metrics must be put in place to ensure that the company is moving in the overall direction of knowledge development.

Information Models in Support of a Knowledge Architecture

Most businesses implementing intranets want solutions that leverage their investments in existing systems and exploit the Internet as another means of increasing business opportunities.

However, most companies plan their first intranet implementation that uses an information model that falls short of supporting a knowledge architecture. In order to start building an intranet that supports a knowledge architecture and provides support to the mission-critical business process of the company, you have to have a vision of where you want to be and what the intranet will be like when it is completed.

This vision must incorporate all aspects of the company's operations, both internal and external, because the business processes of the company do not focus solely on internal activities. Once this vision of the extended enterprise has been created, you can plan how you will grow your intranet to achieve this vision.

Note

> Many books do better justice to the topic of structuring information resources in support of a knowledge architecture than can be done in a single chapter of this book. Please refer to your local bookstore for titles. Paul Strasser's new book, *The Politics of Information*, is an excellent place to start.

Four basic information models have evolved as companies have implemented intranets. They are as follows:

- Simple IntraWeb

- Interactive IntraWeb

- Distributed IntraWeb

- Enterprise Intranet

These models have evolved to match the visions of the people who implemented them. Only one model—the Enterprise Intranet—stretches itself to incorporate the vision of the extended enterprise.

If you start with the vision of the intranet supporting the extended enterprise, you must plan to grow your intranet using the Enterprise Intranet model. The easiest way to approach that growth is to implement the components of the other information models as the stepping stones to the Enterprise Intranet.

The implementation of a Simple IntraWeb and the subsequent progression to Interactive and then, in some cases, Distributed IntraWeb is the growth pattern of many intranets currently in place. However, most of these intranets did not plan to arrive at their eventual destination. This book aims to get you to *plan* to arrive at the Enterprise Intranet by growing quickly through the other models and considering them as stages of growth in the establishment of your Enterprise Intranet, your enterprise knowledge architecture.

The following sections will describe each of these information models and seek to demonstrate the advantages of growing your intranet to the Enterprise intranet. The models will be discussed in ascending growth and complexity.

Simple IntraWeb

The IntraWeb, as discussed in Chapter 1, is really just an internal Web server that publishes static pages of HTML text. The browser opens up a connection to the server, and the server returns the page and closes the connection. If the company's information is relatively stable and does not change, this model may work. A measure of interaction can be added by creating lists of links to sites that the user might be interested in reviewing.

In order to provide the users with all the internal information required to do their jobs, it is possible that an organization could have all staff spending a large part of their day creating the information files that others within the company would re-use.

In research from years ago, it was stated that about 60 percent of the information output of any system, human or machine, was subsequently used as input for another process.

Given the needs of the knowledge architecture and the "knowledge network," the intranet, this model does not really enter into the picture.

Many organizations have users who have put up internal Web sites in order to publish the work they have done. This is usually done by someone with an interest in the technology and is built in their spare time. Once the Web site is up, people will go there as long as there is information of interest. Because these sites are usually not in support of a business process, they are usually short-lived.

In many large organizations, if one group puts up an IntraWeb, another group will put one up as well. And then others will follow. This vanity publishing is able to be corralled if the information technology group offers a centralized IntraWeb where all who wish can have their own space within the guidelines and framework. As a general rule, there is very little done in the way of updating the information in this type of scenario. The tools and methodologies to support such initiatives are lacking.

An example of the model would be the finance department putting up the Policies and Procedures manual. This is a big undertaking if it is to be converted to HTML, and it can take some time to prepare. If a user wanted to request a report from the financial system, he or she could look up the appropriate financial coding online but would have to e-mail or write a request to the folks over in accounting to run the report and send it back to the user.

Interactive IntraWeb

This model extends the first model wherein the resources are centralized and all requests pass through one point. While it enables the user to request information from a variety of back end servers, it is an *information distribution* model. The user formulates a query and inputs the request via the form, the CGI program works its magic, and the data is passed back from the data server (as text or data) to the user.

An interactive IntraWeb contains forms, fields, and buttons (as outlined in Chapter 9, "Beyond Basic HTML: Using Forms to Handle Information") that take input from the user before opening a connection to the server to allow the data and choices to be transmitted. The HTTP server passes the information to a custom server program or script for processing, and then, in turn, a new page is passed back to the browser for viewing. The connection between browser and server is then broken.

This model does seem to provide a foundation for the knowledge network you need to have in place. It is, however, expensive relative to server resources and time because another connection must be established for each communication between browser and server.

By using HTTP as the middleware and the CGI to call the custom server program or script, this model supports simple client/server computing. As long as there is no demand for high levels of interaction between the client and the server, this model works well. Incidentally, there *is* a need for interaction between the client and server, which is why this model is also undesirable for a corporate intranet.

For an example of what is typically implemented at this level, consider the following: a user wants to obtain the latest marketing information and sales numbers for a specific product in relation to a marketing campaign that is being planned. From the intranet, the text documents from marketing are online and available and the financial figures are accessible through a CGI screen, assuming the user has appropriate security levels.

Most companies are at this stage in the implementation of intranet-based technologies in support of the company's business processes.

Distributed IntraWeb

This model attempts to take into account and utilize the current infrastructure of the organization with its data sources distributed throughout the organization. The implementation of technology here attempts to automate repeated functions so that the user does not have to initiate them directly. The simple action of opening an HTML file would invoke the procedure on behalf of the user.

Through the introduction of the Java programming language, small programs, called applets, can be incorporated into the pages sent to the browser. As the browser views the page, the Java applet runs within the browser—in essence there are two technical processes working: the browser is retrieving the information and the Java applet is performing its duties. To date these applets have been used primarily for animation and sound that can be seen on a variety of Internet sites—look for moving graphics, blinking eyes, and so forth.

What might happen within a typical hypothetical insurance company illustrates how a Distributed IntraWeb, if planned and implemented appropriately, could operate: The sales manager arrives in the morning and fires up the browser on the screen. As the manager opens the home page of the intranet, a program sends a query requesting information on the sales of policies from the day before to be delivered to the manager's browser. As the manager starts to skim the latest company news on a sub-page within the intranet, his computer beeps, and a dialog box appears on the screen saying that his daily sales report has arrived. The manager chooses to view the information, and the browser screen is loaded with the report, formatted to the manger's previously defined specifications.

This model provides a richer user interface and can move some of the task processes to the client (for example, parameter checking in the browser—see Chapter 10, "Introduction to CGI," for a refresher on parameter checking) instead of leaving them on the server. However, this model is still tied to the HTTP protocol for communications purposes. Thus, this model is not the most desirable system either; but in the growth stages of the intranet toward the Enterprise intranet, your intranet will pass through it.

You are moving along the road to the required architecture, the road to the Enterprise Intranet. The users must be able to have the intranet do the work for them, not the other way around. Not many companies have been able to reach this far in their intranet, but those who *have* arrived here recognize that they can utilize the functionality inherent in this information model to support most of their business processes.

Enterprise Intranet

As Java programming language matures and companies begin to develop truly useful applications, this model will be replete with true open client/server applications. Picture this: instead of loading an HTML page, the client is coded in downloadable Java and is running in any Java-capable browser.

Note

Java is *the* programming language of the intranet as far as the eyes can see. The Java programming language and environment is designed to solve a number of problems in modern programming practice. Java started as a part of a larger project to develop advanced software for consumer electronics. These devices were to be small, portable, and distributed systems. Within the intranet alone, there has been the growth of multiple incompatible hardware architectures, each supporting multiple incompatible operating systems, with each platform operating with one or more incompatible graphical user interfaces. Creating applications with Java is supposed to allow you to cope with all this and make your applications work in a distributed browser-server environment. The growth of the Internet, the intranet, and "electronic commerce" has introduced new dimensions of complexity into the development process.

For more information on the Java programming language, please refer to *Java!* by Tim Ritchey (New Riders, 1995).

When a page containing a Java applet is downloaded by an HTTP server to the browser, the applet runs in the browser and opens its own communications session with the server. In addition, the applet communicates with another server to provide access to a wide variety of databases, in addition to supporting a variety of middleware, including HTTP, TCP/IP, and Secure Sockets Layer (SSL).

The ability to use protocols other than HTTP is the defining moment. No longer will the information systems be bounded to this particular protocol.

As the new Java Database Connection (JDBC) standards come out, the users will be able to access a variety of database systems. At the time of writing, IBM, Oracle, and Sybase intend to support JDBC.

The implementation of JDBC will permit programmers to develop standalone routines that will work with Java or CGI programs. These routines will take the user's query from an HTTP server and pass it along to the data servers using their respective communications protocols. The results will be returned along the same path for display in the browser.

This seems like a big mouthful and it is. But what it boils down to is this: things are in development that will enable the browser on the desk to connect to a variety of information/data stores; they will not only do retrieval of files known today, but they will be able to do analysis for the user on the data targeted just by opening up the home page on the user's screen.

A hypothetical example of this type of implementation would be an extension of the example used in the Distributed IntraWeb model. Instead of receiving only the sales figures from yesterday, the sales manager is presented a series of information reports to peruse.

For example, after having received the sales figures for the previous day, a series of other actions are performed as follows:

- By using the returned sales figures as input, a report is created showing monthly sales projections by product, complete with variance analysis—using the sales database server

- Projected commissions for the remainder of the month are calculated and results are forwarded to payroll for calculation of mid-month draw for salesmen—using sales, human resources, and accounting database servers

- Meetings are automatically scheduled with sales staff whose sales projections were below normal levels—using sales database and calendaring servers

Quite the little browser page!

In order to get to this Enterprise Intranet model and have it work successfully, wholesale changes are needed in the way in which the information resources of the company are structured. The next chapter will discuss this in more detail.

As you can see, this Enterprise Intranet model is the preferred destination for the intranet. The implementation of the functionality described above enables extensive automated support for the mission-critical business processes of a company and truly supports a knowledge architecture.

Even though the current technology available to the intranet is not capable of delivering this level of functionality, the technological solutions are not far off. By planning to arrive at this level, you can design and prepare for the implementation of this functionality within the design of your support systems to the business processes.

Other Issues to Consider When Establishing a New Information Model

The development and implementation of a new information model is not a trivial task. It requires the analysis and thorough understanding of the following characteristics of the company:

- Vision—its philosophy and driving force for the future

- Mission—its business definition

- Business objectives—how the company measures success

- Critical success factors—the means of achieving success

- Strategies—key decisions, protocols, policies, and plans

- Mission-critical processes—activities performed that are cornerstones of core business processes

In order to establish the required knowledge architecture, two issues that are not specifically focused on the design of the intranet, technicality and time, must be addressed.

Some Organizational Issues

The development and implementation of the intranet as the company's knowledge network will have an impact on the traditional culture and philosophy of the company. The process is going to tear down the silos that have been built, or at least make them transparent so that the people who maintain them will be recognizable. Knowledge manufacturing is not just for people with doctorates—anyone in the organization can add to the corporate knowledge base.

The following organizational questions will be answered in chapters later on within this book. They are listed below to open the reader's thoughts throughout the remainder of the book.

- How does one make the intranet attractive enough to bring everyone in the company to use it as *the* source for information, while not excluding anyone?

- As in any other project, there is a life cycle that must be managed and respected. Have the procedures necessary to sustain the life of the intranet been established?

- Who owns the intranet? Who has control over its direction and policies? Is this a communal project with an oversight committee? Or is it an exit strategy for one individual?

The whole premise of this book is to develop an information resource space that entices users to stay within the "walls" of the intranet to find the answers they seek. Through the development of technologies of the remaining chapters, this book will attempt to provide the technological solutions to these questions. The philosophical part of the answer depends upon the circumstances of the reader and how they respond to the text.

The next chapter will discuss the ownership of the intranet within the structure of the company's information resources.

Some Technical Issues

All the areas of the company need to perform what they do best to help bring about the intranet within the knowledge architecture concept. Some of the issues that are faced in the knowledge architecture's technology component come about when one looks at the intranet as the means of providing the optimal set of tools for the users to do their jobs. It is imperative that the personnel of the company simultaneously get access to all the information they require to perform their duties, and at the same time add to the base of knowledge assets through the use of one single tool.

Companies must change the emphasis of the technologists from tracking projects and writing code to facilitating information and knowledge exchange. They have to optimize the hardware platforms to work with the forms, scripting, and gateway applications that will allow the groupware, conferencing, database access, and other things required to form the technology architecture.

The Human Resources staff must work closely with the intranet in order to develop the training and education programs required to bring people into the fold. Their help is also needed in determining resourcing levels—whom to train for specific jobs or whom to hire in. The implementers of the intranet must also work with the HR folks to understand how to manage the change from the social impact that it will have when the intranet is launched as *the* way in which the knowledge base will be developed.

The intranet must also have the support of those who control the purse strings. Initially, the intranet will be seen as a cost-center by the ROI folks simply because it generates no revenue. However, if the reader agrees on the premise that the company's knowledge assets are the real currency of the company and that the company needs something to maintain and make available these selfsame assets, then the value proposition will have to be the strongest voice for the intranet—at least initially.

To summarize, these are the major issues that must be addressed:

- How to get information to all employees simultaneously

- How to facilitate information and knowledge exchange

- How to change the culture of the organization to handle the new information paradigm

- How to sell the idea of the intranet to those who hold the purse strings

The first two points will be addressed in Chapter 17, "Workflow Software, Groupware, and the Intranet." Changing the culture of an organization is not something this book can do on its own. What this book can do is encourage you to promote the intranet as a means of changing the way work can be done within the organization. If you then demonstrate how the intranet does this through the support of mission-critical business processes, you will see people start to take an interest in the intranet, and this will pull them into changing the organizational culture simply through the use of the intranet.

Chapter 2, "Making Your Case," addressed the last of the points above in its discussion on the value proposition of the intranet.

The Dynamics of Time

Anticipate change. Pretend to be a Boy Scout: "Be prepared." What happens if the intranet is a success and the demand for intranet resources exceeds what has been allocated? Is the intranet an investment or a cost center? Knowing the prejudice of those who hold the purse strings is important. Those who hold the purse strings must be convinced that the intranet is an investment. As an investment "in the way business is done," funding should never be a problem. Just hope that when the funding is needed, it is in the bank.

Status Check

In this chapter, the need for a new information model has been discussed. In order to support the company as it changes its business processes to compete in the global marketplace, the information model of today will have to change. Not only will changing business processes force the change, but the changes in technological capability will permit and require the change.

In the following chapter, the structuring of corporate information resources to prepare for the advent of the "new information model" is discussed. Included in the discussion is a look at the ownership of the intranet.

Constructing Information Resources

13

Structuring Company Information Resources for Intranets

O rganizations today are moving away from the hierarchical models of yesterday and toward leaner, more flexible business models to keep pace with change in the marketplace. The information needs of companies are growing, and this information needs to be shared and disseminated across organizational boundaries. Empowered knowledge workers are pressured to respond to time-sensitive demands of increasing global competition.

The trend today is toward a cross-functional, team-based model that distributes the decision making to empowered employees. The information resources to which these teams require access is not only internal; it is also external. Collaboration on "live" information documents is becoming the norm. There is no longer enough time to distribute a copy to all those concerned and then wait for their answers in order to finalize the documents.

The information that is consumed and generated by these teams tends to be highly re-usable, and there is an inherent demand for the information to be shared throughout the team, the organization, and even organizations outside the company. The needs of these teams require the implementation of technologies that enable the sharing and distribution of the information, but still incorporate:

- Flexible and intuitive access mechanisms

- Dynamic sources of information accessible throughout the entire corporation

- Automated management of the resource set

Note

> Many books do better justice to the topic of structuring information resources than this one can in a single chapter. Please refer to your local bookstore for titles. Paul Strasser's new book, *The Politics of Information*, is an excellent place to start.

The goal of this chapter is to provide an approach to the structuring of an organization's information resources in order to permit the adoption of the Enterprise intranet as the "new information model." The chapter will also discuss the ownership of the intranet within the context of this new information model. The following bullets outline the topics that will be covered in this chapter:

- Developing the rationale for a new information model

- Aligning the new model with business strategies

- Determining who *owns* the intranet

The mission-critical business processes are undertaken to implement the company's business strategies. If the intranet is the new information model to be designed to support the business processes of the company, the information model must be aligned with the business strategies. This chapter will explore this concept in order to ensure that the reader appreciates the importance of aligning the information model with the business strategies.

Rationale for the New Information Model: the Intranet

The demands for information made by company staff are becoming insatiable. Part of the reason this happens is that, often, an employee will obtain a piece of information, read it, digest it, and then file it. It may be filed electronically on a personal computer, filed in a stack of papers in the In/Out pile, in "File 13," or a filing cabinet, or even placed in someone else's possession. The next time the information is needed, it is nowhere to be found.

Following are three types of information that are consumed and generated in the daily lives of a business.

1. Transactional information—sales records, for example, that are typically stored and managed by database software

2. Day-to-day operational information—memos, reports, and "FYI" notices, for example, that are by-products of the office automation tools

3. Mission-critical information—pricing and specifications of a product line, for example, necessary to create a competitive advantage

Most companies tend to have the first and second classes of information under control because they deal with the day-to-day operations of the company. The mission-critical information is often the least managed, even though it is the most important.

Mission-critical information can be characterized as follows:

- It is key to the ability to generate and maintain a competitive advantage in the market; it reflects the core business processes of the company; and it is usually product-, service-, and customer-relevant.

- It is valuable and considered the most important asset.

- It is usually developed over a long time and used over an even longer time. It is often used repeatedly and does not decrease in value, even through reuse.

Managing the information types is discussed in greater detail in the next chapter. The information classes are brought forward here to illuminate the need for a method of structuring the information resources of the company so that it is possible to implement some form of document management.

In order to support the new business models and business processes within those models, an information infrastructure must be put in place. The infrastructure is not only the technology to deliver the information as required, but also the structure of the information itself. The following sections provide a discussion on the steps required to establish a structure for the information resources of the organization.

Alignment with Business Strategies

In order to prepare for the technologies of the coming Enterprise intranet, the company needs to prepare a robust, flexible, and extensive information resource management capacity that will address its current demands and then grow with the organization.

Within the transformation from a simple IntraWeb to an interactive IntraWeb to a distributed IntraWeb to an Enterprise intranet, the ability to access information stored within the walls of the company is enhanced from step to step. To support the mission-critical business processes of the company, it is imperative that those people who are supporting these activities have access to the information resources they need whenever they require it.

The steps covered within the remainder of this section are proposed to assist the organization's decision makers in getting access to the information that is mission-critical. How do companies decide which information is critical enough to collect and store within their information models? Companies must analyze their business strategies to determine the business objectives and critical success factors that will enable them to identify the mission-critical information. The following topics in this section attempt to shed some light on the requirements and the methods of ensuring that the information model is properly aligned with the business strategies:

- The business plan

- Mission-critical processes

- The technical architecture

- The enterprise data model

- The creation of the repository

- The incorporation of legacy data

- The validation process

- The integration of the data model and the business processes

- The integration of the user interface and the *business views* of the data

- The "care and feeding" of the model: supporting staff

Business Plan

A company's business plan is the source outlining where to start defining its mission-critical information components. From the company's vision statement—its philosophy of enterprise and direction for the future—its mission is defined. The mission statement of the company defines the business in which the company finds itself.

In order for a company to measure its success, it establishes business objectives such as profit levels, market share, and turn-over rate. In order to achieve these business objectives, the company has to perform the activities absolutely perfectly in order to achieve the desired levels of success. These critical success factors are implemented through various business strategies, which can be in turn broken down in the mission-critical business processes. These business processes can be further broken down into individual activities that must take place in a specified fashion within the process in order for it, and the chain of elements, to succeed.

The business plan is the starting point. The objectives of the business, the measurable targets, must be identified for all levels of the company in order for the organization to achieve its mission. The critical success factors that outline how these objectives will be reached should also be detailed.

It is possible to dissect the chain from vision into links, individual processes that must be in place in order to achieve the vision. To successfully design and implement the intranet and to ensure that the future growth of the intranet is toward the Enterprise intranet model, the following must be done:

- Identify and analyze those processes which are mission-critical.

- Build a data model that supports these mission-critical processes.

- Build the tools that connect the process to the data.

In order to do these three activities successfully, the business plan must be used as the reference point throughout the exercise.

Read on to find out how to accomplish each task.

Mission-Critical Processes

What activities drive the business? What are the information needs of these activities? When do those responsible need the information? Once these elements have been determined by the company's business analyst(s), the elements must be tracked. The information requirements need to mapped back to the critical success factors. Once this has been done, the company has:

- Mapped the individual activities of mission-critical business processes to the critical success factors that must be met.

- Identified the information needed to perform the activities.

- Distinguished those activities which do not currently support mission-critical goals and objectives of the company.

The first two points will be discussed later; the third provides a list of activities that can be reviewed by the company to determine its value to the company. If no value is added by the activity, and it does not support the mission-critical business processes of the company, a business decision should be made about the life expectancy of the activity. This is not a matter for this book to discuss.

By mapping the information requirements to the activities, the company understands what information is required and at what point. During the analyses of the activities, the specific data entities and their attributes should be identified. Also, the individuals performing the analysis must understand the source, volume, and trends of the information in order to help define the scope and infrastructure that is required.

The last step in the analysis of these mission-critical business processes is to map the data elements of the information requirements back to the legacy data sources from which they originated. Once this has been done, the business analyst can pass the findings to the technical architects.

Technical Architecture

In order to build and design an efficient and effective Enterprise intranet that meets current needs and will handle future expansion, state-of-the-market technology should be employed. The technology to be implemented must support and be integrated with the current technology of the company and any future technology that the company can envision. The building blocks for this architecture include the following:

- A communications infrastructure

- Storage facilities for the data

- A graphical user interface

The technical architecture includes a communications infrastructure that allows the collection, dissemination, and replication of data. The technology for the data warehouse should run on the existing network of the company. In addition, because the intranet model currently runs on TCP/IP, the technology must be accessible from the browser.

The volume of data for storage means that the appropriate storage technology must be in place. Most companies use relational databases such as Oracle or Sybase to store their data. In some large organizations the computing platform may be mainframe or mini-computer, although most companies today are choosing a client/server environment to put the ability to access, manipulate, and present the data at the desktop. With the intranet, the preference at the moment is for client/server (you should already be familiar with how to access information stored within SQL database so this should not present a problem in terms of access to the data).

One key feature of the storage and structuring of the information resources is the ability to get the information into the hands of the people managing and operating the mission-critical business processes. If the business environment is decentralized, the data warehousing solution must be able to get the appropriate information into the hands of the appropriate staff when and where they need it.

Because the intranet provides a single graphical user interface (GUI) to all other information holdings of the organization, access to the database information also must be gained through the browser. As the tools required to create and maintain the physical components are implemented, the interface to these tools must also work through the browser. Thus, a graphical user interface is a requirement because the interface needs to be easy to use and must be accessible from a browser. The user interface tools that exist in the market at this time allow for retrieval, analysis, and transfer of information to the required users.

The result of the creation of this new information model and its actual implementation is a properly designed data warehouse that allows the user to retrieve information easily and quickly. The data warehouse must be able to answer the questions that the process managers ask by providing the ability to drill down from a summary report through to the base data elements. In analyzing the business process and its operations, the process managers must be able to examine the granular details of their processes to determine the effectiveness and efficiency of their operations.

The final point within this discussion of the technical architecture is that the structure of the data model and the user interface must not be developed in isolation. If the goals and objectives of the organization are to be met, the user interface and the data model must be designed to be integral components of the business processes. That can only be done through complete and exhaustive analysis in cooperation with the process managers.

Enterprise Data Model

The data modeling team takes the information needed to support the activities within the mission-critical business processes and builds the data model that supports the processes. In order to properly support the overall goals of the company, the data model must be designed from the top down.

Note

> Data modeling is a discipline within the realm of computer science. Depending upon the size of the organization and the complexities of its data holdings, a data modeller may already be on staff to manage and maintain the structure of the information resources. Consultants can be found who will perform your data modeling for you, leaving you with the model to implement. Some small organizations do not deal with anything more than a desktop computer with Microsoft Access databases. The data modeller in this case may well be the person who put the initial database together.
>
> The size of a company's data modeling team and the skill sets of the individuals involved will vary from organization to organization. However, it is important that the data modeling just gets done and that the resulting model aligns with the business strategies of the company—it is less important *how* it gets done.

Be sure to look at the extended enterprise in which the company finds itself when designing the data model. The inability to get to the data of the entire enterprise from the perspective of customer relationships, products, services, and profitability often leads to a failure in the long run. The integration of the company's legacy applications (the currently existing database applications) into the data model provides the road map that allows the integration of the legacy information into one common enterprise data structure.

Once the model is built for the entire enterprise, it must be validated by the users within the mission-critical activities; then the data from the legacy applications must be mapped to the model and verified again.

Creating an enterprise data model is a significant endeavor. The rationale for creating one is that once all the data elements in all the applications within the company have been mapped to the data model, it is much easier to find, obtain, and deliver information to the user's computer.

Creating the Repository

Once the data modeling is complete, the model, the entities, and all the attributes are transferred into the repository tool selected by the folks who designed the technical architecture. The repository is used to store the model, the legacy application "data dictionaries," data transformation rules, and, finally, the business views of the information and the rules associated with them.

The repository performs the following basic functions with the information infrastructure:

- It defines the target attributers for mapping the data from the legacy applications to the business processes.

- It helps users find information through on-line help and a data dictionary.

- It documents the data model.

The goal of the repository is to provide the company a single point of access and control to the data resources. The repository can be seen to drive the information management process—it is the "font of all knowledge" about the data holdings. The repository tracks where the data came from, how often it is accessed, how it should be translated or transformed, who sees it, what business processes it drives, and which critical success factors it supports. A really well-designed repository makes the complex information holdings of a company seem as simple as an on-line index—browse/search the index to find the description of the information that you want, press a button, and, presto, the requested information appears.

When the data model is completed, the location of the data elements, their attributes, and the business rules and views that are associated with the data element are all entered into the repository. The repository then provides the electronic means to locate the data element the user seeks.

Simply put, the user calls an HTML file that interacts with the repository in order to locate the information resource the user requires. The repository provides the location and the coordinates of the data element for the browser, and the browser then displays the file to the user.

When evaluating repository tools, the following user interface tools are integral components of the product selected:

- Security by user, application, view, entity, or data element level

- Drill-down support through business topics, views, and data elements

Note

For those unfamiliar with the expression "drill-down," the following hypothetical example may help to explain the functional requirement being specified.

The president of ABG Inc. is reviewing the consolidated financial results of the company on his computer screen. He is interested in finding out more about the results coming from one of the plants showing extremely high profitability this month. He points at the plant name, a hyperlink, and retrieves the plant's financial statements.

Here he notices that one of the product lines on the sales portion of the financials shows incredible volume. He clicks on the product line name, a hyperlink, to see the details behind the numbers he sees currently on his screen. The sales breakdown by individual product appears. The president finds the source of the sales volume, a product whose manufacture had been discontinued six months earlier but was still available in inventory.

continues

To find out who bought the product, the president selects the hyperlink of the product in question and the screen displays to him the information contained in the sales register—the invoice number, the customer number, the part number, and the sales rep's number. By selecting the hyperlink of the customer number, the customer profile of the company in question appears on the screen. Satisfied by the details he is able to find, the president closes up the details and returns to his analysis of the consolidated results.

This ability to "drill down" through the layers to the facts at the bottom is the functional requirement which is sought.

- Interfaces to reporting, analysis, and extraction tools (the preference here is for browser-accessible tools)

- On-line help available at all levels

If these functions are present with the implemented repository tool, the users' learning time can be reduced, the complexities of the data model are hidden, and support requirements are minimal. The ability of the users to formulate their own queries is also desirable, although not mandatory.

The last thing to ascertain in implementing a repository is that it must support the data warehouse's user interface. If both the repository and the warehouse support browser access, so much the better. Your intranet objective is to provide the users with a single interface to all the company's data.

Incorporating Legacy Data

Once the data model has been developed and loaded into the repository along with the legacy master file description, the mapping of the data within the legacy applications to the data model entities must take place.

In order to retrieve information that is stored in the legacy applications through the repository, the mapping must incorporate the rules regarding the validation, calculation, and transformation of the data. These rules must also be loaded into the repository along with the structure of the data. The process of mapping the data elements and the rules associated with the data is done from the bottom up because the individual data elements and their attributes must be mapped from the legacy system to the repository.

By establishing the relationship through the repository, the collection, loading, and presentation of data link the business strategies to business views and, in turn, to the actual data. Once this is complete, the information resources of the company that are now "integrated" should be available to all users.

Before the doors can be opened to the users, the validation stage must be completed along with some integration of views to business processes.

Validation Process

The validity of the data mapping must be checked to ensure that the required information elements are available to answer the queries of the process managers. The repository, the supporting modeling tools, and the reporting tools must all be tested in this phase to ensure that the information that is expected is actually delivered.

By testing all the components to see if the information mapping process has been done accurately, you should ensure the desired result of getting the right information to the right people where and when they need it. Because of the intricacies of incorporating legacy data elements into an integrated data model, the following should be reviewed for accuracy during testing, and if there are any discrepancies, should be re-analyzed to correct, before continuing:

- Individual attributes of each data element stored within the repository

- Keys that ensure the proper indexing and relational functions

- Summary levels in which individual elements are accessible for "roll-up"

- Frequencies of update, occurrence, usage, and so on

- Historical data requirements relative to how long the data stays in the system

If there are any discrepancies, bring in the data modellers, the business process managers, and the business analysts who analyzed the information requirements to help work through the problem areas. This is one area of the technology that must be correctly aligned before implementation or else the whole process falls apart.

Integrating Data Model and Business Processes

Now that the data model has been created and validated, including the incorporation of the legacy data systems, the information must be organized in such a fashion as to meet the requirements of the process manager (or any other employee involved in the process). Business views of the data are created by "clustering" data, represented by one or more entities and attributes, to support the measurement of the performance standards as outlined in the business objectives. Because the mission-business process supports a measurable process, the ability to view the data in the fashion that allows comparison with the standards must be implemented.

Note

> For those of a less technical nature, this means that data elements can be pulled from across the breadth of the information resources that are identified in the repository. These elements are grouped in a "virtual table" with which the user may work. The definition of these business views, including access permissions, is also stored within the repository.

Now that the data elements have been pulled together in business views to support the mission-critical processes, what is the next step?

Integration of the User Interface and Business Views

Once the business views have been linked to a mission-critical business process, the participants in that process can get at the data they need to perform their tasks. The last piece in the puzzle is to develop the user interface screens that enable the users to "mine" the data. Designed properly with the incorporation of the repository, the user interface often results in significant productivity gains.

The users should be able to look at summary level data and drill down through the repository to the data stored in the warehouse or in a legacy system. Tools are available that develop user interfaces rapidly. Most of the repository tools provide their own interfaces for smoother integration.

The intranet should ensure that browser access is mandatory. If the business views are accessible to the user, then based on the work done in earlier chapters, forms can be created that use the mapping information from the repository. The simple description of the concept is that because the definition of the business view resides in the repository, the HTML form required would pass the query string to the repository requesting information from the view. The repository in turn would act upon that request, retrieving the data from the various data stores and pass the results back to the user's browser.

Care and Feeding: Supporting Staff

Because of the need to support the mission-critical business processes, the information infrastructure put in place needs very strong people in the various roles. If the activities in the critical processes don't have the resources they require, the goals and objectives will not be met. The basic team members or skill sets that are required to support this infrastructure include, but are not limited to, the following:

- Business analyst—must understand the vision, mission, objectives, and critical success factors thoroughly in order to be successful. This role is crucial because the critical activities must be defined and the information requirements must be detailed.

- Data architect—must maintain the data standards, act as the data steward enforcing the standards, and maintain the data model as more legacy systems are added. Data collection, transformation, distribution, and loading must be defined and monitored by the architects.

- Database administrator—manages the impact on the computers and software upon which the databases run as information resource volumes grow. Performance levels must be monitored to determine when upgrades or other optimization strategies must be implemented.

- Network configuration manager —provides reliable and rapid access to the information resources across internal networks as well as the Internet. Access to information stores will increase as people recognize the strategic value of information.

- End-user support—assists in accessing the data, developing reports, training in the usage of the systems, and supporting the changes that will occur as new information sources are added. This job is important because of the changes in the way people will work and the way in which the tools will be implemented.

In order to maintain the information model, the preceding positions or functions must exist within the support team for the infrastructure. The support of this information infrastructure is mission-critical as it, in turn, supports mission-critical activities.

Note

In Chapter 15, "Role of the IntraMaster," the supporting cast of the intranet is outlined. The people in the IntraMaster's support team are there to provide a delivery service, in simple terms, of critical information to the people who require the information in support of their respective business processes. The supporting cast identified in this chapter is part of those processes in support roles—the strategic planning process and the various processes that create and utilize the databases (sales and marketing, accounting, and human resources, for example). In some cases, when the company is small, there is only one staff person who gets to play all the roles covered here and in

Chapter 15. In most cases, however, there are separate groups, and it is not easy to bridge the two sides of intranet and the data model components.

Over time, companies will understand that the process of providing strategic information to mission-critical business processes is in itself a mission-critical business process. When this occurs, all the personnel dealing with the care and delivery of information will be brought together into a strategic unit. At that time, every single employee in the company becomes a de facto member of the intranet team, because every time they enter a word into the intranet, they are a content provider and part of the "care and feeding crowd." This is a true Enterprise intranet.

A Quick Summary

In order to ensure that the intranet has the ability to support the company in the new business models that it undertakes, the information model in place must align with the business strategies of the company.

By performing the analysis of the processes and activities intended to deliver results that meet the established business objectives, improvement of existing processes or innovative new processes can be implemented.

Starting with the review of the business plan to determine the mission-critical business processes of the company, this chapter has looked at the following:

- Defining the requirements of the technical architecture as a communications infrastructure, data storage facility, and a graphical user interface

- The development of the data model by taking the elements of required information and organizing them into a structure

- The requirement for and functions of the repository in enabling the user to find and access data across all the information resources of the company

- The incorporation and validation of legacy data collections into the repository and data model

- The care and feeding of the information by the supporting staff

It is not the application that will bring about significant change within the organization; the application must change the way in which work is done. The warehouse and repository, within the framework of the Enterprise intranet provide the means to bring to the user all the data resources that support the mission-critical business processes. How the company implements solutions which change the way the users work with the information available to them is the subject of several of the remaining chapters.

Who Owns the Intranet?

Who owns an intranet is the topic of much debate in many organizations and many of the discussions forums on the Internet.

Many Web junkies view the intranet as an extension of the Internet and would prefer to let the relative anarchy of the Internet rule the intranet.

Human Resource groups in other organizations have decided that the intranet is their responsibility and are attempting to impose massive restrictions on the use of the intranet within the organization.

The trend within the marketplace is the effective implementations of intranets that are moving toward the Enterprise intranet model, the model that is recommended within these pages, which is to create a small group—an "oversight committee"—to manage the intranet. This group is a board of directors that is comprised of the managers of the mission-critical business process, the Information Systems manager, the Human Resources manager, Internal Communications (if such a group exists), and the senior manager responsible for Finance.

These representatives and their reasons for existence are outlined in the following list:

- Managers of mission-critical business processes—to get the information they need from the intranet—it is in their best interests to ensure the intranet works well

- Information Systems—to be responsible for the technical direction; to ensure the ability to implement the solutions required and recommended by the others

- Human Resources—to ensure that the human-ware of the company has access to the appropriate training in order to utilize the technology; assist in determining how to deal with the cultural implications of intranet implementation

- Internal Communications—to establish, as professional communicators, a good look and feel; to understand how to prepare and present information

- Senior Finance Manager—to influence the person with the deepest pockets into the direction of the intranet; to understand the requirements of the mission-critical business processes for critical input provided by infrastructure in order to provide the intranet leverage to find funding when required

The functions of this group include the following:

- Development of policies for the intranet, including Acceptable Use, Acceptable Content, and Sub-site Development policies

- Determination of priority applications for inclusion

- Development of design guidelines (establishing the look and feel of the different sites)

- Recommendations and prepared financial requests for additional resources

The policies surrounding the use and provision of content to the intranet should be in place before the intranet is actually in place. This grants users and providers the parameters of the intranet to which they must adhere. Appendix A contains some samples of Acceptable Use Policies.

Although this oversight committee creates a policy on the provision of content, once a group creates a sub-site within the framework of the intranet, that group owns the site and is responsible for maintaining the content on the page. Chapter 15, "Role of the IntraMaster," also discusses the need for this committee with respect to its role in assisting the IntraMaster in the performance of the functions of his office.

In general, most intranets in place today have few or no ownership committees or battles over who controls the content while the intranet in question is in the "simple InfoWeb" phase. Once additional capabilities are developed to access other resources, such as databases or internal discussion forums, battles over control tend to become more frequent.

As the intranet grows into its role of supporting mission-critical functions, there must be an oversight group to ensure that all the mission-critical business processes can be addressed and supported by the intranet.

Status Check

After reviewing the contents of the chapter, you should have an understanding of what is required to structure the company's information resources for the coming of the Enterprise intranet. Through the implementation of a data warehouse and the repository tools on top of the warehouse, the legacy data and the other information holdings of the company are now in a format that can be accessed through the skills already covered and developed in this book.

As the technology matures to the levels outlined in the previous chapter, these tools will be a must for the Enterprise intranet. In any event, the analysis of the business plan to determine the key activities that support the mission-critical business processes provides an excellent understanding of the data resources that are used within the core functions of the company, where they are located, and when and where they are needed. From this base of knowledge the reader can proceed to create applications that support the core business functions, drawing on the key information components, and then provide a solution from within the intranet. This can only enhance the value of the intranet in the eyes of any unbelievers in the reader's organization.

The next chapter deals with the issues of document and content management, moving the discussion here forward in support of the critical activities of the company.

Document Management

When a company leverages its available assets, competitive advantage can be achieved. One of the areas getting a lot of focus in the competitive advantage arena is the leveraging of the information assets of a company. If a company can leverage its stores of valuable mission-critical information, the company has the ability to stay ahead of its competitors.

The unfortunate thing about mission-critical information is that it is usually the least managed information in organizations today. One has the ability within the intranet to seek solutions to this problem through both the use of the client/server nature of the technologies and the desire to leverage all information assets.

This chapter provides an overview of document management technology by exploring documents, the various meanings of document management, what a document management system actually manages, benefits, and choosing a solution. The following questions will be answered:

- What is a document management system?

- What does a document management system manage?

- How do you choose a document management system?

In that last question, a list of vendors has been provided. These vendors offer both product solutions as well as consulting and implementation assistance.

What Document Management Is

A document used to be a piece of paper with something written or printed on it. Document management used to be done through storage boxes, filing cabinets, index cards, card catalogs, and the sweat of the brow. This section establishes an understanding of the current concepts of documents and document management.

Today, document management is not only the technology that manages the documents; it is also the technology that manages the information that resides within the documents. In order to create a competitive advantage from its information resources, a company must have a document management system that manages mission-critical information—from creation, through control, and on to dissemination.

A document management system is required if the company has any of the following:

- Different kinds of information holdings that are not integrated into the intranet computing environment

- Staff spending more time searching for information than using it

- Project teams that cannot access the important information resources held throughout the company

- Mission-critical information stored in desktop computers rather than in LAN file server storage

- The need to reuse information components in a variety of documents

If the preceding points describe the situation in an organization, a document management solution should enable the location and retrieval of accurate and timely information that can be disseminated across the organization more effectively and more efficiently.

What a Document Is

Discussions about documents today tend to focus on the definition of a document as an electronic collection of text, graphics, tables of figures and data, engineering drawings, and even video and audio. A document is some method of getting information into the hands and heads of its reviewers. Coming from multiple sources, documents can either be artifacts of work already complete, or they can contain up-to-the-second information—looking at the same document two minutes later might reveal an entirely different set of information.

Documents are used to communicate and develop information. As a means of communication, "putting it on paper" provides a means of obtaining consensus about the information presented, requiring accurate and timely information in order for people to make informed decisions. Approximately 60 percent of all information created is used as input for another process. For example, the month-end inventory report is created by accounting; the marketing manager reviews it and creates a special promotion program to reduce inventory levels in several products; and the sales manager and finance department work out the pricing levels and inform the sales representatives of the program.

Documents are used as the means of distributing information throughout the organization. Information is captured, managed, and controlled through documents. The information that is mission-critical to the company is contained in the most important documents of all. In the strategic business processes that govern the way the company operates, something has to be moved from stage to stage and from process to process—that something is a document.

For example, branch managers receive year-to-date financial reports, prepare their forecasts for the remainder of the year, and, based on these numbers, prepare their projections for the next year. These branch projections are rolled up into the corporate projections for the coming year. Based on these projections, the financing requirements are developed and submitted to the Board for approval. In each and every case, a document is moved from one stage to the next.

One of the things that any business employee understands from his or her working life is that the closer the business process is to the core business processes of the company, the more essential the document reflecting it becomes.

Two basic types of documents are found within an organization (it is important to understand that they are usually managed by different types of document-management systems):

- Office-automation tools (such as word processors, spreadsheet software, and presentation software) generate memos, letters, briefing notes, and charts that everyone uses.

- Teams or workgroups focus on the mission-critical business processes and tend to create and manage the more strategic, critical documents such as the company's strategic plan or the business case for a new product line.

How these different document types are managed will be touched on later in this chapter.

What a Document Management System Manages

A document management system manages the status of information—where it is located, how to get at it, where it has been used before, how to move the information between people and processes, and how one piece relates to another. The concept is explored a little further in the next section.

Different Kinds of Information

In Chapter 13, "Structuring Company Information Resources for Intranets," three classes of information that need to be made available via the intranet to the users in the organization were identified. They are repeated in the following list (with one slight change) to match the day-to-day operational information with their source applications, the office automation tools. The three classes of information are the following:

- Transaction-based—information stored in and controlled by the SQL databases, coming from interactions with customers, suppliers, and staff

- Office automation-based—information created at the desktop—memos, letters, status reports, presentations, and so on—usually highly unstructured

- Mission-critical—information necessary to create the competitive advantage sought, varying in nature based upon the organization in question (for example, in sales organization, the pricing and specifications of the product line)

Most companies tend to have the first and second classes of information under control because they deal with the day-to-day operations of the company. The mission-critical information is often the least managed even though it is of the most importance.

Mission-critical information can be characterized as follows:

- It is key to the ability to generate and maintain a competitive advantage in the market; it reflects the core business processes of the company; and it is usually product-, service-, and customer-relevant.

- It is valuable and considered the most important asset.

- It is usually developed over a long time and used over an even longer time. It is often used repeatedly and does not decrease in value, even through reuse.

Why You Should Have a Document Management System

Document management technology allows a company's information systems to be used as a key enabler in the competitive global marketplace. By enabling users to access information across platforms and recombine components into new documents, intranets and document management systems reduce the time required to create and disseminate information. Most solutions on the market adhere to such standards as SGML and, therefore, guarantee adherence to standards for interoperability.

Because of its long life, reusability, and significance to the well-being of the company, you need a document management system that will manage the mission-critical information as well as the day-to-day output of the company. You also need to be able to manage the range of data formats in which the information holdings are stored.

Note

Other management systems are sometimes confused with document management. In reality, these systems are components of a corporate document management system:

- Data management system—the relational database systems the company employs and how the contents are managed; the content is often an input into the documents maintained by the document management system.

- Image management system—the scanning of paper documents into a computerized system for search and retrieval based on a few facts about the documents; the contents of the images cannot be indexed and searched for reuse in other documents.

- Office automation systems—these text- and graphics-oriented systems are usually based around individual productivity and cannot manage or assemble information from diverse sources across the company.

The selection of the type of document management system needed for an organization depends upon the type of information to be managed as well as any types of information that might be put in place in the future. Where intelligent assembly, control, reuse, and dissemination of the information is required now or in the future, a document management system is probably required. And in most cases, the output of the other types of information management systems listed above will be included in the document management system.

Due to the length of time required to prepare the mission-critical information documents and its long useful lifetime, the management of the life cycle of important documents needs to be incorporated into the document management system. The majority of documents go through four basic steps:

1. Creation—Documents are created in a variety of ways, from word processing to spreadsheets to engineering drawings in a CAD program. The document is normally placed into a shared workspace.

2. Review—A cycle of review, comment, and edit by others in the project/workgroup takes place until the appropriate approvals are given. The document is placed in a "work-in-process" repository.

3. Assembly—All the information components, having been through their review cycle, are assembled into the final document, which is then stored in a repository of documents available for general consumption.

4. Dissemination—The document is made available to others for use and comment.

As soon as the document is released for dissemination purposes, the whole cycle starts again in preparation for the next release of the document.

The document management system needs to manage the information throughout its life cycle, ensuring that the correct people review the content at the appropriate time. A good document management system manages the interdependencies of information within the documents and notifies the participants, as appropriate, if changes in the information occur. All previous versions of the document must be available for review.

In order to keep track of documents, wherever they are in their life cycle, especially those that are mission-critical, and ensure that the information within those documents is managed properly, some form of document management system needs to be incorporated within the intranet.

Benefits of Document Management

The benefits of implementing a document management system can be summarized in two words: competitive advantage. Combined with the intranet, document management software is the enabler to achieve competitive advantage. By providing immediate access to information sources, increasing the speed and ease of the movement of information within the company, and getting information into the hands of those who need it whenever they need it, a document management system provides one of the keys to reducing the time to market, thereby increasing product quality and customer satisfaction and reducing costs.

Document management systems can enhance the competitive advantage a company enjoys by improving the accessibility, the accuracy, the timeliness, and the velocity of information moving through the organization. Some of the benefits that can be achieved include the following:

- Reduced time to market

- Improved quality

- Increased productivity

- Reduced costs

Reduced Time to Market

A few barriers often stand in the way of getting a new product to the market successfully, quickly, effectively, and efficiently. These barriers include the following:

- Lack of control over the life cycle of the document—Updating the supporting documents for each change in design and data, and seeking the appropriate review and approvals can create havoc at different stages.

- Inability to integrate all the information formats available to the company—Information is drawn from a variety of internal sources as well as from suppliers, vendors, and customers, often with no mechanism for sharing and reuse.

- Inability to find current and accurate information—Companies are often unable to find the latest information available in order to respond to queries in a timely fashion, so they are unable to benefit from the experiences of others.

These barriers to getting new products developed and out the door can be solved by putting in place a document management system. The control over the flow of work throughout the business process and the ability to track who has edited, reviewed, and approved the document provides a means to effectively manage the resources required to complete the task. A proper document management system will provide the means to integrate the information resources from the variety of formats that make up the documentation.

Because the document management solutions available today all tend to have version control mechanisms built into the software, determining the most recent versions of a document is relatively trivial. Most systems also include a search engine to enable the users to search through all the information within the system to maximize the re-use of corporate information.

Improved Quality

Most document management systems incorporate some form of work flow process, enabling the company to establish a review process that ensures the information is delivered to the appropriate people at the appropriate time.

For example, consider the development of the implementation plan of a hypothetical business strategy. This example is simplified for discussion purposes only:

1. The current business processes are analyzed for their ability to implement the strategy—this example assumes that these processes need to be reviewed in order to ascertain their alignment with the strategy. Any documents are submitted to the document management system.

2. The activities that make up the individual business processes are identified and analyzed to determine if the activity adds value to the business process. Any changes or modifications required are noted and the results of the analysis are submitted to the document management system.

3. As the team assigned to prepare the implementation plan is assigned portions of the new plan to create from the research completed in the two previous steps, the review and approval process for these component pieces of the implementation plan is assigned. The final implementation plan cannot be released for review and approval until such time as all the review and approval cycles have been completed to create the component pieces.

By using a document management system to control the preparation of the implementation plan, the manager of this process can, at any point in time, create "the latest version" of the draft plan by having the document management system automatically pull the most recent versions of the component pieces together. Incorporating work flow that provides reminders to participants of commitments and deadlines can ensure that not only is the document presented the most current compilation, but it can route and prompt participants to get their part completed.

This can improve the quality of the overall business plan in that the appropriate information is provided to those people who need it on time and as promised.

Increased Productivity

Most organizations would like to increase the productivity of its workers, especially the knowledge workers. Companies would like to see staff spending more time adding value to information for the purpose of increasing the companys' competitive advantages. In order to do this, employees should not spend their day searching for information.

A document management system provides the ability for staff to find the latest version of documents that the company has in its memory banks. A document management system is especially valuable in large organizations where the internal document collection can be researched to find information that already exists and can be reused.

Reduced Costs

By making certain that the information holdings are accessible and searchable, the reuse of information is feasible. A significant amount of the information that is created becomes input for another document or process. If reuse of existing components can be maximized, the costs associated with the development of redundant components, as well as the cost of the associated processes, can be significantly reduced.

Author's Note

> By way of example, one federal agency spent in excess of $2 million over three years on over 200 studies to define the needs and requirements of its clients. A cursory audit of the studies indicated that approximately 150 of the studies done in years two and three of the period in question would not have been commissioned if the earlier studies had been accessible for review, resulting in a cost reduction of close to $1.2 million.

Some Final Words on the Benefits

Document management technology enables a company to ensure that the right information is in the hands of the appropriate people for review and comment at the right time. The ability to assemble disparate information components to create a complex document that contains the latest information available enables the company to store the various data formats in the most efficient manner and in a place where they are accessible for reuse by all. By combining the intranet for access to database and other information sources with a document management system in order to facilitate the creation and management of the information sources, companies can create a competitive advantage in their marketplace based on their own information.

Calculating the dollar value of the benefits is a bit tricky. The value of the benefits depends upon the document management system implemented, the numbers of seats involved, and so forth. That these systems enable workers to operate more efficiently to produce more in less time and at a lower cost while maintaining or increasing quality levels. Through the elimination of steps that do not add value, the remaining work tasks are provided with prompt and accurate communication of required information, enabling faster decisions and greater throughput.

How to Choose a Document Management System

Documents are information. If you don't manage the documents, you probably do not manage the important information assets of the company. Following is a brief discussion of the things to be considered when evaluating a document management solution.

Evaluation

The document management needs of each company are different based on the size of company, the marketplace it is in, the software and hardware already in place within the company, and a variety of other factors. This section will bring forward some of the key things to keep in the back of your mind as it looks at corporate needs and the solutions available.

The areas that are discussed relative to the evaluation of document management systems include the following:

- Key components required

- Security issues

- Ease of use

- Multiple platform operation

- Ease of configuration

Key Components

Three basic components must be incorporated into the document management system:

- Library management—manages access to all sources and formats of information; manages versions; is searchable; is sometimes called the *repository function* in the structured data world

- Workflow management—automatically routes documents to the appropriate personnel at the appropriate time for review, revision, and approval

- Configuration management—entails that, as key information changes, all dependent information changes as well and the participants should be notified

Two other components that have already been discussed earlier in this chapter within the context of the life cycle management of a document—integrated assembly and automatic distribution—are also desired features.

In determining which document management solution is appropriate for your organization, these solutions are features that *must* be demonstrated by the document management system. Review the product literature of the solutions containing these features to see if the document management solution integrates with the components of your information infrastructure. If a match occurs, at least on paper, ask the vendor of the solution—be it the developer, manufacturer, value-added reseller, or consultant—to put you in contact with sites that match your specific components where the vendor in question has implemented their document management solution.

Security Issues

Because implementing document management software to manage the mission-critical information of the company is recommended, security of the system is an issue. A good document management system provides an audit trail of the usage of the documents, both check-out and check-in, enabling a process manager to review who had what documents, when, and the comments they made.

More importantly, controlled access is an important feature. The software must allow group and individual level controls, as well as different types of access to the content itself. The appropriate levels of content access that should be assigned are *read-only*, *comment*, and *revise content directly*. The terms used for these levels are only descriptive and may not be used by any of the products; they should provide, however, at least the context within which content access permissions should be granted.

Select the document management system software so that it incorporates access control to provide security when and where needed. By using the list of vendors that met the criteria outlined in the previous section, review those vendors' offerings to determine if they incorporate the level of access control that you have determined to be necessary within your information infrastructure.

Figure 14.1 shows the access permissions for document reviewers. If an individual is not included on the list during the review process, he will not know the document exists. Once the document is released for general consumption, it is available for all to view.

Figure 14.1

An example of access permissions for document review.

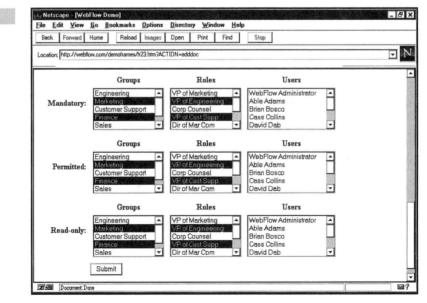

Ease of Use

The information within the system needs to be accessible and easy to use. The ease of information input and retrieval are key factors in the successful implementation of an effective and efficient document management system. Four features make the system easy to use:

- Online help—Users do not have time to wait for a help desk to respond to simple questions about the use of the system and, therefore, context-sensitive online help is required.

- Standard user interface—Because you want to be able to use the document management system within the intranet, a browser should be able to access the system and should be an integral requirement of the product.

- Cross-platform consistency—Regardless of the computer used to access the document management system, the application should look and feel the same.

- User-based environment—The user's workspace should reflect the flow of the business process in which the user is involved; the users should not have to alter their work habits or workspace to use the document management system.

If the users cannot get comfortable with the document management system and if they have to deal with a lot of overhead, the users will not use the system. It must be intuitive and needs to be customizable at the user level if possible.

Use these criteria to continue the development of the list of vendors who meet your circumstances. The more importance that you can attach to any of the features, based on the needs of your organization, the more weight should be given to those features when evaluating the vendor offerings.

Multiple Platforms

The intranet is designed to incorporate information residing on a variety of software platforms on a variety of hardware platforms running under a variety of operating systems. The document management system needs to be able to integrate into the existing environment and must be able to import objects from all the systems within the intranet.

The company must be able to leverage its current investment in hardware and software. The system should run on clients and servers that may be future acquisitions. In addition to just running on these server technologies of the future acquisitions, you must be able to implement the ability of the document management system to import the data that resides in databases on these new servers. In order to enable this flexibility, the document management system needs to be open and fully compatible with these sources. A well-built solution goes beyond the client/server model to provide distributed processing and storage of documents.

In addition, the system should support SGML because of the focus on the structure of the information within the SGML standards. SGML-compliant documents are structured so that their information is interchangeable across systems and organizations as the intranet is opened up to valued customers and suppliers in the future.

Note

HTML and SGML are very similar, with HTML being an instance of SGML. As we move closer to the adoption of HTML 3.0, the distance between HTML and SGML closes, and in the very near future, the two will most likely meld into one suite of standards. HTML 3.0 supports SGML-style Document Type Definitions (DTDs), and many vendors of SGML tools have incorporated a DTD specifically designed for HTML into their products. Because the origin of many of the document management systems was in the publishing world that relied on SGML, the adaptation of these SGML-based document management systems to the HTML world is being undertaken by practically all the vendors. Those vendors that do not currently have a product that works within HTML environment of the intranet are working feverishly to develop and release an intranet-compatible version.

Once again, refine your vendor matrix with the inclusion of the criteria from this section that you feel are be important to your organization.

Ease of Configuration

The company should not have to bend itself as if in a game of Twister just to use the document management application. The product should be configurable to address the business needs of the company. The system must be able to model the information and work processes through the user interface to reflect the company's operating environment. It must have system management/configuration tools that enable the implementation of the company's business logic and the interdependencies of information, documents, business units, and personnel.

The better systems also provide an Application Programming Interface (API) so that the document management system can be integrated directly into other applications. Programming experience with the document management system is required in order to integrate the systems. This experience provides the ability, for example, to store an executable program and create an up-to-the-minute report of sales of product XY within the document management system. When the user chooses to retrieve this document, the application runs in the background and creates the document on the fly for presentation to the user. Chapter 7, "Understanding the Advantages of Browser/Server Communications," provides some more details on the use of APIs in general for your reference.

The last stage in the development of the matrix tells you which vendors meet all the criteria for your organization's information infrastructure. Incorporate the criteria from this section and weigh them as per your needs for these features. This completed matrix will be used in conjunction with the information developed in the next section to help select the appropriate document management system for your organization.

Preparing for a Pilot Project

Before selecting a vendor and going into a full-scale implementation, trying a controlled pilot project before committing to an enterprise solution is always a good idea. This section will cover the steps toward preparing for a pilot project with the product and vendor still to be selected. The following steps pertain to a hypothetical situation and should be used only as a guideline in preparing your own pilot project:

1. Describe the application to be implemented for the pilot project and what will be accomplished functionally, as detailed as possible. (For example, the five customer service representatives will be calling up customer dockets on their browser when they get calls from customers. They add information to each docket while they are on the phone. The manager is notified of any trouble reports.) If the computerized process is not easily visualized, describe the current process on paper.

2. Sketch out the CURRENT location of each person to be working in the pilot. (For example, five customer service representatives located on the fifth floor, two people on the third floor and four people in the accounting department in the basement.)

3. Determine the computing equipment currently being used by the people targeted for the pilot project implementation. Determine the type of computer being used, the network operating system in place, printers available, scanners available, and so on. Are they running Windows? Provide the configuration of each computer (386/33, 486/50, Pentium 100), the amount of RAM, the storage capacity of each computer, and the type of monitor (VGA, SuperVGA, and so forth).

4. Determine if a relational database is being used to perform this application. Also determine the functions performed by the database and how the users interact with the application.

5. Determine the activity volumes of the application. In this example, the number of ACTIVE and INACTIVE dockets. Also determine where both kinds of information are currently stored.

6. Determine the frequency of referral to the ACTIVE dockets and the type of activity, either UPDATEs or READ-ONLY accesses.

7. Determine if the docket in question goes through an APPROVAL process after an UPDATE. List the names of the people who see the docket before it is returned to the file.

8. Determine the number of new ACTIVE dockets created each month. Determine the number of dockets that become INAC-TIVE each month.

9. Determine the events that cause the creation of a new ACTIVE docket and how this trigger is received. Attach a copy of the FORM used to trigger the new ACTIVE docket.

10. Name the project manager responsible for implementation of the pilot program.

By preparing this type of information for a pilot project in advance of selecting a vendor and product, you can focus on a mission-critical business process. This also gives you a sample application to give to the prospective vendors in order for them to make an initial response to your demands for a document management system.

Now that you have a pilot project with which to start, one that incorporates the elements of one of your business processes, a vendor selection can now be started.

Selecting a Vendor

With the pilot project in one hand and the vendor matrix in the other, you can make some final evaluations about which document management system should be chosen for the pilot.

But first, a few words about the vendor. The word "vendor" has been used to represent an organization offering a solution for purchase. This solution may be a product, a service, or a combination of both. The organization offering the solution may be the developer of the product or a re-seller, authorized or not, of the product. The re-seller may also sell its services as part of the solution. The organization could also be a company whose primary business is the services side—they will integrate the product solution that best fits within your needs.

Determining the actual relationship of the organization in question from their marketing literature and advertising can sometimes be very difficult. The vendor matrix now comes in handy.

The matrix that you prepared during the previous sections will work to isolate the product part of the vendor/product/service mix described above. Because the matrix focuses on features, the product determination should be possible now. Cross-referencing the information from the analysis of the pilot project with the vendor offerings from the matrix should provide you with a short list of offerings from which to choose. In the event that none of the offerings from the matrix conforms to all elements of the pilot, choose the offerings that most closely conform to the requirements list of the pilot.

Once you have identified the vendor offerings that seem to be able to meet your pilot project's needs on paper, contact them and present them with your pilot project requirements. After your discussion with these vendors and required demonstrations of the offering's advertised features, you should be able to determine the appropriate vendor and product mix to select.

To summarize, the following are the usual requirements that you will need to ascertain in conjunction with your matrix:

- Browser interface—To ensure that the document management system integrates into the intranet, insist upon a browser-based interface for a look and feel consistent with the rest of the intranet product suite.

- Scalability—The system must be able to grow along with the company and incorporate any foreseen hardware platforms and data formats.

- Open systems/compatibility—The product must be able to integrate with legacy systems and future directions.

- Proven technology—It must be state of the market, not state of the art. The system must work from the beginning.

- Enterprise-wide solution—It must be compatible across all parts of the company, including international parts where foreign language support may be required.

- Support of industry standards—The supplier must support the industry standards to ensure integration of the product with the existing computing environment.

- Industry experience—The vendor must demonstrate an understanding of the company's business needs and should have experience in implementing a solution within the industry.

- Willing partners—The vendor must be willing to work with the company to implement and configure the system to company requirements. The knowledge transfer is both ways—the company understands the document management system better and the vendor understands the business logic and processes which results in better service.

In selecting a product and a vendor, separating one from the other is difficult. The vendor should demonstrate experience in the industry, a track record of success, and implementation experience in a growing, complex environment.

Vendors in the Market

As with any list of vendors of intranet-oriented software, the products and vendors will have changed by the time the reader sees this list.

Not all the companies listed here currently have intranet-compatible solutions, but those who do not are in the final stages of preparing their intranet offerings. The list is a catalog of companies with experience in the implementation of document management systems in a variety of industry settings. Please contact them with these thoughts in mind and ask them for their product literature in order to develop the matrix discussed in this chapter.

The ADM Group
477 Madison Ave.,
17th Floor
New York, NY 10022
Tel: 212-371-4900
Fax: 212-750-7419

Alpharel, Inc.
9339 Carroll Park Dr.
San Diego, CA 92121
Tel: 800-992-6784
Fax: 619-546-7671

Ardilog, Inc.
1000 Boul St. Jean,
Suite 324
Pointe-Claire, Quebec
H9R5P1
Tel: 514-694-9500
Fax: 514-694-3784

Baker & Associates
933 Lorien Dr.
P.O. Box 682
Gwynedd Valley, PA
19437
Tel: 215-643-0908
Fax: 215-643-6686

Byte Ltd.
301 Moodie Dr.,
Suite 410
Nepean, ON
K2H 9C4
Tel: 613-726-9350
Fax: 613-726-1086

CAT-Links, Inc.
2100 N. Broadway,
Suite 200
Santa Ana, CA 92706
Tel: 800-825-4657
Fax: 714-543-2123

CIP Classics
11340 W. Olympic
Blvd., Suite 204
Los Angeles, CA 90064
Tel: 310-445-2767
Fax: 310-445-2766

CMS Automation, Inc.
2215 Tomlynn St.
Richmond, VA 23230
Tel: 804-278-9200
Fax: 804-278-5019

**COM COM Systems,
Inc.,**
2420 Enterprise Rd.,
Suite 201,
Clearwater, FL 34623
Tel: 813-725-3200
Fax: 813-796-6596

COMPINFO, Inc.
381 Park Ave. S.
New York, NY 10016
Tel: 212-532-7777
Fax: 212-685-3341

Chesapeake Interlink/ Pins
8E Music Fair Rd.
P.O. Box 340
Owings Mills, MD 21117
Tel: 410-363-1976
Fax: 410-363-7685

Counselor Systems, Inc.
8820 Business Park Dr., Suite 300
Austin, TX 78759
Tel: 512-338-4531
Fax: 512-338-4681

Excalibur Technologies
9255 Towne Centre Dr., 9th Floor
San Diego, CA 92121
Tel: 619-625-7900
Fax: 619-625-7901

Excelsior Legal
62 White St.
New York, NY 10013
Tel: 212-431-5000
Fax: 212-431-5111

Executive Technologies, Inc.
2120 16th Ave. S.
Birmingham, AL 35205
Tel: 205-933-9311
Fax: 205-930-5517

Folio Legal Views
390 Summit Dr.
Redwood City, CA 94062
Tel: 800-TXT-MGMT
Fax: 415-369-4844

IPRO, Inc.
10801 N. 24th Ave., Suite 101
Phoenix, AZ 85029
Tel: 602-943-5432
Fax: 602-943-4904

Iconovex Corp.
7900 Xerxes Ave. S., Suite 550
Bloomington, MN 55431
Tel: 612-896-5100
Fax: 612-896-5101

Identitech, Inc.
100 Rialto PI
Melbourne, FL 32901
Tel: 407-951-9503
Fax: 407-951-9505

InData Corp.
1478 N. Tech Blvd., Suite 109
Gilbert, AZ, 85233
Tel: 800-828-8292
Fax: 602-497-1833

InMagic, Inc.
800 W. Cummings Park
Woburn, MA 01801
Tel: 617-938-4442
Fax: 617-938-6393

Informative Graphic Corp.
706 E. Bell Rd.
Phoenix, AZ 85022
Tel: 602-971-6061
Fax: 602-971-6061

Intercon Associates, Inc.
95 Allens Creek Rd.,
Building 2
Rochester, NY 14618
Tel: 716-244-1250
Fax: 716-473-4387

Intergrated Information Services
11911 N. Meridian St.
Carmel, IN 46032
Tel: 800-547-8673
Fax: 317-581-7620

Interleaf, Inc.
Prospect Place
9 Hillside Ave.
Waltham, MA 02154
Tel: 800-955-5323

LDSI—Advanced Network Specialist
2021 E. Hennepin Ave.,
Suite LL30
Minneapolis, MN 55413
Tel: 612-378-1108
Fax: 612-378-2264

Legal Edge Software
1150 First Ave.,
Suite 700
King of Prussia, PA 19046
Tel: 610-337-5835
Fax: 610-992-1516

Legal Files Software
129 S. Congress
Rushville, IL 62681
Tel: 217-322-4166
Fax: 217-322-4666

Legal Software Publishing Co.
5715 Johnson St.
Hollywood, FL 33021
Tel: 800-952-9227
Fax: 305-949-4604

MDY Advanced Technologies, Inc.
2100 Rte. 208 S.
Fair Lawn, NJ 07410
Tel: 201-797-6676
Fax: 201-797-6852

PC DOCS, Inc.
124 Marriott Drive
Tallahassee, FL
32301
Tel: 904-942-3627
Fax: 904-656-5559

**PowerLaw Systems,
Inc.**
520 N. Michigan
Ave., Suite 1632
Chicago, IL 60611
Tel: 312-644-1330
Fax: 312-644-1337

**Synaptec Software,
Inc.**
251 Kipling,
Suite 390
Denver, CO 80033
Tel: 303-422-2893
Fax: 303-422-4156

**Technology That
Helps, Inc.**
219 Adams Ave.,
Suite 120
Memphis, TN 38103
Tel: 901-577-5420
Fax: 901-577-5424

**Towery Legal
Solutions**
1835 Union Ave.
Memphis, TN 38104
Tel: 901-725-2400
Fax: 901-725-2401

**World Software
Corp.**
124 Prospect St.
Ridgewood, NJ
07450
Tel: 201-444-3228
Fax: 201-444-9065

**inVzn Development
Corp.,**
1478 N. Tech Blvd.,
#101
Gilbert, AZ 85233
Tel: 602-497-5560
Fax: 602-926-9402

Status Check

You have established your intranet and have provided means to get at the database stores of information through CGI and at text stores through WAIS searching. You have learned about the new model of structuring information resources. This chapter has discussed the need for a document management system to help manage information.

It is true that you pass information among yourselves in the form of documents. You spend enormous amounts of time and effort creating mission-critical documents like sales and marketing plans, annual budgets, and financing requirements. Still, most companies and employees tend to spend little time and effort in the management of the most valuable of assets—information.

This chapter has discussed different types of information to manage, from transaction-based to office automation-based to mission-critical, and has reviewed the rationale for implementing a document management system. With the list of vendors provided and the outline to prepare for a pilot project, you are in a position now to match your corporate needs to vendor offerings and put in place a system that is browser-accessible from the intranet.

The next chapter will cover the role of the "IntraMaster," the ringleader of this circus, and other positions necessary to keep an intranet functional.

15

Role of the IntraMaster

There is a difference between the role of the "Webmaster" and the role of the "IntraMaster." If you search any of the major search engines on the Net for "Webmaster," you will find literally thousands of hits. Each and every site has a Webmaster (a person who modifies and updates a Web site). They range from 13 years of age on up, each with an entirely different skill set.

With many Internet service providers permitting subscribers to set up their own Web home pages, any person can become a Webmaster and call himself the same if he can get a page up on the Net. If you can create a home page and set up navigation between that page and others within the hierarchy of your Web site, does this mean that you really are a Web "master?"

Given that one of the business goals of the intranet is to provide solutions for business processes, the person who is the "IntraMaster" is quite different than being just a Webmaster.

The IntraMaster is, by turns, the janitor, the leader, the manager, and the president of the intranet. He or she will find him or herself in many different positions over the course of the job. This chapter will cover the people, the jobs, and the responsibility areas involved in running an intranet, and how the IntraMaster's job relates to all of those things. The sections of this chapter are as follows:

•The IntraMaster and his or her job

•The people behind the intranet

•Typical responsibility breakdown

•Survival tactics

The Job of the IntraMaster

This section will seek to part the clouds and shed some light on the IntraMaster. The IntraMaster is the person who has to bring all the varied pieces of the organization together to create the intranet. In an attempt to provide you with an understanding of the person called the IntraMaster and the role that individual plays within the company, the following topics will be covered in this section:

• Required skills and abilities

• Job description and duties

Required Skills and Abilities

Juggling the pieces that make up the intranet requires an individual to combine technical, management, planning, and organizational skills into one pot. In order to deal with the complexities of that mix, the person chosen to coordinate and synchronize the pieces, the IntraMaster, needs to be imbued with the qualities listed below:

• A very good grasp of the "business" of the organization—In order to implement the intranet in support of the mission-critical business processes of the company, the IntraMaster must understand the business plan of the company as it is designed to achieve the goals and measurable objectives of the owners. With a review and thorough understanding of the business processes that are to be implemented to achieve these goals, the IntraMaster designs the intranet to get the required information into the hands of those who need it when and where it is required.

- A familiarity with the Internet—With the intranet built upon the technologies developed for the Internet, the IntraMaster must understand the way the standards upon which the technology is based are maintained and modified. With no one individual or organization responsible for the specifications of the standards, the manner in which these standards are derived and maintained must be understood within the intranet model. In the majority of organizations, no one person owns the intranet. How the policies and procedures for the intranet are developed and implemented across the workings of an organization requires a similar approach to that of the Internet. More is discussed about the "ownership" of the intranet later in this chapter and back in Chapter 12, "Alternative Corporate Information Models."

- A background in marketing—The IntraMaster must be able to put in place a sound marketing plan that includes the information products offered, the promotion of the intranet, the people that are required to make a success, and the required selling of the intranet to both management and the masses. In order to accomplish all of that within the marketing plan for the intranet, a background in the marketing discipline helps. Also, because the normal organization usually has to sell products in order to survive, the intranet must support the overall marketing processes. This can best be achieved if the IntraMaster has some marketing experience.

- An understanding of programming languages and technology— The IntraMaster must be familiar with all of the technologies used within the intranet, including TCP/IP, HTTP, CGI programming, server configuration, and HTML authoring. On the programming languages side, the IntraMaster should be familiar with at least Perl, C, Unix shell scripts, and Java. Also, an understanding of the SQL language of the relational database world is recommended. It is not absolutely necessary to know all the intricacies of the languages and the technology, but the IntraMaster does require at least an intermediate understanding of these areas on the whole.

- A big picture view of where the business objectives of the organization specifically, and technology in general, are going—One of the author's research findings is that businesses that are successful in their endeavors have three tendencies:

  - Successful companies implement a state-of-the-art business strategy.

  - Successful companies use state-of-the-market technology in their day-to-day operations.

  - Successful companies have a leading-edge, or as some have called it, a "bleeding-edge," integration of their business strategy and their technology strategy to support the mission-critical business processes.

- Reckless disregard for personal safety and anonymity (most important)—Thick skin helps, at least several layers. Most IntraMasters will tell you that the initial efforts to implement intranets will be cursed, laughed at, and scoffed as "not the way business is done here." Critics will seek every chance to nay-say the intranet. In many cases, the actual implementations of intranets has been undertaken in "skunk works" after having had some form of refusal to sponsor the intranet concept to senior management (the names are being withheld to protect the guilty parties). From many of these *unofficial* intranets came the prototypes that have since met with success—a "damn the torpedoes" approach. Because the intranet will be on constant display and under constant criticism from the nay-sayers, the IntraMaster cannot have a fragile ego—as grandparents are fond of saying, this criticism "builds character!"

If the IntraMaster possesses the skills and abilities listed here, he is well on the way to being able to provide intranet-based solutions to the company in the performance of his job. Speaking of job, the following section provides a sample job description and outlines several of the duties of the IntraMaster.

Job Description and Duties

In this section, you will be presented with a simple example of a job description that was created to hire an IntraMaster. You will also be presented with a list of typical functions and duties that the IntraMaster performs.

Example Job Description

The following is the text of a job posting that was created to hire an IntraMaster. It outlines the basic job description and several of the qualifications that were identified earlier.

> As the IntraMaster you will be responsible for developing the corporate intranet architecture and intranet "starter kits/templates" for application development areas to maintain corporate consistency. You will be responsible for compiling corporate-wide intranet requirements. You will analyze secure-commercial use of intranet/Internet resources to include electronic data interface and digital signatures. You will be responsible for the analysis of *new generation* security standards and protocols. You will be responsible for the evolution of the corporate intranet home page. You will provide support as the central point of contact with the internal content providers.

> To qualify for this exceptional opportunity you should have the following qualifications:

> - Five to ten years of experience in Information Technology Analysis and Planning

> - A proven track record in project planning and project management

> - Experience in computer networking and communications

- Good writing skills and an ability to interface effectively with senior management and diverse user groups, including using oral presentations

- An in-depth knowledge of TCP/IP network and Unix systems administration (firewalls, proxies, HTTP, SSL, packet filtering, DNS, Kerberos, and more)

- An intermediate knowledge of SQL query building using Oracle, Sybase, or Microsoft Access database engines

- An intermediate knowledge of scripting and application development tools such as Perl and C

The Candidate must be able to work independently with minimum supervision and create cross-departmental coalitions to complete projects on time. A bachelor's degree in computer science or software engineering is desirable in conjunction with a master's degree in business administration.

As you can see, there are at least two sides in the life of the Intra-Master—the technical side and the business side.

Functions and Duties of the IntraMaster

The IntraMaster must function upon several levels. The most significant is the business level. The second is that of the community education level. Here the IntraMaster provides outreach and support to encourage and assist the content providers in participating in the intranet.

The next two levels deal with the management of the intranet and the operational duties of the IntraMaster within the intranet.

With respect to the management level, the IntraMaster has the following responsibilities:

- Design and preparation of the intranet home page—This includes the templates that will be used by content providers in maintaining their own sub-sites within the intranet.

- Quality assurance—This is applicable as it pertains to HTML file portability (adherence to HTML standards) and look-and-feel (consistency within the template framework).

- User support—As the primary point of contact with the content providers, the IntraMaster must act as the intermediary between the users and the content providers to ensure ease of use and currency.

- Overall system design at the physical server level as well as the HTTP server level—The design of the intranet must be capable of meeting current needs as well as being scaleable for the future growth in users and traffic.

- Statistics—If the intranet is to support mission-critical business processes by getting the right information to the right people at the right time, you need to know what is being used when and where to see if this matches the analysis of the business processes of the company.

By managing all of these different functions, the IntraMaster is assuming the responsibility of supporting the mission-critical business processes of the company. In order to complete these functions, the following duties need to be performed:

- Check for currency of content—All documents should have a stale date when posted to the intranet in order to "guarantee freshness."

- Ensure that the security of the systems is properly maintained.

- Seek new content providers within the organizations.

- Research and test new software releases as they come to market to determine if they can improve the solutions that are currently provided to users.

- Ensure that CGI programs are created as required to access various databases to meet user demand.

- Respond to user requests for demonstrations and training.

- Ensure that a searchable index of all documents is created and maintained and is available within the intranet.

- Continually assess intranet in terms of meeting the needs of business processes.

The list is neither exhaustive nor is it displayed in a specific order of importance. It is simply a list of some of the duties that need to be performed to ensure that the intranet runs smoothly and provides the necessary support to the organization.

The IntraMaster is the key person in ensuring the intranet meets the needs of the business. However, there are usually several other people or job functions that support the efforts of the IntraMaster. The next section of this chapter discusses the people behind the intranet, the people who make it tick.

The People Behind the Intranet

Launching an intranet can be a big corporate event and can consume large amounts of resources. But the real effort is put forth in keeping the information and the resources up and running in the fashion that they require—in support of the mission-critical business processes. Even though Chapter 2, "Making Your Case," suggests that you start with a pilot project that does not have a huge amount of implementation planning and Return On Investment analysis in the initial stages, that should not diminish the importance of these items. Often in the traditional intranet development life cycle, the person who first champions the intranet within the organization really is the Webmaster—the person who has the energy and desire to pitch the intranet solution up the management line until a sponsor is found.

The combination of the Webmaster and the sponsor usually results in a prototype that is put in front of management for approval to take the next step—usually the value proposition and business case step that was outlined in Chapter 2. This often requires more effort on the part of the Webmaster and the sponsor to bring in whatever resources (computers, people, and dollars) they can beg, borrow, and steal to put up the next version of the prototype.

In some small organizations, the IntraMaster is the only warm body that is available to perform all the tasks required to make the intranet work as advertised. If you have the luxury of having several people allocated to work on the intranet, aside from the role of the IntraMaster, several other jobs need to be carried out by people with different skills and responsibilities.

In order to provide direction to the staff working on the intranet project, it is recommended that you set up a small oversight committee composed of individuals from across the company. The next section will discuss this committee in more detail.

Form an Oversight Committee

After the final decision is made to go ahead and pursue an initial intranet pilot project, the company has to make certain that the required resources are available or obtained to make the project work. With several areas of the company involved, it is usually wisest to work with the strengths of the individual areas of the company in seeking the resources required. But who will coordinate the work of all these people and groups?

There is a need for the company to have a small oversight committee to supervise the politics and to ensure that the directions taken by the intranet are in line with the company's business and strategic objectives. This committee needs to ensure that the resourcing requirements of the intranet are made available. Below, and reporting to this committee, resides the IntraMaster. This reporting structure is a necessity to avoid the small "p" politics of reporting to an individual manager.

It is recommended that the oversight committee be kept small in order for it to be functionally driven, but it needs to represent a cross-section of the organization. The committee should have representation from the users, the content providers, IS, Human Resources, the unions (if applicable), Finance, and Operations. It is recommended that you seek the participation of the VPs (or equivalent) of Finance and Operations to sit on the committee to provide both the input of senior management into the process as well as providing a buffer from the senior management group as a whole. The rationale for bringing the unions to the table is that the changes in the way work may be done in the future may impact job structure and duties. It is felt that the participation of the union in the intranet project will help the union executive understand the nature of the changes and plan for them.

Some of the specific tasks that could be assigned to this oversight committee are listed here:

- Development of intranet usage guidelines and policies

- Approval of content to be provided on the intranet

- Selection and approval of look and feel of the intranet

- Approval and sponsorship to senior management level of the intranet business plan

- Development and presentation of the intranet marketing plan at corporate level

- Periodic validation of the intranet in its support role to business processes

If this were a project to provide information to the outside world, the business objective of the site would determine the "owners." For example, if the objective were to distribute product literature and house a transaction application for product ordering, the Web site might be owned by Marketing.

The intranet is about the company sharing its information across the entire organization. The need for the small oversight committee is to deal with the politics, to clear the way for the IntraMaster to perform the real business of getting knowledge into the hands and heads of the employees. The most crucial task for the committee is to develop the policies and procedures manual that the company will use to provide its information. The manual should include the individual and group responsibilities as well as the approval and evaluation procedures and guidelines. A sample of some these documents can be found in Appendix A, "Acceptable Use and Other Sample Company Policies."

Support Staff Positions

The IntraMaster is the master of ceremonies in the corporate dance of the intranet. If you have the luxury of being the IntraMaster for a large organization, with the resources available to put in place the staff that you need, the following is a list of the staff positions you should fill:

1. User Support—Responsible for user training, development of the system documentation, and answering the phone (until the users get the hang of the feedback forms on the intranet). Good staff are hard to find and keep—their interpersonal skills make them attractive to other areas of the company.

2. Technical Administrator—Needs to know the nuts and bolts of the software, network configuration, and installation, as well as have thorough knowledge of TCP/IP and HTTP protocols. These days it seems as though a Technical Administrator can usually be found in a high school—identifiable by the fact that they can do cube roots on a slide rule while participating in a cafeteria food fight.

3. Intranet Programmer—Adept at using HTML, Java, Visual Basic, Perl, and other programming languages. The intranet programmer will be responsible for putting the code to work on the computers and making the forms talk to the CGI and, in turn, the databases.

Author's Note

Throughout my experiences with intranet implementations, most of the programming staff have done their best coding after hours, away from the distractions of their "real job" and, in many cases after midnight, trying to meet deadlines. Been there, got the T-shirt.

The stereotypical programmer from the early 1980s, when I first started working with computers, learned COBOL or FORTRAN, had a

continues

penchant for Jolt Cola and black coffee, and worked best at night with no lights on. There were many nights returning from post-midnight training runs that the glowing computer screens through the windows were the only lights visible in the university dorms.

I used to joke with my friends, those programmers, about those university-day habits. Now as I sit in a dark basement providing these words to you by the light of my screen, beer mug of black coffee at my elbow, I recall those moments.

4. Webmaster—Responsible for the analysis, design, implementation, and maintenance of the site's interface. Although this may entail an understanding of programming languages, it is important that this person is able to talk with the users of the intranet, to understand how he or she wants the intranet to work for the company, and to sketch out graphically how the solution might work. A good sense of graphic design and a good grasp of HTML coding are minimal requirements. This individual must be able to write pseudocode so that the users can understand what the system will do when the actual coding takes place and so that the programmers can take the pseudocode and make it real. Being able to listen to users comfortably is important. Being afraid of the dark becomes a drawback when trying to explain the users' requirements to the programmers in the programmers' habitats (see Author's Note).

5. Project Manager—Handy in managing the non-technical aspects of intranet development and maintenance cycles, if you have the luxury and budget for these folks. The project manager must have great communications skills, must be able to take charge and make decisions to control the progress of projects. This is also the same basic job description for the IntraMaster, but do not try to take on too many projects as the IntraMaster and project manager. "The devil is in the details" is the favorite expression of a former colleague, and if you try to handle the big picture stuff as well as the details involved in project management, you will be frazzled before long.

Now that you are aware of the different staff you should have for the implementation of your intranet, most of you will be faced with a very limited staff and limited resources. The preceding list should give you an idea of the people you should keep your eyes open for. If you can sell a candidate on the intranet concept, you might be able to borrow some of his or her time to help out in getting things started. You need to convince the candidate that this eventually could be "really big" and provide him or her with a chance to get into something new and exciting.

Typical Responsibility Breakdown

If you have the staff outlined earlier, you can slot them into one of the responsibility areas described in the following list, and then you can think of you and your staff collectively as the IntraMaster. If you are the only resource, the sole IntraMaster, you will be called upon to fill the shoes of each of the following roles: the techie, the salesperson, the baby-sitter, and the futurist. The responsibilities of people who work on the intranet fall into one of four realms:

- The technical realm

- The sales and marketing realm

- The guidance and leadership realm

- The visionary realm

The Technical Realm

The "techie" has a real mix of responsibilities and duties, as referred to previously in the areas of Technical Administration, Programmer, and Webmaster. The following duties fall under the realm of the techie:

- HTTP Server configuration and management (discussed in Chapter 3, "HTTP: Building the Application Layer")

- MIME standardization (discussed in Chapter 6, "Cross-Platform Client Browser Setup") to ensure that all publications and file types required are accessible via the browsers

- Ensuring that all the supporting servers that are put in place to support the intranet are properly installed and configured, including newsgroup, SMTP, FTP, WAIS, proxy, and DNS servers

- Ascertaining that the required security layers are in place to permit access to need-to-know information

- Maintenance of the home page and navigational integrity throughout the intranet

- Development of forms required to pass data from the browser to CGI applications for further processing

- Development, implementation, and maintenance of CGI scripts as required to access the databases storing the raw data

- Development and maintenance, in conjunction with the networking staff, of the routing tables for the intranet servers

- Development, generation, evaluation, and distribution of statistics about the usage of the intranet

- Development and implementation the "really neat stuff" such as JavaScript, imagemaps, and transparent GIFs

Note

The IntraMaster must be able to do all these things alone, yet be willing and unhesitant in delegating these activities, if possible. The technical staff traditionally have somewhat fragile egos and need to be treated with care. Now that the users have the ability to obtain tools that can be used to approximate the work of the techies, the typical intranet techie is much more extroverted and aggressive in dealing with the users in order to solve the user's problem. This tends to keep the user out of the techie's turf and promotes the technical group's ability and willingness to help solve problems quickly.

The IntraMaster must also keep abreast of where the technologies are headed in order to make certain that the intranet is capable of handling the latest and greatest versions. One major issue in this area that sets the IntraMaster apart from the Webmaster is the requirement to keep abreast of and understand the implications of the changes that are happening with other database applications and the hardware on which they run. In order to continue providing access to these systems via CGI programs, the intranet must be continually fine-tuned to keep up with all the various technologies in place.

New business processes or changes to existing ones will probably occur. They will require the IntraMaster to provide technical input into the development of the solution to the business process problem.

The Sales and Marketing Realm

The IntraMaster needs to be the salesperson, the primary marketer, the liaison gaining acceptance of the intranet in all the areas of the company. Following are the primary functions of the salesperson:

- Supplier management—The IntraMaster must continually connect with all the component organizations within the company to convince them to put their information on the intranet, keep it evergreen, and look for new nuggets to put up on the intranet. Any fact that is maintained within the corporation's information systems has the potential to be published.

- New product development—If the IntraMaster hears that a group within the organization is thinking of collecting a new set of facts, immediately the IntraMaster needs to be there to discuss how these facts could be shared with others in the company. Having concrete examples of what others have done in this vein is important.

- Competitive intelligence—The IntraMaster needs to keep abreast of how other companies are using intranets. Several means of doing this can be found on the Internet. Searching for "intranet case studies" will give the IntraMaster a list of sites where case studies are posted about successful intranets. For example, Netscape's Home Page has a section about companies using their servers for intranets. The intranet Journal (http://www.brill.com/intranet/) is another good source for the IntraMaster to keep on a bookmark list.

- Strategic business opportunities—The biggest sales and marketing job the IntraMaster will ever undertake is seeking the approval to take the initial intranet pilot project to full, organization-wide implementation as the primary means of interoperability. The full-blown business case, including ROI, will have to be done, and the support of all the areas of the company will have to be lobbied for ahead of time.

Note

Marketing of the intranet is sometimes difficult—be prepared to use that really thick skin. No matter how much someone wants to do it in a completely different style and format, help them find a way to use the corporate template to give them the desired results. No matter how much people think it won't work, with perseverance and rapid prototyping, the intranet will work.

The Guidance and Leadership Realm

Changing the corporate culture is never easy. Sharing of information is a difficult thing for many people to do. The IntraMaster has a number of "baby-sitting" chores, including the following:

- Getting people to commit to providing information and to provide it continually. Although it is sometimes tedious, it is a big chore and a necessary task.

Note

One method used in many sites is to have an Information Provider Agreement by which all content providers must live. Figure 15.1 shows an example of a "Content Provider's Credo" that was modeled after the Cal Poly Web site (http://www.csupomona.edu) agreement.

Figure 15.1

The "Content Provider's Credo."

Netscape - [Content Provider's Credo]

File Edit View Go Bookmarks Options Directory Window Help

Back | Forward | Home | | Reload | Images | Open | Print | Find | | Stop

Location: file:///C|/Book/Chapters/examples/Credo.htm

Content Provider's Credo

(To be read and acknowledged by persons submitting information to be linked to the Intranet Home Page.)

Thanks for helping us make our Intranet a better place.

Because the quality and timeliness of the information found on theses pages reflects not only on you as provider but also on the company itself, we ask that you observe the following guidelines:

Please

- update the ADDRESS section of the template with the date of last revision as well as your name and e-mail address.
- respond to questions suggestions, and problem reports sent by users of your pages and received via email.
- keep your information up to date and modify or remove it when it becomes obsolete.
- comply with Federal and State law and with corporate policies and regulations.

All information residing on or linked to a corporate Intranet server is accepted at the discretion of the Intramaster and may be moved or deleted at any time.

I acknowledge and agree to the above.

Document: Done

- User support—Training users on how to access the information resources available and manning the Help Desk with user support personnel is a major part of successfully launching the change in culture. If you are not willing to work closely with the user community to help it get the information it wants out of the system, it will be difficult to make the intranet a household word.

This is where the Human Resources people can assist. They can be used to help put in place the training programs required to get the users up to speed. Identify to them the skills and abilities that are needed at the desktop, and they should be able to develop a strategy and an implementation plan for this to work.

The Visionary Realm

The IntraMaster, as "futurist," and his support staff must be adept at looking at the strategic direction of the company and the direction that the applicable technologies are heading. Taking the bearings on where these two tracks will intersect, the IntraMaster must balance short-term needs and demands and those of the longer term. If the two tracks are not headed toward intersection, you will need to force your way into the planning table or find a way to be sponsored in order to get the tracks to intersect.

For example, many organizations need to incorporate a document management system to keep track of their most critical assets. However, document management systems are relatively expensive and take six to eight months to implement properly. In the initial stages of many intranets, senior management is unwilling to earmark the money for the development of such a system to be in operation within the intranet in six to eight months when they have not yet tasted the benefits of the intranet's initial implementation.

As the futurist, the IntraMaster should consider the following concepts:

- Research and development—Some resources must be diverted to ensure that the new technologies are tested and implemented as they become available and are stable enough to incorporate into the intranet.

- Senior management representation—Over the last few years, many Fortune 500 companies have created Chief Information Officers (CIO) and have brought them to the strategic planning table, in recognition of the enabling effect of technology.

- Strategic assets = knowledge—There is a need for the senior management table to include the Chief Knowledge Officer (title per Thomas Davenport) because the knowledge assets of the company are the real currency of the organization. This position is different from the CIO in that knowledge is the new currency of the organization. The understanding of the inventory of knowledge and how it can be re-packaged and leveraged for competitive advantage is more of a business planning function than an enabling function.

The IntraMaster is part of this knowledge base and can provide invaluable feedback and constructive criticism about the strategic plans as they relate to the combination of these knowledge assets into hard business processes and strategies.

Survival Tactics for the IntraMaster

In order to survive, the IntraMaster needs to find people in each area of the company that believe in the concept of knowledge networks or the intranet. After these people have been located and sold on the value of the intranet as a means of working toward the development of the knowledge network, maximize the concurrent development, integration, and application of knowledge. Have them work on creating their knowledge base for access/distribution via the intranet.

The following points are the elements that the IntraMaster must accept as tactics to survive the creation of the intranet as the incarnation of the knowledge network:

- Understanding, developing, and critiquing the intranet's mission—Does the intranet support the current business processes? The role of the intranet is to get mission-critical information into the hands of decision makers when, where, and how they need it. The intranet's performance in this area must be reviewed constantly to make certain that it adds value to the processes.

- Acknowledging the intranet as a system unto itself—Like any other computer system, the intranet has a life cycle and must be rejuvenated, up-graded, and, sometimes, throttled back in order to perform as required.

- Understanding the principles of good intranet design and seeking better ways to design—Using a state-of-the-art business strategy and state-of-the-market technology to provide the means to implement the strategy entails continually re-shaping the intranet to reflect new technologies and methods as they are developed.

- Working directly in creating and maintaining the higher intranet levels which govern the direction it is taking—The knowledge assets of the company are among the most important assets the company has. By ensuring that the intranet's principle functions support the mission-critical business processes that require the knowledge assets, the intranet reflects the alignment with the corporate strategy and vision. If the top of the structure is aligned properly, it is much easier to bring the other participants into alignment even though they are attempting to reach their own objectives. The laws of physics state that it is easier to redirect an object already in motion than it is to start the same object from a dead stop.

- Keeping up with intranet literature and emerging trends and technologies for all points of reference in the intranet—This is a daunting task. There are many stacks of journals and periodicals that have yet to be opened, but make the time to do it. Participate in online discussion groups that permit you to ask questions about specific problems or concerns. Others will be going or have gone through the same process as yourself and can sometimes provide answers.

- Assessing the new trends as they come out and formulating response strategies—Test and pilot everything that you can get your hands on that seems to address the support requirements of current business processes. Use the crystal ball to see where the business processes could be altered "if only technology *x*" were available, and then find and develop that technology.

- Conducting continual experiments with the emerging technologies—As the bumper sticker says, "He who has the most toys, wins." If you test everything that comes out for the appropriate fit within your intranet, you are adding to your knowledge base. It may pay off down the road when you develop a business need for a product that you already tried out last month.

- Assessing strengths and weaknesses of current intranet implementation—Does the critical information arrive on time and where it is needed? How can it be improved? Determine if there are means to improve the process and continually look for innovative methods to do it better and more effectively.

- Listening to the users and making the intranet work for them, while at the same time moving the users and the intranet in the strategic direction the company wishes to take—Keep the intranet aligned with the vision of the company and enable it to support the business processes that enable the achievement of the vision.

Status Check

The IntraMaster role is an important one within the framework of the company. Along with the support staff that sustain and enhance the intranet and its capabilities, the role of the IntraMaster's group is more than simply creating HTML pages and navigation methodologies. In a small company, the IntraMaster's group may be closer to the Webmaster role that is seen everywhere. However, the strategic nature of the IntraMaster role as has been described here makes the position a much richer, more rewarding job than that of a Webmaster.

Be that as it may, the next chapter calls on the technical abilities of the IntraMaster to develop and assist in converting spreadsheet and word-processing documents to HTML automatically. If this can be done with precision and accuracy, groups from across the company should be able to work on, for example, the virtual budget, wherein participants could obtain the file, put their information into the file, and then send it back to the center for roll-up and analysis. Stay tuned!

16

Converting Documents for the Intranet

The key to publishing on an intranet is to realize that the connected computers communicate through standard protocols. HTML is the way text documents are marked up for viewing on the intranet. The transfer protocol (HTTP) and the file format used are independent of each other. The transfer protocol only has to be able to get the required file and deliver it to the browser which, in turn, must be able to interpret the file format and display the document.

Depending upon the connections to the intranet, transfer speeds may vary between remote dial-in users and those directly connected via high-speed cable. Also, different browsers interpret the incoming files in different ways. These varied interpretations may impose some restrictions on the special effects used in the files.

This chapter explores some of the realities of making content available on the intranet. So far, this book has discussed the basics of HTML document creation and then followed that line of work to the creation of forms for access to data stored in relational databases. This book has also discussed the need for document management systems to manage the mission-critical information of the company and the day-to-day information you create. This chapter talks about creating documents and preparing them for inclusion into the intranet through the discussion of the following topics:

- The early stage of intranet popularity

- Principles of reality

- Converting/publishing word processing documents

- Converting/publishing spreadsheets

- Converting other data types for the intranet

The Early Stage of Intranet Popularity

"In the early days of intranet document development, the summer of 1995,"...(only kidding). The intranet phenomenon is young when you look at it from the perspective of Web-like interfaces to corporate data. It has been only in the last 12 to 18 months that the concept of creating Web-based intranets has caught on.

In the early stages of intranet development, relatively few tools were available to assist authors in preparing information for presentation on the intranet in HTML formats. The tools that did exist were so primitive that those who understood HTML used the Windows Notepad or an ASCII text editor to create the HTML files. And the people who actually used these tools often were the IS staff, not the actual authors of the documents!

As the programmers and other IS staff started to wilt under the burden of putting information onto the external Web sites as well as the intranet, authors sought some means of using HTML themselves.

Early tools such as HTML Assistant and Hot Dog were helpful, but they left a lot to be desired in the way they worked. In most companies, the majority of employees could create reasonably complex documents with their word processing software. They had learned how to incorporate images, tables, and spreadsheets into their documents, and they were able to turn out professional-looking documents through their laser printers.

What these users wanted was to be able to take the same document and put it onto the intranet for others to see, read, and use. They wanted these documents to look as wonderful on screen as they did in print. However, early HTML creation applications were so thin on functionality that document authors were unable to create a good on-screen appearance.

Early HTML authors could use Adobe Acrobat to create a file that could be downloaded by the user and reviewed and printed with the Acrobat Reader. The result was a document that was identical to the printed version. The drawback was that the IntraMasters and WebMasters needed to have the document in HTML format in order to have the content indexed for search purposes. WAIS engines could not search the insides of an Acrobat file stored on the server. This inability resulted in having an "ugly" version of the document available on the intranet.

The early technology was inconvenient. First, the user had to convert the document to ASCII text. This meant losing all the wonderful formatting that the authors had worked so hard to establish in the word processing application. The next problem was that the graphic images had to be inserted as an <IMG> tag. By the summer of 1995, tables were still not handled very well by browsers, and they took a long time to create.

Face it. HTML was, and still is, an esoteric language for the non-computer literate to try to figure out from scratch.

Since those early days, entire boat loads of applications have been developed to assist in the creation and authoring of HTML documents. Some applications have a limited set of features; others are full-fledged authoring systems that guide the author through the steps of creating documents.

What has remained evident is that the majority of the users today still prefer to use their word processing system to create their documents. Not every document at every stage in its life will be accessible to the user community on the intranet. But what these users want to be able to do is create their documents using their favorite office automation tools and, once the documents are approved for dissemination, pass them over to the IntraMaster for inclusion on the intranet.

The intranet is supposed to provide a service to the company, getting information into the hands of those who need it when and where required. In terms of providing support to the content providers of the intranet, there are some basic principles of reality that can be established that will facilitate the relationship between the intranet operations and the users and content providers.

Principles of Reality

Following are some of the basic principles of reality that should be kept in mind:

- *You provide a service to the organization and, as such, need to create an environment that is conducive to customer satisfaction.* Because the content providers of the intranet are also the consumers of the goods on the intranet, you need to work with the users to help them understand that they are part of the chain. You must also work with them to eliminate the GIGO (garbage in, garbage out) by establishing service standards to which everyone will abide.

- *You can provide a consistent methodology for users to follow in the creation of their documents.* You understand the technology and the logic behind the business processes; therefore you are uniquely positioned within the organization to establish a well-architected, yet unobtrusive, life-cycle methodology.

- *You will provide and support a toolset to the users for use in their day-to-day activities.* Assuming that you have the luxury of defining the tools that the users will use within the primary computing environment, you have to be certain that the users have the tools and receive the training in how to use them effectively, and you must support them in their activities

- *The users will use any tool they can get their hands on to make their life easier and your life more miserable.* With new products coming to the market almost every day, the users will probably want to try "this product because it's supposed to do that better;" you must keep abreast of the changing market and work with the users to be certain that new products are tested for integration and functionality within your environment.

- *A large number of users, especially new hires and long time staff, want to use the office automation tools that they know and are comfortable with.* You must find a way to bring all the pieces together in order to keep what hair you have left on your head.

- *Users will create most of their documents using the same look and feel, time and time again.* Without even knowing it, a user tends to use the same set of styles and templates for all documents. Only when users work in groups do you see radical changes from one's normal style.

Although these principles may be self-evident, intranet developers often go about looking for the ultimate solution. You can use the principles to create an environment that is effective for the users and efficient for you in the provision of services and information via the intranet.

Converting and Publishing Word Processing Documents

This section will deal with taking the most basic of documents, those created by word processing, and working through the steps of getting them onto the intranet.

The Basics

Many word processing software packages are available on the market, and it is likely that most organizations have at least two within their walls—probably WordPerfect and Microsoft Word. Assume here that companies adopt a single word processing package as their primary standard, but that they recognize that others may exist within the company. This is particularly evident if companies have a mixture of computing platforms.

Two basic methods that convert documents from word processing packages into the format required for the intranet:

- The author does it directly.

- A service bureau does the conversion on behalf of the author. The *service bureau* can be a human who performs the task using a standard toolset, or it can be a mechanical device that accepts the author's input and does the conversion with the push of a button.

In both methods, the same tools can be used. How a company decides to implement the conversion function depends upon internal factors such as *how* the company has established its business processes; but this topic is beyond the scope of this book. What this book will do next is look at the mechanical device and what needs to happen before the document is fed into the machine.

You probably have the luxury of establishing a corporate computing environment, which means that the word processing software is used by almost everyone in the company. Most people never alter the styles that they use within the word processor; you can talk to your users and verify that, but most of your technical support personnel will tell you that the majority of users neither know how to change a style or can't be bothered because the majority of their work fits within the default style sheet.

With these two pieces of information in hand and the knowledge that you need in order to be able to convert these documents to HTML, you can create a style sheet for use within the word processing package, a style sheet that enables you to match the traditional HTML tags to style tags within your word processing. This style sheet can then be integrated into all the computers using the application. The use of the styles in the word processor will result in a document that is displayed approximately as it would be seen in the browser of the intranet.

With this corporate style sheet in hand, you then map the word processor's style sheet to the conversion style sheet within your service bureau, and you will have a consistent set of HTML files coming out every time. Or so the theory states.

There are always exceptions to the rule, and when a user needs to implement a new style or set of styles for a specific document, you can create a new instance of the conversion style sheet for this document. In many cases, series or families of documents will share the same style sheet but are different from the corporate style sheet. What you end up with in the service bureau is a series of word processing style sheets that can be used for a variety of document formats and a series of conversion style sheets.

Once you have been able to implement the style sheets, you will have the users working on providing you the series of documents composed in one of the "standard" formats. If the users can see that their HTML documents look like their word processing documents, they are usually very happy.

Basics of Images

Now what about images? You know the image formats that the intranet supports directly, and you know what helper applications and plug-ins you have implemented. What you need to provide to the user is the understanding of the image types with which you can deal and where to turn to have the non-standard images converted to an acceptable format.

Once you have these basics in place, you can turn to your service bureau. You can establish an entire suite of conversion tools to deal with the various combinations of text format and image format. But it is recommended you look at a solution that is more robust than the txt2html.exe utility of several companies.

You need to work with a product that will accept input from a variety of word processing formats and a variety of image formats. The system has to be able to work with a variety of standard style sheets from the various word processing formats and, ideally, it should be able to save the conversion style sheets as a template to be called up and reused as required.

Several products on the market meet these requirements and more are on the way. Here, the book will work with the HTML Transit program from InfoAccess, Inc. in order to show you the features of these types of products and how they can be used as a service bureau.

An Example: HTML Transit

HTML Transit automatically converts source files into HTML, reading word processing files in their native formats. As you will see, HTML Transit uses a template approach to map the styles from the word processing file to the output styles of the HTML files. The program also creates both an overall and a local table of contents for navigating between the sections of a large document and then within those sections themselves. If the source files contain index entries, HTML Transit creates an index file as well.

Note

A demonstration/evaluation copy of HTML Transit is included on the CD that comes with this book. You can install the program from the CD and work through the examples.

One of the big problems in converting word processing documents to HTML is the fact that most users tend to create one huge document. In the intranet world, a large document takes a long time to download to the browser, and it is even longer if there are a lot of images in the file. HTML Transit provides an easy method to break the word processing file up into manageable, retrieval components, as you will see.

HTML Transit does the following automatically:

- Converts text, images, and tables from multiple sources

- Imports style names and attribute settings

- Permits the creation of hyperlinks to HTML documents, thereby enabling navigation within and between documents

- Creates a table of contents based on user-determined heading levels

- Creates an index file if index markers are present in the source files

- Maintains cross-references and footnotes embedded in the source files

- Avoids altering the source files

How HTML Transit Works on Word Processing Files

When a word processing file is brought into the HTML Transit application, it is associated with an HTML Transit template. The application associates individual styles with Translator Elements that HTML Transit generates automatically. HTML tags are then assigned to the Translator Elements. The template file interprets the Translator elements before the content of the source files are converted into an HTML publication. The template files have an extension of ".hmp" and work in the background to create the .htm files.

The word processing formats that are supported by HTML Transit are as follows:

Text Formats Supported By HTML Transit	Extension
AmiPro	*.sam
ASCII Standard PC	*.txt
Framemaker (MIF)	*.mif
Interleaf	*.doc
MS Word (DOS and Windows)	*.doc
Rich Text Format (RTF)	*.rtf
WordPerfect (DOS and Windows)	*.wpd
Write	*.wri

How HTML Transit Works with Graphics

When graphics are imported into HTML Transit, they are converted into either Graphics Image Format (GIF) by default, or Joint Photographics Experts Group (JPEG) format if specified. The supported file formats are as follows:

Graphics Formats Supported	Extension
Bitmap	*.bmp
Microsoft Paint	*.msp
Paint	*.pcx
Tagged Image File Format (TIFF)	*.tif
Computer Graphics Metafile	*.cgm
Encapsulated PostScript (EPS)	*.eps
Windows Metafile	*.wmf
Corel Draw	*.cdr
Micrografx Designer	*.drw
AutoCAD	*.dxf
Digital Research	*.gem
Graphics Interchange Format	*.gif
Joint Photographics Experts Group	*.jpg
Hewlett Packard Graphics Language	*.plt
WordPerfect Graphics	*.wpg

Now that you see that the program will support the major word processors and image file formats, you can get down to work with the product. Figure 16.1 shows the interface you will be working with once you have obtained and installed the software.

How to Set Up the Interface Parameters

Figure 16.1

User interface.

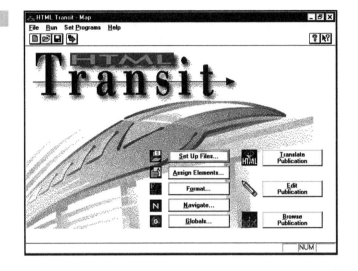

The HTML Transit interface shows a number of buttons in the lower-right corner of the screen and four menu options in the top-left. In terms of preparing for use, you need to specify to the application the browser that you will be using to review the output files and your HTML editor, if you use one.

To set up these two parameters, the following steps are required:

1. Select the Set Programs menu option.

2. Select Set Editor.

3. Enter the name of the editor or use the Browse button to find the name.

4. Click on OK.

5. Repeat the steps above, replacing Set Editor with Set Browser, and entering in the correct name.

How to Create a New HTML Publication Using HTML Transit

When HTML Transit is started, the default template is in use. To create a new HTML publication, follow these steps:

1. Choose File, New. This opens the template map.hmp, a copy of the default template.

2. Save the template file under another name in order to preserve any changes that you make to the template during the course of your work.

3. Choose File, Save As, and then enter the name "transit" (for the sake of this example).

You can now proceed to work with your source file. First, however, take a few minutes to describe what each of the buttons on the HTML Transit interface enables you to do. An understanding of the functions behind each of the buttons is necessary in order to move you up the learning curve.

- Set Up Files—Select source files, establish output files, and identify the output directory.

- Assign Elements—Associate imported styles with Translator Elements, assign HTML tags to Translator Elements.

- Format—Specify format attributes for the Translator Elements.

- Navigate—Add links to the HTML publication for navigation between and within documents.

- Globals—Define global settings such as color.

- Translate Publication—converts the source file into HTML publication.

- Edit Publication—Opens the HTML editor selected to edit HTML directly.

- Browse Publication—Launches the browser to review the publication.

And now to work. You have already saved your copy of the default template file as transit.hmp. Now as you make changes throughout the demonstration, save the changes to the template file periodically.

How to Identify Files to be Converted

The first order of business is to identify to HTML Transit which files you are going to convert for use within the intranet. Ask your content providers for the information that they would like to have on the intranet.

This example uses a simple MS Word file that uses the standard tags Heading 1, Heading 2, and Heading 3 within the style sheet. Figure 16.2 shows the file, transit1.doc, as it appears in its native format.

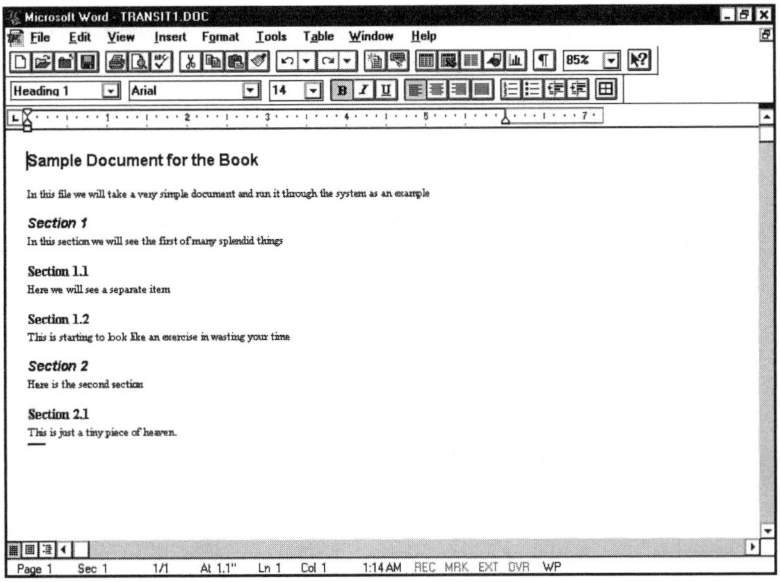

Figure 16.2

MS Word file transit1.doc.

To bring this file into HTML Transit, take the following steps:

1. Click on Set Up Files on the HTML Transit interface.

2. Click on the Select Files tab at the top of the dialog box.

3. Click on Add. The Select Input Files window appears.

4. Ensure that MS Word appears in the List files of Type: window.

5. Find the appropriate file in the directory structure and select the file for translation by double-clicking on the file or by highlighting it and clicking on Insert.

6. Click on OK when the file appears in the Files to Translate box—this returns you to the Set Up Files window

7. In the Page Title box near the top of the window, enter the page title you wish to appear on the HTML file (Book Test for this example).

Figure 16.3 shows the Set Up Files screen to this point.

Figure 16.3

Set Up Files.

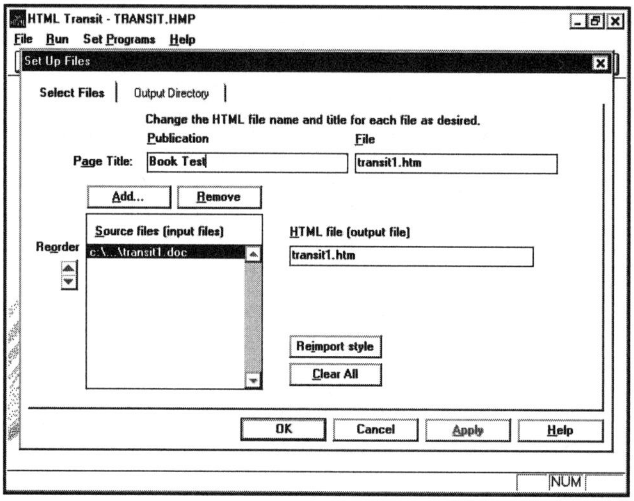

8. Click on the Output Directory tab at the top of the Set Up Files dialog box.

9. Type in or use the Browse button to identify output directory for HTML publication.

10. Make certain that Create TOC is selected.

Figure 16.4 shows the Output Directory information completed for this example.

11. Select OK to accept the settings and return to the main interface.

How to Translate a Document with HTML Transit

At this point you are ready to take your first pass at translating the document. To do this, perform the following steps:

1. Click on the Translate Publication button to translate the source files in conjunction with the template file.

2. Once the program has completed the translation of the document, click on Browse Publication to view the publication that you just created.

3. When you are finished viewing the document, close the browser.

Figure 16.5 shows the results.

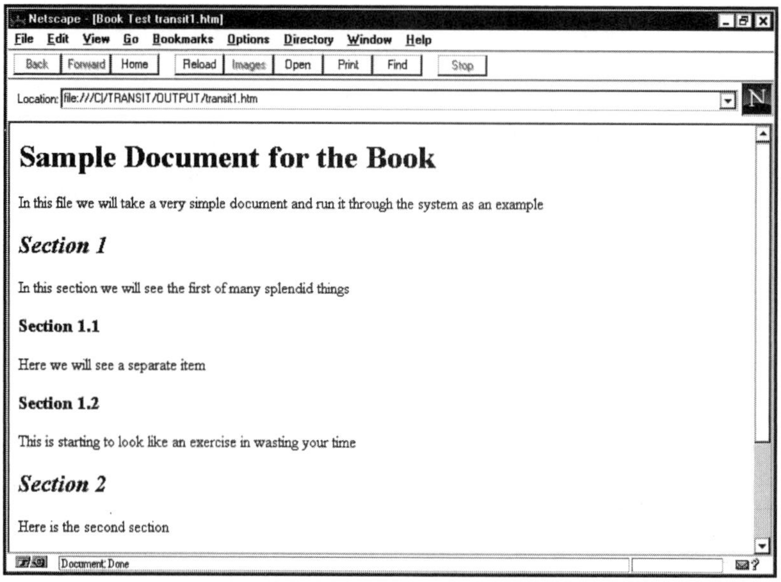

Figure 16.5

HTML results of
conversion.

Figure 16.5 HTML results of conversion.

How to Create a Table of Contents

In the event that the document being converted is relatively long, say
beyond five pages, it is a good idea to create a table of contents that
enables the user to click on an entry and a hyperlink to the appropriate
section of the document. This means that the users do not have to
scroll through the document to get to the section they would like to
read. If the document is over ten pages in length, it is generally a good
idea to break the long document down into a series of smaller documents that are hyperlinked to the table of contents. HTML Transit can
assist you in creating the table of contents and in breaking the document into its component pieces.

The next step is to create a table of contents for the overall document
and then break the document down into smaller components. Because
the document that you are working with is small, please note that the
document is divided into numbered sections with subsections in each.
A quick glance back at figure 16.5 confirms this structure.

In order to implement this feature, you must undertake the following
steps:

1. Click on the Assign Elements button on the main interface.

2. Click on the Place Elements tab at the top of the window.

3. Select Heading 1 and make certain that the Include in TOC and Include in Local TOC boxes are checked.

4. Select Heading 2 and make certain that the Include in TOC and Include in Local TOC boxes are checked.

5. Select Heading 3 and make certain that Include in Local TOC is checked (you do not want them to appear on the main TOC).

Figure 16.6 shows the Assign Elements/Place Elements screen with the Heading 2 information correctly selected for this example.

Figure 16.6

Assign Elements/ Place Elements.

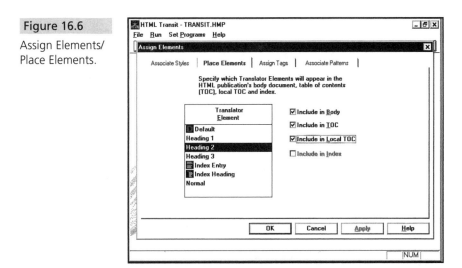

How to View the Table of Contents

To view the implementation of the Table of Contents do the following:

1. Click on OK to close the Assign Elements window and accept the changes.

2. Push the Translate Publication button.

3. When the translation is complete, click on Browse Publication.

4. When finished reviewing the table of contents, close the browser and return to the HTML Transit program.

Figure 16.7 shows the HTML publication with the Table of Contents at the top of the screen. Looking closely at the bottom of the screen, Section 2 still appears in the document. The next step breaks the main document into smaller components based on the headings used for the sections of the document.

Figure 16.7

HTML output with Table of Contents.

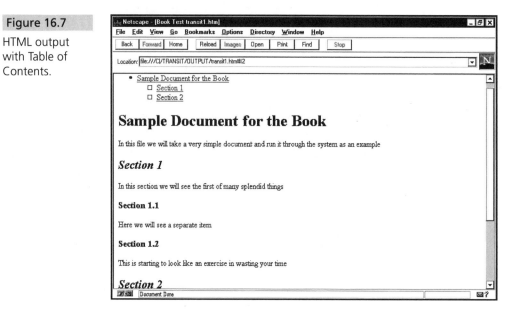

How to Break a Document Down into its Components

Tip

As a rule of thumb, try to keep your documents to five pages or fewer.

In order to break the main document into the component pieces using HTML Transit, you need to do the following:

1. Click on the Assign Element button on the main interface.

2. Select the Assign Tags tab from the window.

3. Select the Heading 2 entry in the Translator Elements box.

4. Ensure the Create New HTML file beginning with this translator element option is selected.

5. Ensure Add the Following to the Page Title is selected.

6. Enter some text indicator into the text box (details for this example).

Figure 16.8 shows the Assign Elements/Assign Tags settings for this example.

7. Click on OK.

To see the output shown in figure 16.9:

1. Click on Translate Publication.

2. Click on Browse Publication.

3. When finished, close the browser.

In the figure you now see the document is broken into components, but you cannot see any means of navigating to them. Two other files were created during the translation—there were two <Heading 2> elements in the document. These two files are currently available in the output directory that you specified and are named with the convention of sourcefilename1.htm, sourcefilename2.htm, and so forth. They can be retrieved and viewed within your browser should you so choose.

Figure 16.9

Breaking the
source file into
components.

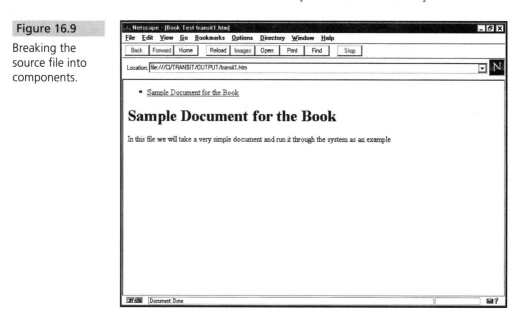

How to Incorporate Navigation Links and Images

So far this chapter has covered the following steps:

1. Identifying the word processing document for conversion

2. Translating the document into HTML

3. Creating a table of contents

4. Breaking the document into smaller components

Now it is time to make certain that the components of the document can be reached from the table of contents via hyperlinks, the navigation method of HTML documents.

Note

> A bitmap (*.bmp) file has been added to the transit1.doc MS Word document to show the graphic file conversion ability of HTML Transit.

In order to implement the navigation, follow these steps:

1. Click on the Navigate button on the main interface.

2. Select the Body Links tab from the window.

3. Check the Previous Page, Next Page, and TOC boxes.

4. For each of the three options, click on Gallery and choose an appropriate graphic.

5. Under Placement, at the bottom of the screen, ensure that the Place at front of page is selected and Place at end of page is cleared.

Figure 16.10 shows the settings for the Navigate/Body Links window for this demonstration.

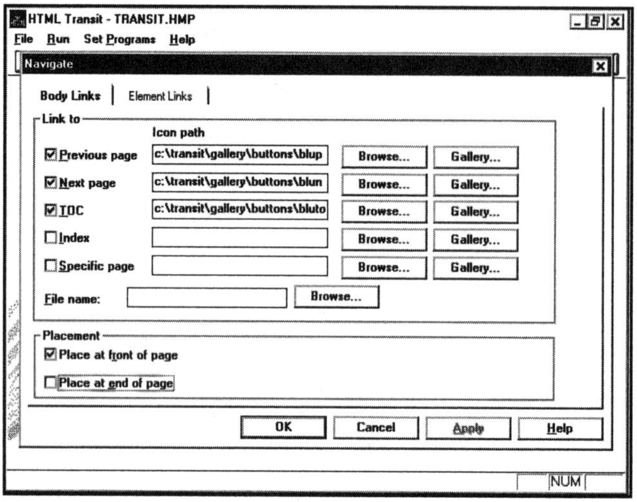

Figure 16.10

Navigate/Body links.

How to View the Results

The final results can be seen by doing the following:

1. Choose OK in the Navigate/Body Links window.

2. Click on Translate Publication.

3. Click on Browse Publication when the translation is complete.

4. Close the browser when you have reviewed the results.

Figure 16.11 shows one of the component documents complete with navigation buttons and graphic.

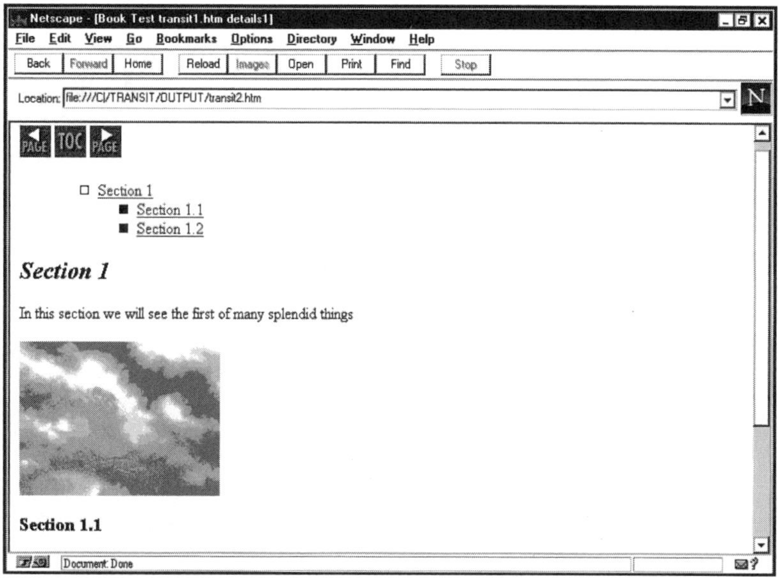

Figure 16.11

Translated document with navigation and image.

Note

Please note that the main Table of Contents is accessed through the TOC image and that the Local Table of Contents is displayed as active hyperlinks. At this point, you have taken the long document, broken it into smaller components, and created an interactive table of contents that allows the user to move between the pages and the table of contents.

Summarizing Your Efforts

Having made it through to the end of the HTML Transit example, you should see that it is quite simple to take a document and walk through the process of creating an interactive table of contents to the component documents that were automatically created by the program.

So there you have it: HTML Transit, a software program that will work as a service bureau for you in the conversion of your word processing documents for the intranet. Remember, however, that you only walked through a simple conversion. Just a couple of final points to bring up and then you will move to the spreadsheet world.

Multiple documents can be selected for conversion at the same time. Keep in mind that in this batch-type mode, the same template will be used for all documents. In order to make the documents adhere to different "look and feel" sets, use the ability to match each source file with the different Translator Element mappings. It is more efficient, however, to translate families of documents, each with one template, instead of fiddling around with the guts of the template. Each document will be incorporated into the table of contents based upon its tagging structure.

Author's Note

I was intrigued when I first encountered the HTML Transit file. I wanted to explore the ability to run multiple files of the same style sheet through the HTML Transit process. With 40 documents of 40 pages on average, I wanted to create a collection of documents driven from one interactive table of contents. It took 20 minutes to install the HTML Transit software, map the style sheet of the Word 6.0 files to the HTML Transit requirements, define the necessary breakpoints, and convert the documents to HTML. Although there was still some work to be done to clean up the look and feel of the documents and table of contents, I was impressed by the speed of the application and the ease of its use.

The conversion was done on a 150 Mhz Pentium with 16 MB Ram and 2 GB hard drive, running Windows 95.

Authors often incorporate tables from spreadsheet files into the word processing documents they translate. How does HTML Transit handle them? As a last example, an MS Excel file was inserted into the transt1.doc. In MS Word, double-clicking on the spreadsheet activates Excel so that the contents of the spreadsheet can be edited. Figure 16.12 shows the translated document, including the spreadsheet. The spreadsheet was converted to a .gif image by HTML Transit and displayed within the HTML publication.

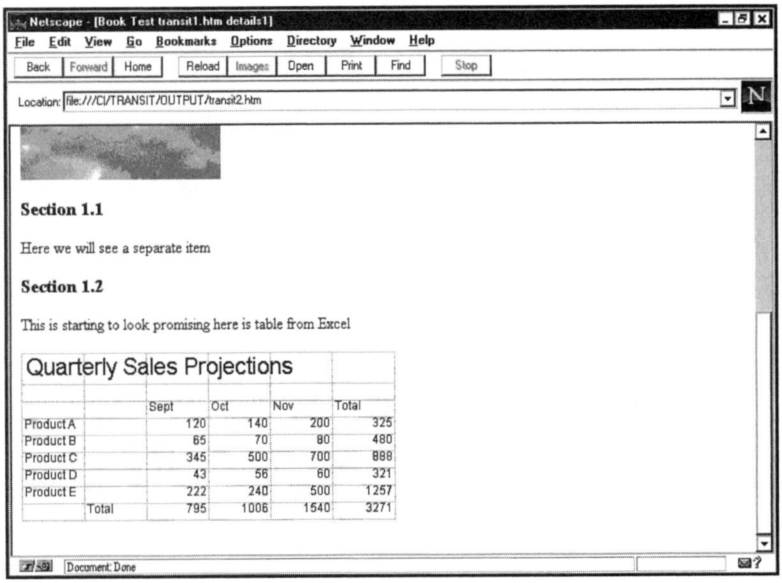

Figure 16.12

HTML publication
showing Excel
spreadsheet.

Converting and Publishing Spreadsheets

Often you want to be able to take a series of spreadsheets and convert them into HTML documents for presentation on the intranet. These spreadsheets could be anything from the latest financial results to the standings in the office baseball league to Quality Assurance results to the annual budget. In the previous section you saw that HTML Transit could take a spreadsheet embedded in a word processing source document and convert it to an image for presentation.

In some cases that may work well. However, there are times when you want the information to be presented as tables within the HTML pages that you love so much or as a page unto itself. Is there some way, other than manual manipulation, to get this information into a reasonable HTML document? The remainder of this section will address two examples of programs that will convert spreadsheets to HTML tables:

- Internet Assistant for Excel

- XTML

Spreadsheet Conversion Programs

Several programs convert spreadsheets to HTML files. Many of them focus on the Microsoft Excel software program, and it is here that a sample demonstration is found.

Microsoft offers a series of Internet Assistants free-of-charge to help users of its software convert data into HTML documents. The Internet Assistant for Microsoft Excel is an "add-in wizard" that works with users to convert their spreadsheet data into HTML format as a separate document or as part of an existing document.

XTML, eXcel Table Markup Language, by Ken Sayward, is a shareware program that creates HTML tables from Microsoft Excel spreadsheets. You can use the normal Excel formatting commands to assign font styles and text alignment, and the XTML add-in produces the HTML tags necessary to reproduce the table for the intranet.

 Note

The CD-ROM that comes with this book includes XTML. See Appendix D, "What's on the CD," for a complete listing of the CD-ROM contents.

Note

It is strongly suggested that you review the discussion of HTML tags and tables in Chapter 8, "Introduction HTML," because you may find you will need to fine-tune your tables once they are converted. It is also important to remember that, at the time of writing, not all browsers support tables.

Creating an HTML Table from a Spreadsheet

In order to move the data from a spreadsheet into the table, you need to devise a macro of some sort that goes row by row, cell by cell through the data, putting the required tags around the contents of each cell. You then have to output the results to an ASCII text file.

Originally, people tried to write the macros to extract information in this fashion. It wasn't pretty, and often things did not quite work as they were intended. The next step along this track was using the report writers (R&R Relational Report Writer, for example) that treated the spreadsheet like a database and enabled them to treat each row as a database record. For each record they defined text strings to precede and follow the individual field contents and print these to a file.

This is the basic concept now at play within the world of conversion utilities. Most of the conversion tools ask the user to define a title for the document, a caption for the table, the row in which the column headings are located, and the rows and columns that make up the body of the table. With this information in hand, it is relatively simple for the tools to create the various tag elements that make up the table.

Take a look at the following examples of conversion utilities that convert spreadsheets into HTML tables:

- Microsoft's Internet Assistant for Excel

- Ken Sayward's XTML

An Example: Internet Assistant for Excel

Microsoft has created Internet Assistant for Excel to provide Excel users the ability to create and distribute Excel documents on intranets (and othernets). It is a no-charge add-in wizard that walks the user through the creation of stand-alone HTML files or a simple HTML table suitable for insertion into an existing document.

The user needs only to download the Internet Assistant from Microsoft and copy it into the EXCEL\LIBRARY directory on the user's computer. This directory may be taken from the root of the computer or under the MSOFFICE directory should the user be a Microsoft Office operator.

How to Install the Internet Assistant:

To install the Internet Assistant:

1. Copy the HTML.XLA (the Internet Assistant) file to the Excel Library directory.

2. Run Microsoft Excel.

3. Select Tools, Add-Ins and check Internet Assistant Wizard.

4. Click on OK to close the window.

Figure 16.13 shows the Add-In window with the appropriate boxes checked.

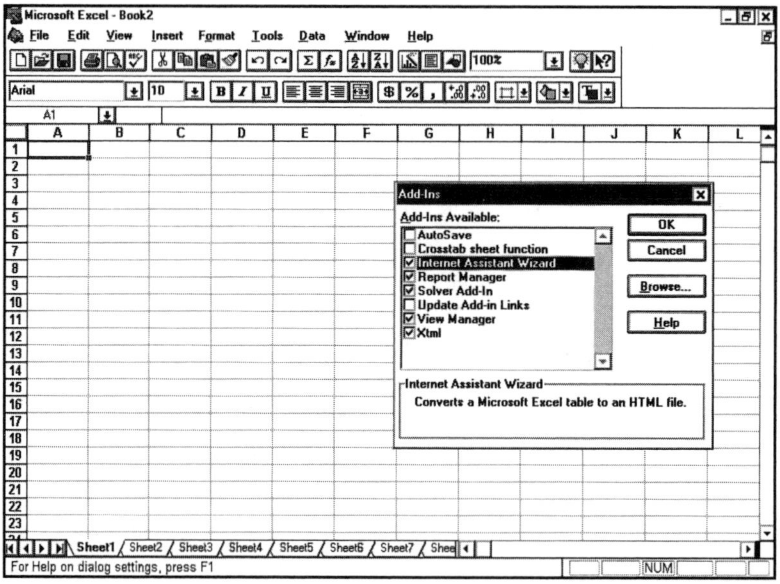

Figure 16.13

Microsoft Excel Add-Ins window.

Retrieving a Sample File

Now that you are all set up to use the tools, retrieve a sample file to work with. Once you have retrieved a sample (or created one for demonstration purposes), the following steps take you through to the creation of your HTML page:

1. Select the cells for conversion to HTML.

2. From the Tools menu choose the Internet Assistant Wizard.

3. Click on Next to continue.

Figure 16.14 shows the first Internet Assistant Wizard screen and the sample data already selected. The range of the data that you wish to convert appears in the input box at the bottom of the Internet Assistant Wizard window.

Figure 16.14

Retrieving a
sample file.

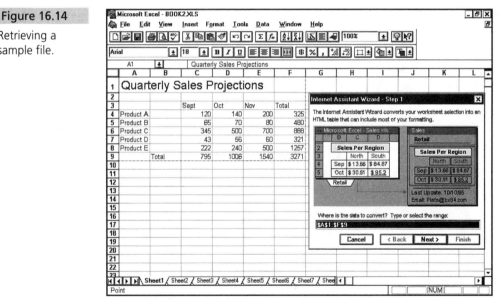

Specifying the Document

The following steps enable the user to specify whether a separate, complete HTML document will be created or the table will be inserted into an existing HTML document, whereby the table itself will be the output:

1. Select the option to create an independent HTML document.

2. Click on Next to continue.

This step is shown in figure 16.15.

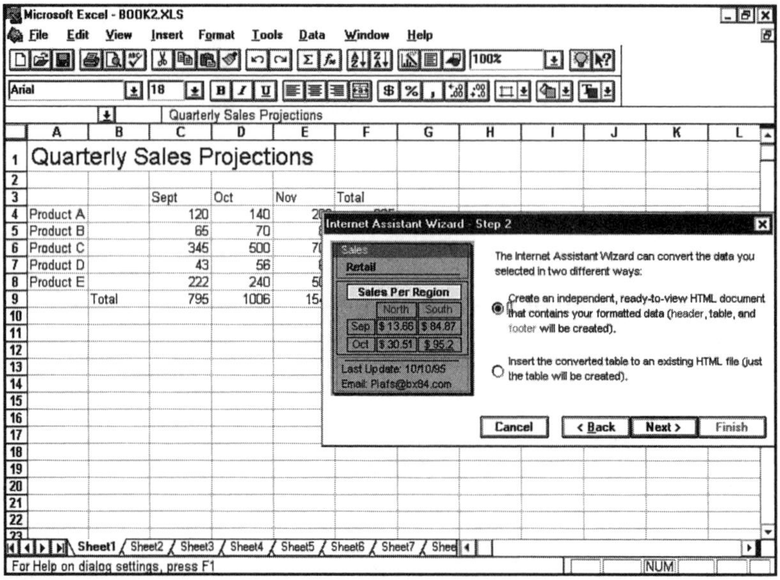

Figure 16.15

Specifying the document.

Permitting the Input of Information

When inputting information, the user is asked to enter a title, a header, and a descriptive paragraph that will appear above the table on the HTML document. The user also has the opportunity to:

- Insert a horizontal line separating the heading information from the body of the table.

- Put in information about the date of last update and an e-mail link to the appropriate person for further information.

- Separate the table from this <address>-like information by inserting a horizontal line after the table.

Figure 16.16 shows the form completed for the example.

Figure 16.16

Permitting the input of information.

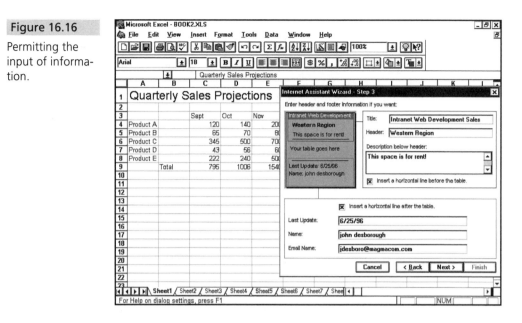

Formatting Options

Step four of the process takes into consideration the formatting that may have been done on the Excel spreadsheet. You can try to convert as much of the formatting as possible or convert only the data.

Figure 16.17 shows the window for this step of the process.

Specifying the Path and Name of the Output File

The fifth and final step of the Internet Assistant Wizard process is to specify the path and name of the HTML output file. Enter the appropriate path and name for the output file and click Finish to create your HTML document.

Figure 16.18 below shows the final step of the Internet Assistant Wizard with the details for this demonstration completed. Figure 16.19 shows the HTML document as it is retrieved in Netscape Navigator.

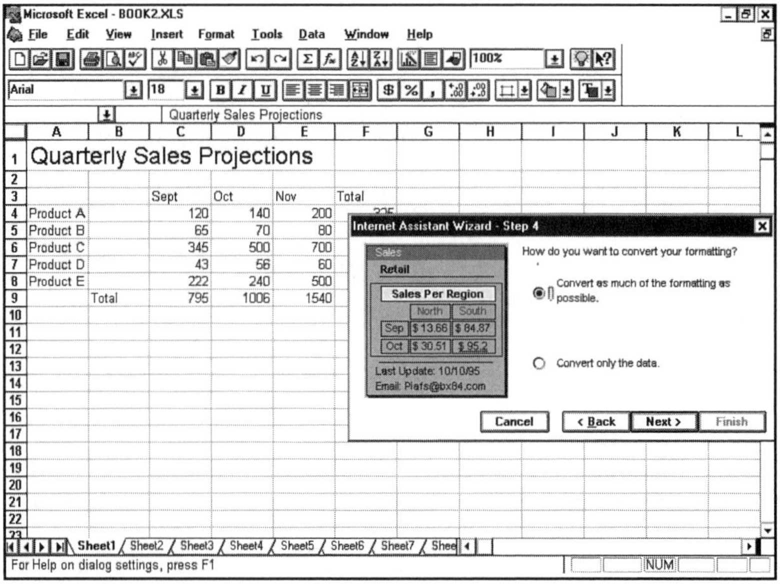

Figure 16.17

Formatting options.

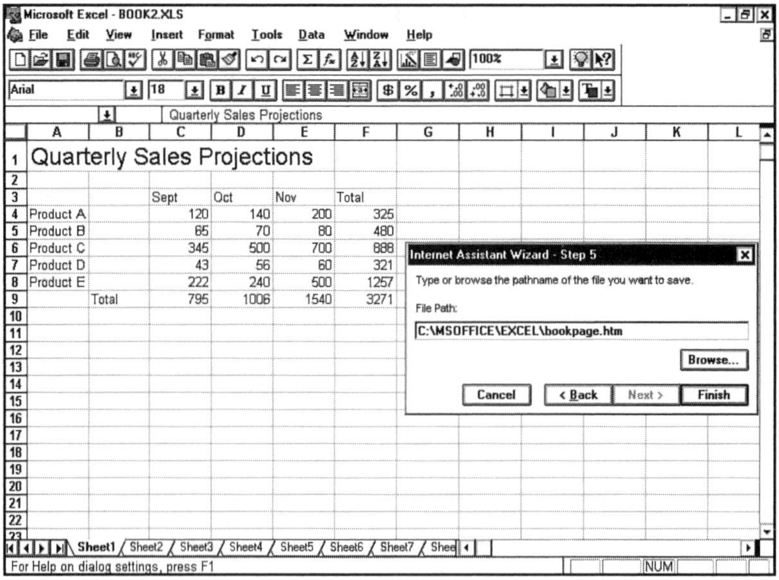

Figure 16.18

Specifying the path and name of the output file.

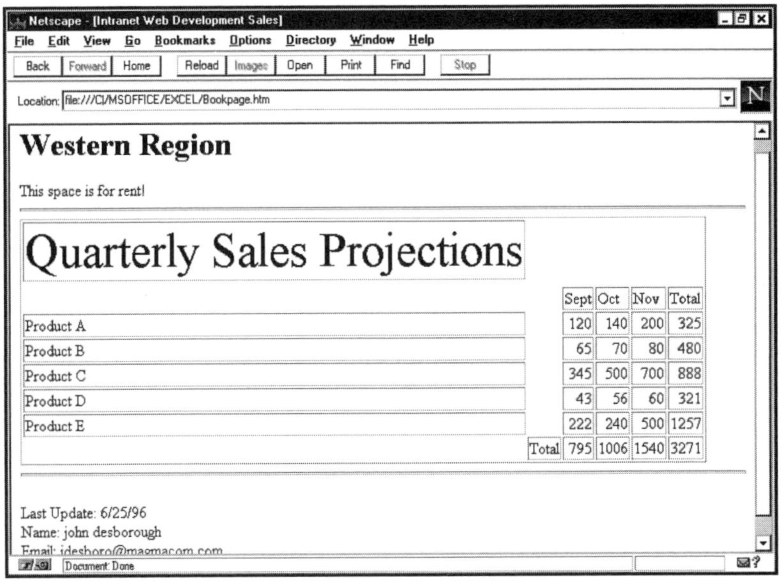

Figure 16.19

Excel file converted to an HTML document.

An Example: XTML

XTML is a shareware add-in for Microsoft Excel that creates HTML tables quickly and easily. These tables can then be used as a very simple standalone HTML document, or they can be integrated into another document.

The reason the program is shown here is that it is very simple to work with—there are only two screens to deal with.

Note

The XTML shareware add-in is available on the CD-ROM that is included with the book. Please see Appendix D, "What's on the CD," for a complete list of what's on the CD.

How to Implement XTML

To install and set up XTML, perform the following steps:

1. Copy the XTML file from the CD-ROM included with this book into the Excel Library directory.

2. Run Microsoft Excel.

3. Select Tools, Add-Ins and check XTML.

4. Click on OK to close the window.

Once again you will use the sample file from the previous section to show how the application works.

Setting the Preferences for Conversion

The first step is to set the Preferences for the HTML conversion. Figure 16.20 shows the Preferences window, which allows you to establish, as best you can, the match between the Excel styles you have used and the HTML output tags.

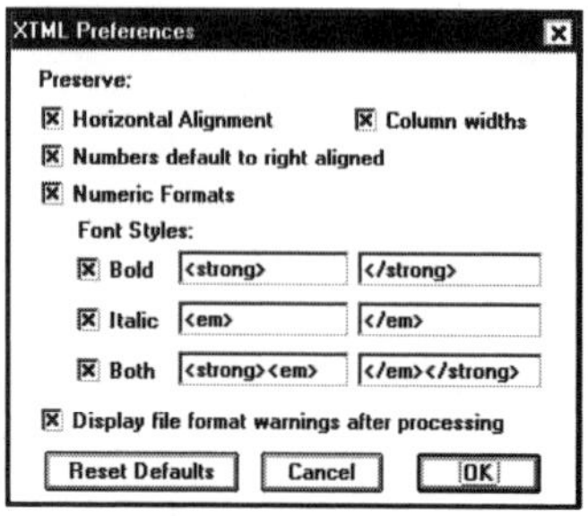

Figure 16.20

XTML Preferences window.

The following is a brief explanation of the XTML preferences:

• Horizontal alignment—Tells XTML to preserve the alignment of cells as formatted in Excel.

• Column widths—Tells XTML to use a <TD WIDTH="x%"> tag. The <TD WIDTH> tag is added in the first table row that does not have any COLSPAN tags. XTML calculates the width of each column as a percentage of the total table width.

- Numbers default to right aligned—Tells XTML to automatically tag numeric cells as right aligned, unless another alignment has been applied to the cell in Excel.

- Numeric Formats—Tells XTML to preserve the formatting of numeric cells, such as currency, commas, percentages, and so on.

- Font Styles—Tells XTML to preserve the font style of cells as formatted in Excel.

- Display file format warnings after processing—Reminds the user about the fact that output files must be saved as formatted text (space delimited). If this is unchecked, no warning dialogs are displayed.

Now that you understand the preferences in XTML, you need only set them once for all your conversions, unless your parameters change over time.

Creating an HTML Table with XTML

In order to create an HTML table using XTML, perform the following steps:

1. Select the range of cells that you wish to include in the table.

2. Select the Tools menu.

3. Select XTML from the bottom of the Tools window.

4. Select Convert to HTML Table from the submenu that appears.

Selecting Convert to HTML Table displays the XTML Table Options screen, as seen in figure 16.21, completed for the example. The input range of cells is already displayed in the Input Range field. You need only complete the remaining fields to conclude your conversion.

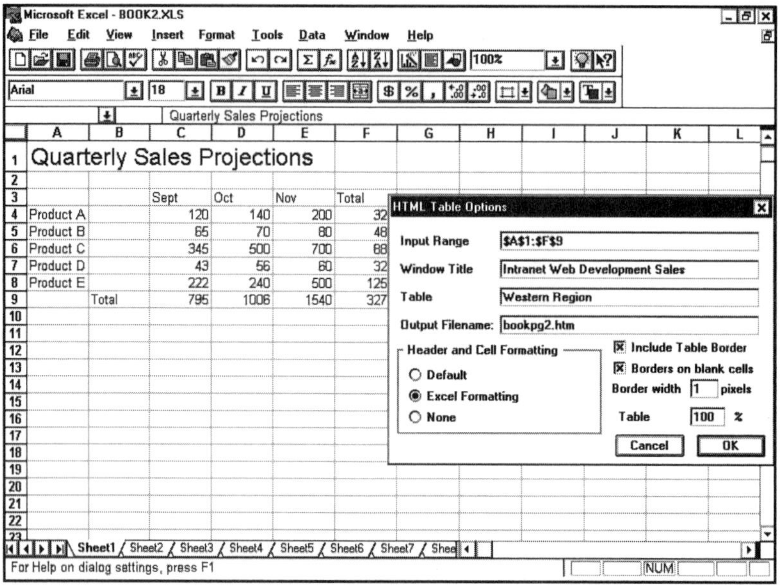

Figure 16.21

HTML Table
Options window.

XTML Options for Conversion

The options available for the conversion are:

- Input Range—the range of Excel cells for which you wish to create HTML output

- Window Title—the window title when the page is viewed with a Web browser (the default is the name of the Excel worksheet)

- Table Caption—the text appears above the table with <CAPTION> & <H2> tags (default is the name of the Excel worksheet)

- Output Filename—the filename for the resulting HTML file (the default is the name of the Excel worksheet, plus the ".HTM" extension)

- Header and Cell Formatting—determines the look of the resulting HTML

- Default—marks up the first row of the table with <TH> tags

- Use Excel Formatting—marks up all cells according to their format and alignment in Excel

- None—marks up only the table with <TR> and <TD> tags

- Include Table Border—includes border as indicated

- Borders on blank cells—forces XTML to insert " " into HTML table cells, so that those cells get borders around them as well (applicable only when the Include Table Border option is selected)

- Border width [ ] pixels—size of the table border (if enabled) in valid range from 1 to 25

- Table Width [ ] %—specifies the percentage of the width of the HTML page to display the table (if 50%, centered on the page but using only half of the current page width—the default is 100%)

Creating the HTML Table

Now comes the hard part: in order to create the HTML table you must do the following:

1. Click on OK and the output file that you specify will be constructed.

2. Retrieve the HTML file just created with your browser.

3. Close the browser when you have reviewed the results.

Figure 16.22 shows the results as seen in the browser.

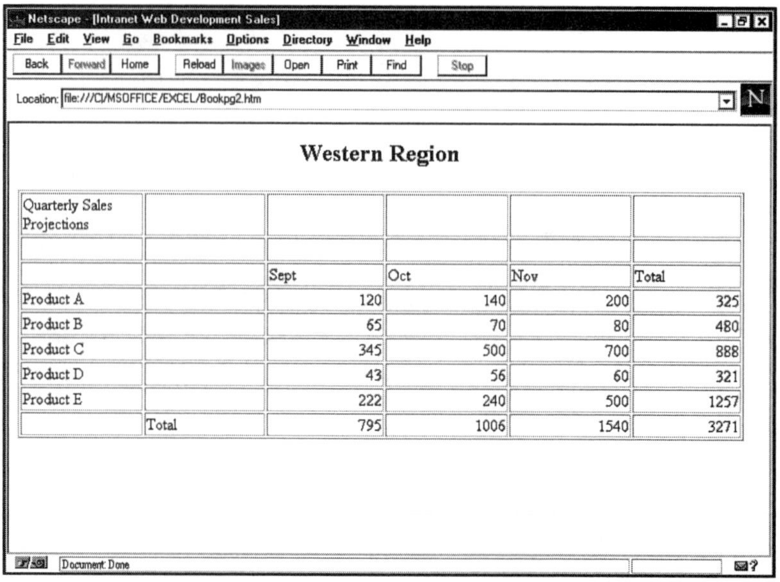

Figure 16.22

HTML output as seen in browser.

Before talking about converting other types of data, this chapter will look back at the output that was created by the XTML program. To fine-tune how the table looks to the users of the intranet, you may want to go in and add some formatting, change the alignment, or have the test span a column or two. Here is the code that was created by the XTML conversion for your review. Review figure 16.23 and fine-tune the code behind the image for use within your intranet. Here is the code:

```
<HTML>
<TITLE>Intranet Web Development Sales</TITLE>
<BODY>
<CENTER>
<TABLE BORDER WIDTH="100%">
<CAPTION><H2>Western Region</H2></CAPTION>
<TR>
<TD WIDTH=<TD"17%">Quarterly Sales Projections</TD>
<TD WIDTH=<TD"17%"> </TD>
<TD WIDTH=<TD"17%"> </TD>
<TD WIDTH=<TD"17%"> </TD>
<TD WIDTH=<TD"17%"> </TD>
<TD WIDTH=<TD"17%"> </TD>
</TR>
```

```
<TR>
<TD> </TD>
<TD> </TD>
<TD> </TD>
<TD> </TD>
<TD> </TD>
<TD> </TD>
</TR>
<TR>
<TD> </TD>
<TD> </TD>
<TD>Sept</TD>
<TD>Oct</TD>
<TD>Nov</TD>
<TD>Total</TD>
</TR>
<TR>
<TD>Product A</TD>
<TD> </TD>
<TD ALIGN=right>120</TD>
<TD ALIGN=right>140</TD>
<TD ALIGN=right>200</TD>
<TD ALIGN=right>325</TD>
</TR>
<TR>
<TD>Product B</TD>
<TD> </TD>
<TD ALIGN=right>65</TD>
<TD ALIGN=right>70</TD>
<TD ALIGN=right>80</TD>
<TD ALIGN=right>480</TD>
</TR>
<TR>
<TD>Product C</TD>
<TD> </TD>
<TD ALIGN=right>345</TD>
<TD ALIGN=right>500</TD>
<TD ALIGN=right>700</TD>
<TD ALIGN=right>888</TD>
</TR>
<TR>
<TD>Product D</TD>
<TD> </TD>
```

```
<TD ALIGN=right>43</TD>
<TD ALIGN=right>56</TD>
<TD ALIGN=right>60</TD>
<TD ALIGN=right>321</TD>
</TR>
<TR>
<TD>Product E</TD>
<TD> </TD>
<TD ALIGN=right>222</TD>
<TD ALIGN=right>240</TD>
<TD ALIGN=right>500</TD>
<TD ALIGN=right>1257</TD>
</TR>
<TR>
<TD> </TD>
<TD>Total</TD>
<TD ALIGN=right>795</TD>
<TD ALIGN=right>1006</TD>
<TD ALIGN=right>1540</TD>
<TD ALIGN=right>3271</TD>
</TR>
</TABLE>
</CENTER>
</BODY>
<HTML>
```

Note

Please note the use of " ". This is a little trick that HTML programmers use in otherwise empty cells to force the HTML border to be displayed around the blank cells.

Converting Other Data Types for the Intranet

A variety of companies and individuals have worked to create applications or components of their applications that convert files of one sort or another to HTML. Several of the applications here are for Apple/Macintosh machines only. And, as always, given the nature of software and the Net, this list is guaranteed to be out of date and missing some of the players in the market. They are provided as examples only. The author has used a number of these and has had the names of some of the applications provided by intranet implementers, but neither he, nor the publisher, warrant the usability of these programs in your environment. Govern for yourself accordingly.

Conversion Utilities for Specific Products

This section has assembled listings of conversion utilities that are designed to convert files of a specific product, MS Word or QuarkXPress, for example, to HTML. They are organized into product-related groupings where possible and, failing this, into program type groupings and word processing in general.

Note

> For more detailed instructions on how to do it yourself, please see New Riders' October 1996 book *Conversion Techniques for Web Publishing*, by Janine Warner, Ken Milburn, and Jessica Burdman.

MS Word Converters

Following is a list of MS Word Converters and the Web sites where they can be found:

HTML Author is a Word for Windows template with macros. It supports non-English versions of Word.

```
http://www.salford.ac.il/iti/gsc/htmlauth/summary.html
```

Logic n.v. is TextToHTML for Macs. It handles rtf as well as plain text.

```
http://www.logic.be/
```

Cyberleaf converts MS Word, WordPerfect, FrameMaker, and more to HTML documents (commercial).

```
http://www.ileaf.com/ip.html
```

WebWizard converts Word 6.0 to HTML (commercial).

```
http://www.w3.org/hypertext/WWW/Tools/WebWizard.html
```

MSWToHTML for Macs requires AppleScript and MS Word 6.0.

```
http://dreyer.ucsf.edu/mswtohtml.html
```

SGML Tag Wizard converts Windows Word 6.0 docs to HTML.

```
http://ourworld.compuserve.com/homepages/nice/
```

CU_HTML.DOT is a template for Word for Windows 2.0 and 6.0 documents.

```
http://www.cuhk.hk/csc/cu_html/cu_html.htm
```

tbl2html converts Word format tables to HTML.

```
http://www.cadd.nps.usace.army.mil/pub/tbl2html.dot
```

GT_HTML.DOT is for Windows MS Word macros.

```
http://www.gatech.edu/word_html/release.htm
```

ANT_HTML.DOT and **ANT PLUS** are for Windows Word 6.0 and Macs.

```
http://www.w3.org/hypertext/WWW/Tools/Ant.html
```

Web Author is for Word 6.0.

```
http://www.qdeck.com/qdeck/demosoft/WebAuthr/
```

EasyHelp/Web 2.31 converts Word 2.0 to Windows help files or Web pages.

```
http://www.eon-solutions.com/easyhelp/easyhelp.htm
```

EasyHelp/Web 2.80c converts Word 6.0 to Windows help files or Web pages.

```
http://www.eon-solutions.com/easyhelp/easyhelp.htm
```

WordPerfect Converters

wpmacro is a WordPerfect 5.1 macro, now largely superseded by WPTOHTML.

```
http://stoner.eps.mcgill.ca/wpmacro/wpmacro.html
```

wpt51d10 converts WordPerfect to HTML.

```
ftp://oak.oakland.edu/pub/msdos/wordperf/wpt51d10.zip
```

WordPerfectInternet Publisher converts WordPerfect to HTML.

```
http://wp.novell.com/elecpub/intpub.htm
```

WordPerfect Macro is DOS macros for WordPerfect5.1.

```
http://www.soton.ac.uk/%7edja/wpmacros/
```

Microsoft Excel Converters

Excel-to-Web from Baarns Publishing is for Excel 5.0 or later.

```
http://www.baarns.com
```

XTML allows you to convert tables in Excel to tables in HTML.

```
http://users.aol.com/ksayward/xtml/
```

XL2HTML.XLS is a Visual Basic Macro for Microsoft Excel 5.0 (Windows and Macintosh versions).

```
http://rs712b.gsfc.nasa.gov/704/dgd/xl2html.html
```

excel-to-html is an Excel 4.0 macro to convert part or all of an Excel spreadsheet to an HTML 3.0 table.

```
http://www.nar.com/people/sib/excel-to-html.html
```

Excel to HTML is a Mac application that converts Excel 4.0 or 5.0 spreadsheets to HTML tables.

```
http://www.rhodes.edu/software/readme.html
```

Quark Converters

E-Gate generates HTML and JPG or GIF files.

```
http://www.rosebud.fr/rosebud/e-gate.html
```

BeyondPress 2/01. needs Mac system 7.1 and QuarkXPress 3.3.

```
http://www.astrobyte.com
```

QuarkImmedia Viewer allows you to interact with multimedia projets created by QuarkImmedia and placed on the intranet. The product includes a royalty-free viewer that can be distributed to all staff.

```
http://www.quark.com
```

Collect HTML converts Quark pages to HTML (commercial).

```
http://www.logic.be/ftpserver/X0001_Collect_HTML_read_me.html
```

HTML XPort is a Quark Xtension.

```
ftp://ftp.uwtc.washington.edu/pub/Mac/Network/WWW/
HTMLXPort1.22.sit.bin
```

qt2www uses Perlscript to convert Quark text files to HTML.

```
http://the-tech.mit.edu/%7ejeremy/qt2www.html
```

FrameMaker Converters

edc2html is a Perl program that generates an HTML document to enable navigation through the structure of a FrameBuilder Element Catalog.

```
http://www.oac.uci.edu/indiv/ehood/edc2html.doc.html
```

Frame to HTML converter converts Frame to HTML.

```
ftp://bang.nta.no/pub
```

WebWorks Publisher converts Frame to HTML.

```
http://www.quadralay.com/Products/WWPub/wwpub.html
```

Miftran is written in C.

```
ftp://ftp.alumni.caltech.edu/pub/mcbeath/web/miftran/miftran.tgz
```

mif.pl uses a Perl library to parse Frame Maker Interchange Format (MIF).

```
http://www.oac.uci.edu/indiv/ehood/
```

www_and_frame converts FrameMaker 3.x to HTML.

```
http://www.w3.org/hypertext/WWW/Tools/www_and_frame.html
```

Webmaker converts FrameMaker to HTML.

```
http://www.cern.ch/WebMaker/whywebmaker/AboutWebMaker.html
```

Fm2HTML converts FrameMaker to HTML.

```
http://www.w3.org/hypertext/WWW/Tools/fm2html.html
```

MifMucker is a Perl application for converting Frame documents.

```
http://www.oac.uci.edu/indiv/ehood/mifmucker.doc.html
```

FrameMaker 5.0 is a built-in HTML converter.

```
http://www.frame.com/
```

HyperCard Converters

HTML Sketcher 1.1 for Macs is a HyperCard stack that provides basic home pages.

```
ftp://ftp.fenk.wau.nl/pub/mac/info-mac/text/html/html-sketche-11-
hc.hqx
```

HomeMaker 1.0b8 for Macs is a HyperCard stack-interactive home page developer.

```
ftp://ftp.fenk.wau.nl/pub/mac/info-mac/text/html/home-maker-10b8-
hc.hqx
```

HyperMarker1.0 for Macs is a HyperCard stack.

```
ftp://ftp.uwtc.washington.edu/pub/Mac/Network/WWW/
HyperMarker1.0Demo.sit.bin
```

Bob HTML Editor is a Mac SuperCard application.

```
http://www.nltl.columbia.edu:3130/bob/home.html
```

HTML TableTool for Macs is a HyperCard stack that converts spreadsheet data to tables.

```
ftp://ftp.fenk.wau.nl/pub/mac/info-mac/text/html/html-table-tool-
111-hc.hqx
```

PostScript Converters

ps2html Classic converts PostScript to HTML.

```
http://stasi.bradley.edu/ftp/pub/ps2html/home.html
```

ps2html Sequel converts arbitrary PostScript text to HTML.

```
http://stasi.bradley.edu/ftp/pub/ps2html/ps2html-v2.html
```

World Wide Web Wonder Widget converts HTML to PostScript using the Mozilla algorithm.

```
http://www.netscape.com/people/mtoy/cgi/www-print.cgi
```

html2ps, compared to Mosaic, can control the layout, sizes of fonts, margins and page, and more.

```
http://www.tdb.uu.se/%7ejan/html2ps.html
```

Other Named Product Converters

Tile converts Lotus Notes to HTML (commercial).

```
http://www.clark.net/pub/listserv/
```

Webify converts PowerPoint to HTML.

```
http://cag-www.lcs.mit.edu:80/%7eward/webify/webifydoc/
```

Web-It for Macs uses Claris Works for HTML development.

```
http://www.umich.edu/%7edemonner/Primer_main/primer_main.html
```

Amiweb is an Amipro v3.0+ HTML converter.

```
http://www.cs.nott.ac.uk/%7esbx/amiweb.html
```

Nisus HTML for Macs is macros for HTML using the Nisus word processor.

```
http://www.unimelb.edu.au/%7essilcot/docs/
SilcotsHTMLMacrosReadMe.html#aa2
```

Websucker 2.5 for Macs is a Pagemaker 5.0 application.

```
http://www.iii.net/users/mcohen/websucker.html
```

HTML+ XTND for Macs outputs HTML text from any XTND word processor (NisusWriter).

```
ftp://ftp.uwtc.washington.edu/pub/Mac/Network/WWW/
HTML+1.0b1.sit.bin
```

Dave for Macs Requires Pagemaker 5.0 and AppleScript.

```
http://www.bucknell.edu/bucknellian/dave/
```

TableScripter for Macs AppleScript, converts a column of items to a table.

http://138.238.21.117/scott/tablescripter.html

Conversion Utilities for Generic Categories

The following listing is several groups of utilities that deal with categories of file types rather than with a specific product. There are many, many more conversion utilities in cyberspace. Most of them are noncommercial. Please be wary of their usage—this book offers no warranty as to the fitness of use within your specific organization.

Text Converters

TexttoHTML for Macs is for rtf and plain text.

http://www.logic.be/ftpserver/index.html#new

txt2html converts text to HTML.

http://www.cs.wustl.edu/%7eseth/txt2html/

txt2html converts AnotherText to HTML.

http://ccat.sas.upenn.edu/mengwong/txt2html.html

Digest had flexibility for dealing with a wide variety of structured files.

http://hopf.math.nwu.edu/docs/utility.html#digest

RTF Converters

TagPerfect converts rtf to SGML.

http://www.jsp.fi/delta/deltatgp.htm

E-Publish converts WinWord or rtf to HTML.

http://www.stattech.com.au/

rtftohtml is for Unix and Macs, but it will translate documents produced in Windows.

```
ftp://ftp.cray.com/src/WWWstuff/RTF/rtftohtml_overview.html
```

RTFTOHTM is a WinWord2.0 template and converter.

```
http://www.w3.org/hypertext/WWW/Tools/RTFTOHTM.html
```

RTF to HTML converter converts rtf to HTML.

```
http://www.ncsa.uiuc.edu/SDG/Software/Mosaic/Notes/rtf-html-con
verter-hector-announce.txt
```

rtftoweb is an extension of the previous converter.

```
ftp://ftp.rrzn.uni-hannover.de/pub/unix-local/misc/rtftoweb/html/
rtftoweb.html
```

eText is for rtf, RTFD, and ETFD and writes to HTML Document, TeXD, C, and formatted ASCII (for NeXTSTEP).

```
http://etext.caltech.edu
```

rtf2html converts rtf to HTML.

```
ftp://oac.hsc.uth.tmc.edu/public/unix/WWW/
```

RTF Tools is for Mac rtf Tools.

```
ftp://ftp.primate.wisc.edu/pub/RTF/index.html
```

Status Check

The long list of conversion utilities makes the mind numb when trying to look for a specific utility to convert a document for the intranet. Rest assured that there is a conversion utility for any file format that you require. It may require a little digging, but you should be able to find it.

Tip

> You may want to check out the major search engines at Yahoo, Alta Vista, or Web Crawler and use the name of the source file format and HTML as your search criteria. The next thing you should do is turn to the discussion groups on the Internet and pose questions there. More than likely someone will have an answer for you.

This chapter has covered the concept of converting files from their native format into HTML for placement on the intranet. The value of software products like HTML Transit lies in the fact that the templates developed to publish a document or a suite of documents today can be saved for use by you or anyone else in the company who needs to publish a document using the same template. Robust tools like this will continue to surface on the market as long as you choose to convert documents for placement on your servers.

By converting them to HTML, you enable search engines to index the text of the documents in order to provide a search and retrieval function. This process does have a cost, however. The source document still exists in its native format and must be managed. You now have a second version of this document on the intranet. Are you certain that the author has not updated the document recently and that the document is not stale?

These are some of the reasons you need to have a document management system that is tied into your publishing process. In order to ensure accuracy and timeliness, the latest version has to be available with little or no delay. The future is bringing interesting technologies to you at an increasingly faster pace.

Soon you will be able to create your documents in your favorite word processing environments and house them in your document management system. The document management system will have an integrated searchable library that will be accessible from the browser of the intranet. The browsers will have plug-ins or helper applications to view the file in its native format. You won't have to convert the documents at all!

Until that comes to pass in full force, as it should by the summer of 1997, you need to get information into the hands of your staff, and that means converting it. Make good use of your time and select robust, supported commercial products that do the job easily, effectively, and efficiently.

17

Workflow Software, Groupware, and the Intranet

Businesses today are being asked to do more, to do it faster, and to do it better in order to survive (let alone compete) in the global marketplace. A shift has taken place in the way businesses operate; "empowered" individuals and teams have replaced bureaucratic hierarchies.

Business process re-engineering, which is a critical examination of the broad business processes in a company, and the implementation of network computing have opened the door to a re-evaluation of the company's information model (see Chapter 12, "Alternative Corporate Information Models" and Chapter 13, "Structuring Company Information Resources for Intranets"). In order to better support the new information model, new software is needed to deal with the business process itself. It is also necessary for integrating information from multiple data sources and input from a variety of individuals within the company.

A business process is defined as a series of activities that are grouped together to achieve a desired result. For example, the publishing of this book is a business process that contains many activities from research to writing to editing to review to layout to printing. Within a business process, there is a flow to the process of activities that are undertaken to achieve the result. For example, this book could not be printed before it was authored. Often, this flow incorporates the receipt of approvals at various stages throughout the process. This organization of the activities and approvals into the proper sequence results in what is called the workflow of the process. *Workflow* consists of (but is not limited to) the following:

- The sequence of tasks and who is to perform them

- Supporting information flow

- Tracking and reporting mechanisms

- Measurement and control systems

Figure 17.1 shows a schematic example of the workflow of a hypothetical process.

Figure 17.1

A Hypothetical process schematic.

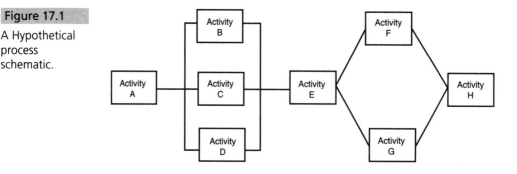

The software category that has evolved to support the operational aspects of the business process is called *workflow software*. The Intranet is proposed as the means to support the information needs of the business processes. Because of this, the Intranet needs to incorporate, or integrate, workflow software into the information infrastructure of the company.

In addition to having defined business processes, organizations today are often required to bring people together on a project basis to perform such tasks as developing a new product or marketing campaign or creating the annual strategic plan. The current thinking of the management gurus, as reflected in the media, is to bring the best and brightest employees that a company has, regardless of their corporate discipline, into a project team to address the issue at hand. Once the project is complete or the individual's skills set is no longer required, the team members return to their home departments.

As these multidisciplinary teams of employees from across the company are assembled to work on projects, new tools are required that enable these people to work together, communicate, and collaborate on the tasks of the project. The software tools that enable groups to work together in this fashion are called *groupware* (short for group software). And in keeping with the theme of the intranet as the means of connecting people with the information that they need, the groupware tools should be browser-based.

As these teams work on projects, many of the tasks that the team members perform are part of a business process as well. An example is, bringing a team together to perform the annual review of the intranet's operations in support of the company's business processes. This annual review is a process and should be supported by a workflow software application. Because a team is performing the review, the team needs groupware tools to enable it to perform its tasks. The end result is clear: there is a need for the integration of groupware tools and workflow software.

Note

Once companies grasp the concept that the intranet's support of their business processes is a mission-critical business process itself, the intranet must be reviewed within the strategic and business planning processes to ensure it performs as required.

In an effort to help you understand how workflow software, groupware, and the intranet relate, this chapter will discuss the following topics:

- The segmentation of the product marketplace

- The "traditional" non-intranet products

- Intranet-compatible products, including an example of a groupware tool and a workflow software product which can be implemented within the intranet

Segmentation of the Product Marketplace for Groupware and Workflow Software

Earlier in the chapter you were introduced to the rationale for groupware, software tools that enable groups to work together, communicate, and collaborate on tasks. The need for workflow software for the support of the operational aspects of the business process was also introduced. It was pointed out earlier in the chapter that there is a need for the integration of groupware tools and workflow software.

This need for the integration of groupware and workflow software within the intranet causes a blurring of lines between the market segments that provide the products. The software products examined later in the chapter will demonstrate their abilities in their separate categories as well as show how the two have been integrated.

The remainder of this section will address the following topics:

- Tools in the workflow software market

- Tools in the groupware market

- Making the decision to incorporate groupware and workflow software into the intranet

Defining the Workflow Software Category

Given the many different types of business processes that have evolved, the workflow software market has segmented itself along the lines shown in figure 17.2. A close examination of the "value" of the business process involved shows how the market is structured to meet processes where significant costs or revenues (high-value processes) or the less expensive (low-value processes) processes that are part of the fabric of the daily office routine are involved. At the same time, figure 17.2 shows the representation of the frequency of the process in question. The focus of software designed for repetitive process is on the aggregate, managing the entire set of work items rather than any single item. At the other end of this spectrum is software designed to coordinate the flow of a single process instance.

Figure 17.2

Value/Frequency breakout of workflow software.

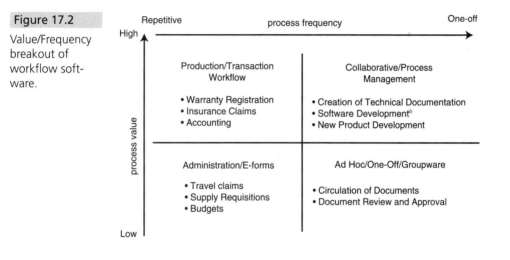

High-value processes tend to be intrinsic to the mission-critical operations of the company. If the efficiency of the process can be improved upon, significant impact on the bottom line usually follows. The lower-value processes, office automation software for example, tend to be those where the impact on the bottom line is negligible.

The following market segments have been identified in figure 17.2:

- The Production Workflow software group

- The Collaborative Workflow software group

The Production Workflow Software Group

The Production Workflow group (the high-value, repetitive quadrant in figure 17.2) is the largest in terms of money and comes with big ticket prices for applications. The most mature part of the group is the document imaging software, which has the embedded workflow to handle the requirements. Many of the companies in this group are starting to expand into the non-imaging Production sub-segments. The next Production sub-segment consists of the client/server companies (for example, SAP, Oracle, ADP, and PeopleSoft) that are incorporating workflow software as a critical part of their component set.

Note

Transaction processing, such as order entry, is a high-value, repetitive element of many companies' business processes. Because these systems are well understood and are developed with relational database software, they fall outside the discussion of workflow software. In many cases, the programs that were written to handle the flow of data through the transaction process were custom-created for the company that required the application.

The Collaborative Workflow Software Group

In terms of expenditures to date, Collaborative Workflow software is the smallest of the market segments described in figure 17.2. This segment is best described as the automation of mission-critical processes that are not transaction-oriented. Both of the market sub-segments here, Collaborative/Process management and Document Management, share workflow-enabling requirements such as document sharing, data, and user comments on work-in-process.

Collaborative/Process Management

Collaborative/Process management focuses on the routing and tracking of work to individuals within the group. This type of management is an extension of the project management software classes. Typical examples include sales force automation and new product development, and they are the target of companies like Action Technologies.

Document Management

Mission-critical document repositories and the needs revolving around *Document Management* business form the second sub-segment of this market grouping. Xsoft, Documentum, Interleaf, Alpharel, and Cimage are some of the companies that find their primary markets within this sub-segment. Included in the base applications of the company you would find the technical document management and product data management systems (product information in a manufacturing environment). These products are generally considered to be *workflow-enabled* because the workflow software is embedded into the management system.

Defining the Groupware Category

In figure 17.2, the products that make up the lower two quadrants of the chart have devolved into one category due to the virtual lack of Ad Hoc workflow-enabled software. What you are left with is an Administrative/Ad Hoc grouping that centers around groupware, electronic forms, and document management for the desktop. The generic name used to represent the market sub-segments discussed here is *groupware* because these products are acquired to automate many different processes, not just one. Most often the products rely on the e-mail system as their transport layer. Thus workflow-enablement becomes the key lever in the vendors' wars for messaging software and message-based applications.

The sub-segments of the groupware market that are briefly discussed include the following:

- Groupware products

- E-forms products

Note

> Document management at the desktop—through software for indexing, retrieving, and managing files on network file servers—is benefiting from the implementation of workflow software. Routing for review, comment, and approval in order to include documents in the collection is becoming a standard feature of products from SoftSolutions, PC DOCS, and Saros.

Groupware Products

Groupware includes the routing and tracking of work that is based on unstructured information; it is the primary vehicle for Lotus Notes and Microsoft Exchange. DEC and ICL are also players in this segment of the workflow market. Because the user has the ability to generate a workflow—a "for your review" memo, meeting schedule, and so forth—at any point in time, the description Ad Hoc is used.

E-forms Products

E-forms started as a print-on-demand replacement for the acquisition of printed forms. With increasing frequency the vendors are incorporating workflow into the routing and processing of the forms instead of the manual re-entry that characterized the early use of e-forms.

Author's Note

The early implementations of e-forms were merely as a replacement for pre-printed forms. The user filled in the blanks of a form displayed on the screen and then, when finished, saved and printed the form. The printed output was a combination of a graphic image (the pre-printed form) with the user input overlaid on the graphic.

The user then e-mailed the electronic version of the completed form to the next person in the process who, in turn, printed out the form and entered the data elements into another application.

Approximately three years ago, this was the e-forms method that was used by my employer at the time. Here are the steps that were in place to complete a travel expense claim:

1. Start WordPerfect software program.

2. Invoke the e-form macro and select Travel Expense Claim.

3. Fill in the blanks in the WordPerfect document that were necessary to input the employee identification information and the travel expenses.

4. Save the file.

5. Invoke the e-form print macro to obtain the seven printed copies required by various branches in the organization.

6. Obtain required signatures on all printed copies.

7. Forward printed copies to Finance Branch.

8. E-mail an electronic version to Finance Branch.

9. Upon receipt of electronic and printed copies, Finance Branch stores the electronic copy in the employee's file along with one copy of printed form.

10. Finance Branch personnel manually enter all fields of information from the printed form into the accounting application available on their desktops.

Things have changed since then. The organization is now in the middle of implementing a solution that is completely automated through the use of groupware (e-form) tools and workflow software.

The key players in the e-forms product marketplace are Jetform, Delrina, Lotus, Banyan, and Reach.

Making the Decision to Incorporate Groupware and Workflow Software Into the Intranet

As the previous sections have outlined, several types of workflow software have been traditionally used within companies to automate the flow of information from one phase of the business process to the next. Other types of groupware tools have been used to assist people in accomplishing the tasks that make up the various business processes.

The first step toward making the decision to implement software from either the groupware or workflow category needs to be an evaluation of the business processes of the organization relative to the demand for information within each business process. Chapter 13, "Structuring Company Information Resources for intranets," discusses the way this activity can be undertaken.

After determining the information needs within the business processes, the method in which the information is delivered and managed *through* the process needs to assessed. If your assessment turns up evidence that the current process could be automated to further enhance the delivery of the information or the management of the information flow, the business process would benefit from the implementation of some form of *workflow* software.

Having looked at the flow of information through the process, turn now to the individual tasks that make up the process. Evaluate the activities by looking at how the work is done. Determine the tools that are used and the information that is used to perform the individual tasks. If some form of automation of the task (or automation of the use of the information) would result in a more efficient or effective completion of the task, some form of groupware should be implemented. If the work is being done by a team or a team member in collaboration with others throughout the organization, it is probable that the staff involved could benefit from some form of *groupware* software.

Once you have looked at the business processes and evaluated your need for workgroup software or groupware, you are ready to proceed to a determination of the product options that are available to you.

Note

When looking to select the appropriate product option, you will have to assess whether the tool will do the job for you. You must determine if you are after *automation* (workflow software products) or *coordination* (groupware products) of a process. If the process involves computer-based tasks, it is probably well-suited to automation. If the users think of the processes in human activity terms, coordination is the answer. In addition, you have to address the value question: is the application for which you want the tool mission-critical (a core operation of the company), or is it part of the regular office routine? Tools for the mission-critical operations tend to be high-priced, and most management groups will want a formal ROI calculation before approval.

The Traditional Groupware Market

In the trade magazines and business press, articles on workflow software and groupware seem to focus on Lotus Notes. As the "grandfather" of groupware applications, Lotus Notes enjoys a market share of about one-third of the combined groupware/workflow software market. In the general purpose groupware category, which is where Lotus Notes fits best, Microsoft and Novell are the other major players. The discussion here will focus on Lotus Notes because of its market position and the fact that most of the business press focuses on "Lotus Notes vs. intranets."

Lotus Notes: The De Facto Standard for the Traditional Groupware Market

One of the key concepts of these traditional groupware products is that they were designed to handle a business process's operational workflow and its workgroup-type applications. The traditional groupware tools use built-in messaging engines to route documents from one stage in the business process to the next.

Lotus Notes works on the metaphor of views and forms to look at the data. A *view* in Lotus Notes can be described as a way of looking at the data held in the Lotus Notes database, a way in which the data is organized for access. In a hypothetical example, the editor's view of the database is different from the contributor's view: the editor's view contains more information than the contributor pertaining to their respective job functions.

A *form* in Lotus Notes is used to look at, modify, or add data to the Lotus Notes database. Within a given view, several forms may be used to perform different activities with the same data records. For example, within the previously mentioned hypothetical example, several forms may exist in the editor's view to look at the same set of data. These forms could include forms that permit the following functions to take place:

- Editing the English version of the document

- Editing the French version of the document

- Editing both documents simultaneously

The use of forms to input and review information within databases is not a new concept within this book. Please refer to Chapters 9 through 11 for discussion on how forms are created and used within the intranet. One of the features of Lotus Notes is that it de-couples the data from the form so that the information may flow from one stage to another and use a different form at each stage.

Note

When the software shows information on the screen where the user can cause some form of activity, a form is being used. It may be called a data entry screen, a launchpad, an interactive document, or a user interface; but it is still a form.

A form in Lotus Notes performs the same function as a form in an HTML document—it displays information on the screen.

Built around client/server architecture, users communicate over a LAN/WAN with document databases or object stores that are housed on single or multiple Lotus Notes servers. The documents within Notes can consist of text, images, sounds, or motion pictures. Databases are also accessible from Notes.

One of the key concepts of Notes is the *synchronized replication* ability that ensures that the data stored across multiple Notes servers is consistent so that everyone is working with the same information. For example, a headquarter's individual places the empty template for the quarterly sales projections, along with instructions, on the Notes server at HQ. The Notes server connects with each of the regional offices to place a copy of the template and instructions on the local Notes server.

How Lotus Notes Works with the World Wide Web

Notes has all the features that are needed to be successful in the traditional groupware/workflow software market. Lotus also saw the development of the Web as both a threat and an opportunity for its Notes product. Built upon proprietary technologies, Notes provided users a graphical interface and hypertext-like links to other documents in the Notes collection (via doclinks) back in the days when these services were not widely available. The difference from the Web paradigm was the open standards of the Web for computing and communication.

Lotus added the InterNotes Web Publisher to its product line to enable HTML-based publishing by companies using Notes to collect and prepare documents in groupware fashion. This product, along with TILE by the Walter Shelby Group, was designed to take Notes data and convert the documents to HTML pages for inclusion in the Web site. This process, though, represented a stop-gap measure in the Notes strategy.

Even though Lotus addressed the initial client demand to be able to move documents to the Web or intranet by publishing the documents in an HTML format, the ability to search through the documents, using the integrated Verity engine, was lost on the Web site. The documents needed to be incorporated into the search engine in place on the Web or intranet. Also, what strategy did the company have in place for re-publishing modified documents, new additions, and deletions from the current set? This was another example of the "timeless" problem of maintaining two sets of information and keeping them in synch—and this was even more critical if the company was using Lotus Notes and an intranet, giving staff the opportunity to use both!

Lotus moved to solve that problem in release 4.0 of Notes by incorporating the InterNotes Web Publisher into the Notes Server product. Lotus also promised to release a version of the Notes Server that would be not only a Notes server, but also an HTTP server. The significance of this dual functionality would be that any Web browser with user access to the Notes database would be able to select and view a document stored there. The conversion from Notes format to HTML would be done on-the-fly by the integrated Web Publisher. In addition, the user would be able to search the Notes database using the search engine built into Notes to find the documents matching the query and subsequent selection of the document could be made.

Announced for release in the second or third quarter of 1996, this version of Notes, code-named "Domino," is in beta at the time of this writing, and the author has seen the results of one organization's work with the beta product. It looks promising. See Chapter 18, "Case Study: Intranet and Lotus Notes Can Coexist," for a detailed case-study of an implementation of an intranet that incorporates Lotus Notes.

Author's Note

It has come to my knowledge that Lotus has approached Netscape and the other major players in the world of Internet technologies with a proposal to provide its replication ability to the Internet world, in return for acceptance of Notes being the Internet standard for replication.

In summary, Lotus Notes is the de facto standard for the traditional groupware market. Although other companies have been mentioned at the beginning of the chapter and in the beginning of this section, this book is about the intranet—it will discuss in more detail the products available at that level.

Workflow Software and Groupware for the Intranet

In the intranet world, the browser is the most desired means of communicating with the server containing the database the user wishes to address (see Chapter 7, "Understanding the Advantages of Browser/Server Communications"). In the discussion about the segmentation of the market early in the chapter, the companies that were identified as providing the software solutions are not all working toward making their products available in the intranet world.

The companies, and their products, are geared for the more traditional client/server implementations. The tools that are used to implement these solutions were not necessarily designed for the intranet and may not necessarily work within the intranet environment. Most of these vendors are re-thinking their business strategies to incorporate tools and solutions designed for the intranet.

In the beginning, intranet-based workflow software applications needed to be developed using CGI programs. Because the intranet supports messaging using e-mail, forms for data input, and CGI programs to develop a custom application, you have the tools necessary to create a "groupware discussion forum." As a matter of fact, in Chapter 20, "Simple Intra-Company Newsgroups," you will learn how to do just that in order to handle internal newsgroups. If you need to brush up on forms and CGI programs, refer to Chapter 10, "Introduction to CGI," and Chapter 11, "Integrating ODBC and CGI."

The market is now starting to fill up with companies providing solutions in both intranet-based workflow software and groupware applications. A list of some of the vendors will be provided later in this chapter.

Introducing Intranet Groupware: Chat, List Servers, and Forums

The software tools that enable groups to work together in this fashion are called *groupware*. Because of its relative youth, the intranet does not enjoy the same breadth of groupware solutions that are available in the traditional marketplace. However, more and more companies are announcing products that work within the intranet and fall into the groupware category. In the following sections, you will be introduced to the following groupware products:

- Chat servers

- List servers

- Discussion forums

Chat

Chat is a real-time discussion. The quality of a chat group, or session, depends greatly upon the participants. Passive participants are often pushed aside by type-A personalities, and one is pressured to respond on the spot even when some consideration may be required. People's personalities tend to play a role in chat sessions similar to the way personalities play off each other in board room meetings. Unless the chat is organized around a topic and has a moderator or expert participant to keep things productive, the review value of the chat transcripts is minimal. It is hard to get into an in-depth discussion in a chat session because typing skills need to be good and the messages short and sweet. Brevity and accuracy do tend to remove some of the thoughtfulness of the reply.

Chat does have a place within the intranet, however, and it will be discussed in more detail in Chapter 21, "Using Chat for Intra-Company Conferencing," where a chat server is set up for conferencing purposes.

List Servers

A *list server* is an e-mail-based server that uses a special address that accepts e-mailed requests for information and then e-mails the information in return. The essential point is the establishment of a mailing list of e-mail addresses that can be reached by sending mail to one address: the *list address*. If a message is sent (posted) to the list address, all the subscribers to the list receive a message via e-mail.

List servers are good for distributing information from a central source to people who want to be notified. New product announcements, company bulletins, and product progress notes are all uses that have been made of list servers. Majordomo and ListProcessor are two automated list server systems that can manage internal (and external) mailing lists.

Two issues come up when considering list servers that need your attention before you decide to embark upon this path:

- If all employees in the organization use the list server to post information, the end result could be a mass of e-mail that arrives at every workstation to be read by the individual. Not only could this bring the e-mail system to a standstill, it could stall the employee who has to sift through the list of e-mails to find the appropriate messages.

- List server software is not easy to run with a big list (approximately 200 people or more) by one individual if you want to offer features beyond automatic subscription management. The features that could require more assistance include dealing with the subscription requests that arrive in non-acceptable format configuration files, log files, and outdated "bouncing" subscriptions that need to be canceled.

List servers do have a place for those who wish to implement them as a very simple, rudimentary form of groupware. For more detailed information on setting up list servers, see *Managing Internet Information Services* (O'Reilly & Associates) by Liu, Peek, Jones, Buus, and Nye.

What is missing from the Chat service is continuity—it is a real-time event and difficult to follow afterwards. List servers require the user to store the e-mail messages locally in order to maintain any semblance of what has happened and what the thread of the discussion has been.

Forums

Forums provide a very good middle ground and are probably the strongest growing section of the market at this time. The forum metaphor can also be described as a discussion group. The typical fashion of these discussion groups is what is called a *threaded forum*—one person posts a comment to which others reply or from which another thread starts. Figure 17.3 shows a sample of a threaded forum.

Figure 17.3

The threaded
forum.

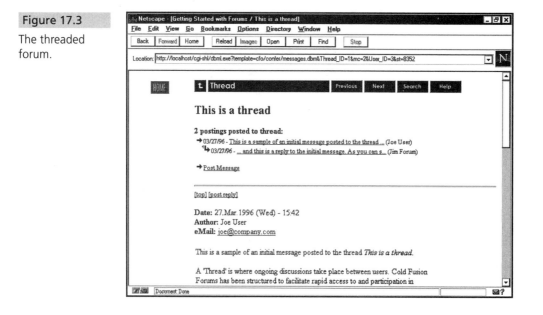

Forums provide a means for public discussion about a topic or series of
topics. Because the individual can compose his or her posting when and
wherever he or she chooses to do so, and then can cut and paste the
content into the body of the message, the user has as much time as he
or she would like to compose the message in the fashion he or she
chooses. The user of the forum can respond to a previously posted message, creating the threaded nature of the forum, or he or she can start a
new thread. Figure 17.3 shows the selection of the thread "This is a
thread," which has two messages—the subject of each posting is a hyperlink to the actual message in the software example shown. Adding a
following new thread creates an opening screen for the forum, as
shown in figure 17.4.

To summarize: at the concept level, chats are like being at a party full of
strangers; forums are like being in a living library; and list servers, well,
they can have the depth of content of a forum, but they lack organization and are impossible to navigate.

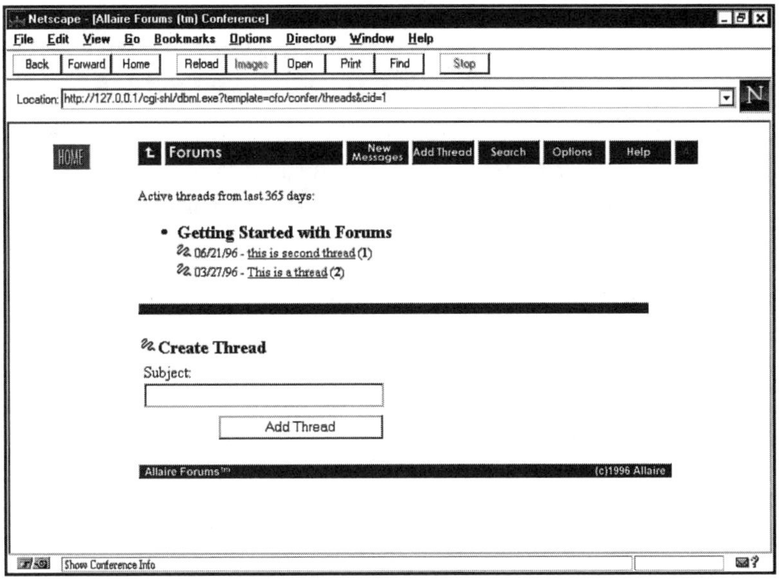

Figure 17.4

Threads to follow in forum.

Groupware Demonstration: Allaire Forums

Allaire Corp., the company that created Cold Fusion, has recently released Allaire Forums. Allaire Forums is a Cold Fusion application that handles threaded discussion forums. Because you should already have some familiarity with Cold Fusion from work in an earlier chapter, Allaire Forums will be used to demonstrate the basic features of this type of groupware. Allaire's Cold Fusion was chosen for demonstration for several reasons other than just having a familiarity with it:

- Its setup and configuration processes are easy to use.

- It allows both private and public discussion groups.

- Several conferences can be established under which any number of forums can be created.

- The forums can be shared across conferences, which reduces the time required to post the same entry in two separate forums located in separate conferences.

- A search facility is built into the program.

Note

The evaluation versions of both Cold Fusion and Allaire Forums can be found on the CD-ROM included with this book.

In order to install and run the Allaire Forums program, you will need to have Cold Fusion installed and running along with your intranet HTTP server. Once you have run the setup.exe program, the application is very easy to configure to work with your organization. The following aspects of the program will be further discussed:

- Creating a conference

- Creating a forum

- Searching the contents of the conference

Creating a New Conference in Allaire Forums

Within the Allaire Forums software, you have the ability to create multiple forums and group them into what Allaire Forums calls a conference. In the actual setup and configuration of Allaire Forums, the person responsible for performing these tasks, usually your systems administrator, must first create the highest level in the hierarchy—the conference.

A *conference* is a broad area of discussion that contains multiple smaller discussion areas. With Allaire Forums you can create multiple conferences on the same system. Each conference has a unique ID and URL. Each conference can also have its own look and feel. Conferences can only be created by administrators.

A *forum* is a discussion area within a conference centered around a particular topic. Within a forum users create and then add postings to the forum. Forums can be shared between conferences, and user access can be set on a forum-by-forum basis. Forums can only be created by administrators.

For example, in your internal conference you may include a forum about a particular product. Within that forum, the people who work on that product can create and post messages to discuss issues that surround the product.

The Allaire Forums software forces you to create a conference first. Under this conference you can create as many forums as you like within the Allaire Forums software. This enables you to choose which of the forums to access from within the Allaire Forums environment without having to create a separate HTML file from which the individual forums would be accessed. Figure 17.5 shows the Allaire Forums Administrator. The Conference Manager and the Forum Manager will be the tools used in this example.

From the Conference Manager Panel that appears in figure 17.6, choose Create New.

Six steps, represented by six different screens within the conference manager, are required to establish a new conference and create the forum that it will be located within. The six steps are as follows:

1. Define location and name information.

2. Configure the look and feel of the user interface.

3. Establish access levels for the conference and its forums.

4. Outline the parameters of the messaging threads.

5. Determine input parameters and procedural work.

6. Outline the search parameters for the database of messages and postings.

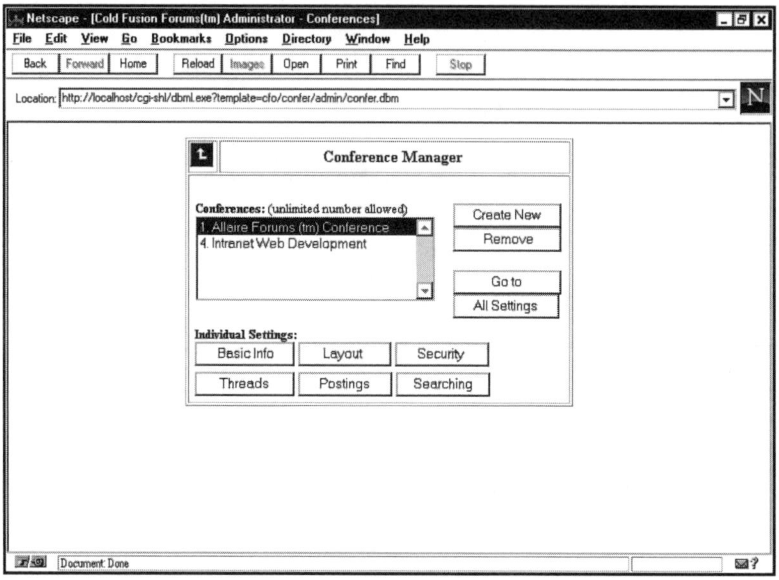

Figure 17.6

The Allaire Forums conference manager.

The following sections will spell out each process for you step by step.

Step 1: Define the Name and Location Information

The first step is to define the following information:

1. Because this may be the only conference that you establish, put in the organization's name.

2. Home/return URL is the location to send users to when they exit this part of the application. Put in the appropriate HTTP address for the intranet page that will be calling this application.

3. Because you want to create new forums, and because there are none currently applicable within the Available Forums selection box, enter the name of the forum to be created into the Add New Forum dialog box. Create a forum to help you with the

Evaluation of this Forum by using those words as the forum name. Click on Add New Forum.

4. Add another new forum called Issues using steps 1 through 3. Both of the forums will now appear in the Selected Forums dialog box. Click on Next.

Figure 17.7 shows this first step completed for a sample company.

Figure 17.7

Creating a new conference— step 1.

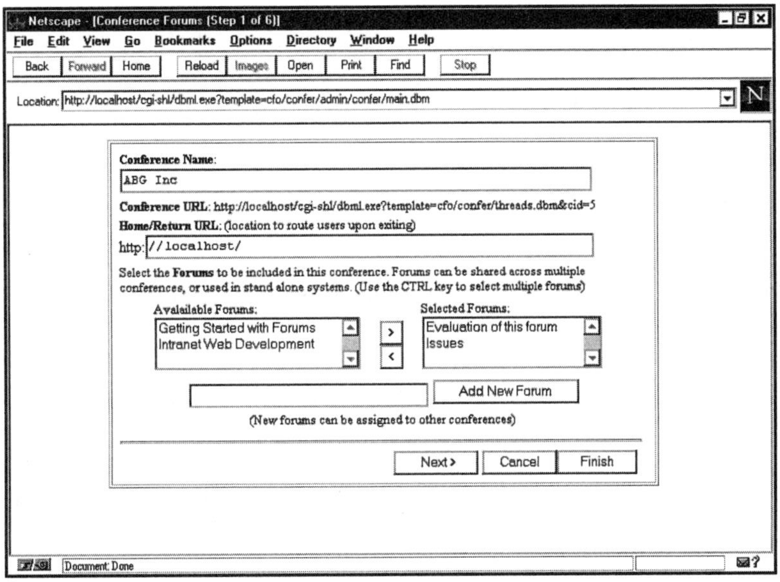

Step 2: Configure the Look and Feel of What the User Sees

The second step involved in creating a new conference enables you to configure the look and feel of the user interface to a certain degree. You can specify the following features:

1. **Banner image**—Appears at the top of the page—use the default for the time being.

2. **Background pattern/image**—Specifies the background image, similar to any HTML page—accept the default for the time being.

3. **Background/font/link colors**—Specifies colors as desired— keep in mind that five percent of the population is red/green color-blind.

4. **Additional Header, Announcement, Bottom Text, and Additional Footer**—Can all be used to provide more information to the users on the page. You can add text to any one of these should you so desire at this time; just push the appropriate button and follow the on-screen prompts.

Click on Next to move to the third step once the features have been determined.

Step 3: Establish Access Levels

Step three deals with the access levels that you may wish to establish for the conference and its forums. Figure 17.8 shows the various options that are available. You need to select the appropriate options for your own organizations.

1. **Access Levels**—Select the appropriate access level from the list presented. Following are the available options:

   - **Automatically Create User Records**—Accepts public access and creates records for each user.

   - **Registration Required, No Session Login**—Forces new users to register, but does not force them to login every session/visit.

   - **Registration Required, Forced Session Login**—Forces new users to register and to login every session/visit.

2. **Session Timeout**—Enter the time in minutes before a non-active session times out.

3. **Password Mail Back**—Choose whether to automatically send new users an e-mail containing their unique password (enables basic user verification).

4. **Guest Login Allowed**—In registration required systems, choose whether to allow users to access the conference as guests.

To start with, it is probably a good idea to set the system to Automatically Create User Records; this allows everyone to have access to the system without having to register. A user's session starts when a user accesses a conference or forum. If there is no activity for more than the number of minutes specified in the session timeout, Forums automatically ends the user's session. It is advised that you make the session time-out be more than 10 minutes because it is normal for a user to either read or write a message over that period of time. Leave the Session timeout at 30 minutes. Click on Next when you are finished.

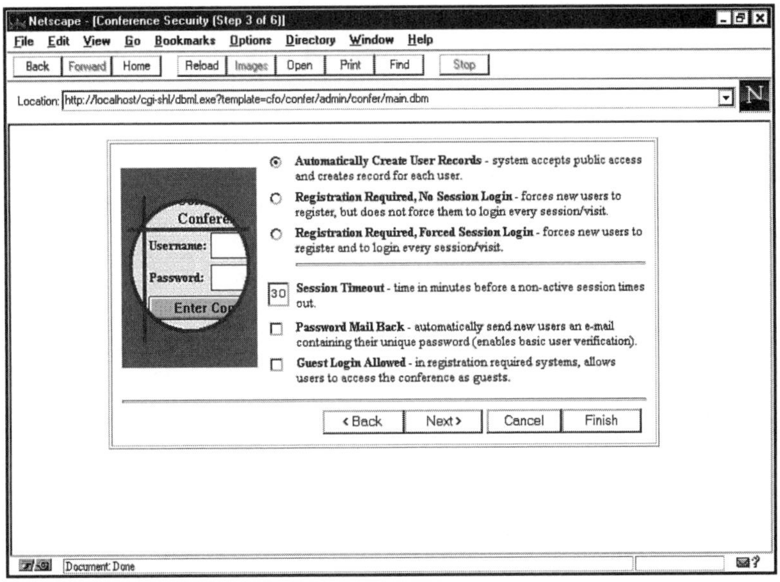

Figure 17.8

Creating a new conference, conference security—step 3.

Step 4: Outline the Parameters of the Messaging Threads

Step four is to outline the parameters of the messaging threads that will be displayed on the screen:

1. **Nested reply levels**—Create the visual and numbered nesting of replies to the original posting. Leave the nesting level at 3 (default and maximum) to provide detail in busy or complex discussions. This will show on the user's screen up to three levels of nesting of responses to a posted message. If a reply is posted to a "3rd level" message, a fourth level is not created. The reply stays at the third level of nesting.

2. **Default age of messages**—Specifies the number of days worth of messages to display to new users. Enter an appropriate time frame—staff tend to take holidays in two week blocks so set the number of days of messages to be shown to something greater than 14 days. However, this depends upon the volume of messages. In a large organization, hundreds of messages could be posted daily, so you may have to fine tune the age of messages over time.

3. **Thread order**—Determines how the threads appear on the main page, last updated on the top or last updated on the bottom. The choice is based on how your users want to see new topic threads—the most recent on the top of the list or the bottom. Choose one of the two options listed below, based on your users' preference.

4. **Message Order**—Specifies the default ordering of postings in each thread. Choose either New Messages at the Top or New Messages at the Bottom.

Once the parameters are selected, click on Next to move to Step five.

Step 5: Determine the Input Parameters and Procedural Work

Step five determines more of the input parameters as well as some of the procedural work. The administrator has the following options to deal with here:

1. **E-mail field**—Displays and requires the users to input their e-mail address. Select this option if you want all messages to contain the e-mail address of the individual who posted the message. Once selected, messages cannot be posted to the forum if no e-mail address is input.

2. **Code display box**—Creates an additional entry box on the form for the user to include HTML or DBML code that will be displayed separately within the e-mail messages. Select this option if you want users to be able to include HTML code within their submissions.

3. **Private e-mail copy**—Enables the user to send a reply both to the forum and the originating author. Select this option if you want to enable this feature that the user can select at his or her option.

4. **Preview message**—Sets the ability of the user to review his or her message before final commitment to the forum. The choices are No, Yes, and User Option (it is recommended that the option be set to Yes to give users a second chance to view the message before posting).

5. **Use fixed-font width**—Provides user with the ability to preserve all spacing and CR/LF if enabled. The choices are No, Yes, or User Option.

Once the parameters are established appropriately for the organization's needs, click on Next to proceed to step six.

Step 6: Outline the Search Parameters

Step six outlines the search parameters that are to be established for the database of messages and postings:

1. **Allow Users to Search for Postings By**—Configures the application to provide the different indexes for searching. Select any or all of the following possible options:

   - Forums

   - Author

   - Keyword

   - Message Age

2. **Search Results**—Permits grouping of retrieved postings by forum. Select this option if you have multiple forums and want the responses to the user's query to be organized by forum.

3. **Messages Sort Order**—Specifies the default ordering of postings in each thread. Choose either New Messages at the Top or New Messages at the Bottom.

4. **Maximum Number of Results**—Specifies the maximum number of hits that will be returned in a query. Select one of the available options based on user demands.

Figure 17.9 depicts the options available for step 6. Once you have selected all the applicable options, click on Finish.

Figure 17.9

Creating a new conference—search parameters.

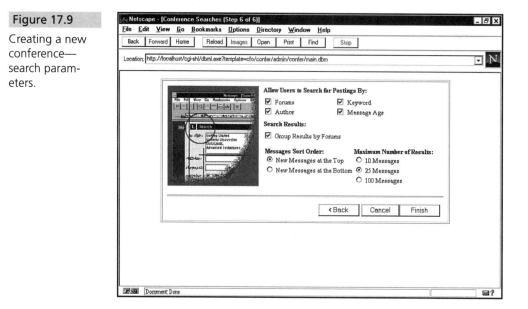

Completing the Conference

Once the Finish button is pushed, you are returned to the Conference Manager. Congratulations, you have just created your first Allaire Forums conference! The following steps can be followed to finish up all the details.

1. Review the look and feel of the conference just created by clicking on the Go To button

2. Create the hyperlink from the intranet to the conference—incorporate the address of the template file into a hyperlink from the intranet in order to enable users to have access to the conference. The conference just created would be called by a code line similar to the following:

```
http://localhost/cgi-shl/dbml.exe?template=cfo/confer/
➥threads.dbm&CID=5
```

3. You need to be certain to change the hostname to that of the server of your intranet. The CID=# parameter at the end is the conference ID number assigned by the Allaire Forums package.

Note

Please be sure to change the URL in step 2 previously to the address of the server where the Allaire Forums template is located. Failure to do so will result in the program not working and an error message will be displayed.

Figure 17.10 shows the opening screen of newly created conference. In the lower half of the screen, in the Create Thread section, you have the option of choosing into which of the forums to put the new thread. Once you establish a new thread and post a few messages, or once the users post a few messages, you see the threading take place.

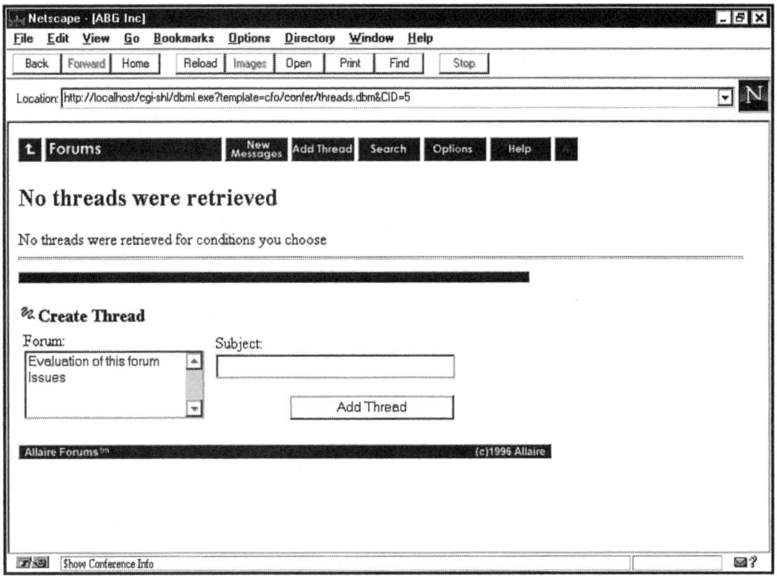

Figure 17.10

Creating a new conference—the results.

Creating a Forum in Allaire Forums

Now that you have created a conference, the next order of business is to use Allaire Forums to create a forum. From the Allaire Forms Administrator, select the Forum Manager option. Once the Forum Manager is started, there are four steps in the process of creating a forum:

1. Enter the basic forum information

2. Identify forum moderators

3. Set full user-level access

4. Set read-only access

Step 1: Entering the Basic Forum Information

The first step is to identify the forum for use within the conference. Click Forum Manager to start the process. The following information must then be entered:

1. **Forum Name**—Identifies the forum in all conferences. Enter the name by which you wish this forum to be known.

2. **Forum Description**—Describes the purpose of the forum. Type in a short description of the forum's purpose.

3. **Conferences**—Identifies the conferences in which the forum will be accessible. Messages posted in forums that are shared will be seen by all users in all selected conferences. Select the conferences from the list of available conferences.

Click Next to move to step 2, identifying forum moderators.

Step 2: Identifying Forum Moderators

In this step you select the groups of users who will have moderator level access to the forum. Moderators have the right to edit thread names and edit and delete messages posted in this forum. Apply the user and group management tools to create moderator groups and assign users to them.

To establish the moderators, perform the following steps:

1   Type in the user name of the moderator in the Add New field and click on the Add New button. The user name is added to the Moderator Groups list.

2. Click on Next to go to step 3.

Note

To create group names, the Allaire Forums Administrator is used to define group membership. See the user documentation that comes with the program for instructions.

Step 3: Setting Full User-Level Access

In this step you select the groups of users who will have full user-level access to the forum. These users will be able to read, post, and reply to messages and create new threads within the forum. The following steps are required to be performed:

1. Select Everyone from the Available Groups list to assign full user-level access to all staff—if the forum is a private forum, select the appropriate group from the list.

2. Click on Next to go to step 4.

Note

To create group names, the Allaire Forums Administrator is used to define group membership. See the user documentation that comes with the program for instructions.

Step 4: Setting Read-Only Access

In this step you select the groups of users who will have read-only access to the forum. These users will only be able to read messages posted to the forum. They will not be able to post and reply to messages or create threads.

To establish this access level, the following steps are required:

1. Select the group(s) of users from the Available Groups list. To create a forum that is exclusively read-only, select the Everyone group from the Available Groups list.

2. Click on Finish—this takes you back to the Forum Manger.

Congratulations! You have just created your first forum. You can now create additional forums as required for your users within the conference you created or under a new conference. Users can now create and post messages in the forum that has been created.

Search Capabilities of the Conference in Allaire Forum

One of the key features that makes a forum like a living library is the ability to store the thoughts and words of people in the organization and search through and retrieve those messages that you need to review at a later date. Instead of you having to review each of the messages on the forum to find the content you are looking for, the Allaire Forums application has a built-in search mechanism—because the data is stored in an ODBC database using the Cold Fusion engine. Figure 17.11 is added to show you the breadth of search capabilities in the application.

Forums can be established for any topic, and membership can be obtained for any or all of the forums available. One of the benefits of forums over list servers is that the individual has to go there to get involved. He or she has to want to participate. Using a forum within a project as the means to post ideas and responses is a viable application of this type of groupware application.

Introducing Intranet Workflow Software

The software category that has evolved to support the operational aspects of the business process is called *workflow software*. The intranet is proposed as the means to support the information needs of the business processes. Because of this, the intranet needs to incorporate, or

integrate, workflow software into the fabric of the information infrastructure of the company.

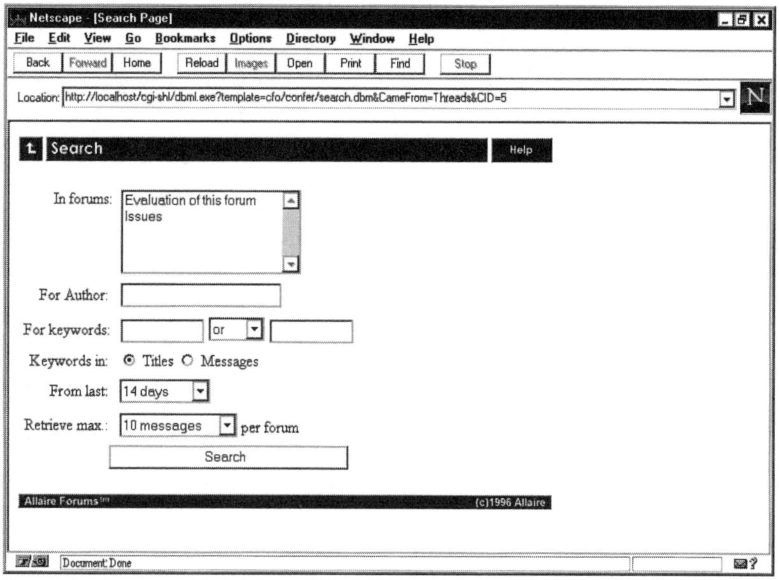

Figure 17.11

The Allaire Fo-
rums search page.

However, given the relative youth of the intranet, the marketplace is
not yet replete with products in the workflow software category. However, WebFlow Corp. has released its SamePage product suite, one of
the first workflow software products available for the intranet. The
following section will take you through a demonstration of how the
WebFlow SamePage software can work in support of your business
processes.

Workflow Software Demonstration: WebFlow SamePage

WebFlow Corp. has released its SamePage product suite of information
and action management tools. Built with intranets in mind, the Same-
Page products enable collaboration on documents and incorporated
workflow through the action item management system.

Note

The software demonstrated in this section is not available on the CD-ROM in the book. Please refer to the WebFlow Corp. Internet site (http://www.webflow.com) for information on how to obtain the software.

An Introduction to WebFlow SamePage

WebFlow SamePage collaboration starts when a document—containing an idea, press release, budget outline, and so forth—is posted to the joint workspace. As you will see later, you can delegate the review task to others on a mandatory, optional, or read-only basis, and the application will notify the others, as appropriate, via e-mail. The reviewers can add comments, insert text into the document, or change views to the information.

In the intranet, SamePage is targeted to support business processes in the managing of the flow of information within and between stages of a process. These features will be discussed shortly. Before you go any further, though, one point has to be established: the person who creates and posts a document to the workspace of the business process is the owner of that document.

It is the premise of this example that the *manager of the business process* is the person who enters the document, such as the concept-piece for the development of a new product, into the workspace. Once this premise is accepted, for the purpose of this example, the reader should be able to follow clearly what is happening.

Note

Workflow software is not necessarily the easiest thing in the world to understand, especially outside the context of your organization. In describing a hypothetical situation to you in this book, you are without the understanding of all the steps that would make up this hypothetical business process. In many cases the operational understanding of the flow of work through a business process is also difficult to understand. This book will attempt to simplify the example used for demonstration purposes in order that you can grasp a basic understanding of what is intended to be shown.

The joint work process needs to be managed by an individual who is responsible for summarizing the comment threads and iterating the material through the use of tools within the product. This document "owner," the business process manager, selects the reviewers and inputs the due dates, and the SamePage application automatically sends reminder notices to the reviewers if they have not participated by the appropriate dates. These functions and features will be demonstrated as the example unfolds.

The Action Item Manager portion of the product suite enables teams to input and manage action items from within the documents as well as in a consolidated action item area. The information views are flexible and can be parameters such as assignee, status, priority, and so on.

Note

The installation and configuration material provided with the product is straightforward and easy to follow, so this chapter will not cover it.

How SamePage Works

The following is a brief demonstration of how the SamePage application works once installed and configured to support the operational aspects of the business process. The demonstration is designed to show how the SamePage product can be used to collaborate on material and assign and monitor activities. The software is not available on the CD included with the book, so the following sections attempt to describe the operations to you and show samples of what you would see on the screen. Figure 17.12 shows the main screen for any individual working within the SamePage application. There are three menus:

- Main Menu—Always at the left, this menu is used to navigate through the workfolders, action items, and user administration.

- Middle Menu—This menu changes depending upon where you are in the system, and the work options available apply only to the current page.

- Preferences Menu—This menu allows the customization of workspace to user preferences.

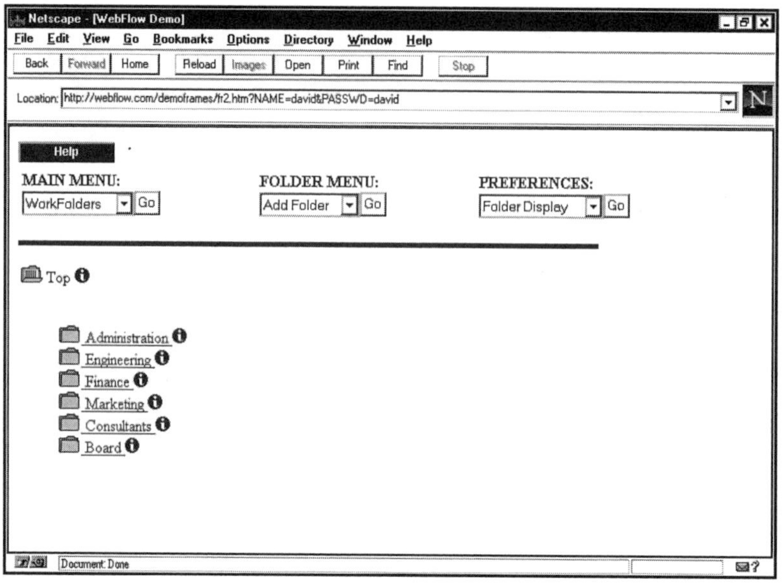

Figure 17.12

WebFlow
SamePage—main
workspace.

Retrieving Documents Within SamePage

The default workspace within SamePage is the WorkFolders option in the Main Menu. The workfolders that are accessible to the user are displayed on the screen. The small "*info*" *dot* is a link to a page that describes the workfolder.

Documents are stored in folders and are retrieved by selecting the folder, and potentially a sub-folder, until you arrive at a document that is already available for review, as shown in figure 17.13. Selecting the link of the appropriate document opens it and puts you into the active WorkSpace.

Features of a Sample Document

Within the document you see on the browser, there are paragraph markers scattered throughout. Each of these points can be clicked to open up a comment window to insert your thoughts/comments. Figure 17.14 shows a sample document with the paragraph markers as well as a comment that has been placed by one of the reviewers. Note the reviewer's name, a one-line summary, the date the comment was made, and the full remark.

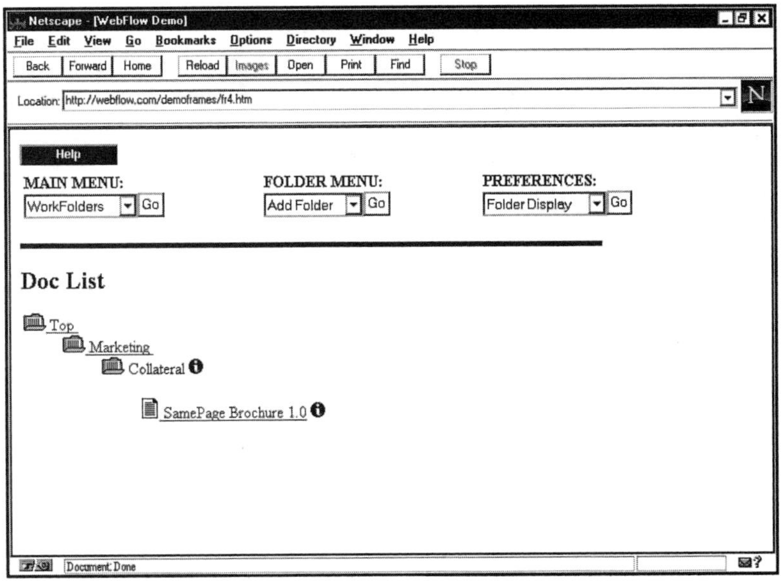

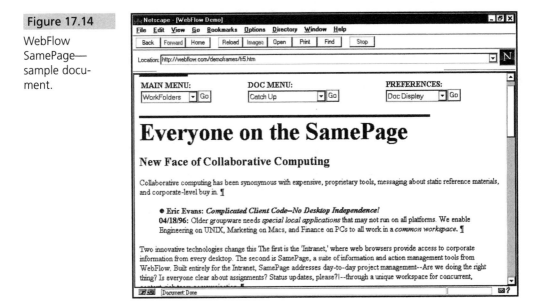

Figure 17.13

WebFlow SamePage—available documents.

Figure 17.14

WebFlow SamePage—sample document.

How to Add a Comment

By clicking on one of the paragraph markers, you can add a comment of your own. The *add comment* screen is displayed, allowing you to do the following:

1. Select positioning of comment. Choose to add a comment onto the material preceding the paragraph marker that was clicked or onto a general comment at the end of the document.

2. Type in a summary line—this is a one-line summary of your comment.

3. Select plain text or HTML as the type of content you will be adding in the comment window.

4. Enter your comment in the window provided.

5. Click on Submit when finished.

Because the default is set to providing a comment on the material preceding the marker, the actual material is displayed on the screen. Figure 17.15 shows an example of a comment page with summary and comment boxes completed.

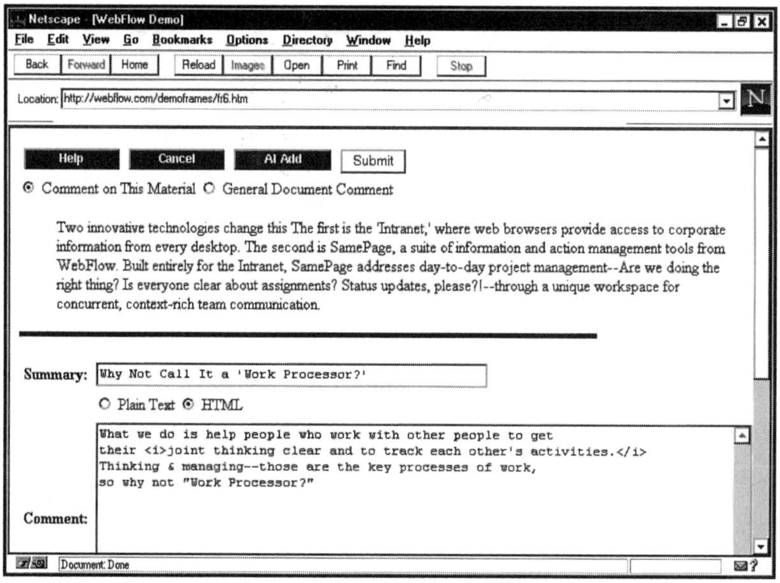

Figure 17.15

WebFlow SamePage—adding a comment.

How to Add an Action Item

In addition to adding comments to the documents, some activities, such as obtaining copyright releases for example, must take place in the business process and must be managed as well. Within SamePage, the facility to provide for including *action items* is called The Action Item Manager. This portion of the product suite allows teams to input and manage action items from within the documents as well as in a consolidated action item area. The information views are flexible and can be parameters such as assignee, status, priority, and so on.

If you look at the buttons at the top of the add comment page, you will see a button labeled "AI Add." Selecting this button enables you to create an *Action Item* for someone to perform. The fields to complete are fairly self-explanatory (see fig. 17.16):

1. **Number**—Leave this field blank—a number will be assigned.

2. **Project**—Type in the name of the project.

3. **Priority**—Assign the appropriate designation from the options Critical, Major, Medium, and Minor.

4. **Owner** — Select the name of the document's owner. The user name will appear by default.

5. **Assignee**—Select the name of the individual to whom the action item is being assigned.

6. **Due Date**—Input the date the action item must be completed.

7. **Task**—Enter the name of the task to be completed.

8. **Notify**—Select the groups, functional roles, and users who can review and comment on the action item.

Click on Submit to move on when complete.

Within the Notify area the owner of the Action Item decides who can view the Action Item and make comments by selecting groups of individuals, specific roles that people might play, or even individual users. Everyone on the list receives an e-mail message when the status of the Action Item changes. Clicking on Submit posts the Action Item.

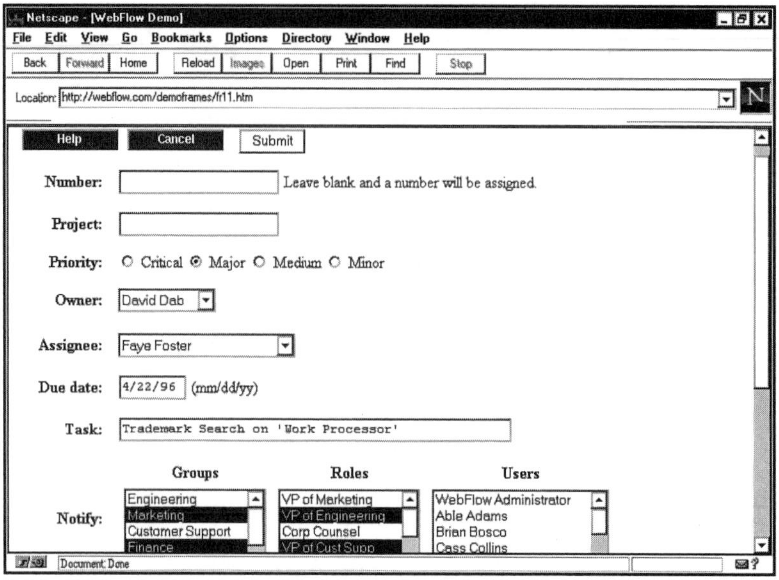

Figure 17.16

WebFlow
SamePage—
adding an action
item.

Action Item Management

The Action Item Management subsystem within SamePage is called "Take Action!" Reports can be customized to track projects, and the lists of activities can be sorted and filtered by any of the variables that are seen in figure 17.17. Full nesting support is also available.

With these abilities to manipulate the action item reports, a team has the tools to do the following:

- Manage what is going on

- Determine who is tasked to do what

- Review the full detailed comments by clicking on the hyperlinked Action Item number

Action Items can also be added from any page within the Action Item Menu by selecting Add AI from the list within the Middle Menu and clicking on the Go button. This can be seen within figure 17.17.

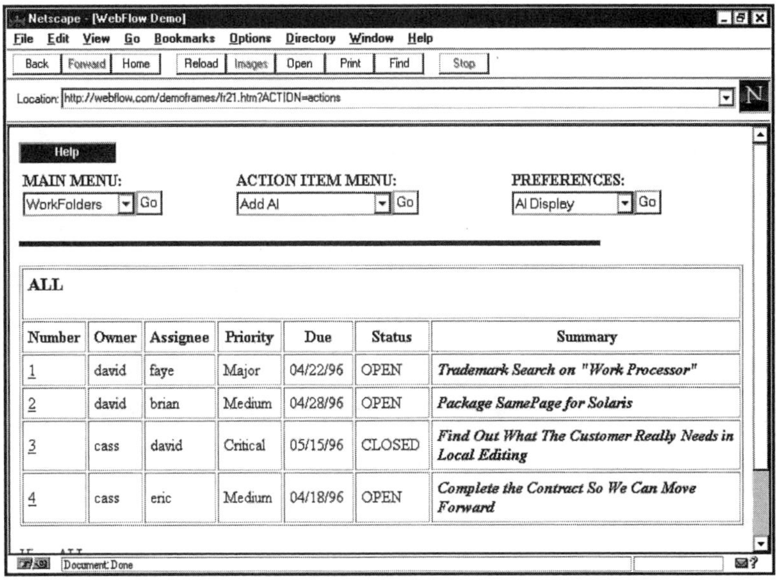

Figure 17.17

WebFlow
SamePage—
action item man-
agement.

How to Add a New Workspace to the Folder

Now that you have seen how to add comments and action items to an existing document, how do you add a new document, or WorkSpace, to the folder? Follow these steps:

1. From the Main Menu, select WorkFolders.

2. Click on Go—this takes you to the main screen that you saw upon entering into the application.

3. Select AddDoc from the Middle Menu.

4. Click on Go—this takes you to the AddDoc work screen.

Creating a New Workspace—Step 1: The Top of the Form

Because of the physical length of the form, the three figures below detail all the fields. Figure 17.18 shows the fields, which are fairly self-explanatory, to complete at the top of the form:

1. **Doc Title**—Enter the title of the document.

2. **Version**—Start with 0.5 because it is the first draft of the document and not really a full version.

3. **Abstract**—Enter the abstract of what the document is about, the topic of "conversation."

4. **Version notes**—The owner or other appointed person who has ownership privileges enters information about the version of the document.

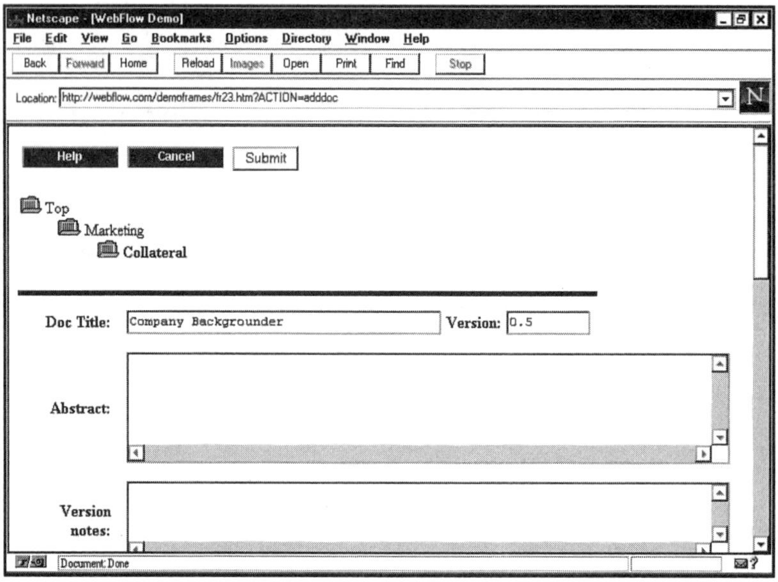

Figure 17.18

Creating a new document with WebFlow SamePage—top of the form.

Creating a New Workspace—Step 2: The Middle Portion of the Form

Figure 17.19 shows the middle portion of the AddDoc form where the source of the information is input.

1. **File**—The initial input into the document can come from a file, HTML or ASCII, whose name is entered into the File input field and requires that the radio button for File be selected. If you wish to enter the text directly yourself, select the Enter Text radio

button to be transported to the text entry page when the Submit button is pushed.

2. **Owner**—The person creating the document comes up as the owner, but the ownership can be assigned to a role, where multiple people under your control have owner privileges.

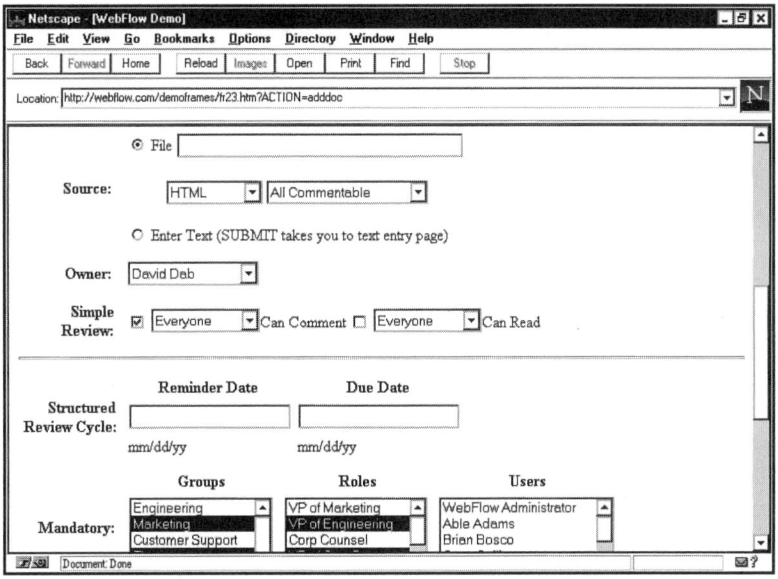

Figure 17.19

Creating a new document with WebFlow SamePage— middle of the form.

Creating a New Workspace—Step 3: The Bottom of the Form

The last section you need to look at in the process of creating a new document is the type of review that you want to have undertaken— Simple or Structured. If you select Simple Review, the material is made available to groups of people for comment and to groups of people for reading. You must decide upon the groups for Can Comment and for Can Read if you choose Simple Review.

If you decide upon a Structured Review, enter a Reminder Date and a Due Date. If the selected reviewers have not reviewed by the Reminder Date, they automatically receive an e-mail notification reminding them of their duties. The document becomes available to everyone on the due date as the review is over. Figure 17.19 shows the fields for the Reminder Date and Due Date. Figure 17.20 shows the selection boxes for the reviewers when you choose a Structured Review. The various categories of reviewers and their associated responsibilities are listed below:

- **Mandatory**—The people selected here must review the document by the mandatory review date. They will be reminded by e-mail of their obligations if they have not completed their review by that time.

- **Permitted**—The reviewers selected here may comment should they choose, but they are not required to do so.

- **Read-only**—"Read-only is as Read-only does" (paraphrase of Forrest Gump).

All participants, regardless of whether the review is Simple or Structured, receive an initial notification of the registration of the document, the key information about the document, and the purpose of this collaborative workspace.

Figure 17.20

Creating a new document with WebFlow SamePage—bottom of the form.

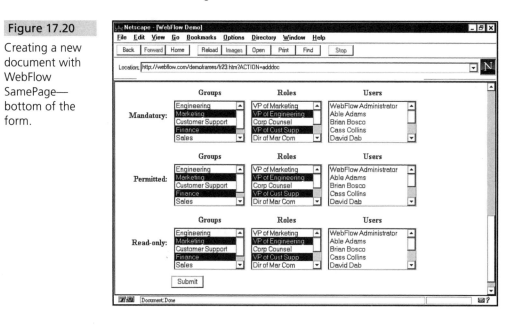

Finishing Up

By pressing the Submit button once all the appropriate information has been entered into the AddDoc form, you add the document to the workfolder space and make it available for others to review as appropriate and required. Figure 17.21 shows the final result of creating the new document.

Figure 17.21

WebFlow SamePage—new document workspace now available.

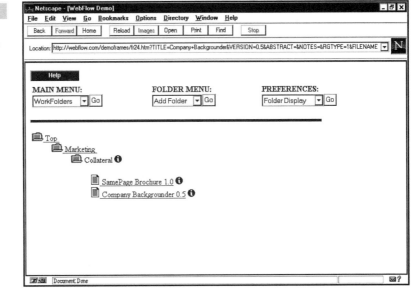

The preceding demonstration gives you a pretty good idea of how the WebFlow SamePage application works. It is somewhat difficult to show all the details, such as the e-mail message notification system, in the framework of a book. The features of the product combine reasonably well to provide you the collaborative aspect of the high-end groupware as well as the actual workflow abilities. It is hoped that the manner in which the product could be used to support business processes is apparent. For more information on the WebFlow SamePage product, including how the product can be applied, visit the Web site at http://www.webflow.com.

Other Products on the Market

At the time of writing, several other products are available on the market, as far as the author is aware. As with any listing of products dealing with the technologies of the intranet, this list will be incomplete by the time it is written, and a second generation will be available by the time the reader sees these words. In any event, here is a listing of some of the products on the market and, where the author has been able to do so, a few words about the product.

Collabra Share

On September 21, 1995, Netscape Communications acquired Collabra Software, signaling the importance and growing use of intranet technologies for collaborative functions. Collabra Share is widely recognized as one the leading conferencing solutions and has won a long list of awards including *PC Magazine's* Editor's Choice award for groupware (1995). This is a very strategic acquisition because Netscape will be able to offer customers an open-systems based, platform-independent, client/server information exchange and messaging solution. For more information, check out the Collabra Web site at http://www.collabra.com.

Action Technologies

On December 4, 1995, Action Technologies (http://www.actiontech.com) released ActionWorkflow Metro, bringing the core functionality of Action's award-winning workflow technology to the intranet and enabling companies to use the intranet to coordinate enterprise business processes through their browser product.

ActionWorkflow Metro allows a browser to become a client for Action's work management services. The product includes 20 customizable applications for customer service, sales and marketing, human resources, finance and accounting, and engineering applications on the intranet—"intranet in a box." Figure 17.22 shows a sample form from the "Technical Support" application within ActionWorkflow Metro. Figure 17.23 is a look at the Metro Application Center of the Action Technologies

Internet site. By exploring the various sample applications that are available here, the user sees that this product could be used both on an external site to kick off internal work processes (Product Order application on figure 17.23) or for intranet activities (Benefits Request).

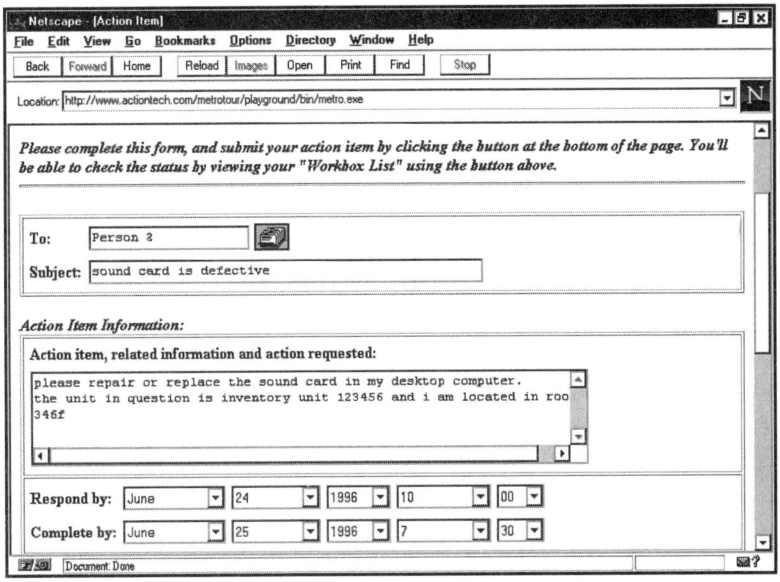

Figure 17.22

Action Technologies Metro— technical support example.

Figure 17.23

Action Technologies Metro— example applications "Playground."

Other Companies with Products

The following is a list of companies whose products are intranet-compatible and exist within the framework of workflow software or groupware, as discussed within this chapter.

Open Text—**LiveLink**

```
http://www.opentext.com/livelink/
```

net.Genesis—**net.Thread**

```
http://www.netgen.com
```

Digital—**Workgroup Web Forum**

```
http://www.digital.com/
```

OS Technologies Corp—**WebNotes**

```
http://www.ostech.com
```

O'Reilly & Associates—**Web Board**

```
http://webboard.ora.com
```

Evaluating a Potential Product Solution

Faced with the decision to implement one form or another of the products described in the preceding pages, a quick method for evaluating the product(s) that you choose to test is needed.

Things to Do Before Starting

The following steps need to be performed to properly look at a solution:

1. Outline your requirements, including potential applications, for the type of product. Include the quadrant-types/market segments from early in the chapter.

2. List the must-haves, would-be-nice-if-it-was-included functions.

3. Read the trade magazines, business press, and on-line discussion groups for user comments.

4. Draft a list of participants who have voiced a need for the application.

Things to Do to Get Started

Once you have prepared your list and checked it twice, you must do the following:

1. Obtain and install the software to be tested.

2. Play with it and run through the tutorial that comes with the application.

3. Create test forums, documents, and action items, depending upon the product and the features it provides.

4. Review the administration utilities to understand how to create groups, implement permissions, moderate the undertakings, and set up user accounts for the participants.

Things to Do to Set up the Pilot

In order to put together a successful pilot, it takes more than slapping the "stuff" together and launching it. In order to set up the pilot properly, you should do the following:

1. Create initial forums, documents, and so on in order to provide instant workspace for participants. Make at least one forum that meets the key business needs of the participants (a discussion forum for Project XYZ, for example).

2. Contact the selected participants outlining the project and why their participation is key.

3. Provide the participants detailed instructions on how to get started, but do not spoon-feed them with buckets of paper outlining the esoteric.

Things to Do to Manage the Pilot

Don't abandon your users while you move onto the next project. A proper pilot project requires that you do the following:

1. Keep the participants involved; designate them to moderate a forum or own a workspace document.

2. Review all areas daily and post comments to all participants about new information if their participation is not noticed.

3. Post new content daily and encourage the others to do so as well.

4. Add new users to bring new blood into the process if it seems to be starting to decrease.

5. Respond quickly to user queries.

6. Create and encourage the users to post feedback to an evaluation forum/workspace.

7. Respond to negative comments privately, not in public view.

8. Wear your thickest skin.

Things to Do When Making a Decision

Now that you have set up and operated the pilot, in order to make a decision, you need to do the following:

1. Gather input from the pilot, including evaluation forum and other critical areas.

2. Prepare a presentation of a real walk-through of the forums/workspaces to show off the knowledge that has been accumulated to date.

3. Present strengths and weaknesses, and evaluate them in light of needs and applicability of the product in question.

4. Make a recommendation, including financial implications, if possible, as well as a value proposition.

Other Things to Consider

The preceding is a quick guide to evaluating a product in the workflow/groupware area where some preliminary research to select the product has taken place. It is offered as a means of starting the evaluation of a product within the specifics of an organization. If several products seem to meet the needs of the company at first read-through, test them first within the technical group of the company before selecting the most promising product for a pilot.

If the plan is to test out several different products, test them at the same time with separate user groups involved in each. However, this simultaneous testing can be very taxing on staff and on computing systems, and it could result in the users of the various groups wanting to continue on with the solution tested. This could leave you with a support mess and some grumpy users if they must switch to a "corporate" program when they were happy with the one they were using. Plan accordingly.

Status Check

There are some significant advantages to implementing some form of workflow or workflow-enabled application within your organizations. And now, within the intranet framework, a variety of types and product offerings meet many of your needs. You have seen how to implement forums for discussion and collaboration and ways to establish required routings and action item delegation and management.

It is up to you to review the needs of your organizations and evaluate the products that will provide you with the appropriate level of functionality.

In the event you are interested in further exploring how Lotus Notes and the intranet can coexist, Chapter 18, "Case Study: Intranet and Lotus Notes Can Coexist," makes for some interesting reading.

Case Study: Intranet and Lotus Notes Can Coexist

D oes one "do Notes" or "do intranet?"

The debate is in the popular press (see "Still Miles to Go," *Web Week*, May 20, 1996; or "Overview: Will Intranets Kill Lotus Notes?" *PC Computing*, May 16, 1996), in the boardrooms, the coffee shops, and even in the newsgroups on the Internet. Passionate debates have been held on the topic over the last year. A good many strained relationships, and battered egos, have come out of the debates.

Can an organization live with both Lotus Notes and an intranet? *Should* an organization live with both? These are two questions the following case study will try to address through a look at a government department's implementation of both.

For the previous five years, the author was involved in the transformation of the department's initiatives relative to information product delivery to its clients. Over the last two years, the author had extensive involvement in the design and development of the initiatives in the following discussion in his roles as Manager, Information Management Architecture, Strategic Technology Directorate and Manager, Electronic and Internet Publishing, Strategic Information Branch. The author left the department at the end of April 1996 to, among other things, write this book.

This case study will review the department's need to change its business strategy and how the information systems support the new direction evolved. This chapter will also review how the convergence of the "separate worlds" of Lotus Notes and intranet was planned and orchestrated. To wrap up the chapter, a brief discussion will be held concerning where the integration of the two worlds (Notes and intranet) is heading within the department.

Organizational Background

Industry Canada is the name of the Canadian federal government's Department of Industry. The current incarnation of the department manifested three years ago with the amalgamation of parts of four distinct governmental organizations: the departments of Industry and Science, Consumer and Corporate Affairs Canada, Investment Canada, and parts of the Department of Communications.

Industry Canada is roughly the equivalent of the U.S. Department of Commerce. The department has three core business functions: marketplace services, policy development, and industrial sector development.

The marketplace services are intended to provide an effective and efficient environment within which small- and medium-sized Canadian companies can flourish. Under this umbrella fall the functions that deal with business registration, bankruptcy, legal metrology, competition policy, foreign investment, intellectual property, and spectrum allocation.

Policy development is done at a micro-economic level. The department plays a role as the flagship department in the development of national industrial policy. The department functions in both the industrial and the science policy arenas.

As the Department of Industry, the major thrust of the industrial sector development is to create jobs and growth in small- and medium-sized businesses. The department works closely with industry associations and the provincial governments to support the needs of industry in the global competitive market.

Previous incarnations of the department supported Canadian industry through the provision of grants and contributions and provided services based upon them. The support infrastructure of the department, both human and technological, was designed around this business strategy.

The Dilemma

The department was faced with implementing the results of the federal government's Program Review immediately after the component organizations had been stuck together. Program Review was the federal government's process of analyzing the programs and services offered to the Canadian people. The goal was to reduce government expenditures and thereby reduce the federal deficit.

For Industry Canada, the impact of Program Review was dramatic. At the time of consolidation, the four component departments had a total human complement of approximately 5,500 in approximately 100 points of presence across Canada and an overall budget of approximately $1.2 billion. Roughly one-half of the budget represented the grants and contributions and the support infrastructure for them.

The target reductions dictated by Program Review meant that Industry Canada would have approximately 4,000 staff, around 80 points of presence, and a budget of somewhere in the neighborhood of $600 million. Those are severe and significant reductions for such an organization.

The dilemma that the executive management of the department faced was how to maintain the same level of utility in the eyes of the department's clients in supporting its three core business functions with the reduced resources.

A small group of individuals, working under the soon-to-become CIO, was tasked to help senior management develop a solution. The results of this solution started the department down the road toward the focus of this case study.

New Business Strategy

Given the need to modify the manner in which the department supported its core business functions, a new set of strategies was needed to enable the department to face the "new reality."

One of the core resources of the department was the store of information it possessed on markets, industry sectors, and impact of policies. This store of information was housed in a wide variety of hardware, software, and humanware. What could the department do to mitigate the effects of the Program Review? A new business strategy was definitely in order.

Rationale for a New Strategy

The results of the research and analysis came to the basic conclusion that the department could take its most valuable resources—its people—and use its knowledge and expertise to create value-added information products in an attempt to maintain current levels of utility with clients of the department.

The wisdom developed over years of interaction with industry would be packaged in a format that was intended to replace the grants and contributions that no longer existed. The basic premise was along the biblical analogy of "teaching a man to fish" instead of just giving the clients fish.

Both the senior and middle management levels had to be convinced of the new "strategic direction," and that information was a strategic product, one that supported the core functions of the department. A presentation of the research and its findings was held, and the following salient points were made:

- The study reviewed a number of organizations who were acknowledged leaders in their industry/field to determine the link between their (perceived) excellence and the combination of business strategy and information technology in support of their strategy.

- The study concluded there were six core themes running through all the organizations that were successful, or perceived to be successful, in achieving their business objectives.

The six core themes that each organization demonstrated are as follows:

- "Know thy business and stick to it."

- It is essential to have an extended view of the enterprise.

- In order to succeed, time and space must be collapsed; it is not "speed kills" but rather "lack of speed kills."

- A *state-of-the-art* integrated business/information technology strategy must be developed.

- The information technology direction must be *state-of-the-market*.

- A tenacious, visionary leader is required to push the strategy through.

The realization was that the department had vast information resources stored in state-of-the-market technology, human resources that understood the needs of its clients, and a clear set of core business functions to support. The information could be harnessed into core products in support of the core business functions.

The next problem facing the department was how to create a "knowledge manufacturing system," combining the information resources and the expertise and experience of its staff, out of an organization that "gave away money and services just for the sake of giving money."

How Was the Technology Component Implemented?

In order to bring together the information and the people to develop the "world class products" of the new strategy, a production methodology was required along with a tool set to enable the work to be done.

Author's Note

> As you will see later in this chapter, the intranet strategy for the department is based on the idea of using the same tool set put into place for the development of externally-oriented products in order to create internally-targeted information. Regardless of the intended audience, the intranet strategy was to leverage the work done in the "world class information products" so that with one publishing application, an internal content provider could have his or her information accessible on the intranet or on the Internet without re-inventing the wheel.
>
> In order to understand how the tool set would be used within the intranet, the development of the application to support "external" publishing will be covered because it is identical to that which would be put in place for the intranet.

Lotus Notes was selected as the tool to link the staff together in order to enable distributed teams of people to work together on their information products. Notes had already been recommended to the senior management as a workgroup tool, but the new business strategy, the "world class information products" strategy, required the implementation of Notes more rapidly than had been initially planned. (See Chapter 17, "Workflow Software, Groupware, and the Intranet," for more information on Lotus Notes.)

One group within the department already had a pilot project underway using Notes to help them develop a portable media-based (disk-based) information collection for an industry sector. This was used as the prototype for the Notes application(s) that would be created in support of other products.

The delivery of the information products was to be accomplished through two principle methods: portable media (CD-ROMs and disks) and online.

The theoretical design of the publishing system required the following components:

- A common set of office automation tools at the user's desktop

- A searchable store of re-usable information components (reports, studies, articles, comments, images, and so forth)

- A workflow application for approvals and publishing

- A single publishing application for all delivery formats

- A distribution facility for online delivery

With all of these elements in place, the information products could be produced, maintained, and updated on a timely and accurate basis—the key to market success.

Strategis: The Distribution Mechanism

The online distribution facility is an Internet site called Strategis (http://strategis.ic.gc.ca) and is built around providing access to text-based information as well as information stored in Oracle databases. The text-based information is retrieved from a Fulcrum SGML-based engine and converted to HTML on-the-fly. Access to the relational data is gained via a series of CGI programs that were optimized for use within the environment.

The specific details of the components and construction of the Strategis site cannot be discussed here. However, one of the biggest obstacles to overcome within the transformation of the information products from the Lotus Notes publishing application to the Internet-delivered products was the requirement to have all the information components stored in an SGML "envelope" on the Fulcrum-powered test server.

The internal content providers, the staff of the department, developed their information content in a variety of methods. Some of the content was created within the user's word in native format. Others had their documents converted to HTML as they were being developed in order to test the look and feel of the documents before they were published.

Much of the content that was collected for the site came, already in HTML format, from other sources such as the World Bank, the U.S.

Department of Commerce, and other international governments. This information came with permissions to publish on the department's site. Some information was obtained, or developed, within an SGML environment.

The application for final publication of the collection of information resources that made up a "world class product" had to deal with these issues. The results were complicated even further when these individual pieces had to be put into the SGML envelope on the Fulcrum server—how does one create a scenario whereby the Fulcrum engine would not have to convert to HTML documents on-the-fly that were already in HTML inside the SGML envelope?

The solution was to place the HTML content document in a field in the Notes application that corresponded to a pre-formatted text field within the SGML envelope. The result is that the SGML structure of the envelope document was converted to HTML on-the-fly while the body of the SGML document, the HTML file, was passed through without any conversion.

To summarize and to provide the impetus for the next section, the Notes publishing application was put in place to enable users to develop their information content. The application, in addition to the actual publishing aspect, permits the users to collect, store, and modify documents within Lotus Notes. The information stored within the Notes application across all the content providers is searchable to allow users in one area to see if there is useful content in another.

The next section discusses where the application is today and provides a few images to help you visualize the process.

Where is the Application Now?

Developed by Aphelion Informatics, Inc. of Ottawa, running under both Lotus Notes 3.x and 4.x, the publishing application has gone through a number of iterations to arrive at what you will see here. One of the key elements is the extension of the Notes application to groups publishing information for internal consumption only.

The application, as it sits today, is designed to allow the content provider to indicate that the information is not to be published on the external Strategis site. If this flag is identified in the document record, instead of being published through the convert-to-SGML application, an HTML-only version of the document is created.

Figure 18.1 shows the main view of the publishing application. The buttons on the left-hand side of the screen show the flavor of the work-flow that has been incorporated into the application. Because of its federal nature, the department must make all its documents available in both official languages of Canada, French and English. The collections of information are visible on the screen. Bear in mind that this is the publishing view of the Notes application. Other views have been created for the individual products, but the base methodology is the same relative to workflow.

Figure 18.1

Lotus Notes publishing application—publisher view.

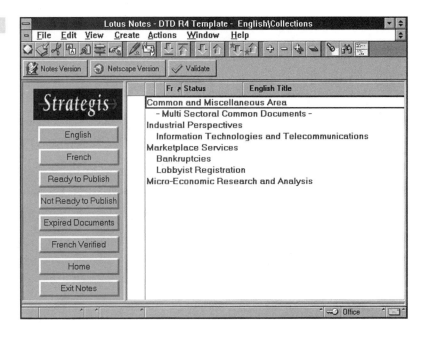

Figure 18.2 shows the section of the form where the content file is included into the Notes application. This is the publisher's view of the form—the content provider's form has only two buttons that appear in this section. The English Filename and Import English HTML Content buttons appear to the user with instructions to input the name of

the English language file. If the file is already in HTML format, the user is instructed to import the document by pushing the button. Figure 18.2 shows a file name that indicates the document was originally in HTML format (the .htm extension) and shows the start of the HTML text at the bottom of the screen.

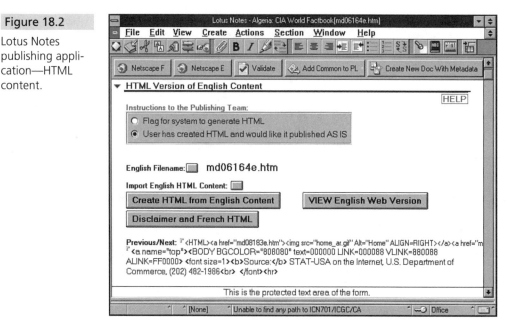

Figure 18.2

Lotus Notes publishing application—HTML content.

As mentioned previously in this section, the ability exists within the application to indicate the target distribution audience, in this case the General Public on Strategis, or, by default, the intranet. Figure 18.3 shows the part of the form where the user has indicated that this document is for the general public. By choosing Do Not Publish On Strategis, the user routes the published version to the intranet.

The next and final figure in this section (figure 18.4) shows a sample of the Not Ready To Publish view of the Notes application. This is part of the workflow procedures that have been incorporated and is shown for this reason. As new documents are added to the individual product collections of the content providers, they appear in this Not Ready to Publish view until such time as all the approvals have been given to the document. Once the document has received final approval for publishing, it appears under the Ready to Publish view.

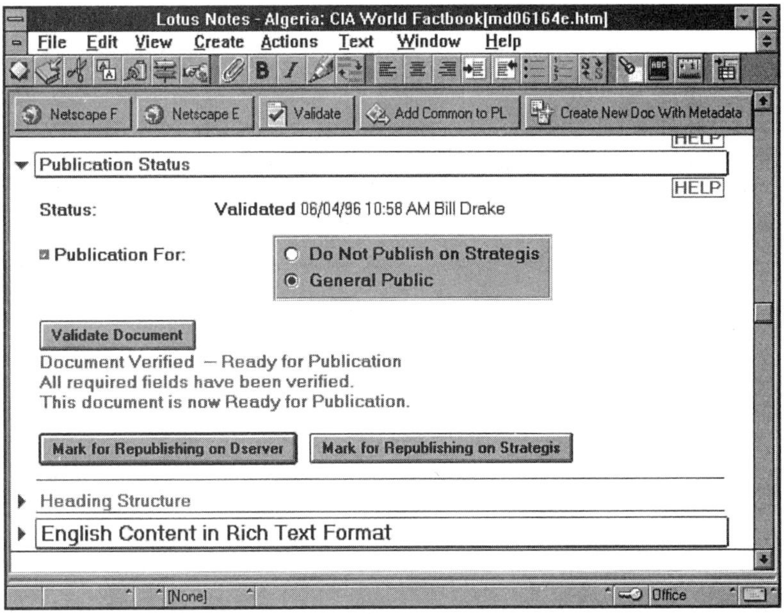

Figure 18.3

Lotus Notes publishing application—Specify Target Distribution.

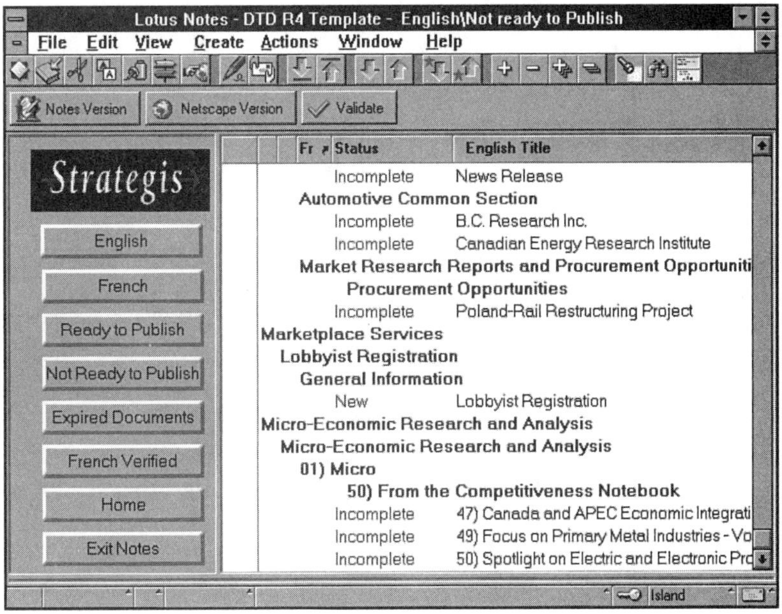

Figure 18.4

Lotus Notes publishing application—Not Ready To Publish.

That provides a brief look at the way in which the Notes publishing application works primarily from the publisher's perspective. This solution to the department's publishing process is not perfect. The data elements must go through a number of hand-offs and procedures before the user finally sees the product when it is retrieved on Strategis.

The important thing to keep in mind for the purposes of this case study is the development of the publishing process that enables the content provider to create documents in native format or in HTML and place them in a Notes application. This application allows them to review, modify, and approve documents for publication.

The last point to be made here is that an estimated 300 to 400 people out of the department's approximately 4,000 employees use the Notes application for the purpose of getting information products onto the external Strategis site.

Intranet Development

At the same time as a core group of individuals focused on the development of the world class information products, others in the department were working to provide for the extension of the same infrastructure and tools to all the employees.

At the time of writing, Lotus Notes was available to every desktop, an office automation suite had been selected and was being rolled out to all those who did not have the components, and Internet access was provided to all staff at the desktop. The department had a Wide Area Network (WAN) connecting all points of presence across the country and was in the process of upgrading to ATM.

Now that the technological infrastructure was in place, the following steps relating to information across that infrastructure needed to be completed:

- Create and publish to an internal audience

- Provide better access to corporate information holdings— CD-ROMs, database applications, legacy data, and so on

- Create an environment conducive to sharing of ideas and experiences

- Reduce noise traffic on e-mail

The decision to implement an intranet was made to address these issues, among others. The remainder of this section will discuss how the department started down the path to solving the problems via the intranet.

The "Corporate Information System" is Dead

The department, like most large knowledge-based institutions, has a large collection of information that needs to be made accessible to all staff. This information comes in a variety of formats: CD-ROMs, optical disks, database applications, text-based documents and reports generated by the department itself, and even Lotus Notes applications. The department has a Notes-based news feed application, Hoover, in place.

In addition to these online resources, the department's library also has CD collections available within its offices as well as online access to information databases such as Dialog.

Before Industry Canada implemented the intranet and Notes, the department made the information holdings available across the WAN from a Saber Menus application. This Corporate Information System (CIS) allowed the user to select the information resource they wished to access, which in turn fired up the application required to view the resource.

The text-based information holdings created by the department were housed within a full-text database retrieval application using the Mega-Text software engine from DataWare.

The departmental management team made the decision in the fall of 1995 that Notes would be used to store the text-based applications in the future. Instead of paying maintenance fees to DataWare for the

MegaText software, in conjunction with the rollout of Notes to the desktop this made inordinate amounts of sense. The conversion of the MegaText-stored data to a format for Notes was started immediately.

All internal information products were to be made available to the users through Lotus Notes. This was the second half of the edict in the fall of 1995.

At that point in time, the "Corporate Information System" as we knew it was dead.

Value Proposition for Intranet

Along with the death of the CIS, outlined above, another phenomenon was sweeping across the department. All of the Regional Offices and many of the individual branches and directorates wanted to create Web sites to distribute their information throughout the department.

The following points were presented as the rational for implementing an intranet within the department as part of a value proposition:

- By creating an intranet and providing space within the intranet framework for groups to maintain their own home pages, the number of individual servers is kept to a bare minimum, and a consistent look and feel can be applied to all sites.

- Employees of the department have commented on the multiple interfaces that they have to use to find information—Notes, Netscape for Web, and the various interfaces of the information products within the CIS. Their demand was to have one interface to get to everything.

- The department had a variety of legacy data systems that each had its own interface—the users were demanding a solution to multiple interfaces.

- Employees wanted an electronic message board wherein they could post quasi-personal messages—for example, "For sale" or "For rent" notices—instead of tacking up notices on the 250 noticeboards spread throughout the headquarters building.

- A significant percentage of the e-mail traffic was considered to be noise.

- The Communications Branch produced a number of internal documents, reports, and newsletters, one of which had an annual printing budget in the $100,000 range—reduction of printing costs alone would provide justification for intranet.

- Lotus Notes announced the integration of Internet technologies into their servers—the announcement was that by fall of 1996, departmental users would be able to use their Netscape browser to access and read, as well as input into, Notes databases directly, and that no conversion of the content to HTML would be necessary.

- Content creators would be able to utilize the Netscape browser to gain access to the Notes publishing application in order to create a new document record, search for information, edit their own documents, and participate in discussion forums without ever really understanding that they were using Lotus Notes.

With all of these points on the table, the first reaction from the Notes supporters was, "Why not wait until Notes is ready? Then you won't have to create an intranet, the users can just use Notes. They don't need to use the browser then." These people had some difficulty in understanding the difference between an "IntraWeb" and an intranet. Please refer to Chapter 1, "Intranet: Building the Corporate-Wide Web," for a discussion of the differences.

In order to satisfy all the demands of all parties within the department, nothing could have been done—it was not possible to satisfy all demands. However, the proposition for the intranet was based on the integration of Notes and the Internet technologies underlying the intranet that was coming in the fall.

It was determined that the implementation of an intranet would address the issues raised here and would prepare all the users of the department for participation in an information product oriented business strategy.

Author's Note

The determination that the intranet would be the answer came about because, along with the director for whom I worked, I hawked the concept up and down the department. In spite of all the focus on external products, our small group recognized the need for and the value that could be provided by the intranet. We repeatedly knocked on doors with our prototype in hand, trying to convince the key internal information providers to participate.

We convinced enough middle managers, in our estimation, to participate so that we could then go to our own management and make the pitch. Grudgingly we were given the OK to proceed, but from within our current resource base.

Design and Development

One of the elements that would require adjustment within the strategy for the development of the intranet was the Notes publishing application. Once the direct access from intranet browser functionality was deployed within Notes, the publishing application would have to be rewritten. It was designed around converting data to another format for publishing (the SGML output required for Strategis or HTML for internal publishing).

The act of publishing the data would no longer be necessary—the Notes files could be read directly by the browser. The developers of the publishing application, Aphelion Informatics, Inc. are currently redesigning the publishing application for this purpose.

The intranet, called Phoenix, was designed on several conceptual levels, to form an integrated solution to the department's internal information distribution needs, including, but not limited to, content collection in Notes, Web-based interface, and planned access to legacy systems. The basic design principles included the following:

- To provide text-based content within the intranet framework, the Phoenix development team worked with content providers to create a customized Notes view that allowed the content provider to get HTML documents into the publishing application. The input form in the Notes view was designed to take the contributor no more than 30 seconds to include the document into the Notes collection.

- To incorporate relational database content into Phoenix, the design was to use the department's SQL database to house the information or to utilize an approved ODBC database as the backend, depending upon volume and planned activity—no new information sources of this nature had been proposed to the Phoenix team before the author's departure, therefore none had been implemented.

- The Phoenix interface would provide access to content items created corporately and would provide the Regional and District Offices, Sectors, and the Branches to have their own home pages, based on templates designed by the Phoenix team—Figure 18.5 shows the current interface to the site.

Figure 18.5

Phoenix interface.

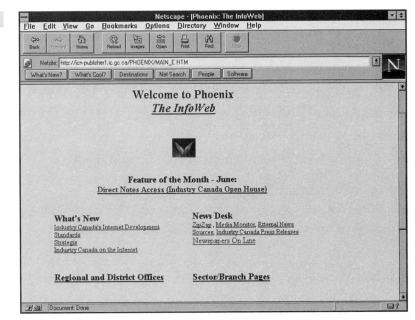

- To provide access to the collection of CD-ROMs and other information applications acquired by the department, a "web launcher" application would be used to invoke the information application across the network, identical to the method previously in place within the Saber Menus solution.

- In order to provide access to information already stored in Notes, and to the data being converted from MegaText to Notes, the Phoenix team would convert the Notes data to HTML in order that it could be retrieved by the browser and in order to create a searchable collection—this was planned as a temporary measure in order to create content for the intranet, the strategy was to use the browser-to-Lotus Notes direct so that no conversion or publishing of the data was required.

- To determine the new content that should be created and made available through Phoenix, a working group was established to review the current holdings and to query the employees of the department as to their needs for internal information resources.

Because of the impending redesign of the publishing application to take advantage of the browser to Notes functionality, no official design drawings or flow charts were created. The Phoenix team was focused on getting the content into the Lotus Notes publishing application and converting the data for access by the Phoenix browser. The remainder of the effort was spent, until the author left at the end of April, in selling the intranet to the middle managers and obtaining their participation as content providers as well as users of the system.

The Phoenix team consisted one person full time (the author) and three others on half-time basis (two for Internet technologies and one working with Notes). The intranet project started in February 1996, and the mentioned developments took place until the end of April 1996.

Author's Note

Why is the intranet called Phoenix?

Unlike some people who have posters and photos on the wall, my wall had a piece of paper that said "The CIS is dead." This was the catch phrase that we were using in discussions with people regarding the development of a new and improved corporate information system.

While building the prototype of the intranet, I was looking for a name that would carry the image of something that was new but also had some founding in the past. The mythical Phoenix rose out of the ashes of its previous incarnation, and, I'm not kidding now, the image and name came to me. It stuck, and through presentations and demonstrations, the users across the department thought it was an apt name.

Where is Phoenix Now?

As an overall set of processes, Phoenix is moving ahead, but at the time of writing, it was moving slowly.

The groups who agreed to provide content are working with the Lotus Notes Development team to create the Notes databases required to store their documents for publishing within and outside the department. More and more groups are using the Notes publishing application to get their information into a publishable format.

With the advent of summer holidays, government slows down. The sense of urgency of projects, time, and spending of year-end resources is not present. It is anticipated that as the fall approaches, the project will pick up steam relative to the further development of content.

Technology of the Future: Notes and Intranet are One and the Same

The technology teams are in process of testing out beta versions of Domino, the version of Notes that will allow users to access Notes databases from a Web browser. If you glance back to figure 18.5, the Feature of the Month for June is a link to Direct Notes Access. By selecting this link, the user accesses the Notes database containing information about the Open House of the department.

The following six images show the reader what is seen in the Netscape browser and source page in the Domino version of Lotus Notes. These show the way in which the browser sees the Notes page that is converted dynamically to HTML by the Domino engine:

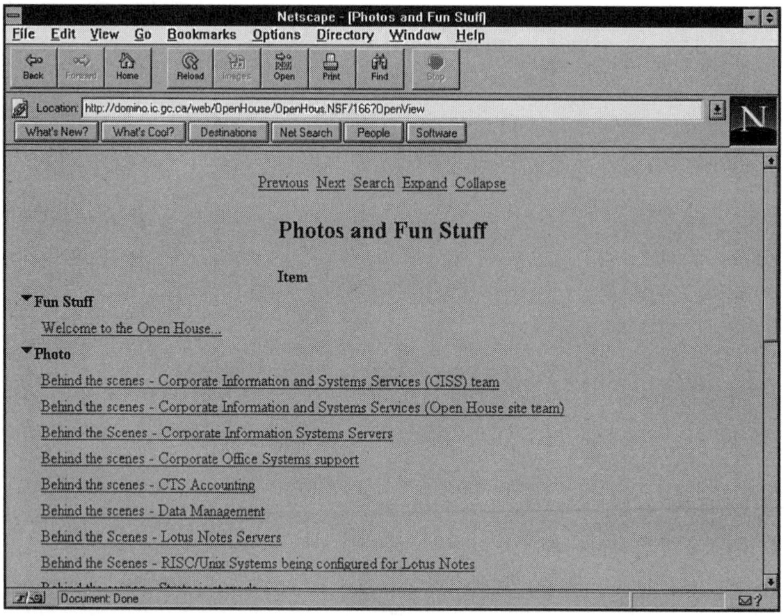

Figure 18.6

Netscape view—menu.

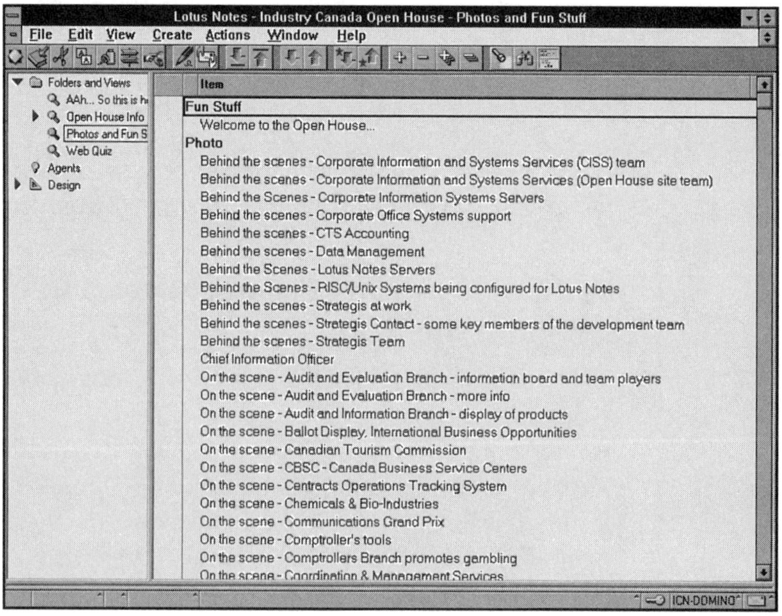

Figure 18.7

Notes view—view list.

Figure 18.8

Netscape view—
document with
digital image.

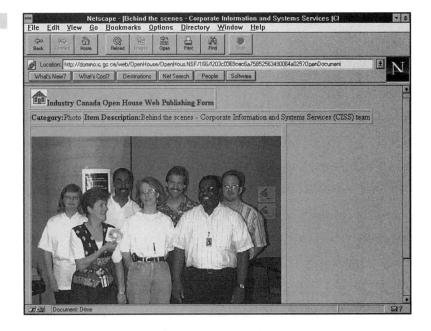

Figure 18.9

Notes view—
document with
digital image.

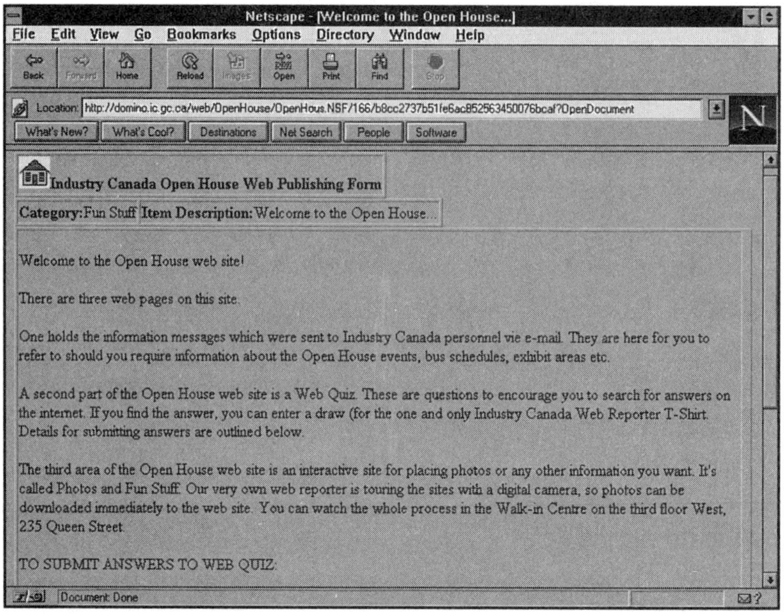

Figure 18.10

Netscape view—
text document.

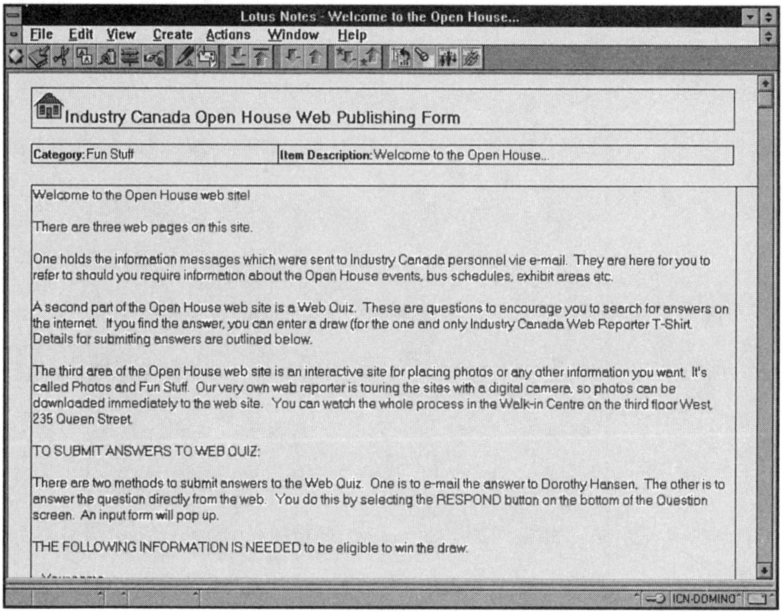

Figure 18.11

Notes view—text
document.

As you can see from the preceding images, the documents as they are created within Notes are displayed almost identically in the browser. The technology team is now working with the developers of the publishing application to ensure that the dynamic conversions of the documents destined for Phoenix retrieval are accessible.

At this time, until the department changes its technology strategy relative to the Strategis server components, the use of the Domino technology for external publishing has not been planned.

In regard to providing access to the legacy systems of the department via the intranet, several groups are working to determine the optimal method and timing for implementation. Decisions will be made in the near future about the viability of some of the information sources, and these may have an impact on the intranet/database connection. In the short term, analyses are under way to determine the priorities for providing access through Phoenix. Even though it has been agreed that the intranet concept is the only way to provide interoperability among the databases, given the nature of the organization, it is unlikely there will be any pilots before the fall of 1996.

In summary, the Phoenix site is up and running. It has HTML content, access to Notes directly for content, and initial pilots for access to data, both in ODBC databases as well as some legacy systems within the department.

Author's Note

At the time these words are written, one of the reasons for a slow-down in the progress on Phoenix is the lack of a full-time project manager. Since my departure from the department, no one has taken the bit between the teeth and run with the project. I firmly believe that by the time you see these words, the Phoenix site will be alive and vibrant and under strong project management. In the meantime, the content providers are making great strides in collecting and preparing information for inclusion on Phoenix and in sourcing new providers to participate in the project.

Convergence of Intranet and Lotus Notes

Within Industry Canada, there is support for both Notes and the intranet. Many see Phoenix as the means of distributing the information in the interface that they wish to use when they hunt elusive facts across the Web. The "Web-junkies" prefer the Netscape browser to the Notes interface, which several have stated is "not intuitive and klunky to use." Notes junkies, on the other hand, prefer the ability to find the resources from that interface.

The major difference will be the ease with which the two solutions provide access to the data stores of the department. Through the gateway products that are on the market today, intranet access to these datasources can be gained with open standards. It is possible to write LotusScripts to access the same datasources, but LotusScript is proprietary and not an industry standard.

This is an issue the department will wrestle with over the coming months as their users demand data that is held in the legacy systems.

The last figures to show in this chapter deal with the Phoenix project and the testing currently being done with the Lotus Domino server.

Gaining access to the data to read from Notes, either dynamically or after conversion to HTML, is only one step for the department in implementing applications on the intranet using Notes as the database. One of the applications currently developed for Phoenix and Lotus Notes combined is the ability to review job openings available within the department that are currently stored in a Notes database. As you have seen in the slides, it is now possible for the staff of the department to see the job openings through Phoenix. What is unique within the department is the ability for a user to apply for that position on-line, from Phoenix.

This Phoenix/Notes application, in beta at the time of writing, allows the user, reading the job posting in the browser, to click a button to apply for the posting. The user is asked for his or her name, coordinates, and ID number, and then prompted to attach a copy of his or her resume to the application. Upon submission, the data is stored in a Notes database that is only accessible to the appropriate Human Resources personnel, who now have a completed application form and résumé.

This application cannot be shown (for legal reasons), but this book still intends to demonstrate the ability to enter data into a Notes database from Phoenix. The technology team within the department implemented a Phoenix-hosted Web Quiz in conjunction with the Open House that was discussed in the images of the previous figures.

Figure 18.12 shows an example response form being filled out in the Netscape browser. Upon submission, the data in the form is input into a Notes database. Figure 18.13 shows the response record from within Lotus Notes.

Figure 18.12

Netscape browser—responding to comment.

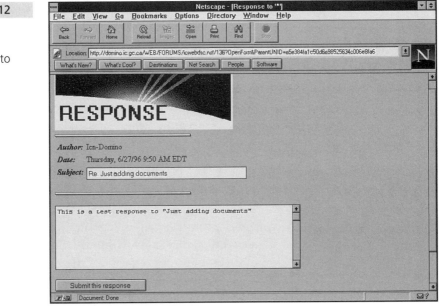

Figure 18.13

Lotus Notes—
viewing response
input from
browser.

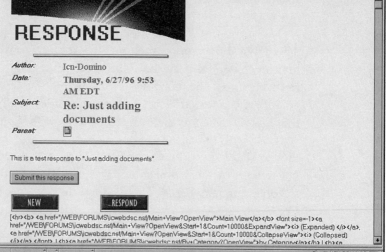

For Industry Canada, the convergence of Notes and intranet may not
have been planned when the decision to roll Notes out to all desktops
was made. The design principles and the business plan for the intranet,
Phoenix, were deliberately based upon the convergence of Notes and
intranet technologies. This feature will greatly enhance the use of Notes
as the collection and preparation tool for internal information products.

What Does the Future Hold?

For the department, the future entails converting the publishing application to a dynamic conversion facility within the Domino server from
Lotus. The core of the publishing application, the collection, preparation, modification, and approval procedures surrounding documents,
will be adapted to work with the new Phoenix/Notes capabilities.

By the end of the department's fiscal year in March 1997, it is anticipated that at least two of the legacy systems will be accessible through
Phoenix, not only for review, but also for update and edit.

The first thing the department needs to do, at the time this is written, is to get a project manager into place that will drive the project as it needs to be driven.

In Summary

The department has made a commitment to both worlds, Lotus Notes and intranet. The implementation of both requires coordination and a focus on the application of the technologies toward supporting the core functions of the department.

The six core themes from the successful companies to use in evaluation of the Phoenix/Notes integration are repeated here:

- "Know thy business and stick to it"—The creation of value-added information products requires that some fact exists to which one can add value. Making the information resources of the department available to the staff through a single interface, regardless of the storage metaphor, can only create richer content.

- It is essential to have an extended view of the enterprise— "World-class information products" for businesses are only one component of the department's overall business strategy. To support the other core functions, access to information is required beyond that of the business community and to other governments, academia, elected officials, and so on. The Phoenix/Notes solution provides access to all potential types of information.

- In order to succeed time and space must be collapsed. It is not "speed kills," but rather "lack of speed kills"—The department must continuously improve and update the information that it provides to its clients. It can only do this if its internal information systems can provide access to the resources required. Phoenix will help to bridge the interoperability gap.

- A *state-of-the-art* integrated business/information technology strategy must be developed—To support the rapid creation of value-added information products that fill gaps in the market, the technology must permit the staff of the department to seek, acquire, modify, and redistribute information easily, effectively, and efficiently. The intranet is a step toward achieving these ends.

- The information technology direction must be *state-of-the-market* —Intranet technologies are based on standards that have been in place for years. It is the application of these technologies to solve the problems facing the core business functions that is key. The Phoenix/Notes combination works to provide the information that is needed in the business process to the right person at the right time.

- A tenacious, visionary leader is required to push the strategy through—The department needs to fill the gap left by the departure of the previous project manager in order to maintain the momentum.

The intranet at Industry Canada will succeed, and one of the main reasons is the integration of Notes and intranet technologies.

19

Human Resources Issues for Intranets

If you have been reading this book in sequence, you are by now familiar with many *technical* aspects of creating an intranet. Although a sound understanding of architecture and development tools is critical, *content* is of at least equal importance in the equation.

Think about a new house. The frame, walls, and wiring are important, but it really isn't a home until you decorate it and add furniture. In this chapter, you'll see that by providing meaningful information in a logical style, all the rooms in your intranet "home" will be places your employees will want to visit.

Note

Some of the material presented in this chapter you may remember encountering earlier. It is repeated here in order to highlight ways in which the utilization of an intranet can benefit a Human Resources Department. At the end of this chapter, you will read about how the Human Resources Department of one company—Silicon Graphics—has benefited from implementing an intranet.

The Evolution of Transactions and Communication in Human Resources

In the crusty old era of corporate behemoths, the pace of business was much more kind and gentle than today. Human resources transactions, burdened with administrative complexity, tended to move slowly. Add to that the high potential for inaccuracy, and many business processes slowed to a crawl.

The Recent Past—The Hands-on Approach

Up until less than a decade ago, when you submitted a dental claim, you could expect to wait weeks for reimbursement because your form found its way slowly from desk to desk, first in your offices, and then in the insurance company's. Enrollment for benefits had to be planned well in advance in order to allow administrative staff sufficient time to key in each employee's information. And employee newsletters disclosed "news" that had already exhausted its value through word of mouth. Because nearly every stage in even the most simple business processes required manual, human involvement, speed was not a major factor or expectation in most of the business world.

In that environment, employee communication could afford to move at more or less the same snail's pace. And today's recognition that better information makes better decisions was a theory limited to the executive suite.

Today's Focus—Good Information, Served Hot

The rapid evolution of information technology has turned this paradigm inside out. Each new iteration of computer hardware and software has opened new channels to speed up transactions within enterprises, while reducing costs.

Organizations have created much of the tremendous stress employees feel today. The slash and burn era of corporate "rightsizing" and re-engineering, along with the relentless pursuit of new ways to reduce costs, has left employees doing much more with much less. Reduced product life cycles have heightened the need for better and faster collaboration. You can alleviate some of this stress by providing better tools for gaining access to and using information through an intranet.

Management teams are finally realizing that holding information close to their chests was creating organizational bottlenecks and slowly burying their competitive advantage.

And yet, although in theory executives have committed to tearing down organizational silos and increasing information flow, they may have created the human resources professional's greatest dilemma: How can you motivate and educate employees and meet their demands for more and better information while time and financial resources are being dramatically pared?

Until recently, there have been few solutions.

Changing Traditional Paradigms of Communication

The traditional model of human resources management and communication depends heavily on print-based media. Employee handbooks are binders with loose-leaf pages. Two- or three-part forms and suggestion boxes are, next to employee meetings, the highest degree of interactivity an employee might expect.

Communication materials rapidly become outdated. A simple change of premium for group life insurance can render a booklet obsolete. Employees receive new inserts for binders that they have long ago misplaced. Employee newsletters, by the time they are written, designed, printed and distributed, provide information that is already weeks old.

To help cope with the increased demands for current information, as well as with escalating costs and declining budgets, human resources executives began to explore the promises of technology.

Early solutions, such as the interactive video kiosks that entered the scene about a decade ago, delivered attractive graphics and a degree of interactivity for the first time. Employees could touch a screen to access information presented as text, animations, audio, and film. However, reaching large numbers of employees meant buying large numbers of expensive units. For most organizations, the costs to place these units in numerous locations, when measured against perceived benefits, were hard to defend.

Interactive voice response (IVR) started as a limited form of interactivity, allowing both the ability to obtain information and complete simple transactions; it has evolved, remaining a useful medium for many activities, such as simple attitude surveys and information updates. If we look beyond human resources, we can see how similar applications have penetrated virtually everywhere we reach by telephone—the automated receptionist being the most obvious example.

The key benefit of IVR is that most employees have access to a touch-tone phone, both in the office and at home. A simple questionnaire of, say, 10 questions, using a nine-point scale, can be conducted with relative ease using IVR. However, you must restrict the range of functions and the amount of information on the system or it will become unwieldy. A complete flexible benefits enrollment could easily become a nightmare if forced on this medium. The key is to take advantage of this medium when it is appropriate, and find another solution when it is not.

Although these new tools opened new doors, one important goal remained: to find a medium that was easy to update and cost-effective, and which would support a vast amount of information and activities across the enterprise.

After years of evolution, the solution has finally emerged—the intranet.

Benefits of Intranet Interactive Communication

Making a shift from a communication strategy focused primarily on traditional media to one which embraces technology is as much cultural as technical. Communicators need to shed the mental model that their employees are "readers" of information, and instead recognize that they are information users.

In the digital world, you need a much more dynamic metaphor—the person must be able to interact with the information, both *gaining* and *adding* value. Employees no longer want information just to read—they want information they can use.

Information That Fits the Individual

Information in print form tends to be static. The focus is on making materials fit with as broad an audience as possible. However, this "one size fits all" mentality also means that employees must sift through material to find what is relevant to them. Employees wanting to check if an expense is covered under the health plan may have to flip through an extensive list of covered items in a hefty binder before finding the one detail they seek.

With an intranet, the organization can build increased interactivity and functionality into the communication process. The same inquiry could be conducted by doing a keyword search of a specific section of an intranet.

Note

> We are barraged with an incredible array of color and movement in nearly all aspects of our lives, from television to educational software. We have seen our comic book heroes come to life in interactive games, where the user controls the action. It should come as little surprise, then, that the traditional static print-focused model is falling flat more and more often. Employees will expect their human resources information to have an "entertainment feel," and they will want to be able to interact with it.

"Pulling" versus "Pushing" Information

Traditional media assume a "push" style, where a more or less common set of materials is presented to all employees, or at least to large groups.

When you push information to employees, you often inundate them with useless information, and real needs are lost in a jungle of paper. Even electronic mail falls largely within the push model. Just as you stuff physical mailboxes with meaningless garbage, so too can you create clutter with e-mail.

By contrast, an intranet places some responsibility on the individual to "pull" information in as much or as little detail as the employee desires.

The organization should re-educate employees to recognize their responsibility to understand their specific information needs. Your role is no longer to spoon-feed information; instead, it is to provide a clear path of access, and then to stay out of the way until needed. The point-and-click method of finding information enables employees to quickly locate what they need and to interact with the content. This is one of the biggest advantages of using an intranet for your organization.

Tip

> Bookmarking features enable the employee to create a profile of those sites that are most meaningful and useful to him or her.

There are many other advantages offered by an intranet. By reducing the number of people involved in the information retrieval process, the

HR department can save both in costs and response time. Adding security features, such as verification of employee numbers and passwords, enables you to provide access to individual information in legacy databases. The employee can update information, add new data, and even perform calculations.

Intranet Benefits

There are many attractive features of an intranet for human resources. This section will discuss the following benefits:

- Cost-effectiveness

- User-friendly interface

- Consistency

- Open architecture

- Timeliness

- Privacy

- Reduced workload

Cost-effectiveness

At the same time as the market demands that employees have access to more information, budget cuts have forced many organizations that communicate primarily by print to reduce the amount of information they provide to employees. Intranets save companies money in two primary ways:

• The cost of materials

• The cost of travel and training

Savings in Materials

Because an intranet requires a relatively small investment both for software and hardware, an organization cannot only retain existing communication materials, but it can also expand the range of information made available to employees.

The costs of producing traditional media can be very expensive, and they are repeated, because materials quickly become dated. A handbook that costs $80,000 to produce one year can easily cost $20,000 or more in subsequent years. The equivalent publication on an intranet generates very few hard-dollar expenses in the first year, and even fewer in subsequent years. Also, the publication's quality can be enhanced on an intranet because, in the digital world, you can produce materials in black-and-white or color with your decision having no bearing on the cost equation.

Savings in Travel and Training

Beyond the savings in print and production costs, intranets can also generate savings in travel and training. For example, newsgroups, chat rooms, and electronic mail discussions dedicated to specific topics can support a degree of collaboration that previously required a face-to-face meeting. Interactive online slide presentations, complemented with hypertext links, enable employees to self-train themselves, reducing the need for trainers to coordinate facilities for a training meeting.

User-friendly Interface

The graphical interface of a Web browser, with its clickable image maps, hypertext links, and in more advanced applications, multimedia tools, makes the process of finding and interacting with information much more palatable for employees. This hyperlinking, when used in a logical file structure, presents information to employees in concise, non-intimidating chunks.

Hypertext links enable you to adopt a "just in time" style of communicating. For example, an employee completing an online enrollment form for flexible benefits may not understand how the number of flex dollars is determined. By providing a link within the form, the employee can find the right amount of information at the time appropriate for it to be meaningful.

Consider another example: An organization has recently phased out an unprofitable division. Fifty jobs have been eliminated. At the same time as the press release is sent to the media, an announcement is made via phonemail, and a complete release is posted on the intranet. But the intranet version is not simply text alone. Within it are links to a video clip of the president, a special newsgroup thread, and a feedback form. Providing these links enables the employee to express ideas—and receive a response—before the rumor mill builds frustration and misconception.

Optimists project that some iteration of the Web browser will emerge as the standard interface from which everyone will conduct nearly all business activity. By familiarizing your employees with this technology early, you contribute to a cultural transformation where your organization is better prepared to deal with new challenges in a digital world.

Note

You have almost total control over your intranet's functionality. You build in only those features in the interface that have value to the user.

Consistency

Even when an organization takes steps to ensure it has updated and distributed traditional communication to employees, it is naive to assume that all employees always refer to the most current materials.

With an intranet, there is only one version of any given document, so the Human Resources Department can take comfort in knowing that employees are gaining access to only the most recent information.

If your strategy calls for a mix of both traditional and new media, as it probably does, you should try to mirror the graphic design and content as much as possible among all media. Consistency within a communication strategy increases the effectiveness of each part.

In fact, applying some of the lessons that come with communicating electronically—such as organizing information in tiers—may benefit your traditional communication media. In the print world, the closest thing to an intranet equivalent is the fractured layout, where the body of the text is almost secondary to numerous sidebars, call-outs and graphics. More and more, this style of publication design is increasing in favor because it makes documents much less intimidating.

Open Architecture

Intranets have helped overcome one of the biggest setbacks to implementation of electronic communication. In the past, accommodating large populations of both PC and Macintosh users was not an easy chore. HR was often forced to choose traditional media because networked communication could not reach all employees. However, because intranets are platform-independent, organizations no longer face the same problems of multiple distributions. A training program developed for PC users works with equal effectiveness on a Mac.

Another advantage of this open-platform architecture is that many add-on applications have been developed, and new options are hitting the market almost daily. HR departments can add functionality to their corner of an intranet whenever new applications become available.

Timeliness

Intranets help remove the "time barrier" from the communication equation. As quickly as you can develop and code new materials, you can provide them to employees. This timeliness is important in a human resources environment, where organizational change issues need to be communicated almost instantly. Even updates in pension formulas and group insurance premiums need to be promptly communicated.

Unlike a human resources department, an intranet is never "closed." Employees can access information from the office during working hours or, if they prefer, from their homes, or while they are staying late in the evening. With increased globalization, sectors of the organization may be working at any time, so leaving an open line to information is essential.

Recognizing that maintaining an intranet is an ongoing commitment is critical. The fact that an intranet site can be easily updated means that it *should* also be frequently updated. Human resources information, particularly details of pension and benefit plans, are often perceived as dry. To maintain interest and content retention, the organization has a responsibility to keep it fresh.

Unlike most systems-based HR applications, an intranet requires little programming expertise to develop content. This moves some responsibility for development and maintenance out of the hands of your systems personnel and into the hands of others. You no longer have to worry that your number-one priority may be just one of many items on the IS department's to-do list.

In fact, most commonly used word processing packages, such as WordPerfect and Microsoft Word, have add-ons that convert their documents into HTML files. With minimal training, a junior assistant can create high-quality materials.

Intranets enable you to prototype training programs and other human resources materials more quickly. Employees in various departments and even remote locations can provide valuable input as you are developing materials. You can make changes easily, so you can realize time savings as new programs are developed.

Privacy

Providing information electronically may open employees' minds to seeking information they may otherwise avoid. For example, if employees seek information about taking an extended personal leave of absence, they may hesitate to directly ask human resources representatives in fear that the information might be passed on to management. However, providing details on an intranet may mean that the employee will locate the information on his or her own.

Critical to effective privacy is ensuring that employees know that the organization is not tracking their personal searches. As your systems administrators review site logs, they should retrieve only top-level information, such as the number of hits, rather than the specifics of who visited where and why. Many servers enable systems staff to disable the tracking of certain areas, particularly where this information would be sensitive.

Reduced Workload

HR departments spend a great amount of time answering routine employee inquiries and inputting minor changes to personal data, such as changes in beneficiaries, addresses, and dependents. Manually entering this data limits the time that human resources staff can spend on more urgent human resources objectives.

Tip

> A frequently asked questions (FAQ) directory can answer many typical queries, and forms linked to databases can be used for routine updates.

The transaction capability of intranets helps you reduce or eliminate much of your routine paper processing, such as flexible benefit enrollments and changes to personal information. Before the electronic world made this possible, these processes occupied much of a department's time.

An intranet can be linked with an organization's "legacy" resources, such as data banks, word processing documents, and groupware databases. Although this connection is not yet in the domain of the novice, you can expect more user-friendly tools to emerge within the next few years.

Building HR Into Your Intranet

If you are your organization's human resources executive and you have been assigned to create an intranet, you should consider one thing before anything else: Do not limit the scope of your ambitions to human resources only. The potential of an intranet is far too broad to restrict it to human resources materials and functions.

As you plan your intranet, consider all potential stakeholders. Marketing, administration, facilities, information systems, production, and other areas may all find value in an intranet's flexibility and "open" style.

As your needs grow, and as your systems architecture and employee culture support this growth, your intranet can evolve. As the capabilities of both servers and software applications expand, more high-bandwidth items, with greater use of audio and video, will mean that you need to consider the technical implications of this growth. Over time, and depending on your employee population, you may need one or many dedicated servers to support the intranet alone.

Ownership of the intranet should be shared among all stakeholders. The key should be to gauge each area's contribution in terms of quality, timeliness, reliability, and, above all, value to the organization in achieving its goals. HR may benefit most from a broader perspective because all employees in other functional areas are "human resources" of the organization.

Having said this, human resources may be an ideal pilot for an intranet. intranets need not be complete from day one. In fact, one great benefit of this medium is that it is scaleable.

By starting small, you can test the effectiveness of various approaches and arrive at what works best with your employees. You can publish and post drafts of information, and then encourage groups of employees to provide feedback. This feedback can be used to continually improve the quality of information provided to employees.

Now examine some issues that will come in to play as you start building human resources into your intranet. This section looks at the following items you should consider:

- Access

- Navigation

- Appropriateness of content

- Education

- Publication strategy

- Access to external Internet

- Integration

- Security

Access

A key factor in the process of educating employees about human resources information is making the right information available at the time it is needed. Undue delays in the access of resources result in employee frustration.

If your workforce connects from remote locations, you may want to consider a direct dial-up approach. The bandwidth of a dedicated server is much faster and more secure than "hiding" your materials within the Internet.

What about providing access to those who do not use a computer daily? One of the most significant arguments organizations make against using an intranet for HR is that some employees do not have easy access to information. In such cases, the organization has three options:

- Limiting the intranet

- Using kiosks

- Creating computer labs

The first option for easier access is to limit the intranet to salaried staff only. Although this simplifies the problem, it may also contribute to an "us and them" mentality, where blue collar workers assume that office staff are getting special treatment. Also, limiting access doesn't really solve communication problems on a universal basis.

The second option is to use kiosks. Unlike the kiosks of old, new kiosks require less sophisticated—and therefore less expensive—hardware.

The third option is to create small computer labs in each location, where employees can visit at their convenience to access the intranet.

Navigation

You will also need to be very thorough in how you structure navigation within the intranet. If your employees need a piece of information, but have difficulty getting to it and then returning to a starting point, they will not make repeated attempts to find it. They will simply get on the phone and seek the information from a live person. A main human resources home page, with a series of well-structured tiers, should prevent confusion.

Navigation must be carefully planned because hypertext is non-linear. Frames are a valuable way to ensure your employees do not become lost when navigating through information. Frames enable employees to explore the various dimensions of the site while always having a logical starting point to which to return.

Also, to get employees to the desired information as quickly as possible, you can build in keyword searches so that users can find an item using concepts rather than specifics.

Appropriateness of Content

Many organizations encourage employees to create their own home pages on the company's intranet. This supports the belief that if employees know each other better, they can also work more effectively together. However, many businesses fear that employees' notions of what is appropriate may not be consistent with the organization's culture or philosophy.

One option may be to establish some ground rules up front about what is inappropriate. Obviously, you will have a concern about pornography, profanity, or racist content. Reasonable corporate standards for creating, storing, and exchanging documents help create an environment in which openness is encouraged—within realistic boundaries.

Education

When rolling out your intranet, computer and Internet literacy becomes a critical issue. Educating employees on the technical side of using online resources may not be as huge a challenge as it may seem at first. More and more people are signing up with online services or Internet access providers from home; Netscape Navigator and other interfaces are familiar to more people.

The real challenge may be in changing the culture to embrace technology. Some employees still have a PC on their desk which is rarely turned on and is used even less. Technology will increasingly become a key competency point for employment and advancement. Those who cling to the belief that they do not need a computer to be effective will simply be unable to evolve with the organization.

Another challenge is also systemic: managers who cling to the clichés of "information is power" and "need to know" may resist more open information sharing. Intranets move beyond the "open door" policy, where employees must rely on managers' willingness to share, to one of "open systems," where much of this information is universally available.

Publication Strategy

Intranets cause HR departments to re-examine publishing strategies in terms of the timeliness factor discussed earlier. The traditional model calls for a master document to be created, with revisions provided at regularly scheduled times. For example, an employee handbook would be provided typically once a year whether or not policies changed to coincide with that publication date. The handbook would quickly become outdated or misplaced, and then it would not be updated for a full year.

The new model is driven much more by events and needs at a given moment in time rather than by the calendar. When a change is made, the online materials can be updated easily and immediately, and then the internal home page can have a brief announcement about the change.

Access to the External Internet

When building an intranet, you need to decide whether to allow employees access to the external Internet. The common mentality is that by opening a gateway to the outside world, employees will fritter away their days visiting inappropriate sites and accessing chat lines. This is tantamount to incorrectly suggesting that all employees reading business documents have an adult magazine tucked inside the cover.

While employees' curiosity and the tremendous media hype may result in some initial exploration, you need to recognize that the downsizing craze has made people far too busy to combine business with pleasure. The important message is to say that you expect the same tact in conducting business over the Internet as you would in managing your other business affairs.

The greater reason for allowing employees through the firewall is that they can use the Internet as an extension of the resources available within the organization. Consider this example: An employee is asked to coordinate an executive board meeting at a remote location. Using the Internet, the manager can do a search and identify several possible meeting sites, request facilities information by e-mail, perhaps even obtain a quote for catering online. This is only a simple example of the value that can be obtained by broadening the tools available to your people.

Integration

An intranet is not something you can drop in to immediately replace all other information sources. For example, by no means should you enable managers to use online training and communication as an excuse to reduce their day-to-day interaction with employees. An intranet is not a salve to cure all that ails human resources departments. It is simply another device—albeit a powerful one—in the HR toolbox.

New technology will be embraced by many and feared by some. However, once employees take the plunge and experiment with the intranet, they will quickly realize how it can increase their efficiency. To get employees to the starting point, you may need to do some marketing. Use your traditional media, including word of mouth, to spread the word. You may also want to consider adding a "hook." Consider periodic contests or other promotions to draw users to your site. Over time, as acceptance grows, start scaling down and phasing out your traditional tools so that employees become dependent on the intranet as an information source.

Security

An effectively designed intranet allows employees access to personalized human resources information. This personal data can be incorporated into documents and enable employees to provide feedback.

For example, the production of employee benefit statements has traditionally been a time-consuming process. By moving this information onto an intranet, you not only ensure accuracy, but you also can provide this information on a current basis instead of just once a year.

On top of this, there is always the danger of providing highly confidential information to the wrong person. Obviously, a special need is created to ensure the information is accessible only to those for whom it is intended. Firewalls within firewalls, and other security features such as encryption and passwords, enable you to maintain confidential information on your intranet while strictly controlling access.

Applications for HR

With a little creativity, a fair amount of elbow grease, and attention to structure, most human resources information can migrate to an intranet. Here is just a partial list of the types of materials that can be integrated into an intranet:

- Policy and procedure manuals

- Personalized benefit statements

- Training programs

- Group insurance and pension booklets

- Organization charts

- Project status reports

- Phone directories

- Speech and article libraries

- Newsletters

- Employee annual reports

- Job listings

- Competitive profiles

- Missions, goals, and corporate philosophy

- Employee recognition

- Information libraries

- Performance management

- Suggestion programs

- Vacation scheduling

Discussing how each of these items could migrate to an intranet would easily fill several chapters. Some of the more powerful ways in which an intranet can support your human resource objectives, and the reasons why the intranet may enhance their effectiveness, are discussed in more detail below.

Information Sharing

Often, materials exist within an organization, but never reach those employees who can benefit from that information. Speeches, proposals, discussion papers, reports, and other informative documents are typically circulated within a narrow distribution list. Within the traditional model, if you do not know who can use the information, the only way to ensure they get it is to distribute it to everyone, which is impractical. By posting these items on an intranet, you ensure that they are accessible to those individuals who will benefit from them.

Knowledge Preservation

We have all long heard the sickly sweet mantra of senior executives who say "Employees are our most important asset." Although this is often a misguided motivator, it does contain more than a grain of truth. Much of the knowledge and experience in an organization is archived not in company files, but rather in the minds of employees. When these employees take other jobs, retire, or die, this information is no longer accessible to the organization.

An intranet enables you to capture much of this knowledge and preserve it for future generations of employees. Important speeches, white papers, reports, and proposals prepared by employees can be made available to a broader audience. Video and audio files can add an extra dimension of usefulness to the information.

While the intranet is great for maintaining expert knowledge of those who have left the organization, it is also valuable for those who are still there. Establishing a searchable skills inventory and an archive of best practices will mean that employees can find and collaborate with those in the organization who have the expertise needed for a given project.

Collaboration

Intranets serve as excellent forums for group interaction. Properly planned and promoted, an intranet can become a laboratory where ideas can be presented and then cultivated.

Here's an example: An HR director plans to introduce a new anti-harassment policy. Conscious that offices in various countries deal with different legislation and cultural mores, the director seeks the input of regional human resources coordinators. A preliminary version is added to the intranet with limited access. Local HR representatives are asked to review the document and provide comments by completing an online form. Using the comments from around the world, the HR director revises the document and posts the final version within the online employee handbook.

Newsgroups can be used to help tackle the rumor mill; by encouraging dialogue about sensitive issues, management can address the issues before the grapevine messages gain strength or become distorted.

Employee Feedback

Intranets can be valuable in getting immediate information about employee perceptions. By distributing a questionnaire via your intranet, you can get quick feedback from your employees on issues. A survey becomes a significant venture using traditional media with a difficult collection and tabulation process. On an intranet you can do employee sensing on current issues and quickly report both on results and planned actions.

One caveat is in order here: Conducting employee research online may compromise the reliability of the data to some degree, unless it is clear to employees that their responses are confidential. The image of "Big Brother" is hard to overcome when you are asking employees to bare their souls.

Intranets can be used to present training information that would previously have required a more involved process, either of classroom training, diskettes, CD-ROMs, or other technology. At the same time, moving some programs online alleviates some of the time and administrative headaches involved in finding a mutually favorable time for dozens of participants to assemble physically. For the first time, programs can be created for the desktop that do not require huge up-front investments in dollars and programming expertise.

Certainly, some programs, such as sensitivity training for cultural diversity, will still require human involvement. However, many skills-based topics lend themselves quite well to an intranet-based approach.

Orientation

An intranet supports overburdened managers in meeting some of their responsibilities with employees, particularly in the critical first weeks with the organization. By providing orientation information online, you can ensure that a manager's good intentions are supplanted with concrete actions.

Think about this example: A manager has hired a new employee who will start the next week. Instead of walking around the office trying to find all the materials an employee will need, she accesses the orientation section of the intranet. There she finds an orientation checklist where she clicks on all the needed items within an online form. When finished, she clicks on the Submit button and goes back to her work. When the employee starts three days later, he arrives to find his desk, complete with a computer and office supplies, waiting.

Into the Future: The Virtual Office

In the future, an intranet's greatest value within an organization may be in extending its borders *beyond* the organization.

Technology has now made it possible to create "virtual offices," where employees of your organization are not actually on the payroll. This model, which is common in the film industry, sees a variety of individual contractors or boutique-sized specialty shops assemble for a project, work closely for a given period of time, and then go their own ways. Corporate culture is not as important a factor in these situations as is rapid, clear, and consistent access to information.

Intranets may be the ideal architecture for these entities because they make it possible to link many organizations who normally use different and proprietary platforms, and because they can be quickly updated to reflect new developments.

The Silicon Graphics Story

"Silicon Junction," the intranet implemented by Silicon Graphics, is an excellent example of how an organization has utilized an intranet for human resources purposes. The rapidly growing company sees its intranet as an important tool for collaboration and for maintaining communication between teams. Silicon Graphics estimates that its intranet,

which has more than 150,000 pages, saves the company $40,000 *every day* by dramatically reducing investments in paper, production, recycling and distribution, as well as in travel and training.

Silicon Graphics has also moved many of its administrative human resources activities to its intranet, including the following:

- A searchable database provides a catalogue of all training programs, many of which can be delivered online. Certification and testing are also managed electronically.

- New employee orientation is simplified using an online form. The manager completes the form, and the ball is in motion to arrange resources for employees.

- Job listings are stored in a searchable database.

- Chat groups, newsgroups, video conferencing, and whiteboards, all tied to the intranet, encourage group collaboration.

- A wide range of databases, operating on different platforms, use the intranet as a front end. This supports easier sharing of data.

On top of the intranet, all employees have access to the external Internet. The company believes that this access is important to competitiveness. The combination of internal and external access to online information has strengthened Silicon Graphics's ability to continue to grow while remaining decentralized and minimizing bureaucracy.

5

Additional Information Servers

20

Simple Intra-Company Newsgroups

In Chapter 17, "Workflow Software, Groupware, and the Intranet," you learned about forums in the concept of groupware and examined a program called Allaire Forums as a commercial example. As you recall, forums provide a tool that directly supports business processes by enabling people to communicate and collaborate on the work that they perform.

In the example application, Allaire Forums used Allaire Corporation's Cold Fusion gateway to store data in an ODBC database. This scenario enables you to further utilize your ability to create intranet-based programs to gain access to the data stored in the ODBC database(s) outside of the Forums implementation.

This chapter will discuss how to provide information through another source—newsgroups—to the users of your intranet. You likely are familiar to some degree with the newsgroups that are accessible on the Internet. Newsgroups can be found that have topics ranging from aviation to data modeling to software patches to zebra mussels in the waterways. By the time you finish reading this chapter, you will understand the rationale for implementing some form of newsgroup service, by using either a commercial product or a simple product that is created with Perl programming. Specifically, the chapter covers the following:

- Defining newsgroups

- Becoming familiar with commercial products

- Creating simple newsgroups with Perl

Defining Newsgroups

Newsgroups are online discussion forums that focus around a specific topic—a definition that sounds much like that of workflow/groupware (or threaded) forums. In reality, the underlying technology supporting these two types of forums are very similar from a conceptual point of view. Depending upon the size of audience and the anticipated volume, one can choose from a variety of technology solutions that exist at each level.

From an industry perspective, Internet newsgroups are inter-company discussion forums where the participants discuss ideas, look for solutions, or even find out the latest software patches from software companies and fellow programmers. Over 15,000 public newsgroups exist on the Internet, and on any given day millions of messages are posted. In order to handle this volume of traffic, robust computers and robust software are necessary.

Intranet newsgroups, those strictly within the company, tend not to have that type of volume or traffic, however. Intranet newsgroups still tend to focus around a topic of conversation, but as you will see, they differ from the groupware forums discussed in the previous chapter.

Justifying Newsgroups?

The biggest difference between newsgroups and groupware forums comes from the perspective of the business process that the discussion forum supports. Working within a project team requires a forum that all participants use as the communications pipeline to success. Staff looking for the latest newspaper articles or competitor news releases have a different reason for using a forum.

Ultimately, the rationale for putting newsgroups in place should be to support a business process. Using newsgroups as a means of reducing e-mail noise and as a repository of information that is organized on a topic basis (postings about the best way to handle an unhappy client or about the undocumented features of a product, for example) can improve the efficiency and effectiveness of an employee.

Reducing E-mail Noise via Newsgroups

Newsgroups support a business process indirectly in reduction of "noise" traffic. In many of the workflow software applications on the market, the notification of activities, reminders, and required events take place through the e-mail system. If the noise traffic is eliminated from the e-mail system, then the employees will know and understand that the e-mail arriving at their workstation is part of the business process. The action taken as a result of the e-mail is part of the business process. If the employee is completing a purchase order, for example, as his or her part in the process, and the computer beeps signaling the arrival of a new message, the employee *knows* it will be another purchase order to complete. The employee does not have to turn to the message and read it right away—the current document should be completed first.

Very few people manage their time effectively when dealing with e-mail (or telephone) interruptions. When the computer beeps, signaling the arrival of a new message, they automatically switch to the e-mail program to see if the message needs to be dealt with now or is just an information item. Often they aren't expecting anything, but they do this out of habit. And in many cases, people respond or react to the information contained in the e-mail immediately, abandoning the task already underway.

Reducing the noise in the e-mail system by creating a "news" forum wherein the FYI-type messages can be posted, for example, increases the effective working time of the average employee. The only requirement is to discipline yourself to review the news forum on a regular (daily?) basis. Of course, if there is a need to find or communicate a particular piece of information, the user is welcome to utilize the "news" forum on an "as required" basis.

> In my previous position within a federal government agency, it was not uncommon to receive upwards of 200 e-mail messages a day. With 85 points of presence across the country and 4,000 plus staff, the Department generated a great deal of "Branch X will be holding a planning session today. For messages...." traffic. Did the offices on the West coast care if 10 people in Ottawa were not at their desks for the day?
>
> Approximately 60 percent of the e-mail traffic to my desk (roughly 120 messages per day) was noise. One of the prime objectives in designing and piloting an intranet was to demonstrate the fact that we could reduce the noise at the desktop and reduce the traffic on the network, increasing efficiency in humanware and hardware.

Other Ways Newsgroups Support Business Processes

Newsgroups also play a role in creating information bases to which staff can turn to find the facts that they are seeking. They are not generally sources of support mission-critical business processes or information stores. They typically play the role as the corporate librarian's assistant—an online reference system that can be referred to and searched as required.

One other possible implementation of a newsgroup within a company that straddles both the intranet and the "othernet" is a full-blown newsgroup on the Internet that the intranet users can gain access to, review, and participate in that is sponsored and operated by the company. This is often one means of communicating with the community at large, and many software companies operate their online customer support facilities in this manner.

If there is a need to reduce noise e-mail traffic that can be posted to a news forum, or newsgroup, as they will now be called, or if there is a need to create a simple online library of information, newsgroups should be implemented.

Becoming Familiar with Commercial Products

Two types of commercial products are available for newsgroups. One kind includes large, robust news servers that function in high-volume Internet-style applications. The other kind is used more often for internal, small-scale newsgroups. The choice is usually based on the number of users and volume of traffic, and the servers on the market are designed with different capacities of these in mind. This section will discuss the use of the first kind of commercial product, which can be used internally as well as externally; this is intentionally planned growth capacity—the company may wish to expand the reach of the intranet newsgroups to clients, vendors, and suppliers at some point in the future.

Note

Several shareware or freeware products also work very well. However, throughout this book the focus has been on products that are commercially available and supported, and this chapter will continue in this vein.

Robust news servers, such as the Netscape News Server or NetWin's DNEWS, provide some of the following features:

- The means to enable Internet-based discussion groups

- Server-to-server replication of data

- Scaleability

- Encrypted interaction with the system

Netscape's product offering in this market is fully integrated into its suite of servers, which provides one Control Panel from which an organization's systems administrator has the ability to control all the various Netscape server types in the company's intranet/othernet.

Access Control Lists that are part of the networking environment of a company enable companies to have wide-open publicly accessible forums as well as restricted access to internal users or groups of users. Using the Access Control Lists of the HTTP server(s) in the intranet in conjunction with the Netscape News Server, for example, allows groupware applications, such as forums or discussion groups, to be put in place.

The robust servers support the major Internet news server protocol, Network News Transport Protocol (NNTP), over TCP/IP networks. The robust servers also are able to communicate with the Usenet news servers on the 'Nets (intra- and Inter-). They also run across many operating platforms so that the company does not have to have different "flavors" of news servers.

One absolute must for companies who want to be able to create internal newsgroups as well as communicate with external newsgroups is the ability to connect to and "feed" other news servers with user postings. The reciprocal function, the ability to "suck" news feeds from a news server directly into the internal news server, is one of the features of the current generation of news servers on the market.

In summary, the commercial products have industrial robustness in their abilities to handle volumes of traffic. They also can handle externally-accessed as well as internal-only newsgroups and can pull news from and push news to external news servers. In many cases these commercial products provide all the room for expansion of a company's newsgroup facilities, but that may be overkill for the moment.

In order to see how one would establish a news server in-house, following is a brief tour of NetWin's DNEWS news server product.

A Brief Tour of a Commercial Product: NetWin's DNEWS

DNEWS meets the requirements of a robust commercial product. Produced by NetWin Ltd. of Auckland, New Zealand, (http://www.netwinsite.com/) the program is available across many platforms and has a dynamic sucking feed feature. This is one of the nicer packages to install and configure via a well-thought out configuration screen. The company provides a trial version of the software which can be obtained for evaluation purposes.

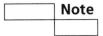

Note

The purpose of demonstrating DNEWS here is not to explore all the details of the software, but rather to demonstrate some of its robust features. DNEWS is available on the CD included with this book in an evaluation/demonstration format.

Configuring DNEWS

Assuming that the software has already been downloaded and is ready for installation, the opening screen of the DNEWS manager is shown in figure 20.1.

Figure 20.1

DNEWS Manager screen.

```
┌─ DNEWS Manager ──────────────────── _ □ ✕ ─┐
│ ┌─Setup DNEWS Server─┐ ┌─Manage Server─┐              │
│ │  [Setup Wizard...] │ │ [Stop Service]│  [ Exit ]    │
│ │                    │ │ [Start Service]│  [ Help ]    │
│ │                    │ │               │              │
│ │  [Main Options...] │ │               │  [Config Files...]│
│ │  [Feeds Out...]    │ │ [View Log]    │  [Register]  │
│ │  [Users & Feeds In...]│ │ [Status]   │              │
│ │                    │ │ [Commands...] │              │
│ │  [Write Changes]   │ │ [Do Reload]   │              │
│ └────────────────────┘ └───────────────┘              │
└──────────────────────────────────────────────────────┘
```

The existence of a Setup Wizard makes the configuration very easy. The system warns the user that the Setup Wizard should only be run once after installation. On a WORKING system, the individual buttons have to be used. Follow these steps to install the news server in your organization:

1. Click on the Setup Wizard button, and then the OK button on the warning screen that follows.

2. Enter the IP name of the news server within the intranet (news.localhost for the purposes here*)*, as seen in figure 20.2, and click on OK.

Figure 20.2

DNEWS Manager
—IP name of
server.

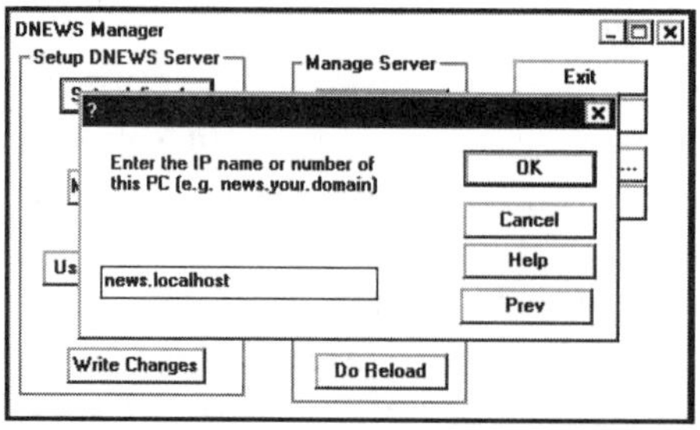

3. Assuming that the server will be "sucking" a news feed from another source, ensure the Yes I'm Going to SUCK News box is
   checked, and then click on OK, as shown in figure 20.3.

Figure 20.3

DNEWS Manager
—the enable
"sucking" fea-
ture.

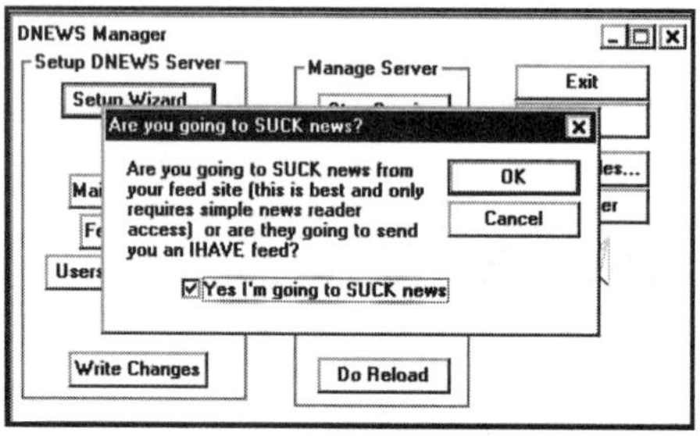

4. Enter the IP name or number of the news server from which the
   DNEWS server will SUCK. Figure 20.4 shows the entry in the
   current example. Click on OK.

Figure 20.4

DNEWS Manager
—the source of
news feed.

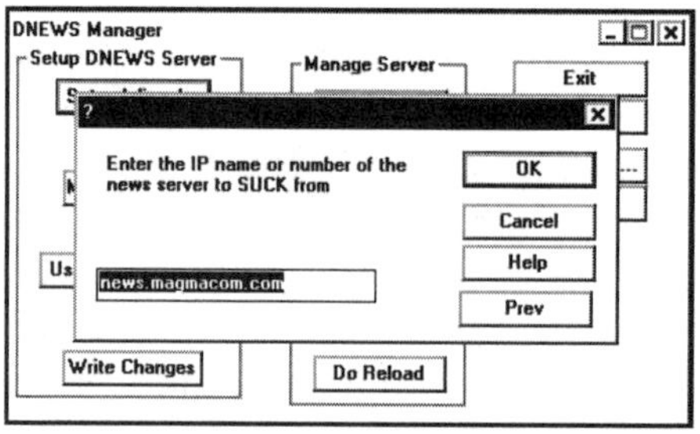

5. Enter the name of the e-mail gateway to the intranet
   (mail.localhost in this example), as seen in figure 20.5, then click
   on OK.

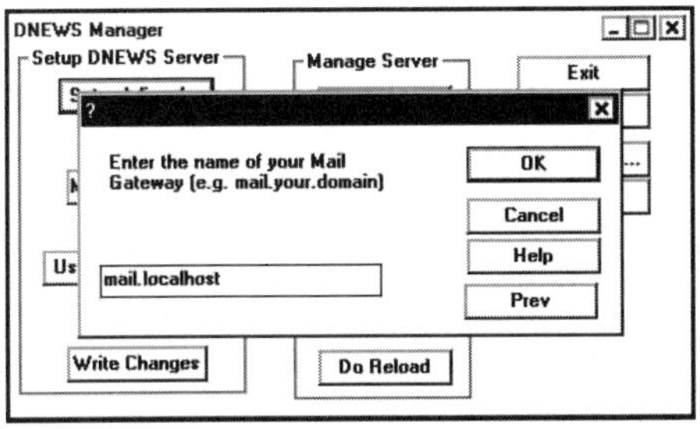

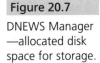

Figure 20.5

DNEWS Manager
—e-mail gateway
name.

6. Enter the name and address of the individual to whom DNEWS
will send reports (john@mail.localhost in this example) and click
on OK (see figure 20.6).

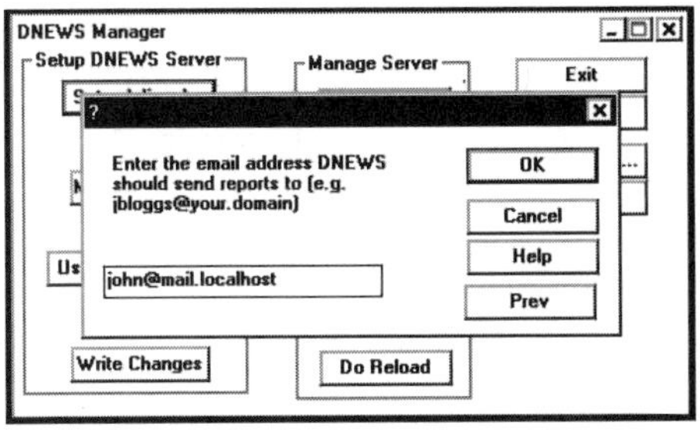

Figure 20.6

DNEWS Manager
—report recipient.

7. Enter the amount of storage space the application may use and
click on OK. The documentation states that 300 MB should be
enough for a relatively active group of 100 users. Figure 20.7
shows that for the sake of this example, 100 MB shall be allocated.

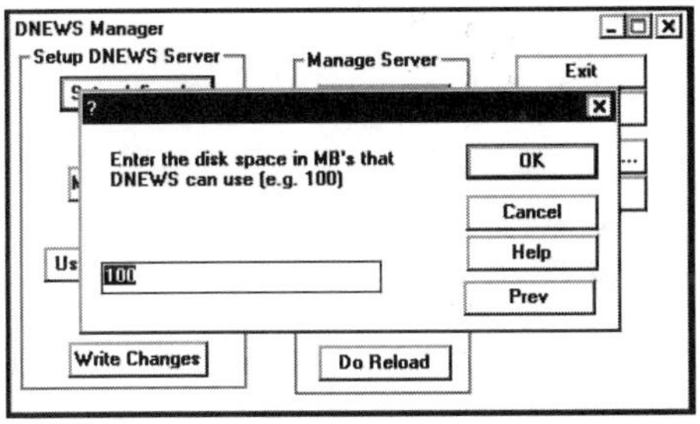

Figure 20.7

DNEWS Manager
—allocated disk
space for storage.

8. In order to confirm postings, DNEWS sends notification to all
users on the identified domains. If your addresses are of the format name@domain, then the domain should be identified as

*domain.where. For this example, see figure 20.8 and note that multiple domains may be identified and are separated by a comma. Click on OK to continue.

Figure 20.8

DNEWS Manager
—confirm
postings.

9. In order to identify the IP addresses of those allowed to gain access to the server, enter the appropriate IP address and click on OK. See figure 20.9 for example results.

Figure 20.9

DNEWS Manager
—access re-
stricted by IP
addresses.

10. Enter the IP names of users allowed to gain access to the system in format *.your.domain, and then click on OK. The example shows *.localhost in figure 20.10.

Figure 20.10

DNEWS Manager
—access re-
stricted to
usernames.

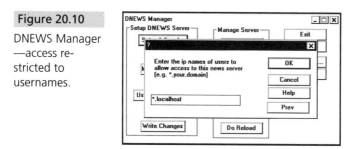

Starting up DNEWS

Once these steps have been completed using the Setup Wizard, the user can start up the DNEWS Server by doing the following:

1. From the DNEWS Manager, click on the Start Service button to invoke the server.

2. The server will initiate and then make contact with the news server from which it was instructed to suck.

3. Users should then be able to gain access to the news server from their browsers (Netscape will enable users to read newsgroups directly).

That concludes the set up and start up of the DNEWS product from NetWin Ltd. It is a very easy product to install and configure from one simple control panel. It is beyond the scope of the book to cover all the details of the program, but through the example, the ability to create a news server and restrict access to IP names and numbers is the means by which you would set up a myriad of internal newsgroups as required.

Commercial News Server Offerings

Any listing of currently available software changes between the time the list is written and the time it is read. A short list of some of the available products is provided, but you should be able to get a more up-to-date listing by connecting to your favorite search engine on the internet and searching for "news server software," "nntp server software," or "nns," which is a new news server protocol created by Microsoft.

The following is a partial list of vendors and their products:

NetManage Inc.—Forum Server

```
http://www.netmanage.com
```

Imagina Inc.—Newstand

```
http://www.imagina.com
```

Netscape Inc.—Netscape News Server

```
http://www.netscape.com
```

NetWin—DNEWS

```
http://www.netwinsite.com
```

Next is a look at a simpler method of creating newsgroups using Perl programs.

Creating Simple Newsgroups with Perl

Although the acquisition of commercial news servers has advantages if the company wants to sponsor and moderate newsgroups in a public forum, it is not always necessary to have such a robust service within the intranet. Assuming that your organization already has Internet access, the responsibility for operating and maintaining the external news server rests within the Internet group and not with the intranet project. The same group may have actual responsibility for both within the company, but ownership will be passed to that group instead of spending more time on the subject.

Netscape's Navigator browser has the built-in ability to gain access to and read newsgroups to which the user has access. As you saw in the chapter dealing with setting up the browser, the user is able to point at external resources to bring information into their workspace by identifying the news server within the Options Menu. Figure 20.11 shows the Netscape News Reader in action, pointed at an external resource; figure 20.12 shows again the Mail and News Preferences screen where the user identifies the resource.

Figure 20.11

Netscape Navigator—reading news.

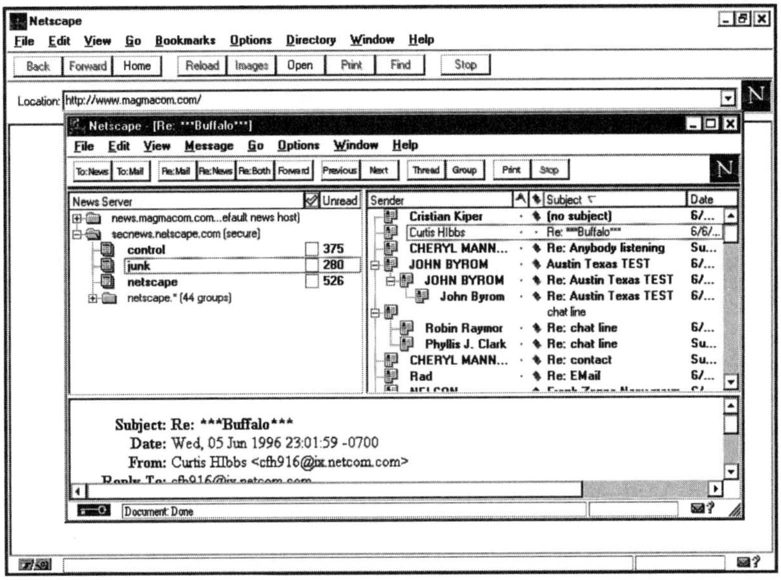

Figure 20.12

Netscape Navigator—Options|Mail and News Preferences.

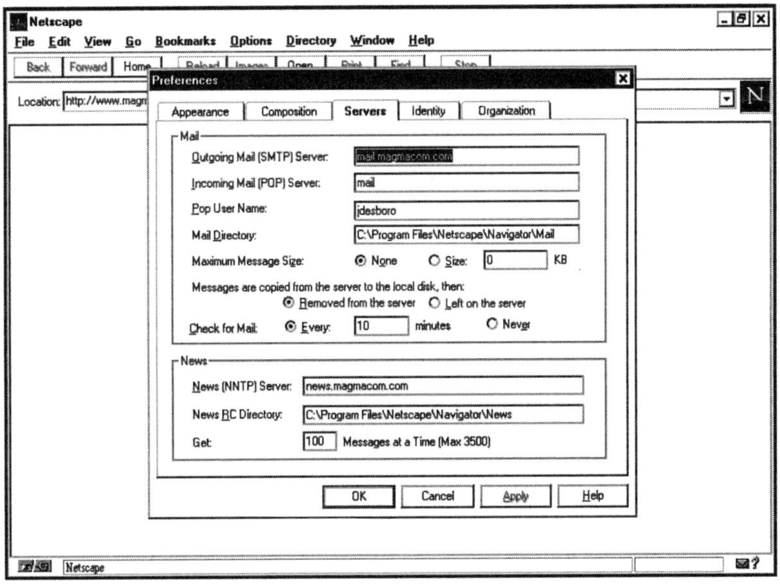

As you can see in figure 20.11, the News Reader has pointed at a news server and shows the three newsgroups to which the author subscribes or from which he reads news from Netscape.

Because your users can gain access to external newsgroups by using only their browser, do not implement a news server on your intranet unless there is a pressing business need for one. The simple example about to be explored will probably handle most internal newsgroups needs as they have been identified.

Why Use A Perl Solution?

As you have already seen in previous chapters, using Perl to create a CGI program is relatively simple. What is even better is when someone else has already done most of the work for you. A number of excellent Perl programmers have created "scripts" that are freely available to others for use. Many of these programmers request only that those who use their scripts keep the copyright and identification information intact and notify the originators so that they can track the usage of their materials. Users are free to modify the code to customize it for their own use, provided the original credit is given.

The Perl solution that will be explored was developed by Matt Wright and is used in several moderated Internet newsgroups.

Note

> Matt has created several excellent scripts for a variety of purposes, and these can be found at "Matt's Scripts Archives" at http://www.worldwidemart.com/scripts/.
>
> Matt is well respected among the Perl programming community, has authored chapters in two books already, and is co-authoring a book on Perl programming due out this fall.

The Perl program that will be employed is called WWWBoard, and you will work through the customization of the program in the subsequent sections of this chapter. The documentation that accompanies the program instructs the users how to configure the program to work within their environment. First, you will build an HTML page to call the Perl program.

Creating the HTML Access Page

Figure 20.13 shows a sample of the "News Group" program at work. The simple beauty of the script is that the initial HTML page that will be discussed hereafter is the working document where the threaded message headings are displayed by the Perl CGI program. More on that later!

Figure 20.13

A sample newsgroup—Perl program example.

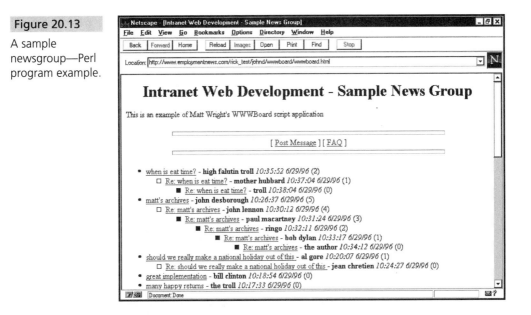

You may also download the WWWBoard program from the script archive mentioned previously and place all the components in a separate directory where you can work on them. Included with the Perl program is the file wwwboard.html that you can modify to create your own page. The code behind figure 20.14, a picture of the HTML file right out of the box, is shown here:

```
<HTML>
<HEAD>
<TITLE>WWWBoard Version 2.0!</TITLE>
</HEAD>
<BODY>
<CENTER>
<H1>WWWBoard Version 2.0!</H1>
</CENTER>
```

```
Below is WWWBoard Version 2.0 ALPHA 1.
<P><HR SIZE=7 WIDTH=75%>
<CENTER>[ <A HREF="#post">Post Message</A> ] [ <A
HREF="faq.html">FAQ</A> ]</CENTER> <HR SIZE=7 WIDTH=75%>

<UL>
<!--begin-->
</UL>

<a NAME="post"><CENTER><H2>Post A Message!</H2></CENTER></A>
<FORM METHOD=POST ACTION="http://your.host.xxx/cgi-bin/wwwboard.pl">
Name: <INPUT TYPE=TEXT NAME="name" SIZE=50><BR>
E-Mail: <INPUT TYPE=TEXT NAME="email" SIZE=50><P>

Subject: <INPUT TYPE=TEXT NAME="subject" SIZE=50><P>
Message:<BR>
<TEXTAREA COLS=55 ROWS=10 NAME="body"></TEXTAREA><P>
Optional Link URL: <INPUT TYPE=TEXT NAME="url" SIZE=45><BR>
Link Title: <INPUT TYPE=TEXT NAME="url_title" SIZE=50><BR>
Optional Image URL: <INPUT TYPE=TEXT NAME="img" SIZE=45><P>
<INPUT TYPE=SUMBIT VALUE="Post Message"> <INPUT TYPE=RESET>
</FORM><P>
Scripts and WWWBoard created by Matt Wright and can be found at <A
HREF="http://worldwidemart.com/scripts/">Matt's Script Archive</A>
</BODY></HTML>
```

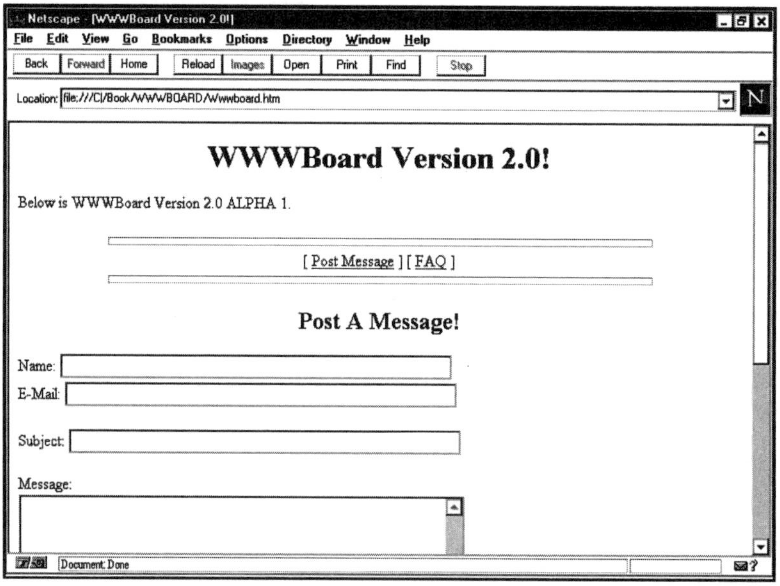

Figure 20.14

WWWBoard.html—right out of the box.

Only the three things listed here must be changed, and then the rest of the customization of the form is up to the imagination of the individual creating the newsgroup page:

- **The <TITLE> content**—Change the content of this tag block to represent the name of the newsgroup being implemented. This example used "Intranet Web Development—Sample News Group" as you can see in figure 20.13.

- **The <H1> content**—Change this to the appropriate heading to appear on the HTML page (see fig. 20.13).

- **The <FORM> action**—In the code example, the address of the CGI script, the Perl application, needs to be changed to point at the correct location. Replace the following:

```
ACTION="http://your.host.xxx/cgi-bin/wwwboard.pl"
```

Insert in its place the appropriate location for the location of the CGI files for your server. Also, make certain that the actual name of the Perl program is set to the extension accepted by the server software—in some cases the programs must end with ".cgi."

Any other customization that the user wishes to make to the HTML file (adding graphics, images, and so on), is at the discretion of the user. The only warning at this point is that this HTML page will display the threaded message headings, as shown in figure 20.13. As users post messages, the HTML file becomes larger and larger. Design the page depending on the expected volume of traffic.

Figure 20.15 shows a sample of the basic wwwboard.html file incorporating an image and the changes detailed above.

Now that you can customize your HTML page from which to call our newsgroup Perl program, you can move on to the actual program to review what modifications need to be done to the script.

Figure 20.15

Basic
WWWBoard.html
file—simple
customization.

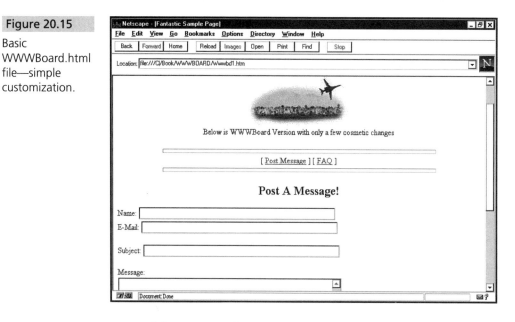

Working With WWWBoard

The changes required to customize WWWBoard for any given installation are outlined in WWWBoard's documentation. For the purposes of examining the code and its required customization, take a look at a portion of the source file, wwwboard.pl.

Note

This Perl program is in use in many locations around the world, including a site called "Intranet Soundings" at http://www.brill.com/intranet/ijx/index.html—a moderated newsgroup where participants can post questions or comments regarding any topic having to do with the intranet.

Following is the portion of wwwboard.pl where you are instructed to change the variables that are specific to your implementation of the application. A closer examination of the code follows.

```perl
#!/usr/local/bin/perl
############################################################################
# WWWBoard                    Version 2.0 ALPHA 2                          #
# Copyright 1996 Matt Wright  mattw@worldwidemart.com                     #
# Created 10/21/95            Last Modified 11/25/95                      #
# Scripts Archive at:         http://www.worldwidemart.com/scripts/       #
############################################################################
# COPYRIGHT NOTICE                                                        #
# Copyright 1996 Matthew M. Wright  All Rights Reserved.                  #
#                                                                         #
# WWWBoard may be used and modified free of charge by anyone so long as   #
# this copyright notice and the comments above remain intact.  By using this #
# code you agree to indemnify Matthew M. Wright from any liability that   #
# might arise from its use.                                               #
#                                                                         #
# Selling the code for this program without prior written consent is      #
# expressly forbidden.  In other words, please ask first before you try and #
# make money off of my program.                                          #
#                                                                         #
# Obtain permission before redistributing this software over the Internet or #
# in any other medium.  In all cases copyright and header must remain intact.#
############################################################################
# Define Variables

$basedir = "/path/to/wwwboard";
$baseurl = "http://your.host.xxx/wwwboard";
$cgi_url = "http://your.host.xx/cgi-bin/wwwboard.pl";

$mesgdir = "messages";
$datafile = "data.txt";
$mesgfile = "wwwboard.html";
$faqfile = "faq.html";

$ext = "html";


$title = "WWWBoard Version 2.0 Test";

# Done
############################################################################
```

```
########################################################################
# Configure Options

$show_faq = 1;                  # 1 - YES; 0 = NO
$allow_html = 1;      # 1 = YES; 0 = NO
$quote_text = 1;      # 1 = YES; 0 = NO
$subject_line = 0;    # 0 = Quote Subject Editable; 1 = Quote Subject
              #   UnEditable; 2 = Don't Quote Subject, Editable.
$use_time = 1;                  # 1 = YES; 0 = NO

# Done
########################################################################
```

In order use the code within your environment, all you need to do is to adhere to the copyright information outlined in the comment area of the program.

You need to make certain that your first line of code is set to the appropriate path for the Perl interpreter. Change the following code line:

```
#!/usr/local/bin/perl
```

The line should reflect the location of the interpreter on the server in question.

Once this is done, you need only configure the defined variable and modify a few options, as appropriate, and then you can implement the code. The following variables need to be defined relative to the newsgroup administrator's specifics:

- **$basedir**—This is the absolute path to the directory where the wwwboard files will be stored and where the HTML file will be located; replace the path in the code block with the correct path, as in the following example:

```
$basedir="/usr/local/newsgroups/marketing/wwwboard";
```

Warning

Don't forget that each Perl command line must end with a semi-colon (;)—this is one of the most common errors in implementation. If you forget, the program will not run until the error is corrected.

- **$baseurl**—This is the URL address for the directory in which the HTML file, among other items, is stored; replace the pertinent code line with the correct URL, as in the following example:

```
$baseurl="http://www.ourhouse.com/marketing/wwwboard";
```

- **$cgi_url**—This is the URL address pointing to the actual CGI program wwwboard.pl and it is used in the follow-up form responses; replace the pertinent code line with the correct URL, as in the following example:

```
$cgi_url="http://www.ourhouse.com/cgi-bin/wwwboard.pl";
```

- **$mesgdir**—This is the directory where all the messages will be created and stored. Create the necessary directory under the wwwboard directory named in the *$basedir* variable. It is recommended that the administrator accept the default of "messages" and create the *messages* directory under *wwwboard* (or whatever name the *$basedir* variable uses).

- **$datafile**—The datafile variable is created to provide a unique and sequential number to each message posted to the newsgroup. The data.txt file included with the application initially contains the number zero, and it is recommended that the administrator accept the default variable name as data.txt and store that file in the directory named in the $basedir variable.

- **$mesgfile**—This is the name of the HTML file that has been created to show the threaded discussion groups and enable users to post to the newsgroup. The default is wwwboard.html, but the user may wish to rename the file index.html to bring up the file automatically within the directory (this also means renaming the HTML file to index.html). For the moment accept the default as has been done within the example and as can be seen by referring to figure 20.13.

- **$faq_file**—A FAQ file has been included with the application. Administrators can use this file or create their own file to answer basic questions about the newsgroup software or the FAQ about the content (requires management by individual to select appropriate content and create file). For the moment, accept the default of faq.html and ensure that the file is located in the directory identified by the $basedir variable.

- **$ext**—This determines what extension should be used to identify the created message files. If it is running on a DOS system, set it to "htm;" otherwise, accept the default of "HTML."

- **$date_command**—This is the path to the server's date command, which is used to time stamp each of the postings to the newsgroup. Change the pertinent code line to the appropriate location.

- **$title**—This variable is displayed on individual message pages as the link text to return to the main HTML file. Change the text to reflect the newsgroup name or topic.

That concludes the journey through the variables. The program can now find its way through the maze of the server's directory structure, provided that you place the files in the correct, and appropriately named, directories.

Following are several options you need to configure in order to customize the file a bit further:

- **$show_faq**—This option decides whether the users should be provided with the opportunity to jump to the FAQ file from individual message pages. For the moment accept the default, but it can be changed easily.

- **$allow_html**—If the administrator wishes to enable users to include HTML markup in their postings (for emphasis, to include images, and so on), set to YES; otherwise, all parts of a message containing text within angle brackets will be eliminated from the message.

- **$quote_text**—This option carries the text from the original posting to the message text of the follow-up, providing a context for the user's posting. Disabling the option presents an empty message text box to the user. Implement it based on the need of a newsgroup.

- **$subject_line**—Three options are available to the administrator for setting the display of the subject text in follow-ups: 0 = carries the original text but enables the user to change it; 1 = displays the original subject, but the user cannot change it; and with 2 =, the user gets an empty subject box and must complete it. Implement it as appropriate for a newsgroup. The default of 0 is the usual implementation.

- **$use_time**—With this option, the *day/month/year* date format is placed with each record. The administrator must decide if time stamping is required as well. Accept the default of YES if the newsgroup gets a lot of postings or to show users activity levels and times of use.

And there it is—the WWWBoard program is now ready for implementation. The files identified need to be placed in the appropriate locations within the server, and the appropriate permissions need to be established. The program documentation outlines the permissions required. For the example, the following shows the status of the files in the wwwboard directory—note that for simplicity's sake the Perl program has been located here as well:

-rwxrwxrwx	1		1	Jun 28	23:43 data.txt
-rwxrwxrwx	1		1955	Jun 28	19:01 faq.html
-rwxrwxrwx	1		1181	Jun 28	19:00 index.html
drwxrwxrwx	2		512	Jun 28	23:43 messages
-rwxrwxrwx	1		2046	Jun 28	23:43 wwwboard.html
-rwxr-xr-x	1		18910	Jun 28	23:38 wwwboard.pl.cgi

Those assignments may curl the hair of the security-minded, but it is for demonstration purposes only. Please establish the appropriate settings for the each individual implementation.

Now that you have the files in the appropriate places and the permissions set, you can test out the program by calling up the modified HTML file. After posting an entry, or six, select a message and review the contents, as shown in figure 20.16.

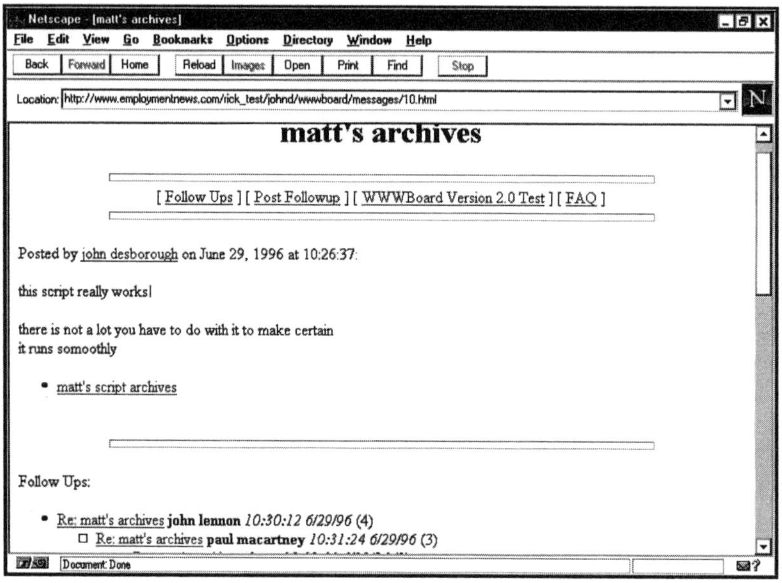

Figure 20.16

WWWBoard—
viewing a
message.

Clicking on the Post Followup link takes you to the part of the message input section of the form. The example program is set to carry the text of messages forward into the follow-ups, as seen in figure 20.17. The lines of text that are carried forward are prefaced by a colon (:), and as the chain of follow-ups increases, so does the number of colons preceding the lines of text. It is easy to tell by the number of colons just where in the sequence of the carry-forward a given message was located. Each response adds a colon to the lines of text to the previous response. If the discussion thread of follow-ups is exceedingly long, entire lines of the message could be filled with colons. Govern the system accordingly.

As the list of messages on the newsgroup grows, the administrator needs to watch the HTML file and, if appropriate, archive older messages. This can be done by making a copy of the HTML file and editing the file to remove the older message lines to create a smaller, "fresher" file. This new file then replaces the larger file that is copied to an archive directory.

Figure 20.17

WWWBoard—posting a follow-up.

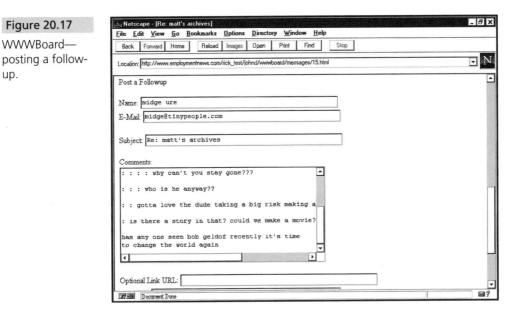

There you have the basic requirements to implement a Perl-based newsgroup system. Multiple groups can be created under different names to permit the creation of any number of newsgroups. In the final analysis, this Perl program could be implemented in place of the Allaire Forums-type products that were suggested for groupware discussion forums. The only disadvantage in this case is that the search functionality that is inherent when one uses an ODBC data storage mechanism is not intrinsic to the Perl environment.

Enhancements for WWWBoard

Many people use and provide support to the scripts written by Matt Wright. One site in particular provides support for Matt's scripts and has developed a series of enhancements for the WWWBoard program. Craig David Horton, who runs Dbasics htmlZine at http://www.dbasic.com/htmlzine/index.html, has a section of his site devoted to the enhancements. Figure 20.18 is a view of the htmlZine page where the enhancements are located. With Craig's permission, several of the enhancements that can be found at htmlZine are highlighted.

Warning

Although Craig Horton is the acknowledged source for the code snippets presented, the author of this book has altered references within the code snippets solely for the purpose of this book. If you choose to utilize these code snippets, please abide by the copyright regulations and stipulations that can be found at the htmlZine site (http://www.dbasic.com/htmlzine/index.html) as it pertains to these files.

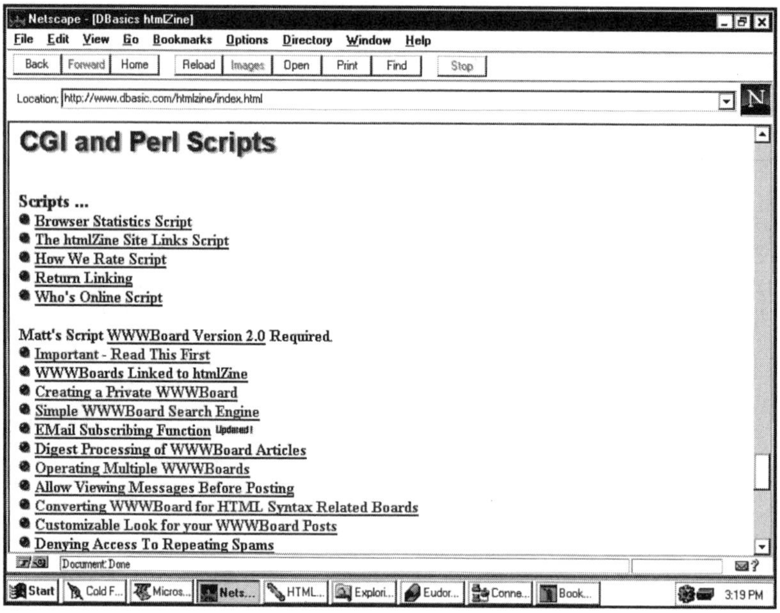

Figure 20.18

htmlZine Site— CGI script enhancements.

Customizing WWWBoard's Background

Horton offers modifications to the wwwboard.pl program to incorporate background colors and images throughout the site.

Within the *Define Variable* section of the program, create a variable called "$background" as follows:

```
$background="<BODY BACKGROUND=\"http://www.your.site/images/
backgrnd.jpg\" BGCOLOR=\"#FFFFFF\" TEXT=\"#000000\"><CENTER><IMG
```

```
WIDTH=300 HEIGHT=50 SRC=\"http://www.your.site/images/header.jpg\"
ALT=\"your text here\"></CENTER><BR>";
```

Even though this appears in this text to be split over several lines, it should all reside on the same line as "$background."

The back slash (\) character is required in front of all quotation marks, or else the server will return an error.

The last step to put this defined variable into use is to edit the wwwboard.pl program and replace "<BODY>" with "$background."

Running Multiple Newsgroups from One Site

Horton offers the following method for running multiple newsgroups from one site:

1. First, create the directory structure for the family of newsgroups that will be maintained—all of them will have a common parent directory. Here is a hypothetical directory structure:

   your.site/newsgroups/home = Parent Directory—Group Index

   your.site/newsgroups/home/marketing = Marketing News

   your.site/newsgroups/home/human = Human Resource News

   your.site/newsgroups/home/finance = Finance News

   your.site/newsgroups/home/technology = Technology News

   your.site/newsgroups/home/general = General Interest News

2. Set up all the files, except the wwwboard.pl file, as specified within the documentation for Matt's application. The appropriate wwwboard.html and data.txt files for each of the newsgroups must be present in each directory, and the messages subdirectory must exist in each.

   The wwwboard.pl program will be placed in the common parent directly to all the newsgroups.

3. You must alter the ACTION within the FORM of each of the HTML files that point to the Perl program. The changes to the ACTION field in each of the newsgroup directories are as follows, using the Human Resources as the example:

```
<FORM METHOD=POST ACTION="http://your.site/newsgroups/home/
➥wwwboard.pl?human">
```

Note the query string added to the end of the wwwboard.pl name. This needs to be repeated in each of the subdirectories within the HTML file that calls the wwwboard.pl program by using the appropriate directory name as the added query string.

4. The last thing to do is modify the wwwboard.pl file. What happens here is that you trap an environment variable, the query string, and add it to the required variables in the following manner:

```
$basedir="/usr/local/your.site/newsgroups/home/
➥".$ENV{'QUERY_STRING'};
```

```
$baseurl="http://www.your.site/newsgroups/home/
➥".$ENV{'QUERY_STRING'};
```

```
$cgi_url="http://www.your.site/newsgroups/home/
➥wwwboard.pl?".$ENV{'QUERY_STRING'};
```

As long as the Perl program shares a common directory with the query string added to the FORM tag and the $ENV{'QUERY_STRING'} added to the end of the script, everything should run smoothly.

Simple Search Engine

The following program was created by Craig Horton, with contributions by Matt Wright, and it is provided to extend the multiple newsgroups example and the functionality of the overall newsgroup facility. This Perl program will create a searchable index of the postings to the newsgroup in order to allow the user to search for previous postings.

With the HTML file to call the wwwboard.pl program, place the following form:

```
<P><CENTER><H2>WWWBoard Message Search</H2></CENTER>
<FORM METHOD=POST ACTION="find.cgi"
<CENTER><B>Search on Keyword(s):</B>
<INPUT TYPE=TEXT NAME="query" SIZE=30>
<INPUT TYPE=SUBMIT VALUE="Search!"></CENTER>
</FORM>
```

The following program, find.cgi, is presented in its original entirety, except for the directory names, which have been changed to reflect the previous, multiple-group example.

```perl
#!/usr/local/bin/perl
###################################################################
# find.cgi  Search WWWBoard Articles
# Created by Craig Horton        (chorton@dbasic.com)
# Contributions by Matt Wright   (mattw@misha.net)
# Created on:  5/4/96
# I can be reached at:           chorton@dbasic.com
# Script Found at:               http://www.dbasic.com/htmlzine/
# This script may be redistributed for non-commericial reasons
# as long as this header remains intact. All copyrights reserved.
###################################################################
# This is the listing of directory/files in relationship to script.
@files = ("messages/*.html",
          "home/marketing/messages/*.html",
          "home/human/messages/*.html",
          "home/finance/messages/*.html",
          "home/technology/messages/*.html",
          "home/general/messages/*.html");

# Print out a content-type for HTTP/1.0 compatibility
print "Content-type: text/html\n\n";


# Get the input
read(STDIN, $buffer, $ENV{'CONTENT_LENGTH'});
```

```perl
# Split the name-value pairs
@pairs = split(/&/, $buffer);

foreach $pair (@pairs) {
   ($name, $value) = split(/=/, $pair);

   $value =~ tr/+/ /;
   $value =~ s/%([a-fA-F0-9][a-fA-F0-9])/pack("C", hex($1))/eg;

   $FORM{$name} = $value;
}

print "<Head><Title>WWWBoard Simple Search</Title></Head><Body>\n";
print "<H2><CENTER>Search Results For $FORM{'query'}</CENTER></
H2>\n";
print "<HR>\n";
   foreach $file (@files) {
      $ls = 'ls $file';
      @ls = split(/\s+/,$ls);
      foreach $filename (@ls) {
        push(@FILES,$filename);
      }
   }
   print "<OL>\n";
   foreach $FILE (@FILES) {

      open(FILE,"$FILE");
      @LINES = <FILE>;
      close(FILE);
      $url = '';
      $detail = '';
      foreach $line (@LINES) {
        if ($line =~ "<TITLE>") {
          $lpos = (index($line,"<T") + 7);
          $rpos = (rindex($line,"/T"));
          $detail = substr($line,$lpos,($rpos-$lpos)-1);
          #$detail = "$line\n";
        }
        if ($line =~ "<TITLE>") {
          $lpos = (index($line,"<t") + 7);
          $rpos = (rindex($line,"/t"));
          $detail = substr($line,$lpos,($rpos-$lpos)-1);
        }
```

```
        if ($line =~ /$FORM{'query'}/i && $line !~ /<HTML>/i) {
          $url = "$FILE";
        }
      }
      if ($url ne '') {
        print "<LI><A HREF=\"$url\"><B>$detail</B></A> - <FONT SIZE=-
➡1>$url</FONT>\n";
      }
    }
print "</OL><FORM METHOD=POST ACTION=\"$ENV{'SCRIPT_NAME'}\">\n";
print "<P><CENTER><B>Search on Keyword: <INPUT TYPE=TEXT
NAME=\"query\" SIZE=30> \n";
print "<INPUT TYPE=SUMBIT VALUE=\" New Search! \"></FORM></
CENTER>\n";
print "</BODY></HTML>";
exit;

#END OF SCRIPT
```

In order to make this work, do the following:

1. Ensure that the first line points properly to the Perl interpreter.

2. Place this program file into the directory referenced within the FORM's action.

3. Make the program file executable with **chmod a+x find.cgi**.

By doing those three things, the administrator of your company's newsgroups should be able to create a customized environment within which the users of the newsgroups can enjoy threaded discussion about articles that are posted.

For more information about other Perl programs that are available from Matt Wright (http://www.worldwidemart.com/scripts) and Craig Horton (http://www.dbasic.com/htmlzine/index.html), check out their Internet sites and enjoy.

Status Check

At this point you should understand the need for providing newsgroups within a company, a commercial product offering, and a Perl-based simple newsgroup solution.

You should review the company's needs relative to the business processes in place to determine the type and format of newsgroup that is available. One of the very nice benefits of the Perl program solution from Wright and Horton is the cost. Only the time and effort of the reader is counted—the programs are provided free of charge.

As a support mechanism, newsgroups provide a means to reduce the noise traffic from e-mail and can provide the company with a means to place information that is less time-critical for distribution.

Next will be a look at providing an online conferencing facility through chat server technology. Online conferencing promises to provide a real-time interactive approach to posting messages.

21

Using Chat for Intra-Company Conferencing

Conferencing technology is used to enable groups of people to interact simultaneously. You are familiar with conferences where people travel to hear presentations and take part in discussions. Alternatives to physical gatherings of people were sought in order to reduce the cost of bringing people together, yet still obtain the synergy of having meetings. In all likelihood you are also familiar with using the telephone for conferencing, having more than one person on the line at a time—not to be confused with the party-line phone system that is still available in some remote rural areas of the country.

Electronic conferencing is a hot topic whose value is debated often. This chapter briefly discusses the types of conferencing that are available for companies. It then examines how to implement a chat server within the organization, and walks you through the installation and operation of this online conferencing solution.

The following list provides a glimpse at the topics that will be covered in this chapter:

- Types of conferencing

- A practical example: The Chat Server by Magma Communications

- A list of vendors for chat servers

Types of Conferencing

In the business press over the last few years, volumes have been written about how companies are trying to reduce the costs involved with meetings. A number of conferencing alternatives are available to companies to reduce costs, yet still hold meetings, including the following:

- Teleconferencing

- Video conferencing

- Online conferencing

Teleconferencing has seen a boom in the amount of traffic as more and more companies have meetings via the phone. The equipment has improved immensely over the last two to three years, so the voice quality is better. But there are still the problems to overcome concerning meeting dynamics. For example, body language tells you a great deal about how a person feels about a given topic; yet you can't see a person's physical reaction across the standard phone line. Also, people with dominant personalities and loud voices often push meeker participants off the phone line and take over the call. This also happens in a physical meeting, but it is much more difficult to control in a teleconferencing situation.

Video conferencing has received lots of press and is used in small segments of the market. The cost of setting up an internal video conferencing system is beyond the means of most companies. Several private sector firms, though, have gone into business providing video conference "boutiques" where one can rent facilities for a video conference. The normal practice is to rent the "boutique" firm's facilities in the cities at both ends (or all ends if at more than two locations) of the video conference. This ensures the compatibility between the technology used in the two locations. Firms that provide this service tend to be located in the larger financial hubs and in most major manufacturing communities.

Video conferencing has come to the desktop in a limited, but improving, fashion. With the aid of software on the workstation and small cameras placed on the top of monitors, users can connect to each other and have onscreen discussions. Many products on the market now enable you to see colleagues at their workstation in a window on the screen while both parties work onscreen within a collaborative application, such as Collabra Share, Lotus Notes, or WebFlow Corp.'s WebFlow product (for more information on collaborative software, see Chapter 17, "Workflow Software, Groupware, and the Intranet"). Note that video and the collaborative application are two mutually exclusive applications—that is, one does not rely upon the other. The brief example used here demonstrates that video conferencing can be used to enhance collaboration among work groups.

What this interactive functionality permits is a visual contact between the two parties trying to solve a problem. The author is familiar with one organization of approximately 60 people that uses this technique to provide software support to end users.

Note

The aforementioned organization does not want to be named because it doesn't want to reveal its competitive advantage. The author has signed a non-disclosure agreement.

Because the organization has over half its staff working from their homes spread across the country, technical support is an issue. The user sends an e-mail or calls the support technician and arranges the conferencing "call." The two parties start their respective video applications, and, using a remote access program, the technician is able to connect to the user's computer and monitor what the user inputs. These two technologies in combination permit the support function to work remotely.

One major issue within several companies is the need to retain a corporate memory of conferences. As you saw in Chapter 20, "Simple Intra-Company Newsgroups," a newsgroup enables people to communicate around a topic with the information posted and retained for viewing. In Chapter 17, you saw the use of a forum to perform much the same functions as a newsgroup, but you may intend to utilize forums to support the business processes of the company such as supporting a project team or a specific work group.

However, there are times when there is a need for real-time conversations or interactions among staff. Whether the need is for remote discussions, meetings, or even an "bear pit" session with the company president, chat servers provide a means for groups of people to hold interactive online conferences.

What is Chat?

Chat is a means of having an online discussion with two or more participants. Like a conversation, it is interactive. Think of chat as e-mail in real-time—one person enters a message that all can see on the screen. Users can respond to that message or post one of their own.

Most chats take place in a *chatroom* or just "room," though it is possible for two individuals to hold a *private chat.* The chat servers in the market today tend to allow for unmoderated or moderated chat sessions. A moderated chat session typically has a topic for discussion, and the moderator is responsible for making sure the line of discussion stays on the topic and encouraging the participants if interest starts to waver.

To date, the primary use for chat servers has been within the Internet world and for entertainment purposes. In numerous sites you can chat about hobbies or other social activities. While some chat server sites are one-room, one-theme sites, many of the chat sites have multiple rooms, providing multiple themes of conversation. For example, a hypothetical chat site could be established to represent a library or bookstore, with each *chatroom* dedicated to discussing a particular type of book: action, mystery, romance, science fiction, or nursery rhymes. Due to the nature of some of the implementations of chat servers, the ability to use an *alias*, or another name, while logged into the chat server has become commonplace to protect the identity of the users.

Chat servers are only now being discovered by companies as an alternative means to bringing their employees together across distances and time zones.

Note

> One of the benefits of a chat conference is that a user who misses the conference can gain access to the transcript of the session to review what was said. Automatic minutes!

Most chat server software enables users to login under the user's ID and name and allows anonymous or alias identification. Internet technology has enabled many companies to reduce long-distance teleconferencing bills by implementing chat servers to hold interactive, keyboard-based conferences online through their intranet.

Many companies have discovered that chat servers can be used to hold meetings with the president, meetings wherein the participants are all anonymous and can put forward their thoughts without fear of embarrassment. Rules of etiquette and conduct are distributed to all via the intranet in order to ensure a civil discussion. The ability to implement these kinds of sessions has provided valuable input into the operations of several of the companies who utilize them on a regular basis.

One company holds weekly "bear pit" sessions online with all the senior management. The employees participate anonymously or with an alias while management is fully identified. Frank discussions can take place, but all participants know that it is an information sharing session, a way to work out problems and grievances in real-time. The company implements these sessions to enable those too shy to say the same things in face-to-face meetings to have a forum where they can be heard.

Note

> Why do you need chat on the intranet? To provide a means for two or more individuals to have an interactive discussion without using the telephone; and to provide a forum for anonymous participation in discussions in which the meek might not otherwise participate.

Now that the conferencing options have been discussed in a bit of detail, here is a look at a chat server program that can be implemented within the intranet to provide the basic facilities for chat sessions.

A Practical Example: The Magma Communications Chat Server

Magma Communications Ltd. is located in Nepean, Ontario, Canada, a suburb of Ottawa, and can be found in cyberspace at http://www.magmacom.com. In the heart of "Silicon Gulch," as the hi-tech corridor is lovingly referred to, Magma Communications has developed The Chat Server for use within intranets (and the "othernets"). The program's continuous stream capability is currently designed for use with a Netscape browser, but other releases forthcoming should work with the major browsers.

One of the key benefits of the product is that The Chat Server has been designed to work across any TCP/IP network, not just the Internet. Demo versions of The Chat Server for the Windows NT and the Linux platforms can be found on the CD-ROM that accompanies this book.

Note

You will find the Chat Server on the CD-ROM that comes in the back of this book. For a complete list of what the CD contains, please see Appendix D "What's on the CD."

Note

The Chat Server from Magma Communications is similar to the majority of chat servers on the market. One key feature that sets this product apart from the others is the *continuous stream capability* that currently works with the Netscape Navigator browser. This eliminates the need for the chat participants to reload or refresh their browser screen after every entry, making the chat conference smoother and easier to use.

The installation, setup, and operations of The Chat Server are similar to that for other chat servers on the market, a list of which is provided later in the chapter. The products, along with their implementation procedures and features, may have some differences; but, for the most part, the chat servers work in much the same fashion.

The author likes The Chat Server from Magma Communications because of the continuous stream capability and the ease with which
the software can be customized for implementation within an intranet.

Following is a further look at how the system is installed, configured,
and operated.

The Chat Server

Like any of the other major chat server products, The Chat Server enables a company to hold moderated information/discussion sessions
with internal employees and host virtual meetings on the intranet. And,
if the company is connected to the Internet, it can use the product to
host meetings or discussions with suppliers, vendors, and clients, or
conduct interviews with potential job seekers.

The Chat Server Features

The Chat Server is used to run *L'Hotel Chat*, which has been voted as
one of the top Chat sites in the Internet world. The site is located at
http://chat.magmacom.com/lhotel/hotel.html

L'Hotel Chat is the largest continuous stream chatting server currently
running on the othernet. A visit to L'Hotel Chat is a good way to see
how the product works in a full-scale public implementation.

Following are the basic features of The Chat Server engine:

- Continuous streaming—When a user submits a message to the
  Chat Server, it is automatically posted to the screen—the user
  does not have to "RELOAD" the screen to see the message.

- Frame support for Netscape 2.0—This reduces the amount of text
  that needs to be reloaded and enables users to read new messages
  while they compose their own.

- Actions—Users can shout, whisper, or throw things through menu-based interface; all actions are customizable by the system administrator.

- Private messages—Participants can send private messages to each other while the rest of group continues a virtual meeting. The private messages can, for example, assist in negotiating a sharing of resources in return for support of a proposed project.

- HTML code in messages—Participants can place HTML code into their messages, adding images, sounds, video, or links to another page.

- Moving from room to room—If a multi-room environment is in place, users can move from room to room, simulating real life.

- Customizing—Most features can be customized for the specifics of the company employing the server.

These features make for a very robust application. The ability to move from room to room permits "virtual breakout sessions" at a virtual meeting, whereby the user can check in on the progress of other groups.

Chat Server Requirements

The Chat Server currently runs on the following operating systems: Linux, Solaris/SunOS, BSD, HP-UX, SGI's IRIX, and Windows NT or 95.

Each chatroom setup requires approximately 300 K of RAM, and each participant in the room requires approximately 8 K of RAM. These numbers are approximate and vary depending upon the operating platform of the server.

The Chat Server needs no special software to run on the server. It is not necessary to be running an HTTP server on the Chat Server machine. An HTTP server, however, is required to host the HTML pages that provide the user the link to the chatrooms. Within the example to be demonstrated here, the chat server will be made accessible from the intranet pages.

Installing The Chat Server

The Chat Server program is very simple to obtain and install. As mentioned earlier, the CD included with this book contains the demo versions of The Chat Server for the Windows NT and the Linux. Demo versions of one of the other available operating systems can be obtained at http://chat.magmacom.com.

"UnZip-ing" or "untar-ing" the downloaded file provides you with the executable or binaries, a "datafile," and a README file containing the latest information.

Once the software has been obtained and uncompressed, the procedures to get the system up and running are very simple. They will be covered shortly, but first, some planning should be undertaken before actually beginning to set up the software.

Planning The Chat Server Setup

Before The Chat Server is installed, you need to spend a few moments planning how it will be implemented within the intranet. A simple demonstration can be found in this chapter, but here are some of questions to be answered before a full-scale implementation takes place:

- What business processes need the support of online conferencing?

- Is there a need for single-room conferences? For multiple-room conferences?

- Will you implement moderated conferences, complete with topics and time frames? If so, how will you advertise these to your staff?

The basic technology-related information questions to answer are as follows:

- What is the name of the machine upon which the server will run? For the purposes here, the name is *localhost*, but normally the name of the server would be more along the lines of *chat.domain.net*, to represent your domain and net extensions.

- How many rooms will be operated? What port number will be assigned to each room? The port number for each room should be a unique number between 1001 and 30000. For the purposes here, use *Lobby*: port *9696*.

- What is the file name for each of the conference logs? One file is required for each room. For the purposes here, the Lobby conference will be logged in */tmp/chat.9696*.

- Where will the HTML pages that point to The Chat Server be located? This requires the full directory path name, */book/research/website/htdocs/chatserver*, and the introductory page will be *lobby.html* for the example.

- What is the URL for the page? For our purposes here, *http://localhost/chatserver/lobby.html* will be used; use the appropriate name for your server.

Now that you have organized how you are planning to set up your chat server, you are ready to create the introductory page.

Creating the Introductory Intranet Page

You need to create a page that invokes the chat session for the user from your intranet. The code for the HTML file that has been developed for the sample follows. Figure 21.1 shows this entry page as seen in the browser.

```
<HTML>
<HEAD>
<TITLE>intranet Chat Facility - Lobby</TITLE>
</HEAD>
<CENTER>
<H2>Welcome to the Conference Centre</H2>
</CENTER>
```

Pushing through the revolving doors leading into ABG Inc
headquarters, you leave the hot, humid New York air behind. The
cool, air-conditioned atmosphere that you expect to find
here is on the blink and it is even stuffier
inside than out.
<P>
As you walk through the lobby you glance to the right
and see a security guard in his uniform. He greets you with
a friendly smile. The lobby itself is adorned with large potted
palms.
You continue to take in your new surroundings as you stroll
over to the main desk.<P>

In the distance, you notice the elevator waiting to take you
to the upper floors of ABG Inc headquarters.<P>
Finally, you arrive at the main desk, where you are greeted
by one of the receptionists.
<P>
<HR>
<FORM ACTION="http://localhost:9696/" METHOD=POST>
Name: <INPUT NAME="USER" VALUE="Anonymous" SIZE=25>
<INPUT TYPE=HIDDEN NAME="SAYS" VALUE="&lti&gtEnters the
lobby...&lti&gt">
<INPUT TYPE=HIDDEN NAME="HISTORY" VALUE="4">
<INPUT TYPE=SUBMIT VALUE="Chat in the Lobby">
</FORM>
You may sign in under your own name or you can remain
anonymous if you would rather not say.<P>
<B>If you're having problems reaching someone from the
lobby... head over to the lab and see if things are working better
there. </B>
<A HREF="lab.html">Enter the Lab</A>
<P>
<A HREF="intranet.html">Exit Chat and return to intranet</A>
<P>
<HR SIZE=7>
<CENTER>
<FONT SIZE=2>Chat technology by <B><A
HREF="http://www.magmacom.com/">
Magma Communications Ltd.</B></A>
</CENTER>
<ADDRESS>

```
filename: lobby.html
last updated: June 27, 1996
</ADDRESS>
</HTML>
```

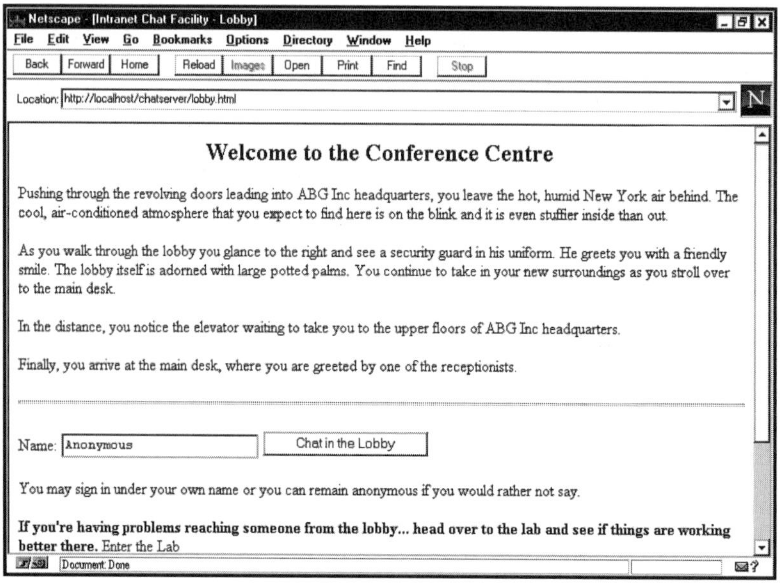

Figure 21.1

Entry point for
The Chat Server—
Lobby.html.

Before users enter The Chat Server, they must register their name with
the server. You do that in this file using a form within the HTML page.
The user has the option of using the default name "anonymous" or
entering a real name. The essential part of the HTML file is repeated
below in order to make a few important comments.

```
<FORM ACTION="http://localhost:9696/" METHOD=POST>
Name: <INPUT NAME="USER" VALUE="Anonymous" SIZE=25>
<INPUT TYPE=HIDDEN NAME="SAYS" VALUE="&lti&gtEnters the
lobby...&lti&gt">
<INPUT TYPE=HIDDEN NAME="HISTORY" VALUE="4">
<INPUT TYPE=SUBMIT VALUE="Chat in the Lobby">
</FORM>
```

1. The first line is the link to The Chat Server on the server *localhost*,
    running on port *9696*. The lobby chatroom would run on that
    particular port, as stated earlier.

2. The second line prompts the user to identify himself or accept the default of anonymous.

3. The third line, containing the hidden input field SAYS, is used to let participants know that a new person has joined the chat.

4. The HISTORY field outlined in the fourth line of the code block specifies the number of messages to keep visible on the screens when a new user enters the room. In this case, the last four sent on The Chat Server will be displayed in this room.

5. The SUBMIT VALUE line you recognize as the definition of the submit button to invoke the form.

6. The last line is the closing tag.

In implementing this example within an intranet, please adjust the values according to the specifics of the local network and intranet parameters.

You have also created a sample page for the Lab, a second room within the chat environment. The code for the inclusion of this second room is displayed below and is followed by figure 21.2, which shows you the Lab page in the browser. In reality, this second chat room will be running a separate Chat Server session on another port, but more about this will be explained later.

```
<HTML><HEAD>
<TITLE>intranet Chat Facility - The Lab</TITLE></HEAD>
<H2>The Lab</H2>
"What is this doing in a downtown high-rise?", you ask the
person standing next to you.<P>
"Don't ask... he's mad... completely insane...", he whispers
quietly.<P>
"But why..."<P>
"It's the CEO... he's working on something he says will
improve the intranet for everyone..."<P>
"But what is it for?"<P>
"If ever you are having a problem with the Chat Rooms, you simply
enter this room and try to chat with the people here... this room is
```

```
constantly being rearranged, so you'll want to wear a hard-hat... if
you're not having a
problem with the Chat Room... you're better stick to
Lobby."<P>
"Hmmm... I think I'll take a look....", you mutter as you
are drawn towards the lab.<P>
<Hr>

<FORM ACTION="http://localhost:9999/" METHOD=POST>
Name: <INPUT NAME="USER" VALUE="Anonymous" SIZE=25>
<INPUT TYPE=HIDDEN NAME="SAYS" VALUE="&lti&gtWanders into the
lab...&lt/i&gt">
<INPUT TYPE=HIDDEN NAME="HISTORY" VALUE="4">
<INPUT TYPE=SUBMIT VALUE="Chat in the Lab">
</FORM>
<A HREF="lobby.html">Return to the Lobby</A>
<Hr>
<CENTER>
<FONT SIZE=2>Chat Technology by <B><A
HREF="http://www.magmacom.com/">Magma Communications
Ltd.</A></B>

</CENTER><BR>
<ADDRESS>
filename=lab.html  last update June 27, 1996
</ADDRESS>
</HTML>
```

Editing The Chat Server Datafile

The Chat Server datafile contains customizations for the rooms that are operated within the chat facility. Before looking at the datafile in place for the example, a discussion about the components of the datafile is in order. Following is an examination of how the rooms are specified within the datafile.

Tokens Understood by The Chat Server

The Chat Server uses *tokens* to define activities and parameters. The following section describes the tokens understood by The Chat Server. Tokens are variables which are passed to the server by the datafile so that The Chat Server can establish the appropriate environment.

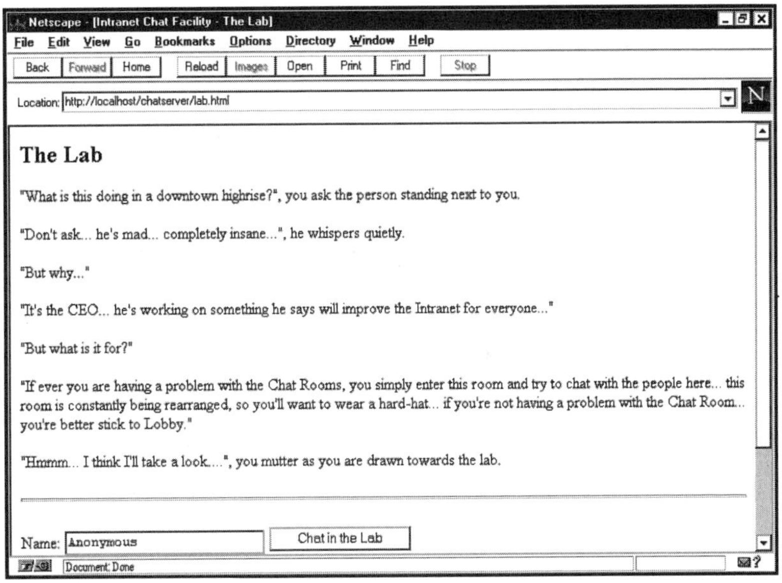

Figure 21.2

A second room within The Chat Server—the lab.

Tokens Common to both Single- and Multiple-Room facilities:

- [PORT]—A port number is required for each individual room and must be the first token listed for a room. The next line must contain only the appropriate port number.
  All other tokens in the datafile following the [PORT] statement are assumed to be part of this [PORT] until another [PORT] token is issued.

  ```
  [PORT]
  9696
  ```

- [TITLE]—The title must be a one line statement containing the name of the room and cannot have HTML code embedded in title. This title tells other Chat Server datafiles (there is one created for each room) how this particular room should be referenced in the datafiles of the other rooms. This title appears in the list of rooms to which the user can move.

  ```
  [TITLE]
  The Lobby
  ```

- [ACTIONS]—This is a required part of the datafile and lists the actions which the user can perform in this room. This is the most complex part of the datafile but permits customizing the Chat Server room to meet the needs of the user. A sample from the datafile follows:

```
[ACTIONS]
says to¦<I>says to $1</I>: $2¦DEFAULT
shouts to¦<I>shouts to $1 (and draws a glare from the
receptionist)</I>:<B> $2</B>¦
scowls at¦<I>scowls at $1</I>: $2¦
winks at¦<I>winks at $1</I>: $2¦
nudges¦<I>softly nudges $1</I>: $2¦
nods to¦<I>nods knowingly to $1</I>: $2¦
inquires to¦<I>inquires to $1</I>: $2¦
smirks at¦<I>smirks at $1</I>: $2¦
kicks¦<I>kicks $1's leg</I>: $2¦
agrees with¦<I>agrees with $1</I>: $2¦
PRIVATELY whispers to¦<I>PRIVATELY whispers to $1</I>:
$2¦PRIVATE
```

The format of the action line is as follows:

```
<action displayed in list>¦<action printed as
message>¦[options]
```

An example from earlier would be this:

```
nods to¦<I>nods knowingly to $1</I>: $2¦
```

This is a standard action line in the datafile. The action selected by the user, nods to, results in a message being printed on the screen *"nods knowingly to username."* The variable $1 in the code line is replaced by the name of the user to whom the action is intended. The message being sent by the person initiating the action is $2.

If anonymous executed the *nods to* action above to Thad with the message "g'day mate," the resulting line in the chat screen would be this:

```
Anonymous: nods knowingly to Thad: g'day mate
```

Under the heading of options, in the code block, DEFAULT is used to associate an action to the default person (ALL). This broadcasts the message to all participants if selected by the user.

The PRIVATE option, when used with an action item that incorporates the option, sends the message so that the only participants who see the message are the sender and the recipient.

- [TALKONLYTO]—This token forces everything said to be directed to the named individual but is not used very often.

  ```
  [TALKONLYTO]
  Al Gore
  ```

- [HEADER]—Any text on the line following the [HEADER] token will be sent to browser before any other text. The information to be sent must be on one line or it will not be recognized by the chat server. The default, if nothing else is specified, is the title of the room and the number of current users in room (more details on what can be used here are in the "How To..." section of this chapter).

  ```
  [HEADER]
  <BODY BACKGROUND="http://localhost/chatserver/logo.jpg">
  ```

- [HEADER2]—If frames are used (and supported by the browser) to separate the browser's screen into two halves, this token writes data to the output portion of the frame, and [HEADER] writes to input portion (see [HEADER] above for example).

- [SCROLLING]—The use of this token forces the output area in a frames-based browser (see [HEADER2] above) not to scroll when new messages are displayed. This is not used often.

  ```
  [SCROLLING]
  noscroll
  ```

- [FULLURL]—The inclusion of this token redirects the users to another HTML page when the room they are entering is full—that is, when the maximum number of participants has been reached. The file identified on the following line is a file that needs to be created by the chat server administrator and usually tells people that the room is full, come back again later.

```
[FULLURL]
http://localhost/chatserver/full.html
```

- [SECUREURL]—If the security features have been implemented, this token redirects the users to another HTML page if the room they tried to enter did not accept their password, they are using a user ID already in use within the room, or they have been booted from the room (by the moderator). The file indicated in the address following the token needs to be created and placed within the intranet.

```
[SECUREURL]
http://localhost/chatserver/invalid.html
```

- [SLEEP]—Each time Chat Server checks for input/output from users, it pauses or sleeps for one second. This may cause noticeable delays for users even though this improves CPU usage. A value of zero stops the server from sleeping and may improve performance.

```
[SLEEP]    0
```

- [TIME]—This token is used to turn the display of the time within the chat server on or off.

```
[TIME]
none
```

- [OPTION]—This token turns on or off the options for a particular room; each defined option must appear on separate lines. The available options are as follows:

  - nosecure—The Chat Server does not watch the IP addresses from which a user is chatting. With low traffic, a user who comes back later with a different IP address but the same username may be bounced for "impersonation." The nosecure option turns off that feature.

- striphtml—With this option, users are not able to place HTML within their messages. This prevents images, large text, and so on.

- fair—This changes security from none to fair, allows users with valid IDs and passwords to enter a room even when the room is at capacity, and guarantees access for the Systems Administrator.

- strict—The highest security level, it requires valid user identification and a password to enter the room.

- noconfig—This removes the config button from user's browser page.

```
[OPTIONS]
nosecure
fair
striphtml
```

- [READFILE]—This token specifies the file that will be monitored by The Chat Server for new messages which are displayed whenever text is appended to the file and a new message is posted. The default is */tmp/chatfile.<port>* where <port> is the port number specified under the [PORT] token.

```
[READFILE]
/tmp/chat.9696
```

- [WRITEFILE]—This specifies the file to which the new messages will be written and is usually the same file as the [READFILE].

```
[WRITEFILE]
/tmp/chat.9696
```

- [FRAME]—This token enables the chat server administrator to customize layout of screen by creating frames, which must be supported by the users' browsers; BOTTOM means that control frame is at bottom of window and NONE turns off the frame feature of The Chat Server.

  ```
  [FRAME]
  BOTTOM
  ```

- [FRAMESIZE]—This token enables the administrator to determine the frame sizes that user sees; the following example shows upper frame at 130 pixels with the remainder of the Netscape window available for the bottom frame.

  ```
  [FRAMESIZE]
  130,*
  ```

- [MAIN]—This token overrides settings in [HEADER] and allows total customization of the input area of the room. The Administrator can add links to other pages, pictures, and text, and can customize the layout of the various input entities. Any of the following variables embedded in this area will act as a flag to The Chat Server to insert the item as described. (The [MAIN] functions are more completely detailed within the program's manuals, and the absolute granularity of their workings is beyond the scope of the book at this point. They are highlighted here merely to show the ability to customize a variety of features from one token.)

  - $FORM =

  - $USER = user's name...

  - <ACTIONLIST>—list of possible actions in the room

  - <USERLIST>—list of users in the room

  - <GOTOLIST>—list of other rooms to go to

  - <IGNORELIST>—list of users to ignore

  - $NOPIC—status of picture option (config option)

- $VERBOSE—status of verbose (config option)

- $HISTORY—value of history (config option)

- $CONFIG—used to carry user's settings from room to room; this single token could be substituted by the following:

```
USER=$USER&VERBOSE=$VERBOSE&HISTORY=$HISTORY&USERPASS=
$USERPASS&LOGIN=$LOGIN&PASSWORD=$PASSWORD&NOPIC=$NOPIC
```

- $PASSWORD—user's room password

- $USERPASS—member's password

- $LOGIN—member's customer number

- $1—the title of the room

- $2—the number of users in the room

For moderated rooms:

- $MODNAME1—the moderator's first name

- $MODNAME2—the moderator's second name

- $MODNAME—the moderator's only name when being a single user

- $MODPWD—the moderator's, guests', or administrator's password

- $QUEUE—the moderator's queue of messages

- [CONFIG]—This token is used to override the settings the users can select by clicking the Config button on their browser. This feature is generally used in multiple-room chat environments where the administrator wants to control the settings, such as in a room where the chat is not monitored but is established for private conversations between two people. The syntax for this token is the same as the [MAIN] token.

- [BODY]—This token used only for Java-only output windows. Refer to The Chat Server manuals for Java implementation.

Tokens for Single-Room Sites Only:

- [LEAVEHTML]—If there is only one room in the chat facility, include this entry so that users can leave the room and return to the specified URL.

```
[LEAVEHTML]
http://localhost/intranet.html
```

Tokens for Multiple-Room Sites Only:

- [HTML]—Only one line is expected (and allowed) containing an URL and is used by chat servers on other ports as specified in the same datafile in multiroom implementation. The [TITLE] token is used in conjunction with this token to assist the other Chat Servers in understanding the title of the room as well as how to get there. Below are two examples; the first points to the introductory HTML page, the second points directly to the port of the room.

```
[HTML]
http://localhost/chatserver/lobby

[HTML]
http://localhost:9696/
```

Creating the Datafile of the Chat Rooms

Now that you have strained your eyes to review these tokens, take a look at the datafile that will be used for this example. The second room has been identified as The Lab in the datafile so that you can see how the choice of rooms can be implemented.

```
[PORT]
9696
[TITLE]
Lobby
[HTML]
http://localhost/chatserver/lobby.html
```

```
[ACTIONS]
says to¦<I>says to $1</I>: $2¦DEFAULT
shouts to¦<I>shouts to $1 (and draws a glare from the
receptionist)</I>:<B> $2</B>¦
scowls at¦<I>scowls at $1</I>: $2¦
winks at¦<I>winks at $1</I>: $2¦
nudges¦<I>softly nudges $1</I>: $2¦
nods to¦<I>nods knowingly to $1</I>: $2¦
inquires to¦<I>inquires to $1</I>: $2¦
smirks at¦<I>smirks at $1</I>: $2¦
kicks¦<I>kicks $1's leg</I>: $2¦
agrees with¦<I>agrees with $1</I>: $2¦
PRIVATELY whispers to¦<I>PRIVATELY whispers to $1</I>:
$2¦PRIVATE
[OPTIONS]
fair
[FULLURL]
http://localhost/chatserver/soldout.html

[PORT]
9999
[TITLE]
The Lab
[HTML]
http://localhost/chatserver/lab.html
[ACTIONS]
says to¦<I>says to $1</I>: $2¦DEFAULT
shouts to¦<I>shouts to $1 (and draws a glare from the
receptionist)</I>:<B> $2</B>¦
scowls at¦<I>scowls at $1</I>: $2¦
winks at¦<I>winks at $1</I>: $2¦
nudges¦<I>softly nudges $1</I>: $2¦
nods to¦<I>nods knowingly to $1</I>: $2¦
inquires to¦<I>inquires to $1</I>: $2¦
smirks at¦<I>smirks at $1</I>: $2¦
kicks¦<I>kicks $1's leg</I>: $2¦
agrees with¦<I>agrees with $1</I>: $2¦
PRIVATELY whispers to¦<I>PRIVATELY whispers to $1</I>:
$2¦PRIVATE
[OPTIONS]
fair
[FULLURL]
http://localhost/chatserver/soldout.html
```

```
[PORT]
0
[TITLE]
Leave the intranet Chat Facility
[HTML]
http://localhost/intranet/chatserver.html
[ACTIONS]
asfsadf
[OPTIONS]
```

The file that is shown here is called datafile. Please note that there is a [PORT] of 0 at the end. This is a little trick that allows the user to leave the chat facility. You will notice that two [PORT] tokens define two distinct rooms. This datafile would be used by the chat room specified at the top of the file on the port specified. A second instance of The Chat Server would be run on the port specified for the second room, and the datafile for that particular room would be similar to the one shown here, except that the detailed information for that chat room would be placed at the beginning of the file.

Starting The Chat Server

The example that has been developed for demonstration here uses the metaphor of an office tower with the lobby of the building being the chat room where the initial conversations take place. A second room, The Lab, has been established as a room that is intended to be monitored by the chat server administrator to provide assistance to those users who are having trouble using the chat environment. Within this second room, all the traffic is logged in order to debug the chat server and the user's problems with using the chat facility.

In order to do this, two instances of The Chat Server will be established and run, one for each of the rooms.

The tutorial that comes with The Chat Server extends this demonstration to show you how to include additional rooms to the site.

Setup for Session One: The Lobby

To start The Chat Server and incorporate the two room environment and the logging features in The Lab, the second room, this example starts one session as follows:

```
chatserver -c <config file> -p <port> [-m <max users>]
```

<config file> is the datafile, <port> is the port number, and <max users> sets the maximum number of users allowed within the room (default is 25).

Note

The version of The Chat Server included on the CD-ROM is limited to a maximum of five participants in a room.

Setup for Session Two: The Lab

Because the second room is designed for the administrator to monitor and respond to requests for assistance from inexperienced chat users or from those who are experiencing difficulty in getting the chat to work, the second session started is slightly different. This session uses a version of The Chat Server executable that contains a great deal of logging and debugging information.

```
chatserverlog [-v] [-l <logfile>] -c <config file> -p <port>
[-m <max users>]
```

"-v" is for "verbose" messages that will be displayed to stdout, indicating the status of The Chat Server. Use this option only for rooms with low traffic—there is a lot of output!

Startup of Sessions One and Two

The actual code lines to start up these two sessions are as follows:

```
chatserver -c datafile -p 9696 -m 25

chatserverlog -v -l /tmp/chatlog -c datafile -p 9999 -m 20 &
```

The ampersand (&) is standard Unix syntax for running the server in the background. The Windows command does not require the & character—the process will run in the background automatically.

Now start it up and test the program.

Testing the Chat Server

By entering the commands to start up the Chat Server at the end of the previous section, you should now be able to connect to the chat server from your HTML page. You can also type in directly the URL of the chat server as follows:

```
http://<URL of server running the Chat Server>:9696/
```

This is the address used by the server that has been used and identified in earlier examples:

```
http://localhost:9696/
```

You should now be connected. First you go directly to the chatroom and leave a message there. After that is done, open your introductory HTML page and return to the chatroom. Figure 21.3 shows the chat screen through the browser as you first come to the chatroom.

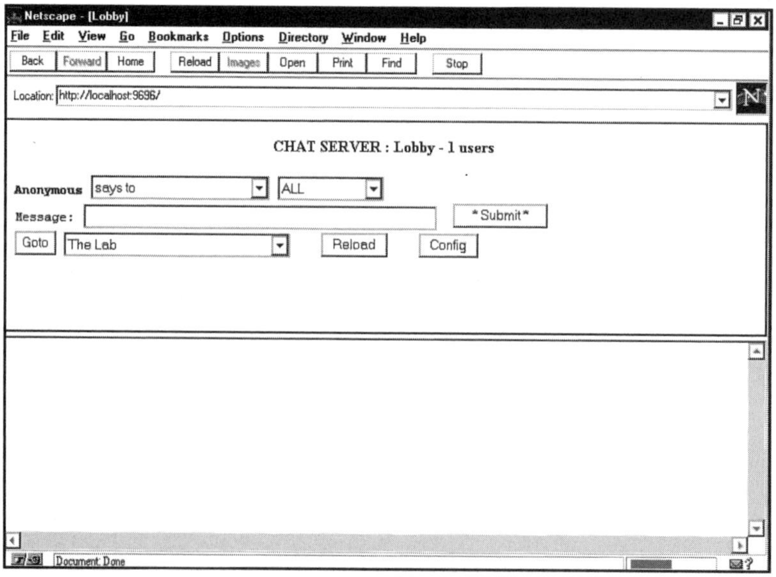

Figure 21.3

Entering The Lobby chatroom.

In figure 21.3 the Goto button enables the user to jump from room to room; you can see "The Lab" displayed in the window. The user has been identified as "anonymous" and the first of the actions shows in "Says To."

To change the user's identification, the user presses the Config button shown in the browser. Figure 21.4 shows the screen that appears when users desire to change a variety of user-related information, including the identification name by which they will be known throughout their chat session. The information items that can be changed by the users in this configuration area are relatively self-explanatory.

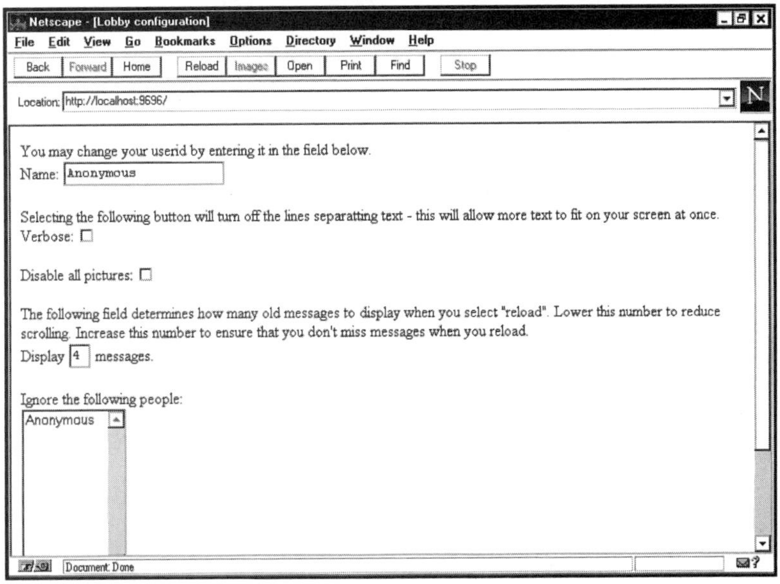

Figure 21.4

Changing user information by using the config button.

Now input some information to test that the chat server is functioning properly before trying it from the HTML page created earlier. Figure 21.5 shows the results within the browser after entering a few sample messages.

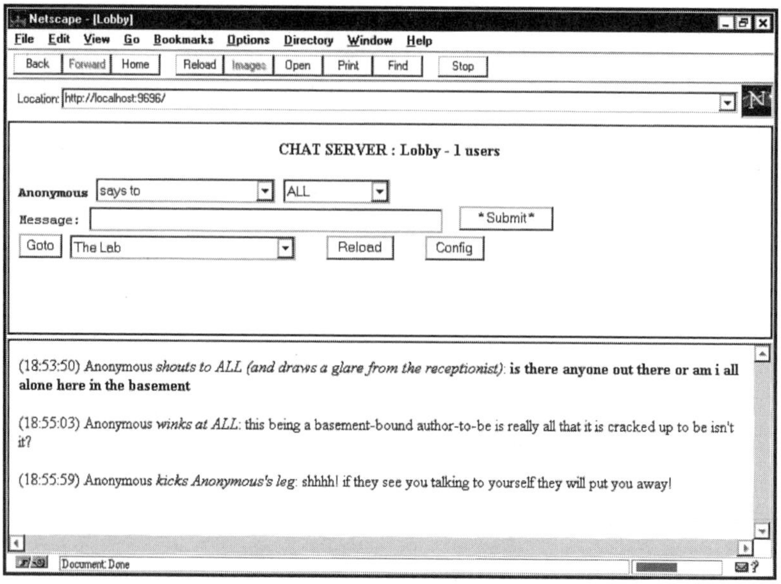

Figure 21.5

Testing The Chat Server.

Next, examine what happens when someone leaves and then another enters from an HTML page. You can review the HTML code that was written previously and recall that when the Submit button was clicked on, a hidden field called "Says To" captured the value "Enters the lobby..." and passed it to the server. You can see the results in figure 21.6, where a user who registered in the lobby as "high falutin' troll" entered and left a message.

So the software works. You have The Chat Server up and running. The next section goes over some of the "how to..." items that you should understand.

"How To..."

This section covers how to customize a couple of Chat Server features. These features, which appeared on the chat screen and are identified within the datafile, include the following:

- Customizing the background of the room

- Customizing the actions

- Adding Config and Reload buttons

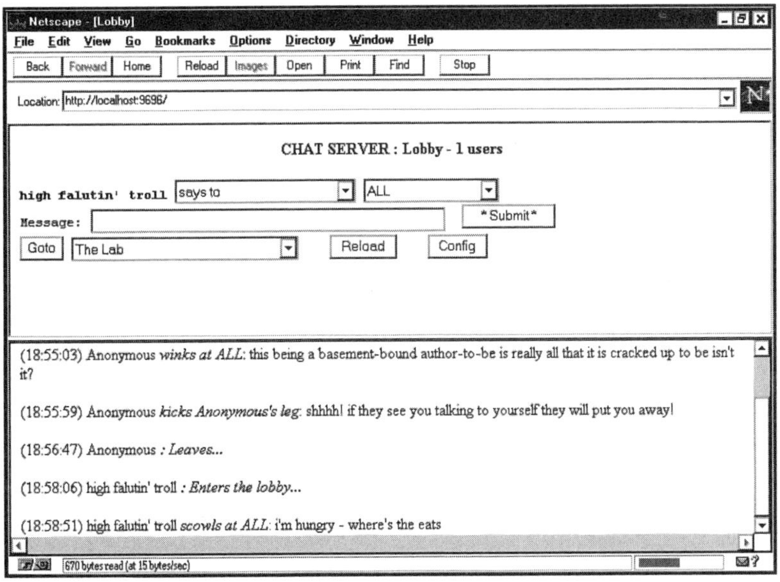

Figure 21.6

A hungry client
arrives.

Figure 21.6

A hungry client
arrives.

Customizing the Background of the Room

All of the customizing for a particular room is done within the configuration file. The basic way to customize is through the implementation of HTML at the top of the page. The only restriction about including HTML elements is that they must, repeat, MUST appear on a single line following the [HEADER] token in the configuration file. The Chat Server is programmed to receive a single line of instructions for this token and will not operate properly if the instructions span more that one line. The length of the one line does not matter.

The following three code lines grow from the first to the third and give you a idea of how you can customize the chat site.

First:

```
[HEADER]
<BODY BGCOLOR="#00FF00">
```

Next:

```
[HEADER]
<BODY BGCOLOR="#00FF00"><IMG SRC="http://localhost/troll.jpg">
```

Then:

```
[HEADER]
<BODY BGCOLOR="#00FF00"><IMG SRC="http://localhost/troll.jpg"><A
HREF="http://localhost/survey.html>Chat User Survey</A>
```

Warning

> Be aware that each of the preceding code sets are actually only 2
> lines. If your code sets don't stick to only two lines, you will receive
> an error message.

And so on.

Customizing the Actions

The actions that were included on the form are limited in nature. The
Systems Administrator can create the appropriate actions that are required for a site and then implement them. For example, in a meeting
where resolutions or motions are put forward and voted upon, the actions for a chatroom called "The Boardroom" may be Move, Second,
Vote Aye, Vote Nay, Throw Ash Tray, Snickering Behind Hand, and so
on. This ability to customize enables a chatroom full of people to hold
a meeting and cut and paste their resolutions right into the message
window. If people had these prepared in advance, it would be rather
easy to cut and paste them in. In fact, figure 21.7 shows a message
from "the troll" where he pasted a message containing most of this
paragraph, just for demonstration's sake.

Figure 21.7

The Chat Server—
cut and paste is
possible into
message window.

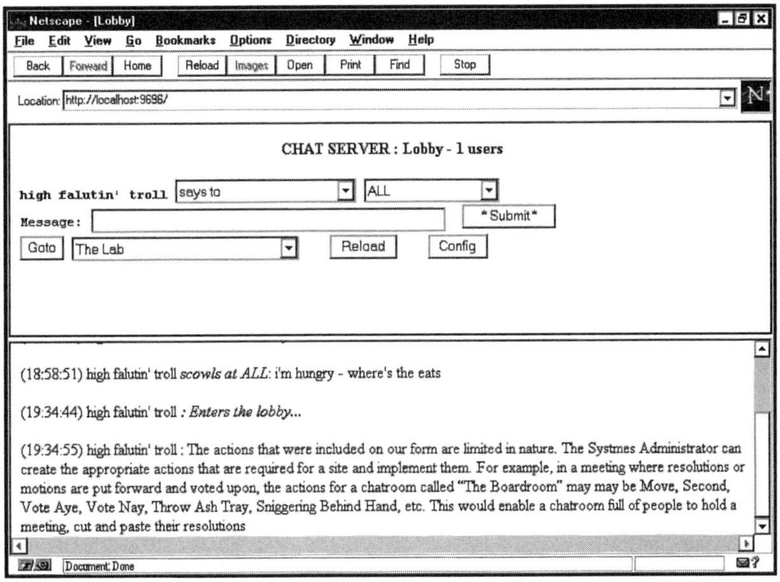

Adding Config and Reload Buttons

The Config button allows the users to jump to a page where they can change their login name and customize their interface to the room. For example, they can choose to ignore people in the room or set how many messages to start with in the room when it is reloaded. The Config page link can be represented either by the button or by a hyperlink. A sample datafile containing a Config button is shown here:

```
[PORT]
9696
[FRAMESIZE]
100,*
[MAIN]
<B>$USER</B> says: <INPUT NAME="SAYS" SIZE=20>
<INPUT NAME="SUBMIT" TYPE="SUBMIT" VALUE="Submit Message">
<INPUT NAME="HISTORY" TYPE="HIDDEN" VALUE="$HISTORY">
<INPUT NAME="NOPIC"   TYPE="HIDDEN" VALUE="$NOPIC">
```

```
<INPUT NAME="USER"    TYPE="HIDDEN" VALUE="$USER">
<INPUT NAME="VERBOSE" TYPE="HIDDEN" VALUE="$VERBOSE">
</FORM><FORM ACTION="/BANNER" METHOD="POST" TARGET="_top">
<CENTER>
<INPUT NAME="HISTORY" TYPE="HIDDEN" VALUE="$HISTORY">
<INPUT NAME="NOPIC"   TYPE="HIDDEN" VALUE="$NOPIC">
<INPUT NAME="USER"    TYPE="HIDDEN" VALUE="$USER">
<INPUT NAME="VERBOSE" TYPE="HIDDEN" VALUE="$VERBOSE">
<INPUT NAME="CONFIG"  TYPE="SUBMIT" VALUE="Config">
</CENTER>
```

The Reload button simply reloads the chatroom page, clearing the list of messages if it is exceedingly long. Only the number of messages that are specified in the Config button is maintained.

A sample datafile to include a Reload button is shown here:

```
[PORT]
9696
[FRAMESIZE]
100,*
[MAIN]
<B>$USER</B> says: <INPUT NAME="SAYS" SIZE=20>
<INPUT NAME="SUBMIT" TYPE="SUBMIT" VALUE="Submit Message">
<INPUT NAME="HISTORY" TYPE="HIDDEN" VALUE="$HISTORY">
<INPUT NAME="NOPIC"   TYPE="HIDDEN" VALUE="$NOPIC">
<INPUT NAME="USER"    TYPE="HIDDEN" VALUE="$USER">
<INPUT NAME="VERBOSE" TYPE="HIDDEN" VALUE="$VERBOSE">
</FORM><FORM ACTION="/BANNER" METHOD="POST" TARGET="_top">
<CENTER>
<INPUT NAME="HISTORY" TYPE="HIDDEN" VALUE="$HISTORY">
<INPUT NAME="NOPIC"   TYPE="HIDDEN" VALUE="$NOPIC">
<INPUT NAME="USER"    TYPE="HIDDEN" VALUE="$USER">
<INPUT NAME="VERBOSE" TYPE="HIDDEN" VALUE="$VERBOSE">
<INPUT NAME="CONFIG"  TYPE="SUBMIT" VALUE="  Config  ">
<INPUT NAME="RELOAD"  TYPE="SUBMIT" VALUE="Reload">
</CENTER>
```

These simple techniques enable the Systems Administrator to customize The Chat Server so that any type of conference room can be created.

Moderated Rooms

It is possible to have moderated rooms where discussions are guided by the moderator and usually focus around a guest of some sort.

The moderator acts as a filter in the room and must approve all messages, except for postings by the guest, before they are visible to everyone. The moderator has the ability to submit, discard, and reply to users' messages.

The Administrator has the ability to remove users from a room as well as the ability to close down a room and restart it.

Note

Both moderated and unmoderated rooms can have administrators.

To enable administration, moderation, and guest functionality, the follow tokens are needed in the datafile for the room in question:

```
[ADMIN]
password
[MODERATOR]
password
[GUEST]
password2
```

In the preceding list, the passwords that are shown should be replaced by the chat server administrator for security reasons.

The regular users of the room enter as normal, but the moderator and guest enter from a slightly different angle. An HTML page can be created for the moderator which contains code similar to the following:

```
<FORM ACTION="http://localhost:9696/" METHOD=POST>
Moderator's Name: <INPUT NAME="MODNAME" VALUE="" SIZE=25><BR>
Moderator's Password: <INPUT NAME="MODPWD" VALUE="" SIZE=25><BR>
<INPUT TYPE=HIDDEN NAME="HISTORY" VALUE="6">
```

```
<INPUT TYPE=SUBMIT NAME="SUBMIT" VALUE="Enter Room">
</FORM>
```

This enables the moderator to do the following:

- Submit the message to all

- Discard the message

- Shuffle the message back into the queue

- Reply by submitting the user's message as well as one by the moderator

- Send a message on his or her own

- Reload the screen and display the first queued message

Figure 21.8 shows the moderator's screen called from a simple HTML page.

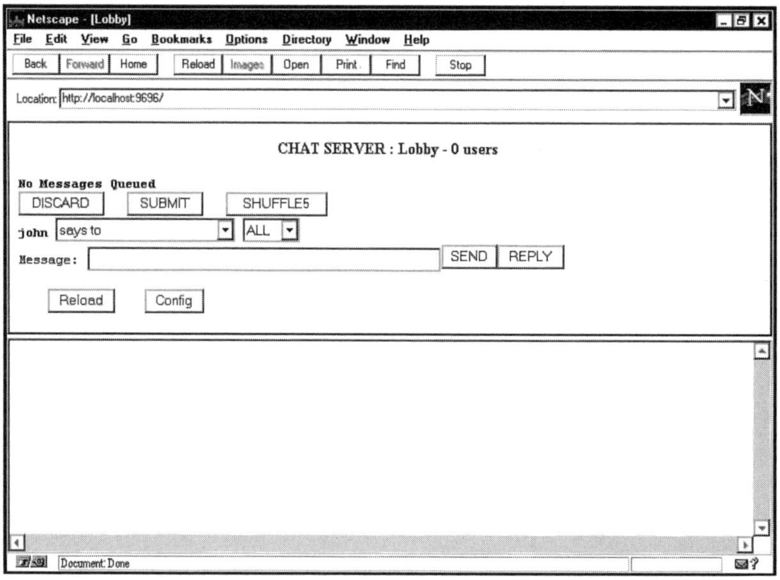

Figure 21.8

The Chat Server—the moderator's screen.

Maintaining The Chat Server

Aside from moderating the rooms and the creation and maintenance of new rooms and their configuration files, little work is involved in running The Chat Server. Once the server is up and running, however, the log files need to be maintained.

When The Chat Server is started, the name and location of the log file is entered on the command line, as demonstrated earlier. The file can safely be renamed and moved while The Chat Server is running because the program will automatically create a new log file under the original name.

The log file can be erased, reviewed, and could even be indexed within a text search engine for search and retrieval processes. Because these files tend to be quite large, it is recommended you use a tool such as a text editor or HTML Transit (see Chapter 16, "Converting Documents for the Intranet"), to break them down into smaller, more manageable chunks.

Security Documentation

The Chat Server supports password protection either by user identification or by room. The two methods are exclusive of each other initially, but they can be combined to force users to obtain the appropriate membership to participate in conferences. The user needs to have an entry in the password file as well as know the password for a particular room in order to "pass Go."

The format for The Chat Server password file is as follows:

```
<login>@<password>
```

<login> is the user's login name, which can be made up of any character except for (@), and <password> is the user's password.

The passwords are not encrypted—that would impair performance. The password file should be owned by the user account running The Chat Server, and it should be readable only by that account.

To enable passwords within a room, the [PASSWORDFILE] token must be in the configuration/datafile as well as the appropriate entry under the [OPTIONS] heading.

```
[PASSWORDFILE]
/book/research/website/htdocs/chatserver/passwd
[OPTIONS]
fair
```

The absolute path to the password file must be given, as in the example code. The security levels available under options are as follows:

- default—The default security level is *none* and any passwords entered are ignored.

- fair—A password file is used. When the chatroom is full, users with passwords are allowed in, but those without are turned away. Thus, the size of the room is stretched beyond the maximum limits set in the startup command line.

- secure—"No ticket, no laundry!"

There is a difference to keep in mind here. The user's online name is not necessarily the user ID. The following code block is an example of what could be used on an HTML entry page to the chat facility:

```
<FORM ACTION="http://localhost:9696/">
Who Are You?: <INPUT NAME="USER" VALUE="Anonymous" SIZE=20>
<I>As the B52's said, "Bang Bang on the Door Baby":</I>
Login:    <INPUT NAME="LOGIN" VALUE="" SIZE=10>
Password: <INPUT NAME="USERPASS" VALUE="" SIZE=10>
<INPUT TYPE="SUBMIT" VALUE="Chat">
</FORM>
```

Figure 21.9 shows a variation of that code to create an HTML page that requires the user to enter the information. The NAME entry would be the user's online name. The others are self-explanatory.

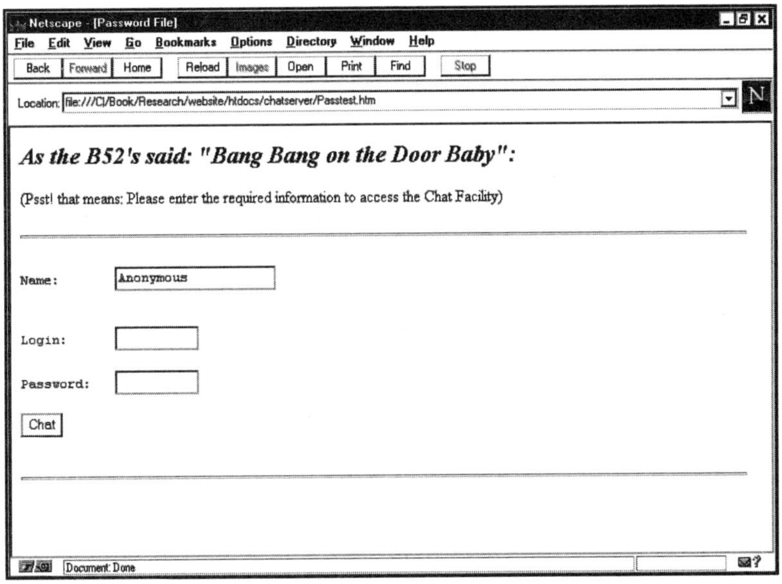

Figure 21.9

The Chat Server— sample password form.

If the users do not put in the correct password information, they should be routed the HTML file listed under the [SECUREURL] token in the datafile.

Password protection of the room can be done by entering the [PASSWORD] token in the datafile with the appropriate password underneath.

```
[PASSWORD]
hunkydory
```

The password for the room is "hunkydory." Creating the HTML entry form for the room is similar to that for the entry page in figure 21.9. Simply remove the Login field from the entry form.

Vendor List

The following short table is a list of vendors of chat server products. This list, like any other in the book, is bound to be incomplete—both at the time of writing and the time of reading. The author has not tested all of these products, but provides the list for comparison sake.

The Chat Server—Magma Communications

http://chat.magmacom.com

EZIRC Server—Surfing Squirrel Products

http://www.surfingsquirrel.com

KeepTalking—UNET2 Corporation

http://www.keeptalking.com

Webline95—company uncertain

http://x.gen.il.us/webline95/

Global Stage Chat Server—Prospero Systems Research

http://he.net/~prospero/globalchat/download.html

Netscape Chat—do I have to put in the name?

http://home.netscape.com

Channels—TEAM Software Inc

http://www.channels.com

iChat Server—iChat

http://www.ichat.com

CommunityAct—Amicus Networks

http://www.amicus.com

Status Check

After having run through the sample application solution for a chat server, you should be able to quickly and easily put in place an instance of this type of online conferencing system.

You must keep in mind the differences between these real-time conferences and the business processes that they support; and the forums described in the chapter on workflow, groupware, and the intranet. Both can support different facets of the same business process, but they tend to provide different methodologies that may have markedly different acceptance levels within an organization.

This chapter has covered the installation, configuration, and maintenance of a chat facility. The uses for and types of conferences that can be held within this type of software are limited only by the imagination.

22

Simple Intra-Company ftp Servers

T he File Transfer Protocol (ftp) service provides a means for you to collect your files; put them into an archive, a storage space for the documents; and make them available for retrieval.

This book focuses on the most familiar method of ftp on the Internet—anonymous ftp. This method enables people to log on by providing a username and a password whether or not they have an actual user account on the server. By specifying *anonymous* as the username, users can log onto the ftp server. The convention is to ask people for their e-mail address as the password so that the server administrator can find out who has been using the system. Typically, the server administrator will not permit access to people who do not enter an e-mail address that has a valid e-mail format (xxx@yyy.zzz).

Because your intranet has security features built into the systems via the routers (assuming routers have filtering abilities) as well as at the server, you can be comfortable knowing that the users coming into the intranet systems are from your organization. (For a review of intranet security, refer to Chapter 5, "Intranet Security," or to *Internet Security Professional Reference* by Chris Hare, et al. [New Riders].) Because almost any computer system can be compromised, it is recommended that you keep sensitive materials off the ftp server.

For security purposes, the anonymous ftp users are restricted to seeing only part of the file structure on the actual server. The ftp server allows the users to only view directory listings, upload files to designated areas, and download files to their workstations from designated areas. You do not want to allow users to have access to the areas of the machine such as the place the executable files for the server operations are kept—you do not want to take the chance that someone may accidentally corrupt or erase any files. Because you can restrict the ftp access to certain areas of the server, it is relatively safe to set up and use.

Ftp will store data in any format. It takes a bit of effort to set up the server itself and maintain the lists of available files. Following is more information on setting up the server and managing the service. Here are the topics that will be covered in this chapter as the ftp server is established:

- What an archive is and why you need one

- Setting up the ftp service

- Maintaining the ftp archive

Warning

This chapter is predominantly technical in nature and requires that you understand the basics of Unix and/or Windows NT. For more detailed information on the work that is being done here, or if you have difficulty in following the information presented, please consult with your systems administrator. You can also refer to the following books for excellent advice: George Eckel's *Building a Unix Internet Server* (New Riders, 1995); and *Building a Windows NT Internet Server* by Eric Harper, Matt Arnett, and R. Paul Singh (New Riders, 1995).

The first step is to define the need for an archive of documents housed within an ftp server.

Note

> You may ask why the ftp server is covered in this book when Chapter 14, "Document Management," discusses the need for a document management system. An organization with the resources to implement a document management system may choose to do so. But at some point, there may be some rationale, perhaps stale dating, extraneous versions, or space availability on the main server, for moving some of the company's information into an archive that can allow access should an organization feel the need. The ftp server can provide the means to store and retrieve those documents. It is also possible to create a WAIS index of the text-based files that the users could search to find text documents they seek.
>
> In some small organizations without the resources to implement a document management system, the ftp server can serve as a proxy. It can work if you incorporate a searchable index of the text files and create (perhaps with Cold Fusion) a searchable database of document titles that is accessible for user input via a form within an intranet HTML document.
>
> Because there may be an occasion for the implementation of an ftp server, this chapter will take you through the development of a Windows NT and a Unix ftp server.

What an Archive Is and Why You Need One

You have almost developed a three-phase information model, relative to the currency and timeliness of the facts and documents in the intranet. The phases are as follows:

- Phase 1—The inclusion of documents, reports, and the like that are created by the content providers of your organization for dissemination by the intranet. The current versions of the documents are displayed when the user selects the hyperlink that provides access to the file that was perhaps converted using the tools outlined in Chapter 16, "Converting Documents for the Intranet."

- Phase 2—The implementation of group work tools such as discussion forums or workflow tools that provide dynamic discussion about current projects and events, such as was described in Chapter 17, "Workflow Software, Groupware, and the Intranet," and in Chapter 20, "Simple Intra-Company Newsgroups."

- Phase 3—The outdated versions of documents that have been superseded by a new edition or just plain, stale data, with no demand from anyone within the company. These documents are the ones that no one wants to throw away because some day....

Your intranet server, HTML-based, provides you the latest facts, figures, images, sounds, and, maybe some day, smells (scratch-and sniff-cards that are bundled with your software?). "What's New" sections, project and corporate newsgroups, and a large amount of other information that users need to know are presented now through the intranet HTML pages.

At some point in the life cycle of a document, its facts may no longer be current. Another version of the document may be created, superceding the current version. Marketing promotions may have ending dates that are past and have been replaced by newer promotions.

Even though, for example, Caterpillar, the heavy equipment manufacturer, prides itself on being able to meet the demand for parts 96 percent of the time for every machine model ever sold, the drawings of those machines (which are probably older than you or I) may no longer be required in today's intranet. However, they do need to be available for review should someone have the need to see them.

Thus, the ftp server can provide the means for the storage and retrieval of large quantities of information, an archive, that may be needed, however infrequently.

Role of the Data Librarian

Someone has to take care of the information that is stored within the ftp server. Many organizations refer to the manager of the ftp archive as the "data librarian" because much of the activity that goes on within the archive is the classification, categorization, and storage of the files. Putting the information into the appropriate locations within the directory structure and providing the necessary links to the documents from within the ftp server is a necessary function. In many cases, the role of the data librarian falls to the systems administrator, who ends up maintaining the service by default because it runs on the server that he or she operates.

The documents that fall into the third phase of this model are not so much time-related as they are volume-related. The difference in the port numbers where the ftp server and the HTTP server are located are important factors when establishing document retrieval mechanisms, as discussed later. Large files require a longer connection time between the browser and the server when downloading files. By bringing down a 10 MB file through the HTTP server, you are occupying that resource for the length of time of the transfer. If the HTTP server is a busy one, and you should certainly plan for your intranet server to be very active, you do not want people "hogging" the bandwidth from your showpiece.

The use of ftp servers within the intranet (and you may need multiple servers in some cases, depending upon the amount of data and the frequency of access) provides a means to place a hyperlink on the HTML page of the intranet server pointing at a large file for retrieval. However, instead of starting the file transfer process from the HTTP server, the link takes you to the ftp server where you select the document and initiate the download. Using the Back button on your browser, you can return to the intranet pages and continue to search the sites while the ftp server continues the download in the background. This does not impede the intranet server unless you have the ftp server running on the same physical machine as the the intranet main server (the HTTP server).

It is recommended that you use another computer to run the ftp site if you are going to have any large volume of traffic or files to transfer.

The ftp Service

In order to establish an information archive using the ftp server for the delivery of the information, the ftp server session must be set up and configured. The following sections discuss the requirements for doing the following:

- Setting up a Unix-based ftp server

- Setting up a Windows NT-based ftp server

Setting Up a Unix-based ftp Server

The ftp service, ftpd, comes with most brands of Unix and can be found in the */etc* or */usr/etc* directory. Following are the two parts of the ftp archive of documents:

- The server that responds to client requests for files

- A filesystem that the ftp server scans

The standard Unix implementation of the ftp server is *ftpd* or *in.ftpd*.

Author's Note

> The following discussion runs a little heavy on the actual Unix side of things, more so than earlier in the book. However, this chapter doesn't delve too deeply into the topic. I would recommend that you refer to *Intranet Working* by George Eckel (New Riders, 1996) for a fuller discussion of how to set up the Unix server in a more complete fashion.

When you set up the server, ftpd runs under the Unix superserver, inetd, which then listens to TCP port 21, the ftp control port. As described earlier in the book, based on the type of protocol in the URL, the packet will get sent to the appropriate port of the inetd server. For ftp the default port is 21 on the destination host. Please refer to Chapter 3, "HTTP: Building the Application Layer," if you feel the need to review the HTTP server (the intranet server) and ports.

Note

> IP numbers identify specific computers; port numbers identify specific services running on the same computer. Because you may have more than one service running on the computer, the port number makes sure the message gets to the right service.
>
> HTTP servers are usually located at port 80 while port 21 is used for the ftp services within this example. These are the de facto standards.

When the TCP packet is received at port 21, a new fptd service is started to handle the request. This will happen for each request that arrives at port 21. Because you have the ftp server running under inetd, you need to add an ftp user to the host's */etc/passwd* file. Before allowing the anonymous user to connect to the system the following occurs:

1. The server checks to see that the user *anonymous* is allowed to use the service.

2. The ftp user's entry in the */etc/passwd* file is verified—the password should be " * " to prevent any password from matching the encrypted password.

3. The server checks to see if the user has permissions to gain access to the directories of the ftp service. The password entry should also contain the login directory name, which becomes the user's root directory using the chroot( ) system call.

This restricts the users to the specific area you would like them to see.

Many server administrators also establish a standard domain name for the ftp site, (for example *"ftp.inforium.com"*). This makes it relatively easy for people to find the ftp site within the intranet. Please refer to Chapter 3, or Chapter 4, "Fundamentals of TCP/IP: Understanding the Transport Layer," if you feel the need to review domain names and how they work within the intranet.

The filesystem to which the ftp server restricts the anonymous logins, via chroot( ), must have a special structure, contain certain files, and contain certain executables. Because the ftp user's login directory has become the root directory for the ftp server, the files are copied to the appropriate place under the */users/ftp/* directory. You need to perform the following steps to establish the required structure:

1. Create the ftp user's login directory and three directories underneath that one: *bin, etc,* and *pub.*

2. Copy the host's ls program into the *bin* subdirectory just created.

3. Assign minimal password and group information to the files to provide ftpd with the information to map user and group IDs back to names, but omit dangerous encrypted password data; password information should never be made available—avoid any chances of the system being compromised.

4. Set the appropriate permissions using the chmod( ) command (refer to the Unix manual for a complete discussion of the modes described here, should you so desire) for the directories listed here:

   • The login directory should be owned by the root user and should be readable and executable by all users (mode 555).

   • The *bin* subdirectory should be owned by *root* and group *wheel* or *other.* This directory should be executable but unreadable and unwritable by all users (mode 111). This enables the anonymous users to execute ls.

   • The *etc* subdirectory should be owned by root and should be executable but not unreadable and unwritable (mode 111).

   • The *pub* subdirectory should be owned by root or the user who administers the archive and should be readable and executable by all users (mode 555).

You could set up some optional subdirectories, including an *incoming* directory to allow users to upload the file. If you intend to allow people to upload files, and this certainly should be the case, the incoming subdirectory should be owned by *root*, group *wheel* or *other*, with write and execute permissions set for group and other (mode 733). In order to protect the files in the directory from being deleted or renamed by other users of the host (other than the ftp users), set the sticky bit on the directory with **chmod 1733 incoming.**

Note

> If you are getting stuck here, please refer to your systems administrator or the Unix manual for an explanation. As was indicated at the beginning of the chapter, this information is highly technical and will require such assistance.

Testing Your ftp Service

Test your service out by connecting with your favorite ftp client. Most Web browsers will allow you to use ftp—in fact, Netscape Navigator now allows ftp file upload as well as download.

1. From a plain vanilla Unix ftp client, ftp, enter this:

   ```
   % ftp 0
   ```

2. If everything works, you will see a message on the screen that contains the following lines (and probably more):

   ```
   Connected to 0
   Name(0:user):
   ```

3. Now try logging in as the anonymous user by entering the following:

   ```
   Name(0:user): ftp
   ```

4. You will see a message like the following if you have successfully logged in:

   ```
   331 Guest login ok, send ident as password
   Password:
   ```

5. Enter your e-mail address as the password, and you should see the following, if successful:

   ```
   Password:
   230 Guest login ok, assess restrictions apply
   Remote system type is UNIX
   Using binary mode to transfer files
   ftp>
   ```

6. By entering the ls command, you will get a listing of all the sub-directories created as well as any files in the directory. The syntax is as follows:

```
ftp>ls
```

7. In order to obtain a file that you see, use the following syntax:

```
Get filename pathname_for_storage
```

8. Enter the following from the ftp> prompt to get the file and place it into the *\data\temp* subdirectory on your hard disk:

```
ftp> get i_want_this_file c:\data\temp
```

If this works and it provides you with a confirmation message and the file in the *\data\temp* directory, you are ready to try to upload a file to the incoming subdirectory.

9. After connecting and changing to the incoming directory, try to send a file to the ftp server using the following:

```
ftp> put /data/temp file_for_upload
ftp> ls
```

10. The ls command is used to test the incoming directory to see if the file is there. If the read permissions have been turned off, as suggested earlier, and this is the only file to have been uploaded to the directory, the ls command would have sent the following message back:

```
ftp> ls
200 PORT command successful
150 Opening ASCII mode data connection for /bin/ls
. unreadable
total 2
226 Transfer complete.
ftp>
```

What you see is actually what you are supposed to see—nothing. Because you don't want people to see the files that have been listed here

in the upload, all you can do is judge by the number of files. The "."
file is there, as you can see in the message. It is the only file that is actually in the directory at all times.

Tip

> Here's a little tip that you can use to double-check if you were suc-
> cessful in uploading files under the preceding conditions. Before you
> use the put command, enter the ls command and make note of the
> number of files that are currently in the directory. Then put the file
> onto the ftp server and enter the ls command one more time. The
> number should have been incremented by one.

If these simple tests have worked, you are now ready to get the ftp archive up and running.

Setting Up a Windows NT-based ftp Server

In the Windows NT software, an ftp client is included to facilitate file
transfers between machines in the network. NT also provides an ftp
server so that other machines can initiate the file transfers.

For security reasons, Microsoft recommends that you install the ftp
Server service on an NTFS (NT File System) partition so that the files
and directories available through ftp can be secured. The security model is integrated with the NT security model, with access to the directories and files maintained by the Windows NT security structure.

To install the ftp Server services, perform the following steps:

1. From the Control Panel, choose the Network icon.

2. In Network Settings, select Add Software.

3. Select TCP/IP Protocol and Related Components to bring up the
   NT TCP/IP Installation Options dialog box.

4. Select the ftp Server Services option.

5. Click on OK, and then Yes, to initiate the copying of files.

After the files have been copied and the software is installed, you can configure the services through the ftp Service dialog box.

Configure the service for the maximum number of connections and the home or root directory you want the users to see when they log in. This is based on the directories that provide them the ability to read and download files and, if you provide them permissions, to upload files. To configure the anonymous connections, you can allow the users to employ the username Anonymous. The password is the user account name and, by default, has the same privileges as user Guest. To review the privileges associated with the Guest account, please review the Windows NT Server documentation or check with the Systems Administrator.

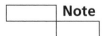 **Note**

It is recommended that you create a default Anonymous user by using the User Account Editor of Windows NT and entering the username and rights you choose to provide in the appropriate field.

Select the option to allow anonymous connections to enable only the ftp service and maintain some measure of security. The only passwords that are unencrypted across the network are the usernames of the people logging in with the Anonymous account. To complete the configuration process, click on OK.

Note

Normally when you log into a server on a network, you are asked for two things: your username and your password. Any time you enter your password into a network, a potential exists that someone is out there trying to obtain passwords by "sniffing" the network, sort of like a phone tap. In the anonymous ftp world, the username is always anonymous, and the password that you are asked to enter is a password that you should never tell to anyone. The de facto standard on the Internet is to have the users enter their e-mail address. Within the intranet, you can have the users enter their e-mail address or, because the users are all employed by the same firm, just their usernames.

This provides a measure of security because at no time is the password ever entered into an ftp site.

After the ftp Server services start, an ftp Server icon appears for managing the server. Activate the icon, and the ftp User Sessions dialog box appears. The users currently connected to the ftp service appear, complete with IP address, how long they have been connected, and if they logged in using the Anonymous account, the passwords they used. This information is available to the IntraMaster to help in the evaluation of the site's usage and performance and helps in the determination of the value of the service in supporting business processes.

If you feel like the "Supreme Ruler of the Earth/Intranet," you can disconnect all the users with the push of a button at the bottom of the dialog box. This allows you a measure of control over people who abuse the service, though it is unlikely there would be any.

By selecting the Security button, you can review and configure each partition on the system for read and write access. To increase the security of the system for ftp purposes, place all the sensitive documents on a separate partition and grant neither read nor write access to that partition. To allow users to download files only, select the Allow Read but not the Allow Write checkbox.

To allow users to upload files, create an incoming subdirectory on the server under each branch of the directory structure where it is applicable, and select the Allow Write checkbox. Leave the Allow Read checkbox blank so that users cannot see what has been uploaded.

Maintaining the ftp Archive

Once you have the ftp sever up and running, you will need to organize the information and get it up into the archive.

Remember that most browsers used in the intranet enable users to graphically click and select files for download. The ftp archive gives the user another option for retrieving files. For example, in your intranet example, you can provide access to the collection of CAD drawings that you have in one of two fashions:

- Create an HTML page with a link to the file in which the URL will instruct the browser to ask the user what to do with the file (including saving the file to disk).

- Create an ftp archive with a subdirectory full of the drawing files for the users to "get" and copy to the (current) directory on their hard drive.

One of the big differences here is the port number that is used—the ftp service example here uses port 21 while the HTTP server uses port 80. As the demands on the intranet HTTP server increase, especially with the use of forms and CGI scripts, the use of port 80 for file transfer will slow the HTTP server down. Thus, you can use the ftp service to move larger files between computers in the intranet. If you have a busy intranet, you do not want the users to find access slow or unavailable because someone is trying to access the large CAD files referred to in the example via the intranet HTTP server. Use the ftp port, which is designed for file transfer and is in most cases going to be used less than your HTML site.

Note

This is sort of like having a service entrance to an office tower. The clients and people working can get in through the front door and up the passenger elevators (the intranet server). At the same time, the service entrance and freight elevator (the ftp server) can be used to get the tools that people need to operate their businesses in and out of the building.

A directory structure will need to be created to enable the organization and storage of files in logical groups. The ftp manager can and should delegate the authority to maintain the subdirectories to the appropriate staff member—if maintaining on a divisional or project basis. Transferring the ownership of a directory is as easy as having the systems administrator entering the chown command as follows:

```
chown userid subdirectory_name
```

The new owners would be responsible for keeping the files current and organized, creating their own subdirectories, and maintaining a README file that outlines what is in the directory. The README file should contain a list of the standard filename extensions that are used, and any non-standard extensions that are present in the directory should be identified here.

In the Windows NT environment, use the User Account Editor to set up the rights of ownership for the users.

Status Check

At this point you should have an understanding of the way an ftp server can be used as a place to archive documents—both from the perspective of the "old and ancient" documents that are not used regularly but still required occasionally and the perspective of reducing the traffic of large files being retrieved through the "front door" of the HTTP server.

You should now also understand how to set up the ftp server on both a Unix platform and the Windows NT server.

Author's Note

> Considering the ease of implementation and server maintenance, the graphic front end offered by Windows NT is certainly nicer, in my opinion, to work with, but both platforms work terrificly.

Should you need any more assistance on setting up the ftp server in your environment, refer to George Eckel's *Intranet Working* (New Riders, 1996). It is an excellent book and a very good reference for all your networking questions as they relate to intranets, in addition to the sections dealing with the ftp server.

Know Thyself

And thus the reader has arrived at the final chapter of this book. It is definitely not the last of the intranet.

In the last chapter of a book of this nature, the reader is usually provided with a summary of what went on during the book and what it means to the reader. This book uses a slightly different tack.

This book assumes that, if you have read this far without turning here to see "whodunnit," you have an interest in establishing an intranet that meets the current needs of your organization. This chapter assumes that you need to make certain that your intranet is also built with the future in mind. In order to build for the future, as the architect of the organization's intranet, you should review the following sections of this chapter:

- Know Thyself

- Peering into the Crystal Ball

- Places to "Play and Learn"

Know Thyself

"Know Thyself" is the translation for the Greek, "Gnothe Seauton"— a good approach to the implementation of an intranet.

This book stresses the need to implement the intranet in support of the mission-critical business processes that drive the organization's efforts to achieve its objectives, goals, and vision. Before one can start to put in place the means to support these business processes, a thorough understanding of the company's vision, and how this is to be achieved, is required.

The company's business plan is the starting point. The objectives of the business, the measurable targets, are identified here for all levels of the company. The critical success factors that outline how these objectives will be reached are also detailed. By breaking these critical success factors into the series of activities that need to be performed, an analysis of the information requirements at every point along the various processes provides the foundation for the intranet.

Knowing what information needs to be in whose hands when and where it's needed should be the result of the above analysis. Ensuring that the information is delivered as mentioned is the job of the intranet.

Understanding the Organization

In order to create an intranet necessary to meet the outlined requirements, it should be built to support the business processes that currently drive the company. In order to support those business processes as the company evolves toward the future, an understanding of the organization and its reason for existence is required. This requires the analysis and thorough understanding of the company's following:

- Vision—its philosophy and driving force for the future

- Mission—its business definition

- Business objectives—how the company measures success

- Critical success factors—the means of achieving success

- Strategies—key decisions, protocols, policies, and plans

- Mission-critical processes—activities performed

Once the company has been reviewed from the vision, at the top, to the individual activities that are grouped together to make up the mission-critical processes, an intranet can be designed and the implementation begun.

In designing the intranet, you must consider the current needs of the organization and the resources that are available to implement the intranet. In some cases, the current needs of the company can be handled by the implementation of an internal Web site. However, because businesses operate in an ever-changing global marketplace, the ability to scale up the intranet to meet the information demands that will be caused by changes in the way the company does its business is of paramount importance. This is why the following section on the evolution of the "internal Web site" to "Enterprise intranet," as described more fully in Chapter 12, "Alternative Corporate Information Models," is repeated in brief.

An Evolving Intranet

Four basic models of the intranet are in and of themselves solutions for an organization. In order for the intranet to offer itself as an enterprise alternative to client/server computing, the progression from "Simple IntraWeb" toward "Enterprise intranet" must occur. The models through which the typical evolution of the intranet takes place are listed here:

- **Simple IntraWeb**—The IntraWeb, as discussed in Chapter 1, "Intranet: Building the Corporate-Wide Web," is really just an internal Web server that publishes static pages of HTML text. The Browser opens up a connection to the server, and the server returns the page and closes the connection. A measure of interaction can be added by creating lists of links to sites that the user might be interested in reviewing. This model serves as the first step in most organizations that try to demonstrate the ability to incorporate an electronic distribution facility for static documents.

- **Interactive "IntraWeb"**—This model contains forms, fields, and buttons (as outlined in Chapter 9, "Beyond Basic HTML: Using Forms to Handle Information") that take input from the user before opening a connection to the server to allow the data and choices to be transmitted. The HTTP server passes the information to a custom server program or script for processing and then, in turn, a new page is passed back to the browser for viewing. The connection between browser and server is then broken.

  This model increases the ability of the intranet to extract information from databases and text collections based on the user's criteria and returns that information to the user. Not knowing what the user requires in terms of specific data, the intranet provides the facility for the user to specify the criteria and retrieve the information from the stores held within the intranet server and its databases.

- **Distributed "IntraWeb"**—This takes into account and utilizes the current infrastructure of the organization with its distributed data sources throughout the organization. The simple action of opening an HTML file invokes the procedure on behalf of the user. Through the introduction of the Java programming language, small programs, called applets, can be incorporated into the pages sent to the browser.

  Even though the browser/server model has been used for the initial internal Web site, all the processing is done by the server. With the advent of Java, it is now possible to move some of the processing work to the browser to relieve some of the workload of the server. The distributed IntraWeb provides the ability to incorporate access to all the legacy data. This is achieved through the implementation of a more structured means of documenting where the data is located and how the data is stored.

- **Enterprise intranet**—As the Java programming language matures and companies begin to develop truly useful applications, this model will be replete with true open client/server applications.

Picture this: instead of loading an HTML page, the client is coded in downloadable Java and is running in any Java-capable browser. When a page containing a Java applet is downloaded by an HTTP server to the browser, the applet runs in the browser, opening its own communications session with the server.

In plain English, the retrieval of a file from the intranet causes a whole series of other activities to take place. For example, pulling in the baseball scores of the previous day from the newspaper available in the intranet causes the intranet, through a Java program, to recalculate the statistics of all the players in the league based on the information in the statistics from the game. If this is important for your organization, the fact that it functions as advertised when the link is selected is the sign of a job well done.

Knowing the company's core business functions and knowing every last detail about the mission-critical business functions can help the user decide the level of support at which the intranet will be operated. The more the intranet is highly involved with and closely integrated into the mission-critical business process, the more the company will tend to move toward the Enterprise intranet model.

If a company makes the decision that it will implement client/server technology through the intranet, then by default, the full-scale Enterprise intranet will be developed. The combination of a state-of-the-art business strategy with state-of-the-market technology creates the competitive advantage the company seeks only if the current critical processes are understood. To be successful in the future, the company must continually evaluate its vision, mission, goals and objectives, critical success factors, and the business processes that are required to meet the moving target that *is* the future of the company.

It is difficult to project exactly where a company will be relative to its vision at the end of a given period of time. All that the truly enlightened companies do, relative to this futuristic vision, is make certain that the process of reviewing their operations and mission-critical business processes *becomes* one of the mission-critical business processes. If the ability to adapt to the future market conditions and requirements and thereby achieving competitive advantage is a critical issue for the company, it must be built into the business processes of the company and must be supported by the intranet.

How should an organization address the future of the intranet? What will happen to the technology? How can you keep abreast of the changes? These are a few of the questions that the next sections of this chapter will attempt to answer.

Peering into the Crystal Ball

The future of the intranet is in your hands.

The implementation of intranets in support of business processes demands new solutions and new technologies be put in place as the business models of the company change. It may be impossible to gaze into the crystal ball and predict the future of the company; but it *is* possible to establish business processes that evaluate the current and planned activities that the company performs or plans to perform. Analyzing the activities within a business process identifies the information required to complete the individual activities, and, hence, the objectives of the business processes.

One of the recommendations that does come out of this book is that companies consider the review of the information needs of their mission-critical business processes as a critical process that must be undertaken. This forces the improvement of the intranet to deliver the information as required.

There is no harm in *planning* the migration to the Enterprise intranet model and putting the infrastructure in place to fully implement the technologies should the business processes demand it. Stopping short of moving the intranet out of the IntraWeb format into the Enterprise intranet may constrain the company's ability to compete in the marketplace in the future.

In the hope that this book can help to point you in the direction of the future, the remainder of this section will cover the following topics briefly:

- Where the hardware and software vendors are heading

- What applications will drive the intranet of the future

- How you can influence the direction

Where the Hardware and Software Vendors Are Heading

This chapter might just be the start of the "yellow brick road" in the development of the perfect intranet. Intranets are relatively young, just starting upon the growth curve in terms of market potential. Most of the pundits feel that the growth in the marketplace will not come necessarily from the sale of HTTP server software but rather from the software applications that will run on the intranet and the information industry to fill the data needs of those new applications.

And now, turn the Tarot cards over and see what is in store for you in the form of

- The future of intranet-related hardware

- The future of intranet software

The hardware used on the intranet will change. It will become bigger, faster, and be able to do more on its own. These changes are not due to the intranet in and of itself. These changes are and will be a *result* of the intranet. The intranet enables companies to change the way work is done. These changes drive the demand for the new hardware. This section will talk about some of the changes that will be seen in the hardware arena.

Computers on the desktop are getting faster, have more memory, and can store large amounts of data at a relatively inexpensive level. New models of machines with the same price as old models but with an increased capacity seem to appear in a three to four month cycle. What this means to the intranet is that greater processing power and a greater capability to take advantage of the new software applications such as Virtual Reality Modeling are available at the same prices as last year's model. The paradigm seems to have changed from reducing the price on the current model to holding the price and providing "more bang for the buck."

Author's Note

> I remember buying the Canadian Region of Consolidated Fibres first microcomputer, an IBM XT, back in February of 1985. It had 640 KB of RAM, a 10 MB hard disk, a monochrome monitor, and a 360 KB floppy diskette drive. Add to that an Epson wide carriage dot-matrix printer and a copy of dBASE II and the bill came to just under $15,000 Canadian.
>
> Four months ago I bought a 100 MHz Pentium with 16 MB of RAM, 1.6 GB hard drive, 4X CD-ROM, and a 15-inch monitor for $3,500 Canadian. Last week I replaced that machine with a 150 MHz Pentium with 16 MB of RAM, 2 GB hard drive, 6X CD-ROM and a 15-inch monitor for the same $3,500 Canadian.
>
> Moral of my story: technology and its price will constantly change.

The processing power available at the desktop will increase as long as the users need to be able to use personal productivity tools.

The development of new network terminals by Oracle, Wang, and others will create a demand for the applications on the network—the intranet. One vision of these new computers is that they will have "no guts;" they are designed to connect to and use the applications of the Internet and the intranet. This means that the software applications must be developed for the terminals to use. Another vision is that the new computers will have enough capacity to run applications internally, but the applications will be stored in a central server and downloaded to the user's computer as required. The data would be stored somewhere else within the intranet.

Both of the preceding visions require a fundamental change in the computing model that exists today but are compatible with the Enterprise intranet model that has been discussed within this book.

The intranet is poised to replace the interconnectivity strategy of many organizations with disparate locations. Using the technologies of the intranet, these "dumb computers" are built to operate as terminals on TCP/IP networks. For more information on these network terminals, please refer to the following articles that discuss the pros and cons of these new proposed computers:

- "The H-Report: Attack of the $500 Killer Network Computers," CMP Media, Inc.

     http://192.21.6.71/techweb/nc/616/616robb.html

- "Web Terminal: Expensive Toy or Cheapest Personal System?" Inteco Corp.

     http://www.inteco.com/inin6.html

One of the latest announcements at the time this is written is about the "embedded Java" chips coming out of the Far East. Instead of Java running within the browser, the chip set on the circuit boards will be able to perform in the same way Java applets do.

Computer manufacturers are now starting not only to create the physical computer to be used as servers, but they also are starting to offer "all-in-one" servers—the intranet server software already bundled with and optimized for the hardware. The hardware vendors will likely be approached by the developers of intranet/Internet server software to form strategic alliances to create these types of bundles.

Another hardware trend is in the offing: currently the portable computer market is pushing out notebooks at record rates. Many business people are willing to plug in an external monitor, mouse, and keyboard or use a docking station in order to have the flexibility to travel with their office computer. With professionals now more mobile, the demands for intranet solutions to keep these travelers in touch with the office and synchronized with the tasks they need to perform in their part of the business processes will drive a whole series of changes in the notebook hardware market, from faster modems to wireless network connections.

The manufacturers are making CD-ROMs part of the integral configuration of the notebook more often. There seem to be two reasons for the inclusion of the CD:

- Gone are the days when software came on a single high density disk. With all their internal functionality and complexities, the majority of software now comes on CD-ROM. The notebooks of today require a CD-ROM in order to install the software.

- Multimedia presentations can be burned onto a CD-ROM and used for demonstration purposes. In-house creation of CD-ROMs is relatively inexpensive for prototypes, but not for mass production.

What this means to a company is that it can use the CD-ROM technology to cut its CD-ROMs to do the following:

- Create a presentation complete with multimedia that takes up the entire CD storage space. With up to 600 MB of storage space on a CD, you can create large presentations that may not fit on the hard drive of the notebook.

- Users in remote areas with no access to the intranet can cut the data they need to gain access to, such as the sales data for the previous month, onto a CD and take the data with them. This enables the user to perform analysis without access, which can then be posted back to the intranet once a communications link can be reached.

- Applications can be cut into and run from the CD-ROM, leaving all the available hard disk space for analytical workspace and data storage.

The CD-ROM has its place in the technology suite of the intranet. By acquiring the capability to create your own CD-ROMs in-house, you can expand what can be done with the notebook computer.

Note

> However, today, the notebook CD-ROM seems to be more of an enter-tainment device than a work tool for the traveler; the capability to play the user's favorite audio CD while on a plane or in a hotel room is the main reason. There are not a lot of business process-related uses for the CD-ROM that have been implemented in most companies.

With the advent of the intranet and the ability to distribute software over the network, users no longer require the CD-ROM drive to install the software—they simply connect to the intranet and click on a link or two. This can be done across the phone lines or from the desktop docking station. The software will still be purchased in CD-ROM format for installation onto the intranet. The licenses for all staff will be purchased without the media, and staff will download the software to their desktops. It may also be cut onto a CD-ROM in-house so that it runs from the CD of a notebook.

As for multimedia presentations, notebooks have playback capability while the CD-ROM is used to store and play back the data.

What companies need to do to justify the acquisition of notebooks with CD-ROM drives is obtain the means to create CD-ROMs in-house in order to create data-packs, presentations, or application-packs that are related to the business processes of the user.

Another piece of technology that provides for storage of data and programs is the PCMCIA card. With the improvement in PCMCIA card disk storage capacity and pricing, the capability to re-use the storage space on the PCMCIA card-mounted storage space becomes very attractive. Storing a 300 MB presentation on the $450 PCMCIA card means that it can be played back in the same fashion as on the CD-ROM. Look for software companies to start using these cards to ship their wares in addition to continue providing the software on CD-ROM.

The Future of Intranet Software

The intranet enables companies to change the way work is done. This means changes in the business processes of the company. The intranet is intended to support the information needs of the business processes as they change over time.

The software companies are driving the intranet bus at the moment. Netscape has the biggest share of the browser market any way you slice it. With its large base of browsers in corporations, Netscape is looking to leverage its servers into those companies based on a "same manufacturer on both ends" basis as well as on the quality and variety of functions that their servers are able to provide. By blanketing the server market with a Netscape server option for all possibilities, companies with a larger user base of Netscape Navigator browsers are starting to turn to Netscape for this one-vender solution.

On the other side of the field, Microsoft is throwing the gauntlet down at the feet of just about everyone. By entering the market with its Internet/intranet technology products, the sheer weight of Microsoft will force some competitors to seek other markets. With the in-house capability to optimize its productivity suite software to Microsoft intranet technologies, Bill Gates, the founder of Microsoft, has provided a one-stop shopping venue for organizations to rely solely on Microsoft for their solutions. The one foreseeable drawback of the Microsoft technology solution is the implementation of proprietary file types within the intranet—as opposed to the traditional, open standards of the intranet technology.

What Applications Will Drive the Intranet of the Future

As more companies move toward using the intranet to support business processes in general, and mission-critical business processes in particular, more emphasis will be placed on the applications that permit collaboration, group work, and document management. The intranet applications that support these business processes today and will enable these business processes to become more efficient and effective in the future will be the next "killer applications" in the intranet world.

Businesses are forced to create virtual teams to work on a project, and then they re-organize the teams for the next go-around. As many of these people become increasingly mobile, the ability to participate in discussions and share the work as it flows among the team members is imperative.

The primary driver as far as applications are concerned is the groupware segment. Groupware applications will be designed to enable group work while simultaneously handling document management requirements for versioning and indexing, as well as routing required information.

Domino, the version of Lotus Notes in its beta tests at this time, is a product to watch coming out of the more traditional side of the groupware market. Pricing and policy issues still need to be worked out relative to the integration of Notes and the intranet, but Domino shows promise. Please see Chapter 17, "Workflow Software, Groupware, and the intranet," to review how Notes fits within the groupware market segment; and Chapter 18, "Case Study: Intranet and Lotus Notes Can Coexist," for a review of how Notes and the intranet can go hand in hand.

The Domino product is a combination of the Notes server that is currently available, the Lotus InterNotes Web Publisher, which converts Notes data to HTML, and an HTTP server all rolled up into one product. Notes users interact with the databases on the Domino server as though they were a Notes database, while users gaining access to the Domino databases from the intranet see the retrieved documents as HTML files. It is realistic that users from both Notes and the intranet could be reading the same document at the same time in their separate formats without any interference from each other.

Keep an eye on companies like WebFlow Corp., maker of the WebFlow SamePage software product, and OpenText, maker of the Livelink product. These two companies should capture different levels of the marketplace, but they both will be key players in the workflow game. OpenText will also be in the picture with its search engines. Netscape's purchase of the Collabra Share groupware/workflow software product keeps Netscape in the workflow software ballpark and provides Netscape with an entrance to the value-added functions world beyond the servers and browsers.

How You Can Influence the Direction the Intranet Takes

Unless you are dealing with a frictionless surface, the laws of physics state that it is easier to change the direction of a moving object than a stationary object—it requires less force. This part of the "laws of inertia" is presented in the hope that if your intranet is constantly looking to improve the service it provides in support of the business processes of the company and is moving forward, any changes in the technology external to the company can be incorporated into the intranet direction fairly easily.

If you can convince your company to incorporate the business process of reviewing the information required to support the mission-critical business processes, significant gains will have been made. This would indicate the acceptance of the strategic value of the company's information. That is the essence of the intranet.

And that is the internal influence that you can have on the development of the intranet. To influence the software and hardware vendors and the service providers that deal in the establishment and delivery of the intranet, you are encouraged to participate in the locations identified in the next section.

Places to Play and Learn

Where can you go to learn about the intranet? To find the answer to a particular problem you are having with hardware or software? To see how other companies are using the intranet?

There are opportunities to play with software at demo sites and learn from the experience of others. The following sections highlight several places on the Internet where you can go to find large amounts of information. These sites range from providers of white papers offering their interpretation of the direction of the intranet, to discussion forums, and to jumpstations that have listed numerous sites and resources for you to visit. White papers are the position papers of the persons or organizations who write them and provide their views on the future direction of the intranet.

The discussion forums that are listed below are excellent places to start. Ask a question. Respond to previous postings. Many of the vendors of intranet products read these forums and participate—they are looking for clues as to what the next release of their software should contain. When someone leaves a "how do I" question on these boards, it is unlikely that no one will respond—although there may be occasional derisive laughter. Generally, questions are answered by the participants. In fact, there are several unofficial competitions going on among participants to continuously "one-up" the other in terms of providing responses to questions.

The following is a list of discussion forum categories:

- Big impact vendors

- White papers (and other things)

- Discussion groups

- E-zines and jumpstations to intranet information

- Articles and news items to ponder

- "Last but not least"

The discussion forums in these categories are described and evaluated below.

Big Impact Vendors

Netscape's Internet Solutions

http://home.netscape.com/comprod/at_work/index.html

This is Netscape's source for case histories that use their products, on-line resources, and other information, including their white paper (http://home.netscape.com/comprod/at_work/white_paper/

intranet/vision.html). Although it is focused on Netscape products, this is the biggest collection of Internet examples in one place.

Microsoft's Intranet Strategy

```
http://www.microsoft.com/intranet/documents/msinswp/intranetTOC.htm
```

Microsoft has published its white paper that outlines where Microsoft is headed as a corporation in terms of intranet technology. The incorporation of Web technology in all Microsoft user products is targeted to bring into the Microsoft world corporations seeking one-stop solutions to all office technology.

White Papers (And Other Things)

"The Intranet Information Page"

```
http://www.strom.com/pubwork/intranet.html
```

David Strom's white paper, "Creating Private Intranets: Challenges and Prospects for IS," is a good starting point for those interested in some of the challenges faced in starting an intranet.

"Tap Into the Power of Intranets and the Internet!"

```
http://www.novell.com/icd/nip/nbg2ii1.html
```

Novell gets into the act by explaining how you can use intranet technologies to link all areas of your company on a global basis.

"Product review of Cold Fusion, Sapphire/Web, and NetDynamics in Web Developer"

```
http://www.webdeveloper.com/current/review.html
```

In this review, Web Developer takes a look at three packages—Cold Fusion™ Professional 1.5, Sapphire/Web 2.0, and NetDynamics 1.0 beta—that let you connect your database to the Web so that you can decide for yourself which tool is best suited to your task.

NetDynamics White Paper

```
http://www.w3spider.com/products/ndwhite.html
```

This white paper presents NetDynamics, a next-generation application builder from Spider Technologies. It explores the technical requirements of the Web/database application environment, presents the NetDynamics solution, and discusses the architectural tradeoffs of solutions in the marketplace and of languages underlying those solutions.

Allaire Corp. Announces Intranet Strategy

```
http://www.allaire.com/cgi-shl/dbml.exe?template=/Allaire/news/re-
leases/intranet.dbm
```

Corporate intranets are growing extremely fast, and there is a demand for solutions that offer an easy way to integrate emerging Internet protocols with traditional database technologies to deliver interactive Web applications that go beyond static HTML pages. Allaire is the developer of Cold Fusion and Allaire Forums.

Developing and Deploying World Wide Web Applications

```
http://www.bluestone.com/papers/whitepapers/www_app_devel.html
```

This is Bluestone's white paper. Sapphire/Web is an application development tool for creating inter- and intra-enterprise applications that use Web browsers. This paper discusses one of the newly emerging uses of the Web, with a view to stimulating the thinking of managers responsible for developing and implementing software in their organizations. It also explains how organizations can use Web technology to disseminate information more easily, efficiently, and cost-effectively. It is hoped that this paper will stimulate its readers into thinking about how they can leverage Web technology to give their organizations the competitive advantage they must have if they are to survive and prosper.

Discussion Groups

Intranet Soundings

`http://www.brill.com/intranet/ijx/index.html`

This is a threaded message exchange that is focused on the intranet. It is a very active site with an active core of participants. Questions run from "What is an intranet?" to "Has anyone tried to do this with the latest release of product XX?" Seldom do newbies' queries go unanswered here.

IntraNut

`http://www.intranut.com/`

This is a newer site that has been up since the beginning of July 1996. At the time of this writing, the site is primarily a discussion forum that is just getting started. By the time you see this, the site should be expanded to a weekly publication regarding all aspects of the intranet. Looks to be a good place to find lots of user tales.

The Intranet Exchange

`http://www.innergy.com/ix/index.html`

This is a new moderated message exchange dedicated to the intranet. The participants to date seem to be the same people as those who use the Intranet Soundings site above. You'll have to see what themes the moderators follow.

E-Zines and Jumpstations to Intranet Information

Intranet Journal

`http://www.brill.com/intranet/`

This is the home page for a number of sub-offerings, including the Intranet Soundings discussion group. Excellent product listings,

Expert's Corner, the Opinion page, and a set of links to other sites can be found here.

Webmaster Intranet Resource Center

`http://www.cio.com/webmaster/wm_irc.html`

This site is one of the best all-around sites for Web technology and information. In addition to the preceding information set, it has an area dedicated to the intranet. It's well worth the effort to browse through the seminar on what setting up an intranet requires from a company.

Intranet Design Magazine(sm)

`http://www.innergy.com/`

IDM will start out bi-weekly, featuring articles by some of the industry's brightest practitioners. "This Old Web," a how-to section, Up-to-date News & Trend Analysis—insight, not hype—for the busy IS professional, and a definitive Internet FAQ (Frequently Asked Questions) are among the features at this site.

WebWeek On-line

`http://www.webweek.com/`

This site is the online version of *Web Week Magazine* and is one of the best sites around to keep up on what is new in the Internet market-place. The site is broken down into several topical areas, including in-tranets; there is usually at least one case study in the Internet section. This is a Mecklermedia site linked in with their other online offerings. It is one of the author's "must-reads" and is in his electronic calendar with a reminder.

Web Developer On-line

`http://www.webdeveloper.com/`

This site is targeted at the WebMasters to ensure that they are kept abreast of the latest technologies that affect their line of work. From design issues to code samples to band-aids, this is one of the sites that is tough not to include in the look toward the future.

Articles and News Items to Ponder

"The Internet Rolls In"

http://techweb.cmp.com/iw/564/64iuint.htm

From *Information Week Magazine* Jan. 29, 1996: "Even as the Net alters Sun's orbit, it's also changing the way business shares data with employees. Internal Nets are cheap, easy, and safe."

"Internet Products: Content and Collaboration"

http://www.pcmag.com/issues/1508/pcmg0045.htm

From *PC Magazine*, April 23, 1996: "Products for accessing group discussions and gigantic document databases via a Web browser are here, but how do they measure up to their legacy competitors?"

"Cheap & Efficient Intranets Flourish"

http://www.sun.com/sunworldonline/swol-05-1996/swol-05-intranet.html

From a May 1996 *SunWorld* article: "Encouraged by low cost, ease of use, short development cycles, and the utilization of existing hardware and network infrastructure, users in the U.S. and Europe—and to a lesser degree in Asia—are rapidly deploying intranets in an effort to streamline internal communications."

"New Breed: Internet Champions"

http://pubs.iworld.com/ww-online/96Mar/news/breed.html

This is a March 1996 *Web Week* article on how to make your case for a corporate Internet to management, examples of companies who are developing intranets, and ideas on whom to approach to approve an Internet project.

"Last But Not Least"

Books available on the Internet and Internet technologies

`http://www.mcp.com/newriders`

New Riders Publishing has a site that lists the books that are available from its presses, as well as hosting information on the books that it has published, including data examples.

The Author's Humble Site

`http://www.intranomics.com`

The author is in the process of refining his Internet jumpstation to the available resources on the Internet that deal with intranets. The problem for the author is keeping the list current; it changes on an hourly basis these days. In addition, the author maintains a discussion forum on his site regarding the applications that have been and are being developed for Internet implementations. The author's biggest challenge is to provide the visitors to his site an up-to-date listing of conferences and seminars regarding intranets and their technologies around the globe. Please post a notice on the site if you discover a conference in your area, and the author will add it to the list.

Author's Note

Because I am an avid runner, having completed five marathons the same day that I started them, I am very keen on trying to combine travel for business with major running events (marathons preferably—everyone goes too fast in the shorter stuff), as well as running through the various locations in which I find myself. If you happen to have information about upcoming running events in your area, regardless of timing with a conference or seminar, please post that information as well. The author would appreciate any information about running trails in cities and towns around the world, especially digitized (scanned) maps/brochures. As soon as he recovers from an August 1996 arthroscopy, he will be back on the roads again.

part

6

Appendices

Acceptable Use and Other Sample Company Policies

What You Need to Know about Acceptable Use Policies

Author's Note

Several examples are included here to provide you with a framework to develop your own policy. For more information on acceptable use policies, please check out my site at http://www.intranomics.com/policy/aup/. I will keep an updated list of acceptable use policies at this location from Sept 1, 1996 forward. Other types of intranet policies are housed on my site.

It is very important that you develop an acceptable use policy for your intranet. Acceptable use policies are necessary for several reasons:

- They help educate your staff about the kinds of tools they will use on the network and what they can expect from those tools (in a very general way).

- They help to define boundaries of behavior, and more critically, specify the consequences of violating those boundaries.

- They specify the actions that a system administrator might take in order to maintain or "police" the network—so there are no surprises at the office. The policies may outline general worst case consequences or responses to specific policy violation situations.

- One of the most important things to understand about these policies is that none of them are perfect. You will undoubtedly encounter situations that you could not have predicted. Still, these documents should not become instruments of paranoia. The vast majority of staff will not do anything to cause difficulty for themselves or others on the network. Remember, the biggest problem that your staff will face on the intranet stems from the cultural clash they will encounter between their familiar ways of talking to each other and the way people communicate in virtual environments.

Acceptable Intranet Guidelines Draft — John Desborough

Network

1. All use of the system must be in support of corporate business and consistent with the mission of the company. Company reserves the right to prioritize use and access to the system.

2. Any use of the system must be in conformity to state and federal law and district policy. Use of the system for commercial solicitation is prohibited.

3. The system constitutes public facilities and may not be used to support or oppose political candidates or ballot measures.

4. No use of the system shall serve to disrupt the operation of the system by others; system components including hardware or software shall not be destroyed, modified, or abused in any way.

5. Malicious use of the system to develop programs that harass other users or gain unauthorized access to any computer or computing system and/or damage the components of a computer or computing system is prohibited.

6. Users are responsible for the appropriateness and content of material they transmit or publish on the system. Hate mail, harassment, discriminatory remarks, or other antisocial behaviors are expressly prohibited.

7. Use of the system to access, store, or distribute obscene or pornographic material is prohibited.

8. Subscriptions to mailing lists, bulletin boards, chat groups, and commercial online services and other information services must be pre-approved by the company.

Security

9. System accounts are to be used only by the authorized owner of the account for the authorized purpose. Users may not share their account number or password with another person or leave an open file or session unattended or unsupervised. Account owners are ultimately responsible for all activity under their account.

10. Users shall not seek information on, obtain copies of, or modify files, other data, or passwords belonging to other users, or misrepresent other users on the system, or attempt to gain unauthorized access to the system.

11. Communications may not be encrypted so as to avoid security review.

12. Users should change passwords regularly and avoid easily guessed passwords.

Personal Security

13. Personal information such as addresses and telephone numbers should remain confidential when communicating on the system.

14. Staff should never make appointments to meet people in person who they have contacted on the system.

15. Staff should notify the administrator whenever they come across information or messages that are dangerous, inappropriate, or make them feel uncomfortable.

Copyright

16. The unauthorized installation, use, storage, or distribution of copyrighted software or materials on corporate computers is prohibited.

General Use

17. Diligent effort must be made to conserve system resources. For example, frequently delete e-mail and unused files.

18. No person shall have access to the system without having received appropriate training, and a signed and received approval in the form of an Individual User Release Form must be on file with the intranet supervisor.

Harris Corporation Electronics System Sector

(used with permission)

WORLD WIDE WEB USAGE — GUIDELINES FOR USE

A. GENERAL ITEMS

AWARENESS:

- Usage is monitored automatically

- Resource usage (e.g. network) is regularly monitored

- Assume all Web communications are insecure

- External site visits are typically registered; Harris "stamp" is always left behind

- Harris culture promotes empowerment; freedom to use or misuse resources exists

- An enormous amount of data exists; potential for significant time drain

- May inadvertently enter foreign sites which may pose export issues

- Hidden costs may exist based on information requested/ gathered from external sites

- Formal releases of Harris-related information must first be cleared as per Harris command media directives

DOS AND DON'TS:

- DO comply with Harris Corporation Standards of Business Conduct.

- DO use in fashion and with discretion similar to other Harris resources; e.g., phones, e-mail.

- DO see Business Standards Advisor (BSA) on ethical questions.

- DO refer to recently-distributed "Harris Communications Guidelines" pamphlet.

- DO refer to evolving Harris security guidelines related to the Web.

- DO adhere to copyright laws.

- DON'T use resources improperly.

- DON'T invite risk; avoid foreign sites, gambling, games, contests, pornography, commerce (i.e., don't buy/sell over the Web).

B. EXTERNAL USAGE

BUSINESS DEVELOPMENT/INTELLIGENCE:

Web usage as a marketing and information dissemination/gathering tool to enable rapid, effective communication in support of pursuits of viable new business opportunities.

WEB-BASED OFFERINGS:

Incorporation of Web technologies into Harris product/service offerings.

TROUBLESHOOTING:

Web usage in search for resolution to specific, well-defined problems where logical Internet paths exist and alternative approaches are significantly more cumbersome.

BENEFITS:

- Time savings

- Generally current, accurate, complete, reliable information

- Feedback mechanism to information source typically provided

- Non-Harris experiences often available

- Relative ease in information gathering and implementation of solution from proper sources (e.g., Microsoft patches, drivers)

AWARENESS:

- No guarantees of data currency, accuracy, completeness, and reliability

- Hidden costs/charges may exist

- Viruses may exist on downloaded executables

DOS AND DON'TS:

- DO validate and pre-test solutions derived via the Web.

- DO assess credibility of information source.

- DO start with logical sites (e.g., software supplier) rather than third parties.

- DO utilize electronic feedback process.

- DO share results with appropriate Harris community.

- DO perform virus scans on downloaded executables.

- DON'T distribute solutions internally prior to adequate testing and verification.

- DON'T overlook issues of licensing, compatibility, software expiration, etc.

NEWS GROUPS:

Web usage for the sake of staying current on items of topical interest; e.g., NetNews.

BENEFITS:

- Time savings

- Information available from a wide range of sources; diversity of opinions including those from "user" perspectives

- Emergency information readily available, e.g. hurricane preparedness

AWARENESS:

- All opinions are subjective

- Entries are uncensored

- "Flame wars" are common

- Comments/opinions on products/companies may put you and Harris at risk

DOS AND DON'TS:

- DO respect the Harris reputation; remember that your entries may be viewed as Harris statements.

- DON'T submit inflammatory remarks; instead stick to the facts; stay constructive.

PRODUCT/MARKET DATA:

Web usage to gather specific data as supplied by product providers and independent organizations (educational nature).

BENEFITS:

- Time savings

- Data available from product/market sources

- See "Troubleshooting" benefits

AWARENESS:

- Information may be subjective (e.g., from the suppliers' perspective)

- Independent opinions subject to verification

INFORMATION SERVICES:

Web usage for industry data access to supplement existing toolsets; e.g., IHS data sheets; Commerce Business Daily.

BENEFITS:

- Ease of access and use

- Elimination of purchased/leased product scenarios

- Enormous data volume available

- Automatic data "upgrades"

AWARENESS:

- Limited opportunities at present

- Check for Web data and capabilities prior to purchasing from third parties

PUBLIC RELATIONS:

Use of the Web to enhance Harris's image in the marketplace and business communities.

BENEFITS:

- Can be kept current and dynamic

- Can be responsive to market dynamics

- Can reach all Harris stakeholder communities including shareholders, customers, and suppliers

AWARENESS:

- Must only originate from authorized Harris organizations

PARTNERSHIPS:

Web usage to facilitate necessary communication within multiple company arrangements; includes subcontracting, consortia, industry groups.

BENEFITS:

- Ease of use

- Timeliness

- Interactive nature

- Accommodates dissimilar computing environments

- Facilitates "greater than two party" communication

- Cost savings/avoidance

AWARENESS:

- Arrangements must be sanctioned by management

- Be careful not to share proprietary or classified information; refer to security guidelines

RECREATION/PERSONAL:

Web usage, of a limited nature, for other than ESS business purposes during non-work hours.

BENEFIT:

- Personal time savings

AWARENESS:

- Use common sense and remember that Harris monitors use of its systems

SOFTWARE DOWNLOADS:

Download and use of public domain (usually free) software.

BENEFITS:

- Availability of potentially good products

- Cost savings as compared with similar products that must be purchased

- Time savings; avoidance of procurement cycle

- Easily accessible

RISKS:

- Potential application compatibility issues

- Virus potential

- Requires management sanction; must adhere to enterprise system guiding principles for software selection and use

- Potential network compatibility issues

- May be hidden costs or licensing implications

- Application support may be lacking

AWARENESS:

Familiarize yourself with policies and procedures governing the use of software found on public networks (e.g., Redbook policy 561).

C. INTERNAL USAGE

COMMAND MEDIA:

Web usage as a vehicle for electronic access to ESS internal command media.

BENEFITS:

- Accessible via standard client

- Ease of distribution and management

- Cost savings

BULLETIN BOARDS:

Web usage for internal "news group" style communication among employees.

BENEFITS:

- Offload from e-mail services; disk space savings on mail servers

- Fosters internal communication

AWARENESS:

- Need browsers for all employees

- Value based on quality of individual postings

- "Migration" from e-mail bulletin boards will be centrally managed

SYSTEM FRONT-ENDS:

Web usage as the client side of enterprise client-server applications.

BENEFITS:

- Inherently client-server, GUI, open

- Ease in distribution and management

- Future includes multimedia (e.g., Java) and sophisticated RDBMS links

AWARENESS:

- Rapidly advancing technology yet still relatively immature

WORKFLOW POTENTIAL:

Web usage as an enabler for workflow engine implementation and access.

BENEFITS:

- Common "communication" system; i.e., tool, access, knowledge

- Enabler for business process re-engineering (e.g., InForms)

AWARENESS:

- Security risks

- Immature technology

INTER-SECTOR COMMUNICATIONS:

Web usage as an information dissemination vehicle for Harris employee population.

BENEFITS:

- Enables cross-sector synergy

- Provides access to wealth of Harris information

- Vehicle for capturing informal knowledge base

PROFESSIONAL HOME PAGES:

Web usage as a vehicle for employees to communicate and participate in professional organizations.

AWARENESS:

- Not intended for personal home pages

- Specific corporate-wide guidelines being defined

END OF DOCUMENT

current as of 6/10/96

Intranet Server

These are sample additional guidelines for branch intranet servers that are not accessible from the Internet.

1. Each intranet WWW server must have a link back to the corporate home page—http://.

2. Material placed on intranet WWW server must comply with the Acceptable Use policy of the company.

3. Branches are responsible for their own standards for their intranet WWW Server content.

Proposed Computer and Network Policy University of Miami School of Law

I. Introduction

II. Rights and Responsibilities

III. Existing Legal Context

IV. Conduct That Violates This Policy

V. Enforcement

I. Introduction

This acceptable use policy governs the use of computers and networks at the University of Miami School of Law. As a user of these resources, you are responsible for reading and understanding this document. This document protects the consumers of computing resources, computing hardware and networks, and system administrators.

Computer facilities and infrastructure are provided for meeting academic goals and to provide access to local, national, and international facilities to aid in the achieving of those goals. Those using the facilities and services must respect the intellectual and access rights of others locally, nationally, and internationally. Students should be aware that any use of the facilities or infrastructure that is in violation of the guidelines listed below may be considered an Honor Code violation.

The School of Law is committed to intellectual and academic freedom and to the application of those freedoms to computer media and fora. The School of Law is also committed to protecting the privacy and integrity of computer data and records belonging to the School of Law and to individual users.

II. Rights and Responsibilities

Computers and networks can provide access to resources on and off campus, including the ability to communicate with other users world-wide. Such open access is a privilege, much like access to books in the library, and requires that individual users act responsibly. The School of Law is committed to protecting the rights of students, faculty, and staff to freedom of expression and to free academic inquiry and experimentation. Users must respect the rights of other users, respect the integrity of the systems and related physical resources, and observe all relevant laws, regulations, and contractual obligations.

Because electronic information is volatile and easily reproduced, users must exercise care in acknowledging and respecting the work of others through strict adherence to software licensing agreements and copyright laws.

III. Existing Legal Context

All existing laws (federal and state) and University regulations and policies apply, including not only those laws and regulations that are specific to computers and networks, but also those that may apply generally to personal conduct. These include but are not limited to the Family Educational Rights and Privacy Act of 1974 (Title 20 U.S.C. section1232[g]), the Electronic Communications Privacy Act of 1986 (Title 18 U.S.C. section 2510 et. seq.), and the Florida Computer Crimes Act (FS Chap. 815). Illegal reproduction of software and other intellectual property protected by U.S. copyright law is subject to civil damages and criminal punishment including fines and imprisonment. The UM School of Law supports the policy of EDUCOM on "Software and Intellectual Rights."

Users do not own accounts on University computers, but are granted the privilege of exclusive use of their accounts. Use of the network does not alter the ownership of data stored on the network. Users are entitled to privacy regarding their computer communications and stored data. However, system administrators may access user files in the normal course of their employment when necessary to protect the integrity of computer systems or the rights or property of the University or other users. For example, system administrators may examine or make copies of files that are suspected of misuse or that have been corrupted or damaged. Copies of all user files stored on the network are routinely backed up for disaster recovery purposes.

Subject to the exceptions set out above, users have reason to expect the same level of privacy in personal files on the Law School's computers (e.g., files in a user's home directory) as users have in any other space assigned to them by the Law School (e.g., a locker or an office). Private communications by computer are entitled to the same degree of privacy as private communications via telephone. User files may be subject to search by law enforcement agencies or under court order if such files contain information which may be used as evidence in a court of law.

Other organizations operating computing and network facilities that are reachable via the UM School of Law network may have their own policies governing the use of those resources. When accessing remote resources from UM School of Law facilities, users are responsible for obeying both the policies set forth in this document and the policies of the other organizations.

In addition to possible federal and state legal controls, and applicable University and School of Law policies and procedures, misuse of computing, networking, or information resources may result in the loss of computing and/or network access.

IV. Conduct That Violates This Policy

Conduct that violates this policy includes, but is not limited to, the activities in the following list.

- Use of a computer account that belongs to another person or department, except for diagnostic testing by an authorized member of the Computer Resources department.

- Use of accounts in such as way as would violate the School of Law's contracts with data service providers (e.g. use of an academic Lexis or Westlaw account as a research tool in the course of employment outside the law school).

- Giving access to a computer account, through sharing of passwords or otherwise, to any person other than the assigned user or an authorized member of the Computer Resources staff. Project or group accounts must be approved by the Computer Resources department prior to use.

- Using the Network to gain unauthorized access to any computer system.

- Connecting unauthorized equipment to the network for purposes inconsistent with the academic purposes of the law school.

- Unauthorized attempts to circumvent data protection schemes or uncover security loopholes. This includes creating and/or running programs that are designed to identify security loopholes and/or decrypt intentionally secure data.

- Knowingly or recklessly performing an act that will interfere with the normal operation of computers, terminals, peripherals, or networks.

- Knowingly or recklessly running or installing on any computer system or network, or giving to another user a program intended to damage or to place excessive load on a computer system or network. This includes, but is not limited to, programs known as computer viruses, Trojan Horses, and worms.

- Deliberately wasting/overloading computing resources.

- Violating terms of applicable software licensing agreements or copyright laws.

- Violating copyright laws and their fair use provisions through inappropriate reproduction or dissemination of copyrighted text, images, and so forth.

- Using system resources to harass, threaten, defraud, or otherwise harm another. This includes sending repeated, unwanted e-mail to another user.

- Initiating or propagating electronic chain letters.

- Inappropriate mass mailing such as multiple mailings to newsgroups, mailing lists, or individuals; e.g., "spamming," "flooding," or "bombing."

- Forging communications to make them appear to originate from another person.

- Attempting to monitor or tamper with another user's electronic communications, or reading, copying, changing, or deleting another user's files or software without the express agreement of the other user.

V. Enforcement

The system administrator is responsible for protecting the system and users from abuses of this policy. Pursuant to this duty, the system administrator may informally or formally communicate with offending parties. In more extreme cases, the system administrator may temporarily revoke or modify use privileges. Temporary suspension decisions are reviewable by the system administrator's supervisor(s) and ultimately the Dean and/or the Dean's designee.

In addition, offenders may be referred to their supervisor, the Dean, or other appropriate disciplinary authority for further action. If the individual is a student, the matter may be referred to the Honor Council for appropriate disciplinary action.

Any offense that violates local, state, or federal laws may result in the immediate loss of all University computing privileges and may be referred to appropriate University disciplinary authorities and/or law enforcement authorities.

This document is adapted, with permission, from the UC Davis Computer and Network Use Policy, ©1993-1995 Regents of the University of California. This draft will be presented to the Faculty of the University of Miami School of Law. The faculty may accept, amend, or reject it.

Thus, this draft does not necessarily state the current policy of the School of Law.

er. 1.02 Rev. Jan 18, 1996.

This text is online at `http://www.law.miami.edu/~froomkin/` `aokuse3.htm`. This document may be reproduced for any non-commercial use.

Business Case Study: Intranet Information Server

Within the last six months, Microsoft has changed the Internet products market. With the introduction of its Intranet Information Server into the marketplace, Microsoft has made the competition in the Windows NT Web server market much tougher for the other top players: Netscape, O'Reilly, and Progress. The reactions of these companies have varied.

What Does Microsoft Say?

Microsoft's strategy points toward the extension of the generally accepted Internet standards to include the potential that exists within the Microsoft product suite—both in terms of currently available products and those products that are on the workbench.

By working toward the integration of its productivity tools with Internet technologies, Microsoft plans to enable decision support through easy communication, collaboration, and workflow tools. Microsoft plans not only to link employees within a company, but to embrace the concept of extended organization between companies by implementing Electronic Data Interchange functionality within the suite. Through the implementation of the new Point-to-Point Tunneling protocol, a virtual secure connection can be put in place between two different companies across the Internet.

The Intranet Information Server (IIS) forms an integrated part of Windows NT Server 4.0's operating system. The fact that Microsoft includes in its "Intranet Strategy Whitepaper," released in June of 1996, a discussion about the other network protocols that exist and must be incorporated into the overall strategy means that Microsoft is moving toward the Enterprise Intranet model discussed earlier in this book.

Microsoft has already released into the market its Internet Assistant applications for its MS Office product. These applications assist companies to convert their data to HTML for placement on the Web. As well, it has released several viewer applications that can be employed as helper applications in the browser.

In the area of browser technology, Microsoft's NT and 95 operating systems already ship with Internet Explorer. Soon the Windows Explorer and the Internet Explorer will be merged into one product. Version 3.0 of the Internet Explorer will handle Java, Netscape extensions, and plug-ins that had previously run only within Netscape.

To bring the whole package together and put a bow on it:

- Microsoft plans to make NT 4.0 not only a Windows server but also an intranet server.

- Until IIS ships and the bugs are worked out, Microsoft has been providing it free of charge to those who want to implement it on NT servers. This is a "bait and switch" strategy—by getting the companies to put the freebie in place while they are waiting to migrate to the more robust NT 4.0 server, Microsoft is building a base of installed servers from which to grow.

- Giving away the browser for free—with the integrated enhancements for the IIS servers— and providing it with every "box" that ships, puts the browser in front of people.

- By distributing Viewers and Internet Assistants, Microsoft is keeping the users of its productivity tools happy until all the components of its entire strategy are developed.

- As businesses discover the intranet is a means to provide interoperability between the productivity suite and the legacy systems, Microsoft recognizes that the market for internal servers will be equal or greater than that for the external servers.

Microsoft has been placating its customers with throw-aways until such time as the core components of the overall business strategy are in place. If Microsoft can give companies the means to publish, collaborate, and route information through a business transparently—from the information's desktop creation to its distribution on the servers— businesses will continue to buy Microsoft's back-end storage facilities (Exchange and Access) as well as the rest of Microsoft's business productivity tools.

In essence, Microsoft provides one-stop shopping for all your integrated tools.

What Does the Market Say?

The market is reacting diffidently at the time of this book's writing. One of the big NT Web server companies, Process Software, provides its Purveyor server primarily to the intranet market. After Microsoft entered the server market with IIS, Process started to focus on its intranet/groupware strategy to leverage the power of its server.

O'Reilly has made its WebSite 1.1 personal Web server freely available for NT and 95. O'Reilly is not worried about Microsoft's offering at this time because its market primarily consists of external server implementations.

Netscape has revised its pricing strategy in order to compete, but has been hitting back at Microsoft by pointing out the "hidden costs" of running Microsoft's IIS.

Analysts feel that the Web software market will involve $4 billion a year in the year 2000, but only about 10 percent of that will be for actual Web servers. The rest of the market will consist of software that builds applications, manages content, and lets workers collaborate. Some analysts hold the view that now that Microsoft has entered the game, no one will be able to integrate a server into NT better than Microsoft. Their advice is to find another market that they are not in and win there.

It will be a while until the market shakes out.

What Does the Author Think?

Microsoft will build the best NT Web server in the game. They can't help but do this. By giving away its IIS software now, Microsoft gives companies the chance to get their systems into place and create the applications that support their core business functions. When the new version of the IIS program comes out—bundled with NT 4.0 and a flock of tightly integrated productivity tools—Microsoft's combination of intranet technology with productivity tools will be too much for corporate America to pass up.

Microsoft 1, The Others 0

Intranet-Compatible HTTP Server Products

Alibaba:
http://www.csm.co.at/csm/

Amiga Web Server:
http://www.phone.net/aws/

Apache:
http://www.apache.org/

Apache-SSL-US:
http://apachessl.c2.org/

Common Lisp Hypermedia Server:
http://www.ai.mit.edu/projects/iiip/doc/cl-http/home-page.html

Commerce Builder:
http://www.ifact.com/ifact/inet.htm

COSMOS Web Server:
http://www.ris.fr/

OSU DECthreads server:
http://kcgl1.eng.ohio-state.edu/www/doc/serverinfo.html

EMWAC Freeware HTTPS:
http://emwac.ed.ac.uk/html/internet_toolchest/https/contents.htm

EnterpriseWeb:
http://www.beyond-software.com

Esplanade:
http://www.ftp.com/esplanade

ExpressO HTTP Server:
http://www.capitalcity.com:4321/

Fnord Server:
http://www.wpi.edu/~bmorin/fnord/

GN:
http://hopf.math.nwu.edu:70/

GNNserver:
http://www.tools.gnn.com/

GoServe for OS/2:
http://www2.hursley.ibm.com/goserve/

IBM Internet Connection Server:
http://www.ics.raleigh.ibm.com/

IBM Internet Connection Secure Server:
http://www.ics.raleigh.ibm.com/

JSB INTRAnet Jazz Server:
http://www.intranet.co.uk/

MacHTTP from Quarterdeck:
http://www.starnine.com/

Microsoft Internet Information Server:
http://www.microsoft.com/infoserv

NCSA HTTPd:
http://hoohoo.ncsa.uiuc.edu/

NetPresenz:
http://www.share.com/stairways/

Netscape Enterprise Server:
http://home.netscape.com/

Netscape FastTrack Server:
http://home.netscape.com/

NetWare Web Server from Novell:
http://www.novell.com/

OmniHTTPd:
http://www.fas.harvard.edu/~glau/httpd/

Open Market Secure WebServer:
http://www.openmarket.com/

Open Market WebServer:
http://www.openmarket.com/

Oracle WebServer:
http://www.oracle.com

Purveyor WebServer:
http://www.process.com/

Quarterdeck WebServer:
http://www.quarterdeck.com/

Spinnaker Web Server:
http://www.searchlight.com

Spinner:
http://spinner.infovav.se/

SPRY SafetyWeb Server:
http://server.spry.com/

SPRY Web Server:
http://server.spry.com/

Stairways Web Server:
http://www.share.com/stairways/

SU/httpd:
http://www-swiss.ai.mit.edu/scsh/contrib/net/sunet.html

TECWeb Server:
http://www.tecs.com/

thttpd:
http://www.acme.com/software/thttpd/

VBServer:
http://wwwdev.com/products/vbserver/vbserve.htm

Web Commander from Luckman Interactive:
http://www.luckman.com/WebCommander/webcom.html

Web Server/400:
http://www.inetmi.com/products/webserv/webinfo.htm

Webshare:
http://www.beyond-software.com/Software/Webshare.html

WebSite from O'Reilly & Associates:
http://website.ora.com/

WebSTAR 95/NT from Quarterdeck:
http://www.quarterdeck.com/

WebSTAR Mac from Quarterdeck:
http://www.starnine.com/

Webware Commercial Edition:
http://www.edime.com.au/webware/

WN:
http://hopf.math.nwu.edu/

Zeus Serve:
http://www.zeus.co.uk/

What's on the CD

cgi-lib.pl version 2.12

by Steve Brenner

S.E.Brenner@bio.cam.uk

www.bio.cam.ac.uk

The cgi-lib.pl library has become the de facto standard library for creating Common Gateway Interface (CGI) scripts in the Perl language.

Welcome to the official Web site for cgi-lib.pl, with the most up-to-date releases of the library. The cgi-lib.pl library makes CGI scripting in Perl easy enough for anyone to process forms and create dynamic Web content.

It is extremely easy to use cgi-lib.pl, and most people can pick it up from just a few examples. The following scripts work equally well under Perl4 and Perl5.

(This information taken from the Web site.)

WWWWAIS 2.5

A Product of Enterprise Integration Technologies (EIT)

`www.eit.com`

WWWWAIS by Kevin Hughes acts as gateway between programs that create indexed catalogs of files and forms-capable World Wide Web browsers. With the freely distributable freeWAIS or SWISH packages and WWWWAIS, you can do the following with your Web site:

- Create searchable databases of the information on your Web site.

- Allow users to search multiple databases via their Web browser with customizable options.

- Create a custom pop-up menu of servers to search through.

- Produce hypertext search results, with file information and links directly to the relevant HTML documents.

- Retrieve WAIS source descriptions and files—specify URLs and filters to map results to.

- Only allow users from certain sites to search documents.

This program runs on a Unix server.

(This information taken from the Web site.)

Cold Fusion 1.5

A Product of Allaire Corp.
7600 France Avenue South, Suite 552
Minneapolis, MN 55435

Phone: 612-831-1808
Fax: 612-830-1090
E-mail: info@allaire.com

`www.allaire.com`

Cold Fusion is a Web Application Development (WAD) platform for Windows NT and Windows 95. Cold Fusion can be used to create a wide variety of applications that integrate relational databases with the Web on intranets and the Internet. Applications range from dynamic Web sites to enterprise-wide groupware. Cold Fusion enables dynamic, data-driven Web sites that use pages that are generated on-the-fly from information stored in databases and provided by users. Page content can be instantly customized based on user requests. Dynamic sites enable users to enter and retrieve information and offer unparalleled ease of maintenance and administration.

More complicated applications include online customer feedback, order entry, event registration, bulletin-board style conferencing, technical support, interactive training, and a wide variety of information publishing applications. Advanced applications include internal client/server systems and Web-based groupware. These applications can be used on the Internet or as part of enterprise-wide networks (intranets).

Developing applications with Cold Fusion does not require coding in a traditional programming language like Perl, C/C++, Visual Basic, Java, or Delphi. Instead, developers build applications by combining standard HTML with high-level database commands stored in templates. This method of web application development is simpler, faster, and more flexible than first generation, code-intensive techniques. With Cold Fusion, developers can leverage the power of the Web and relational databases to create dynamic Web sites and full-scale Web applications.

(This information taken from the Web site.)

Allaire Forums

A Product of Allaire Corp.
(see previous entry for address
information)

Allaire Forums is a flexible Web conferencing system that enables online discussions via the Web on intranets and the Internet. With Allaire
Forums you can create conferences where people can easily communicate and share information with each other using their Web browser.
Allaire Forums offers a wide range of options for configuring discussions and managing access and security, with all administration and
configuration through the Web.

(This information taken from the Web site.)

HTML Transit 2.0

A Product of About InfoAccess
Phone: 800-344-9737 or 206-747-3203
Fax: 206-641-9367

http://www.infoaccess.com

Headquartered in Bellevue, Washington, InfoAccess (formerly OWL
International) has been producing hypertext-based electronic publishing software for government and Fortune 500 customers for over 10
years. In addition to HTML Transit, InfoAccess also offers the GUIDE
family of electronic publishing products for organizations with advanced information distribution requirements.

HTML Transit 2.0 eases conversion of documents to HTML for serious information publishers. The new version 2.0, scheduled for release
in September 1996, will offer more design control over the look and
feel of converted Web pages.

(This information taken from the Web site.)

XTML 1.3.0

by Ken Sayward
155 Flanders Rd.
Niantic, CT 06333

sayward@ae.vitro.com

http://users.aol.com/ksayward/xtml/

XTML enables you to maintain your tables in Microsoft Excel, then quickly and easily produce the HTML code required to publish the data on the Web. The formatting from the Excel worksheet is preserved.

XTML was created for one basic purpose: to create HTML Tables quickly and easily. If you have data in a Microsoft Excel spreadsheet, XTML can convert it into a table ready for inclusion in your Web site with one command. You can use the normal Excel formatting commands to assign font styles and text alignment, and XTML will produce the necessary HTML tags to reproduce the table on the Web. The resulting HTML source is saved into a text file, where you can edit and fine-tune it just as you would any of your other Web files.

XTML Runs on Macintosh and PC and requires Excel. It is compatible with Microsoft Excel version 5.0 or later (Macintosh or Windows versions).

It costs only $7.00. This is shareware.

(This information taken from the Web site.)

DNEWS News Server

by Chris Pugmire

netwin@world.std.com

www.netwin.com/denws

DNEWS News Server has been called the most advanced commercially supported news server on the market today.

DNEWS is an easy-to-use, high speed, fully functional, standards-based NNTP news server for Windows NT, Windows 95, Linux, Solaris, Polaris, and VAX. Save thousands of dollars in installation, ongoing management time and cost, and disk space and bandwidth.

Netwin LTD is a world leader in Internet Software design dedicated to being number one in their field.

(This information taken from the Web site.)

Chat Server

A Product of Magma Communications, Ltd.
Unit 201, 52 Antares Drive
Nepean, Ontario, Canada K2E 7Z1
Phone: 613-228-3565 or 613-228-8313

chatserver.sales@magmacom.com

www.magmacom.com

The Chat Server is the only continuous stream, real-time, multimedia-capable, Web-based communication server on the planet (as far as we know).

The Chat Server is the perfect tool for quickly setting up virtual meetings and discussions between people located throughout the world.

The Chat Server works with practically all Web browsers. To take advantage of the continuous-stream capabilities of the Chat Server, though, the Netscape browser is required.

(This information taken from the Web site.)

HTML Code Samples

by John Desborough, author

jdesboro@magmacom.com

Chapter 8

basic.html
subhome.html
homepage.html
homepg2.html
docshome.html
deflist.html
doctable.html

Chapter 9

form1.html
form2.html
form3.html
form4.html
form5.html
form6.html
form7.html
rollbar.html

Chapter 10

9form1.html
cgitemp.html
getfeed.html
postfeed.grml
getbreak.html
postbrk.html
lastform.html
index.html
firstscript.perl.cgi
printvars.perl.cgi
feedback.perl.cgi
breakout.get.perl.cgi
breakout.post.perl.cgi
intranet.feedback.perl.cgi

Index

CHECK OUT THESE RELATED TOPICS OR SEE YOUR LOCAL BOOKSTORE

CAD and 3D Studio

As the number one CAD publisher in the world, and as a Registered Publisher of Autodesk, New Riders Publishing provides unequaled content on this complex topic. Industry-leading products include AutoCAD and 3D Studio.

Networking

As the leading Novell NetWare publisher, New Riders Publishing delivers cutting-edge products for network professionals. We publish books for all levels of users, from those wanting to gain NetWare Certification, to those administering or installing a network. Leading books in this category include *Inside NetWare 3.12*, *CNE Training Guide: Managing NetWare Systems*, *Inside TCP/IP*, and *NetWare: The Professional Reference*.

Graphics

New Riders provides readers with the most comprehensive product tutorials and references available for the graphics market. Best-sellers include *Inside CorelDRAW! 5*, *Inside Photoshop 3*, and *Adobe Photoshop NOW!*

Internet and Communications

As one of the fastest growing publishers in the communications market, New Riders provides unparalleled information and detail on this ever-changing topic area. We publish international best-sellers such as *New Riders' Official Internet Yellow Pages, 2nd Edition*, a directory of over 10,000 listings of Internet sites and resources from around the world, and *Riding the Internet Highway, Deluxe Edition*.

Operating Systems

Expanding off our expertise in technical markets, and driven by the needs of the computing and business professional, New Riders offers comprehensive references for experienced and advanced users of today's most popular operating systems, including *Understanding Windows 95*, *Inside Unix*, *Inside Windows 3.11 Platinum Edition*, *Inside OS/2 Warp Version 3*, and *Inside MS-DOS 6.22*.

Other Markets

Professionals looking to increase productivity and maximize the potential of their software and hardware should spend time discovering our line of products for Word, Excel, and Lotus 1-2-3. These titles include *Inside Word 6 for Windows*, *Inside Excel 5 for Windows*, *Inside 1-2-3 Release 5*, and *Inside WordPerfect for Windows*.

Orders/Customer Service **1-800-653-6156**   Source Code **NRP95**

New Riders Publishing   201 West 103rd Street ◆ Indianapolis, Indiana 46290 USA

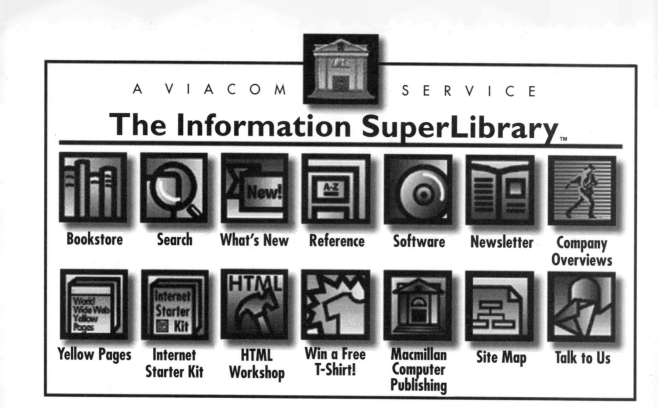

A VIACOM SERVICE

The Information SuperLibrary™

Bookstore	Search	What's New	Reference	Software	Newsletter	Company Overviews
Yellow Pages	Internet Starter Kit	HTML Workshop	Win a Free T-Shirt!	Macmillan Computer Publishing	Site Map	Talk to Us

CHECK OUT THE BOOKS IN THIS LIBRARY.

You'll find thousands of shareware files and over 1600 computer books designed for both technowizards and technophobes. You can browse through 700 sample chapters, get the latest news on the Net, and find just about anything using our

We're open 24-hours a day, 365 days a year.

You don't need a card.

We don't charge fines.

And you can be as **LOUD** as you want.